P9-DNP-729

Ethical Dilemmas and Decisions in Criminal Justice

7th EDITION

Ethical Dilemmas and Decisions in Criminal Justice

Joycelyn M. Pollock
Texas State University—San Marcos

WADSWORTH
CENGAGE Learning

Australia • Brazil • Japan • Korea • Mexico • Singapore • Spain • United Kingdom • United States

Ethical Dilemmas and Decisions in Criminal Justice, Seventh Edition
Joycelyn M. Pollock

Senior Publisher: Linda Schreiber-Ganster

Senior Acquisitions Editor: Carolyn Henderson Meier

Senior Developmental Editor: Robert Jucha

Senior Assistant Editor: Erin Abney

Editorial Assistant: Virginette Acacio

Media Editor: Ting Jian Yap

Senior Marketing Manager: Michelle Williams

Marketing Assistant: Sean Foy

Senior Marketing Communications Manager: Heather Baxley

Senior Content Project Manager: Christy Frame

Creative Director: Rob Hugel

Senior Art Director: Maria Epes

Senior Print Buyer: Mary Beth Hennebury

Rights Acquisitions Account Manager: Tom McDonough

Production Service: Kalpana Venkatramani, PreMediaGlobal

Photo Researcher: Josh Brown, PreMediaGlobal

Text Designer: Diane Beasley

Copy Editor: Lunaea Weatherstone

Cover Designer: Riezebos Holzbaur Design Group

Cover Image: Nathan Griffith/Corbis Images

Compositor: PreMediaGlobal

For product information and technology assistance, contact us at
Cengage Learning Customer & Sales Support, 1-800-354-9706

For permission to use material from this text or product, submit all requests online at **www.cengage.com/permissions**
Further permissions questions can be e-mailed to
permissionrequest@cengage.com

Library of Congress Control Number: 2010939923

ISBN-13: 978-1-111-34642-3

ISBN-10: 1-111-34642-9

Wadsworth
20 Davis Drive
Belmont, CA 94002-3098
USA

Cengage Learning is a leading provider of customized learning solutions with office locations around the globe, including Singapore, the United Kingdom, Australia, Mexico, Brazil, and Japan. Locate your local office at **www.cengage.com/global**

Cengage Learning products are represented in Canada by Nelson Education, Ltd.

To learn more about Wadsworth, visit **www.cengage.com/wadsworth**

Purchase any of our products at your local college store or at our preferred online store **www.cengagebrain.com.**

TO GREG AND ERIC, AS ALWAYS

About the Author

Joycelyn M. Pollock received her Ph.D. in Criminal Justice at the State University of New York at Albany. She also obtained a J.D. at the University of Houston, and passed the Texas Bar in 1991.

The first edition of *Ethics in Crime and Justice: Dilemmas and Decisions* was published in 1986 and continues to be one of the leading texts in the field. Dr. Pollock has also published *Crime and Justice in America: An Introduction* (2008); *Criminal Law, 8th Ed.* (2009); *Morality Stories, 2nd Ed.* (with Michael Braswell and Scott Braswell, 2007); *Prisons and Prison Life: Costs and Consequences* (2003); *Women, Prison and Crime, 2nd Ed.* (2002); *Sex and Supervision: Guarding Male and Female Inmates* (1986); *Counseling Women Prisoners* (1999); *Criminal Women* (2000); *Prison: An American Institution, 2nd Ed.* (Editor, 2006); and is co-editor with Alida Merlo of *Women, Law and Social Control, 2nd Ed.* (2004). In addition to publishing these texts, she maintains an active research agenda, primarily in the areas of police ethics and women's prisons. Most recently she has worked with Barbara Owen, James Wells, and Bernadette Muscat on an NIJ-funded research project exploring the nature of violent victimization in women's prisons.

In addition to teaching at Texas State University (formerly Southwest Texas State University), Dr. Pollock has delivered training to police officers, probation officers, parole officers, constables, and other groups in the areas of sexual harassment, ethics, criminology, and other subjects. She has taught at the Houston Police Academy and the Bill Blackwood Law Enforcement Management Institute, and has been a guest speaker for the International Association of Policewomen, the Texas Juvenile Justice Association, and the Southwest Legal Institute, among other groups. In 1998, she was awarded a Fulbright Teaching Fellowship to Turku School of Law in Turku, Finland. She was also a recipient of a Senior Scholar Justice award from the Open Society Institute. She has served as president of the Southwest Association of Criminal Justice and a trustee-at-large for the Academy of Criminal Justice Sciences. In 2007, she was awarded the Bruce Smith Award from ACJS for outstanding contributions to the field of criminology, and in 2008, she was awarded the Distinguished Alumni award from the State University at Albany, School of Criminal Justice.

Brief Contents

Contents

Preface

The first edition of this book was published in 1986, when there were very few texts for a course covering criminal justice ethics. Over the many years and editions, the book has been shaped by current events, reviewers' comments, and the many individuals who have read the book and provided feedback. I want to thank each and every person who has contacted me through e-mail, letters, or personally at conferences. I welcome and appreciate all feedback. Please continue to let me know what you think and help me make the book better and more accurate.

This text provides a balance between the philosophical material necessary to analyze ethical dilemmas and a discussion of research and current events relevant to ethics in the criminal justice field. While balancing philosophical background and current issues, *Ethical Dilemmas and Decisions in Criminal Justice* remains a highly applied text in that the major focus is on how individuals perceive and resolve ethical dilemmas. The book is designed to be used in undergraduate criminal justice ethics courses; however, it would not be inappropriate for a graduate level course as well. It has also been used in law enforcement training academies.

One of the central features of this book is the inclusion of current news events to show that these are not simply "ivory tower" discussions. In this edition, some of the news stories are continuing to unfold as the book goes to press; therefore, instructors will need to update these stories. In addition to real-life examples of misconduct, the book discusses the effects of misconduct, academic research, and the ethical implications of various policy issues in criminal justice. The book also identifies themes, such as discretion and due process, that run through the entire criminal justice system.

IN THIS EDITION

In this edition, I have reworked the chapters to provide a more organized and symmetrical presentation of each of the sub-areas of criminal justice (police, courts, corrections). In response to reviewers' requests, there are now 14 chapters—a better fit for most classes today. Even more important, there are also fewer introductory chapters, so students get to the more concrete, applied material sooner; the book's section on law enforcement professionals, for instance, now starts with Chapter 5 instead of Chapter 7.

As noted, there are three chapters each allocated to law enforcement professionals, legal professionals, and correctional professionals. These chapters follow the same general organization with the first chapter presenting general background issues relevant to that professional field (i.e., the role of law enforcement in Chapter 5, the function of law in Chapter 8, and the rationale for corrections in Chapter 11). Also included in each of the first chapters is a discussion of the formal codes of ethics, and a discussion of the occupational subculture and how it may conflict with the formal code of ethics. The second chapter in each set discusses issues that create dilemmas for the professional (i.e., use of the taser in Chapter 6, attorney–client privilege in Chapter 9, and the tension between treatment and custody in Chapter 12). Echoing the title of the book, there are several highlighted dilemmas in these chapters that receive an extended analysis. The third chapter in each set of three provides definitions and examples of misconduct (i.e., the latest police scandals in cities such as Tulsa and Philadelphia in Chapter 7, the prosecutorial misconduct in the Ted Stevens case in Chapter 10, and the indictments of correctional officers affiliated with criminal gangs in Baltimore in Chapter 13). Also included in these chapters are the explanations for and suggestions on how to reduce misconduct in each professional field. As in the 6th edition, the final chapter uses the war on terror as a backdrop to discuss ethical reasoning, concluding with some final thoughts on how to resolve ethical dilemmas.

FEATURES

There are several boxed features found in *Ethical Dilemmas and Decisions in Criminal Justice*, 7th Edition, which highlight and provide real-world examples of key concepts and issues.

IN THE NEWS This feature has been present since the earliest editions of this book. Each chapter presents news items that relate to the discussion. In every edition, some of the news stories are kept, but most are cycled out to make room for current events. Examples include:

Pact with the Devil?

Conduct Unbecoming?

In His Heart, There Is Forgiveness

QUOTE AND QUERY Another long-time feature of the book, the quote and query boxes offer some classic and current quotes meant to illustrate a point or issue from the chapter's discussion. There is a query following the quote that spurs the reader to think about the quote in the context of the discussion.

POLICY These boxes provide an overview of a current debate as well as a discussion centered on the law, policy, and ethics of the topic. Many of these topics have foreshadowed changes in the law or new developments, such as the policy box offered in the last edition on racial profiling, which has been updated to include a discussion of Arizona's new law requiring police officers to investigate the citizenship of anyone they have reasonable cause to believe is an illegal alien. Examples include:

The Future of Affirmative Action

Medical Use of Marijuana

Racial Profiling

WHITE COLLAR CRIME The white collar crime boxes were introduced in the 5th edition and their number has been increased in this 7th edition. The boxes focus the issues discussed in some chapters to white collar crime. For instance, the discussion of justice in Chapter 3 is supplemented with a box that discusses what justice means for white collar offenders. In later chapters, a white collar crime box shows the punishments received by notorious white collar offenders. Other chapters also are enriched with white collar crime boxes where relevant.

WALKING THE WALK Introduced in the last edition, these boxes describe individuals who display ethical courage. This has become a popular feature of the book, and in this edition there is a Walking the Walk box for each chapter. Readers are invited to contact the author and offer suggestions of individuals for these boxes for future editions of the book.

CHAPTER DILEMMAS A new feature to this edition is a number of highlighted dilemmas in Chapters 6, 9, and 11. The dilemmas are followed by an extended analysis under law, policy and ethics. The feature makes more explicit the focus of the book, illustrated by its title, "Dilemmas and Decisions."

PEDOGOGICAL AIDS

In addition to the boxed features, *Ethical Dilemmas and Decisions in Criminal Justice*, 7th Edition, has several pedagogical aids designed to enhance student learning and comprehension.

KEY TERMS As in previous editions, key terms are highlighted and defined. In this edition, the definitions are provided within the chapter rather than at the end of the chapter.

STUDY QUESTIONS These questions identify important points and concepts in the chapter and can be used for test reviews or test questions.

WRITING/DISCUSSION QUESTIONS These questions cover more abstract concepts and are designed to provide an opportunity to employ critical thinking skills in a writing or discussion exercise.

ETHICAL DILEMMAS Since the first edition of this book, dilemmas have been provided at the back of each chapter that are designed to be representative of what criminal justice professionals might face in the field. Many of the dilemmas describe true incidents and have been provided by police officers, probation officers, lawyers, and other criminal justice professionals. Others have been gleaned from news events or the media.

NEW TO THIS EDITION

CHAPTER OBJECTIVES New to the 7th edition are chapter objectives that preview the key content in each chapter for the reader.

CHAPTER REVIEW At the end of each chapter, the chapter objectives are presented again, but there is also a short summary of content. These reviews summarize the key content of the chapter for the reader.

CHAPTER-BY-CHAPTER CHANGES

- **Chapter 1, Morality, Ethics, and Human Behavior:** Chapter 1 provides the introduction to the study of ethics, with definitions and a discussion of the parameters of ethical analysis. For the most part, this chapter has remained the same as previous editions, with slight modifications, such as new In the News boxes, and the addition of Chapter Objectives and Review.

- **Chapter 2, Determining Moral Behavior:** This chapter presents the major ethical systems (utilitarianism, ethical formalism, religion, ethics of care, virtue ethics) and remains relatively unchanged, except that, in response to reviewers' concerns, egoism has been given its own section, and some topics have been slightly shortened. There is a new In the News box on Pat Robertson's comments regarding Haiti's "pact with the devil."

- **Chapter 3, Justice and the Law:** This chapter begins a major restructuring of chapters. I have combined Chapter 4 (justice) and part of Chapter 5 (law) from the last edition to form this new chapter on justice and law. The remainder of the old Chapter 5 on law has been moved to become the introductory chapter on legal professionals (Chapter 8). The discussion of distributive justice has been reduced, as have issues of culpability and other purely legal topics in order to accommodate new information in more directly relevant areas. The chapter order was changed so that justice and law now come *before* the discussion of how individuals develop their moral sense and how they decide moral issues (old Chapter 3) so that these topics can serve as the lead-in chapter to the remainder of the book. There is a new white collar crime box focused on justice issues, new In the News boxes, a new Walking the Walk box on Nelson Mandela, and the discussion of restorative justice has been moved here.

- **Chapter 4, Becoming an Ethical Professional:** This chapter consists of the old Chapter 3 (Determining Moral Behavior) and Chapter 6 (Ethics and the Criminal Justice Professional). The discussion of moral development and the discussion of training and education have been combined and condensed with a focus on criminal justice professionals. I have added an expanded discussion on how leadership affects ethics in an organization. There are new In the News boxes on corruption at the border and corruption in politics, and there is a new Walking the Walk box on Thomas Tamm, a whistleblower in the FBI. The number of introductory chapters has been reduced so that the first chapter dealing with law enforcement professionals begins with Chapter 5 in this edition instead of Chapter 7 as in the last edition.

- **Chapter 5, The Police Role in Society:** This chapter includes much of the same material as Chapter 7 in the last edition. I have added a new Quote and Query box on community policing, and new In the News boxes on police investigations of misconduct. The discussion on police subculture has been condensed, with findings from recent research added. This chapter begins the template for the organization for the remainder of the book. I have provided three chapters each for law enforcement, legal, and correctional professionals. In the first chapter, major issues of the field are discussed, as are the source of formal ethics and any subcultural elements that impact ethical behavior.

- **Chapter 6, Police Discretion and Dilemmas:** This chapter has been rearranged to focus on the dilemmas faced by law enforcement officers in the course of their duties. A new feature is highlighting a few dilemmas in the body of the chapter with an expanded discussion of the dilemma applying the law, policy, and ethics analysis. Much of the discussion from old Chapter 9 is revised and included here (i.e., dilemmas that arise in proactive and reactive investigations, possible racism in the system, the use of force, and interrogation methods). There are new In the News boxes, a discussion of the Arizona immigration law, an updated discussion of the William Jefferson case, an expanded discussion of the Jon Burge case, expanded information about informants along with news items related to their use, a new Walking the Walk box on Frederick Whitehurst, and a revised discussion of the use of force, adding an expanded section on tasers.

- **Chapter 7, Police Corruption and Misconduct:** In this edition, the third chapter in each of the sub-areas (law enforcement, courts, and corrections) focuses on misconduct and ways to reduce it. Chapter 7 uses much of the same material as Chapter 9 in the last edition, but also includes the explanations for misconduct and suggested methods to reduce it, which came from other chapters. I have added an expanded discussion of Frank Serpico, added a bulleted list of news stories of police committing crimes across the country, including incidents in New Orleans, Tulsa, Philadelphia, Baltimore, and other locations, and In the News boxes on corruption in the Mexican police force, police gratuities, and professional courtesy. The discussion of various methods to reduce corruption has been expanded with new research findings presented.

- **Chapter 8, Law and Legal Professionals:** Reviewers have raised concerns that legal professionals received fewer chapters than either law enforcement or correctional professionals. This wasn't exactly true because the law chapter (Chapter 5) in the old edition was, in many ways, similar to the general discussion offered in the first chapters of the other two sub-areas, it just wasn't placed next to the legal professionals chapters. This organizational issue has been addressed in this edition, and the old law chapter has now been moved to introduce the chapters concerned with legal professionals. This chapter includes the justification for law, the role of law in society, the various perceptions of the system, and the idea of the attorney as legal agent or moral agent. It also includes discussions concerning the source of legal ethics for attorneys, as well as subcultural elements in the profession that are inconsistent with formal ethics. This chapter serves as a parallel to Chapter 5. New elements include an expanded discussion of new ethics rules for prosecutors, a discussion of the same-sex marriage legal debate, and relevant news items such as the BP Gulf of Mexico oil disaster and the Massey Mining Company explosion.

- **Chapter 9, Discretion and Dilemmas in the Legal Profession:** In the last edition, judges were covered in a separate chapter. This edition discusses issues for defense attorneys, prosecutors, and judges in this chapter under the same organization as presented in Chapter 6 for law enforcement professionals. Similar to the 6th edition, the ABA Criminal Justice Standards are used to present ethical issues, but in this edition, certain dilemmas are highlighted and analyzed under law, policy, and ethics. New to this edition are updated discussions of the Cameron Todd Willingham case, the ethical issues facing defense attorneys in drug courts, the 2009 report of the National Academy of Sciences on forensic science lab procedures, the use of jailhouse informants, the Supreme Court holding in *Holland v. Florida* as well as other cases dealing with procedural versus substantive issues of justice, and the new legislation reducing the 100:1 drug sentencing ratio for crack compared to cocaine. An In the News box on the activities of police and prosecutors in Tenaha, Texas, is also offered.

- **Chapter 10, Ethical Misconduct and Responses:** This chapter parallels Chapter 7 and offers examples and explanations of misconduct in the legal profession. There is an expanded discussion of the Clarence Brandley case as well as other cases of exonerated individuals. There are new In the News boxes on misconduct incidents, and possible intimidation of Innocence Project volunteers. Also included are expanded descriptions of prosecutorial misconduct in the Ted Stevens case and incidents of judicial misconduct by state and federal judges, including ex-judges Porteous, Kent, Spargo, and DeLaughter. There is also a new Walking the Walk box on federal judge William Wayne Justice. New to this edition are sections on explaining misconduct and reducing misconduct of legal professionals. The recent case of *Garcetti v. Ceballos* is discussed as a barrier to whistleblowers in government.

- **Chapter 11, The Ethics of Punishment and Corrections:** This is substantially the same as Chapter 12 in the old edition with the addition of sections on formal ethics and subcultural elements that were in other chapters in the old edition. It parallels Chapters 5 and 8 in its organization. There is a new In the News box on Bernard Madoff, and a new Walking the Walk box on Tom Murton. Also included are expanded discussions of supermax prisons, new Supreme Court cases on the death penalty, and new sections on formal ethics codes for correctional professionals not covered in the last edition.

- **Chapter 12, Discretion and Dilemmas in Corrections:** This chapter parallels Chapters 6 and 9 and covers ethical issues and dilemmas for all correctional professionals. While in the last edition, institutional and community corrections professionals were separated into different chapters, they have been combined in this chapter. As in Chapters 6 and 9, certain dilemmas are highlighted with an analysis provided by law, policy, and ethics. Much of this chapter comes from Chapters 13 and 14 from the last edition. New In the News boxes on correctional officer misconduct in New York and Virginia are included. There is an expanded discussion of the ethics of correctional psychologists using new sources, and a discussion of shackling pregnant prisoners.

- **Chapter 13, Correctional Professionals: Misconduct and Responses:** This chapter is a parallel to Chapters 7 and 10 and offers examples of misconduct in corrections as well as a discussion of how to reduce corruption and misconduct. There is a new Walking the Walk box on D. J. Vodicka, a former correctional officer, and a new In the News box on corruption by a prison purchasing agent, Also in this edition are an expanded discussion of the Prison Rape Elimination Act and the various forms of sexual relationships between guards and inmates, descriptions of incidents in Florida and Maryland prisons involving smuggling by correctional officers and other staff members, and a discussion on alleged abuses in immigration facilities. New to this edition are examples of misconduct in probation and parole, and the sections on explaining misconduct and suggested ways to reduce it in community corrections.

- **Chapter 14, Making Ethical Choices:** While much of the material in Chapter 15 of the last edition has been included here (i.e., the just war/just means discussion, the responses to 9/11, rights-based policing), the material has been condensed with a greater emphasis on how the threat of terrorism and the responses taken illustrate the importance of ethics in current events. Also, there is a greater emphasis on how these issues affect professionals in the justice system. A new Walking the Walk box on Mary McCarthy is offered in conjunction with an expanded discussion of whistleblowers.

SUPPLEMENTS

A number of supplements are provided by Cengage Learning to help instructors use *Ethical Dilemmas and Decisions in Criminal Justice* in their courses and to aid students in preparing for exams. Supplements are available to qualified adopters. Please consult your local sales representative for details.

FOR THE INSTRUCTOR

INSTRUCTOR'S EDITION Designed just for instructors, the *Instructor's Edition* includes a visual walk-through that illustrates the key pedagogical features of the text, as well as the media and supplements that accompany it. Use this handy tool to quickly learn about the many options this text provides to keep your class engaging and informative.

INSTRUCTOR'S RESOURCE MANUAL WITH TEST BANK An improved and completely updated *Instructor's Resource Manual with Test Bank* has been developed by Paulina Ruf at Lenoir-Rhyne University. The manual includes learning objectives, detailed chapter outlines, key terms, suggested readings, questions for review and discussion, and Internet assignments. Each chapter's test bank contains questions in multiple-choice, true–false, fill-in-the-blank, and essay formats, with a full answer key. The test bank is coded to the chapter objectives that appear in the main text and includes the page numbers in the main text where the answers can be found.

EXAMVIEW® COMPUTERIZED TESTING

The comprehensive *Instructor's Resource Manual* described above is backed up by ExamView, a computerized test bank available for PC and Macintosh computers. With ExamView you can create, deliver, and customize tests and study guides (both print and online) in minutes. You can easily edit and import your own questions and graphics, change test layouts, and reorganize questions. And using ExamView's complete word-processing capabilities, you can enter an unlimited number of new questions or edit existing questions.

LESSON PLANS From Michael Whalen, South University, the instructor-created lesson plans bring accessible, masterful suggestions to every lesson. Each lesson plan includes a sample syllabus, learning objectives, lecture notes, discussion topics, in-class activities, tips for classroom presentation of chapter material, a detailed lecture outline, and assignments. Lesson plans are available on the instructor website.

PPTS These handy Microsoft PowerPoint slides, prepared by Cheryn Rowell of Stanley Community College, which outline the chapters of the main text in a classroom-ready presentation, will help you in making your lectures engaging and in reaching your visually oriented students. The presentations are available for download on the password-protected website and can also be obtained by e-mailing your local Cengage Learning representative.

WEBTUTOR™ ON BLACKBOARD® AND WEBCT® Jump-start your course with customizable, rich, text-specific content within your Course Management System. Whether you want to web-enable your class or put an entire course online, WebTutor delivers. WebTutor offers a wide array of resources, including media assets, test bank, practice quizzes linked to chapter learning objectives, and additional study aids. Visit www.cengage.com/webtutor to learn more.

THE WADSWORTH CRIMINAL JUSTICE VIDEO LIBRARY So many exciting new videos—so many great ways to enrich your lectures and spark discussion of the material in this text. Your Cengage Learning representative will be happy to provide details on our video policy by adoption size. The library includes these selections and many others:

- *ABC® Videos.* ABC videos feature short, high-interest clips from current news events as well as historic raw footage going back 40 years. Perfect for discussion starters or to enrich your lectures and spark interest in the material in the text, these brief videos provide students with a new lens through which to view the past and present, one that will greatly enhance their knowledge and understanding of significant events and open up to them new dimensions in learning. Clips are drawn from such programs as *World News Tonight, Good Morning America, This Week, PrimeTime Live, 20/20,* and *Nightline,* as well as numerous ABC News specials and material from the Associated Press Television News and British Movietone News collections.

- *Cengage Learning's "Introduction Criminal Justice Video Series"* features videos supplied by the BBC Motion Gallery. These timely, engaging clips from CBS and BBC news programs—everything from nightly news broadcasts and specials to CBS News Special Reports, *CBS Sunday Morning, 60 Minutes,* and more—are perfect classroom discussion starters. Designed to enrich your lectures and spark interest in the material in the text, the brief videos provide students with a new lens through which to view the past and present, one that will greatly enhance their knowledge and understanding of significant events and open up to them new dimensions in learning. Clips are drawn from BBC Motion Gallery.

- *Films for the Humanities.* Choose from nearly 200 videos on a variety of topics such as elder abuse, supermax prisons, suicide and the police officer, the making of an FBI agent, and domestic violence.

CRIMINAL JUSTICE MEDIA LIBRARY

Cengage Learning's Criminal Justice Media Library includes nearly 300 media assets on the topics you cover in your courses. Available to stream from any Web-enabled computer, the Criminal Justice Media Library's assets include such valuable resources as Career Profile Videos featuring interviews with criminal justice professionals from a range of roles and locations, simulations that allow students to step into various roles and practice their decision-making skills, video clips on current topics from ABC® and other sources, animations that illustrate key concepts, interactive learning modules that help students check their knowledge of important topics, and Reality Check exercises that compare expectations and preconceived notions against the real-life thoughts and experiences of criminal justice professionals. The Criminal Justice Media Library can be uploaded and used within many popular Learning Management Systems. You can also customize it with your own course material. You can also purchase an institutional site license. Please contact your Cengage Learning representative for ordering and pricing information.

FOR THE STUDENT

COURSEMATE Cengage Learning's Criminal Justice CourseMate brings course concepts to life with interactive learning, study, and exam preparation tools that support the printed textbook. CourseMate includes an integrated e-book, quizzes mapped to chapter learning objectives, flashcards, videos, and more, and EngagementTracker, a first-of-its-kind tool that monitors student engagement in the course. The accompanying instructor website offers access to password-protected resources such as an electronic version of the instructor's manual and PowerPoint® slides.

CLEBOOK Cengage Learning's Criminal Justice e-books allow students to access our textbooks in an easy-to-use online format. Highlight, take notes, bookmark, search your text, and, for most texts, link directly into multimedia. In short, CLeBooks combine the best features of paper books and e-books in one package.

CAREERS IN CRIMINAL JUSTICE WEBSITE

AVAILABLE BUNDLED WITH THIS TEXT AT NO ADDITIONAL CHARGE. Featuring plenty of self-exploration and profiling activities, the interactive Careers in Criminal Justice website helps students investigate and focus on the criminal justice career choices that are right for them. Includes interest assessment, video testimonials from career professionals, résumé and interview tips, and links for reference.

To access additional course materials, please visit www.cengagebrain.com. At the CengageBrain.com home page, search for the ISBN of your title (from the back cover of your book) using the search box at the top of the page. This will take you to the product page where these resources can be found.

CURRENT PERSPECTIVES: READINGS FROM INFOTRAC® COLLEGE EDITION These readers, designed to give students a closer look at special topics in criminal justice, include free access to InfoTrac College Edition. The timely articles are selected by experts in each topic from within InfoTrac College Edition. They are available free when bundled with the text and include the following titles:

- Cyber Crime
- Victimology
- Juvenile Justice
- Racial Profiling
- White-Collar Crime
- Terrorism and Homeland Security
- Public Policy and Criminal Justice
- Technology and Criminal Justice
- Ethics in Criminal Justice
- Forensics and Criminal Investigation
- Corrections
- Law and Courts
- Policy in Criminal Justice

ACKNOWLEDGMENTS

I thank the reviewers for this new edition. They are:

Susan Brinkley, University of Tampa

Duane Everhart, Wayne Community College

Lori Guevara, Fayetteville State University

Stephen L. Mallory, University of Mississippi

Rebecca Anne Mercier, Bluegrass Community and Technical College

Thomas Nolan, Boston University

Angela C. Simon, University of Dubuque

The staff members at Cengage Learning have been integral to the development of this edition as well. They are: Carolyn Henderson Meier, Senior Acquisitions Editor; Robert Jucha, Senior Development Editor; Michelle Williams, Marketing Manager; Christy Frame, Senior Content Project Manager; Tom McDonough, Rights Acquisitions Specialist; and Rachel McDonald, Assistant Editor. Thanks also to Kalpana Venkatramani at PMG. I especially want to thank Lunaea Weatherstone, the best copy editor this book has ever had.

Joycelyn Pollock
jpl2@txstate.edu

PART I

Ethics and the Criminal Justice System

Clark Brennan / Alamy

1

Morality, Ethics, and Human Behavior

Chapter Objectives

1. Give examples of how discretion permeates every phase of the criminal justice system and creates ethical dilemmas for criminal justice professionals.
2. Explain why the study of ethics is important for criminal justice professionals.
3. Learn the definitions of the terms *morals*, *ethics*, *duties*, *superogatories*, and *values*.
4. Describe what behaviors might fall under moral/ethical judgments.
5. Explain the difference between ethical issues and ethical dilemmas.

Consider the following dilemma: You are a police officer patrolling late at night and see a car weaving back and forth across lanes of traffic. You turn on your siren, and the car pulls over. The driver stumbles out of the car, obviously intoxicated. There is no question that the driver meets the legal definition of intoxication. He also happens to be your father. What would you do?

Or decide what you would do in this case: You are a correctional officer working the late-night shift. Your sergeant and another officer from the day shift come onto the tier where you are working and ask you to open up an inmate's cell. After you do so, they enter the cell. Then you hear a series of grunts, cries, and moans. They leave, muttering about how the inmate has been taught a lesson. You believe that you have been a party to an assault, but you say nothing. The next night you find out that the inmate did not report the incident, nor did any other inmate. You believe that if you come forward and report what you saw, you will be severely ostracized. You may not be believed (especially if the inmate doesn't back you up). You might even lose your job. What would you do?

Finally, consider this scenario: You are a student interning in a criminal defense lawyer's office. As part of your duties, you sit in court with the lawyer you are working with, help her with legal research, and assist in interviewing witnesses. During the course of the internship, you conclude that the lawyer, in your opinion, is extremely negligent. She does not return clients' calls, she misses appeal deadlines, and she ignores or does not follow up on promising leads that might lead to exculpatory evidence. You are appalled that several of her clients are advised to plead guilty even though you think that the evidence against them is weak. When you bring up these issues with her, she fires you on the spot and tells you that all her clients are guilty anyway and that she is just another "cog in the wheel" of the justice machine. What, if anything, would you do?

Why Study Ethics?

How would you go about deciding what to do in these situations? Learning how to determine the "right thing to do" is the central purpose of this book. We make ethical decisions all the time, whether we recognize them or not. Think about some ethical choices you have been faced with in the last couple of weeks or months. Perhaps you have been faced with one of the following ethical choices:

- A fellow student offered you a paper purchased from an Internet site. You believe that you could turn it in as your own and never be caught.

- A co-worker took something from the store where you both work and expected you to say nothing.

- A friend asked you to lie for him to his girlfriend to cover up the fact that he went out with another girl.

- You felt compelled to tell a professor a "white lie" when asking for an extension on an assignment.

All of us make choices that can be judged under ethical standards. Further, we frequently judge other people's behaviors as right or wrong. Those who work in the criminal justice field must be especially sensitive to the ethical issues that may arise in their professional lives. Criminal justice professionals, whether they work in law enforcement, the courts, or corrections, encounter a multitude of situations in which they must make choices that affect people's lives.

The criminal justice system can be examined using political, organizational, or sociological approaches. Let us shift the lens somewhat and look at the system through an ethics perspective. Asking whether something is legal, for instance, is not necessarily the same question as asking whether something is right. Actors at every stage in the justice process make decisions that can be analyzed and judged as ethical or unethical. Although the decisions faced by these professionals—ranging from legislators who write the laws to correctional professionals who supervise prisoners—may be different, they also have similarities, especially in that these professionals all experience varying degrees of **discretion**, authority, and power.

discretion The authority to make a decision between two or more choices.

Legislators have the power to define behavior as illegal and, therefore, punishable. They also have the power to set the amount of punishment. They criminalize behavior usually because it threatens public safety, but sometimes also employ moral definitions for deciding which behaviors should be legal and which should be illegal. "Protection of public morality" is the rationale for a number of laws, including those involving drugs, gambling, and prostitution. How do legislators use their great discretion to balance the rights of *all* people? We explore these questions in more detail in Chapter 3, which covers the concept of justice, and in Chapter 8, which begins our discussion of the law and legal professionals.

Police officers, who enforce the laws created by legislators, have a great deal of discretionary power. For instance, they have the power to deprive people of their liberty (through arrest), the power to decide which individuals to investigate and perhaps target for undercover operations, and the power to issue a ticket or let a driver off with a warning.

Police serve as the interface between the awesome power of the state and the citizenry governed. In some countries, police operate as a fearsome coercive force for a controlling political body. In the United States, we enjoy constitutional protections against untrammeled police power, and police act as the guardians of the law, not merely enforcers for those in power. In Chapters 5, 6, and 7, the ethical use of police discretion is discussed in more detail.

Prosecutors probably face the least public scrutiny of all criminal justice professionals—which is ironic because they possess a great deal of discretion in deciding who and how to prosecute:

- They decide which charges to pursue and which to drop.
- They decide which cases to take to a grand jury.
- They decide how to prosecute a case and whether to pursue the death penalty in homicide cases.

Although prosecutors have the ethical duty to pursue justice rather than conviction, some critics argue that at times their decision making seems to be influenced by politics or factors other than the goal of justice. Defense attorneys have ethical duties similar to prosecutors in some ways; however, they also have unique duties to their client.

Judges also possess incredible power, typically employed through decisions to deny or accept plea bargains, decisions regarding rules of evidence, and decisions about sentencing. Chapters 8, 9, and 10 explore the ethical issues of legal professionals in the criminal justice system.

Finally, correctional officials have the following immense powers over the lives of some citizens:

- Probation officers make recommendations in presentence reports and violation reports that affect whether an individual goes to prison.
- Prison officials decide to award or take away "good time," and they may punish an inmate with segregation; both types of decisions affect the individual's liberty.
- Correctional officers make daily decisions that affect the life and health of the prisoners they supervise.
- Parole officials decide when to file a violation report, and make other decisions that affect a parolee as well as his or her family members.

In short, all correctional professionals have a great deal of discretion over the lives of those they control. The ethical issues of correctional professionals are discussed in Chapters 11, 12, and 13.

Although the professionals discussed face different dilemmas, they also have the following common elements:

- *They each have discretion—that is, the power to make a decision.* Although the specific decisions are different, they all involve power over others and the potential deprivation of life, liberty, or property.
- *They each have the duty of enforcing the law.* Although this concept is obvious with police, it is also clear that each of the professionals mentioned has a basic duty to uphold and enforce all laws; they serve the law in their professional lives.
- *They must accept that their duty is to protect the constitutional safeguards that are the cornerstone of our legal system—specifically, due process and equal protection.* Due process protects each of us from error in any governmental deprivation of life, liberty, or property. We recognize the right of government to control and even to punish, but we

have certain protections against arbitrary or unlawful use of that power. Due process protects us against such abuses. We also expect that the power of our government will be used fairly and in an unbiased manner. Equal protection should ensure that what happens to us is not determined by the color of our skin, our gender, nationality, or the religion we practice. Laws are for everyone, and the protection of the law extends to all of us. Although a fair amount of evidence indicates that different treatment does exist, the ideal of equal protection is an essential element of our legal system and should be an operating principle for everyone working in this system.

- *They are public servants.* Their salaries come from the public purse. Public servants possess more than a job; they have taken on special duties involving the public trust. Individuals such as legislators, public officials, police officers, judges, and prosecutors are either elected or appointed guardians of the public's interests. Arguably, they must be held to *higher standards* than those they guard or govern. Temptations are many, and, unfortunately, we find examples of *double standards*, in which public servants take advantage of their positions for special favors, rather than higher standards of exemplary behavior.

The Josephson Institute (2005), which is heavily involved in ethics training for corporations and public agencies, identifies the ethical principles that should govern public servants: public service (treating the office as a public trust), objective judgment (striving to be free from conflicts of interest), accountability (upholding open decision making), democratic leadership (observing the letter and spirit of the law), and respectability (avoiding the appearance of impropriety). It cannot be over-emphasized that the ethical demands placed upon public servants are different than those placed upon the rest of us. Edwin Delattre (1989b: 79) argued that:

> Part of what is needed [for public servants] is a public sense of what Madison meant by wisdom and good character: balanced perception and integrity. Integrity means wholeness in public and private life consisting of habits of justice, temperance, courage, compassion, honesty, fortitude, and disdain for self-pity.

It would be ideal if all public servants possessed the characteristics identified by Delattre; however, even public servants of good character are sometimes perplexed as to the right course of action in situations they encounter in their professional duties. Obviously, the law governs many of the decisions that public servants make, but because of the discretion that exists at every stage of the criminal justice process, the possibility of an unethical use of such discretion remains. Understanding the ethical issues involved in one's profession might help to guide such discretion and prevent abuse. Therefore, all professionals in the criminal justice field must be sensitive to ethical issues. These issues may involve their relationships with citizens and others over whom they have power, their relationship with their agency, or their relationships with one another.

Felkenes (1987: 26) explained why the study of ethics is important for criminal justice professionals:

1. Professionals are recognized as such in part because [a] "profession" normally includes a set of ethical requirements as part of its meaning.... Professionalism among all actors at all levels of the criminal justice system depends upon their ability to administer policy effectively in a morally and ethically responsible manner.
2. Training in critical ethics helps to develop analytical skills and reasoning abilities needed to understand the pragmatic and theoretical aspects of the criminal justice system.

in the NEWS

TRANSPARENCY INTERNATIONAL

Every year, this international organization publishes their list of the most corrupt and least corrupt nations in the world. The information is drawn from surveys of ordinary citizens, who are asked to describe the honesty and practices of public officials. Not surprisingly, in the 2009 results, countries such as Somalia, Afghanistan, Myanmar, Sudan, Iraq, and Chad are identified as the most corrupt countries in the world. Perhaps surprisingly, the United States is not ranked in the top 10 least corrupt countries. While New Zealand, Denmark, Singapore, Sweden, Switzerland, Finland, and the Netherlands rank as the least corrupt countries, the United States comes in at number 19.

SOURCE: Transparency International web site, available at www.transparency.org/policy_research/surveys_indices/cpi/2009/cpi_2009_table (accessed June 27, 2010).

3. Criminal justice professionals should be able to recognize quickly the ethical consequences of various actions and the moral principles involved.

4. Ethical considerations are central to decisions involving discretion, force, and due process which require people to make enlightened moral judgments.

5. Ethics is germane to most management and policy decisions concerning such penal issues as rehabilitation, deterrence, and just deserts.

6. Ethical considerations are essential aspects of criminal justice research.

In answer to a similar question, Braswell (1996/2002: 8) explained the following five goals of a study of ethics:

- Become aware of and open to ethical issues.

- Begin developing critical thinking skills.

- Become more personally responsible.

- Understand how the criminal justice system is engaged in a process of coercion.

wholesight Exploring issues with one's heart as well as one's mind.

- Develop **wholesight** (which roughly means exploring with one's heart as well as one's mind).

The comprehensive nature of these two lists requires few additions; however, we also could note that individuals who ignore ethics do so at their peril. They may find themselves sliding down a slippery slope of behaviors that threaten their career and personal well-being. Even if their actions are not discovered, many people suffer from personal crises when their actions are in conflict with their conscience. Three basic points are reiterated below:

- We study ethics because criminal justice is uniquely involved in coercion, which means there are many and varied opportunities to abuse such power.

- Almost all criminal justice professionals are public servants and, thus, owe special duties to the public they serve.

- We study ethics to sensitize students to ethical issues and provide tools to help identify and resolve the ethical dilemmas they may face in their professional lives.

Defining Terms

morals Principles of right and wrong.

ethics The discipline of determining good and evil and defining moral duties.

The words **morals** and **ethics** are often used in daily conversations. For example, when public officials use their offices for personal profit or when politicians accept bribes from special interest groups, they are described as unethical. When an individual does a good deed, engages in charitable activities or personal sacrifice, or takes a stand against wrongdoing, we might describe that individual as a moral person. Often, the terms *morals* and *ethics* are used interchangeably. This makes sense because they both come from similar root meanings. The Greek word *ethos* pertains to custom (behavioral practices) or character, and *morals* is a Latin-based word with a similar meaning.

MORALS AND ETHICS

Morals and morality refer to what is judged as good conduct. (Immorality refers to bad conduct.) The term *moral* also is used to describe someone who has the capacity to make value judgments and discern right from wrong (Souryal, 1992/2007: 12). The term *ethics* refers to the study and analysis of what constitutes good or bad conduct (Barry, 1985: 5; Sherman, 1981: 8).

There are several branches, or schools, of ethics:

meta-ethics The discipline of investigating the meaning of ethical terms, including a critical study of how ethical statements can be verified.

normative ethics What people ought to do; defines moral duties.

applied ethics The study of what is right and wrong pertaining to a specific profession or subject.

professional ethics Applied principles of right and wrong relevant to specific occupations or professions.

- **Meta-ethics** is the discipline that investigates the meaning of ethical systems and whether they are relative or are universal, and are self-constructed or are independent of human creation.

- **Normative ethics** determines what people ought to do and defines moral duties based on ethical systems or other means of analysis.

- **Applied ethics** is the application of ethical principles to specific issues.

- **Professional ethics** is an even more specific type of applied ethics relating to the behavior of certain professions or groups.

To many people, ethics has come to mean the definition of specific behaviors as right and wrong within a profession. Often, in common usage, *morality* is used to speak of the total person, or the sum of a person's actions in every sphere of life, and *ethics* is used to refer to behaviors relating to a profession and is an analysis of behavior relevant to a certain profession. For instance, the medical profession follows the Hippocratic Oath, a declaration of rules and principles of conduct for doctors to follow in their daily practices; it dictates appropriate behavior and goals. In fact, most professions have their own set of ethical standards or canons of ethics.

Even though professional ethics typically restricts attention to areas of behavior relevant to the profession, these can be fairly inclusive and enter into what we might consider the private life of the individual. For instance, doctors are judged harshly if they engage in romantic relationships with their patients, as are professors if they become involved with their students. These rules usually are included in codes of ethics for these professions. We are very much aware of how politicians' private behavior can affect their career in politics. When John Edwards was exposed in 2009 as attempting to cover up fathering a child with his mistress, his presidential aspirations were destroyed. Clearly, in professions involving the public trust, such as politics, education, and the clergy, there is a thin line between one's private life and one's public life.

For our purposes, it does not make a great deal of difference whether we use the formal or colloquial definitions of *morals* and *ethics*. This text is an applied ethics text, in that we will be concerned with what is defined as right and wrong behavior in the professions relevant to the criminal justice system and how people in these professions make decisions in the course of their careers. It also is a professional ethics text, because we are concerned primarily with professional ethics in criminal justice.

DUTIES

duties Required behaviors or actions, i.e., the responsibilities that are attached to a specific role.

The term **duties** refers to those actions that an individual must perform to be considered moral. For instance, everyone might agree that one has a duty to support one's parents if able to do so; one has a duty to obey the law (unless it is an immoral law); and a police officer has a moral and ethical duty to tell the truth on a police report. Duties are what you must do in order to be good.

superogatories Actions that are commendable but not required in order for a person to be considered moral.

Other actions, considered **superogatories**, are commendable but not required. A Good Samaritan who jumps into a river to save a drowning person, risking his or her own life to do so, has performed a superogatory action. Those who stood on the bank receive no moral condemnation, because risking one's life is above and beyond anyone's moral duty. Of course, if one can help save a life with no great risk to oneself, a moral duty does exist in that situation.

Police officers have an ethical duty to get involved when others do not. Consider the 2001 attack on the World Trade Center. One of the most moving images of that tragedy was of police officers and firefighters running toward danger while others ran away. This professional duty to put oneself in harm's way is why we revere and pay homage to these public servants. Many civilians also put themselves in harm's way in this disaster, and because they had no professional duty to do so, they could be said to be performing superogatory actions.

imperfect duties Moral duties that are not fully explicated or detailed.

There are also **imperfect duties**, general duties that one should uphold but do not have a specific application as to when or how. For instance, most ethical systems support a general duty of generosity but have no specific duty demanding a certain type or manner of generosity. Another imperfect duty might be to be honest. Generally, one should be honest, but, as we will see in Chapter 2, some ethical systems allow for exceptions to the general rule.

VALUES

values Judgments of desirability, worth, or importance.

Values are defined as elements of desirability, worth, or importance. You may say that you value honesty; another way of saying that is that one of your values is honesty. Others may value physical health, friendships, material success, or family. Individual values form value systems. All people prioritize certain things that they consider important in life. Values only become clear when there is a choice to be made; for instance, when you must choose between friendship and honesty, or material success and family. Behavior is generally consistent with values. For instance, some individuals believe that financial success is more important than family or health. In this case, we may assume that their behavior will reflect the importance of that value and that these persons will be workaholics, spending more time at work than with family and endangering their health with long hours, stress, and lack of exercise. Others place a higher priority on religious faith, wisdom, honesty, and/or independence than financial success or status.

Values as judgments of worth are often equated with moral judgments of goodness. We see that both can be distinguished from factual judgments, which can be empirically verified. Note the difference between these factual judgments:

- "He is lying."
- "It is raining."

and these value judgments:

- "She is a good woman."
- "That was a wonderful day."

The last two judgments are more similar to moral judgments, such as "Lying is wrong" or "Giving to charities is good." Facts are capable of scientific proof, but values and moral judgments are not.

Some writers think that value judgments and moral judgments are indistinguishable because neither can be verified. Some also think that values and morals are relativistic and individual. In this view, there are no universal values; values are all subjective and merely opinions. Because they are only opinions, no value is more important than any other value (Mackie, 1977: 22–24).

In contrast, others believe that not all values are equal, and that some values, such as honesty, are always more important than other values, such as pleasure. In this view, values such as charity, altruism, integrity, knowledge, and responsibility are more important or better than the values of pleasure or wealth. You may value personal pleasure over charity or honesty, but to someone who believes in universal values, you would be wrong in this view. This question is related to a later discussion in Chapter 2 concerning whether ethics are relative or absolute.

As stated earlier, values imply a choice or a judgment. If, for instance, you were confronted with an opportunity to cheat on an exam, your values of success and honesty would be directly at odds. Values and morals are similar, although values indicate the *relative* importance of these constructs, whereas morals prescribe or proscribe behavior. The value of honesty is conceptually distinct from the moral rule against lying.

Messner and Rosenfeld's (1994) theory of crime utilizes the concept of values. In their explanation of why the United States has a higher rate of violent crime than other Western countries, they propose that the U.S. value system, which emphasizes consumerism over family and financial success over honesty, creates an environment in which crime results. In the United States, success is defined almost exclusively by the accumulation of material goods, not by doing good. Because behavior is influenced by one's value system, individuals who place material success over any other value will behave dishonestly or even violently in the pursuit of such goods.

An explicit value system is part of every ethical system, as we will see in Chapter 2. The values of life, respect for the person, and survival can be found in all ethical systems. Certain values hold special relevance to the criminal justice system and those professionals who work within it; privacy, freedom, public order, justice, duty, and loyalty are all values that will come up again in later discussions.

Making Moral Judgments

We make moral or ethical judgments all the time: "Abortion is wrong." "Capital punishment is just." "It's good to give to charity." "It's wrong to hit your spouse." These are all judgments of good and bad behavior. We also make choices, knowing that they can be judged as right or wrong. Should you call in sick to your boss, even though you aren't sick, to get a day in the sun? Should you give back extra change that a clerk gave you by mistake? Should you tell a friend that her husband is having an affair even though he asked you not to tell? Should you cut and paste sections of Wikipedia into your term paper?

Not all behaviors involve questions of ethics. To draw the boundaries of our ethical discussion more specifically, we need to know which behavioral decisions might be judged under ethical standards. Decisions that can be judged involve four elements: (1) acts that are (2) human and (3) of free will (4) that affect others.

ACT First of all, some act must be present to judge. For instance, we are concerned with the *act* of stealing or the *act* of contributing to charity, rather than an idle thought that stealing a lot of money would enable us to buy a sailboat or a vague intention to be more generous. We are not necessarily concerned with how people feel or what they think about a particular action unless it has some bearing on what they do. The intention or motive behind a behavior is an important component of that behavior. For instance, in ethical formalism (which we will discuss in Chapter 2), one must know the intent of an action to be able to judge it as moral or immoral, but one also must have some action to examine before making a moral judgment.

ONLY HUMAN ACTS Second, judgments of moral or ethical behavior are directed specifically to human behavior. A dog that bites is not considered immoral or evil, although we may criticize pet owners who allow their dogs the opportunity to bite. Nor do we consider drought, famine, floods, or other natural disasters immoral even though they result in death, destruction, and misery. The devastating earthquake that hit Haiti in 2010 is not considered immoral; although individuals who could have helped victims and did not might be. Philosophers widely believe that only humans can be moral (or immoral) because of our capacity to reason. Because only humans have the capacity to be good—which involves a voluntary, rational decision and subsequent action—only humans, of all members of the animal kingdom, have the capacity to be bad.

There is much more to this argument, of course, and there are those who argue that some mammals show moral traits, if not moral sensibilities. Shermer (2004: 27–28), for instance, recognizes a pre-moral sense in animals, including shame or guilt in dogs, food sharing in bats, comforting and cooperative behaviors in chimpanzees, life-saving behaviors in dolphins and elephants, and defending behaviors in whales. Mammals, especially apes, monkeys, dolphins, and whales, exhibit attachment and bonding, cooperation and mutual aid, sympathy and empathy, direct and indirect reciprocity, altruism and reciprocal altruism, conflict resolution and peacemaking, deception and deception detection, community concern and caring about what others think, and awareness of and response to the social rules of the group.

Does this mean, then, that these mammals can be considered moral or immoral? Although they may be placed on the continuum of moral awareness closer to humans than other species, one could also argue that they do not possess the moral rationality of humans. They do not, as far as we know, freely choose to be good or bad, nor do they judge their fellow animals as right or wrong.

FREE WILL In addition to limiting discussions of morality to human behavior, we usually further restrict our discussion to behavior that stems from free will and free action. Moral culpability is not assigned to persons who are not sufficiently aware of the world around them to be able to decide rationally what is good or bad. The two groups traditionally exempt from responsibility in this sense are the young and the insane, similarly to what occurs when ascribing legal culpability.

Arguably, we do not judge the morality of their behavior because we do not believe that they have the capacity to reason and, therefore, cannot choose to be moral or immoral. Although we may punish a 2-year-old for hitting a baby, we do so to educate or socialize, not to punish, as we would an older child or adult. We incapacitate the violent mentally ill to protect ourselves, but we consider them sick, not evil. This is true even if their actual behavior is indistinguishable from that of other individuals we do punish. For example, a murder may result in a death sentence or a hospital commitment, depending on whether the person is judged to be sane or insane, responsible or not responsible.

AFFECTS OTHERS Finally, we usually discuss moral or immoral behavior only in cases in which the behavior significantly affects others. For instance, throwing a rock off a bridge would be neither good nor bad unless you could possibly hit or were aiming at a person below. If no one is there, your behavior is neutral. If someone is below, however, you might endanger that person's life, so your behavior is judged as bad.

All the moral dilemmas we will discuss in this book involve at least two parties, and the decision to be made affects at least one other individual in every case. In reality, it is difficult to think of an action that does not affect others, however indirectly. Even self-destructive behavior is said to harm the people who love us and who would be hurt by such actions.

We sense that these elements are important in judging morality when we hear the common rationale of those who, when judged as doing something wrong, protest, "But nobody was hurt!" or "I didn't mean to." Indeed, even a hermit living alone on a desert island may engage in immoral or unethical actions. Whether he wants to be or not, the hermit is part of human society; therefore, some people would say that even he might engage in actions that could be judged immoral if they degrade or threaten the future of humankind, such as committing suicide or polluting the ocean.

One's actions toward nature also might be defined as immoral, so relevant actions include not only actions done to people but also to animals and to the environment. To abuse or exploit animals can be defined as immoral. Judgments can be made against cockfighting, dog racing, laboratory experimentation on animals, and hunting. The growing area of environmental ethics reflects increasing concern for the future of the planet. The rationale for environmental ethics may be that any actions that harm the environment affect all humans. It also might be justified by the belief that humankind is a part of nature—not superior to it—and part of natural law should be to protect, not exploit, our world.

Thus far, we know that morality and ethics concern the judgment of behavior as right or wrong. Furthermore, such judgments are directed only at voluntary human behavior that affects other people, the earth, and living things. We can further restrict our inquiries regarding ethics to those behavioral decisions that are relevant to one's profession in the criminal justice system. Discussions regarding the ethics of police officers, for instance, would concern issues such as the following:

- Whether to take gratuities
- Whether to cover up the wrongdoing of a fellow officer
- Whether to sleep on duty

Discussions regarding the ethics of defense attorneys might include the following:

- Whether to devote more effort to private cases than appointed cases
- Whether to allow perjury
- Whether to attack the character of a victim in order to defend a client

Of course, all of these actions affect other people, as do most actions taken as a professional. Most behaviors that might be judged as ethical or not for criminal justice professionals fall into four major categories:

- Acts involving citizens/clients (i.e., misuses of authority, harassment, malfeasance or misfeasance)
- Acts involving other employees (i.e., harassment, gossip, lying)

- Acts involving one's organization (i.e., theft, work ethic, filing false reports)
- Acts involving those one supervises (i.e., arbitrary discipline, unrealistic demands, discouraging honest criticism)

In this text, we will present some of the unique issues and dilemmas related to each area of criminal justice. It is important, first, however, to explore the means available for analyzing and evaluating the "right" course of action.

Morality and Behavior

One of the most difficult things to understand about human behavior is the disjunction between moral beliefs and behavior. We all can attest to the reality that believing something is wrong does not always prevent us from doing it. Often, we engage in acts that we believe are bad, such as lying, stealing, and cheating. Some individuals, such as the ones highlighted in the White Collar Crime box, engage in very wrong acts, despite their great wealth. It seems obvious that these successful, educated men knew their conduct was wrong, but this knowledge did not stop them.

Why do people engage in behavior that they believe to be wrong? Criminology attempts to explain why people commit unlawful acts, but the larger question is this: why do any of us engage in wrongful acts? Unfortunately, even though over 80 percent of college students believe cheating to be wrong, most have cheated on tests or papers (McCabe

White Collar Crime: How Much is Enough?

While one might be able to understand why someone who is poor may shoplift or commit burglary, it is much harder to understand why those who seem to have plenty of money commit crimes to get even more. We have seen a steady stream of individuals convicted and punished for white collar crimes involving millions of dollars. The question is evidently not whether they knew what they were doing was wrong, but rather, how much money is ever enough

Allen Stanford The most recent king of the Ponzi schemes, Stanford has been charged with running a $7 billion scheme. A Ponzi scheme is when an offender convinces investors that they can make large returns on their money and uses subsequent investors to pay earlier ones. As long as new investors are convinced to put in their money, the scheme continues. It collapses when investors want to withdraw their principal—because there isn't any. This flamboyant businessman, who was awarded a knighthood in the tiny Caribbean country of Antigua, is believed to have defrauded thousands of investors, using the money to fund a profligate lifestyle.

Bernard Madoff Madoff obtained notoriety in one of the largest Ponzi schemes ever uncovered, stealing between $10 and $20 billion. He defrauded thousands of investors, including many charitable organizations. Madoff is serving a 150-year sentence for his crimes.

Dennis Kozlowski The former head of Tyco International was convicted and sentenced to 8 to 25 years for misappropriating more than $400 million from the company.

Lord Conrad Black This newspaper magnate was convicted in 2007 of diverting funds from his company to his personal use. He was sentenced to 78 months.

Andrew Fastow and Jeffrey Skilling The former Enron CFO and CEO were sentenced for fraud, insider trading, money laundering, and conspiracy for concealing the company's true financial situation from federal regulators and shareholders. They are currently in federal prison.

Bernard Ebbers This former WorldCom CEO was convicted of an $11 billion fraud against investors.

Source: BusinessWeek Online, July 6, 2006, www. businessweek.com/magazine/content/06_06/b3970083. htm (accessed June 28, 2010).

and Trevino, 1996). Some looters in New Orleans after Hurricane Katrina may have been stealing food as a matter of necessity, but many others exploited the natural disaster to take what belonged to others. Theories abound endorsing everything from learning and role modeling to biological predisposition, but we still haven't answered fundamental questions of causation. Even with all the scientific and philosophical attempts to explain human action, we are left with troubling questions when we read or hear about people who kill, steal, or otherwise offend our sense of morality. Evil is still one of the great mysteries of life.

In discussions concerning these questions, basic beliefs about the nature of humankind must be considered. Are people fundamentally bad and held in check only by rules and fear of punishment? Or are people fundamentally good and commit bad acts because of improper upbringing or events that subvert their natural goodness? Or are there fundamentally bad and fundamentally good people who are just "born that way" for no reason? An applied ethics approach, as we will illustrate below, presumes that individuals generally prefer to do what is right. In those circumstances where the right thing to do is unclear, there are steps to take to help make the decision easier.

Analyzing Ethical Dilemmas

ethical issues Difficult social questions that include controversy over the "right" thing to do.

Ethical discussions in criminal justice focus on issues or dilemmas. **Ethical issues** are broad social questions, often concerning the government's social control mechanisms and the impact on those governed—for example, what laws to pass, what sentences to attach to certain crimes, whether to abolish the death penalty, and whether to build more prisons or use community correctional alternatives. The typical individual does not have much control over these issues. The ethical issues that arise in relation to criminal justice are serious, difficult, and affect people's lives in fundamental ways. These are just a sample of some criminal justice issues that have ethical implications:

- Decriminalization of soft drugs
- Megan's Law and other sex-offender registry statutes
- The death penalty
- Mandatory DNA registries
- Three-strikes legislation
- Racial profiling
- Law-enforcement corruption
- Waiver of juveniles to adult courts
- Citizen oversight committees for police departments
- The Patriot Act and other challenges to civil liberties in the wake of terrorism

Periodically we will highlight a criminal justice policy issue in this text to illustrate the relationships among law, policy, and ethics. The issue of the medical use of marijuana is examined in this chapter's Policy Box.

ethical dilemmas Situations in which it is difficult to make a decision, either because the right course of action is not clear or the right course of action carries some negative consequences.

While ethical issues are broad social questions, **ethical dilemmas** are situations in which one person must make a decision about what to do. Either the choice is unclear or the right choice will be difficult because of the costs involved. Ethical dilemmas involve the individual struggling with personal decision making, whereas ethical issues are topics for which one might have an opinion but rarely a chance to take a stand that has much impact (unless one happens to be a Supreme Court judge or a state governor).

POLICY ISSUES   Medical Use of Marijuana

Controversy exists over whether marijuana should be legalized for the limited use of pain relief and nausea control for seriously ill individuals, including cancer patients and those individuals suffering from AIDS. Many medical professionals have testified in state and federal hearings that they believe that marijuana is more effective and has fewer side effects than other forms of legal pain relief. Others dispute the findings. There has been a move recently in several states to pass medical marijuana laws that allow for limited use of small amounts of marijuana if it is medically prescribed.

Laws

The federal government's drug laws do not make an exception for the medical use of marijuana. California passed a law allowing medical uses of marijuana to be regulated but decriminalized. The Supreme Court held that the federal laws "trumped" California law. As of 2010, there are 10 states that have passed some version of a medical marijuana law, allowing for some limited prescription of marijuana, but federal laws against any use still remain.

Policy

Federal drug officials under President George W. Bush made it clear that they would enforce the federal laws against doctors and medical co-ops that distribute marijuana. In a new development, after President Obama took office, the Justice Department has indicated that they will not pursue these types of cases in states that have laws allowing for the use of medically prescribed marijuana. This constitutes a substantial change in policy for the Justice Department.

Individual ethics

Doctors, and others, must decide whether to violate the federal law regulating the use of marijuana, even if they happen to be in a state that has passed a medical use law. Personal ethical systems determine whether these individuals will risk arrest for their actions. Personal ethical systems may also influence individuals to seek a change in the law (in either direction) to match their own personal views on the issue (see *Raich v. Ashcroft*, 248 F.Supp. 2d 918 [N.D. Cal. 2003]; also see www.drugpolicy.org/marijuana/medical/).

At times, one's belief regarding an ethical issue gives rise to a personal dilemma. In 2000, George Ryan, then governor of Illinois, declared a moratorium on use of the death penalty in his state when at least five individuals on death row were exonerated through the use of DNA evidence. One of his last acts as he left office in 2003 was to commute the sentences of all 160 prisoners on death row to life without parole.

Governor Ryan faced a difficult personal dilemma because he was in a position to do something about his belief that the death penalty was implemented in a way that could never be just. The strong support *and* strong opposition to his action indicate the depth of his dilemma and the seriousness of the issue. In a sad and ironic footnote to this story, Ryan ended up in prison himself after being convicted of federal racketeering charges and sentenced to a six-and-a-half-year sentence in a federal prison. Evidence proved that he had been involved in a system of "sweetheart deals" and backroom bribes selling government contracts since he had been secretary of state (Schaper, 2007).

Sadly, there are additional examples of public figures whose private lives aren't consistent with their public actions. Eliot Spitzer, governor of New York who was elected on a law-and-order platform, resigned in March 2008 after it was revealed that he had paid thousands of dollars to prostitutes. Even though he consistently took courageous stands to promote the public good as part of his professional duties, his private decisions led him to break the law and engage in marital infidelity. Then, Lieutenant Governor David Paterson, who stepped in as governor after Spitzer's resignation, admitted that both he and his wife had engaged in extramarital affairs, and that he had tried marijuana and cocaine in the 1970s when he was in college. Later it was revealed that he helped his lover get a government job.

Although most of us do not have the power to commute death sentences or sign laws into effect, we can also act upon our beliefs. Writing letters, petitioning our legislators, marching in demonstrations, and working to pass (or overturn) laws are examples of acting on our moral beliefs. Personal ethical dilemmas arise when the individual is forced to choose between two or more behaviors. In applied ethics texts, various authors set out the steps to take when facing ethical dilemmas. For instance, Ruggiero (2001) advises us to study the details of the case, identify the relevant criteria (obligations, ideals, consequences), determine possible courses of action, and decide which is the most ethical.

Here are the steps we will use throughout this book to clarify any dilemma:

1. *Identify the facts.* Make sure that one has all the facts that are known—not future predictions, not suppositions, not probabilities.

2. *Identify relevant values and concepts.* Concepts are things that cannot be proven empirically.

3. *Identify all possible moral dilemmas for each party involved.* This can help us see that sometimes one's own moral or ethical dilemma is caused by others' actions. For instance, a police officer's ethical dilemma when faced with the wrongdoing of a fellow officer is a direct result of that other officer making a bad choice. It is helpful to see all the moral issues involved to be able to address the central issue.

4. *Decide what is the most immediate moral or ethical issue facing the individual.* This is always a behavior choice, not an opinion. For example, the moral issue of whether abortion should be legalized is quite different from the moral dilemma of whether I should have an abortion if I find myself pregnant. Obviously, one affects the other, but they are conceptually distinct.

5. *Resolve the ethical or moral dilemma by using an ethical system or some other means of decision making.* (Ethical systems will be discussed in Chapter 2.)

Let us refer to the dilemma, at the beginning of this chapter, of the correctional officer who must decide what to do about the possible beating he observed.

1. This officer has to make sure that he has all the facts. Was the inmate hurt? Did his injuries occur during the time the two other officers were in his cell? Is the officer sure that no one reported it? Would the inmate come forward if he believed that someone would testify against the other two officers, or would he deny the assault (if there was one)? What other facts are important to know? Remember that facts are those things that can be proven; however, this does not necessarily mean that the individual facing the dilemma knows what the facts are.

2. The officer might examine the relevant values. In this situation, one can identify duty, legality, honesty, integrity, safety, protection, loyalty, self-preservation, and trust. Are any other values important to resolve the dilemma? Concepts also are important. They are like values in that they are not susceptible to empirical proof, but they are not necessarily values. Although this dilemma may not have any relevant concepts, others do. For instance, the issue of abortion revolves around the value of life, but it is also a concept in that there is no proof of when life begins or ends (although there are facts regarding respiration, brain activity, etc.). Many arguments surrounding ethical issues are really arguments about concepts, not necessarily values or ethical judgments.

3. Several ethical issues come into play here. The first is whether the other officers should have entered the prisoner's cell. There is probably an earlier issue involving whatever the prisoner did to warrant the visit. There is obviously the issue of whether the officer should have let off-duty officers into the cell in the first place. Finally, there is the issue of what the officer should do now that he believes an injustice may have taken place.

4. The most immediate dilemma for the officer is whether or not to come forward with the information.

5. To resolve the dilemma, it is helpful to work through Chapter 2 first because one way to resolve ethical dilemmas is to decide on an ethical system. If the officer was a utilitarian, he would weigh the costs and benefits for all concerned in coming forward and in staying quiet. If he followed duty-based ethics (ethical formalism), he would find the answer once he determined his duty.

CONCLUSION

In this chapter, we defined the terms *morals* and *ethics* as both relate to standards of behavior. We explained why a study of ethics is especially important to criminal justice professionals. It also was noted that not all behaviors would be subject to ethical judgments—only those that are performed by humans who are acting with free will and that affect others.

WALKING THE WALK

Scott Waddle was the captain of the *U.S.S. Greenville* in 2001, a former Eagle Scout whose career in the Navy saw a steady progression of successes resulting in his command of the *Greenville*. A tireless promoter of the Navy and the giant submarine he captained, Waddle sent autographed pictures of the sub to schoolchildren, and he enthusiastically participated in the "distinguished visitor" program, which allowed civilians to accompany the submarine crew on cruises.

During one of these public relations cruises, on February 9, 2001, the submarine captain gave the order for an "emergency blow," a maneuver in which the submarine comes up out of the depths at great speed, breaking the surface of the water like a breaching whale before settling back onto the surface. In a tragic accident, the probabilities of which boggle the mind, the submarine came up under a Japanese trawler carrying students and their teachers, as well as a crew. The submarine smashed it to bits and sent the crew and passengers who survived the initial impact into the ocean. The accident killed nine people and cost more than $100 million in damages and compensation costs.

The ensuing investigation and testimony determined that the person in charge of the radar deferred to Waddle's visual inspection of the surface and didn't tell him of a sonar contact that was within 4,000 yards. Waddle and other officers who manned the periscope had scanned the surface too quickly and missed the small ship in the turbulent swells. Testimony indicated that

after the crash Waddle grimly kept the crew focused, and instructed them over the intercom, "Remember what you saw, remember what happened, do not embellish. Tell the truth and maintain your dignity."

Against his lawyer's advice, Waddle gave up his right to silence in the military tribunal that was held to assess whether to court martial him. He was reported to have said, "This court needs to hear from me—it's the right thing to do." In his testimony, he refused to shift responsibility to others and accepted all blame for the accident. He said, "I'm solely responsible for this truly tragic accident, and for the rest of my life I will have to live with the horrible consequences."

A father of one of the victims was sitting in the room when Waddle testified, and his anger was overcome by Waddle's tearful apology. Waddle ultimately accepted a letter of reprimand that ended his career with the Navy. Then he went to Japan to apologize to the victims' families personally.

In the aftermath of his decision to testify and not fight to keep his career, Waddle reported that he considered suicide, but he moved past his shame and guilt. Today he gives speeches on the experience and advises others of the importance of dealing with failure honestly, one of which was to a Boy Scout awards ceremony in Chattanooga, Tennessee. Speaking to the 500 attendees, he said that the values of honesty and responsibility he learned in Scouting helped him make the decisions he did during the aftermath of the accident.

Sources: Hight, 2005; Putman, 2008; *Newsweek*, 2001.

Professional ethics deals with only those behaviors relevant to one's profession. We make ethical judgments (what we consider right and wrong) using rationales derived from historical and traditional ethical systems. These ethical systems will be described in Chapter 2.

The most important thing to remember is that we all encounter situations where we must determine the ethical or moral course of action among several choices. In the boxes throughout the book titled Walking the Walk, we will offer real-life examples of individuals who faced ethical dilemmas. It is clear that in many of these situations, the easier decision would have been to avoid responsibility, transfer blame, hide behind rationalizations, or refuse to stand up for what is right. By becoming aware of those who uphold ethics in their professional decision making, we can honor them for doing what is right.

This chapter closes with a chapter review, followed by study questions to answer in class or in a journal. These can be helpful to check your understanding of the issues. These are followed by writing/discussion exercises, which have no right or wrong answers and can be the basis for classroom discussions or individual writing assignments. Finally, ethical dilemmas are presented to encourage the reader to practice ethical analysis.

CHAPTER REVIEW

1. Give examples of how discretion permeates every phase of the criminal justice system and creates ethical dilemmas for criminal justice professionals.

Discretion can be defined as the power and authority to choose one of two or more alternative behaviors. At each stage of the criminal justice system, professionals have such discretion: legislators make decisions regarding the creation of laws, police make decisions on the street in their enforcement of those laws, prosecutors make decisions about which arrests to formally prosecute, judges make decisions about which evidence to allow, and correctional professionals make decisions that affect the lives of offenders.

2. Explain why the study of ethics is important for criminal justice professionals.

First, we study ethics because criminal justice is uniquely involved in coercion, which means there are many and varied opportunities to abuse such power. Second, almost all criminal justice professionals are public servants and, thus, owe special duties to the public they serve. Finally, we study ethics to sensitize students to ethical issues and provide tools to help identify and resolve the ethical dilemmas they may face in their professional lives.

3. Learn the definitions of the terms *morals*, *ethics*, *duties*, *superogatories*, and *values*.

The terms *morals* and *ethics* come from Greek and Latin words referring to custom or behavioral practices. Morals refer to what is judged as good conduct. Ethics refers to the study and analysis of what constitutes good or bad conduct. Duties are obligatory acts (by law, practice, or morals). Superogatories are those acts that go above and beyond duties. Values are statements of worth or importance.

4. Describe what behaviors might fall under moral/ethical judgments.

Behaviors that can be adjudged under moral criteria are those that are acts (not thought), committed by humans (not animals), of free will (not by those judged as incompetent), and that affect others.

5. Explain the difference between ethical issues and ethical dilemmas.

Ethical issues are broad social questions, while ethical dilemmas are situations in which one person must make a decision that can be judged as right or wrong, and where what is right is difficult to decide or is hard to do for some other reason.

KEY TERMS

applied ethics
discretion
duties
ethical dilemmas
ethical issues

ethics
imperfect duties
meta-ethics
morals
normative ethics

professional ethics
superogatories
values
wholesight

STUDY QUESTIONS

1. Define a public servant and why public servants should be especially sensitive to ethical issues.

2. Discuss Felkenes's reasons for why it is important for criminal justice professionals to study ethics.

3. Define *morals, ethics, values, duties, superogatories, imperfect duties, meta-ethics, normative ethics,* and *applied ethics.*

4. What are the four elements that specify the types of behaviors that are judged under ethical criteria? Which groups traditionally have been exempt from legal and moral culpability? Why?

5. What are the steps in analyzing an ethical dilemma?

WRITING/DISCUSSION EXERCISES

1. Write an essay about (or discuss) a difficult ethical dilemma that you faced. What was it? What were the options available to you? Who was affected by your decision? Were there any laws, rules, or guidelines that affected your decision? How did you make your decision?

2. Write an essay (or discuss) whether public servants should be held to higher standards than the rest of us. Touch on the following questions in your response: Should we be concerned about a politician who has extramarital affairs? Drinks to excess? Gambles? Uses drugs? Abuses his or her spouse? What if the person is a police officer? A judge? Should a female police officer be sanctioned for posing naked in a men's magazine, using pieces of her uniform as "props"? Should a probation officer socialize in bars that his or her probationers are likely to frequent? Should a prosecutor be extremely active in a political party and then make decisions regarding targets of "public integrity" investigations of politicians?

3. Write an essay (or discuss) the issue of the medical use of marijuana. What do medical studies indicate regarding whether or not it is necessary or the best medical alternative for certain patients? What do critics argue in their opposition to the medical use laws? If you or a loved one were suffering and someone told you that marijuana could ease your pain, would you violate the law or not? Why?

ETHICAL DILEMMAS

Situation 1

A rich businessman's daughter, Patty, had the best of everything all her life. Her future would have included college, a good marriage to a successful young man, and a life of comparative luxury—except that she was kidnapped by a small band of radical extremists who sought to overthrow the government by terror, intimidation, and robbery. After being raped, beaten, and locked in a small, dark closet for many days, continually taunted and threatened, she was told that she must participate with the terrorist gang in a bank robbery; otherwise, she and her family would be killed. During the course of the robbery, a bank guard was shot.

Was her action immoral? What if she had killed the guard? What if the terrorists had kidnapped her mother or father, too, and told her if she didn't cooperate, they would kill her parents immediately? What would you have done in her place? (Readers might recognize this dilemma as the Patty Hearst case. In 1974, the Symbionese Liberation Army, a terrorist group, kidnapped the daughter of Randolph Hearst, the tycoon of a large newspaper chain. Her subsequent capture, trial, conviction, and prison sentence have been portrayed in books and movies and provide ripe material for questions of free will and legal and moral culpability.)

Situation 2

You are taking an essay exam in a college classroom. The test is closed-book and closed-notes, yet you look up and see that the person sitting next to you has hidden under his blue book a piece of paper filled with notes, which he is using to answer some questions. What would you do? Would your answer change if the test was graded on a curve? What if the student were a friend? What would you do if the student was flunking the course and was going to lose the scholarship he needed to stay in school? What about a situation of plagiarism? Would you turn in a student if you knew they turned in a plagiarized paper? Why or why not? If someone cheats in school, isn't it likely that they will be less honest as a criminal justice professional?

Situation 3

You are selected for a jury in a trial of a 64-year-old mother who killed her two adult sons. The two men had Huntington's disease, a degenerative brain disease, and were institutionalized. They were certain to die and would endure much pain and suffering before they expired. The defendant's husband had died from this same disease, and she had nursed him throughout his illness until his death.

The defendant took a gun into the nursing home, kissed her sons good-bye, and then shot them both through the head. She was arrested for first-degree murder. The prosecutor informs you that there is no "mercy killing" defense in the law as it is written.

If you were on the jury, how would you decide this case? What punishment does she deserve? (See "Justice Tempered with Mercy," by K. Ellington, *Houston Chronicle*, January 30, 2003: 10A. The prosecutor accepted a plea of guilty to assisting suicide.)

Situation 4

You are completing an internship with a juvenile probation agency and truly have enjoyed the experience. Although working with the kids is challenging, you see many rewards in the job, especially when you sense that you are reaching a client and making a difference. Mr. Childers, the probation officer with whom you work, is less optimistic about the kids and operates in a strictly by-the-book legalistic manner. He is burned out and basically does his job without getting too involved. Although you respect him, you know you would approach the clients differently if you were to be hired full-time.

One weekend, you are out with friends in a downtown bar frequented by college students. To your surprise, you see Sarah, a 16-year-old probationer, dancing. In watching her, you realize that she is drunk and, in fact, is holding a beer and drinking it while she is dancing with a man who is obviously much older than she is. You go over to her, and she angrily tells you to mind your own business and immediately leaves with the man. Later she comes back into the bar and pleads with you to keep quiet. She is tearfully apologetic and tells you that she already has had several violations of her probation and at the last hearing was told that if she has one more violation, she will be sent to a juvenile detention center. You know that Sarah has been doing much better in school and plans to graduate and even go to college.

On Monday morning, you sit in Mr. Childers's office. What should you tell him?

Situation 5

All your life you have played by the rules. When you went to college, you studied hard and didn't party to the extent that it hurt your grades. During your senior year, you began to make plans to graduate and begin your career. One Friday night, you were in a car with four other students heading home from a bar. Before you knew what happened, the car was hit head on, and all of you were injured seriously. You now are paralyzed and face the rest of your life in a wheelchair. The car that hit you was driven by a drunken student who, coincidentally, was in several of your classes. Several days after you return home from the hospital, he wants to see you. Despite your anger, you do see him, and he begs for your forgiveness. He breaks down and cries and tells you that he had never done anything like that before and wishes he were dead.

Can you forgive him? When he is prosecuted, what would your sentence recommendation be? Would your answers be different if someone had died? What if he had prior drunk-driving incidents? What if he also had committed other crimes and was not a fellow college student?

2

Classic Image/Alamy

Determining Moral Behavior

CHAPTER OBJECTIVES

1. Define deontological and teleological ethical systems, and explain ethical formalism and utilitarianism.
2. Describe how other ethical systems define what is moral—specifically, religion, natural law, ethics of virtue, and ethics of care.
3. Discuss the argument as to whether egoism is an ethical system.
4. Explain the controversy between relativism and absolutism.
5. Identify the three consistent elements of most of the approaches to resolving ethical dilemmas.

Detective Russell Poole was a Robbery-Homicide Division investigator with the Los Angeles Police Department. In 1998, he was assigned an investigation regarding the alleged beating of Ismael Jimenez, a reputed gang member, by LAPD officers, and a suspected cover-up of the incident. In his investigation, he uncovered a pattern of complaints of violence by the anti-gang task force in the Ramparts Division. Gang members told Poole and his partners that a number of officers harassed them, assaulted them, and pressured them to provide untraceable guns. The beating occurred because Jimenez would not provide the officers with a gun. In a search of the house of Officer Rafael Perez, a member of the anti-gang task force, Poole found a box with a half-dozen realistic replica toy guns. He concluded that a number of the officers in the division were "vigilante cops" and requested that the investigation proceed further.

After Poole informed his superiors of what his investigation had uncovered, Bernard Parks, the LAPD chief at the time, ordered Poole to limit his investigation solely to the Jimenez beating. Poole prepared a 40-page report on the Jimenez case for the district attorney's office, detailing the pattern of complaints, alleged assaults, and other allegations of serious wrongdoing on the part of the Rampart officers. Poole's report never reached the district attorney's office because his lieutenant, enforcing the chief's orders, replaced his detailed report with a two-page report written by the lieutenant and another supervisor. Poole knew that in not providing the district attorney's office with all the information he uncovered, he could be charged with obstruction of justice, and the report provided so little information that the officer probably would not even be charged. Poole's lieutenant then asked him to put his name on the report (Golab, 2000).

How did Detective Poole decide what was the right thing to do in this situation? He had conflicting duties and conflicting values. He knew that not signing the report might have serious consequences for his career. How would you determine the right thing to do if you were in a similar situation?

As discussed in Chapter 1, if confronted with an ethical dilemma, one can follow a series of steps to come to an ethical resolution:

1. *Identify the facts*. Identifying all relevant facts is essential as a first step. Most of the important facts in this dilemma are presented in the preceding paragraphs. Sometimes individuals facing a dilemma do not know all the facts, and sometimes the decision to find the facts is an ethical dilemma unto itself.

2. *Identify relevant values and concepts*. One's values of duty, friendship, loyalty, honesty, and self-preservation are usually at the heart of professional ethical dilemmas. In this case, what is Poole's duty? His decision may hinge on his value system; for instance, whether he values his career over honesty or loyalty to his supervisors over law.

3. *Identify all possible moral dilemmas for each party involved*. Recall that this was to help us see that sometimes one's own moral or ethical dilemma is caused by others' actions. Obviously, Poole is in the situation he is in because his supervisor asked him to do something that was unethical and probably illegal. Neither would have been in the situation if the officers who were the target of the investigation had not violated the law. The officers may not have felt compelled to violate the law if they had not been attempting to control criminal gang activity. Thus, we see that usually one's ethical dilemma is prefaced upon others' ethical (or unethical) decisions.

4. *Decide what is the most immediate moral or ethical issue facing the individual*. This is always a behavior choice, not an opinion. Poole's immediate decision is whether to sign the report, despite his misgivings as to its truthfulness.

5. *Resolve the ethical or moral dilemma by using an ethical system or some other means of decision making*.

In this chapter, we will concentrate on the fifth step in the sequence above and present several ethical systems that can help us identify the right thing to do when faced with an ethical dilemma.

Ethical Systems

Our principles of right and wrong form a framework for the way we live our lives. But where do these principles come from? Before you read on, answer the following question: If you believe that stealing is wrong, why do you believe this to be so? You probably said it is because your parents taught you or because your religion forbids it—or maybe because society cannot tolerate people harming one another. Your answer is an indication of your **ethical system**.

ethical system A structured set of principles that defines what is moral.

Ethical systems have a number of characteristics. First, they are the source of moral beliefs. Second, they are the underlying premises from which you make judgments. Third, they are beyond argument. That is, although ethical decisions may become the basis of debate, the decisions are based on fundamental truths or propositions that are taken as a given by the individual employing the ethical system.

C. E. Harris (1986: 33) referred to such ethical systems as *moral theories or moral philosophies* and defined them as a systematic ordering of moral principles. To be accepted as an ethical system, the system of principles must be internally consistent, must be consistent with generally held beliefs, and must possess a type of "moral common sense." Baelz (1977: 19) further described ethical systems as having the following characteristics:

- *They are prescriptive.* Certain behavior is demanded or proscribed. They are not just abstract principles of good and bad but have substantial impact on what we do.

- *They are authoritative.* They are not ordinarily subject to debate. Once an ethical framework has been developed, it is usually beyond question.

- *They are logically impartial or universal.* Moral considerations arising from ethical systems are not relative. The same rule applies in all cases and for everyone.

- *They are not self-serving.* They are directed toward others; what is good is good for everyone, not just the individual.

We don't consciously think of ethical systems, but we use them to make judgments. For instance, we might say that a woman who leaves her children alone to go out drinking has committed an immoral act. That would be a *moral judgment.* Consider that the moral judgment in any discussion is only the tip of a pyramid. If forced to defend our judgment, we would probably come up with some rules of behavior that underlie the judgment. Moral rules in this case might be:

"Children should be looked after."

"One shouldn't drink to excess."

"Mothers should be good role models for their children."

But these moral rules are not the final argument; they can be considered the body of the pyramid. How would you answer if someone forced you to defend the rules by asking "why?" For instance, "Why should children be looked after?" In answering the "why" question, one eventually comes to some form of ethical system. For instance, we might answer, "Because it benefits society if all parents watched out for their children." This would be a utilitarian ethical system. We might have answered the question, "Because every parent's duty is to take care of their children." This is ethical formalism or any duty-based ethical system. Ethical systems form the base of the pyramid. They are the foundation for the moral rules that we live by.

The ethical pyramid is a visual representation of this discussion. In Figure 2.1, the moral judgment discussed above is the tip of the pyramid, supported by moral rules on which the judgment is based. The moral rules, in turn, rest upon a base, which is usually one of the ethical systems that we will cover in this chapter.

deontological ethical system The study of duty or moral obligation emphasizing the intent of the actor as the element of morality.

We will not discuss all possible ethical systems, nor are the brief descriptions here enough to fully explain each of the systems mentioned. The reader would be well advised to consult texts in philosophy and ethics for more detail. However, we will explore and provide brief summaries of the most often used ethical systems.

Deontological and Teleological Ethical Systems

teleological ethical system An ethical system that is concerned with the consequences or ends of an action to determine goodness.

A **deontological ethical system** is one that is concerned solely with the inherent nature of the act being judged. If an act or intent is inherently good (coming from a good will), it is still considered a good act even if it results in bad consequences. A **teleological ethical system** judges the consequences of an act. Even a bad act, if it results in good consequences, can be defined as good under a teleological system. The saying "the end justifies the means" is a teleological statement. The clearest examples of these two approaches are ethical formalism (a deontological or "nonconsequentialist" system) and utilitarianism (a teleological or "consequentialist" system).

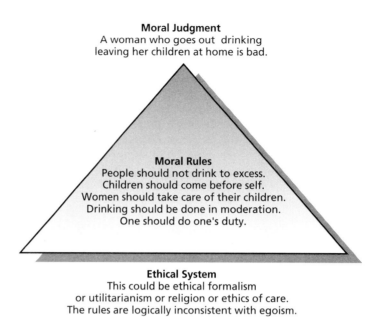

Moral Judgment
A woman who goes out drinking
leaving her children at home is bad.

Moral Rules
People should not drink to excess.
Children should come before self.
Women should take care of their children.
Drinking should be done in moderation.
One should do one's duty.

Ethical System
This could be ethical formalism
or utilitarianism or religion or ethics of care.
The rules are logically inconsistent with egoism.

FIGURE 2.1 ETHICAL PYRAMID: EXAMPLE

ETHICAL FORMALISM

ethical formalism The ethical system espoused by Kant that focuses on duty; holds that the only thing truly good is a good will, and that what is good is that which conforms to the categorical imperative.

Ethical formalism is a deontological system because the important determinant for judging whether an act is moral is not its consequence, but only the motive or intent of the actor. According to the philosopher Immanuel Kant (1724–1804), the only thing that is intrinsically good is a *good will*. On the one hand, if someone does an action from a good will, it can be considered a moral action even if it results in bad consequences. On the other hand, if someone performs some activity that looks on the surface to be altruistic but does it with an ulterior motive—for instance, to curry favor or gain benefit—that act is not moral. Gold, Braswell, and McCarthy (1991) offer the example of a motorist stranded by the side of the road; another driver who comes along has a decision to help or to pass by. If the driver makes a decision to stop and help, this would seem to be a good act. Not so, according to ethical formalism, unless it is done from a good will. If the helper stops because he or she expects payment, wants a return favor, or for any reason other than a good will, the act is only neutral—not moral. Only if the help springs from a good will can we say that it is truly good.

Kant believed that moral worth comes from doing one's duty. Just as there is the law of the family (father's rule), the law of the state and country, and the law of international relations, there is also a universal law of right and wrong. Morality, according to Kant, arises from the fact that humans, as rational beings, impose these laws and strictures of behavior upon themselves (Kant, trans. Beck, 1949).

The following constitute the principles of Kant's ethical formalism (Bowie, 1985: 157):

- *Act only on that maxim through which you can at the same time will that it should become a universal law.* In other words, for any decision of behavior to be made, examine whether that behavior would be acceptable if it were a universal law to be followed by everyone. For instance, a student might decide to cheat on a test, but for this action to be moral, the student would have to agree that everyone should be able to cheat on tests.

- *Act in such a way that you always treat humanity, whether in your own person or that of any other, never simply as a means but always at the same time as an end.* In other words, one should not use people for one's own purposes. For instance, being friendly to someone so that you can use her car is using her as a means to one's own ends. Even otherwise moral actions, such as giving to charity or doing charitable acts for others, would be considered immoral if done for ulterior motives such as self-aggrandizement.

- *Act as if you were, through your maxims, a lawmaking member of a kingdom of ends.* This principle directs that the individual's actions should contribute to and be consistent with universal law. However, the good act must be done freely. If one is compelled to do a good act, the compulsion removes the moral nature of the act. Only when we freely choose to abide by moral law and these laws are self-imposed rather than imposed from the outside are they a reflection of the higher nature of humans.

hypothetical imperatives Statements of contingent demand known as if-then statements (if I want something, then I must work for it); usually contrasted with categorical imperatives (statements of "must" with no "ifs").

categorical imperatives The concept that some things just must be, with no need for further justification, explanation, or rationalization for why they exist (Kant's categorical imperative refers to the imperative that you should do your duty, act in a way you want everyone else to act, and don't use people).

These are absolute commands—together, they form the categorical imperative. According to Kant, **hypothetical imperatives** are commands that designate certain actions to attain certain ends. An example is, "*If* I want to be a success, *then* I must do well in college." By contrast, **categorical imperatives** command action that is necessary without any reference to intended purposes or consequences. The "imperative of morality" according to Kant needed no further justification (Kant, trans. Beck, 1949: 76).

A system such as ethical formalism is considered to be an *absolutist system*—if something is wrong, it is wrong all the time, such as murder or lying. To assassinate evil tyrants such as Adolf Hitler, Saddam Hussein, or Osama Bin Laden might be considered moral under a teleological system because ridding the world of dangerous people is a good end. However, in the deontological view, if the act and intent of killing are wrong, then killing is always wrong; thus, assassination must be considered immoral in all cases, regardless of the good consequences that might result.

This absolute judgment is criticized by those who argue that there are sometimes exceptions to any moral rule such as "one should not lie." In a well-known example, Kant argued that if someone asked to be hidden from an attacker in close pursuit and then the attacker asked where the potential victim was hiding, it would be immoral to lie about the victim's location. This seems wrong to many and serves to dissuade people from seeing the value of ethical formalism. However, according to Kant, an individual cannot control consequences, only actions; therefore, one must act in a moral fashion without regard to potential consequences. In the example, the attacker may not kill the potential victim; the victim may still be able to get away; or the attacker may be justified. The victim may have even left the place you saw them hide and move to the very place you offer to the attacker as a lie. The point is that no one person can control anything in life, so the only thing that makes sense is to live by the categorical imperative.

Kant also defended his position with semantics—distinguishing untruths from lies with the explanation that a lie is a lie only when the recipient is led to believe or has a right to believe that he or she is being told the truth. The attacker in the previous scenario or an attacker who has one "by the throat" demanding one's money has no right to expect the truth; thus, it would not be immoral not to tell this person the truth. Only if one led the attacker to believe that one were going to tell the truth and then did not would one violate the categorical imperative. To not tell the truth when the attacker doesn't deserve the truth is not a lie, but if one intentionally and deliberately sets out to deceive, then that is a lie—even if it is being told to a person who doesn't deserve the truth (Kant, ed. Infield, 1981).

This ethical framework follows simply from the beliefs that an individual must follow a self-imposed moral law and that one is capable of using reason to determine right actions because any action can be evaluated by using the principles just listed. Criticisms of ethical formalism include the following (Maestri, 1982: 910):

- *Ethical formalism seems to be unresponsive to extreme circumstances.* If something is wrong in every circumstance regardless of the good that results or good reasons for the action, otherwise good people might be judged immoral or unethical.
- *Morality is limited to duty.* One might argue that duty is the baseline of morality, not the highest aspiration of it. Further, it is not always clear where one's duty lies. At times one might face a dilemma where two duties conflict with each other.
- *The priority of motive and intent over result is problematic in some instances.* It may be seriously questioned whether the intention to do good, regardless of result or perhaps with negative result, is always moral. Many would argue that the consequences of an action and the actual result must be evaluated to determine morality.

How would ethical formalism help resolve the dilemma faced by Detective Poole, the LAPD officer we discussed in the opening of this chapter? When he was asked to sign the "doctored" report for the district attorney's office, what was his duty? His duty was obviously to uphold the law. Did he also have a duty to obey his superiors? Did he have a duty to protect the police department from scandal? Did he have a duty to serve the public? Could he perform all these duties at the same time, or are they inconsistent with one another?

Applying the principles of ethical formalism to the dilemma, we can make the following observations:

- *Act in such a way that the behavior could be universal.* Would covering up potential police misconduct be a rule that we would want to endorse universally? Probably not. It seems that if evidence is routinely held back from prosecutors, they would not be able to do their job.
- *Do not treat others as a means to an end.* It seems clear that Poole's superiors were attempting to use him to further their own interest. Would he be using someone as a means to an end by signing the shortened report? Would he be using someone as a means to an end by not signing the shortened report?
- *Behavior must be autonomous and freely chosen to be judged as moral.* If Poole were frightened or pressured into doing something, then the action would not be moral regardless of what it was. If, for instance, he believed that the district attorney would find out and come after him for falsifying a legal document, then he might not sign it, but it would not be because of a good will and, therefore, could not be considered a moral act.

Other writers present variations of deontological ethics that do not depend so heavily on Kant (Braswell, McCarthy, and McCarthy, 2002/2007). The core elements of any deontological or duty-based ethical system are the importance placed on intention and the use of a predetermined set of principles to judge morality rather than looking at the consequences of an act.

UTILITARIANISM

utilitarianism The ethical system that claims that the greatest good is that which results in the greatest happiness for the greatest number; major proponents are Bentham and Mill.

Utilitarianism is a teleological ethical system: what is good is determined by the consequences of the action. Jeremy Bentham (1748–1832), a major proponent of utilitarianism, believed that the morality of an action should be determined by how much it contributes to the good of the majority. According to Bentham, human nature seeks to maximize pleasure and avoid pain, and a moral system must be consistent with this natural fact.

The "utilitarian doctrine asserts that we should always act so as to produce the greatest possible ratio of good to evil for everyone concerned" (Barry, 1985: 65). That is, if one can show that an action significantly contributes to the general good, then it is good. In situations where one must decide between a good for an individual and a good for society, then society should prevail, despite the wrong being done to an individual. This is because the utility or good derived from that action generally outweighs the small amount of harm done (because the harm is done only to one, whereas the good is multiplied by the many). For instance, if it could be shown that using someone as an example would be an effective deterrent to crime, whether or not the person was actually guilty, the wrong done to that person by this unjust punishment might be outweighed by the good resulting for society. This assumes that citizens would not find out about the injustice and lose respect for the authority of the legal system, which would be a negative effect for all concerned.

Although utilitarianism is quite prevalent in our thinking about ethical decision making, there are some serious criticisms of it:

- *All "pleasures" or benefits are not equal.* Bentham did not judge the relative weight of utility. He considered pleasure to be a good whether it derived from vice, such as avarice or greed, or from virtue, such as charity and kindness. Later utilitarians, primarily John Stuart Mill (1806–1873), believed that utilities (benefits) had different weights or values. In other words, some were better than others. For instance, art offers a different utility for society than alcohol; altruism carries more benefit than pleasure, and so on. But who is to determine which is better? Determining what is good by weighing utilities makes sense, but the actual exercise is sometimes very difficult.

- *The system presumes that one can predict the consequences of one's actions.* In the well-known "lifeboat" dilemma, five people are in a lifeboat with enough food and water only for four. It is certain that they will survive if there are only four; it is also certain that they will all perish if one does not go overboard. What should be done? Under ethical formalism, it would be unthinkable to sacrifice an innocent, even if it means that all will die. Under utilitarian ethics, it is conceivable that the murder of one might be justified to save the others. But this hypothetical situation points out the fallacy of the utilitarian argument. In reality, it is not known whether any will survive. The fifth might be murdered, and five minutes later a rescue ship appears on the horizon. The fifth might be murdered, but then the remaining four are eaten by sharks. Only in unrealistic hypothetical situations does one absolutely know the consequences of one's action. In real life, one never knows if an action will result in a greater good or ultimate harm.

- *There is little concern for individual rights in utilitarianism.* Ethical formalism demands that each individual must be treated with respect and not be used as a means to an end. However, under utilitarianism, the rights of one individual may be sacrificed for the good of many. For instance, in World War II, Winston Churchill allowed Coventry to be bombed so the Germans would not know the Allies had cracked the Germans' secret military radio code. Several hundred English people were killed in the bombing raid of Coventry. Many might have been saved if they had been warned. It was a calculated loss for greater long-term gains—bringing the war to an end sooner. This could be justified under utilitarianism but perhaps not under ethical formalism.

Utilitarianism has two forms: act utilitarianism and rule utilitarianism. The basic difference between the two can be summarized as follows: In **act utilitarianism**, only the basic utility derived from an action is examined. We look at the consequences of any action for all involved and weigh the units of utility accordingly. In **rule utilitarianism**, one judges that action in reference to the precedent it sets and the long-term utility of the rule set by that action.

On the one hand, act utilitarianism might support stealing food when one is hungry and has no other way to eat because the utility of survival would outweigh the loss to the store owner. On the other hand, rule utilitarianism would be concerned with the effect

act utilitarianism The type of utilitarianism that determines the goodness of a particular act by measuring the utility (good) for all, but only for that specific act and without regard for future actions.

rule utilitarianism The type of utilitarianism that determines the goodness of an action by measuring the utility of that action when it is made into a rule for behavior.

that the action would have if made into a rule for behavior: "Any time an individual cannot afford food, he or she can steal it" would contribute to a state of lawlessness and a general disrespect for the law. Such a rule would probably not result in the greatest utility for the greatest number. With rule utilitarianism, then, we are concerned not only with the immediate utility of the action but also with the long-term utility or harm if the action were to be a rule for all similar circumstances. Note the similarity between rule utilitarianism and the first principle of the categorical imperative. In both approaches, one must judge as good only those actions that can be universalized.

Applying utilitarianism to Detective Russell Poole's dilemma, it seems clear that his superiors were engaged in damage control. They did not want a scandal, especially considering that it had not been that long since the Rodney King incident. By suppressing evidence of further wrongdoing, they probably assumed that they could keep the information from the public and deal with it internally. In fact, Chief Parks fired more than 100 officers during his time as chief, but he did so in a way that the district attorney's office was unable to prosecute any of the officers for their alleged crimes. Internal Affairs routinely used a practice of compelling testimony without reading the officer his rights before questioning. This meant that the evidence obtained could be used to discipline the officer but not to prosecute him or her. The result was that officers were fired, but their cases never ended up in court—or in the newspaper.

If Detective Poole used utilitarian reasoning, where did the greatest benefit lie? Was there greater benefit to all concerned in opposing his superiors' attempts to suppress the investigation, or with going along with the cover-up? Actually, the attempt to suppress the actions of the Ramparts Division officers was unsuccessful anyway. A year after Poole refused to sign the report that protected Officer Rafael Perez, Perez was prosecuted for stealing a large amount of cocaine from the evidence room. In a plea arrangement, he told investigators from the D.A.'s office the whole story of the Ramparts Division officers, leading to the biggest scandal in LAPD's history (Golab, 2000; Boyer, 2001). This illustrates one of the problems with utilitarianism: if people sacrifice their integrity for what they consider is a good cause, the result may be that they lose their integrity and still do not achieve their good cause.

In summary, utilitarianism holds that morality must be determined by the consequences of an action. Society and the survival and benefit of all are more important than any individual. Something is right when it benefits the continuance and good health of society. Rule utilitarianism may be closer to the principles of ethical formalism because it weighs the utility of such actions after they have been made into general laws. The difference between ethical formalism and rule utilitarianism is that the actions themselves are judged right or wrong depending on the motives behind them under ethical formalism, whereas utilitarianism looks to the long-term consequences of the prescribed rules to determine their morality. Which of the ethical systems support Joseph Darby's decision described in the Walking the Walk box?

Other Ethical Systems

Utilitarianism and ethical formalism are the two best representatives of deontological and teleological ethics. It should be noted, however, that the discussion of ethics existed before Kant and Bentham; for instance, we haven't discussed the views of Socrates, Plato, or Epicurus and, unfortunately, have no space to do so in this text. The debate has also continued into modern times through the work of Friedrich Nietzsche, Jean-Paul Sartre, John Rawls, Alasdair MacIntyre, John Finnis, Nel Noddings, and many others. We continue to ponder the ancient questions of what it means to be a good person. A few additional ethical systems will be described below, but the interested reader is urged to supplement this reading with any standard ethics text.

WALKING THE WALK

Joe Darby was a military reservist from a low-income family who grew up in Pennsylvania and settled in Maryland. The 372nd was a military police unit based in his town, and almost everyone had some ties to the military. Darby's unit was deployed to Iraq.

One fateful day in January 2004, Darby began his march into the history books by asking Specialist Charles Graner for some pictures of the surrounding countryside. Graner gave him a CD of pictures. Clicking through the pictures to decide which ones to send home, he stumbled on some that, at first, made him laugh; then, as others appeared on the computer screen, he grew more and more disgusted. "They just didn't sit right with me," he said later.

The pictures were the infamous torture photos taken in the Abu Ghraib prison by Graner and others. Whether Graner didn't remember that they were on the CD or didn't care will never be known; however, once Darby saw the pictures, he couldn't stop thinking about them. He had not been present and did not know that soldiers had been posing the prisoners nude, forcing them to simulate masturbation and homosexual acts, using dogs to intimidate and attack the naked prisoners, and placing them on stools and telling them if they fell off they would be electrocuted.

Darby had seen other things at the prison, though, which he related years later in news accounts—things like a helicopter flying into the prison grounds in the middle of the night with a prisoner being hustled into the interrogation room by men who not only were nameless but who never revealed whether they were military intelligence, CIA, or civilian contractors. When they left the next morning, the prisoner was dead and the soldiers were told to "clean it up."

The pictures of Charles Graner and Sabrina Harmon (another military police specialist) posing next to the body of this man are part of the group of photos that were plastered across newspapers, shown on televisions, and appeared on Internet sites around the world. The scandal tarnished the reputation of the United States, probably contributed to an increase in the Iraqi insurgency, ruined careers, and ended up with the soldiers in the pictures serving prison time.

So why did Darby do it? Why did he burn copies of the pictures onto a disk and give them to the Criminal Intelligence Division (CID) rather than to his commanding officer? He said later that it was because things had been reported to his superiors before and nothing happened, and, besides, Ivan Frederick, one of those who appeared in the pictures, was the commanding officer of the night shift. Darby first turned in the envelope with the photos to CID investigators and said he didn't know where it came from, but then he admitted that he had gotten the pictures from Graner. He was promised that his name would be kept confidential.

Once investigators obtained the photos, they immediately began an investigation and questioned all those in the pictures who were then, inexplicably, allowed to remain in the compound. Tension and paranoia were intense, and Darby said he literally feared for his life, hoping that no one would discover that it was he who had turned them in. "I'm not the kind of guy to rat somebody out," he said later. "I've kept a lot of secrets for soldiers…but this crossed the line to me. I had the choice between what I knew was morally right and my loyalty to other soldiers. I couldn't have it both ways."

At some point, his name was leaked to the press, and then Secretary of Defense Donald Rumsfeld announced in the congressional hearing about Abu Ghraib that Darby was the one who turned in the photos. Darby was sitting in a crowded mess hall in Iraq when the hearing was being aired on the television. The room became quiet. Although some soldiers shook Darby's hand, many regarded him as a traitor. So did most of his neighbors and even some of his family. His wife endured weeks of threats and vandalism before she was taken into protective custody by the military. Neighbors said he was a rat, a traitor, and should fear for his life. Darby, too, was removed from Iraq ahead of his unit and reunited with his wife in seclusion and under heavy guard. He was told that it wasn't safe to return to their hometown, and he didn't. They are not welcome there. His tour of duty was extended through the trials, which lasted through 2006. In 2005, Darby received the John F. Kennedy Profile in Courage Award.

Today, the media storm that Darby created has finally died down and he is a civilian trying to create a new life. He does not regret what he did. "I've always had a moral sense of right and wrong. And I knew that, you know, friends or not, it had to stop," Darby says.

Sources: Hylton, 2006; CBS.news.com, 2005; CBS.news.com, 2007; Gourevitch and Morris, 2008.

RELIGION

Probably the most frequently used source of individual ethics is religion. Religion might be defined as a body of beliefs that addresses fundamental issues such as "What is life?" and "What are good and evil?" A religion also provides moral guidelines and directions on how to live one's life. For instance, Christians and Jews are taught the Ten Commandments, which prohibit certain behaviors defined as wrong. The authority of **religious ethics**, in particular Judeo-Christian ethics, stems from a willful and rational God. For believers, the authority of God's will is beyond question, and there is no need for further examination because of His perfection. The only possible controversy comes from human interpretation of God's commands. Indeed, these differences in interpretation are the source of most religious strife.

religious ethics The ethical system that is based on religious beliefs of good and evil; what is good is that which is God's will.

Religious ethics is, of course, much broader than simply Judeo-Christian ethics. Religions such as Buddhism, Confucianism, and Islam also provide a basis for ethics because they offer explanations of how to live a "good life" and address other philosophical issues, such as "What is reality?" Pantheistic religions—such as those of primitive hunter-gatherer societies—promote the belief that there is a living spirit in all things. A basic principle follows from this belief that life is important and one must have respect for all things, including trees, rivers, and animals. A religion must have a willful and rational God or god figure before there can be a judgment of right and wrong, thus providing a basis for an ethical system. Those religions that do have a god figure consider that figure to be the source of principles of ethics and morality.

It is also true that of the religions we might discuss, many have similar basic moral principles. Many religions have their own version of the Ten Commandments. In this regard, Islam is not too different from Judaism, which is not too different from Christianity. What Christians know as the Golden Rule actually predates Christianity, and the principle can be found in all the major religions, as well as offered by ancient philosophers:

- Christianity: "Do unto others as you would have them do unto you."
- Hinduism: "Do naught to others which, if done to thee, would cause thee pain: this is the sum of duty."
- Buddhism: "In five ways should a clansman minister to his friends and familiars… by treating them as he treats himself."
- Confucianism: "What you do not want done to yourself, do not do unto others."
- Judaism: "Whatsoever thou wouldst that men should not do unto thee, do not do that to them." (Reiman, 1990/2004: 147)
- Isocrates: "Do not do to others what would anger you if done to you by others." (Shermer, 2004: 25)
- Diogenes Laertius, *Lives of the Philosophers:* "The question was once put to Aristotle how we ought to behave to our friends; and his answer was, 'As we should wish them to behave to us.'" (Shermer, 2004: 25)
- The Mahabharata: "This is the sum of all true righteousness, deal with others as thou wouldst thyself be dealt by. Do nothing to thy neighbor which thou wouldst not have him do to thee hereafter." (Shermer, 2004: 25)

A fundamental question discussed by philosophers and religious scholars is whether God commands us not to commit an act because it is inherently wrong (e.g., "Thou shalt not kill"), or whether an act acquires its "badness" or "goodness" solely from God's definition of it. This is a thorny issue and one that continues to be debated.

Another issue in Western religious ethics is how to determine God's will. Some believe that God is inviolable and that positions on moral questions are absolute. This is a legalist position. Others believe that God's will varies according to time and place—the situationalist position. According to this position, situational factors are important in determining the rightness of a particular action. Something may be right or wrong depending on the circumstances (Borchert and Stewart, 1986: 157). For instance, lying may be wrong unless it is to protect an innocent, or stealing may be wrong unless it is to protest injustice and to help unfortunates. Some would say that it is impossible to have an *a priori* knowledge of God's will because that would put us above God's law: we ourselves cannot be "all-knowing." Thus, for any situation, if we are prepared to receive God's divine commands, we can know them through faith and conscience. Box 2.1 briefly describes some of the major world religions other than Judeo-Christianity.

BOX 2.1

Overview of Major World Religions

Islam

One of the newest, yet largest, religions is Islam. Like Christianity, this religion recognizes one god, Allah. Jesus and other religious figures are recognized as prophets, as is Muhammad, who is considered to be the last and greatest prophet. Islam is based on the Quran, which is taken much more literally as the word of Allah than the Bible is taken by most Christians. There is a great deal of fatalism in Islam: *Inshallah*, meaning, "If God wills it," is a prevalent theme in Muslim societies, but there is recognition that if people choose evil, they do so freely. The five pillars of Islam are (1) repetition of the creed (*Shahada*), (2) daily prayer (*Salah*), (3) almsgiving (*Zakat*), (4) fasting (*Sawm*), and (5) pilgrimage (*Hajj*).

Another feature of Islam is the idea of the holy war. In this concept, the faithful who die defending Islam against infidels will be rewarded in the afterlife (Hopfe, 1983). This is not to say that Islam provides a legitimate justification for terroristic acts. Devout Muslims protest that terrorists have subverted the teachings of Islam and do not follow its precepts, one of which is never to harm innocents.

Buddhism

Siddhartha Gautama (Buddha) attained enlightenment and preached to others how to do the same and achieve release from suffering. He taught that good behavior is that which follows the "middle path" between asceticism and hedonistic pursuit of sensual pleasure. Essentials of Buddhist teachings are ethical conduct, mental discipline, and wisdom. Ethical conduct is based on universal love and compassion for all living beings. Compassion and wisdom are needed in equal measures. Ethical conduct can be broken into right speech (refraining from lies, slander, enmity, and rude speech), right action (abstaining from destroying life, stealing, and dishonest dealings, and helping others lead peaceful and honorable lives), and right livelihood (abstaining from occupations that bring harm to others, such as arms dealing and killing animals). To follow the "middle path," one must abide by these guidelines (Kessler, 1992).

Confucianism

Confucius taught a humanistic social philosophy that included central concepts such as *Ren*, which is human virtue and humanity at its best, as well as the source of moral principles; *Li*, which is traditional order, ritual, or custom; *Xiao*, which is familial love; and *Yi*, which is rightness, both a virtue and a principle of behavior—that is, one should do what is right because it is right. The *doctrine of the mean* exemplifies one aspect of Confucianism that emphasizes a cosmic or natural order. Humans are a part of nature and are included in the scheme of life. Practicing moderation in one's life is part of this natural order and reflects a "way to Heaven" (Kessler, 1992).

Hinduism

In Hinduism, the central concept of *karma* can be understood as consequence. Specifically, what one does in one's present life will determine what happens in a future life. The goal is to escape the eternal birth/rebirth cycle by living one's life in a moral manner so no bad karma will occur (Kessler, 1992). People start out life in the lowest caste, but if they live a good life, they will be reborn as members of a higher caste, until they reach the highest Brahman caste, and at that point the cycle can end. An early source for Hinduism was the Code of Manu. In this code are found the ethical ideals of Hinduism, which include pleasantness, patience, control of mind, refraining from stealing, purity, control of the senses, intelligence, knowledge, truthfulness, and non-irritability (Hopfe, 1983).

According to Barry (1985; 51–54), human beings can "know" God's will in three ways:

- *Individual conscience.* An individual's conscience is the best source for discovering what God wants one to do. If one feels uncomfortable about a certain action, it is probably wrong.
- *Religious authorities.* These authorities can interpret right and wrong for us and are our best source if we are confused about certain actions.
- *Holy scriptures.* The third way is to go directly to the Bible, Quran, or Torah as the source of God's law. Some believe that the written word of God holds the answers to all moral dilemmas.

Strong doubts exist as to whether any of these methods are true indicators of divine command. Our consciences may be no more than the products of our psychological development, influenced by our environment. Religious authorities are, after all, only human, with human failings. Even the Bible seems to support contradictory principles. For instance, advocates of capital punishment can find passages in the Bible that support it (such as Genesis 9:6: "Whoever sheds the blood of man, by man shall his blood be shed…"), but opponents to capital punishment argue that the New Testament offers little direct support for execution and has many more passages that direct one to forgive, such as Matthew 5:38–40: "…Offer no resistance to injury. When a person strikes you on the right cheek, turn and offer him the other."

The question of whether people can ever know God's will has been explored through the ages. St. Thomas Aquinas (1225–1274) believed that human reason was sufficient not only to prove the existence of God but also to discover God's divine commands. Others believe that reason is not sufficient to know God and that it comes down to unquestioning belief, so reason and knowledge must always be separate from faith. These people believe that one can know whether an action is consistent with God's will only if it contributes to general happiness, because God intends for us to be happy, or when the action is done through the *holy spirit*—that is, when someone performs the action under the influence of true faith (Borchert and Stewart, 1986: 159–171).

To summarize, the religious ethics system is widely used and accepted. The authority of the god figure is the root of all morality; basic conceptions of good and evil or right and wrong come from interpretations of the god figure's will. Many people throughout history have wrestled with the problem of determining what is right according to God. Religion continues to dominate national conversations, as the In the News box illustrates.

in the NEWS

PACT WITH THE DEVIL?

After the devastating earthquake that hit Haiti in 2010, the televangelist Pat Robertson created a type of media earthquake himself when he explained that Haiti's problems were due to a pact with the devil. He declared on national television that Haitian voodoo priests had made a deal with the devil to gain their independence and that, because of this rejection of God, the small country has been battered by hurricanes and other natural disasters, and suffered extreme poverty and other problems. The firestorm that erupted condemned Robertson's lack of compassion for the victims, and caused him to retract his statements. The incident created an interesting national debate about religion, causation, and God's judgments, and shows us the central place religion continues to have in our national conversations about good and evil.

SOURCE: Fletcher, 2010.

NATURAL LAW

natural law The idea that principles of morals and rights are inherent in nature and not human-made; such laws are discovered by reason but exist apart from humankind.

The **natural law** ethical system holds that there is a universal set of rights and wrongs that is similar to many religious beliefs, but without reference to a specific supernatural figure. Originating most clearly with the Stoics, natural law is an ethical system wherein no difference is recognized between physical laws—such as the law of gravity—and moral laws. Morality is part of the natural order of the universe. Further, this morality is the same across cultures and times. In this view, Christians simply added God as a source of law (as other religions added their own prophets and gods), but there is no intrinsic need to resort to a supernatural figure because these universal laws exist quite apart from any religion (Maestri, 1982; Buckle, 1993).

The natural law ethical system presupposes that what is good is what is natural, and what is natural is what is good. The essence of morality is what conforms to the natural world; thus, there are basic inclinations that form the core of moral principles. For instance, the preservation of one's own being is a natural inclination and thus is a basic principle of morality. Actions consistent with this natural inclination would be those that preserve one's own life, such as in self-defense, but also those that preserve or maintain the species, such as a prohibition against murder. Other inclinations are peculiar to one's species—for instance, humans are social animals; thus, sociability is a natural inclination that leads to altruism and generosity. These are natural and thus moral. The pursuit of knowledge or understanding of the universe might also be recognized as a natural inclination of humans; thus, actions that conform to this natural inclination are moral. St. Thomas Aquinas, in *Summa Theologiae*, distinguished natural law from God's law, and placed reason at the epicenter of the natural law system: "Whatever is contrary to the order of reason is contrary to the nature of human beings as such; and what is reasonable is in accordance with human nature as such" (Aquinas as cited in Buckle, 1993: 165).

Souryal (2007: 86) described natural law as the "steward" of natural rights. At least some of the U.S. founders might be described as natural law theorists. The Constitution recognizes "natural rights" endowed by the Creator. However, the idea of natural law originally was more concerned with duties than rights. Fishman (1994) explained that Thomas Hobbes and John Locke transformed the original natural law theory that emphasized duties or obligations of humans in the natural order to one that emphasized "natural" human rights. To stay true to the internal consistency and historical legacy of natural rights theory, one must balance the emphasis on rights with an emphasis on obligations. For instance, the protection of individual freedoms as natural rights is an important component of any democracy, but democracy can exist only when citizens accept and perform the obligations of citizenship. Citizens who are not vigilant in protecting their freedoms through the political process risk losing them. In this sense, natural law theory echoes the emphasis on duty found in ethical formalism.

Natural law theory defines good as that which is natural. The difficulty of this system is identifying what is consistent and congruent with the natural inclinations of humankind. How do we know which acts are in accordance with the natural order of things? Who determines the natural laws?

Natural law has been employed to restrict the rights and liberties of groups of people. So-called "natural" laws regarding the superiority of whites were also used to support and justify slavery. In *Bradwell v. Illinois* 83 U.S. 130 (1873), the Supreme Court upheld Indiana's right to prevent Myra Bradwell from becoming a member of the bar. The state's argument, which the Supreme Court endorsed, was the woman's "natural" role was child-bearer. In their famous "mother of the species" holding, the Court decided that women's childbearing role was a natural destiny and that the sordid world of the courtroom was no place for women. Today, natural law is sometimes employed to oppose same-sex marriage. The fundamental problem with this ethical system is: how does one know whether a moral rule is based upon a true natural law or a mistaken human perception?

THE ETHICS OF VIRTUE

ethics of virtue The ethical system that bases ethics largely upon character and possession of virtues.

Each of the foregoing ethical systems asks, "What is a good action?" The **ethics of virtue** instead asks, "What is a good person?" This ethical system rejects the approach that one might use reason to discover what is good. Instead, the principle is that to be good, one must do good. Virtues that a good person possesses include thriftiness, temperance, humility, industriousness, and honesty. It may be considered a teleological system because it is concerned with acting in such a way as to achieve a happy life (Prior, 1991). The specific "end" pursued is happiness, or *eudaimonia*, but the meaning of this word is not the same as the meaning given by utilitarians. This version of happiness does not mean simply having pleasure, but also living a good life, reaching achievements, and attaining moral excellence.

The roots of this system are in the work of Aristotle, who defined virtues as "excellences." These qualities are what enable an individual to move toward the achievement of what it takes to be human. Aristotle distinguished intellectual virtues (wisdom, understanding) from moral virtues (generosity, self-control). The moral virtues are not sufficient for "the good life"; one must also have the intellectual virtues, primarily "practical reason." Aristotle believed that we are by nature neither good nor evil, but become so through training and the acquisition of habits:

principle of the golden mean Aristotle's concept of moderation, in which one should not err toward excess or deficiency; this principle is associated with the ethics of virtue.

> [T]he virtues are implanted in us neither by nature nor contrary to nature: we are by nature equipped with the ability to receive them and habit brings this ability to completion and fulfillment. (Aristotle, quoted in Prior, 1991: 156–157)

Habits of moral virtue are obtained by following the example of a moral *exemplar*. These habits are also more easily instilled when "right" or just laws also exist. Moral virtue is a state of character in which choices are consistent with the **principle of the golden mean**.

BOX 2.2

Catalog of Virtues

Area	Defect	Mean	Excess
fear	cowardice	courage	recklessness
pleasure	insensitivity	self-control	self-indulgence
money	stinginess	generosity	extravagance
honor	small-mindedness	high-mindedness	vain
anger	apathy	gentleness	short temper
truth	self-depreciation	truthfulness	boastfulness
shame	shamelessness	modesty	self-hate

Source: Aristotle's virtues, adapted from Prior (1991: 165).

This principle states that virtue is always the median between two extremes of character. For instance, proper pride is the mean between empty vanity and undue humility, and so on. The Catalog of Virtues derived from the writings of Aristotle lists others (Box 2.2).

Moral virtue comes from habit, which is why this system emphasizes character. The idea here is that one does not do good because of reason; rather, one does good because of the patterns of a lifetime. Those with good character will do the right thing, and those with bad character usually will choose the immoral path. Every day we are confronted with numerous opportunities to lie, cheat, and steal. When a cashier looks the other way, we could probably filch a $20 bill from the cash drawer; or when a clerk gives us a $10 bill instead of a $1.00 bill by mistake, we could keep it instead of hand it back. We don't because, generally, it does not even occur to us to steal. We do not have to go through any deep ethical analysis in most instances when we have the opportunity to do bad things, because our habits of a lifetime dictate our actions.

Somewhat related to the ethics of virtue ethical system are the 6 Pillars of Character promulgated by the Josephson Institute of Ethics (2008). The 6 Pillars of Character echo Aristotle's virtues.

1. *Trustworthiness*. This concept encompasses honesty and meeting one's obligations. Honesty means to be truthful, forthright, and sincere, and the pillar also involves loyalty, living up to one's beliefs, and having values.

2. *Respect*. This pillar is similar to the second portion of the categorical imperative, which admonishes to treat each person with respect and not as a means to an end. It also encompasses the Golden Rule.

3. *Responsibility*. This means standing up for one's choices and being accountable. Everyone has a moral duty to pursue excellence, but, if one fails, the duty is to take responsibility for the failure.

4. *Fairness*. This concept involves issues of equality, impartiality, and due process. To treat everyone fairly doesn't necessarily mean to treat everyone the same, but rather, to apply fairness in one's dealings with everyone.

5. *Caring*. This pillar encompasses the ideas of altruism and benevolence.

6. *Citizenship*. This includes the duties of every citizen, including voting, obeying the law, being a good steward of the natural resources of one's country, and doing one's fair share.

It should also be noted that most of us have some virtues and not others. There are many other virtues besides those already mentioned, including compassion, courage, conscientiousness, and devotion. Some of us may be completely honest in all of our dealings but not generous. Some may be courageous but not compassionate. Therefore, we all are moral to the extent that we possess moral virtues, but some of us are more moral than others by having more virtues. One difficulty is in judging the primacy of moral virtues. For instance, in professional ethics there are often conflicts that involve honesty and loyalty. If both are virtues, how does one resolve a dilemma in which one virtue must be sacrificed?

The ethics of virtue probably explains more individual behavior than other ethical systems because most of the time, if we have developed habits of virtue, we do not even think about the possible bad acts we might do. For instance, most of us do not have to analyze the rightness or wrongness of stealing every time we go into a store. We do not automatically consider lying every time a circumstance arises. Most of the time we do the right thing because of our habits and patterns of a lifetime. However, when faced with a true dilemma—that is, a choice where the "right" decision is unclear—the ethics of virtue may be less helpful than other ethical systems.

Alasdair MacIntyre (1991: 204), a contemporary philosopher who promotes virtue ethics, defines virtues as those dispositions that will sustain us in the relevant "quest for the good, by enabling us to overcome the harms, dangers, temptations and distractions which we encounter, and which will furnish us with increasing self-knowledge and increasing knowledge of the good." MacIntyre (1999) also seems to endorse an ethics-of-care approach because he discusses virtue as necessary to care for the next generation. He sees life as one of "reciprocal indebtedness" and emphasizes "networks of relationships" as the locale of giving and receiving the benefits of virtues. This language is similar to the ethics of care, which will be discussed next.

In our opening case, Detective Poole reported that he never considered putting his name on a report he knew was wrong. His superiors, co-workers, and colleagues describe him as "professional," "hard working," "loyal, productive, thorough, and reliable," "diligent," "honest," and "extremely credible." He was known as a first-rate investigator and trusted by the D.A.'s office to provide thorough and credible testimony. In other words, his habits in his professional life were directly contrary to participating in a cover-up. Those who advocate the ethics of virtue would predict that Poole would not participate in a cover-up because of his character—and they would be right, because he did not sign the report (Golab, 2000).

THE ETHICS OF CARE

ethics of care The ethical system that defines good as meeting the needs of others and preserving and enriching relationships.

The **ethics of care** is another ethical system that does not depend on universal rules or formulas to determine morality. The emphasis is on human relationships and needs. The ethics of care has been described as a feminine morality because women in all societies are the childbearers and consequently seem to have a greater sensitivity to issues of care. Noddings (1986: 1) points out that the "mother's voice" has been silent in Western, masculine analysis: "One is tempted to say that ethics has so far been guided by Logos, the masculine spirit, whereas the more natural and perhaps stronger approach would be through Eros, the feminine spirit."

The ethics of care is founded in the natural human response to care for a newborn child, the ill, and the hurt. There are similarities in the ethics of care's idea that morals derive from natural human impulses of compassion and Jean-Jacques Rousseau's (1712–1778) argument that it is humans' natural compassion that is the basis of human action and the idea that morality is based in emotion rather than rationality, i.e. "What I feel is right is right, what I feel is wrong is wrong" (Rousseau, as cited by Ruggiero, 2001: 28).

Carol Gilligan's work on moral development in psychology identified a feminine approach to ethical decision making that focused on relationships and needs instead of rights and universal laws. The most interesting feature of this approach is that while a relatively small number of women emphasized needs over rights, no men did. She attributed this to Western society, in which men and women are both socialized to Western ethics, which are primarily concerned with issues of rights, laws, and universalism (Gilligan, 1982).

Applying the ethics of care does not necessarily lead to different solutions, but perhaps to different questions. In an ethical system based on care, we would be concerned with issues of needs rather than rights. Other writers point to some Eastern religions, such as Taoism, as illustrations of the ethics of care (Gold et al., 1991). In these religions, a rigid, formal, rule-based ethics is rejected in favor of gently leading the individual to follow a path of caring for others. In criminal justice, the ethics of care is represented to some extent by the rehabilitative ethic rather than the just-deserts model. Certainly the "restorative justice" movement is consistent with the ethics of care because of its emphasis on the motives and needs of all concerned, rather than simply retribution. In personal relationships, the ethics of care would promote empathy and treating others in a way that does not hurt them. In this view, meeting needs is more important than securing rights.

peacemaking justice
An ancient approach to justice that includes the concepts of compassion and care, connectedness and mindfulness.

In their text, Braswell and Gold (2002) discuss a concept called **peacemaking justice.** They show that the concept is derived from ancient principles, and it concerns care as well as other concepts: "Peacemaking, as evolved from ancient spiritual and wisdom traditions, has included the possibility of mercy and compassion within the framework of justice" (2002: 25). They propose that the peacemaking process is composed of three parts: connectedness, caring, and mindfulness:

- *Connectedness* has to do with the interrelationships we have with one another and all of us have with the earth.

- *Caring* is similar to Noddings's concept that the "natural" inclination of humans is to care for one another.

- *Mindfulness* involves being aware of others and the world in all personal decision making (Braswell and Gold, 2002: 25–37).

To summarize, the ethics of care approach identifies the needs of all individuals in any ethical situation and attempts to maximize them. It is different from utilitarianism, however, in that one person cannot be sacrificed for others. Also, there is an attempt to resolve situations through human relationships and a sense that decisions should come from compassion rather than attention to rights or duties.

Egoism: Ethical System or Not?

egoism The ethical system that defines the pursuit of self-interest as a moral good.

Very simply, **egoism** postulates that what is good for one's survival and personal happiness is moral. The extreme of this position is that all people should operate on the assumption that they can do whatever benefits themselves. Others become solely the means to ensure happiness; there is no recognition of the rights of others under this system. For this reason, some have rejected egoism as an ethical system entirely, arguing that it is fundamentally inconsistent with one of the elements ("they are not self-serving") (Baelz, 1977).

psychological egoism
The concept that humans naturally and inherently seek self-interest, and that we can do nothing else because it is our nature.

Psychological egoism is a descriptive principle rather than an ethical prescription. Psychological egoism holds that humans are naturally egoists and that it would be unnatural for them to be any other way. All species have instincts for survival, and self-preservation and self-interest are merely part of that instinct. Therefore, it is not only moral to be egoistic, but it is the only way we can be, and any other explanations of behavior are mere rationalizations. In behaviors that appear to be altruistic, such as giving to charity or volunteering, the argument goes that these acts provide psychic and emotional pleasure to the individual and that is why they do them, not for some other selfless reason. Even though acts such as running into a burning building or jumping into a river to save victims seem altruistic, psychological egoists believe that these acts occur because of the personality make-up of individuals who derive greater pleasure from being considered heroes, or enjoy the adrenalin rush of the dangerous act, more than the feeling of security derived from staying on the sidelines.

enlightened egoism
The concept that egoism may appear to be altruistic because it is in one's long-term best interest to help others in order to receive help in return.

Enlightened egoism is a slight revision of this basic principle, adding that each person's objective is long-term welfare. This may mean that we should treat others as we would want them to treat us to ensure cooperative relations. Even seemingly selfless and altruistic acts are consistent with egoism because these acts benefit the individual by ensuring reciprocal assistance. For instance, if you help your friend move when he asks you to, it is only because you expect that he will help you when you need some future favor. Under egoism, it would be not only impossible but also immoral for someone to perform a completely selfless act. Even those who give their lives to save others do so perhaps with the expectation of rewards in the afterlife. Egoism completely turns around the priorities of utilitarianism to put the individual first, before anyone else and before society as a whole; however, because long-term interests often dictate meeting obligations and helping others, enlightened egoists might look like altruists.

Adam Smith (1723–1790), the "father" of free enterprise, promoted a type of practical egoism, arguing that individuals pursuing their own personal good would lead to nations prospering as well. Capitalism is based on the premise that everyone pursuing self-interest will create a healthy economy: workers will work harder to get more pay; owners will not exploit workers too badly because they might quit; merchants will try to get the highest price for items whereas consumers will shop for the lowest price; and so on. Only when government or liberal do-gooders manipulate the market, some argue, does capitalism not work optimally. Ayn Rand (1905–1982) is perhaps the best-known modern writer/philosopher associated with egoism. She promoted both psychological egoism (that humans *are* naturally selfish) and ethical egoism (that humans *should be* self-interested). Libertarians utilize Rand's writings to support their view of limited government and fierce individualism.

Most philosophers reject egoism because it violates the basic tenets of an ethical system. Universalism is inconsistent with egoism, because to approve of all people acting in their own self-interest is not a logical or feasible position. It cannot be right for both me and you to maximize our own self-interests because it would inevitably lead to conflict. Egoism would support exploitative actions by the strong against the weak, which seems wrong under all other ethical systems. However, psychological egoism is a relevant concept in natural law (self-preservation is natural) and utilitarianism (hedonism is a natural inclination). But if it is true that humans are *naturally* selfish and self-serving, one can also point to examples that indicate that humans are also altruistic and self-sacrificing. One thing seems clear: when individuals are caught doing illegal acts, or acts that violate their professional codes of ethics, or acts that harm others, it is usually only egoism that can justify their behavior.

Other Methods of Ethical Decision Making

Some modern writers present approaches to applied ethics that do not directly include the ethical systems discussed thus far. For instance, Krogstand and Robertson (1979) described three principles of ethical decision making:

imperative principle The concept that all decisions should be made according to absolute rules.

- The **imperative principle** directs a decision maker to act according to a specific, unbending rule.

- The **utilitarian principle** determines the ethics of conduct by the good or bad consequences of the action.

utilitarian principle The principle that all decisions should be made according to what is best for the greatest number.

- The **generalization principle** is based on this question: "What would happen if all similar persons acted this way under similar circumstances?"

These should sound familiar because they are, respectively, religious or absolutist ethics, utilitarianism, and ethical formalism. Ruggiero (2001) proposes that ethical dilemmas be evaluated using three basic criteria. The first principle is to examine one's obligations and duties and what one has promised to do by contract or by taking on a role (this is similar to ethical formalism). The second principle is to examine moral ideals such as how one's decision squares with prudence, temperance, justice, honesty, compassion, and other ideals (this is similar to Aristotle's ethics of virtue). The third principle is to evaluate the act to determine if it would result in good consequences (this is utilitarianism).

generalization principle The principle that all decisions should be made assuming that the decision would be applied to everyone else in similar circumstances.

Close and Meier (1995: 130) provide a set of questions more specific to criminal justice professionals and sensitive to the due-process protections that are often discarded in a decision to commit an unethical act. They propose that the individual decision maker should ask the following questions:

1. Does the action violate another person's constitutional rights, including the right of due process?

2. Does the action involve treating another person only as a means to an end?

3. Is the action illegal?

4. Do you predict that your action will produce more bad than good for all persons affected?

5. Does the action violate department procedure or professional duty?

There are three general principles that can be drawn from all of the approaches above. Think of them as the three "F's." First, we are interested in attaining all the *facts* of the situation; this includes the effects of the decision on oneself and others. We can't make good decisions unless we know all the facts, or, at least, as many as we can know. Second, the so-called *"front page"* test asks us to evaluate our decision by whether or not we would be comfortable if it was on the front page of the newspaper. Public disclosure is often a good litmus test for whether something is ethical or not. Finally, the concept of a *formula* or rationale indicates that individual decisions should be based on a set of moral or ethical principles that would apply to all situations, rather than made ad hoc in each situation.

Most of us seek to make good decisions when confronted with moral or ethical dilemmas, and we believe that our decisions can be judged as good or bad. There is a school of thought, however, that holds that such judgments are purely subjective. We turn now to relativism, the idea that there can be no universal judgments of good or bad because there is no universal truth.

Relativism and Absolutism

Ethical relativism describes the position that what is good or bad changes depending on the individual or group, and that there are no moral absolutes. What is right is determined by culture and/or individual belief; there are no universal laws. There are two main arguments for relativism. The first argument is that there are many different moral standards of behavior. According to Stace (1995: 26), "We find that there is nothing, or next to nothing, which has always and everywhere been regarded as morally good by all men." The second argument is that humans are incapable of determining what, if anything, is an absolute rule of morality. Who is to say what is right and what is wrong?

One may look to anthropology and the rise of social science to explain the popularity of moral relativism. Over the course of studying different societies—past and present, primitive and sophisticated—anthropologists have found that there are very few universals across cultures. Even those behaviors often believed to be universally condemned, such as incest, have been institutionalized and encouraged in some societies (Kottak, 1974: 307). Basically, **cultural relativism** defines good as that which contributes to the health and survival of society. As examples, societies where women are in ample supply may endorse polygyny, and societies that have a shortage of women may accept polyandry. Hunting and gathering societies that must contend with harsh environments may hold beliefs allowing for the euthanasia of burdensome elderly, whereas agricultural societies that depend on knowledge passed down through generations may revere their elderly and accord them an honored place in society.

cultural relativism
The idea that values and behaviors differ from culture to culture and are functional in the culture that holds them.

In criminology, cultural differences in perceptions of right and wrong are important to the subcultural deviance theory of crime, wherein some deviant activity is explained by subcultural approval of that behavior. The example typically used to illustrate this concept is that of the Sicilian father who kills the man who raped his daughter, because to do otherwise would violate values of his subculture emphasizing personal honor and retaliation (Sellin, 1970: 187). A more recent case of subcultural differences involves a father who sold his 14-year-old daughter into marriage. Because he lived in Chicago, he was arrested; if he had lived in his homeland of India, he would have been conforming to accepted norms of behavior. In a recent case in Texas, state officials seized all the children of a polygamous religious sect called the Fundamentalist Church of Jesus Christ of Latter Day Saints, because they allegedly required underage girls to be married to the men in the sect. Because neither consent nor marriage is a defense to statutory rape, Texas laws were allegedly broken by the religious and cultural practices of the sect (Associated Press, 2008e).

We should also note how governments attempt to change culture through the criminal law. The cultural support in India for killing wives whose families do not provide a dowry is being slowly eroded by the current legal system that (albeit halfheartedly) investigates and punishes those responsible. Cultural relativists recognize that cultures have very different definitions of right and wrong, and moral relativists argue that there are no fundamental or absolute definitions of right and wrong. In opposition to this position, absolutists argue that just because there may be cultural norms endorsing such things as cannibalism, slavery, or having sex with 6-year-olds, the norms do not make these acts moral.

Although cultural relativism holds that different societies may have different moral standards, it also dictates that individuals within a culture conform to the standards of their culture. Therein lies a fundamental flaw in the relativist approach: If there are no universal norms, why should individuals be required to conform to societal or cultural norms? If their actions are not accepted today, it might be argued, they could be accepted tomorrow—if not by their society, perhaps by some other.

An additional inconsistency in cultural relativism is the corresponding prohibition against interfering in another culture's norms. The argument goes as follows: Because every culture is correct in its definitions of morality, another culture should not step in to change those definitions. However, if what is right is determined by which culture one happens to belong to, why then, if that culture happens to be imperialistic, would it be wrong to force cultural norms on other cultures? Cultural relativism attempts to combine an absolute (no interference) with a relativistic "truth" (there are no absolutes). This is logically inconsistent (Foot, 1982).

Cultural relativism usually concerns behaviors that are always right in one society and always wrong in another. Of course, what is more common is behavior that is judged to be wrong most of the time, but acceptable in certain instances. As examples: killing is wrong except possibly in self-defense and war; lying is wrong except when one lies to protect another. Occupational subcultures also support standards of behavior that are acceptable only for those within the occupation. For instance, some police officers believe that it is wrong to break the speed limit unless one happens to be a police officer—even an off-duty one. Some politicians believe that certain laws don't apply to them because they are the ones who create the laws or because they can substitute their own judgment about what is best for the country. Some of these decisions may be justified, but others may not be by any of the ethical decision-making methods we have discussed in this chapter.

It must be noted that even absolutist systems may accept some exceptions. The **principle of forfeiture** associated with deontological ethical systems holds that people who treat others as means to an end or take away or inhibit their freedom and well-being forfeit the right to protection of their own freedom and well-being (Harris, 1986: 136). Therefore, people who aggress first forfeit their own right to be protected from harm. This could permit self-defense (despite the moral proscription against taking life) and possibly provide justification for lying to a person who threatens harm. Critics of an absolutist system see this exception as a rationalization and a fatal weakness to the approach; in effect, moral rules are absolute *except* for those exceptions allowed by some "back-door" argument.

Alan Dershowitz, a well-known criminal defense attorney, has written a book of ethics in an attempt to explain how one should determine right and wrong. He argues that rights do not come from God because He does not speak to everyone in a single voice; they are not derived from natural law because nature is value-neutral; and they do not come from positive (man-made) law because it is subject to political influence. Dershowitz further disputes whether absolute rules can ever be sufficient to answer the questions of right and wrong. His conclusion is that our morals come from our experiences: morality is evolving and changes when major events change our thinking about actions. His example is that when something like the Holocaust occurs, there is an evolution of rights such that new and greater rights are recognized for everyone.

According to Dershowitz, this moral evolution occurs in fits and starts and is not gradual or consistent; however, once something has been lived through, there is a new way of thinking about rights. He uses the example that because of World War II and the after-the-fact recognition that we were wrong to place Japanese-American citizens in internment camps, after 9/11 we didn't put Middle Eastern visitors and citizens of Middle Eastern heritage in similar camps (Dershowitz, 2004: 9, 94). One might argue

principle of forfeiture
The idea that one gives up one's right to be treated under the principles of respect for persons to the extent that one has abrogated someone else's rights; for instance, self-defense is acceptable according to the principle of forfeiture.

with his facts, however, in that after 9/11 many people did advocate internment and thousands of Middle Easterners who were in this country on visas or green cards were detained by authorities. Furthermore, it is interesting that Dershowitz has come out more recently in support of torture in certain circumstances, arguing that it is better to have rules and laws allowing torture in limited circumstances than to let it occur with no legal authority and, therefore, no legal oversight. His rationale, of course, is based on act utilitarianism: there is a greater good for everyone if the torture may reveal information that could save large numbers of people from harm. Perhaps he would also agree that in the future we may look back at waterboarding and other coercive interrogation techniques, and recognize the essential human right of everyone not to be tortured.

Absolutists would argue that the reason that things like the Holocaust, slavery, the slaughter of Native American Indians, the Armenian genocide, Japanese-American internment, the Bataan Death March, and torture in Abu Ghraib and Guantanamo happen is because people promoting what they consider to be a good end (security or progress) do not apply absolute rules of morality and ethics and, instead, utilize relativism: It is okay for me to do this, at this time, because of what I consider to be a good reason.

Relativism allows for different rules and different judgments about what is good. Universalists would argue that if moral absolutes are removed, subjective moral discretion leads to egoistic (and nationalistic) rationalizations.

Toward a Resolution: Situational Ethics

situational ethics The philosophical position that although there are a few universal truths, different situations call for different responses; therefore, some action can be right or wrong depending on situational factors.

Situational ethics is often used as a synonym for *relativism*; however, if we clarify the term to include certain fundamental absolute elements, it might serve as a resolution to the problems inherent in both an absolutist and a relativist approach to ethics. Recall that relativism, on the one hand, is criticized because it must allow any practice to be considered "good" if it is considered good by some people; therefore, even human sacrifice and cannibalism would have to be considered moral—a thoroughly unpalatable consequence of accepting the doctrine. Absolutism, on the other hand, is also less than satisfactory because we all can think of some examples when the "rule" must be broken. Even Kant declined to be purely absolutist in his argument that lying isn't really lying if told to a person who is trying to harm us. What is needed, then, is an approach that resolves both problems.

moral pluralism The concept that there are fundamental truths that may dictate different definitions of what is moral in different situations.

Hinman (1998) resolves this debate by defining the balance between absolutism and relativism as **moral pluralism**. In his elaboration of this approach, he stops short of an "anything goes" rationale but does recognize multicultural "truths" that affect moral perceptions. The solution that will be offered here, whether one calls it situational ethics or some other term, is as follows:

1. There are basic principles of right and wrong.

2. These principles can be applied to ethical dilemmas and moral issues.

3. These principles may call for different results in different situations, depending on the needs, concerns, relationships, resources, weaknesses, and strengths of the individual actors.

Situational ethics is different from relativism because absolute laws are recognized, whereas under relativism there are no laws. What are absolute laws that can be identified as transcendent? Natural law, the Golden Rule, and the ethics of care could help us fashion a set of moral absolutes that might be general enough to ensure universal agreement. For instance, we could start with the following propositions:

- Treat each person with the utmost respect and care.
- Do one's duty or duties in such a way that one does not violate the first principle.

These principles would not have anything to say about dancing (as immoral or moral), but they would definitely condemn human sacrifice, child molestation, slavery, and a host of other practices that have been part of human society. Practices could be good in one society and bad in another. For instance, if polygamy was necessary to ensure the survival of society, it might be acceptable; if it was to serve the pleasure of some by using and treating others as mere objects, it would be immoral. Selling daughters into marriage to enrich the family would never be acceptable because that is not treating them with respect and care; however, arranged marriages might be acceptable if all parties agree and the motives are consistent with care.

To resolve the dilemma from Chapter 1 of the police officer who stops his father for driving while intoxicated, one might argue that the officer can do his duty and still respect and care for his father. He could help his father through the arrest process, treat him with care, and make sure that he receives help, if needed, for his drinking. Although this might not be enough to placate his father and the father might still be angry with him, as would others, their reaction could then be analyzed: Are they treating the officer with care and respect? Does the father respect his son if he expects him to ignore a lawful duty?

This system is not too different from a flexible interpretation of Kant's categorical imperative, a strict interpretation of rule-based utilitarianism, or an inclusive application of the Golden Rule. All ethical systems struggle with objectivity and subjectivity, along with respect for the individual and concern for society. Note that egoism does not pursue these goals and that is why some believe it cannot be accepted as a legitimate ethical system. Interestingly, situational ethics seems to be entirely consistent with the ethics of care, especially when one contrasts this ethical system with a rule-based, absolutist system. In the ethics of care, you will recall, each individual is considered in the equation of what would be the "good."

Resulting Concerns

Ethical systems provide the guidelines or principles to make moral decisions. Box 2.3 ("The Major Ethical Systems") summarizes the key principles of these ethical systems. It can happen that moral questions are decided in different ways under the same ethical system. For instance, if facts are in dispute, two people using utilitarianism may "weigh" the utilities of an act differently. Capital punishment is supported by some because of a belief that it is a deterrent to people who might commit murder; others argue it is wrong because it does not deter (this is an argument about facts between two utilitarians). Others believe that capital punishment is wrong regardless of its ability to deter. Most arguments about capital punishment get confused during the factual argument about the effectiveness of deterrence. "Is capital punishment wrong or right?" is a different question than "Does capital punishment deter?"

Another thing to consider is that none of us is perfect; we all have committed immoral or unethical acts that we know were wrong. Ethical systems help us to understand or analyze morality, but knowing what is right is no guarantee that we will always do the right thing. Few people follow such strong moral codes that they *never* lie or *never* cause other people harm. One can condemn the act and not the person. The point is that just because some behaviors are understandable and perhaps even excusable does not make them moral or ethical. Finally, few people consistently use just one ethical system in making moral decisions. Some of us are fundamentally utilitarian and some predominantly religious, but we may make decisions using other ethical frameworks as well.

BOX 2.3

The Major Ethical Systems

Ethical formalism. What is good is that which conforms to the categorical imperative.

Utilitarianism. What is good is that which results in the greatest utility for the greatest number.

Religion. What is good is that which conforms to God's will.

Natural law. What is good is that which is natural.

Ethics of virtue. What is good is that which conforms to the Golden Mean.

Ethics of care. What is good is that which meets the needs of those concerned.

Egoism. What is good is that which benefits me.

Most of us try to behave ethically most of the time. Dilemmas arise when we are confused about the right thing to do or when the right thing to do carries considerable cost. Detective Poole knew what the right course of action was. He also knew that he would pay a price for doing it. In fact, he was transferred to a less prestigious position and denied a promotion. He was vilified and treated as a traitor by some officers when he went public with his evidence of a cover-up. Ultimately, he resigned from the Los Angeles Police Department (Golab, 2000). This illustrates the sad fact that doing the right thing sometimes comes at a price.

CONCLUSION

In this chapter, we have explored some of the major ethical systems. Ethical systems are ordered principles that define what is right or good. Each of these ethical systems answers the question "What is good?" in a different way. Sometimes the same conclusion to an ethical dilemma can be reached using several different ethical systems, but sometimes using different ethical systems can result in contradictory answers to the determination of goodness.

Ethical systems are more complex to apply than they are to explain. For instance, utilitarianism is fairly easy to understand, but the measurement of utility for any given act is often quite difficult. Ethical formalism says to "do one's duty," but it does not help us when there are conflicting duties. The ethics of care emphasizes relationships but is vague in providing the steps necessary to resolve ethical dilemmas. More applied approaches utilize steps one can take to resolve ethical dilemmas. These steps often include the ideas of obtaining all facts, applying a "front page" test (or exposing the decision to outside scrutiny), and applying a formula or set of principles. Whether morals are relative or absolute has been debated throughout time. The concept of situational ethics may help to reconcile the question as to whether ethics are ultimately subjective or universal.

CHAPTER REVIEW

1. Define deontological and teleological ethical systems and explain ethical formalism and utilitarianism.

A deontological ethical system is one that is concerned solely with the inherent nature of the act being judged. If an act or intent is inherently good (coming from a good will), it is still considered a good act even if it results in bad consequences. A teleological ethical system judges the consequences of an act. The saying "the end justifies the means" is a teleological statement. Kant's ethical formalism defines good as that which conforms to the categorical imperative, which includes the universalism principles, the idea that we shouldn't use people, and the stricture that we must do our duty through a free will in order to be considered moral. Utilitarianism, associated with Jeremy Bentham, defines good as that which contributes to the greatest utility for the greatest number.

2. Describe how other ethical systems define what is moral—specifically, religion, natural law, ethics of virtue, and ethics of care.

Under Judeo-Christian religion, what is good is determined by God's will. One can know God's will through one's religious leaders or the Bible. Other religions also have statements of good and evil and sources to use to determine what is good. Under natural law, good is determined by what is natural. Moral rules are considered similar to other natural laws, such as gravity. Even if humans have not discovered these moral rules, or disagree about what they are, they still exist. Under the ethics of virtue, goodness is determined by the virtues. Aristotle and others have identified what are considered to be moral virtues. Those who possess such virtues will make the right decision when faced with a moral dilemma. The ethics of care is based on the emotions of relationships. Caring is the basis of this morality.

3. Discuss the argument as to whether egoism is an ethical system.

Most who write in the area of applied ethics reject egoism as an ethical system because it is self-serving and logically inconsistent. It doesn't make sense to have a universal rule that everyone should pursue self-interest, because our self-interests will inevitably conflict. Proponents of ethical egoism also believe in psychological egoism, the idea that we are, by nature, purely self-interested. Under this view, we are egoists and, therefore, to pursue our self-interest is a good.

4. Explain the controversy between relativism and absolutism.

Absolutist ethics allow no exceptions to moral rules for exceptional circumstances. Relativism seems to allow individuals to define anything as morally acceptable, even acts that would be considered wrong under universal moral rules. The compromise is situational ethics, which propose a very few absolute rules that will support different decisions in different circumstances.

5. Identify the three consistent elements of most of the approaches to resolving ethical dilemmas.

Most of the step-based approaches include the following: one must know the *facts* of the situation; one should apply the *"front page"* test; and one should use a *formula* or set of moral or ethical principles to resolve any ethical dilemma.

KEY TERMS

act utilitarianism
categorical imperatives
cultural relativism
deontological ethical
  system
egoism
enlightened egoism
ethical formalism
ethical system
ethics of care

ethics of virtue
generalization principle
hypothetical imperatives
imperative principle
moral pluralism
natural law
peacemaking justice
principle of forfeiture
principle of the golden
  mean

psychological egoism
religious ethics
rule utilitarianism
situational ethics
teleological ethical system
utilitarianism
utilitarian principle

STUDY QUESTIONS

1. What are the elements of any ethical system, according to Baelz? What are the three parts of the ethical pyramid?

2. What are the three parts of the categorical imperative? What is the difference between act and rule utilitarianism.

3. What are the three ways to know God's will? What are the 6 Pillars of Character?

4. What are Krogstand and Robertson's three principles of ethical decision making?

5. Explain the differences between situational ethics and relativism.

WRITING/DISCUSSION EXERCISES

1. Write an essay (or discuss) the ethical systems in regard to the following situations:

   a. In the movie *Sophie's Choice*, a woman is forced to choose which one of her children to send to the gas chamber. If she does not decide, both will be killed. How would ethical formalism resolve this dilemma? How would utilitarianism resolve it?

   b. There is a continuing debate over whether the United States had to bomb Hiroshima and Nagasaki at the end of World War II. Present the arguments on both sides. Now consider this: Are they utilitarian arguments, ethical formalist arguments, or some other?

2. Write an essay on (or discuss) the basic nature of humans. Are we basically altruistic? Basically egoistic? Include in this essay responses to the following and examples to support your answer: What are the "natural" inclinations of human beings? Do you think most people do the right thing out of habit or out of reason?

3. Write an essay (or discuss) whether ethics and morals are relative or absolute. Are there absolute moral truths, or is morality simply an individual's definition of right and wrong? Should everyone have the right to decide which behaviors are acceptable for them? Should all cultures have the right to decide what is right? If you believe there are absolute definitions of right and wrong, what are they?

ETHICAL DILEMMAS

Situation 1

You are the manager of a retail store. The owner of the store gives you permission to hire a fellow classmate to help out. One day you see the classmate take some clothing from the store. When confronted by you, the peer laughs it off and says the owner is insured, no one is hurt, and it was under $100. "Besides," says your acquaintance, "friends stick together, right?" What would you do?

Situation 2

You are in a lifeboat along with four others. You have enough food and water to keep only four people alive for the several weeks you expect to be adrift until you float into a shipping lane and can be discovered and rescued. You will definitely all perish if the five of you consume all the food and water. There is the suggestion that one of you should die so the other four can live. Would you volunteer to commit suicide? Would you vote to have one go overboard if you choose by straws? Would you vote to throw overboard the weakest and least healthy of the five? If you were on a jury judging the behavior of four who did murder a fifth in order to stay alive, would you acquit them or convict them of murder? Would your answer be different if the murdered victim was your son or daughter?

Situation 3

You aspire to be a police officer and are about to graduate from a criminal justice department. Your best friend has just been hired by a local law enforcement agency, and you are applying as well. When you were freshmen, you were both caught with marijuana in your dorm room. Although you were arrested, the charges were dismissed because it turned out that the search was illegal. The application form includes a question that asks if you have ever been arrested. Your friend told you that he answered no because he knew this agency did not use polygraphs as part of the hiring process. You must now decide whether to also lie on the form. If you lie, you may be found out eventually, but there is a good chance that the long-ago arrest will never come to light. If you don't lie, you will be asked to explain the circumstances of the arrest, and your friend will be implicated as well. What should you do?

Situation 4

You have a best friend who has confessed a terrible secret to you. Today the man is married and has two children. He has a good family, a good life, and is a good citizen. However, 14 years earlier he killed a woman. A homeless person was accused of the crime but died before he could be tried and punished. Nothing good can come of this man's confession. His family will suffer; and no one is at risk of being mistaken as the murderer. What would you advise him to do? (Some may recognize this dilemma as coming from Dostoyevsky's *The Brothers Karamazov*.)

Situation 5

You are working in internal affairs, and in the course of another investigation, you discover disturbing evidence regarding the police chief's son, who is also an officer in the department. Several informants have confided in you that this individual has roughed them up and taken their drugs, yet you find no record of arrest or the drugs being logged in the evidence room. When you write your report, your sergeant tears it up and tells you that there is not enough evidence to justify an investigation and for you to stick to what you are told to do. What would you do? What would you do if the chief calls you into his office the next day and offers you a transfer to a high-status position that will definitely lead to a promotion?

3

Steve Petteway, Collection of the Supreme Court of the United States.

Justice and Law

Chapter Objectives

1. Describe the three themes included in the definition of justice.
2. Define the three types of justice described in the chapter.
3. Under corrective justice, distinguish between substantive and procedural justice.
4. Describe civil disobedience and when it may be appropriate.
5. Explain the concept of restorative justice and the programs associated with it.

What is justice? Harold Hall would argue that he didn't receive justice by spending 20 years in a California prison for a crime he didn't commit. In 1985, at the age of 18, he was arrested for a double homicide and rape. He was interrogated for 17 hours, hand-cuffed to a chair, and denied food and water. The police told him that they had evidence linking him to the crime. Finally he told police what he thought they wanted to hear. That confession and the perjured testimony of a jailhouse informant was enough for a jury to convict him to life in prison. After 20 years in prison, Hall was finally released after an appellate court finally agreed to his pleas for a test of the DNA collected from the crime scene. The testing led to his exoneration and release (Hall, 2008).

Hall had been subjected to a lawful arrest; he had the benefit of a trial during which time he was defended by an attorney; and he had the right to appeal. Some would say that the legal system worked as it was supposed to have worked, but did he receive justice?

Professionals in the criminal justice system serve and promote the interests of law and justice, and before we explore the ethical dilemmas that confront them, this chapter begins with a discussion of justice itself. An underlying theme is that the ends of law and justice are not always the same. Although *law* is often defined as "the administration of justice," it may very well be the case that law forces consequences that many might conclude are unjust. Legal rights might be different from moral rights, rights might be different from needs, and needs may not be protected under either the law or justice.

According to Lucas (1980: 3), justice "differs from benevolence, generosity, grati-tude, friendship, and compassion." Justice is not something for which we should feel grateful, but rather, something upon which we have a right to insist. Justice should not be confused with "good." Some actions may be considered good but not demanded by justice. For instance, the recipients of charity, benevolence, and forgiveness do not have a right to these things; therefore, it is not an injustice to withhold them. Justice concerns rights and interests more often than needs. Although the idea of need is important in some discussions of justice, it is not the only component or even the primary one. It is important to understand that what is just and what is good are not necessarily the same.

People can be described as displaying unique combinations of generosity and selfishness, fairness, and self-interest. Some writers insist that the need for justice arises from the nature of human beings and that we are not naturally generous, open-hearted, or fair. On the one hand, if we were to behave all the time in accordance with those virtues, we would have no need for justice. On the other hand, if humans were to always act in selfish, grasping, and unfair ways, we would be unable to follow the rules and principles of justice. Therefore, we uphold and cherish the concept of justice in our society because it is the mediator between people's essential selfishness and generosity. In other words, justice is the result of a logical and rational acceptance of the concept of fairness in human relations.

Anthony Walsh (2000) presents the interesting idea that justice is a biologically adaptive trait. He uses evolutionary psychology to argue that the sense of justice is emotional rather than rational and is the result of natural selection. His argument, simplified, is that humans, similar to other animal species, have "cheaters" and "suckers." Cheaters are those who do not engage in "reciprocal altruism" (basically, cooperation). Suckers are those who are continually taken advantage of by cheaters. They are not optimally adapted for survival, and if they perish, cheaters would perish as well because they need victims to take advantage of. Thus, "grudgers" evolve as a response; they may be fooled once by cheaters, but they are outraged and demand punishment when they are victimized. This adaptation successfully ensures the continued existence of grudgers as well as cheaters. Our "moral outrage," in other words, is an evolutionary response, as is our emotional demand for justice.

Galston (1980: 282) described justice as

> …more than voluntary agreement, [but] … less than perfect community. It allows us to retain our separate existences and our self-regard; it does not ask us to share the pleasures, pains, and sentiments of others. Justice is intelligent self-regard, modified by the requirements of rational consistency.

Any discussion of justice includes at least three continuing themes: fairness, equality, and impartiality. *Fairness* is related to equal treatment. Parents ordinarily give each child the same allowance unless differences between the children, such as age or duties, warrant different amounts. Children are sensitive to issues of fairness long before they grasp more abstract ideas of justice. No doubt every parent has heard the plaintive cry, "It's not fair—Johnny got more than I did" or "It's not fair—she always gets to sit in the front seat!" What children are sensing is unequal and, therefore, unfair treatment. The concept of fairness is inextricably tied to equality and impartiality.

- *Equality* refers to equal shares or equal treatment as well. There is a predisposition to demand equity or equal shares for all. In contrast to the concept of equal shares is the idea of needs or deserts; in other words, we should get what we need or, alternatively, what we deserve by status, merit, or other reasons. The concept of equality is also present in retributive justice in the belief that similar cases should be treated equally—for instance, that all individuals who commit a similar crime should be similarly punished.

Impartiality is also related to the concept of equal treatment. At the core of our system of criminal justice is the theme of impartiality. Our symbol of justice represents, with her blindfold, impartiality toward special groups and, with her scales, proportionally just punishments. Impartiality implies fair and equal treatment of all without discrimination and bias. It is hard to reconcile the ideal of "blind justice" with the individualized justice of the "treatment ethic" because one can hardly look at individual circumstance if one is blind toward the particulars of the case. Indeed, most would argue, individual differences and culpabilities should be taken into consideration—if not during a finding of guilt or innocence, then at least when sentencing occurs. The blindfold may signify no special treatment for the rich or the powerful, but then it must also signify no special consideration for the young, for the misled, or for extraordinary circumstances.

Origins of the Concept of Justice

justice The quality of being impartial, fair, and just; from the Latin "jus." concerning rules or law.

Justice originated in the Greek word *dike*, which is associated with the concept of everything staying in its assigned place or natural role (Feinberg and Gross, 1977: i). This idea is closely associated with the definitions of justice given by Plato and Aristotle. Even today, some writers describe justice as "the demand for order: everything in its proper place or relation" (Feibleman, 1985: 23).

According to Plato, justice consists of maintaining the societal status quo. Justice is one of four civic virtues, the others being wisdom, temperance, and courage (Feibleman, 1985: 173). In an ordered state, everyone performs his or her role and does not interfere with others. Each person's role is the one for which the individual is best fitted by nature; thus, *natural law* is upheld. Moreover, it is in everyone's self-interest to have this ordered existence continue because it provides the means to a good life and appropriate human happiness. Plato's society is a *class system*, based on innate abilities, rather than a *caste system*, which differentiates purely by accidents of birth.

Aristotle believed that justice exists in the law and that the law is "the unwritten custom of all or the majority of men which draws a distinction between what is honorable and what is base" (Feibleman, 1985: 174). Aristotle distinguished *distributive justice* from *rectificatory justice*:

- *Rectificatory justice*, or *commutative justice*, concerns business deals where unfair advantage or undeserved harm has occurred. Justice demands remedies or compensations to the injured party.

- *Distributive justice* concerns what measurement should be used to allocate society's resources. Aristotle believed in the idea of proportionality along with equality.

In Aristotle's conception of justice, the lack of freedom and opportunity for some people—slaves and women, for instance—did not conflict with justice, as long as the individual was in the role in which, by nature, he or she belonged. In other words, unequal people should get unequal shares.

In this chapter, we will not discuss rectificatory/commutative justice; however, we will discuss various viewpoints concerning distributive justice. The debate in distributive justice is: what do people deserve? Then, we will turn our attention to corrective justice. This type of justice is also concerned with desert; however, in corrective justice, the question is what punishment is deserved, rather than societal goods or opportunities.

DIstributive Justice

The concept of the appropriate and just allocation of society's goods and interests is one of the central themes in all discussions of justice. According to one writer, justice always involves *rightful possession* (Galston, 1980: 117–119). The goods that one might possess include:

- Economic goods (income or property)
- Opportunities for development (education or citizenship)
- Recognition (honor or status)

If there was enough of everything (goods, opportunity, status) for everyone, issues of distributive justice would not arise; it is only because there is usually a condition of scarcity that a problem arises with the allocation of goods. Two valid claims to possession are *need* and *desert*. The principles of justice involve the application of these claims to specific entitlements. Different writers have presented various proposals for deciding issues of entitlement.

Lucas (1980: 164–165) identified distributions based on need, merit, performance, ability, rank, station, worth, work, agreements, requirements of the common good, valuation of services, and legal entitlement. Despite differences, all schemes include some concept of need and merit (also see Raphael, 1980: 90). A major conflict in distributive justice is between need and merit. Consider the following: An armored car spilled its load of cash in a very poor neighborhood in Miami. People scooped up the cash and ran away. Police went door to door, asking people to turn in the half million dollars that was taken, and telling them that it was theft to keep the money. One resident was quoted as saying, "This couldn't have happened to a more *deserving* neighborhood" (Associated Press, 1997: A7). This is an interesting comment in that the people who took the cash did nothing to earn it. What type of distribution system could justify the statement that they "deserved" the cash? Obviously, need rather than merit was the criterion for the person speaking.

The difficulty in distributing society's goods lies in deciding the weight of each of the criteria discussed above. The various theories can be categorized as egalitarian, Marxist, libertarian, or utilitarian, depending on the factors that are emphasized (Beauchamp, 1982):

- *Egalitarian theories* start with the basic premise of equality or equal shares for all.
- *Marxist theories* place need above desert or entitlement.
- *Libertarian theories* promote freedom from interference by government in social and economic spheres; therefore, merit, entitlement, and productive contributions are given weight over need or equal shares.
- *Utilitarian theories* attempt to maximize benefits for individuals and society with a mixed emphasis on entitlements and needs.

How do the theories apply to the wide disparities in salaries found in the United States? For instance, a professional athlete's salary is sometimes one hundred times greater than a police officer's salary. The average CEO's salary of the *Forbes* top 100 companies runs in the millions of dollars. The bonuses proposed for the Wall Street bankers who were partially responsible for the economic collapse in 2008–2009 were higher than most of us make in a year (or a decade!). The White Collar Crime box shows some of these salaries. Which distribution principle justifies such extreme discrepancies? Libertarian theorists would shrug at such disparity; Marxist theorists would not.

White Collar Crime: Salaries on Wall Street

Stanley O'Neal (Merrill Lynch) — $172 million (over 4 years)

James Cayne (Bear Stearns) — $161 million

Lloyd Blankfein (Goldman Sachs) — $57.6 million

The average pay for Wall Street firms in 2007 was $353,089 and the average bonus was $211,849. Even after the dramatic economic collapse that affected home prices, unemployment, the national debt, and the gross national product, salaries and bonuses were in the millions of dollars. To date, no one has been punished for the risky loans and business practices that led to the necessity of a bailout for many of the biggest banks and businesses in the United States by American citizens. Instead, Wall Street rewards individuals with salaries that most of us can only dream about. Is there a crime here? If so, what is it?

Source: Associated Press, 2008f: H6.

Obviously, few would agree that workers in all jobs and all professions should be paid the same amount of money. First, not many people would be willing to put up with the long hours and many years of schooling needed in some professions if there were no incentives. Second, some types of jobs demand more responsibility and involve greater stress than others. However, most of us would agree that some remuneration is entirely out of proportion to an objective analysis of worth.

Should workers be paid based on their production? If so, how would one pay secretaries, teachers, or customer service workers, whose production is more difficult to measure? How would one pay police officers—by the number of arrests? Thus far, we have discussed only salaries, but in the workplace other goods are also distributed, such as promotions, merit increases, job postings, desirable offices, and parking places. How should these "perks" be awarded if production isn't easily measured?

Marxist distribution systems propose that we pay people according to need. This sounds fair in one sense because people would get only what they need to survive at some predetermined level. In that case, a person with two children would earn more than a person with no children. In the past, this was the argument used by employers to explain why they would favor men over women in hiring, promotions, and pay increases—because men had families to support and women did not. Two arguments were used against this type of discriminatory treatment: The first was that women deserve as much pay as men if they are of equal ability and performance. The second was that women also, more often than not, have to support families. These two arguments emphasize different principles of justice. The first is based on an equal-deserts argument; the second rests on an equal-needs argument.

Just distribution of other goods in society is also problematic. There are perennial arguments over how much people should receive in entitlement programs, such as food stamps and TANF (Temporary Assistance for Needy Families, formerly Aid to Families with Dependent Children [AFDC]). The principle of need is the rationale we use to take from the financially solvent, through taxes, and give to those who have little or nothing. There is always some resentment over this redistribution because of the belief that some people choose not to work and take advantage of governmental "handouts." If cheaters were dropped from such programs, what about their children? Do they also deserve to be punished? What do children deserve from the state?

Since the 2008 presidential election cycle, the issue of universal health care has become a divisive controversy in this country. Proponents argue that the United States stands alone among Western countries in its refusal to ensure universal health care (basic health care for everyone in society regardless of their ability to pay) for its citizens. Opponents argue that the free market should provide such coverage and any move toward universal health care will put this country on the path to socialism. Note that the argument as to whether the federal government can provide better and less costly health coverage than private enterprise is a much different argument than whether or not people deserve universal health coverage paid for through others' taxes. One is an empirical argument, but the other is a moral argument and one squarely in the center of this discussion over distributive justice. What do people deserve *vis-à-vis* health care when others have to pay for it?

Another "good" that society distributes to its members is opportunity. Many people would argue that education (at least at the university level) is a privilege that should be reserved for those few who have the ability and the drive to succeed. However, the educational system in the United States is fundamentally democratic. Not only do we have guaranteed—in fact, compulsory—education at elementary and secondary levels, we also have open admission to some universities. Moreover, remedial courses are available to help those without the skills to meet college standards. Massive amounts of time and money are devoted to helping some students improve their skills and ultimately graduate from college. Some might argue that this system wastes resources. Other countries "track" students very early and identify those who have natural skills, then allow only that selected group to take advantage of state-supported higher education. Is this a more efficient use of state resources?

There is also a compelling argument that although the *ideal* of education is democratic, the *reality* is that because of unequal tax bases, school districts are incredibly unequal and distribute the opportunity of education unequally. While some school districts have swimming pools, computers in every classroom, and teachers with specialized education, other school districts make do with donated textbooks and buildings that are poorly heated and ventilated. Likewise, there are vast differences in the quality and status of higher education, with degrees from some universities worth much more than others. Who deserves to go to these better universities? If you said "those with better grades," do you also agree with the process whereby high schools are ranked by admissions committees so that a 4.0 GPA in one high school is ranked lower than a 4.0 GPA from another high school?

Affirmative action programs were designed to provide opportunities to groups that historically have been discriminated against—blacks, women, and Hispanics, among others. Some believe that taking affirmative steps to increase opportunities for minority groups has simply transferred unfair treatment to white males. What is acceptable to overcome previous discrimination? The accompanying Policy Box addresses this distributive justice issue.

The fact that everyone is not equal, in terms of ability, performance, motivation, need, or any other measure, is easy enough to agree on. On the one hand, few people would argue that everyone in every position should receive the same salary, get the same education, and achieve the same status in society. On the other hand, to acknowledge inequality puts us in the position of distributing goods and other benefits on the basis of other criteria, and it is here that problems arise. When injustice occurs, we sense it on the basis of fairness. We think that it is not fair that there are starving children and conspicuous wealth in the same country or the same world. We sense unfairness when people work hard yet still struggle to get along on poverty wages, while star actors or athletes make millions of dollars largely through luck or for contributions to societal welfare that seem trivial in comparison.

John Rawls's theory of justice is perhaps the best-known modern conception of justice. He elegantly combines utilitarian and rights-based concepts in his theory. Basically, he proposes an equal distribution unless a different distribution would benefit the

POLICY ISSUE   The Future of Affirmative Action?

Should members of minority groups that historically have been discriminated against receive special privileges in hiring decisions in police departments? This question is extremely controversial. One argument is that preferential hiring of minorities strengthens police departments by helping the department more closely reflect the neighborhoods it polices and increases the skill sets of the officers. Another argument is that quota systems and the pressure to hire minorities made hiring standards go down and that unfit people have been hired as police officers. Further, even those who are qualified and good candidates are stigmatized because of a perception that they were hired only because of their gender, race, or ethnicity. How should hiring decisions be made when applicants are roughly similar in education, background, and civil service test scores?

Law

In *Ricci v. DeStefano* (129 S.Ct. 2658[2009]), the Supreme Court held, in a 5–4 decision, that the city of New Haven's decision to throw out firefighters' promotion test results because no blacks scored high enough to be promoted was discriminatory. City officials feared that the test itself would be ruled invalid because of the disparate impact, prompting them to ignore the test scores that placed only whites and two Hispanics in the eligible category for promotion. The Supreme Court held, in a suit brought by white firefighters who scored highly on the exam, that the city had failed to show a strong basis of evidence that there had been disparate treatment of minorities in the past that needed to be overcome. The case signals the continuing trend in the law

to look disfavorably upon affirmative action programs if they impose disparate impact on any race (white included) and/or that are not created to overcome clear evidence of historical discrimination toward minorities. Proponents of killing affirmative action argue that the usefulness of such programs has passed and that such actions should be ruled illegal because they discriminate against whites. Supreme Court decisions have struck down broad-based affirmative action programs but have held that race can be *one* factor in decisions regarding admitting students to universities or hiring. Opponents would argue that race should *never* be used in such decisions.

Policy

Agencies differ on their policies regarding affirmative action. Some agencies continue to aggressively recruit minorities and may have policies that favor minority and female applicants, but it may be the case that affirmative action programs are simply policy choices today and not legally mandated. In fact, policy choices that attempt to promote the interests of minorities may be the subject of discrimination suits themselves, as was seen by the *Ricci* case above.

Individual Ethics

Individual ethics arise for those who are doing the hiring and those who are hired. If individuals know that they have been hired solely because of their gender, race, or ethnicity, what should they do? Should the hiring decision makers consider these elements, even though there is no formal policy to do so?

---

disadvantaged. Rawls believes that any inequalities of society should be to the benefit of those who are least advantaged (Rawls, 1971: 15):

veil of ignorance
Rawls's idea that people will develop fair principles of distribution only if they are ignorant of their position in society, so in order to get objective judgments, the decision maker must not know how the decision would affect him or her.

- Each person is to have an equal right to the most extensive total system of basic liberties compatible with a similar system of liberty for all.

- Social and economic inequalities are to be arranged so that they are both reasonably expected to be to everyone's advantage and attached to positions and offices open to all (except when inequality is to the advantage of those least well-off).

So, for instance, Rawls may argue for a purely objective hiring scoring system except when they give extra points for those who are least well off, and tax rebates that are equally distributed except if they are a bit more favorable for those in the lower income brackets. Rawls uses a heuristic device that he calls the **veil of ignorance** to explain the idea that people will develop fair principles of distribution only if they are ignorant of their position in society, for they just as easily may be "have-nots" as "haves" (Rawls, 1971: 12). Thus, justice and fairness are in everyone's rational self-interest because, under the veil of ignorance, one's own situation is unknown, and the best and most rational distribution is the one that is most equal to all.

Rawls's theory of justice has been criticized. First, some argue that the veil of ignorance is not sufficient to counteract humanity's basic selfishness: given the chance, people would still seek to maximize their own gain, even if doing so involves a risk (Kaplan, 1976: 199). Second, Rawls's preference toward those who are least well-off is contrary to the good of society. Rawls states that "all social values—liberty and opportunity, income and wealth and the bases of self-respect—are to be distributed equally unless an unequal distribution of any, or all, of these values is to the advantage of the least favored" (quoted in Sterba, 1980: 32). This may be ultimately dysfunctional for society, for if those who are least well-off have the advantages of society preferentially, there will be no incentive for others to excel. Also, some argue that Rawls is wrong to ignore desert in his distribution of goods (Galston, 1980: 3).

Let us now turn to how these theories of distributive justice relate to the ethical systems discussed in Chapter 2. The ethics of care is consistent with a Marxist theory of justice, for both emphasize need. Utilitarian theories try to maximize societal good, so some balance of need and merit would be necessary to provide the incentive to produce. Ethical formalism is concerned solely with rights; thus, issues of societal good or others' needs may not be as important as the individual's rights (however those might be defined). Rawls's theory is both utilitarian and Kantian because it demands a basic level of individual rights but also attempts to establish a preference toward those who have less, for the good of all society.

How are these concepts of distributive justice relevant to criminal justice? First, the discussion illuminates the issues regarding the appropriateness of affirmative action in the hiring and promotion of police officers and other criminal justice professionals. Should your race give you special hiring privileges? What if the profession is one such as policing, which has been historically closed to minorities? Another issue that is related to distributive justice is how much to pay police officers or correctional officers compared to other professions. Most people believe that police are underpaid. If so, how much is a fair salary, and how does that salary compare to others, such as elementary school teachers? The criteria you used to determine these answers should have some basis in the distribution systems discussed above.

Finally, there is a connection between distributive justice and corrective justice, which will be discussed next. If it is true that socioeconomic status predicts criminal predisposition, should we care? Is it fair that poor people tend to end up in prison and those with more resources usually receive a lesser form of punishment? Further, should we consider issues of distributive justice (i.e., what someone has by accident of birth) in any discussion of corrective justice (i.e., what people deserve when they commit a crime)? Reiman (1984/2005/2007), for instance, argues that economic power affects lawmaking, lawbreaking, enforcement, and punishment practices; literally, he argues that the rich get richer and the poor get prison under our system of justice. Clearly, distributive justice is an important concept in any discussion of the criminal justice system.

Corrective Justice

substantive justice Concerns *just deserts*—in other words, the appropriate amount of punishment for a crime.

Recall that corrective justice is concerned with dispensing punishment. As with distributive justice, the concepts of equality and desert, fairness and impartiality are important. Two components of corrective justice should be differentiated. **Substantive justice** involves the concept of just deserts, or how one determines a fair punishment for a particular offense, and **procedural justice** concerns the steps we must take before administering punishment.

● ● ● ● ● ● ● SUBSTANTIVE JUSTICE

procedural justice The component of justice that concerns the steps taken to reach a determination of guilt, punishment, or other conclusion of law.

What is a fair punishment for the crime of murder? Many believe that the only just punishment is death because that is the only punishment of a degree equal to the harm caused by the offender. Others might say that life imprisonment is equitable and fair. Since the beginning of codified law, just punishment has been perceived as proportional to the degree of harm incurred. This was a natural outcome of the early, remedial forms of justice, which provided remedies for wrongs. For instance, the response to a theft of a slave or the killing of a horse involved compensation. The only just solution was the return or replacement of the slave or horse. This remedial or compensatory system of justice contrasts with a punishment system: The first system forces the offender to provide compensation to the victim or the victim's family, and the second apportions punishment based on the degree of harm suffered by the victim. They both involve a measurement of the harm, but in the first case, measurement is taken to adequately compensate the victim, and in the second it is to punish the offender. In a punishment-based system, the victim is a peripheral figure. The state, rather than the victim, becomes the central figure—serving both as victim and as punisher. Two *philosophies* of corrective justice can be identified: retributive justice and utilitarian justice.

retributive justice The component of justice that concerns the determination and methods of punishment.

lex talionis A vengeance-oriented justice concerned with equal retaliation ("an eye for an eye; a tooth for a tooth").

lex salica A form of justice that allows compensation; the harm can be repaired by payment or atonement.

RETRIBUTIVE JUSTICE The concept of **retributive justice** is one of balance. The criminal must suffer pain or loss proportional to what the victim was forced to suffer. In an extreme form, this retribution takes the form of *lex talionis*, a vengeance-oriented justice concerned with equal retaliation ("an eye for an eye; a tooth for a tooth"). A milder form is *lex salica*, which allows compensation; the harm can be repaired by payment or atonement (Allen and Simonsen, 1986: 4). A life for a life might be easy to measure, but most cases involve other forms of harm. How does one determine the amount of physical or mental pain suffered by the victim, or financial loss such as lost income or future loss, in most crimes? And if the offender cannot pay back financial losses, how does one equate imprisonment with fines or restitution?

Historically, corporal and capital punishment were used for both property crime and violent crime. With the development of the penitentiary system in the early 1800s, punishment became equated with terms of imprisonment rather than amounts of physical pain. The greater ease of measuring out prison sentences probably contributed to the rapid acceptance of those sentences. An offender might be sentenced to one, two, or five years, depending on the seriousness of the crime. Imprisonment had several advantages over earlier forms of punishment:

- It was considered more humane than corporal punishment.
- It was incapacitating (preventing offenders from committing further crime).
- It allowed offenders to reflect on their crime and repent.
- It did not elicit sympathy for the offenders from the populace.

However, a term of imprisonment is much harder to equate to a particular crime. Although one can intuitively understand the natural balance of a life for a life, $10 for $10, or even a beating for an assault, it is much harder to argue that a burglary of $100 is equal to a year in prison or that an assault is equal to a term of two years. A year in prison is hard to define. Research on prison adjustment indicates that a year means different things to different people. For some, it might be no more than mildly inconvenient; for others, it might lead to suicide or mental illness (Toch, 1977).

In addition to retribution, imprisonment was tied to the reform of the criminal offender. Reform or rehabilitation may be a laudable goal, but it has no place in a retributive scheme of justice. Retributive punishment is based on balancing the victim's harm with the offender's pain or suffering. Treatment involves no such balance; therefore, there is no retributive rationale for its existence. Philosophical support for rehabilitative treatment of criminal offenders is found in utilitarianism.

In earlier systems of justice, the status of the victim was important in determining the level of harm and, thus, the punishment. Nobles were more important than free men, who were more important than slaves. Men were more important than women. Punishment for offenders was weighted according to these designations of the worth of the victim. Although we have no formal system for weighting punishment in this way and have rejected the worth of the victim as a rationale for punishment (except in a few cases, such as assaulting a police officer), many believe that our justice system still follows this practice informally. People argue that harsher sentences are given when the victim is white than when the victim is black and when the victim is rich as opposed to poor. In a similar manner, many argue that the justice system discriminates unfairly and unjustly against characteristics of the offender. Many believe that offenders receive harsher sentences because of their race, background, or income.

Whether or not these charges are true, it is important to recognize that earlier systems of justice, including the Greek and Roman, approved of and rationalized such different treatment as perfectly fair and just. Our system of justice has rejected these discriminations even while holding on to others—specifically, intent, partial responsibility, and, to some extent, victim precipitation. It is difficult, if not impossible, for everyone to agree upon a fair and equitable measurement of punishment when one allows for exceptions, mediating factors, and partial responsibility. That is why there is so little agreement on what is fair punishment. Even when two defendants are involved in a single crime, our system of justice can support different punishments under a retributive rationale.

In Rawls's (1971) theory of justice, retributive punishment is limited in such a way as to benefit the least advantaged, similarly to the distributive justice scheme discussed earlier. In this philosophy of justice, the offender is punished until the advantage changes and the offender becomes the least advantaged. What is a just punishment for any offense should be considered using the veil of ignorance so one does not know whether one is the offender, the victim, or a disinterested bystander. Critics argue that Rawls's system would create a situation wherein an offender may victimize a large corporation or a well-off victim and still be more disadvantaged, dictating that no punishment is due him or her. Most of us would not countenance this definition of justice.

One other issue that must be addressed here is the concept of mercy. Seemingly inconsistent with any definition of retributive justice, mercy is, nevertheless, always associated with the concept. From the very beginnings of law, there has been the element of forgiveness. Even tribal societies had special allowances and clemencies for offenders, usually granted by the king or chief. For instance, the concept of **sanctuary** allowed offenders respite from punishment as long as they were within the confines of church grounds. Benefit of clergy, dispensation, and even probation are examples of mercy by the court. However, it must be made clear that mercy is different from just deserts. If, on the one hand, because of circumstances of the crime, of the criminal, or of the victim, the offender deserves little or no punishment, then that is what he or she deserves, and it is not mercy to give a suspended sentence or probation. On the other hand, if an offender truly deserves the punishment and is instead forgiven, then the individual has been granted mercy. The In the News box shows that sometimes mercy and forgiveness are offered despite great harm.

Murphy (1985/1995) proposes that retributive emotions derive from self-respect, that it is a healthy response to an injury to feel angry, resentful, and, yes, even vengeful.

sanctuary Ancient right based on church power; allowed a person respite from punishment as long as he or she was within the confines of church grounds.

in the **NEWS**

IN HIS HEART, THERE IS FORGIVENESS

In 2009, Catholic priest Shaji Varghese was stabbed nearly 20 times by a mentally disturbed man, who was caught shortly afterward. Varghese was given last rites because he was not expected to live. However, he did live and says he has no anger toward his attacker. He said the attack brought the church members together. As he was an immigrant from India, parishioners had been initially wary of him until the attack. He believes that their prayers for his recovery were instrumental in his survival. He said that in his heart, there is nothing but forgiveness for David Rodriquez, who faced attempted murder charges.

SOURCE: Powell, 2009: B6

However, it is also acceptable to forgive and extend mercy to one's assailant if the forgiveness extends not from a lack of self-respect but rather from a moral system. For instance, he points out that many religions include the concept of "turning the other cheek" and extending mercy to enemies. Mercy is appropriate when the offender is divorced in some way from his or her offense. One way to this separation is true repentance.

Murphy (1988: 10) summarizes the points of mercy as follows:

1. It is an autonomous moral virtue (separate from justice).
2. It is a virtue that tempers or "seasons" justice—something that one adds to justice.
3. It is never owed to anyone as a right or a matter of desert or justice.
4. As a moral virtue, it derives its value at least in part because it flows from love or compassion while not losing sight of the importance of justice.
5. It requires a generally retributive outlook on punishment and responsibility.

Therefore, mercy is related to justice but is not necessarily a part of it. It is connected with a change in the offender because, typically, there must be repentance before mercy is extended. Also, it is connected with the compassion, charity, or benevolence of the victim.

Other questions of mercy remain, however. Who has the right to extend mercy? At times, victims or the families of victims are upset with a sentencing judge because of the lenient sentence administered to the offender. Should victims be the only ones who have the right to give the gift of mercy?

utilitarian justice The type of justice that looks to the greatest good for all as the end.

UTILITARIAN JUSTICE We have been discussing retributive justice as a rationale for and as a means to determine punishment. However, **utilitarian justice** also supports punishment. Whereas the goal of a retributive framework of justice is to restore a natural balance by righting a wrong or neutralizing criminal gain with an equal amount of loss or pain, the goal of utilitarian justice is to benefit society by administering punishment to deter offenders from future crime.

Cesare Beccaria (1738–1794) and Jeremy Bentham (1748–1832) provided a utilitarian rationale for proportionality in punishment. Punishment should be based on the seriousness of the crime: the more serious the crime (or the greater the reward the crime offered the criminal), the more serious and severe the punishment should be to deter the individual from committing the crime. A utilitarian framework of justice would determine punishment on the basis of deterrence.

hedonistic calculus Jeremy Bentham's rationale for calculating the potential rewards of a crime so the amount of threatened pain could be set to deter people from committing that crime.

Bentham's **hedonistic calculus**, for instance, is concerned with measuring the potential rewards of the crime so the amount of threatened pain could be set to deter people from committing that crime. The use of proportionality in this scheme is deterrence, not balance. In a retributive system, we measure to determine the proportional amount of punishment to equalize the wrong; in a utilitarian system, we measure to determine the amount of punishment needed to deter. We see that under the utilitarian framework, there is no necessity for perfect balance. In fact, one must threaten a slightly higher degree of pain or punishment than the gain or pleasure that comes from the criminal act; otherwise, there would be no deterrent value in the punishment.

In some cases, retributive notions of justice and utilitarian notions of justice may conflict. If a criminal is sure to commit more crime, the utilitarian could justify holding him in prison as a means of incapacitation, but to hold him past the time "equal" to his crime would be seen as an injustice under a retributive system. We might punish an offender more seriously than he "deserves" under a utilitarian system if it could be shown to deter many others. Deterrence is the primary determinant of justice under a utilitarian system, but desert is the only determinant of a retributive system of justice. Correctional rehabilitation is prevention, not deterrence per se, but it is also acceptable under a utilitarian justice system and irrelevant and unsupported by a retributive one.

PROCEDURAL JUSTICE

We turn now to the procedure of administering punishment—our legal system. Law includes the procedures and rules used to determine punishment or resolve disputes. It is a system of rules for human relations—the "whole field of the principles laid down, the decisions reached in accordance with them, and the procedures whereby the principles are applied to individual cases" (Raphael, 1980: 74). There can be a difference between justice and law. You might think of justice as the concept of fairness, while law is a system of rules.

The law is an imperfect system. Fuller (1969: 39) explored the weaknesses of law and described ways that the procedure of law may fail to achieve justice. Generally, there is a tension between having no rules and making ad hoc decisions for each individual case, and a system of rules that is too stringent with no exceptions made for extraordinary circumstances.

Some have argued that property and interest cases can be decided by legal rule, but that those cases involving conflicts of human conduct cannot. Even this bifurcation is criticized, however, because the most straightforward contract disagreements may involve human action, misinterpretation, and interest (Wasserman, cited in Feinberg and Gross, 1977: 34).

We are left to assume that although a system of law is necessary for the ordered existence of society, it sometimes does not result in justice. "Moral rights" may differ from "legal rights," and "legal interests" may not be moral. Shakespeare's *The Merchant of Venice* (excerpted in the Quote and Query box) addresses many of the issues discussed in this chapter. Here the plea for mercy emphasizes the relationship between justice and mercy. Shylock's demand for the court's enforcement of his legal right (his pound of flesh) and the unwillingness of the court to deny it, despite the clear implication that it would be a tragedy, illustrate how law sometimes has little to do with justice. Then Portia's surprise argument—that because Shylock's contract mentioned only flesh and not blood, so no blood could be spilled, and thus Shylock is denied his compensation—is a superb illustration of the law's slavish devotion to technical rules over substance. As a legal trick, this interpretation of a contract has not been improved upon yet, in fiction or in reality.

QUOTE & QUERY

The quality of mercy is not strained;
It droppeth as the gentle rain from heaven
Upon the place beneath. It is twice blest;
It blesseth him that gives and him that takes.
…
It is an attribute to God himself,
And earthly power doth then show likest God's
When mercy seasons justice. Therefore, Jew,
Though justice be thy plea, consider this,
That, in the course of justice, none of us
Should see salvation. We do pray for mercy,
And that same prayer doth teach us all to render
The deeds of mercy. I have spoke thus much
To mitigate the justice of thy plea,
Which if thou follow, this strict court of Venice
Must needs give sentence 'gainst the merchant there.

WILLIAM SHAKESPEARE, *THE MERCHANT OF VENICE*, ACT 4, SCENE 1

What is the magistrate in this passage asking Shylock to do? How do you believe mercy should "season" justice? What would be procedural justice in this case? What would be substantive justice?

due process
Constitutionally mandated procedural steps designed to eliminate error in any governmental deprivation of protected liberty, life, or property.

In our system of justice, **due process** exemplifies procedural justice. Our constitutional rights of due process require careful inquiry and investigation before punishment or forfeiture of any protected right can be carried out by the state. One has the right to due process whenever the government seeks to deprive an individual of protected rights of life, liberty, or property. Due process is the sequence of steps taken by the state that is designed to eliminate or at least minimize error. Procedural protections include:

- Notice of charges
- Neutral hearing body
- Right of cross-examination
- Right to present evidence
- Representation by counsel
- Statement of findings
- Appeal

These protections do not eliminate deprivation or punishment, but they do result in more accurate and just deprivations and punishments. Thus, if due process has been violated—by use of a coerced confession, tainted evidence, or improper police or court procedures—an injustice has occurred. The injustice does not arise because the offender

in the **NEWS**

DEADLINES AND JUSTICE

In *Holland v. Florida* (No. 09-5327 [June 2010]), the Supreme Court held that the time for filing a federal habeas corpus petition could be extended by "equitable tolling" when the conduct of an attorney was sufficiently egregious to warrant the extension. Holland had lost two direct appeals and had one year to file a federal habeas corpus appeal. Despite his many pleas to his attorney to get an appeal in before the deadline, the attorney failed to do so. Because of the deadline, Holland was barred from appealing his death sentence under a habeas petition. He filed his own pro se (without legal assistance) petition arguing that the deadline be waived because of the attorney's negligence. The Eleventh Circuit denied relief, but the Supreme Court held that courts must look at the totality of circumstances on a case by case basis to determine whether or not the deadline should be extended. Since Holland had exercised due diligence by reminding his attorney of the deadline to no avail, the Court sent the case back to the lower court to determine, on the facts of this case, whether equitable tolling should apply.

does not deserve to be punished, but rather, because the state does not deserve to do the punishing, having relied on unfair procedures.

We have been discussing legal procedures for determining punishment, but in some cases legal procedures may be strictly followed and injustice still occurs. For instance, it is unlikely that anyone would argue that Nelson Mandela (described in the Walking the Walk box) when he was imprisoned in South Africa, or Andrei Sakharov, a Soviet dissident, received *just* punishment even though the legal procedures of their respective countries might have been scrupulously followed. These are clear examples that illustrate the difference between procedural justice and substantive justice. The In the News box describes a recent Supreme Court case that distinguishes between rules and justice.

Immoral Laws and the Moral Person

In this discussion, we have argued that procedural justice may not be equivalent to substantive justice. As noted, Nelson Mandela was tried by a court of law before he was imprisoned, but that legal system was part of a brutal regime of oppression. In his trial, he argued that the process was illegitimate because it did not conform to principles of natural laws of justice. What is the moral duty of individuals when laws and governmental edicts are themselves immoral? Examples might include the laws of the Spanish Inquisition in the 15th century that resulted in large numbers of people being tortured and killed for having dissenting religious beliefs, and the Nuremberg laws of Nazi Germany stripping Jewish citizens of their citizenship, as well as later laws requiring Jews to give themselves up to be transported to concentration camps and often to their death. Examples in the United States might include the internment laws during World War II that forced U.S. citizens of Japanese descent to give up land and property and be confined in camps until the end of the war, and the segregationist laws that once forced blacks to use different doors and water fountains than whites.

These laws are now thought of as immoral, but they were not considered so by many people at the time. The most common example of immoral laws are those that deprive

 **WALKING THE WALK**

Nelson Mandela was imprisoned in South Africa for 27 years. He began fighting apartheid in the 1940s. In 1964, he was convicted of sabotage and treason and sentenced to a life term of imprisonment for his activities in the African National Congress Party, which had been outlawed by the government. Throughout his decades in prison, he refused to compromise his position in order to gain his release, arguing that "only free men can negotiate." However, he did begin secret talks in the late 1980s when he was approached by the ruling white party leaders, who gradually came to the realization that apartheid could not continue as South Africa became in danger of being torn apart by race-based violence. Eventually Mandela's reputation grew to worldwide proportions, and he was released in 1990. In 1991, he was elected president of the African National Congress when the ban against the political party was lifted. In 1994, black South Africans voted for the first time and Mandela was elected as president of a democratic South Africa, formally bringing to an end the era of apartheid. He was awarded the Nobel Peace Prize in 1993 along with Frederik de Klerk, the South African president who released him from captivity.

After apartheid ended, Mandela was instrumental in averting a civil war between blacks and whites. There was a strong possibility that it might happen; small numbers of blacks began a pattern of violence toward those who had cooperated with the separatist government. "Necklaces" made of burning rubber were used to burn victims alive in a pattern of retaliation. This violence was condemned by Mandela and others, and, instead, Truth and Reconciliation panels were created. These panels brought out into the open the horrors of apartheid and the brutal system that developed to protect it, but promised amnesty for those who admitted their wrongdoing. The Truth and Reconciliation panels, as well as earlier conciliatory gestures, such as Mandela congratulating the white rugby team during his only term (1994–1998) as president (memorialized in the movie *Invictus*), and his refusal to use his power to attack and punish the vanquished white ruling party, led to South Africa coming out of a brutal, repressive regime to a democracy with minimal civil strife.

Throughout his life, Mandela's principles served as the guiding light for his actions and, because of those actions, a whole country was changed.

Sources: Nelson Mandela Foundation web site, www.nelsonmandela.org (accessed July 1, 2010); Bryson, 2010.

certain groups of liberty or treat some groups differently, giving them either more or fewer rights and privileges than other groups. Boss (2001) has described unjust laws as having the following characteristics:

- They are degrading to humans.
- They are discriminatory against certain groups.
- They are enacted by unrepresentative authorities.
- They are unjustly applied.

Most ethical systems would condemn such laws, and an objective ethical analysis would probably prevent the passage of such laws in the first place. The example of Japanese American internment can be used to illustrate how one might use ethical systems to judge a specific law. The religious ethical framework would probably not provide moral support for the action because it runs contrary to some basic Christian principles, such as, "Do unto others as you would have them do unto you." Ethical formalism could not be used to support this law because it runs counter to the categorical imperative that each person must be treated as an end rather than as a means, and to the universalism principle. The principle of forfeiture could not justify the action because these were innocent individuals, many of whom were fiercely loyal to the United States. The only ethical framework that might be used to support the morality of this law is utilitarianism. We must be able to show that the total utility derived from internment outweighed the negative effect it had on the Japanese Americans who lost their land and liberty. Did it save the country from a Japanese invasion? Did the benefits outweigh the harm to Japanese Americans? If you cannot answer these questions in the affirmative, then internment cannot be justified under utilitarianism either.

Are there any laws today that might be considered immoral? After 9/11, there was some discussion of deporting all those of Middle Eastern origin, regardless of their immigration status. This idea was rejected, perhaps partly because moral hindsight has shown that the Japanese internment was a flawed response to the fear created by World War II. However, thousands of Middle Easterners were required to register with Immigration, and many were detained for expired visas and other minor immigration irregularities. The detainees in Guantanamo have been held for years without any due process, in violation, many argue, of the Geneva Convention. Defenders argue that our actions have been necessary and morally justified as self-defense. Unfortunately, actions that may seem reasonable when in the grip of fear, in retrospect, may not be legally or morally justifiable.

In some countries, the legal climate has allowed torture and death squads to be used. If you lived in a South American country and knew of assassinations by government police and nighttime kidnappings and disappearances, would you follow a law requiring you to turn in political subversives? If you were living in a country divided by warring factions, would you support a law that dispossessed members of a rival faction of their property? These issues are at the heart of our next discussion. Can one be a moral person while enforcing or obeying an immoral law?

Martin Luther King, Jr., Mahatma Gandhi, and Henry David Thoreau agreed with St. Augustine that "an unjust law is no law at all." There is a well-known story about Thoreau, jailed for nonpayment of what he considered unfair taxes. When asked by a friend, "What are you doing in jail?" Thoreau responded, "What are you doing out of jail?" The point of the story is that if a law is wrong, a moral person is honor-bound to disobey that law. Box 3.1 addresses civil disobedience. If moral people were to disobey laws, what would happen to the stability of society?

Another story concerns Socrates. About to be punished for the crime of teaching radical ideas to youth, he had the opportunity to escape and was begged by his friends to leave the country, yet he willingly accepted his death by hemlock because of a fundamental respect for the laws of his country. This position supports the notion that one should never place one's own moral code above the duly enacted laws of the land. One should change

BOX 3.1

Civil Disobedience

1. It must be nonviolent in form and actuality.
2. No other means of remedying the evil should be available.
3. Those who resort to civil disobedience must accept the legal sanctions and punishments imposed by law.
4. A major moral issue must be at stake.
5. When intelligent men [sic] of good will differ on complex moral issues, discussion is more appropriate than action.
6. There must be some reason for the time, place, and target selected.
7. One should adhere to "historical time."

Source: Hook, quoted in Fink (1977: 126–127).

the laws, if believed to be wrong, through the process of legislation and appeal, not by committing unlawful acts, because the latter is dangerous to the stability of society.

If we agree with the proposition that an unjust law is no law at all, we may set up a situation in which all citizens follow or disobey laws at will, depending on their own conscience. If one holds a relativist view of morality—specifically the belief that one can intuit morals and decide morality on an individual basis—two people holding different moral positions could both be right even though one position might be inconsistent with the law. An absolutist view holds that there is only one universal truth, which would mean that if one knew a law to be wrong based on this universal truth, that person would be morally obliged to disobey the law. Evidently, either relativism or absolutism could support civil disobedience. The Quote and Query box presents quotes on just and unjust laws, by Henry David Thoreau and Martin Luther King, Jr.

QUOTE & QUERY

Under a government which imprisons any unjustly, the true place for a just man is also a prison....

HENRY DAVID THOREAU, "CIVIL DISOBEDIENCE (RESISTANCE TO CIVIL GOVERNMENT)," 1849

[T]here are two types of laws[:] just and unjust. I would be the first to advocate obeying just laws. One has not only a legal but a moral responsibility to obey just laws. Conversely, one has a moral responsibility to disobey unjust laws.

MARTIN LUTHER KING, JR., "LETTER FROM BIRMINGHAM JAIL," 1963

Do you believe that a just person has a moral obligation to disobey an unjust law?

civil disobedience
Voluntarily breaking established laws based on one's moral beliefs.

Civil disobedience is the voluntary disobedience of established laws based on one's moral beliefs. Rawls (1971) defined it as a public, nonviolent, conscientious, yet political act contrary to law and usually done with the aim of bringing about a change in the law or policies of the government. Many great social thinkers and leaders have advocated breaking certain laws thought to be wrong. Philosophers believe that the moral person follows a higher law of behavior that usually, but not necessarily, conforms to human law. However, it is an exceptional person who willfully and publicly disobeys laws that he or she believes to be wrong. Psychological experiments show us that it is difficult for individuals to resist authority, even when they know that they are being asked to do something that is wrong.

The Milgram experiments are often used to show how easily one can command blind obedience to authority. In these experiments, subjects were told to administer shocks to individuals hooked up to electrical equipment as part of a learning experiment (Milgram, 1963). Unbeknownst to the subjects, the "victims" were really associates of the experimenter and faked painful reactions only when the subjects thought they were administering shocks. In one instance, the subject and the "victim" were separated, and the subject heard only cries of pain and exclamations of distress, then silence, indicating that the "victim" was unconscious. Even when the subjects thought they were harming the "victims," they continued to administer shocks because the experimenter directed them to do so and reminded them of their duty (Milgram, 1963).

Although it is always with caution that one applies laboratory results to the real world, history shows that individual submission to authority, even immoral authority, is not uncommon. Those who turned in Jewish neighbors to Nazis and those who participated in massacres of Native Americans in this country were only following the law or instructions from a superior authority.

To determine what laws are unjust, Martin Luther King, Jr., used the following guidelines: "A just law is one that is consistent with morality. An unjust law is any that degrades human personality or compels a minority to obey something the majority does not adhere to or is a law that the minority had no part in making" (quoted in Barry, 1985: 3). Remember that civil disobedience occurs when the individual truly believes the law to be wrong and therefore believes that the enforcement of it or obedience to it would also be wrong. We are not referring to chronic lawbreaking because of immediate rewards. Indeed, most criminals have a fairly conventional sense of morality. They agree with the laws, even though they break them. Even those gray-area laws that involve disagreement over the "wrongness" of the behavior are not proper grounds for disobedience unless one believes that the government is immorally oppressing certain people.

There is a widespread belief that law is synonymous with morality and that as long as one remains inside the law, one can be considered a moral person. Callahan (1982: 64) points out the following:

> We live in a society where the borderline between law and ethics often becomes blurred. For many, morality is simply doing that which the law requires; a fear of punishment is the only motivation for behavior in some minimally acceptable way.

Obviously, Callahan is concerned with the false perception of law as a total representation of morals. Most of us struggle to achieve goodness using the definitions of the society we live in, represented in our laws; very few apply a higher standard of morality that conflicts with existing law. Luckily, most of us are rarely faced with circumstances where we have to do so.

Restorative Justice

Our current system of law and justice is oriented completely to the offender. What would a system of justice be like if the emphasis were on the victim's rights, needs, and compensation? In a system with a primary emphasis on the victim rather than the offender, money would be spent on victim services rather than prisons. It would be victims who would receive job skills training, not offenders. Some of the money that now goes to law enforcement and corrections would be channeled to compensation programs for victims of personal and property crimes. Victims would be helped even if their offenders were not caught. The major goal would not be punishment, but service. Offenders would be peripheral figures; they would be required to pay restitution to victims, and punishment would occur only if they did not fulfill their obligation to their victims. Could such a system work? Would such a system provide better justice?

restorative justice An approach to corrective justice that focuses on meeting the needs of all concerned.

Although the restorative justice movement does not propose quite this level of radical restructuring, it does dramatically redesign the justice system and offers a new alternative to retributive justice. **Restorative justice** is a term used to describe a number of programs that seek to move compensation back to center stage in the justice system, instead of retribution. A similar, but not identical, philosophy has been called "peacemaking justice" by Braswell and Gold (2002). Programs that require the offender to confront the victim and provide compensation, and programs that place the victim in the middle of the process of deciding what to do about the offender, can be categorized under the restorative justice rubric. The propositions of the movement are as follows (Van Ness and Strong, 1997):

1. Justice requires restoring victims, offenders, and communities who have been injured by crime.

2. Victims, offenders, and communities should have the opportunity to be a fully active part of the justice process.

3. Government should restore order, but the community should establish peace.

The roots of restorative justice can be found as far back as Roman and Grecian law. Both were based on repayment to victims. Recall that Aristotle's "rectificatory justice" was concerned with ill-gotten gains in contract and business relationships that had to be remedied. In a similar manner, other offenses were also considered compensatory, and only when the offender refused to provide compensation was physical punishment employed.

In the 1970s, a trend toward "community justice" was part of the larger movement of community empowerment and development. Community justice boards or local justice committees were created as part of the justice system (Schweigert, 2002). This model actually comes from earlier examples of tribal justice, such as the Maori tribal council of New Zealand, which involves members of the families of both the victims and the offenders. The model uses reintegrative shaming, and responsibility for the crime is shared by the offender's family. Another example is the Skokomish Community Peacemaking Panel. Tribal peacemakers are selected from community members, and an adversarial system is specifically rejected in favor of one that seeks to solve the issue rather than simply to assess punishment.

Hallmarks of community justice models include the following (Schweigert, 2002: 25):

1. The process of justice employs local leadership, is informal, and invites participation from community members.

2. The goal is to repair the harm done to a community member by another community member in a way that will restore the health of the community relationship.

3. The authority of the justice is through the customs and traditions accepted by all members.

In community or restorative justice models, crime is viewed as a natural human error that should be dealt with by the community. Offenders remain a part of the community. Some writers make distinctions between restorative justice and community justice models.

> Restorative justice is a philosophical approach to correctional intervention, in which crime is seen as a conflict between individuals and their community whereby the party that causes the injury incurs an obligation to make things right—whenever and however possible…. Community justice is similar to restorative justice but with a stronger emphasis on prevention. Community justice involves a partnership between the justice system and community organizations to control crime and social disorder. (Carey, 2005: 5)

More generally, however, community and restorative justice can be distinguished from retributive justice in fundamental ways. Carey (2005: 25) details the differences between retributive justice and restorative justice. In retributive justice, the question is "Who did it?" while in restorative justice, the question is "What is the harm?" In retributive justice, the question is "Which laws were broken?" while in restorative justice the question is "What needs to be done to repair the harm?" In retributive justice the question is "What should the punishment be?" while in restorative justice, the question is "Who is responsible for this repair?"

Types of restorative justice programs include victim-offender mediation (or victim-offender reconciliation programs), whereby victims and offenders get together so the victim can make it clear to the offender what harm has occurred and they can decide together how to make it right. Reparative boards have community members (rather than justice officials) decide what should happen after a crime has been committed and an offender identified. Family group conferencing and circle sentencing include family members and other interested parties in the decision on what should happen to an offender (Braithwaite, 2002). It has been found that victims are more satisfied in restorative justice programs than with traditional sentencing (79 percent compared to 57 percent). Offenders were also more likely to successfully satisfy their restitution orders in such programs (Braithwaite, 2002: 71).

Community reparative boards are more common with youthful offenders. They are also called youth panels, neighborhood boards, or community diversion boards, and they have been in use since the 1920s. These boards reemerged in the mid-1990s, especially in Vermont. The goals are (Braithwaite, 2002: 73):

- Promote citizen ownership of process
- Provide opportunity for victims and community members to confront offenders in a constructive manner
- Provide an opportunity for the offender to take personal responsibility
- Generate meaningful community-based responses to crime and reduce dependence on formal justice processing

Family group conferencing comes from the Maori tribal model and was made a part of national legislation in New Zealand in 1989. The Wagga Wagga model in Southern Australia employs police to set up conferences of offenders, victims, families, and interested or involved others to resolve the problem. The goals of this type of program are as follows (Braithwaite, 2002: 76):

- Provide an opportunity for the victim to be directly involved in the decisions of sanctions
- Increase the offender's awareness of the human impact of his/her behavior and give an opportunity for the offender to take responsibility for it
- Engage the collective responsibility of the offender's support system
- Allow both offender and victim to reconnect to key community support systems

Circle sentencing, a similar model, comes from the Navajos in North America. Everyone involved directly in a criminal offense sits in a circle and gets a turn to speak. The entire circle decides what should be done. The goal is not to respond only to the current offense but also to heal the community. The goals of this type of sentencing are the following (Braithwaite, 2002: 77):

- Promote healing
- Provide the offender an opportunity to make amends
- Empower victims, community members, families, and offenders
- Address underlying causes of criminal behavior
- Build a sense of community and promote and share community values

There are potential problems with, and some criticisms of, these types of programs (Braithwaite, 2002; Dzur and Wertheimer, 2002). For instance, victims may feel pressured to forgive before they are ready. Less due process may be given to offenders because the goal is not to punish; thus, issues of guilt or innocence may be unresolved. However, restorative justice seems to offer an alternative to our traditional retributive justice system that can be supported by ethics of care, utilitarianism, religion, and possibly other ethical systems. It is more akin to older systems of law that focused on compensation rather than punishment. While legal sanctions usually do not make the victim "whole" or change the offender, restorative justice attempts to do both.

CONCLUSION

In this chapter, we have explored the origins and components of justice. Typically, justice includes the concepts of fairness, equality, and impartiality. Whereas justice is a philosophical concept concerned with rights and needs, law is the administration of justice. Justice can be further differentiated into rectificatory/commutative justice, distributive justice, and corrective justice. Corrective justice is the central concern of the criminal justice system and can be further divided into substantive and procedural issues. Substantive justice is concerned with the fairness of what we do to offenders; procedural justice is concerned with the procedures that must be undertaken before punishment occurs. A special concern is when the legal system or a law can be considered to be unjust and immoral. Principles of civil disobedience allow us to provide guidance as to when a moral person might legitimately oppose a law. Restorative justice is a new approach that actually has ancient roots. It focuses attention on the victim rather than the offender.

CHAPTER REVIEW

1. Describe the three themes included in the definition of justice.

Most definitions of justice include the concepts of fairness (equal treatment), equality (equal shares), and impartiality (absence of bias). Justice acts to mediate our impulses of selfishness and fairness. Justice is distinguished from goodness.

2. Define the three types of justice described in the chapter.

The three types of justice described are rectificatory or commutative justice (which concerns fairness and rights in business dealings and contracts), distributive justice (which concerns the fair distribution of goods and opportunities in society), and corrective justice (which concerns the fair application of the law and punishment).

3. Under corrective justice, distinguish between substantive and procedural justice.

Substantive justice concerns the inherent fairness of a law or punishment. Substantive justice can be supported by either retribution or utilitarian rationales. Under retribution, we are only concerned with desert; under utilitarianism, we are concerned with a justice system that results in the greatest good for the greatest number. Procedural justice is concerned with legal administration or the steps taken before punishment is administered. For instance, a substantive justice question would be "Is capital punishment just?" while a procedural justice question would be "What due process should apply before a decision of capital punishment is just?"

4. Describe civil disobedience and when it may be appropriate.

Laws that may be subject to civil disobedience must be immoral and unjust. For instance, they could be degrading, discriminatory, enacted by unrepresentative authorities, or unjustly applied. Civil disobedience must be nonviolent, there should be no other alternative, one must accept the legal consequences, and there should be a major moral issue at stake. If people of good will disagree on the matter, then civil disobedience is not appropriate.

5. Explain the concept of restorative justice and the programs associated with it.

Restorative justice puts the emphasis on making the victim whole and maintaining bonds between the community, the victim, and the offender. Types of restorative justice programs include victim–offender mediation (or victim–offender reconciliation programs), reparative boards, family group conferencing, and circle sentencing.

KEY TERMS

civil disobedience
due process
hedonistic calculus
justice
lex salica

lex talionis
procedural justice
restorative justice
retributive justice
sanctuary

substantive justice
utilitarian justice
veil of ignorance

STUDY QUESTIONS

1. Explain how Plato and Aristotle associated status with justice. Define rectificatory or commutative justice.

2. Describe distributive and corrective justice. Identify how different systems under distributive justice would allocate the resources of society.

3. Describe Rawls's system of distributive and corrective justice.

4. Describe retributive and utilitarian rationales for punishment, which is a substantive justice issue. Explain due process and how it fits with procedural justice. What are the elements of due process?

5. Describe some types of restorative justice programs. What ethical systems support restorative justice?

WRITING/DISCUSSION EXERCISES

1. Write an essay on (or discuss) how the government should distribute societal resources such as education and health care. How would you answer the argument of a couple who did not believe they should have to pay school taxes because they have no children? What about the argument that rich school districts should share their wealth with poor districts (keeping in mind that those who pay higher taxes in that district might have moved there because of the reputation of the school)? What are the arguments for and against universal health care?

2. Write an essay on (or discuss) the following issues under substantive and procedural justice:

   a. What is the proper punishment for a burglary, for a murder in an armed robbery, and for a million-dollar embezzlement? If you were being punished for a crime, would you rather receive a year in prison or 50 lashes? Why do we not use corporal punishment for criminal offenders? Do you think we should? Are there situations in our justice system where victims or offenders are treated differently than others because of who they are?

b. An 87-year-old man living in Chicago is exposed as a soldier who took part in killing hundreds of Jewish concentration camp victims. U.S. extradition procedures are followed to the letter, and he is extradited to Israel to stand trial, as Israeli law determines that courts in Israel have jurisdiction over Nazi war crimes. Israeli legal procedure is followed without error, and he is convicted of war crimes and sentenced to death.

c. Federal law enforcement agents determine that a citizen of another country participated in a drug cartel that sold drugs in the United States. A small group of agents goes to the foreign country, kidnaps the offender, drugs him, and brings him back to the United States to stand trial. Upon challenge, the government agents explain that, although these actions would have been unconstitutional and illegal against a citizen of the United States in this country, because they were conducted on foreign soil against a non-U.S. citizen, they were not illegal.

3. Write an essay on (or discuss) whether civil disobedience is ever justified. Discuss war protesters, anti-abortion activists who burn down clinics, protestors who are arrested for trespassing, and so on. If you believe that civil disobedience might be justified, when and in what circumstances would it be acceptable?

ETHICAL DILEMMAS

Situation 1

Two individuals are being sentenced for the exact same crime of burglary. You are the judge. One of the individuals is a 20-year-old who has not been in trouble before and participated only because the other individual was his friend. The second person has a history of juvenile delinquency and is now 25. Would you sentence them differently? How would you justify your decision?

Situation 2

In your apartment building there lives a young man who appears to be of Middle Eastern descent. You notice that other young men often visit him and that they come and go at odd hours of the day and night. You engage in a conversation with him one day, and during the course of the conversation, he states that "the United States deserved what happened on September 11 because of their imperialistic actions across the world and their support for the oppression of the Palestinian people." You think it is your duty to report him to the local police, and they appear to be interested in your report. One day, you observe him being taken away in handcuffs, and you never see him again. Several weeks later, his apartment is vacant, and you do not know what happened to his belongings. Would you attempt to find out what happened to him? Do you believe you should investigate further?

Situation 3

You are serving on a jury for a murder trial. The evidence presented at trial was largely circumstantial and, in your mind, equivocal. During closing, the prosecutor argues that you must find the defendant guilty because he confessed to the crime. The defense attorney immediately objects, and the judge sternly instructs the jury to disregard the prosecutor's statement. Although you do not know exactly what happened, you suspect that the confession was excluded because of some procedural error. Would you be able to ignore the prosecutor's statement in your deliberations? Should you? Would you tell the judge if the jury members discussed the statement and seemed to be influenced by it?

Situation 4

You are a probation officer who must prepare sentencing recommendation reports for the judge. The juvenile defendant to be sentenced in one case grew up in a desperately poor family, according to school records. He had a part-time job in a local grocery store, stocking the shelves and providing general cleanup. The store owner caught him stealing meat. Actually, this is the second time he has been caught stealing food. The first time he shoplifted at the store, the deferred adjudication included his commitment to work for the store owner. He explained that he was trying to help his mother, who could not provide enough food for his family. In general, failure to succeed at deferred adjudication results in a commitment to a juvenile facility. What would you recommend to the judge?

Situation 5

You are an ardent tea-party activist who believes the government has encroached unlawfully upon the sovereign rights of the state and the privacy rights of individuals. You do not believe that your taxes should go to anything other than national security and a few restricted activities, such as the federal highway system. Any other governmental programs are theft as far as you're concerned. Your group has organized a sit-in, and you discover that they plan to block the entrance to a publicly funded health clinic to demonstrate their ire at the federalization of health care. You know that the planned activities will constitute trespass and you may get arrested. Would you participate? Why or why not?

David Gard/Star Ledger/Corbis

4

Becoming an Ethical Professional

Chapter Objectives

1. Be able to describe the three major theories (and theorists) that attempt to explain behavior.
2. Become familiar with Bandura's idea of self-regulation and how it can be "turned off."
3. Describe what is necessary for moral growth according to Kohlberg.
4. Be familiar with the necessary elements for criminal justice ethics courses according to Sherman.
5. Become familiar with what steps organizational leaders should take to encourage ethical decision making on the part of employees.

In 2008, New York was rocked with a series of articles concerning Eliot Spitzer, a law-and-order governor who was caught on tape setting up a liaison with a high-priced call girl. His "fall from grace" was precipitous; he quickly resigned in the wake of a firestorm of publicity and faced potential federal charges because he allegedly wired money across state lines for illegal activity (prostitution). Critics were stunned because Spitzer's career had been a steady series of successes, first at Princeton, then Harvard, where he obtained his juris doctorate. He spent several years as a district attorney in Manhattan, then ran for and was elected attorney general in 1998. He honed his political reputation as a fearless advocate for justice who targeted white collar criminals on Wall Street and in the banking industry.

When Spitzer was elected governor in 2006, he pledged to clean up the corruption in Albany and alienated opponents and supporters alike with his "take no prisoners" approach to changing the back-scratching and questionable ethics of the capital city. How could a moral crusader, who campaigned on the promise to end corruption and who tirelessly prosecuted criminal offenders, betray his wife, lie to the voters, and break federal and state laws? Was he a good man who made mistakes or a bad man who did good things? Or are moral character and moral behavior much more complicated than simple dichotomies of good and bad?

In this chapter, we shift from the discussion of "What is good?" to "How does one become a good person?" More specifically, we are interested in how can we ensure that criminal justice professionals will uphold the ethics of their profession and not abuse their power. Why people act the way they do has been the question for philosophers, religious scholars, psychologists, sociologists, psychiatrists, economists, and, more recently,

in the **NEWS**

CORRUPTION AT THE BORDER

One of the inescapable facts of policing the border is that there are border agents who can be bought to look the other way and allow guns, drugs, or illegal aliens across. In 2006 alone, more than 600 criminal investigations were opened on U.S. immigration officials accused of corruption-related charges. In 2006, nine officers were arrested or sentenced for charges such as bribery and smuggling. Texas cases include David Duque (bribery; selling identification documents), Lizandro Martinez (allowing drugs to pass through his inspection lane; money laundering), Fabian Solis (smuggling undocumented migrants for money), Juan Alfredo Alvarez (bribery; drug conspiracy), and Aldo Manuel Erives (allowing drugs and immigrants through checkpoint). Officers who give in to the temptation to accept money in return for looking the other way could earn as much as $60,000 in a single shift—the equivalent of a year's salary.

The Department of Homeland Security's Office of Inspector General and the Office of Professional Responsibility at Immigration and Customs Enforcement (ICE) investigate corruption complaints. The two agencies have only about 300 investigators to follow up on complaints for 72,000 immigration employees. Incredibly, only about 10 percent of new job applicants are given polygraph exams because of the cost.

In a more recent story, it is noted that some Mexican smuggling cartels groom their workers to apply for border patrol jobs as part of a long range plan to smuggle. Luis Alarid, who faces seven years in prison, evidently researched how much prison time he would get before taking $200,000 for waiving through cars packed with marijuana. Others recently sentenced included two female border agents who were romantically involved with drug smugglers. Prosecutions have increased over 40 percent in the last several years.

SOURCES: Arrillaga, 2006: A13; Archibold, 2009.

criminologists. There is an obvious overlap between the question we ask in criminology—"Why do people commit crime?"—and the one we ask here: "Why do people commit unethical acts?" In some cases, when the unethical acts are also crimes, the question is exactly the same. For instance, the In the News box describes many individuals who committed both unethical and illegal acts. Do you think these individuals went into the border patrol intending to commit crime?

We should also recognize that there is a tension between the attempt to discover the causes of human behavior and the belief of some that explanations of behavior mask moral responsibility. Is sin (immorality) a character disorder that should be treated? Karl Menninger (1973), a psychiatrist, argued in the 1970s that the fields of psychiatry and psychology usurped and undercut earlier beliefs and judgments of sin. He wrote then that the moral decay of society was accelerating because we excused sins with psychiatric explanations. The sins he described included group sins of slavery, corporate greed, and environmental damage; and individual sins of pride, sensuality (adultery and pornography), gluttony (excessive food, drugs, and drink), sloth, envy, affluence, waste, cheating and stealing, lying, and cruelty. One might argue, 40 years later, our society continues to be described as in a state of declining morals, so it could be the case that every generation despairs when faced with obvious evidence of human weaknesses. Whether true or not,

in the **NEWS**

WILL THE HONEST POLITICIAN PLEASE STAND UP?

It seems to be a race among states as to who has the most dishonest politicians. Unfortunately, in this kind of race, there are no winners.

New York

Ex-Governor Eliot Spitzer (transferring money across state lines for prostitutes, possibly misusing state police powers); current Governor David Paterson (use of office to influence witness in criminal case, possible misuse of state police, use of drugs); Representative Charles Rangel (accepting corporate junkets, misreporting income on tax forms); Representative Eric Massa (sexual harassment). Also, a state senate majority leader convicted of federal corruption charges; a New York City Council member indicted for federal corruption; an assemblyman sentenced to prison for stealing from Little Leaguers; a state senator expelled from Congress for assault against his girlfriend.

Illinois

Ex-Governor Rod Blagojevich (attempting to "sell" President Obama's Senate seat); also (since 1972) three governors, two congressmen, 19 judges, 30 aldermen, and many others convicted of corruption.

Massachusetts

State Speaker of the House Salvatore DiMasi (violation of lobbying rules); former Speaker Thomas Finneran (convicted for obstructing justice); former Speaker Charles Flaherty (tax fraud); state Senator Dianne Wilkerson (bribery); Boston City Councilor Chuck Turner (bribery); state Senator James Marzilli (prostitution); Governor Deval Patrick (patronage); state Treasurer Timothy Cahill (patronage).

New Jersey

Forty-four people arrested in one case—three mayors (including Jersey City Deputy Mayor Leona Beldini), two state assemblymen, and five rabbis (money laundering and sale of black-market body parts); state Senator Wayne Bryant (extortion).

SOURCES: Gershman and Saul, 2010; Lendman, 2009; Pierce, 2009; CourierPostOnline, 2010.

there is a widespread perception that the United States is at a new low in levels of ethics and morality. The reasons given for this perceived decline include the following:

- We have eliminated many of the opportunities for the teaching of morals.

- The community is no longer a cohesive force.

- The authority of religion is not as pervasive as it once was.

- The family is weakening as a force of socialization.

- Educators have abdicated their responsibility for moral instruction in favor of scientific neutrality.

One of the most interesting findings regarding behavior is that what people believe isn't necessarily what they do. Thieves believe it is wrong to steal, but do it anyway. Students know it is wrong to cheat, but do it anyway. In a survey of 1,139 students at 27 universities, no less than 60 percent admitted cheating (Ryan, 2002: A11). One assumes politicians know it is wrong to take bribes, but, unfortunately, there is daily evidence to indicate that they do it anyway, as the In the News box illustrates.

Some studies do find beliefs and actions to be correlated. In one study, "honesty scores" for people in three organizations were compiled from an attitudinal questionnaire about beliefs. It was found that the organization with the highest average honesty score had the least employee theft, and the organization with the lowest average honesty score had the most employee theft (Adams, 1981). Other studies have found that instruments measuring the "ethical climate" in an organization accurately predict the relative levels of illegal or unethical behaviors of employees (for review, see Pollock, 2010). In contrast, other studies have found no correlation between honesty scores and behavior, and female prisoners were found to have the same rank orderings of values as female college students (Kohlberg and Candel, 1984: 499–503).

Part of the problem is the difficulty of measuring moral beliefs and the validity of the instruments used. It has been determined that so-called "**recognition tests**" that require the subject merely to recognize and identify certain moral principles and agree with them are less helpful in predicting behavior than "production" measures, which require the subject to actually reason through a dilemma and provide some rationale (Gavaghan, Arnold, and Gibbs, 1983; Aleixo and Norris, 2000). One would assume that criminal offenders would have lower morality scores than non-criminals, but that has not necessarily been the case. Studies have, however, shown that correctional programs can raise morality scores of offenders (Hickey and Scharf, 1980; Gibbs et al., 1984; Wiley, 1988; Arbuthnot and Gordon, 1988; Buttell, 2002; Pearson, 2002). Whether increasing morality scores will subsequently affect behavior is still undetermined.

recognition tests Paper-and-pencil tests that measure an individual's ability to recognize and/or agree with moral terms.

Theories of Moral Development

Important contributions to the discussion of why people behave unethically involve biological factors, learning theory, and Kohlberg's moral stage theory.

BIOLOGICAL FACTORS

The most controversial theories of human behavior point to biological predeterminers. Biological criminologists have discovered correlations between delinquency/criminology and a range of human traits, including impulsivity and aggressiveness (Fishbein, 2000). Researchers who study the brain have also discovered a possible linkage between the brain and the development of moral behavior. The frontal lobes of the brain seem to be implicated in feelings of empathy, shame, and moral reasoning. Ellis and Pontius (1989: 6) presented a theory postulating the influence of the frontal lobe and the limbic system on the individual's capacity for moral reasoning, in which individuals with frontal-lobe damage display characteristics that may be related to unethical behaviors, including increased impulsiveness, decreased attention span, tendency toward rude, unrestrained, tactless behavior, and a tendency to not be able to follow instructions, even after verbalizing what is required. Moll et al. (2005) presented a much more detailed explanation of brain activity in moral cognition. They showed that moral cognition is not limited to the limbic region but stems from the integration of content- and context-dependent representations in the cortical-limbic networks. Three components that form the structure of brain activity are structured event knowledge, social perceptual and functional features, and central motive and emotional states. The work of these researchers indicates that moral decision making is influenced by different regions of the brain responsible for emotional reactions and rational thinking. Injury to any of the regions will have different effects on one's abilities to respond to ethical dilemmas.

Ellis and Pontius (1989) proposed that biological sex differences in brain activity support the notion that women are more inclined to empathy and sensitivity to human relationships. More than 70 studies examining sex differences in brain functioning found evidence that men are more antisocial, commit more serious types of offenses, and more often have serious childhood conduct disorders. There are also sex differences in delinquency, school performance, hyperactivity, impulsivity, and attention deficit disorders. Some analysts propose that these differences are associated with sex-linked brain activity, specifically in the frontal lobes and limbic regions. They claim that males' sex hormones influence brain development prenatally and during puberty. Further, although there is a great deal of overlap between male and female populations in brain development and activity, there are also distinct and measurable differences; specifically, these differences may influence the brain's ability to absorb "moral messages" or act upon them. This research offers intriguing explanations of why some people (more often men) act in ways that are harmful to others.

Wilson (1993) has argued that values such as sympathy, fairness, self-control, and duty are moral "senses" that are inherent in humans and arise through a combination of genetics and socialization. Shermer (2004) also argues that these traits are inherited, although he supports a group selection argument—specifically, eons ago human groups that held these traits were more likely to survive than groups that did not.

In an interesting twist to the debate as to whether morals exist apart from humans or are created by them, Shermer argues that they are both: They transcend humans in the sense that our moral senses have been created by evolutionary factors that have taken place over the millennia; however, they are "of us" in the sense that they are human emotions, sentiments, and behaviors.

Shermer (2004: 37) states that asking why humans should be moral is like asking why we should be hungry or jealous. We are because we are hardwired for these feelings and emotions. Drawing a parallel between humans and foxes, he relates research that showed breeding foxes for docility also resulted in other physical changes, including more juvenile features and smaller jaws and teeth. Shermer argues that the same evolutionary trend occurred with humans. He compared humans to bonobos (a type of chimp that is much less aggressive, more sexual, and more social than its close genetic cousins). He suggested that the different behavioral patterns may be a result of their higher levels of serotonin than their more aggressive cousin chimps. More sexual activity is said to generate oxytocin (OT), a feel-good hormone that increases with sexual activity, and oxytocin is related to serotonin production (2004: 227)

Shermer also places morality in the intuitive and emotional capacities of humans, rather than the rational (2004: 177, 257). He points out research showing that moral emotions activate the amygdale, the emotion module in the brain, as well as the orbital and medial prefrontal cortex, which is the center of cognitive processing. Arguably, dilemmas arise when these two areas of the brain are in conflict. For instance, in a well-known hypothetical moral dilemma, a woman is hiding from enemy soldiers with others in a cellar when her baby starts crying. When test subjects are asked to imagine what they would do in this situation, two areas of the subjects' brains in MRIs light up—the inferior parietal lobe, which is related to rational, but impersonal, thinking, and the emotion centers of the brain, which evidently react with horror to the alternative of smothering the baby as a solution (Vedantam, 2007).

Researchers found that when subjects performed altruistic acts, their behavior triggered the pleasure center of the brain, connected with food and sex. This indicates that moral behaviors are hardwired into humans' basic impulses. Other research indicated that those with damage to the ventromedial prefrontal cortex, which is related to emotions, were unable to have any feelings regarding moral judgments (e.g., sympathy for others' pain and suffering or good feelings from altruism), although they were quite able to impersonally and coldly evaluate costs and benefits. The argument of some researchers is that morality lies in empathy, which derives from the emotional center of the brain. They say that only much later in evolution did the reasoning area of the brain become developed and involved in moral decision making (Vedantam, 2007).

This area of research is fascinating, not only to help us understand why humans act the way we do but also to help us understand in what specific ways we are similar to and different from other species in the animal kingdom. With continuing research in brain chemistry and with the work of the human genome project that has been mapping human DNA to discover our genetic heritage, fundamental questions of morality, culpability, and responsibility will arise.

LEARNING THEORY

Learning theorists believe that children learn what they are taught, including morals and values as well as behavior. In other words, right or wrong is not discovered through reasoning; rather, all humans are shaped by the world around us, and we form completely subjective opinions about morality and ethics. This learning can take place through modeling or by reinforcement.

modeling Learning theory concept that people learn behaviors, values, and attitudes through relationships; they identify with another person and want to be like that person and pattern themselves after the "model."

In **modeling,** values and moral beliefs come from those whom one admires and aspires to identify with. If that role model happens to be a priest, one will probably develop a religious ethical system; if the role model happens to be a pimp or a sociopath, an egoistic ethical system may develop. If the identification is broken, moral beliefs may change. It is no surprise that, when asked who has been important in their moral development, most people say it is their parents, because primary caregivers are the most significant people in life during the important formative years. Although we may not hold exactly the same views and have exactly the same values as our parents, they are influential in our value formation.

reinforcement Rewards.

Another way that learning theorists explain moral development is through **reinforcement**. This theory holds that behaviors and beliefs that are reinforced (either through material rewards or through more subjective rewards, such as praise) are repeated and eventually become permanent. Behavior is completely neutral; an infant can be taught any behavior desired, and the moral beliefs consistent with that behavior. In one experiment, children were told a hypothetical story in which an adult punished a neutral act, such as a child practicing a musical instrument. The children later defined that act as bad, despite the intrinsic neutrality of the action. This indicates the power of adult definitions and punishment in the child's moral development (Boyce and Jensen, 1978: 133–170).

cognitive dissonance Psychological term referring to the discomfort that is created when behavior and attitude or belief are inconsistent.

Quite a bit of research supports a learning theory of moral development. For instance, it was found that large gains in moral maturity (at least as measured by paper-and-pencil tests of expression of beliefs) could be achieved by direct manipulation of rewards for such beliefs (Boyce and Jensen, 1978: 143). Contrary to the view that an individual comes to a realization of moral principles through cognitive development, this theory proposes that one can encourage or create moral beliefs simply through rewards.

When behavior is not consistent with beliefs, the discomfort that results is called **cognitive dissonance**. This leads to the development of attitudes to support one's behavior. The child who is constantly told to share toys and is disciplined upon refusing to do so is learning not just the desired behavior, but also the values of cooperation and charity. In an adult these values may be manifested by lending one's lawn mower to a neighbor or by contributing to charities. In contrast, if a child is never punished for aggressive behavior and instead is rewarded by always getting the desired object, aggressiveness and the accompanying moral principle of "might makes right" develop. If we do acts that are contrary to the beliefs that we have been taught, we will feel discomfort. Therefore, we will either stop doing the acts or change our beliefs to reduce the dissonance.

Albert Bandura (born 1925), one of the most cited psychologists of this era, developed social learning theory and the idea of modeling as the mechanism of development. In his early career, he described how the successful use of rewards is related to the child's age. As the child matures, concrete rewards and external sanctions are replaced by symbolic and internal controls (one's conscience) (Bandura, 1964). Eventually Bandura described the individual as not simply a passive recipient of rewards, but rather, as an active participant in the construction and meaning of rewards (Bandura, 1969, 1971). In this view, individuals are active, not passive; self-reflective, not merely acted upon; and self-regulating, not merely controlled by external forces. Bandura's later work revolved around his development of the concept of self-efficacy. **Self-efficacy** can be defined as the individual's feelings of competence, and this sense is developed by comparing the self to others.

self-efficacy
Individuals' feelings of competence and confidence in their own abilities and power, developed by comparing self to others.

Bandura believes that moral values can be most effectively instilled by a combination of direct influence (modeling) and reinforcement. Further, he argues that reinforcement (negative sanctions), accompanied by reasons that encourage empathy for the victims, produce greater abilities to self-regulate than utilizing negative sanctions alone (1991: 53). Bandura sees social and moral maturity as constantly changing, reacting to outside influences (involving family, peers, and social institutions). Self-regulation occurs through a process of anticipatory sanctions—that is, the individual perceives how bad they would feel if they did the act (2002).

Bandura argues that this self-regulation can be "turned off," leading to inhumane acts, through cognitive restructuring via several different mechanisms, as follows (1990, 1991, 2002):

- *Moral justification.* This is an appeal to a higher or more important end to justify the act (e.g., terrorists who are fighting for a cause). Similar to utilitarianism, the idea here is that the end justifies the means.

- *Euphemistic labeling.* By using words that downplay the seriousness of actions, the true moral nature of such actions is ignored (e.g., sanitizing language, such as "wasting" or "whacking" instead of killing, and the term "collateral damage" for killing civilians in times of war).

- *Advantageous comparison.* This is an argument that the action may be wrong, but it isn't as bad as some other actions (e.g., "What was done at Abu Ghraib wasn't as bad as the actions of insurgents who cut off the heads of civilian contractors").

- *Displacement of responsibility.* This argument basically removes the individual as a free-thinking agent of his or her own actions in order to deny culpability (e.g., "I was only following orders").

- *Diffusion of responsibility.* In this situation, the individual can redefine his or her responsibility for an action by diffusing it among a number of people (e.g., when a number of people are engaged in morally questionable behavior such as a mob action).

- *Disregard or distortion of the consequences.* By misidentifying the consequences of one's actions, one can deny one's responsibility for harm (e.g., when the executioner is hidden behind a curtain or when the CEO who gives the order to pollute merely requests that the problem be "taken care of").

- *Dehumanization.* Humans feel the most sympathy/empathy for those who are most like us and who are closest to us, and we feel the least for those who are most unlike us. Therefore, dehumanization is a process to strip the victim of any qualities of similarity that may create sympathy (e.g., the use of terms such as gooks, slant-eyes, pigs, wetbacks, and other dehumanizing references).

Bandura argues that it takes a certain constellation of conditions to create human atrocities, not necessarily "monstrous" people (Bandura, 1991: 89). Also, he purports that the shift to immoral acts and attendant justifications is probably gradual, not immediate. Inhibitions are lessened when there is social support for inhuman acts. Finally, external conditions are not all-powerful; the individual adapts and reinterprets them within his or her own internal cognitive processes (Bandura, 2002).

Learning theory leaves little room for universalism, absolutism, or the idea that a moral truth exists apart from humans that is not of their construction but that awaits their discovery. The theory is completely humanistic in that morality is considered to be a creation of humans that explains and provides a rationale for learned behavior.

KOHLBERG'S MORAL STAGE THEORY

developmental theories
Approaches to behavior proposing that individuals have normal growth phases in areas such as morality and emotional maturity.

Developmental theories propose that individuals mature physically, cognitively, and emotionally. Physical development—such as height and weight—can be charted by a pediatrician. Intellectual development is measured by a variety of intelligence tests and is charted against a normal curve of development. Emotional or social development also progresses at a predictable and normal pace, although it may be more difficult to measure. Social maturity is marked by the ability to empathize with others and a willingness to compromise one's desires with others' needs. An emotionally mature person neither abandons self for others nor puts oneself above others, but rather, balances individual needs with others' demands; however, that development might be stunted by negative environmental influences.

The contributions of Jean Piaget and Lawrence Kohlberg have become essential to any discussion of moral development. Piaget believed that we all go through stages of cognitive, or intellectual, growth. These stages parallel moral stages of development, and together they describe a systematic way of perceiving the world. Piaget studied the rules that children develop in their play. These rules reflect the perceptions that children hold of themselves and others and move from egocentrism to cooperativeness.

Kohlberg carried on with Piaget's work and more fully described the stages that each individual passes through in moral and cognitive development (Kohlberg, 1984). In this conception, 2-year-olds do not understand the world in the same way as 20-year-olds do. This difference in understanding affects their moral reasoning ability. The infant lacks sensitivity toward others and is supremely selfish regarding his or her needs and wants. Infants are not concerned with others because they are only vaguely aware of their existence. The infant's world is confined to what is within reach of his or her hands and mouth. Even a mother is important only as the source of comfort and food. Slowly the infant becomes aware that others also have feelings and needs. This awareness leads to empathy and the recognition of right and wrong.

Kohlberg's moral stages The view that moral development is hierarchical; each higher developmental stage is described as moving away from pure egoism toward altruism.

At later stages, abstract reasoning develops, which leads to the ability to understand more difficult moral concepts. **Kohlberg's moral stages** consist of three levels of moral reasoning, with two stages in each level. According to Kohlberg and his colleagues, each stage involves qualitative differences in the way the individual sees the world. Cognitive development and moral development are integrated—that is, one must grow intellectually in order to achieve a higher moral stage. One cannot skip stages, they are hierarchical; however, some people will not advance to the highest stages (Hersh, 1979: 52).

At the *pre-conventional level*, the person approaches a moral issue motivated purely by personal interests. The major concern is the consequence of the action for the individual. For instance, young children do not share toys with others because they see no reason to do so. They derive pleasure from their toys, so to give the toys to others does not make sense to them. Even if the toys belong to others, children are predisposed to appropriate them. Parents are aware of the tears and tantrums associated with teaching a child that toys belonging to others must be given back. Young children first start sharing when they perceive benefit to themselves, such as giving someone their doll in exchange for a game or a ball, or they grudgingly share because they fear punishment from an adult if they do not.

Stage 1 has a punishment and obedience orientation. What is right is that which is praised; what is wrong is that which is punished. The child submits to an authority figure's definition and is concerned only with the consequences attached to certain behaviors, not with the behavior itself.

Stage 2 has an instrument-and-relativity orientation. The child becomes aware of and is concerned with others' needs. What is right is still determined by self-interest, but the concept of self-interest is broadened to include those who are within the child's sphere of relationships. Relationships are important to the child, and he or she is attached to parents, siblings, and best friends, who are included in the ring of self-interest. There is also the emerging concept of fairness and a recognition that others deserve to have their needs met.

At the *conventional level*, people perceive themselves as members of society, and living up to role responsibilities is paramount in believing oneself to be good. Children enter this level when they are capable of playing with other children according to rules. Games and play are training grounds for moral development because they teach the child that there are defined roles and rules of behavior. For instance, a game of softball becomes a microcosm of real life when a child realizes that he or she is not only acting as self but also as a first baseman, a role that includes certain specific tasks. Before this stage, the child runs to the ball regardless of where it is hit. Thus, in a softball game with very young children playing, one may see all the players running after the ball and abandoning their bases because they have difficulty grasping the concept of role responsibilities. Further, although it would be more expeditious to trip the runners as they leave the base so they can be tagged out, the child learns that such behavior is not fair play and is against the rules of the game. Thus, children learn to submerge individual interest to conform to rules and role expectations.

Stage 3 has an interpersonal concordance orientation. The individual performs conventionally determined good behavior to be considered a good person. The views of "significant others" are important to self-concept. Thus, individuals will control their behavior so as to not hurt others' feelings or be thought of as bad.

Stage 4 has a law-and-order orientation. The individual is concerned not just with interpersonal relationships but also with the rules set down by society. The law becomes all-important. Even if the laws themselves are wrong, one cannot disregard them, for that would invite social chaos.

At the *post-conventional level*, a person moves beyond the norms and laws of a society to determine universal good—that is, what is good for all societies. Few people reach this level, and their actions are observably different from the majority. For instance, Mahatma Gandhi might be described as having a post-conventional morality. He did not subscribe to the idea that laws must be obeyed, and he carried out peaceful noncompliance against established laws to conform to his belief in a higher order of morality. At this level of moral development, the individual assumes the responsibility of judging laws and conventions.

Stage 5 has a social contract orientation. The person recognizes interests larger than current laws. This individual is able to evaluate the morality of laws in a historical context and feels an obligation to the law because of its benefits to societal survival.

Stage 6 centers on universal ethical principles. The person who has reached this stage bases moral judgments on the higher abstract laws of truth, justice, and morality.

A seventh stage? Kohlberg advanced the possibility of a seventh stage, which has been described as a "soft" stage of ethical awareness with an orientation of cosmic or religious thinking. It is not a higher level of reasoning, but is qualitatively different. According to Kohlberg, in this highest stage individuals have come to terms with questions such as "Why be just in a universe that is largely unjust?" This is a different question than the definition of justice that forms the content of the other stages. In this stage, one sees oneself as part of a larger whole, and humanity as only part of a larger cosmic structure. This stage focuses on *agape*—a nonexclusive love and acceptance of the cosmos and one's place in it (Kohlberg, 1983; Power and Kohlberg, 1980).

Critics of Kohlberg Some believe that Kohlberg's theory of moral development has several serious flaws. For instance, he has been criticized for focusing too much on the concept of justice, ignoring other aspects of morality. In fact, it is argued that the way he defines moral development is culturally based, reflecting the Judeo-Christian heritage of Kohlberg and his followers. He has also been criticized for focusing too much on rational thinking as opposed to emotional aspects of morality (Levine, Kohlberg, and Hewer, 1985: 99). There has also been research that indicates the stages are not necessarily invariant or form a coherent explanation for people's moral beliefs (Boyce and Jensen, 1978; Bandura, 1991: 49). As mentioned before, there is a disturbing lack of correlation between moral stage scores and behavior (Lutwak and Hennessy, 1985).

Another criticism is that Kohlberg's research can be described as sexually biased because he interviewed only boys in early research. Carol Gilligan (1982, 1987), one of Kohlberg's students, researched an apparent sex difference in moral reasoning and proposed that women may possess a morality *different* from men. Most men, it seems, analyze moral decisions with a rules or justice orientation (Stage 4), whereas many women see the same moral dilemma with an orientation toward needs and relationships (Stage 3). Gilligan labeled this a *care perspective.* A morality based on the care perspective (which is similar to the ethics of care system described in Chapter 2) would be more inclined to look at how a decision affects relationships and addresses needs, whereas the justice perspective is concerned with notions of equality, rights, and universality.

In Gilligan's study, although both men and women raised justice and care concerns in responses to moral dilemmas, among those who focused on one or the other, men focused exclusively on justice whereas half of the women who exhibited a focus did so on justice concerns and the other half on care concerns (Gilligan, 1987). She also found that male and female respondents alike were able to switch from a justice perspective to a care perspective (or back again) when asked to do so; thus, their orientation was more a matter of perspective than an inability to see the other side. What Gilligan points out in her research is that the care perspective completely drops out when one uses only male subjects— which is what Kohlberg did in his early research for the moral stage theory.

Later studies have obtained results consistent with Gilligan's findings. However, the content of the dilemma also evidently influences whether care considerations will be found. The dilemmas involving interpersonal relationships were more likely to stimulate care considerations than those without interpersonal relationships (Rothbart, Hanley, and

Albert, 1986; Flanagan and Jackson, 1987). More recent studies have continued to investigate sex differences in measurements of moral development. A study of male and female Coast Guard members revealed that, when utilizing an identification measure of morality, women scored statistically higher than men (White, 1999); and a study of lawyers revealed that women were significantly less likely to be brought up on disciplinary charges (Hatamyar and Simmons, 2002).

Other studies have failed to find any differences between men and women in their responses to moral dilemmas (see reviews in Walker, 1986; Thoma, 1986; Loo, 2003). Critics of Gilligan argue that her work is more art than science in that she used small sample sizes, and her results have not been widely replicated in larger studies. Further, similar to the criticisms directed at Kohlberg, the approach of measuring one's morality as a hierarchical stage, regardless of whether Stage 4 is higher or lower than Stage 3, has been criticized by those who argue that there is not necessarily a linear progression in one's moral development. Gilligan's most extreme critics, however, have been largely polemical, accusing her of stereotyping women by describing them as being more emotional and nurturing than men, which, critics argue, hark back to the days of stereotyping women as being "naturally" suited only to motherhood (Larrabee, 1993).

The importance of Kohlberg's work is the link he makes between moral development and reason. Although this concept originated with Kant and even earlier philosophers, Kohlberg provides a psychological analysis that sheds light on *how* reason influences moral judgments. Also important in Kohlberg's work is the guidance it provides to education. According to the theory of moral stages, one can encourage movement through the stages by exposing the individual to higher-stage reasoning. The procedures for encouraging moral growth include presenting moral dilemmas and allowing the individual to support his or her position, thereby spurring an intellectual challenge and consequent mental growth. Through exposure to higher reasoning, one sees the weaknesses and inconsistencies of lower-level reasoning and, theoretically, abandons it for higher-level reasoning (Hersh, 1979).

Ethics Teaching/Ethics Training

Can one teach ethics? Can one train employees to act ethically? Or, as many people presume, is one's character pretty well established by the time of young adulthood? Kohlberg (1976) described the following as necessary for moral growth:

- Being in a situation where seeing things from other points of view is encouraged

- Engaging in logical thinking, such as reasoned argument and consideration of alternatives

- Having the responsibility to make moral decisions and to influence one's moral world

- Being exposed to moral controversy and to conflict in moral reasoning that challenges the structure of one's present stage

- Being exposed to the reasoning of individuals whose thinking is one stage higher than one's own

- Participating in creating and maintaining a just community whose members pursue common goals and resolve conflict in accordance with the ideals of mutual respect and fairness

Even if one does not adhere to the other principles of Kohlberg's moral stage theory, these elements of what is necessary for moral growth seem logical. For instance, a child growing up in a family that repeats moral judgments with little attempt to explain or defend them will learn to be closed to other viewpoints. A child who is never forced to take responsibility for his or her own actions will have difficulty developing moral reasoning skills and will not advance to higher stages. These children will be stunted, in a sense, at the Kohlberg pre-conventional level of an infant, constantly fed and cared for, but not allowed to discover that other people exist and must be considered.

A different question, however, is whether the moral belief systems or behaviors of young adults can be changed. We can probably agree that, as adults, if we surround ourselves only with people who think as we do, we are unlikely to change our moral belief systems, but is it possible to change people's attitudes and behavior through education or training?

In most colleges in the 1800s, a course in moral philosophy was required of all graduates. This class, often taught by the college president, was designed to help college students become good citizens. The goal of college was not only to educate as to facts, but also to help students attain the moral sensibility that would make them productive, worthy citizens. As it was taught, ethics involved not only the history of philosophical thought but also a system of beliefs and values and the skills to resolve moral or ethical dilemmas.

Most professional schools today (in law, medicine, and business) require at least one class in professional ethics. Typically, these classes present the opportunity to examine the ethical dilemmas that individuals may encounter as members of that profession and help students discover the best way to decide ethical issues. Usually the classes combine discussion and instruction. Although some class time is devoted to having students discuss their views, certainly part of the task is to provide what might be called indoctrination to the values and codes of behavior of that profession.

It is possible that you are reading this book for a college ethics course in a criminal justice or criminology department. As such, your exploration of ethics is akin to a professional responsibility course for law students or a medical ethics class for medical students. Your instructor may take an issue-based approach, exploring or evaluating issues such as the definition of justice; the appropriate use of force; the relative importance of due process over efficiency; the ethical use of technology to control the populace; the variables used to determine responsibility and punishment; the right of society to treat (or punish); and the limits that should be placed on treatment (or punishment). But your course may also include more applied discussions of how professionals should make decisions when faced with ethical dilemmas. Applied courses attempt to provide the analytical tools available for determining ethical actions.

According to Sherman (1982: 17–18), the following elements are necessary for any ethics course relating to criminal justice:

- Stimulating the "moral imagination" by posing difficult moral dilemmas

- Encouraging the recognition of ethical issues and larger questions instead of more immediate issues such as efficiency and goals

- Helping to develop analytical skills and the tools of ethical analysis

- Eliciting a sense of moral obligation and personal responsibility to show why ethics should be taken seriously

- Tolerating and resisting disagreement and ambiguity

- Understanding the morality of coercion, which is intrinsic to criminal justice

- Integrating technical and moral competence, especially recognizing the difference between what we are capable of doing and what we should do

- Becoming familiar with the full range of moral issues in criminology and criminal justice in the study of criminal justice ethics

in the NEWS

ETHICS CLASSES: SOLUTION OR SCAM?

In an editorial poking fun at the recent rise of ethics classes, Joan Ryan of the *San Francisco Chronicle* writes that Raytheon, a defense contractor, has produced a video in which the company's vice president, along with film critic Roger Ebert, gives thumbs-up or thumbs-down to a series of behaviors. Ryan wonders if Bert and Ernie of *Sesame Street* might have done a better job. An attempt to improve the ethics of a work force is laudable, but the approach may be patronizing or even cynical, depending on the company's motivation.

Ryan points out that businesses that have ethics programs in place are eligible for reduced fines if they are found guilty of corporate wrongdoing. The behavior of leaders and the values of the company are more important determiners of employees' behaviors than whether or not they sat through a class. She says, "[T]he post-Enron era is much like the pre-Enron. Companies were cooking the books, faking transactions, lying to shareholders. The problem was about perpetuating a sham. Now so, too, is the solution."

SOURCE: Ryan, 2002: A11.

Teaching ethics, which may have focused solely on issues, is replaced with training for ethics once in the field, with an almost exclusive applied focus. Training can be purely informational—that is, instructors telling employees what is and is not acceptable in the organization. More often, however, ethics training includes elements to help professionals approach ethical dilemmas. In the growing field of ethics instruction, businesses are hiring "ethics officers" to ensure that their workers behave honestly and ethically, and ethics centers are offering training to state and private organizations of every type. The Josephson Institute is a training center that markets to a broad range of businesses and organizations. Neil Trautman's National Ethics Institute in Mississippi and the Center for Law Enforcement Ethics in Texas are two centers that offer ethics training to law enforcement and correctional agencies. In fact, ethics training is a growth industry, as the In the News box points out, with somewhat mixed reviews.

Many believe that it is much more effective to target new members of a profession with ethics training before these individuals are faced with real-life dilemmas. Socio-moral reasoning opportunities could exist in academies to encourage "higher stage" thinking. Of course, what often happens is that once students leave this setting, they are often told to forget what they've learned in the classroom. This happens often in police and correctional academies, where cadets are taught "the book," and then learn "the street" when they are paired with an older officer. This also happens when lawyers realize that the high ideals of justice they learned in law school have little to do with the bargaining and bureaucratic law of the courthouse. Learning theorists would argue, alternatively, that the most effective way to change the ethics of a profession is to utilize rewards and punishments to change behaviors; in other words, supervision and discipline are the vehicles to creating an ethical organization. Of course, both training and supervision/discipline together may be more effective than concentrating on either to the exclusion of the other. Also, many argue that ethics training is not as important in creating an ethical organization as the behavior of administrators and supervisors.

Leadership and the Ethical Organization

Can anyone argue against the idea that if leaders are honest, ethical, and caring, there is a good chance that those who work for them will also be ethical? If administrators and/ or managers are hypocritical, untruthful, and use their positions for personal gain, workers often march in these same footsteps. If the business itself is premised on misleading the consumer and perpetrating fraud to secure higher profits, why should business leaders expect that workers would behave any differently? Trautman (2008) offers the "Corruption Continuum," which details how organizations can become corrupt through (1) administrative indifference toward integrity, (2) ignoring obvious ethical problems, and creating a (3) hypocrisy and fear dominated culture, all leading to (4) a survival of the fittest approach by individual employees (who will commit unethical acts to protect themselves).

In any organization, there are those who will almost always make ethical choices, those who will usually make unethical ones, and those who can be influenced one way or the other. The best course of action is to reward those in the first group and identify those in the second group and encourage them to find other employment or at least remove them from temptation. Then organizational leaders must create an atmosphere for the third group that encourages ethical decision making. This can be done by promoting ethical administrators, rewarding morally courageous behavior, and providing clear and powerful organizational policies that emphasize worthwhile goals and honest means.

Gardner (2007) discusses the GoodWorks Foundation, a private foundation that does research and advises businesses on how to achieve excellence through ethical practices and principles. In his work, Gardner argues that in order to meet future challenges, companies and organizations will have to recognize responsibilities to the greater community. Workers will need the following five types of cognitive capabilities:

- *The disciplined mind:* The ability to focus and learn a field of study

- *The synthesizing mind:* The ability to integrate diverse ideas into a coherent whole

- *The creating mind:* The ability to recognize and solve problems

- *The respectful mind:* The ability to form and maintain good relationships with other people

- *The ethical mind:* The ability to fulfill one's responsibilities as a citizen and to identify with fellow human beings

Basically, Gardner argues, much like Aristotle, that to be an excellent person or organization, there is an essential element of ethics that must be a part of the beliefs, values, and principles of the organization (or individual's self-definition). For an organization to be excellent and succeed in the future, individuals in the organization must be more than intelligent and educated; they must be ethical.

An ethical organization must have ethical administrators and managers. They are responsible not only for their personal conduct but also for the actions of those they supervise. What does it mean to be an ethical leader? Obviously, one first has to be sure that one is not personally engaged in unethical and corrupt behaviors. Unfortunately, in many recent examples, leaders cannot pass even this first test. In the White Collar Crime box, the failings of these organizations' leaders led to ethical scandals, but, more importantly, the financial victimization of thousands of people, including their own employees.

Administrators and managers do not necessarily ensure that an organization will be free from corruption merely by not engaging in corrupt practices themselves; they must take affirmative steps to encourage ethical actions. Issues that could be examined in a

White Collar Crime Lack of Ethical Leadership

Hewlett-Packard Spy Scandal This so-called boardroom spying scandal erupted in 2006, when it was discovered that detectives hired by officials at Hewlett-Packard investigated who was leaking confidential information by spying on board members. This included using pretexting—using the target's Social Security number to convince telephone companies to release the telephone records of the person. The head of HP, Patricia Dunn, resigned, and she and other top officials, as well as the detectives, faced state and federal charges of identity theft, fraud, and wiretapping.

Chicago's Hired Truck Scandal State and federal investigations began in 2002 and are ongoing into a corruption scheme in city government. The core of the corrupt activities lies in the hiring practices of city officials who allocated jobs and contracts to those who would pay kickbacks and/or campaign for the political figures who approved the position or contract. The resulting investigations concern how high up the corrupt scheme went, some arguing that even Mayor Richard Daley was involved.

Bernie Madoff and Allen Stanford's Ponzi Schemes Both of these Ponzi schemes involved billions of dollars and thousands of victims. Both men took money and spent it lavishly while assuring investors that they would receive substantial returns on their money. Madoff has been convicted and is serving a 150-year prison sentence. Stanford is in jail awaiting trial.

Ivan Boesky Boesky was the king of insider trading in the 1980s and served three years in federal prison.

Dennis Kozlowski The head of Tyco International, Kozlowski was convicted of misappropriating over $400 million of his company's funds. He was sentenced to eight years in prison.

Conrad Black Black was convicted in 2007 of diverting funds from his newspaper companies for his own personal use.

The Enron Felons Andrew Fastow (former CFO of Enron) pleaded guilty to fraud, money laundering, and conspiracy. He will be released from prison in 2013. Jeffrey Skilling (CEO) was convicted of fraud, insider trading, and other crimes. His release date is 2028. Kenneth Lay, the head of Enron, died of a heart attack before being brought to trial.

HealthSouth CEO Richard Scrushy was found guilty of bribery and mail fraud in relation to a scheme to get himself appointed to a regulatory panel. He will be released from prison in 2014.

Adelphia Communications John Rigas and his sons embezzled $2.3 billion from the company. Rigas was convicted of bank, wire, and securities fraud. He will be released from prison in 2018 and his son, Timothy Rigas, will be released in 2022.

WorldCom Bernard Ebbers (former CEO of WorldCom), after bilking investors of $11 billion, was convicted of false financial reporting and fraud. He won't be released until 2139.

Sources: Associated Press, 2007a; Von Bergen, 2006: Al, A13; Sallah and Barry, 2009; BusinessInsider.com, 2009.

discussion of ethical leadership include the practice of recruitment, training, discipline and reward structures, and evaluation of performance.

Souryal (1992: 307) offers advice to leaders who would like to advance ethical decision making and emphasizes the importance of organizational support for ethical actions. Ethical leaders should do the following:

1. Create an environment that is conducive to dignified treatment on the job.
2. Increase ethical awareness among the ranks through formal and informal socialization.
3. Avoid deception and manipulation in the way officers are assigned, rewarded, or promoted.
4. Allow for openness and the free flow of unclassified information.
5. Foster a sense of shared values and incorporate such values in the subculture of the agency.

6. Demonstrate an obligation to honesty, fairness, and decency by example.

7. Discuss the issue of corruption publicly, expose corrupt behavior, and reward ethical behavior.

Metz (1990) offers a similar set of advice. He proposes that ethical administrators follow these steps:

1. Establish realistic goals and objectives.

2. Provide ethical leadership (meaning, set a moral tone by actions).

3. Establish formal written codes of ethics.

4. Provide a whistleblowing mechanism.

5. Discipline violators of ethical standards.

6. Train all personnel in ethics.

When top leaders take responsibility for their subordinates' behavior, they will lead and administer with greater awareness, interaction, and responsibility. Because of this responsibility, a supervisor or administrator must be concerned with how the workplace treats the worker, how the worker views the mission, and how the public views the organization. A concern for one's public image may be shared by ethical leaders and egoistic bureaucrats, but the first group has a sincere desire to understand the public's complaints and respond to them, and the second group is concerned solely with protecting the image of the organization—a stand that may mean punishing whistleblowers rather than appreciating them for bringing problems out in the open.

A strong ethical leader would have a personal relationship with subordinates—without showing favoritism. This personal relationship is the foundation of modeling, identification, and persuasive authority. Strong leadership involves caring and commitment to the organization. A strong leader is someone who is connected with others but also has a larger vision, if you will, of goals and mission.

Delattre (1989b) describes a *realistic idealist*—and it's possible that he would also be content with the term *idealistic realist*. What he is referring to is the capacity for good leaders to understand social realities, but to avoid cynicism in the face of such social realities. For instance, in the use of force, a realistic idealist would understand that force is necessary at times, but would attempt every alternative means to protect all human life, including the offender's life. Leaders must never lose sight of the organizational mission; for public servants, the mission is public service.

The Criminal Justice Professional

For the criminal justice professional who must uphold and enforce the law, the discussion of morality, justice, and law is not just academic. Line officers often face questions of individual morality versus obedience and loyalty to one's superiors or the organization. One thing that every professional must understand is that they alone are morally and ethically responsible for their decisions and actions. It is for this reason that the study of ethics is so important.

The My Lai incident in Vietnam has almost passed out of this nation's consciousness, but at the time, there was great debate over whether soldiers should follow their superiors' orders blindly or make an independent assessment of the morality of the action. In this case, several officers were prosecuted by a military court for killing women and children in a village during the Vietnam War without any evidence that they were a threat to the unit's safety. The officers' defense was that their superiors gave the orders to take the village

WALKING THE WALK

Thomas Tamm grew up with the FBI in his blood. Both his father and uncle were highly regarded ranking officials in the bureau. His brother became an FBI agent. It is said that, as a child, Tamm played in J. Edgar Hoover's office. Thus, you would not have expected that in the early morning hours of August 1, 2007, a squad of heavily armed FBI agents would roust his family from bed with a search warrant, seizing his and his children's computers and other personal items. His alleged crime? He leaked the fact that the federal government was engaged in spying on its own citizens, against the laws of the land.

Tamm, like his relatives, had pursued a career in public service, as a prosecuting attorney in the Department of Justice. In his job with the Department of Justice's Office of Intelligence Policy and Review, he had access to highly classified wiretap transcripts of suspected terrorists. In 2004, he discovered evidence that the National Security Agency was gathering domestic intelligence illegally without going through the Foreign Intelligence Surveillance Court for warrants. At first, Tamm tried to use accepted channels to address the problem, but when superiors and others in the government did not seem to be interested in investigating the acts of illegal spying, he met with Eric Lichtblau, a *New York Times* reporter. The explosive story of illegal domestic spying won Lichtblau a Pulitzer Prize, raised the important question of the extent of presidential power, spurred Congress to change the Foreign Intelligence Surveillance Act to retroactively make the wiretapping legal so that the acts of the president would not be attacked as illegal, and left Tamm with a federal indictment over his head for divulging national secrets.

Tamm had been subject to increasing depression and anxiety after leaking the story and eventually resigned from the Department of Justice under a cloud of suspicion in 2006. When he became the target of the investigation, he was pressured to plead guilty to one felony count of revealing classified information, but he refused. Since then he has lived under a potential indictment, even though those who were involved in the illegal spying have been promised immunity for their actions. When asked why he did it, he responded, "I had taken an oath to uphold the Constitution." In 2009, he received the Ridenhour Truth-Telling Prize from the Nation Institute and Fertel Foundation (the honor is named for Ron Ridenhour, the soldier who was instrumental in bringing the My Lai massacre to the public's attention). Still, the cost of Tamm's action is high: he has lost his career, suffers from depression, and is over $30,000 in debt due to legal fees. Eric Holder, the current U.S. Attorney General, has not yet indicated whether an indictment against Tamm is forthcoming.

Source: Isikoff, 2008.

without regard to whether the inhabitants were civilians or guerrillas. The rationale was that often there wasn't time to establish whether a civilian was friendly or not, and that, in any event, civilians often carried grenades or otherwise harmed U.S. troops. There was heated public discussion in support of and against the soldiers' actions. Is an individual excused from moral culpability when following orders, or should one disobey orders that one believes to be illegal or immoral? Generally, military justice does not allow a defense of "following orders" if the order is against a treaty or law.

In the Abu Ghraib prison scandal, soldiers argued that they were only following orders when they abused the detainees. Joseph Darby (profiled in the Walking the Walk box in Chapter 2) was so distressed by the pictures showing various types of abuse that he turned them in to the Army's CID, and the resulting investigation led to indictments and resignations. Some, however, blamed Darby and held the position that he should not have exposed what the other soldiers had been doing. Some condemned Darby as a traitor to his country, and he and his family received death threats and were not able to return to their hometown to live because of the town's hostility to him.

A soldier's dilemma is not all that different from a police officer's dilemma in that both organizations place a great emphasis on chain of command and loyalty. It is possible that police officers may receive orders that they know to be illegal and/or unethical from their field training officer (FTO) or other supervisor. Do police officers or other criminal justice professionals have a duty to substitute their personal moral judgments when presented with an unlawful or unethical order, or is obedience to superiors mandatory? In these circumstances, one has to depend on the law rather than the chain of command. If the action is clearly illegal, there will be no legitimate defense if the individual officer follows orders; he or she is as guilty as any other officer who engages in the act. If the action is not against the law but is against policy, departmental sanctions may be applied. If the action is not against the law and not against departmental policy, it is a much grayer area as to which, if any, ethical system would support going against one's superior. The stronger ethical position in this case may be to follow appropriate grievance procedures if something seems to be wrong. As discussed in the Walking the Walk box, Thomas Tamm was faced with a dilemma when he believed that government actors were breaking the law.

Some of the hardest decisions one will be faced with in the course of a career involve going against superiors or colleagues. Even if the behavior is obviously illegal, it is difficult to challenge authority. **Whistleblowers** are those who risk their career to expose wrongdoing in their organization. Of course, some may have purely egocentric reasons for exposing wrongdoing, but many whistleblowers do so because their principles and individual ethical system will not allow them to stand quiet when others in the organization are committing unethical and/or illegal acts. Box 4.1 gives some examples of whistleblowers.

whistleblowers
Individuals, usually employees, who find it impossible to live with knowledge of corruption or illegality within a government or organization and expose it, usually creating a scandal.

Although professionals and practitioners may get bogged down with day-to-day problems and bureaucratic agendas may cause them to lose sight of larger goals, foremost in their minds should always be the true scope and meaning of the power inherent in the criminal justice system. It is people who make a *justice* system just or corrupt.

To protect the citizenry from misuse and abuse of power, personnel in the criminal justice system must have a strong professional identity. There is continuing debate over whether police officers can be described as professionals, and there is even more debate over whether correctional officers can be described as such. These arguments miss a central point: Whether one calls the men and women who wear these uniforms professionals, practitioners, or some other term, they have immense power over other people's lives. This power must be recognized for what it is and held as a sacred trust.

Criminal justice professionals are public servants and, as such, should aspire to a higher standard of behavior. They have a duty to the citizenry they serve, but even more than that, they must possess the moral and ethical sense to prevent the power inherent in their positions from being used for tyranny. Education isn't enough. Learning a body of knowledge and acquiring essential skills do not give individuals the moral sense necessary to use those skills wisely. Witness the recurring scandals involving lawyers and business professionals. A highly educated group is not necessarily free from corruption.

Criminal justice practitioners find themselves faced with a wide spectrum of ethical choices, including:

- Balancing friendship against institutional integrity—that is, when friends and colleagues engage in inappropriate or illegal behavior or rule breaking

- Balancing client (offender) needs against bureaucratic efficiency and institutional goals

- Balancing personal goals or biases that conflict with fair and impartial treatment of the public and the clients served.

BOX 4.1

Blowing the Whistle on Wrongdoing

Many people risk their careers, their livelihood, and even, in some cases, their safety by coming forward when they believe their organization and/or superiors are committing unethical or illegal acts. Often, despite whistleblower laws that protect individuals who work in governmental agencies from retaliation, the individual pays a heavy price.

Mathew Zipoli

Zipoli was a police officer at the Lawrence Livermore National Laboratory. He contacted federal officials in 2001 to report safety and security lapses at the nuclear weapons facility. Although a federal investigation confirmed Zipoli's allegations, he was fired by the University of California, which ran the lab. He ultimately received a $175,000 settlement but had to give up his job and agree to a permanent ban on employment there.

Donna Trueblood

Trueblood told state and federal environmental officials that her employer, a waste incineration plant, was not handling toxic chemicals correctly. Although Trueblood received a settlement that was sealed by the court, she also had to agree to a lifetime employment ban at the company.

Coleen Rowley

Rowley, an FBI agent, wrote a widely publicized memorandum to FBI Director Robert Mueller, describing in detail how the agency had mishandled information concerning alleged terrorist Zacarias Moussaoui. She was named as one of the "Persons of the Year" by *Time* magazine in 2002, retired from the FBI in 2004, and ran an unsuccessful campaign for Congress in 2006.

Babak Pasdar

Pasdar was a computer security analyst who discovered a mysterious "Quantico circuit" in a major telecommunications company that he was hired to review for security problems. The circuit was a transmission conduit for all information that flowed through the company; anyone with access could peek into citizens' phone and e-mail transmissions. He was told to leave the circuit alone, and his urgent advice that it at least should have a log to determine who accessed it resulted in his being pulled from the project.

Richard Conrad

Conrad was a Navy officer who warned his superiors that proper repair procedures were not being followed in the Navy aviation base in San Diego. In return for his persistent reporting to his superiors that the Navy was endangering pilots by not following current procedures, he was isolated, his work duties were drastically curtailed, and he was forced to accept an early retirement. Then, after an Inspector General report, the Navy awarded Conrad a commendation.

Sources: Whistleblowers Australia, 2007. Also see the Government Accountability Project web site, www.whistleblower.org.

Most people in the criminal justice field (or, indeed, any profession) have basically good character. However, it can be argued that in some situations even those who have formed habits of honesty, truthfulness, and integrity are sincerely perplexed as to the correct course of behavior. These situations arise because the behavior choice seems so innocuous or trivial (e.g., whether to accept free coffee) or so difficult (e.g., a partner or friend wants you to cover up something she did wrong). In these instances, where basically good people have trouble deciding what to do, the ethical systems might help them analyze their choices.

It must also be accepted that in some dilemmas there are going to be costs involved in making the right decision. For instance, an officer who knows it is his duty to provide evidence against his brother-in-law who is a major drug dealer may lose his wife's and children's love. There is no assurance that doing the right thing will not come at a high cost. The ethical person may not necessarily be honored; some have been heavily sanctioned. However, those who do not expose wrongdoing and/or go along with it in an effort not to "rock the boat" often find that their long-term peace of mind pays the price for their silence.

AVOIDING CYNICISM AND BURNOUT

burnout The condition in which a worker has abandoned the mission of the organization and is just "going through the motions."

Two of the greatest dangers in criminal justice are cynicism and **burnout**. Cynical leadership, cynical instructors, and overwhelming evidence that we live in an imperfect world create the all-too-common occurrence of workers who are cynical, who are burned out, and who have abandoned the ideals that led them to the profession in the first place. Cynicism and burnout lead to unethical actions. As mentioned before, ethical leaders should be able to transmit a vision and be committed to the mission of the organization, but many administrators and managers exhibit only pessimistic cynicism over the potential for change, the worth of humanity, and the importance of doing what is right.

How does one avoid cynicism and burnout? First, adopt realistic goals before entering the profession. A police officer cannot expect to save the world, and a treatment professional should not expect to find success with every client. A more realistic career goal might be a resolution to do one's best and to always follow the law.

The second element in avoiding burnout and cynicism is to find and nurture a network of mentors and colleagues who promote ethical values. Cynical people are contagious, and cynicism breeds rationalizations for committing unethical behavior—from leaving work early or falsifying overtime records to violating the rights of suspects or defendants. In every department that has a corruption scandal, however, there are also those who have managed to avoid participating in such activity.

The third element is to seek self-fulfillment and personal enrichment. This could be by gaining higher education, reading self-help books, attending church, joining interest clubs, participating in charitable activities, volunteering to coach community sport teams, or becoming involved in the PTA. Note that these activities all have the element of communication and interaction with others. Such activities promote connectedness with the community at large and counteract the negativity that pervades the criminal justice field. Unfortunately, criminal justice professionals see humanity at its worst, and there is a great need to see the best of the human spirit as well.

CONCLUSION

This chapter shifted the focus from "What is ethical or moral?" to "Why do people act in ethical or unethical ways?" More specifically, we are interested in any findings that shed light on how to ensure that criminal justice professionals act ethically. Philosophers, religious scholars, biologists, psychologists, sociologists, and criminologists have all tried to explain why people do bad things. Biology, learning theory, and Kohlberg's moral stages were used to explain why people behave the way they do, but it was also noted that research finds that people's beliefs sometimes do not match their behavior.

We then turned to issues concerning ethics teaching and training. Research indicates that one's moral beliefs can mature given certain environmental elements, although, as noted, we have weaker evidence that these beliefs will affect behavior. This leaves a large question for organizations as to how best to ensure ethical behavior by professionals and other employees in the organization. It seems clear that training alone is not sufficient and must be combined with ethical leadership.

Ethical leadership is absolutely essential for the ethical organization. Ethical leaders owe a duty to their employees to take responsibility for their own behavior and to create an environment conducive to employees acting ethically, which includes open communication and the use of fair and appropriate discipline.

How criminal justice professionals perform their job determines whether justice is a reality or an illusion. The greatest protection against corruption of power is a belief in and commitment to the democratic process and all it entails. If one desires a career in criminal justice, one must ask these questions:

Do I believe in the Constitution?

Do I believe in the Bill of Rights?

Do I truly believe in the sanctity and natural right of due process?

If one views these protections as impediments, nuisances, or irrelevant, that person should not be a public servant. In the chapters to follow, we examine in greater detail the issues that criminal justice professionals face.

CHAPTER REVIEW

1. Be able to describe the three major theories (and theorists) that attempt to explain behavior.

Biological theories propose that we commit good or bad acts because of biological predispositions, which may be inherited or not. *Learning theory* argues that our behavior is based on the rewards we have received in our past. Albert Bandura's more sophisticated social learning theory presents the individual as an active participant in adapting and interpreting the rewards of his or her environment. Lawrence Kohlberg's *moral stage theory* explains that people's behavior is influenced by the intellectual and emotional stage of development, and that one reaches or does not reach higher stages of development based on environmental factors. Kohlberg's theory proposes a hierarchy of moral stages, with the highest stage holding the most perfect moral principles, which are universalistic. Carol Gilligan found that women were more likely to have a Stage 3 relationship orientation to ethical judgments, while men were more likely to have a Stage 4 "law and order" orientation.

2. Become familiar with Bandura's idea of self-regulation and how it can be "turned off."

Bandura explained that individuals behaved ethically through self-regulatory mechanisms (conscience), but that these mechanisms could be "turned off" through cognitive restructuring using the following: moral justification (appealing to higher principles), euphemistic labeling (downplaying the seriousness of the act), making comparisons (arguing it isn't as bad as something else), displacing responsibility (arguing someone else is at fault), diffusion of responsibility (by acting in a mob), disregarding the consequences (acting in such a way to ignore the effect of one's action), and dehumanization (pretending one's victims are less than human).

3. Describe what is necessary for moral growth according to Kohlberg.

According to Kohlberg, the following are necessary for moral growth: being in a situation where seeing things from other points of view is encouraged; engaging in logical thinking; having the responsibility to make moral decisions and to influence one's moral world; being exposed to moral controversy and to conflict in moral reasoning that challenges the structure of one's present stage; being exposed to the reasoning of individuals whose thinking is one stage higher than one's own; participating in creating and maintaining a just community whose members pursue common goals and resolve conflict in accordance with the ideals of mutual respect and fairness.

4. Be familiar with the necessary elements for criminal justice ethics courses according to Sherman.

Sherman believed that the following should be present in criminal justice ethics courses: stimulating the "moral imagination" by posing difficult moral dilemmas; encouraging the recognition of ethical issues; helping to develop analytical skills and the tools of ethical analysis; eliciting a sense of moral obligation and personal responsibility; tolerating and resisting disagreement and ambiguity; understanding the morality of coercion; integrating technical and moral competence, especially recognizing the difference between what we are capable of doing and what we should do; becoming familiar with the full range of moral issues in criminology and criminal justice in the study of criminal justice ethics.

5. Become familiar with what steps organizational leaders should take to encourage ethical decision making on the part of employees.

According to Sam Souryal and other authors, leaders should create an environment that treats employees with dignity and respect, set realistic goals, increase ethical awareness through training and having a formal written code, avoid deception, allow for openness and transparency, foster a sense of shared values, present an example of honesty and fairness, and expose corrupt behavior (and provide a whistleblowing mechanism) and reward ethical behavior.

KEY TERMS

burnout	Kohlberg's moral stages	reinforcement
cognitive dissonance	modeling	self-efficacy
developmental theories	recognition tests	whistleblowers

STUDY QUESTIONS

1. Briefly explain how biological approaches might explain antisocial behavior. What are some differences between males and females noted by biological researchers? Explain modeling and reinforcement.

2. Explain Kohlberg's moral development theory. What problems do critics have with his theory? How does Carol Gilligan disagree with Kohlberg's stage theory?

3. What necessary elements did Sherman identify for teaching ethics in criminal justice?

4. What are some standards that can be applied to good leadership? What advice do Souryal and Metz offer to those who desire to be good leaders?

5. How does one avoid cynicism and burnout?

WRITING/DISCUSSION EXERCISES

1. Develop an essay on (or discuss) the development of morality. Who has been the greatest influence on your moral development? Why? How? Why do you think people behave in ways that hurt other people? Have you ever done something you knew to be wrong? Why did you do it?

2. Develop an essay on (or discuss) the relationships between morality, moral/ethical teaching, and criminality. Do thieves have the same moral beliefs as others? Do they know that stealing is wrong? Can we successfully predict which individuals will perform unethical or immoral actions?

3. Develop an essay on (or discuss) what an ideal ethical organization would be. What would be the characteristics of leadership? Training? Employees? How does one create such an organization as a change agent if the existing organization is rife with corruption?

ETHICAL DILEMMAS

Situation 1

You are a prosecutor trying your first case. You are thrilled with how well it is going. Every objection you make is upheld, and every objection the defense makes is overruled. The judge shakes her head affirmatively every time you make a point and scowls and makes disparaging comments about and to the defense attorney. As the trial proceeds, you begin to see that it is going so well not because of your legal expertise, but rather, because the judge is obviously and seriously biased against the defense. You do not know if she simply does not like the defense attorney or if she does this in all the trials, but you do know that she is making it extremely difficult for the jury to ignore her and, thus, is violating the due process rights of the accused. Should you be grateful for your good luck and accept an easy conviction or make a stand against the judge's actions?

Situation 2

You are a police officer assigned to the juvenile division. For the most part, you enjoy your job and believe that you have sometimes even made a difference when the juvenile has listened to you and stayed out of trouble (at least as far as you knew). One day you are told repeatedly by your captain to pick up a juvenile, even though you don't think there is any probable cause to do so. This is the third time you have been ordered to pick him up and bring him into the station. You discover that the detectives are trying to get the juvenile to become an informant because he is related to a suspected drug dealer. Should you participate in the attempt to intimidate him or refuse to do so?

Situation 3

Your partner has been on the force 25 years, and you value her opinion greatly. However, you have noticed that she has become progressively more lethargic and unenthusiastic about the job. When dispatch asks for available cars, she won't let you respond. When you see accidents on the highway, she instructs you to go around the block so that you won't have to stop. Even when you receive calls, she tells you to advise dispatch that you are otherwise occupied. You believe that she has become burned out and isn't performing up to the standard that you know she is capable of. What, if anything, would you do about it?

Situation 4

You are a rookie police officer and are riding with a field training officer (FTO). During your shift, the FTO stops at a convenience store and quickly drinks four beers in the back room of the store. He is visibly affected by the beers, and the smell of alcohol is noticeable. What should you do? What if the FTO had just written a favorable evaluation of you even though you should have received a reprimand for an improper disposition of a traffic accident?

Situation 5

You are a senior getting close to graduation and are taking too many classes during your last semester. You find yourself getting behind in class and not doing well on tests. One of the classes requires a 30-page term paper, and you simply do not have the time to complete the paper by the due date. While you are on the Internet one day, you see that term papers can be purchased on any topic. You ordinarily would do your own work, but the time pressure of this last semester is such that you see no other way. Do you purchase the paper and turn it in as your own?

PART II

Police

5

Mikael Karlsson / Alamy

The Police Role in Society

Chapter Objectives

1. Describe the two different missions of law enforcement in a democracy.
2. Explain the types of control that police have at their disposal.
3. Provide the justification for police power and the basic ethical standards that derive from this justification.
4. Identify the differences between the formal ethics of law enforcement and the values of the police subculture.
5. Describe recent research findings on the police subculture.

It began as a typical drug investigation. It ended in the death of an elderly woman and prison sentences for the officers involved. In 2006, officers received a tip from an informant that drugs were being sold out of a house. Instead of following protocol by sending in an informant to buy drugs and confirm the tip, they filed an affidavit for a no-knock search warrant, falsely stating that they had done so. When the raid team burst into her home, the startled 92-year-old woman believed she was under attack and shot at the police officers. She was killed in a hail of bullets. When the officers did not find any drugs in her house and realized the depth of their mistake, they planted marijuana and heroin and falsely claimed they found the drugs to justify the raid. They also forced one of their informants to lie about buying drugs from the woman at her house, in an effort to cover up the tragic error.

Two of the three officers eventually confessed and pleaded guilty to involuntary manslaughter. The lead officer, Gregg Junnier, received a six-year sentence. Their sergeant pleaded guilty in 2009 to federal charges of violating the dead woman's civil rights, for knowingly allowing the perjured affidavit to be submitted to the court, and received 18 months in a federal prison. After the scandal erupted, the district attorney expressed his distrust of officer testimony and initiated a wide-ranging review of criminal cases where officers might have employed similar tactics (Dewan and Goodman, 2007: A18; Visser, 2009).

This case is a cautionary tale for officers who may be tempted to take shortcuts in their mission of crime fighting. In some people's minds, perhaps, the officers were caught up in a "war" and Kathryn Johnston, the woman killed, might be considered collateral damage in that war. In another view, however, the officers forgot their mission of public service and ignored the premise that allegiance to the law is more important than catching lawbreakers.

Crime Fighter or Public Servant?

In Chapters 5, 6, and 7, we will discuss ethics as it relates to policing in the United States. In this chapter, we begin with some overarching issues that relate to the profession itself; specifically, we explore the role of law enforcement in a democracy, the extent of police officer discretion, and the manner in which police discretion is guided and controlled by formal ethics and the police occupational subculture. Chapter 6 presents and explores several controversial issues in law enforcement and how these issues translate into dilemmas for individual officers. In Chapter 7, the parameters and prevalence of police corruption and misconduct are described, along with measures that have been suggested to reduce them.

As we discuss issues of law enforcement ethics in these chapters, we must keep in mind that the majority of officers are honest and ethical. We focus on the few officers who abuse their position or forget their mission; however, this in no way should be taken as a criticism of the thousands upon thousands of officers who do good work, every day, in every city in the country. In order to understand the few deviant officers, we must focus on their actions and the elements of the profession that open the door to such behaviors.

Harsh scrutiny is often directed at police actions, and officers think they are treated unfairly by the public and the media. However, there is an important reason for such scrutiny. The police represent the "thin blue line" between disorder and order, between the "war of all against all" and lawful order. No other criminal justice professional comes under as much constant and public scrutiny—but no other criminal justice professional wields as much discretion in so many situations. The scrutiny is understandable when one realizes that the police are power personified. They have the choice to arrest or not to arrest, to mediate or to charge, and in decisions to use deadly force, they even hold the power of life and death.

We will approach these chapters with an underlying premise that what drives individual decisions on the part of law enforcement officers and society's reactions to them are derived from a perception of the law enforcement mission. Two different missions—crime fighting and public service—can be identified as having quite different implications for decision making. We do not, of course, mean to say that these missions are necessarily contradictory or exclusive; however, it is important to note the history and present-day influence of these different roles.

CRIME FIGHTER

When one asks most people what the role of policing is in society, the response is some version of "catch criminals" or "fight crime." If one views police as crime control agents, these presumptions may follow:

- Criminals are the enemy, and fundamentally different from good people.
- Police are the "army" that fights the enemy, using any means necessary to control, capture, and punish them.
- Good people accept and understand that police are in a "war" and must be allowed deference in their decision making because they—not us—are the experts and only they know the enemy.

This model is obviously based on Herbert Packer's (1968) crime control model (which he contrasted with the due process model discussed below). According to Packer, the crime control model operates under the following principles:

1. Repression of criminal conduct is the most important function.
2. Failure of law enforcement means the breakdown of order.
3. Criminal process is the positive guarantor of social freedom.
4. Efficiency is a top priority.
5. Emphasis is on speed and finality.
6. A conveyor belt is the model for the system.
7. There is a presumption of guilt.

Police perception of their role as crime fighters will lead to certain decisions in their use of force, their definition of duty, and their use of deception and coercion. Public perception of the police mission as primarily crime fighting leads to a willingness to accept certain definitions and justifications of behavior: that drug addicts are crazed, that individuals who are beaten must have deserved it, that all defendants must be guilty, and so on.

Typically, members of the public who have a crime control outlook show outrage only when police accidentally violate the rights of the "good" guys instead of the "bad" guys: when the victim of deadly force turns out to be a middle-class insurance agent, when the evening news shows police officers hitting someone who doesn't look like a criminal, or when an innocent person is exonerated. In most cases, police actions are rationalized or excused by the belief that people "get what they deserve."

PUBLIC SERVANT

public servants
Professionals who are paid by the public and whose jobs entail pursuing the public good.

If one views police as **public servants**, other presumptions follow:

- Criminals are not a distinct group; they shop, pay taxes, have kids and parents, and often are one's next-door neighbor.
- Police have limited ability to affect crime rates one way or the other because crime is a complex social phenomenon, and the history of law enforcement originates in order maintenance, not crime control.
- Police as public servants serve *all* people, including criminals, and therefore should not make quick judgments about an individual's worthiness to receive their services.

Under Packer's (1968) due process model, the following principles stand out in contrast to those described above as representing the crime control model:

1. There is a possibility of error.
2. Finality is not a priority.
3. There is insistence on prevention and elimination of mistakes.
4. Efficiency is rejected if it involves shortcuts.
5. Protection of process is as important as protection of innocents.
6. The coercive power of the state is always subject to abuse.

Packer's original model of due process is somewhat different from our description of the public service mission because, rather than just an emphasis on rights, law enforcement is perceived as "owned" by all people, so service is foremost. Police must respond to all constituencies, including groups that may be less supportive of the police than

WALKING THE WALK

Anthony Bouza, a Spanish immigrant, entered police work for economic security. He obtained a bachelor's degree and a master's degree during 12 years of night school in New York while working as a police officer in the Bronx. He initiated early police–community contacts that predated community policing and was a vocal critic of social inequality.

In 1976, he quit before he was fired after making some ill-advised comments that the middle and upper class only wanted the police to make the problems of the lower class invisible. He was asked to be chief of police in Minneapolis, where he continued to make waves. During the 1980s, his officers sometimes arrested his wife, an activist who was an ardent opponent of the military. He butted heads frequently with the city council, but his most vocal opponents were his officers, who did not like his position, expressed frequently to the media, that he owed his loyalty to the citizens of Minneapolis, not his fellow police officers. He voluntarily stepped down in 1989 and went on to run unsuccessfully for governor of Minnesota.

Bouza is not a perfect man. He may be described as "full of himself." He may be criticized for having a flip and indiscreet tongue. But one thing that most people, even his critics, will admit is that he acts as he believes, and he believes in the values of public service and integrity.

Source: Bouza, 2001.

white middle-class communities. It is an enlarged view of the police officer role in society. Rather than simply catching criminals, officers are perceived to be peace keepers and service providers.

A perception of the police officer as public servant implies a much more restrictive view of the use of force and police power. The utilitarian idea that the "end" (crime control) justifies almost any "means" is rejected in favor of an approach that is more protective of due process and equal protection. Anthony Bouza, as described in the Walking the Walk box, might be seen as reflecting these concepts of allegiance to public service. Note his perception that he owed loyalty to the public he served, even over loyalty to his fellow police officers. In the public service mission, law enforcement, above all, protects the rights of every citizen and—only in this way—escapes the taint of its historical role as a tool of oppression for the powerful. These two models are better understood if we take a brief look at the history of law enforcement in the United States.

HISTORY OF POLICING: FROM PUBLIC SERVANT TO CRIME FIGHTER

Kappeler, Sluder, and Alpert (1984/1994) have discussed the early origins of law enforcement as a model of service. Police were involved in social service activities: they ran soup kitchens, provided lodging for indigents, and spurred moral reform movements against cigarettes and alcohol. Of course, early law enforcement personnel were also involved in social control and employed utilitarian violence—that is, they acted as the force for power holders in society and were union busters and political-machine enforcers. Such force was frequently used against immigrants, labor organizers, and the poor (Alpert and Dunham, 2004; Harris, 2005). Researchers note that early law enforcement even used undercover agent provocateurs in the 1800s, placing them in anarchist groups to incite violence to justify using official violence against them. Two incidents of this are the 1874 Tompkins Square riot, where 7,000 were injured, and the Haymarket incident in 1886 (Donner, 1992: 13).

Early police departments also were marred by frequent graft and other forms of corruption. Crank (2003), for instance, discusses how police were involved in local political machines. They stuffed ballot boxes and coerced votes. Their graft was widely tolerated because of their meager salaries. Donner (1992: 62) called this the "dialectic of the bargain," referring to police pursuing and harassing dissenter groups in exchange for the power holders' toleration of police corruption.

The move toward police "professionalism," starting in the 1920s, was spurred by several factors, one of which was to improve the image of police as *objective* enforcers of the law rather than enforcers for whomever happened to be in power. In effect, there was a real or perceived shift of police loyalty from political bosses to the law itself (Kappeler et al., 1994: 49; Fogelson, 1977). Part of this transformation involved the idea that police were crime fighters—professional soldiers in the war on crime—a concept that implies objectivity, professional expertise, and specialized training. This role deemphasized the social service role and ultimately led to policing characterized by detachment from the community being policed instead of integration in that community. In this new role, police were proactive rather than simply reactive to public demands (Payne, 2002; Crank and Caldero, 2000/2005).

Even though the professional crime fighter role of the police officer has been well established for more than 70 years, we can see remnants of the legacy of both the early political enforcer role and the public service role. Some continue to see the police as enforcers for those who hold financial and political power and point to their continuing role in investigating and monitoring dissident groups. The so-called "Red Squads" in some police departments infiltrated and spied on organizations believed to be sympathetic to socialism from the 1930s to the 1960s (Donner, 1992). Then, in the 1960s and 1970s, police turned their attention to antiwar groups and others that expressed opposition to the government. At one point the Chicago police department had files on 117,000 individuals and 14,000 organizations (Donner, 1992: 92). In fact, these activities were what led to more stringent wiretapping laws and legal decisions that ruled such activities improper infringements on citizens' privacy rights (Donner, 1992: 103).

In 2004, New York City police were widely criticized for mass arrests of those who wanted to protest in front of the Republican National Convention. Although 1,800 were arrested and held in makeshift detention facilities until the convention was over, 90 percent of the arrests led to dismissals. Critics argue that police utilized their power not for the enforcement of the law, but rather, to restrain the freedom to exercise political beliefs (Dwyer, 2005). In May 2007, LAPD officers used rubber bullets and batons against what was described as a peaceful demonstration in support of illegal immigrants in MacArthur Park. Although the police resort to force was prompted by the actions of the demonstrators, Chief William Bratton ended up sanctioning the commanders in charge that day, indicating that the police use of force was inappropriate and against policy, if not illegal (Steptoe, 2007). The point is, to some people, police continue to be the enforcers for those who are in power against those who have none.

In other countries, this perception of police as "muscle" for the power holders is present as well, in greater or lesser degrees. Although British police are widely respected as professional and measured in their use of force, London police are engaged in an ongoing scandal due to an alleged illegal use of force during their suppression of demonstrators during a G20 meeting in 2009 (Edwards and Smith, 2009). In other countries, the image of police as corrupt and in league with the powerful is much more pronounced. For instance, in the fall of 2009, Alexey Dymovsky, a Russian police officer, posted a YouTube video alleging rampant corruption, including being told to make false arrests. The video resulted in Major Dymovsky's arrest, but also spurred other officers to make their own videos. They echoed the widespread belief that police in Russia often do the bidding of corrupt politicians and businessmen, including arresting rivals on trumped-up charges and intimidating labor organizers. Police have even been implicated in the unsolved murders of crusading journalist Anna Politkovskaya, human rights lawyer Stanislav Markelov, and journalist Anastasia Baburova. Wendle (2009) points out that a new code of conduct has been established and circulated to all police in Russia. Rashid Nurgaliyev, head of the Ministry of Internal Affairs, was quoted as saying that the moral education of officers was far from ideal. Russian President Dmitry Medvedev has called police corruption a threat to national security and, indeed, it can be said that when 40 percent of a nation's population don't trust the police and almost a quarter say they are afraid of them, there is a threat of political destabilization (Schreck, 2009).

Military officials indicate that one of the challenges in Afghanistan is that police (along with government officials) are so corrupt that the people do not trust them to provide order or enforce the law and, therefore, turn to the Taliban for protection. Evidently, police are known to steal truckloads of gasoline; and judges, prosecutors, and police routinely solicit and/or accept bribes. Although the United States has sent more trainers to help police become more professional, the culture of corruption is so pervasive that it is almost impossible to overcome (Oppel, 2009). It is not an overstatement to say that a nation's police force is part of the foundation of a secure government. When police act as the enforcers for a small group of the powerful, or utilize their position purely for self-interest, rather than act as agents of the law, there is no law and the very stability of the country is at risk.

community policing A model of law enforcement that creates partnerships with the community and addresses underlying problems rather than simply enforcing the law.

The other historical role of police is that of public service. The early role of social service has been resurrected in the **community policing** movement, which involves having officers develop closer relationships with community leaders to help them solve some of the social problems that are believed to be associated with the development of disorder and lead to crime. Police officers may be involved in cleaning up parks, getting the city to raze abandoned houses, cleaning up graffiti, helping to start youth programs, and having community meetings to listen to what citizens think are the problems of the community (National Institute of Justice, 1992: 3). Patrol officers' resistance to community policing models may make sense if one views neighborhood policing as trading in the "crime fighter" role for a much less esteemed "social worker" role. However, even those who resisted the community policing model admitted that the role of law enforcement has always included community relations and community service—what some have called "order maintenance."

Schafer (2002) argues that community policing is not a panacea for problems related to police misconduct. He offers some potential issues for community policing strategies as they relate to corruption. Gratuities may be more of an issue for officers who are expected to create and maintain close ties to the community. Gratuities then may create the slippery-slope slide into more serious forms of misconduct. Officers may be exposed to wider corruption among city employees, such as building inspectors, and, by such exposure, have a harder time withstanding minor transgressions themselves. In addition to those issues, close relationships with the community blur the lines so that lawbreakers may become friends, and the police officer's discretion regarding when to enforce the law is compromised by personal relationships. Finally, increased freedom and autonomy and decreased supervision provide more opportunities for misconduct. On a positive note, Schafer observes that because community policing seems to lessen cynicism and burnout and reduces the anonymity of individual police officers, it may act as an insulator against misconduct. Further, because officers share a closer relationship with community members, the possibility of brutality may be decreased.

FUTURE OF POLICING: THE END OF COMMUNITY POLICING?

While some aspects of the community policing approach have been institutionalized, observers note that 9/11 has led to a retrenchment in policing and a return to more traditional crime fighting elements (Murray, 2005; Brown, 2007). Because one might argue that aspects of the police culture never fully fit with the community policing approach, it is not hard to understand why the threat of terrorism might have derailed the success and acceptance of community policing. Problem-solving policing and zero tolerance for community disorder seem to have remained as current elements of law enforcement management; however, community–police partnerships and police as troubleshooters for purely social problems may be a trend that has come and gone.

Harris (2005) echoes much of this discussion in his description of how 9/11 has led to sweeping reforms that have changed the face of federal law enforcement and influenced change in state and local law enforcement as well. He makes an analogy between the current shift in focus of the law enforcement mission to what occurred in the 1960s and 1970s when law enforcement became involved in counterintelligence and control efforts against war demonstrators. Today, there is pressure for local law enforcement to involve itself in immigration control and counter-terrorism efforts. Harris documents the opposition (including from local police administrators) to such demands immediately after 9/11 (2005: 7) and, generally, discusses how such efforts damage the trust and communication between the community and the police department. He promotes the view that the centralized, top-down, "crime control" approach is counterproductive in meeting the challenges of the 21st century and that what law enforcement should do is improve communication and trust between the police and the community. This focus was the hallmark of community policing; in fact, he presents what he calls a "preventive policing" model, which includes the concepts of community policing, problem-oriented policing, and accountability mechanisms (2005: 24).

QUOTE & QUERY

Departments must evolve from the simplistic view of their mission as "locking up the bad guys" to one in which police departments make communities safe in collaboration with those they serve.

—SOURCE: HARRIS, 2005, P. 14.

Why do you think Harris does not endorse the "crime fighter" role of the police?

It is important to understand that both the crime fighter role and the public servant role have the potential and capacity for wrongdoing. The professional crime fighter may trample rights in the interest of efficiency in catching criminals, and community police officers may be too eager to do the bidding of community members in controlling those who upset the "order" of the community (for example, by over-enforcement of noise ordinances or loitering laws). The point cannot be overemphasized that police officers have powers unlike any other group. In the next section, we examine police power more carefully, but before we do, the Policy Box examines one particular example of how the perceived mission affects police policy.

POLICY ISSUES — Racial Profiling

There is widespread public opinion condemning racial profiling, and departmental policies have seen some changes over the last several years in their endorsement of such practices.

Law

Many states now have laws mandating that police collect demographic information on stops. Case law is somewhat contradictory, but it seems clear that the courts will not allow police stops based solely on race, although race can be one element that makes up reasonable suspicion. Searches must be based on probable cause unless consent is given. Border searches (including airports and port entries to the United States) are different, with different legal parameters. In effect, border agents do not need any level of suspicion to search or require identification. Note that a recent Arizona law now requires officers (anywhere in the state, not just near the border) to inquire about one's immigration status if there is reasonable suspicion that the person is here illegally. Critics contend that this law will lead to profiling of Latinos even though the law explicitly states that there must be some cause other than ethnicity to justify the questions. Attorney General Eric Holder has indicated that he will legally challenge the law as usurping federal authority. Recent polls indicate a majority of Americans favor this type of law and many states evidently plan to pass similar laws.

Policy

After federal and public scrutiny, most police departments created formal policies that discourage and/or prohibit stops based solely on race. However, informal policies in departments must still support such stops, as recent studies continue to show disproportionate stops of minorities. But it seems to be the case that such policies vary by city; thus, departments must have either formal or informal policies that support such stops. Cities that have policies that encourage close ties to the community would probably not also have policies that encourage racially based stops since they tend to hamper creating good will with community members. Departments that emphasize the crime control mission may endorse such stops.

Ethics

An officer has a duty to prevent crime. If he or she feels that an individual is very likely a criminal, based on race, then formal policies are going to conflict with personal ethics and the perception of duty. Some argue that police officers' informal decisions to stop will not change until they are educated as to the evidence that stops and searches of blacks are less likely to result in a discovery of contraband than stops based on more sophisticated, behavioral-based criteria. As long as police officers believe that racial profiling is effective policing, formal policies that prohibit it will be contrary to their individual ethics and perception of duty (as a crime fighter). If, on the other hand, the police officer emphasizes a public service mission, then such stops would be seen as infringing on the individuals' rights in an unacceptable way unless there is stronger evidence to stop.

Power and Discretion

authority
Unquestionable entitlement to be obeyed that comes from fulfilling a specific role.

power The right inherent in a role to use any means to overcome resistance.

persuasion The use of signs, symbols, words, and arguments to induce compliance.

Klockars (1984) describes police control as consisting of the following elements: authority, power, persuasion, and force. **Authority** is the unquestionable entitlement to be obeyed that comes from fulfilling a specific role. Neither persuasion nor force is needed to achieve domination when one possesses authority. Police officers are usually obeyed simply when they tell a citizen to do something. We do what they tell us because of their uniform. A teacher has this type of authority in the classroom, and parents have authority over their own children (but not over other people's children).

Power is similar to authority in that it is inherent in the role and the individual merely draws upon it, but it is different from authority in that power implies that there might be resistance to overcome. It also implies that if there is resistance, it will be crushed. Power is the means to achieve domination. The baton, the handcuffs, and the power of arrest symbolize police power.

Persuasion may also be used in response to resistance, but seeks to overcome it "by mobilizing signs, symbols, words, and arguments that induce in the mind of the person persuaded the belief that he or she ought to comply" (Klockars, 1984: 530), and may even involve the use of deception to gain compliance. Although those who have power don't have to use persuasion, they often do, to avoid the use of force.

force The authority to use physical coercion to overcome the will of the individual.

Force is different from the previous three means of control in that it is physical, whereas the other three are exercised through mental domination and control. When force is used, "the will of the person coerced is irrelevant" (Klockars, 1984: 532). Police show their ability to use force when they use their arrest power, or when they physically restrain and subdue an individual. Force is ultimately behind every position of authority.

Any police officer at any time might have the need or opportunity to exercise one of these four different types of domination, from unquestioned authority to physical force. Why does law enforcement have the right to employ these types of control? "We give it to them" is the easy answer. Police power is a governmental right invested in federal, state, and local law enforcement agencies. It means that these organizations, unlike almost any other except perhaps the military, have the right to control citizens' movements to the point of using physical and even deadly force to do so.

social contract The concept developed by Hobbes, Rousseau, and Locke in which the state of nature is a "war of all against all" and, thus, individuals give up their liberty to aggress against others in return for safety. The contract is between society, which promises protection, and the individual, who promises to abide by laws.

Cohen and Feldberg (1991) developed a careful analysis of, and justification for, police power and proposed that it stems from the **social contract**. Thomas Hobbes (1588–1679) and John Locke (1632–1704) created the concept of the social contract to explain why people have given up liberties in civilized societies. According to this theory, each citizen gives up complete liberty in return for societal protection against others. Complete freedom is given up in return for guaranteed protection. Police power is part of this *quid pro quo*: we give the police these powers in order to protect us, but we also recognize that their power can be used against us.

This general idea has corollary principles. First, each of us should be able to feel protected. If not, we are not gaining anything from the social contract and may decide to renegotiate the contract by regaining some of the liberties given up. For instance, vigilante movements arise when the populace thinks that formal agents of social control do not protect them, and isolationist groups "opt out" of most traditional societal controls because they believe that they can create a better society.

Second, because the deprivations of freedoms are limited to those necessary to ensure protection against others, police power should be circumscribed to the minimum necessary to meet the goals of protection. If police exceed this threshold, the public rightly objects.

Third, police ethics are inextricably linked to their purpose. If the social contract is the basis of their power, it is also the basis of their ethics. Cohen and Feldberg (1991) propose five ethical standards that can be derived from the social contract:

- Fair access
- Public trust
- Safety and security
- Teamwork
- Objectivity

Delattre (1989b) approaches police authority and power from a slightly different point of view. He asserts that police, as public servants, need those qualities that one desires in any public servant. He quotes James Madison, who stated that essential to any public servant are these characteristics: wisdom, good character, balanced perception, and integrity.

Only if the person entrusted with public power has these qualities can we be assured that there will be no abuse of such authority and power: "Granting authority without expecting public servants to live up to it would be unfair to everyone they are expected to serve" (Delattre, 1989b: 79). In this proposition, the right to authority lies in the character of the person. If one has those virtues necessary to be a public servant, one has the right to use the authority invested in the role; if one does not have those virtues, one should not be in that position to begin with. It would be nice if we could be sure that every police officer hired has the qualities of wisdom, good character, and integrity; unfortunately, that is probably not the case. Therefore, we must take a closer look at the way officers utilize their discretion.

DISCRETION AND DUTY

discretion The authority to make a decision between two or more choices.

duty Required behavior or action—i.e., the responsibilities attached to a specific role.

Discretion can be defined as having the authority to choose between two or more courses of behavior. Law enforcement professionals have a great deal of discretion regarding if and when to use their authority, power, persuasion, or force—more specifically, when to enforce a law, how to enforce it, how to handle disputes, when to use force, and so on. Every day is filled with decisions—some minor, some major. Discretion allows officers to choose different courses of action, depending on how they perceive their duty. **Duty** can be defined as the responsibilities that are attached to a specific role. In the case of police officers, myriad duties are attached to their role; however, there is a great deal of individual variation in how officers perceive their duty.

Patrol officers are the most visible members of the police force and have a duty to patrol, monitor, and intervene in matters of crime, conflict, accident, and welfare. Patrol officers possess a great deal of discretion in defining criminal behavior and deciding what to do about it. When police stop people for minor traffic violations, they can write tickets or give warnings. When they pick up teenagers for drinking or other delinquent acts, they can bring in the teens for formal processing or take them home. After stopping a fight on the street, they can arrest both parties or allow the combatants to work out their problems. In many day-to-day decisions, police hold a great deal of decision-making power over people's lives because of their power to decide when to enforce the law. Studies indicate that police do not arrest in a large number of cases where they legally could. For instance, Terrill and Paoline (2007) found that officers in their sample made arrests in less than a third of the cases. The decision to arrest was influenced by seriousness of the offense, the city (there were two cities in their sample), whether they were responding to a citizen call for service, suspect resistance, suspect disrespect, and suspect intoxication (2007: 319). What is clear from many studies focused on police discretion is that police do not arrest, nor do they ticket, in every case where they have a legal right to do so.

Discretion also comes into play when the officer is faced with situations that have no good solutions. Many officers agonize over family disturbance calls where there are allegations of abuse, or when one family member wants the police to remove another family member. Other calls involve elderly persons who want police to do something about the "hoodlums" in the neighborhood, homeless people with young children who are turned away from full shelters, and victims of crime who are left without sufficient resources with which to survive. A very problematic call is when family members call concerned over a mentally ill person. In these cases, officers often face extremely difficult decisions over whether to arrest or not, and/or the use of force (Wells and Schafer, 2006; Finn and Stalens, 2002). These types of "messy" social service calls are probably much more common than the exciting crime control calls that characterize cop shows on television. In many cases, there are no good solutions to the misery and problems of the citizenry. In response to each of these calls, officers must decide what course of action to take or can sometimes decide to do nothing at all because they do not perceive it as a crime problem.

Police officers perceive their duty in different ways. Officers may respond to a domestic dispute and find a wife who is not seriously injured, but is bruised, upset, and without money or resources to help herself or her children. One officer may ascertain that departmental policy or law does not dictate any action and that the woman is afraid to press charges, so the officer can leave with a clear conscience that official duties have been completed. However, another officer might take the woman to a shelter, drive her to a relative's home, or wait with her until friends or family members arrive.

Law enforcement's response to domestic violence calls historically has been noninterference, with the perception that domestic violence was not a crime control matter unless it involved injury amounting to felony assault, so women who were battered received different treatment depending on whether their batterer was their intimate partner or a stranger and whether the crime was determined to be a felony or a misdemeanor. This situation is personified most dramatically by *Thurman v. City of Torrington*, 595 F. Supp. 1521 (D. Conn. 1984), which involved a woman who was beaten, stomped, and stabbed by her ex-husband on the front steps of her mother's house while a police officer sat in a car and watched.

Some police departments began a more service-oriented approach to domestic violence in the late 1970s and 1980s with the presence of crisis intervention units with officers who were trained to counsel the parties involved or refer them to social service agencies. Interestingly, contemporaneous with such public service approaches was a crime control approach. Mandatory arrest policies were instituted in the 1980s after research indicated that arrest was associated with reducing domestic violence, even though subsequent studies failed to replicate such findings. Mandatory arrest was supposed to protect victims of domestic violence by forcing police to take action by arresting the perpetrator. However, what seems to have happened in the intervening years is a greater likelihood that both parties will be arrested when there is evidence of injuries, regardless of who is the aggressor. Thus, in an attempt to control individual officers' discretion in domestic violence situations, a crime control response (mandatory arrest policies) has been instituted which may have resulted in worse consequences for the victims it was supposed to help.

An altruistic, involved style of interaction in which the police officer would be compelled to help the victims in any way possible is supported by the ethics of care, the ethics of virtue, utilitarianism, religious ethics, and ethical formalism. But a more self-protective standard, in which the actions mandated would be only those necessary to maintain a self-image consistent with the police role as crime fighter, might also be justified using utilitarianism or ethical formalism.

It is important to note that if police were to become personally involved in every case and go out of their way to help all victims, they would exhaust their emotional reserves in a short time. As a matter of psychological survival, police must develop an emotional barrier between themselves and the victims they encounter. It is virtually impossible to observe suffering on a consistent basis if one does not create some type of emotional shield. So-called "morgue humor" is most prevalent with police officers, medical personnel, and the military because these individuals must find a way to tolerate seeing suffering on a level most of us never do.

The amount of discretion and how it is used depend on the style of policing that is characteristic of a certain area. Various researchers have developed typologies of policing that help us understand how different officers view and utilize their discretion. For instance, Wilson (1976), in one of the classic typologies, described policing styles as follows:

- The *legalistic* style of policing is described as the least amenable to discretionary enforcement.

- The *watchman* style describes police who define situations as threatening or serious depending on the groups or individuals involved, and act accordingly.

- The *caretaker* style treats citizens differently, depending on their relative power and position in society.

Muir's typology (1977: 145) included the *professional* (balancing coercion with compassion), the *reciprocator* (who had citizens solve problems and made deals to keep the peace), the *enforcer* (who used coercion exclusively), and the *avoider* (who avoided situations where they might be challenged). Finally, Brown (1981: 224) presented a typology that shared some of the same elements as those above:

- *Old-style crime fighters* are concerned only with action that might be considered crime control.

- *Clean-beat officers* seek to control all behavior in their jurisdiction.

- *Service-style officers* emphasize public order and peace officer tasks.

- *Professional-style officers* are the epitome of bureaucratic, by-the-book policing.

Each of these descriptions is obviously more detailed than our binary model of the crime control versus public servant mission. However, all illustrate that different beliefs about their mission and their role in society will affect officers' use of their discretion.

Discretion is by no means limited to law enforcement. In subsequent chapters, we will see that discretion is an important element in every subsystem, from lawmaking to the courts and corrections. Discretion in criminal justice has been attacked as contributing to injustice. A long line of researchers has explored the parameters of discretion (McAnany, 1981; Davis, 1980), concluding that the presence of discretion creates the opportunity for power to be abused, with certain groups (the poor, the powerless, and minorities) more likely to be subject to discriminatory treatment. Some solutions to control discretion are unsatisfactory because absolute rules, guidelines, and standards either limit decision making to mechanistic applications of given rules or provide only rhetorical ideals with little or no enforcement capability. Cohen (1983, 1985) described discretion as balancing justice for the individual against justice for the group and pointed out that full enforcement would be unfair to individuals at times. Unbound discretion is not acceptable either since officers are only human and their personal biases and prejudices should not guide their decision making. How is the discretion invested in the law enforcement officer role guided and controlled?

In the next two sections, we will look at how individual officers are influenced by both the formal ethics of the agency and the informal culture that exists. These two sources arguably promote somewhat different views of the mission, values, and ethical actions for individual officers.

Formal Ethics for Police Officers

A professional code of ethics exists for most professions. For instance, doctors pledge allegiance to the Hippocratic Oath, lawyers are taught their professional code of responsibility, and psychiatrists subscribe to the code promulgated by their professional organization. In fact, having a professional code of ethics seems to be part of the definition of a profession. Sykes (1989) writes that a profession includes the following:

- A body of specialized, internationally recognized knowledge

- A pre-professional education and continuing education

- Legal autonomy to exercise discretionary judgment

- Lateral movement

- Authorized self-regulation (which includes a code of ethics and disciplinary mechanisms)

A code of ethics helps engender self-respect in individual officers; pride comes from knowing that one has conducted oneself in a proper and appropriate manner. Further, a code of ethics contributes to mutual respect among police officers and helps in the development of an *esprit de corps* and common goals. Agreement on methods, means, and aims is important to these feelings. As with any profession, an agreed-upon code of ethics is a unifying element. A code can help define law enforcement as a profession, for it indicates a willingness to uphold certain standards of behavior and promotes the goal of public service, an essential element of any profession.

Police officers generally pledge an oath upon graduation from an academy, and many police agencies have adopted a code of ethics. Other agencies cover similar ground in a value or mission statement that identifies what values are held to be most important to the organization. These documents may be mere wall hangings, forgotten once an officer has graduated from the academy, or they might be visible and oft-repeated elements in the cultures of the agencies, known by all and used as guides for behavior by administrators and officers alike.

THE LAW ENFORCEMENT CODE OF ETHICS

The International Association of Chiefs of Police (IACP) promulgated the Law Enforcement Code of Ethics and the Canons of Police Ethics, and many departments have used these or adapted them to their own situations. More recently, the IACP has endorsed the Oath of Honor (displayed in the Quote and Query box). This oath, developed by a committee of the IACP, is offered as a shortened version encapsulating the contents of the Code of Ethics.

QUOTE & QUERY

IACP Oath of Honor
On my honor,
I will never betray my badge,
my integrity, my character,
or the public trust.
I will always have
the courage to hold myself
and others accountable for our actions.
I will always uphold the Constitution,
my community, and the agency I serve.

—INTERNATIONAL ASSOCIATION OF CHIEFS OF POLICE, 2008.

Does this oath emphasize a crime fighter or public service mission?

The IACP code or other codes of ethics for law enforcement have at least four major themes.

The principle of justice or *fairness* is the single most dominant theme in the law enforcement code. Police officers must uphold the law regardless of the offender's identity. They must not single out special groups for different treatment. Police officers must not use their authority and power to take advantage, either for personal profit or professional goals. They must avoid gratuities because these give the appearance of special treatment.

in the NEWS

CONDUCT "UNBECOMING"?

A Pennsylvania state trooper who worked for Pittsburg Steelers quarterback Ben Roethlisberger was investigated for unspecified ethics violations after a 20-year-old college student alleged he did nothing when Roethlisberger sexually assaulted her in a bar. Although the prosecutor in Georgia has declined to file charges against Roethlisberger, the Pennsylvania State Police investigated the trooper for unspecified ethical violations stemming from his outside employment as a "personal assistant" to Roethlisberger and concluded that he must quit the outside job if he wanted to continue to be a trooper. Even though outside employment is not prohibited, troopers (as all law enforcement officers) are expected to conduct themselves in a manner consistent with high professional standards.

SOURCE: Mandak, 2010a, 2010b.

A second theme is that of *service*. Police officers exist to serve the community, and their role appropriately and essentially concerns this idea. Public service involves checking on the elderly, helping victims, and, in the community service model, taking a broad approach to service by helping the community deal with problems such as broken street lights and dilapidated buildings.

Still another theme is the *importance of the law*. Police are protectors of the Constitution and must not go beyond it or substitute rules of their own. Because the law is so important, police not only must be concerned with lawbreakers, but also their own behavior must be totally within the bounds set for them by the law. In investigation, capture, and collection of evidence, their conduct must conform to the dictates of law.

The final theme is one of *personal conduct*. Police, at all times, must uphold a standard of behavior consistent with their public position. This involves a higher standard of behavior in their professional and personal lives than that expected from the general public. "Conduct unbecoming" is one of the most often cited discipline infractions and can include everything from committing a crime to having an affair or being drunk in public (Bossard, 1981: 31). The In the News box shows that formal ethics cover behaviors that are not necessarily illegal.

The emphasis on service, justice for all groups, and higher standards for police behavior is consistent with the public service mission more so than the crime fighting mission. One might also argue that while the code promotes a public servant ideal, police are, for the most part, socialized and rewarded for actions consistent with the crime fighter role.

The Police Subculture

Research has described an occupational culture that is at odds with the formal ethics and values of the police organization. Some early research indicated that police officers were significantly different from others in their values and characteristics. Scheingold (1984) described the factors that lead to the extreme nature of the police subculture:

- Police typically form a homogenous social group.
- They have a uniquely stressful work environment.
- They participate in a basically closed social system.

THEMES AND VALUE SYSTEMS

In one of the classic pieces of research on the police subculture, Van Maanen (1978) discussed how police operate with stereotypes of the people with whom they come into contact. The individual who does not recognize police authority is "the asshole." Other names for this type of person include creep, animal, mope, rough, jerk-off, clown, wiseguy. The idea is the same—that some individuals are troublemakers, not necessarily because they have broken the law, but rather, because they do not recognize police authority (1978: 227). Others have identified the same concept in terms such as bad guy, punk, idiot, knucklehead, terrorist, predator (Herbert, 1996). Herbert further points out the problem whereby officers are so quick to identify these types of individuals as threats to safety that they may overgeneralize and identify, for instance, everyone living in a neighborhood in the same way.

Van Maanen (1978: 226) observed that "certain classes in society—for example, the young, the black, the militant, the homosexual—are . . . 'fixed' by the police as a sort of permanent asshole grouping." He argued that the professionalism movement of law enforcement might widen the distance between the police and the community they served, and further allow them to be "moral entrepreneurs" who were even more likely to define some groups as bad simply because they did not conform to some preconceived standards of behavior (1978: 236).

Sherman (1982: 10–19) also described some common themes running through police attitudes and values of the police culture. First, loyalty to colleagues is essential; second, the public, or most of it, is the enemy (echoing, to some extent, van Maanen's research). Sherman explained that police use their discretion in a way that takes into account the identity of the victim and offender (attitude, class, and race impact decisions of how to enforce the law). Disrespect for the authority of police (POPO or "pissing off a police officer") is especially important in how police choose to deal with situations. Further, Sherman argued that police officers believe in the use of force for those who deserve it. Other elements described by Sherman include disparagement of due process as a barrier to doing the job and the value of deception and lying, even on the witness stand, if it means getting a bad guy. Finally, Sherman described a priority of "real" policing (crime control) over "garbage calls" (social service) (1982: 10–19). Scheingold (1984: 100–104) highlighted police cynicism (the idea that everyone is weak or corrupt), the use of force (as justified in the face of any opposition), and the idea of the police officer as a victim (of low pay and public antipathy).

Herbert (1996) discusses six concepts or what he calls "normative orders" of policing, including law, bureaucratic control, adventure/machismo, safety, competence, and morality. Morality is related to the idea that police draw on moral definitions to justify their actions. Herbert's observational study allowed him to draw on field experiences to present examples whereby officers would continually be told and express the view that they were the "good guys" against the "evil out there."

Crank (1998) also discussed a number of themes of policing. These themes are not values per se, but rather, elements of police work and/or shared perceptions of police officers, and include coercive territorial control, force, illicit coercion, the importance of guns, suspicion, danger, uncertainty, "maintaining the edge," solidarity, masculinity, and excitement and crime.

Zhao, He, and Lovrich (1998) examined police officers' values compared to those of the general population. They described a value as an "enduring belief that a specific mode of conduct or end-state of existence is personally or socially preferable" (1998: 23) and reported that individuals' values (specifically, freedom and equality) have been shown to affect their political preferences. They found that police exhibited similar value preferences across time (comparing 1961 to 1997) and across place (comparing Tacoma, Washington, to Spokane, Washington). In their study, they found that police rated equality significantly lower than did the general public and, in general, were more conservative than the general public in their viewpoint. Crank and Caldero (2000/2005) also have discussed the values of police, reporting on other research showing that police officers place less emphasis on independence and more emphasis on obedience.

THE COP CODE

Many authors present versions of an informal code of conduct that new officers are taught through informal socialization that is quite different from the formal code of ethics described above. Reuss-Ianni (1983: 14) presented the most complete "cop code":

- Watch out for your partner first and then the rest of the guys working that tour.
- Don't give up another cop.
- Show balls.
- Be aggressive when you have to, but don't be too eager.
- Don't get involved in anything in another guy's sector.
- Hold up your end of the work.
- If you get caught off base, don't implicate anybody else.
- Make sure the other guys know if another cop is dangerous or "crazy."
- Don't trust a new guy until you have checked him out.
- Don't tell anybody else more than they have to know.
- Don't talk too much or too little.
- Don't leave work for the next tour.

The informal code also specified conduct indicating that management was not to be trusted. Those code rules that are specific toward management included these (Reuss-Ianni, 1983: 14):

- Protect your ass.
- Don't make waves.
- Don't give them too much activity.
- Keep out of the way of any boss from outside your precinct.
- Don't look for favors just for yourself.
- Don't take on the patrol sergeant by yourself.
- Know your bosses.
- Don't do the bosses' work for them.
- Don't trust bosses to look out for your interest.

What is obvious is that the informal code of behavior, as described above, is different from the formal principles as espoused by management. Some principles of the informal code directly contradict the elements in formal codes of ethics.

Scheingold (1984: 97) described the police subculture as no more than an extreme of the dominant U.S. culture and argued that it closely resembles a conservative political perspective. In other words, we all agree with certain elements of the police value system and, if the general public is less extreme in its views, it is only because we have not had a steady diet of dealing with crime and criminal behavior as have the police.

POLICE CULTURE AND "NOBLE CAUSE"

One aspect of police culture that has received recent attention is what has been called noble-cause corruption. This refers to the utilitarian concept that the "end" of crime fighting justifies "means" that might otherwise be illegal, unethical, and/or against rules or regulations (such as lying on an affidavit or the witness stand or planting evidence). Arguably, the police culture, at least in some locales, endorses or tolerates this type of activity. Klockars (1983) presented us with a type of noble-cause corruption in the "Dirty Harry problem" (from the Clint Eastwood movie), asking whether it was ethically acceptable for a police officer to inflict pain on a suspect in order to acquire information that would save an innocent victim. Crank and Caldero (2000/2005) are noted for their expanded discussion of noble-cause corruption. They argue that practices such as "testilying" (lying to get a warrant or a conviction) are not caused by selfishness, but rather, by ends-oriented thinking. McDonald (2000) offers a detailed study of the practice of testilying, which includes reordering facts, adding details, or omitting information. It is also referred to as shading, fluffing, firming up, or shaping and occurs in sworn affidavits for arrest or search warrants, in reports, or in testimony. The most notorious example of exposed testilying is the O.J. Simpson case. The defense attorney used a tape of LAPD officer Mark Fuhrman saying 17 times that he and other police officers "regularly" manufactured and planted evidence, and when asked if he had done so in the Simpson case, he pleaded the Fifth Amendment (refusing to answer because it might incriminate him) (McDonald, 2000: 3, 9). In McDonald's study of one police department, he found that officers were more likely to testilie when there was a differential emphasis on goal (crime control) over means (2000: 13). McDonald notes that, according to his sample, police perceive that some prosecutors "wink at" deception or encourage it to get a win (2000: 28).

In McDonald's study, the two most frequently given reasons for testilying was that legal technicalities made their job impossible to do, and the belief that the offender

in the **NEWS**

NOBLE CAUSE?

Austin, Texas

An officer lied in a police report, stating that he had seen a crack pipe in the defendant's car (to justify a car search). Although this officer was fired for lying, the grand jury refused to issue an indictment for false swearing.

Camden, New Jersey

At least four Camden police officers have been the target of an investigation that uncovered evidence that they stole drugs and planted the drugs on suspects to make cases, threatened individuals with arrests in order to coerce them to become informants, traded drugs for information from prostitutes, filed false police reports, and lied on the witness stand to obtain convictions. At least 30 convictions based on these officers' testimonies have been vacated and charges have been dropped in at least 185 cases with the expectation that there will be many more. The city is also bracing itself for a number of civil rights lawsuits based on the officers' behavior.

SOURCE: Plohetski, 2008; Philly.com, 2010; Katz, 2010; Katz, Boyer, and Anastasia, 2010.

was guilty. The least most common reason was "pressure for productivity" (2000: 106). When asked how often do police officers they know personally engage in testimonial deception, the majority indicated they did not know anyone, but substantial numbers agreed that they knew officers who rarely or sometimes used deception when testifying (2000: 114). McDonald concluded that police officers from large agencies were more likely to use testimonial deception, as were police officers who perceived their jurisdiction as having high crime, and officers who believed there were too many legal technicalities (2000: 238–239).

The noble cause of police officers is "a profound moral commitment to make the world a safer place to live" (Crank and Caldero, 2000: 9). Officers will do what it takes to get an offender off the street, even if means employing a "magic pencil"—that is, making up facts on an affidavit to justify a warrant or to establish probable cause for arrests. Arguably, they are inclined to behave this way because we hire those who have values that support such actions, train and socialize them to internalize these values even more deeply, and then put them in situations where their values dictate doing whatever it takes to "make the world safe" (2000: 88). The In the News box offers several instances of what might be called noble-cause corruption. One might argue that the officers involved emphasized the crime fighting mission over the public service mission in their choices, but the end result of such actions is usually not helpful to the crime fighting mission either.

Police are not the only actors who subscribe to noble-cause values. Crime lab investigators and prosecutors also engage in shortcuts and magic pencils in order to convict the perceived guilty. Prosecutors have been known to suppress evidence and allow perjured testimony, so it is not only police officers who feel compelled to break the law in order to further the noble cause of crime control (Crank and Caldero, 2000: 134). How pervasive is this tendency? Studies show that about 60 percent of rookies support mild lies to achieve a conviction (2000: 157).

Other authors argue vehemently that noble-cause corruption is a dangerous concept because it gives credence to illegal behavior on the part of officers. Alderson (1998: 68), for instance, protests that

> … noble-cause corruption … is a euphemism for perjury, which is a serious crime…. In ethical police terms justice is not divisible in this way into means and ends, and the peddlers of this perversion of justice are guilty of the immorality of the totalitarian police state, and their views stand to be roundly condemned.

However, it may be that Alderson misunderstands those who present the noble-cause concepts. Crank and Caldero (2000/2005), for instance, do not seem to be supporting the rationale; rather, they argue that "noble cause" is the underlying reason for much of officers' unethical behaviors, so efforts to control corruption must take cognizance of this motivation in order to be effective. If selfishness and personal gain are not the motives for misdeeds, then monitoring and punishments may not work if the underlying culture is not addressed.

The occupational subculture of policing is not supportive of egoistic corruption like bribery or abuse of authority, such as when officers engage in sexual misconduct, but it may be supportive of "catching the criminal—whatever it takes." If we want to change this attitude, we must address it directly. Further, Crank and Caldero argue that such an attitude must change because we are increasingly living in a world where pluralism is the reality and the values of the police organization may not be reflective of the citizenry they police. As multiculturalism becomes the dominant reality, police must learn to adapt and accommodate the needs and priorities of different groups.

POLICE CULTURE AND THE BLUE CURTAIN OF SECRECY

code of silence The practice of officers to not come forward when they are aware of the ethical transgressions of other officers.

blue curtain of secrecy Another name for the code of silence or the practice of police officers to remain silent when fellow officers commit unethical actions.

Another element of the police code is absolute loyalty to other officers, even if it means not coming forward to expose a wrongdoer. Variously described as the **code of silence**, **blue curtain of secrecy**, or other terms, it refers to the subcultural code of "Don't give up another cop" (Skolnick, 2001). It should also be noted that a **code of silence** is present in other occupations and groups as well. For instance, very few college students say they would report a fellow student for cheating even if they see it happen. Other groups show varying degrees of loyalty to members of the group, even when such members engage in incompetent or corrupt activities.

The books *Serpico* (Maas, 1973) and *Prince of the City* (Daley, 1984) describe two examples of police officers who chose to challenge the "blue curtain" of secrecy and testify against their fellow officers in corruption hearings. In the Quote and Query box, Serpico's statement to the Knapp Commission illustrates the problem of police loyalty when officers are willing to cover up corruption. The later statement indicates that nothing much had changed in the decades between the Knapp Commission and the Mollen Commission. David Durk's statement to the Knapp Commission (cited in Menninger, 1973) is eloquent in his plea for the commission to understand that the problem was not only with the police department.

QUOTE & QUERY

The problem is that the atmosphere does not yet exist in which honest police officers can act without fear of ridicule or reprisal from fellow officers....

—FRANK SERPICO, KNAPP COMMISSION, 1971, AS REPORTED IN HENTOFF, 1999

Cops don't tell on cops.... [I]f a cop decided to tell on me, his career's ruined.... [H]e's going to be labeled as a rat.

—POLICE OFFICER TESTIMONY, MOLLEN COMMISSION, 1992, AS REPORTED IN WALKER, 2001

I saw that happening to men all around me; men who could have been good officers; men of decent impulse, men of ideas, but men who were without decent leadership, men who were told in a hundred ways every day, go along, forget about the law, don't make waves and shut up....

So your report has to tell us about the district attorneys and the courts and the bar; and the mayor and the governor and what they have done, and what they have failed to do, and how great a measure of responsibility they also bear. Otherwise, if you suggest or allow others to suggest that the responsibility belongs only to the police, then for the patrolmen on the beat and in the radio cars, this commission will be just another part of the swindle.

—DAVID DURK, 1972, CITED IN MENNINGER, 1973

How would you create an atmosphere in a police department wherein officers would feel more comfortable reporting the misdoings/criminality of other officers? Or would you even want to?

Quinn (2005) describes many cases in his career when he stood up to unethical and illegal police practices such as using excessive force, accepting gratuities, and engaging in other misconduct. He describes how reporting such actions to supervisors led to threats and retaliation, but that the illegal or unethical behavior also did not continue to happen in his presence. He argues that good officers are sucked into the corrupt cover-ups because of the nature of policing. Every officer does something wrong, and the most common mistake, perhaps, is using too much force. When an officer has just experienced a life-threatening event, such as a high-speed chase, a foot chase, or a fight for his weapon, the adrenalin "hijacks" reason, according to Quinn, and some officers overreact. When co-workers cover for the officer, the officer who made the mistake is indebted and trapped in a situation where the officer thinks he or she must do the same. Even if the offending officer would have told the truth about his or her mistake, the officer who covered up has lied and, therefore, it is almost impossible to "sacrifice" that loyal officer by churlishly telling the truth and calling him or her a liar.

Skolnick (2001) explored how the blue curtain of secrecy affected the case of Norman Batista, who was arrested buying drugs. By the time the police were able to enter the barricaded house, all drugs had been flushed away and, allegedly, narcotics task force officers beat the dealer and Batista in frustration. When Batista was transported to the hospital for his injuries, the doctor referred the case to the prosecutor's office. Testimony indicated he had suffered six broken ribs, injuries to chest, sternum, testicles, and knees. He ended up spending six days in the hospital. No officer was willing to testify that officers used excessive force. Most said they hadn't seen anything. The ADA charged two officers with assault with the legal argument that all officers were culpable if they didn't stop the assault. The indicted officers opted for a bench trial, and 75 off-duty police officers filled the court during the trial. The judge acquitted the two officers (Skolnick, 2001: 15). Skolnick called it a "culture war" where police officers viewed the beating as extra-legal justice and deserved, while the prosecutor and emergency room physician viewed the beating as a corrupt use of power. What is also important to note is the lack of any officer willing to break the code of silence over the incident and, in this way, no officer was held responsible. Skolnick also points out that even in the Abner Louima case (discussed more fully in the next chapter), which involved an anal assault with a broomstick, no officer came forward until they were forced to by threats of prosecution (2001: 16).

There is also evidence that officers will ostracize and sanction the person who does expose the wrongdoing of his or her peers. In their large attitude survey of police officers, Weisburd and Greenspan (2000) discovered that, although 80 percent of police officers did not think that the code of silence was essential for police trust and good policing, fully two-thirds reported that a whistleblower would encounter sanctions. Further, more than half agreed that it was not unusual for police to ignore improper conduct on the part of other officers, and 61 percent indicated that police officers do not always report even the most serious violations/crimes of other officers.

Special problems are involved when police officers protect one another. One of the greatest harms of cover-ups is the damage inflicted on the department's credibility. The O. J. Simpson trial has become the classic example of what happens when a jury loses confidence in police testimony. Prosecutors ordinarily can rely on a jury to take police testimony as fact and even believe police testimony over non-police witnesses. When police testimony is given no greater weight than any other witness—indeed, when jury members believe that police are prone to lie on the stand—the justice system itself is at risk.

Is there an ethical rationale that justifies protecting a fellow officer who engages in misconduct? Obviously, the type of misconduct makes a difference. Misconduct ranges from accepting a gratuity to murder. Generally, however, for types of misconduct such as use of excessive force, we can identify ethical rationales both for not exposing the officer and for coming forward.

in the NEWS

I THOUGHT I SAW A KITTY CAT! I DID. I DID.

The most recent scandal to hit the Hollywood, Florida, police department was the "cat" incident, where officers conspired to blame an accident victim for a traffic accident involving a patrol car and arrested her for DUI. An officer collided with a woman who was stopped at a traffic stop, and then the officers involved developed a story that the woman stopped suddenly when her cat jumped out of the car window. Unfortunately for the officers, the dashboard video camera caught them constructing the story. One officer was heard saying, "I'm gonna tell you exactly how to word this so we can get him off the hook" and "I don't like making things up ever because it's wrong, but if I have to bend it a little to protect a cop I'm gonna." The officers talked about doing a little "Walt Disney." The woman's charges of DUI were dropped and five officers were ultimately fired, as well as one civilian crime scene employee. The union vows to help officers appeal the firing, saying that they were politically motivated and the punishment is too severe.

SOURCE: Smith, 2009; Sherman and Moskovitz, 2009.

Recall that teleological ethical rationales are concerned with the consequences of an action. Egoism may support not coming forward because it may not be in one's best interest: An officer might say, "I don't want to get involved." "I don't want to go against everyone." Or, "It's the sergeant's (or lieutenant's or captain's) job, not mine." These are all egoistic reasons for not coming forward. Utilitarian reasons to keep quiet also look at the consequences (or utility) of the action. If one engaged in "the end justifies the means" thinking, described above as noble-cause corruption, some activities that are labeled corrupt may actually further the ends of justice, at least in the short term. Also, the loss of a skilled police officer, even though that officer may be moderately corrupt, is a loss to society. One may believe that the harm to the police department in exposing the deviance of one officer is greater than the harm to society created by what that officer is doing, or that there is greater utility in stopping the officer without making the issue public.

There are also teleological arguments for coming forward. Egoism may dictate that an individual has to come forward to protect himself from being accused of wrongdoing. The police officer may also endure such a crisis of conscience or fear of being punished that she can attain peace of mind only by "coming clean." Utilitarian arguments for coming forward are offered as well. The harm that comes from letting the individual carry on his misdeeds or not forcing the individual to a public punishment may be greater than the harm that would come from the scandal of public exposure. This is especially true if one is forced to either tell the truth or lie; in this case, the harm to police credibility must be taken into account.

Recall that deontological arguments look at the inherent nature of the act. Arguments against exposing other officers include the idea that one's duty is to the police force and one's fellow officers so one should protect them from exposure. Arguments for coming forward are much stronger, including the argument that a police officer has a sworn duty to uphold the law. Also, one cannot remain silent in one situation unless one could approve of silence in all situations (Kant's categorical imperative), and one must do one's duty, which involves telling the truth when under an oath (Wren, 1985: 32–33).

It should be noted that, in general, deontological ethics support whistleblowing because it is a higher duty to uphold the law than it is to defend one's fellow officers. This argument also depends on whether the primary role of officers is as crime fighter or as public servant. If one perceives oneself as primarily a crime fighter, the duty to the law becomes subservient to the duty to fight crime; however, if one primarily sees one's duty to be a public servant sworn to uphold the law, then crime fighting is subservient to the law and the legal process.

When one considers whether to come forward to expose the wrongdoing of others, external moral philosophies, such as utilitarianism, are rarely articulated. What tends to be the impetus for covering up for other officers is an internal mechanism—loyalty. While the prime motivator for coming forward and/or truth-telling is personal integrity, the individual often feels great anguish and self-doubt over turning in or testifying against friends and colleagues. That is understandable because "a person's character is defined by his commitments, the more basic of which reveal to a person what his life is all about and give him a reason for going on" (Wren, 1985: 35). Loyalty is a difficult concept that others have written about extensively; it can be a vehicle of both ethical and unethical behavior (Fletcher, 1993).

Loyalty in police work is explained in that police depend on one another, sometimes in life-or-death situations. Loyalty to one's fellows is part of the *esprit de corps* of policing and is an essential element of a healthy department. Ewin (1990) writes that something is wrong if a police officer doesn't feel loyalty to fellow officers. Loyalty is a personal relationship, not a judgment. Therefore, loyalty is uncalculating. We do not extend loyalty in a rational way or based on contingencies. Loyalty to groups or persons is emotional, grounded in affection rather than reflection.

Loyalty refers to a preference for one group over another (Ewin, 1990: 13). Loyalty always involves some exclusion: one is loyal to X rather than to Y, so Y is thus excluded. At times the reverse can also be true: if a group of people is excluded (whether or not they are properly excluded), they can feel a common cause in response to what they see as oppression, which can result in the growth of loyalty among them. That loyalty, provoked by a dislike and perhaps distrust of the other group, is likely to be marked by behavior that ignores legitimate interests and concerns of the other group.

The application to policing is obvious. If police officers feel isolated from the community, their loyalty is to other police officers and not to the community at large. If they feel oppressed by and distrust the police administration, they draw together against the "common enemy." To address abuses of loyalty, one would not want to attack the loyalty itself because it is necessary for the health of the organization. Rather, one would want to encourage loyalty beyond other officers to the department and to the community. Permeability rather than isolation promotes community loyalty, just as the movement toward professionalism promotes loyalty to the principles of ethical policing rather than to individuals in a particular department.

Wren (1985) believes that police departments can resolve the dilemma of the individual officer who knows of wrongdoing by making the consequences more palatable—that is, by having a fair system of investigation and punishment, by instituting helping programs for those with alcohol and drug problems, and by using more moderate punishments than dismissal or public exposure for other sorts of misbehavior. This is consistent with the ethics of care, which is concerned with needs and relationships.

Delattre (1989a) handled the problem differently, but came to somewhat similar conclusions. He turned to Aristotle to support the idea that when a friend becomes a scoundrel, the moral individual cannot stand by and do nothing. Rather, one has a moral duty to bring the wrongdoing to the friend's attention and urge him or her to change. If the friend will not, then he or she is more scoundrel than friend, and the individual's duty shifts to those who might be victimized by the person's behavior. We see here not the ethics of care, but rather, a combination of virtue-based and deontological duty-based ethics.

Souryal (1996, 1999b) discussed loyalty to superiors or to fellow officers as misplaced. He argued that there are different kinds of loyalty: personal loyalty, institutional loyalty, and integrated loyalty (which relates to the ideal values of the profession). Loyalty to superiors is traced back to *divine right*—the idea that persons are indistinguishable from their office (1996b: 48). Today, however, we are governed by laws, not kings, and such loyalty should be properly placed in our laws and our values rather than an individual. Souryal noted that personal loyalties often lead to unethical actions and that loyalty to values or organizations has a stronger ethical justification. One might argue that even loyalty to a police organization may be misplaced if it leads to lying to protect the organization against scandal.

The informal practice of punishing individuals who come forward is an especially distressing aspect of loyalty and the police culture. Individual police officers have been ostracized and have become the target of a wide variety of retaliatory gestures after "ratting" on another officer. Reports include having equipment stolen, threats made to the officer and his family members, interfering with radio calls and thereby jeopardizing his safety, scrawling the word "rat" on his locker, putting cheese or dead rats in his locker, vandalizing his patrol car, or destroying his uniform. The Quote and Query box has one account of what happened to a whistleblower.

As distressing as these acts are, the more incomprehensible reaction is that of administrators. Administrators sometimes tell the accused officer who informed on them, or support the retaliation against the officer who came forward implicitly or explicitly. Instead of rewarding officers who expose wrongdoing, administrators sometimes punish them by administrative sanctions, transfers to less desirable positions, or poor performance reports. More than 40 Los Angeles police officers filed a class action suit against such administrative sanctions for whistleblowers (Johnson, 2005). This retaliation is not just true of law enforcement agencies. Sanctions against whistleblowers are so common that most states and the federal government now have laws designed to protect whistleblowers.

QUOTE & QUERY

…Two nights later I was walking through the courthouse, in uniform. One of the officers I had accused of assault grabbed me by the front of my jacket and pushed me into a corner. With his face touching mine he whispered …, "If you ever snitch us off again I will kill you." Then he walked away.

[The incident occurred after Officer Quinn had reported to the deputy chief and his lieutenant that a prostitute in his district had been beaten up by a police officer.]

—Quinn, 2005: 41

Why do you think police officers have similar ("don't snitch") subcultural prohibitions as criminals?

POLICE CULTURE TODAY

Our descriptions of the police culture date back more than 40 years and so a legitimate question is whether or not modern police officers subscribe to the same set of values and whether the "cop code" still exists. Arguably, the subculture and the values described above may be breaking down in police departments today. Several factors contribute to the possible weakening of the subculture:

- *Increasing diversity* of police recruits has eliminated the social homogeneity of the workforce. Many diverse groups are now represented in police departments, including African Americans, Hispanics, other ethnicities, women, and the college-educated. These different groups bring elements of their own cultural backgrounds and value systems into the police environment.

- *Police unions*, with their increasing power, formalize relationships between the line staff and the administration. Subcultural methods for coping with perceived administrative unfairness are giving way to more formal rather than informal means of balancing different objectives of management and line staff.

- *Civil litigation* has increased the risk of covering for another officer. Although police officers may lie to internal affairs or even on a witness stand to save a fellow officer from sanctions, they may be less likely to do so when large monetary damages may be leveled against them because of negligence and perjury.

One might add that many of the authors who described the police culture did so in the 1970s and 1980s, during a time of great social change when the Supreme Court recognized groundbreaking due process protections. Older police officers who had not been socialized to give *Miranda* warnings or obtain search warrants were understandably slow to adapt to the new order. Today's recruit officers were born after the *Miranda* warning was institutionalized as a standard arrest element and have never known a time when police did not need a search warrant. Today's recruit is also more likely to have been exposed to community policing and its tenets of community–police partnership and other progressive police practices through television, education, or other means. Thus, for younger police officers, these due process protections may be seen as normal and expected elements of the job rather than barriers to good police work.

It is also no doubt that the police subculture varies from department to department. Size, regional differences, and management may influence the strength of the subculture. The make-up of the department, its relationship with the community, and training may also influence the type of occupational culture found in any department.

In an incomplete measurement of police subculture, Paoline, Myers, and Worden (2000) found that the police subculture is by no means monolithic. Using responses from officers in a survey research project, they were able to measure seven outlooks that they believe were associated with the informal subculture described in the literature:

- Orientation to law enforcement
- Orientation to order maintenance
- Orientation to community policing
- Aggressiveness
- Selectivity
- Distrust of citizens
- Perceptions of citizen cooperation

They found substantial variation among the officers and differences in their cultural views. Further, no factors emerged as strong predictors of officers' values. There were weak and inconsistent associations between sex and cultural values. There were some expected associations between race and cultural values, with minority officers having more positive orientations than white officers toward order maintenance and community policing concepts; however, the associations were not strong. The association between aggressive patrol and race was stronger, with minority officers displaying less support than white officers for aggressive patrol. In general, most of the associations were of small magnitude. The authors conclude that the police culture may be less uniform and less powerful than other researchers have portrayed. They admit, however, that their measures did not directly or comprehensively measure police culture as described in earlier research.

Greene et al. (2004: 60–63) examined attitudinal data from a sample drawn from the Philadelphia police department. A series of questions measured their attitudes toward ethics and some elements of the police culture. The percentage who disagreed with each statement is indicated below:

- It is not really wrong for an officer to accept small gifts from the public. (43.6 percent disagreed)

- Sometimes an officer has to use methods prohibited by directives to enforce the law or make an arrest. (46.5 percent disagreed)

- Most officers would take action if they knew of misconduct, even if it was a friend. (39.2 percent *agreed*—note, this item is reversed)

- An officer cannot be consistently productive unless he/she bends or breaks the rules from time to time. (68.5 percent disagreed)

- Sometimes officers use methods prohibited by directives to achieve arrest of a criminal, if it's the only way that it can be done. (52.3 percent disagreed) (Note that this item seems to be problematic as a measure of ethical attitudes in that officers may know that this behavior exists but not agree with it.)

- Unless it is an extremely serious matter, officers should protect each other when misconduct is alleged. (60.7 percent disagreed)

- It is sometimes necessary to be verbally disrespectful or abusive to a person because that is the only way they will understand or comply. (56.5 percent disagreed)

- Professional courtesy (excusing a fellow officer for minor violations of the law) is generally okay. (29.8 percent disagreed)

- Most supervisors agree that rules must be broken or bent to get the job done, but wouldn't admit it. (47.9 percent disagreed)

- Sometimes officers have to exaggerate probable cause to get a crook off the street. (63.3 percent disagreed)

- An officer occasionally has to bend the facts a little in court or in a report in order to get a criminal convicted. (74.4 percent disagreed)

- An officer's personal life is his/her business, and the department shouldn't care what we do as long as we do our jobs. (41.5 percent disagreed)

- Taking care of errands while working (like picking up dry cleaning) is generally okay. (39.3 percent disagreed)

- Some people should get "street justice" after hurting a police officer because that is the only real punishment they will get. (65.1 percent disagreed)

- Officers should never go on strike no matter how unfair the working conditions or wages. (41.8 percent disagreed) (This item is problematic as a measure of ethical attitudes.)

Research continues to support the idea that there is a police culture, albeit one that is more fragmented and weaker than in earlier decades (Murray, 2005; Conti, 2006). Academy training of recruits, for instance, is reported to pay formal attention to community policing and public service elements, but the informal message of instructors and the academy experience tends to promote the "warrior" role that can lead to ends-based policing (Conti and Nolan, 2005; Quinn, 2005). Payne and Guastaferro (2009) found that police chiefs were much more likely to believe that the Supreme Court should overturn *Miranda* (40 percent) than a civilian sample (14 percent). They also were more likely than civilians to believe that offenders sometimes "got off easy" because of *Miranda* (2009: 97). These views, one presumes, trickle down in the form of subcultural socialization to the rank and file.

Regarding the "blue curtain of secrecy," research indicates that this practice may be breaking down. Barker (2002), for instance, reported on some research indicating that the addition of minorities and women has led to a less homogenous force and a weaker subcultural norm of covering up wrongdoing, as evidenced by the proliferation of complaints against fellow officers. Barker notes that there were more than 30 cases in Los Angeles where officers were the primary witnesses against other officers. Another survey (Rothwell and Baldwin, 2007) found that police respondents were more likely to report misdemeanors and felonies of their fellow officers than were civilian employee-respondents in other agencies. An additional factor that was substantially related to reporting was whether or not the agency had a mandatory reporting policy.

Another study found that police officers were more likely to report wrongdoing of other officers if it involved acquisition of goods or money (except for gratuities) rather than excessive force or bending rules. In this study, even though almost all respondents thought that stealing from a burglary scene was very serious, about a quarter thought that their colleagues would not report it (Westmorland, 2005).

In a survey sponsored by the National Institute of Justice, police respondents indicated that support for the use of force was still modestly present (about a quarter agreed or strongly agreed that sometimes illegal force was acceptable), but a much larger percentage (67 percent) agreed that someone who reported another officer's misconduct would be ostracized, and 50 percent disagreed that police officers would always report serious criminal violations of other officers (Weisburd and Greenspan, 2000: 2, 5). In another study using hypotheticals, about one-third of officers responded that they would not report an incident depicting a clear case of excessive force. In this study, newer officers, supervisors, and those with many years of experience were more likely to report, while those least likely to report were mid-career officers (Micucci and Gomme, 2005: 493, 499).

In an exploration that attempted to measure noble-cause values and their relationship to crime, researchers defined noble cause as a utilitarian value of approving of illegal means to convict criminals. In a small sample of sheriffs' deputies, the researchers found that there were wide variations in support for noble-cause statements and that adherence to noble cause did not seem to be related to a perception of level of crime (Crank, Flaherty and Giacomazzi, 2007).

Generally, police, like any occupational group, are socialized to some type of informal value system that guides and provides a rationale for decision making. This value system may be as—or in some cases, more—influential than the police rulebook or code of ethics. It is also true that the police culture is not now, or perhaps never was, as monolithic as early writers indicated and the strength of it is affected by the size of the department and other variables.

Crime Fighter and Public Servant?

Police hear mixed messages from the public regarding certain types of crime. They are asked to enforce laws against gambling, pornography, and prostitution, but not too stringently. They are expected to enforce laws against drunk driving but also to be tolerant of individuals who aren't really "criminal." They are expected to uphold laws regarding assault unless it is a family or interpersonal dispute that the disputants want to settle privately. In other words, we want the police to enforce the law unless they enforce it against us.

We also ask the police to take care of social problems, such as the homeless, even if they have to step outside the law to do so. Extra-legal means are acceptable as long as they are not used against us. Citizens who want police to move the transients out of a park or get the crack dealers off the corner aren't concerned with the fact that the police might not have the legal authority to do so. If a little "informal" justice is needed to accomplish the task, that is fine with some people, as long as it is used against those we don't like.

When we accept and encourage such extra-legal power in some situations, we shouldn't be surprised when it is used in other situations as well. The police role as enforcer in a pluralistic society is problematic. The justification for police power is that police represent the public: "The police officer can only validly use coercive force when he or she in fact represents the body politic" (Malloy, 1982: 12). But if the police do not represent all groups, their authority is seen as oppressive. It should be no surprise that police were seen as an invading army in the ghettos of the 1960s. They were not seen as representing the interests of the people who were the target of their force. The Los Angeles riots that erupted after the acquittal of the officers who were charged with beating Rodney King illustrate the tension between minority communities and police departments. More recent disturbances have occurred in other cities, sparked by perceived police abuses.

Police take their cue from the community they serve. If they serve a community that emphasizes crime control over individual rights or other public service, we will see the results of that message in the way laws are enforced. An example of a crime control approach is the **zero-tolerance policy**, implemented when William Bratton was police chief of New York City in the 1990s. Police officers were instructed to take an aggressive stance against street people and minor criminals, especially those who roamed the downtown Manhattan business area and subway system.

zero-tolerance policy The law enforcement approach whereby small violations and ordinances are enforced to the maximum with the expectation that this will reduce more serious crime.

The dramatic decline in crime enjoyed by New York City was touted as the result of the zero-tolerance policy. When the little criminals are arrested, so goes the theory, the big crimes don't happen. It was true that frequently the minor offenders arrested had outstanding warrants for more serious crimes. From 1993 to 1997, felony complaints dropped by 44.3 percent. Murder and non-negligent homicide dropped 62 percent, forcible rape dropped 12.4 percent, robbery dropped 48 percent, and burglary rates dropped 45 percent (Greene, 1999: 176). However, critics argued that New York's success might have had something to do with the 40 percent increase in sworn officers that also occurred during this time. Further, the decline of crime was felt all over the country, not just in New York City. For instance, in San Diego, a city that did not see an increase in sworn officers, the crime rate declined by almost as much as New York's (Greene, 1999).

The problematic issue regarding zero tolerance is the effect it had on police–community relations. Citizen complaints against New York City police went up 75 percent in the four-year period between 1995 and 1999 (Greene, 1999: 176). Even downtown merchants, who were thrilled with the effects of the crackdown when the Times Square area was described as "safe for tourists" again, were now feeling the effects of the pervasive police influence. Some complained that police were harassing them by enforcing trivial ordinances (such as placement and size of window signs or sidewalk sales). The most serious charge was that the aggressive policing policies of zero tolerance led to some police officers employing an "anything goes" philosophy, and contributed to extreme cases such as the Abner Louima assault (1997) and the Amadou Diallo shooting (1999), even though Bratton was gone by the time these incidents occurred, as his tenure in New York City lasted only from 1994 to 1996.

There are indications that the NYPD continues to utilize a model of policing that encourages officers to employ a heavy-handed policing approach, and critics continue to argue that it comes at a cost of community relations. In a study reported in 2009, it was found that only 1.3 percent of nearly 600,000 stops in that year resulted in a weapon and only 6 percent resulted in an arrest. There is a concern expressed in newspaper editorials and by human rights organizations that the police department has exceeded the benefit of the zero-tolerance policing model (*New York Times*, 2010a).

Bratton's legacy in the form of the Compstat program, a computerized crime-counting method that emphasizes accountability of middle managers, is in the center of a recent scandal involving an alleged downgrading of crime statistics. Adrian Schoolcraft, an officer in the 81st precinct, came forward in 2009 to report that supervisors and commanders routinely downgraded crime reports and even called victims to encourage or coerce them to withdraw their report or change the facts so that it could be reported as a lesser crime. He first made his concerns known to the Quality Assurance division of the NYPD and provided them with examples of victims whose crimes were misrecorded. Subsequently, Schoolcraft received a poor work review and was put on desk duty and then suspended for leaving work an hour early. At one point, officers went to his home to bring him back to the stationhouse and then forcibly took him to a mental ward in a Queens hospital; it took him six days to obtain his release. Schoolcraft has been suspended from the NYPD and now lives in upstate New York. He reports that he is still harassed by NYPD officers and plans to sue the city and the police department. After he decided that the department was not going to deal with his allegations, he went to the *New York Daily News*, which published the allegations (Rayman, 2010a, 2010b).

Schoolcraft has more recently revealed that he had been taping roll calls and interactions with other police officers for over a year and provided the tapes to the *Village Voice* newspaper, which posted them on their website. The tapes capture commanders exhorting police officers to make their quotas of tickets and to employ a zero-tolerance policy for those who live in a high crime area of the precinct, especially one particular housing project. Commanders instructed police officers to arrest anyone on the sidewalk and think of a reason later—obviously, a practice not consistent with law or public policy. The tapes show that, at least in this precinct, zero tolerance has slid into abuses of police power (Rayman, 2010).

In 2002, William Bratton became the chief of Los Angeles, a city that had experienced serious tension between the minority community and the police department. By most accounts, Bratton has been successful in achieving his goal of reducing crime. Between 2002 and 2007, Los Angeles experienced a 31 percent decrease in serious crimes and a 44 percent decrease in homicides. Further, civil lawsuits against the department declined. Bratton has been successful in wresting the money from the city council to hire hundreds of new police officers and was applauded for taking swift action against officers in the "May Day Melee" in 2007, when officers fired on demonstrators with rubber bullets (Steptoe, 2007).

Bratton was sworn in for a second five-year term in 2007, the first chief since the 1980s to survive to a second term (Buntin, 2007). By 2009, citizen satisfaction with the LAPD had risen dramatically. Nearly 8 in 10 citizens said they strongly approved of the force, as compared to only 4 in 10 in 1991 after the Rodney King and Rampart scandals. Interestingly, community leaders say that Bratton's success was due not to his crime-fighting mandates or accountability measures such as Compstat, but to his regular meetings with community leaders and transparency regarding incidents between police officers and citizens (Wood, 2009). In 2009, the LAPD was released from the consent decree that had been in place for eight years after incidents such as the Rampart scandal and the Rodney King incident. A federal judge ruled that the department had made substantial reforms, but also mandated more training and reforms (Moore, 2009). One could argue that accountability, as long as it covers the means as well as the ends of law enforcement, is the key to an efficient and ethical police department. In 2009, Bratton resigned and, in 2010, he became the head of Altegrity Risk International, an international security firm.

Whereas the formal code of ethics emphasizes the public servant role of law enforcement, the informal subculture emphasizes the crime fighter role. The public expects the police to live up to the crime fighter role, but also expects more. The public expects the police to be problem solvers and supermen (and superwomen). From noisy neighbors to incest, we expect the police to have the answers to our problems—to be the one-stop shop for solving problems. The surprising thing is that the police do so well at this impossible task.

The Gallup Poll has measured respect for police since 1965. In a 2005 poll, 56 percent of Americans indicated that they had "great" respect for police. This is down from about 70 percent in the 1960s, but when those who answered with "some" respect is added, 89 percent of the population has some or a great deal of respect for police (Gallup Poll, 2005).

Public perceptions of police misconduct have been linked to the public's trust in the police and the recognition of police as agents of legal and moral authority (Tyler, 1990; Tyler and Wakslak, 2004). Interestingly, at least one study found that while extensive media coverage of a police scandal influenced the public's belief about the guilt of the officers involved, it did not seem to affect the public's general perceptions of respect for the agency (Chermak, McGarrell, and Gruenewald, 2006). Another study found that public attitudes about police misconduct are separate and distinct from their attitudes about police effectiveness. The most influential factors on public attitudes about police misconduct were personal experiences of self, family and friends, neighborhood characteristics, and media coverage, while public attitudes of police effectiveness were influenced by other factors (Miller and Davis, 2007).

Public attitudes toward police misconduct/police legitimacy have even been linked to violent crime (Kane, 2005). Therefore, it is important for police departments to set and maintain high standards of conduct not only for their own professional pride, but also because it seems that police ethics impact public safety in a more general sense. Police officers who ignore the law evidently give others the green light to do so as well.

CONCLUSION

In this chapter, we have identified two "missions" of law enforcement. We looked at the parameters of police discretion and how researchers have drawn typologies to describe the way individual police officers navigate their multifaceted role by emphasizing certain duties over others. Officers' discretion is controlled and guided by both formal ethics and the informal culture of law enforcement officers. The police subculture is not monolithic and may be different from when the early researchers described it. There does seem to continue to be support for what has been called "noble-cause corruption" and "the blue curtain of secrecy." Throughout this discussion and the chapters to follow, the mission and role of police as crime fighters or public servants is a pervasive theme.

CHAPTER REVIEW

1. Describe the two different missions of law enforcement in a democracy.

The two missions of law enforcement are crime fighting and public service. Under the crime fighting mission, criminals are the "enemy," and fundamentally different from "good" people. Police are the "army" that fights the enemy, and various means that might otherwise be illegal or against the rules are excused or justified because of the importance of the mission of crime fighting. Under the public service mission, police are seen as serving the needs of all the public. This role is more expansive than the crime fighter role and includes other types of public service. Furthermore, it involves the idea of public service to all people, not just law-abiding "good" citizens.

2. Explain the types of control that police have at their disposal.

Authority is the unquestionable entitlement to be obeyed that comes with certain roles, such as police officer. We do what they tell us because of their uniform. Power is also inherent in the role but implies that force will be used against resistance. Persuasion uses signs, symbols, words, and arguments (and possibly deception) to induce action. Force is the use of physical coercion to subdue the will of the individual.

3. Provide the justification for police power and the basic ethical standards that derive from this justification.

The social contract is the basis of police power. We basically give up some rights in return for protection (by police). Part of that agreement is that they have the right to utilize power in order to protect the populace against aggressors. The social contract is also the basis of police ethics. Cohen and Feldberg (1991) propose five ethical standards that can be derived from the social contract: fair access, public trust, safety and security, teamwork, and objectivity.

4. Identify the differences between the formal ethics of law enforcement and the values of the police subculture.

Formal law enforcement ethics promote the principles of fairness, service, the importance of the law, and upstanding personal conduct. The police subculture, on the other hand, has been described as endorsing stereotyping ("assholes"); absolute loyalty to colleagues (blue curtain of secrecy); the use of force for those who don't respect police authority; and noble-cause corruption (testilying and other "means").

5. Describe recent research findings on the police subculture.

In a research study, two-thirds reported that a whistleblower would encounter sanctions, more than half agreed that it was not unusual for police to ignore improper conduct on the part of other officers, and 61 percent indicated that police officers do not always report even the most serious violations/crimes of other officers. About 60 percent of rookies support mild lies to achieve a conviction. However, substantial variation exists among officers in their cultural views, according to survey studies. Current researchers conclude that the police culture is not monolithic and is perhaps more fragmented today than in the past.

KEY TERMS

authority
blue curtain of secrecy
code of silence
community policing

discretion
duty
force
persuasion

power
public servants
social contract
zero-tolerance policy

STUDY QUESTIONS

1. What are Klockars's descriptions of police authority, power, persuasion, and force?
2. Describe Wilson and Brown's typologies of police, and explain how each might use discretion.
3. Describe the elements of the formal code of ethics, and contrast them with the values of the police subculture.
4. Describe Sherman's police "values" and Herbert's normative orders.
5. Explain why some people think the police subculture is breaking down.

WRITING/DISCUSSION EXERCISES

1. Write an essay on (or discuss) discretion in policing. In this essay, define discretion, give examples, and discuss unethical and ethical criteria for the use of discretion. Find newspaper articles illustrating police use of discretion. Analyze the officer's use of discretion in relation to the ethical systems described in earlier chapters.
2. Write an essay on (or discuss) community policing and whether it is likely to reduce or to encourage unethical actions by police officers. Utilize current research to illustrate whether or not community policing is growing or declining in popularity.
3. Write an essay on (or discuss) the two perceptions of the police officer—crime fighter or public servant. Consider various police practices and innovations as supporting one or the other role.

ETHICAL DILEMMAS

Situation 1

As a patrol officer, you are only doing your job when you stop a car for running a red light. Unfortunately, the driver of the car happens to be the mayor. You ticket her anyway, but the next morning you get called into the captain's office and told in no uncertain terms that you screwed up, because of an informal policy extending "courtesy" to city politicians. Several nights later, you observe the mayor's car weaving erratically across lanes and speeding. What would you do? What if the driver were a fellow police officer? What if the driver were a high school friend?

Situation 2

There is a well-known minor criminal in your district. Everyone is aware that he is engaged in a variety of crimes, including burglary, fencing, and drug dealing. However, you have been unable to make a case against him. Now he is the victim of a crime—he reports that he is the victim of theft and that his neighbor stole his riding lawnmower. How would you treat his case?

Situation 3

You are completing an internship with a local police agency. The officers you ride with are great and let you come along on everything they do. One day, the officer you are riding with takes you along on a drug raid. You are invited to come in when the house is secure, and you observe six young men sitting on two sofas in the living room. The officers are ransacking the house and asking the young men where they have hidden the drugs. Four of the youths are black and two are white. One of the officers walks behind the sofa where the black youths are sitting and slaps each one hard on the side of the head as he walks past. He ignores the two white youths sitting on the other sofa. You are shocked by his actions, but you know that if you say anything, your chance of being hired by this agency will be very small. You desperately want a good recommendation from the officers you ride with. What would you do?

Situation 4

You are a police officer in New Orleans. During the flood following Hurricane Katrina, you are ordered to patrol a section of the downtown area to prevent looting. The water is waist high in some places, and sections of blocks are, for the most part, inundated with floodwater. You come upon one shop where the plate-glass window has been broken, and about a dozen people are coming out of the shop with clothing in their arms. The stores' contents will be written off anyway by the owners and covered by insurance. Should that make a difference in your decision? What if the store was in an area of the city that wasn't flooded and the contents were not ruined? What if the people said they were desperate and didn't have any clothes because their belongings were under water? What if the items being taken were televisions and other electronics?

Situation 5

You and your partner have been working together for more than five years. He has seen you through the serious illness of your young child, and you have been there for him during his divorce. After the divorce, though, you have become increasingly anxious about him. He is obviously not taking care of his health, he drinks too much, and he has been consistently late to roll call. Now you can smell alcohol on his breath during the day and suspect that the ever-present cup of coffee he carries has more than a little whiskey in it. You've tried talking to him several times, but he just gets angry and tells you to mind your own business. Today, when the two of you responded to an accident scene, a witness drew you aside and said, "Aren't you going to do something about him?" pointing to your partner. Unfortunately, you knew what she meant, for he was literally swaying, trying to keep his balance in the hot sun. To make matters worse, he insists on driving. What would you do?

Zigy Kaluzny/Stone/Getty Images

6

Police Discretion and Dilemmas

Chapter Objectives

1. Provide any evidence that exists that law enforcement officers perform their role in a discriminatory manner.
2. Present the ethical issues involved in proactive investigations.
3. Present the ethical issues involved in reactive investigations.
4. Present information concerning the prevalence of and factors associated with the use of force by police officers.
5. Enumerate predictors associated with the use of excessive force.

The selection of Joseph Pistone as an undercover agent to infiltrate the Mafia made sense. He was Sicilian and grew up on the mean streets where Mafia "wiseguys" drove the big cars and had the most money. In 1976, after he had been with the FBI for seven years, he was selected to work undercover to bust a truck hijacking ring. His success in that role led his FBI supervisors to decide that he would make a good small-time jewel thief in order to get close to Mafia members. He became Donnie Brasco. His six years as Donnie Brasco meant that he lived the life of the "wannabe wiseguy," with visits to his wife and daughter, who were moved to another state, limited to a day or so every three or four months. Eventually he got close to some of the most powerful organized crime figures in New York.

When his Mafia friends decided that he had to be "made"—an honor that meant he would be a full member of the family, but only after he completed a hit on someone they targeted—the FBI decided to pull him out. Brasco's information led to 200 indictments, 100 convictions, and a $500,000 contract on his head. Later, the FBI convinced organized crime figures to rescind the contract, but Brasco continues to travel and live in a way that protects his identity. A movie based on his book about the experience, called *Donnie Brasco*, was a hit in the late 1990s (Pistone, 1987; Pistone and Brandt, 2007).

Brasco's story is the iconic image of law enforcement—a lone "warrior," who, at great risk to self, investigates and ultimately catches bad guys. While most police officers in the United States do not have a career that becomes the plot for a Hollywood movie, every officer has probably at times felt as alone as Brasco was working undercover. In many situations, police officers have to make decisions on their own, with only their own moral compass to guide them.

Most ethical dilemmas that police officers face derive from their powers of discretion. These ethical dilemmas are part and parcel of the job. Muir describes moral dilemmas of the police officer as frequent and unavoidable, not academic, always unpopular with some groups, usually resolved quickly, dealt with alone, and involving complex criteria (Muir, 1977: 211). In this chapter, we will discuss three topics: discrimination, investigative practices, and the use of force. Each of these topics has been the center of controversy. Each also can be thought of as representing Klockars's descriptions of the types of control possessed by law enforcement described in the last chapter: authority, power, persuasion, and force. Authority and power represent the idea that police officers can tell us what to do and we usually do it. We all know that if we don't do it, there is the threat of more coercive control to come. What if the police officer exercises this control in an unfair and discriminatory way? This is the topic in the first section, where we discuss discretion and discrimination. Persuasion is the type of control that allows police officers to use non–physically coercive means to achieve their goal, including the use of deception. We discuss various forms of deception in the section on discretion and criminal investigations. Finally, the most coercive control is physical force, and the last section in this chapter describes the issues concerning discretion and the use of force. In each of these sections, we describe the issues generally, but also try to show how individual officers might be faced with dilemmas related to the issue. It is helpful to approach individual decisions by asking the following questions:

- What must the officer do under the law?
- What does departmental policy dictate?
- What do individual ethics dictate?

Discretion and Discrimination

When individuals have discretion, individual prejudices and perceptions of groups such as women, minorities, and homosexuals can influence their decision making. Officers' views of the world affect the way they do their job. If these views include prejudicial attitudes toward groups, and such prejudices affect decisions, those groups may not receive the same protections as "good" citizens. The point is not that police officers are more prejudiced than the rest of us; it is that their special position creates the possibility that their prejudices could cause a citizen to receive less protection from the law than other citizens would. This becomes even more of a problem when the police occupational culture reinforces prejudicial views of groups of citizens. Essentially, when police act on prejudices while performing their jobs, they discriminate either in the allocation of services or enforcement of the law. Discrimination often takes the form of either enforcing the law differentially or withholding the protections and benefits of the law (Kappeler, Sluder, and Alpert, 1994: 175). As the In the News box illustrates, some police officers may express extremely negative stereotypes of certain groups. Administrators cannot take the chance that such views may translate into differential enforcement of the law.

As has been discussed before, officers form viewpoints regarding certain groups of people, and these viewpoints affect officers' behaviors and decision making. The "assholes" in Van Maanen's description of the police culture, by whatever name, comprise one group that may be the target of discrimination because police may behave differently once a citizen is labeled as such. Other groups that may be treated differently are gays and

in the **NEWS**

OFF THE RECORD?

A Temple University journalism student became news when she wrote an article after riding along with a Philadelphia police officer. During the few hours she rode with him, she heard a display of derogatory language and expressions of racism that became the focus of her article (titled "Black and Blue"). Then her news article became news itself as it spawned a heated controversy over whether police were racist, and whether she should have printed the negative article. In the article, she relates how the officer explained a range of calls involving assaults, rapes, and other crimes as "TNS" ("typical n----- shit"), and told her that the people living in the all-black neighborhood were "like animals." The journalism student couldn't understand why the officer was using such offensive language to her, and one must conclude that it was because he didn't see it as such. The officer was relegated to desk duty pending an investigation; the student worried about getting a job.

AND ELSEWHERE...

A police officer was fired during his probationary period, partly because he felt comfortable expressing stereotypical attitudes such as, when asked what the occupation of a witness was, he responded, "Well, she's Asian, so she's either a manicurist or a whore." Supervisors decided this officer was not equipped with the right personality characteristics to enforce the law.

SOURCE: John-Hall, 2009; personal communication, 2010.

the poor, and obviously there is the long-standing, pervasive—some may say endemic—issue of discrimination toward minorities, especially African Americans.

Kappeler, Sluder, and Alpert (1994: 176–184) discuss the case of Konerak Sinthasomphone—one of Jeffrey Dahmer's victims—as an example of police bias and discriminatory treatment of homosexuals and racial minorities. Sinthasomphone was the Laotian boy who was found wandering the streets, incoherent, naked, and bleeding from the rectum. He had escaped from Dahmer's apartment after he had been drugged, tortured, and sexually abused. Two African American women called the police. When the police arrived, the women tried to tell them that Sinthasomphone was an injured boy and that Dahmer was the one who hurt him. Despite the women's attempts, police officers on the scene helped Dahmer take Sinthasomphone back to his apartment and waved away emergency medical technicians who were starting to examine him. If they had examined him, they would have discovered the holes that Dahmer had already drilled into his skull and the acid that he had poured into the holes. Dismissing the incident as a "homosexual thing," the officers left Sinthasomphone with Dahmer, who strangled him shortly after they left.

This case is not about a simple mistake in judgment on the part of police officers. Their conduct represents a pattern of enforcement that allots police protection based on membership in certain categorical groups. If the Laotian boy had been white, if he had been a she, if Dahmer had been a minority member instead of a Caucasian, if the two women who requested assistance had not been African American, we might have seen a different response. Even though the police chief suspended the officers involved, they were supported by the police union and were ultimately reinstated with back pay. No further sanctions were taken against them. Obviously, the case is an extreme example of what happens when police allow their prejudices to influence their decision making when responding to a call for assistance. In other, less dramatic, cases that occur every day, how much do individual biases affect police officers' decisions? It seems the answer depends on whom you ask.

Another case that illustrates elements of discrimination, the blue curtain of secrecy, and the culture of force is the beating of undercover officer Mike Cox in Boston. Lehr (2009) has chronicled the incident where Cox, working undercover, was chasing a suspect and ended up almost being killed by other officers. Officers came up behind Cox, assumed he was the suspect, and pulled him backwards off the fence he was climbing and brutally beat him, despite his protestations that he was an officer. This was not the first time that a black undercover officer was mistaken for a suspect. Cox received severe head injuries and still suffers from speech and memory problems. In the ensuing investigation, "no one saw anything." It is not coincidental in this case that Cox was black. To the police officers who pulled him down and beat him, it was a natural reaction to assume a black man running ahead of them was a suspect instead of a fellow officer. It might be argued that the fact that no one admitted their mistake in beating him indicates both the strength of the blue curtain of secrecy and the fact that black officers still are not entirely part of the "brotherhood" in some departments.

Elsewhere, one sees that black officers resent this "otherness." A group of five black officers in the Minneapolis police department sued over alleged discrimination in the department and won a $740,000 settlement. More troubling, a joint city/federal probe of corruption in the department was scuttled, arguably due to a decision that the department's internal policies tainted the investigation because the only officers targeted in the corruption probe were black (*Star Tribune*, 2009; Kennedy and McEnroe, 2009). Even after many decades of black and white officers working together, there is an uneasy tension between them in some departments across the country.

More clearly, there is a pervasive sense among minority groups in the United States that law enforcement is fundamentally racist (Cole, 1999; Walker, Spohn, and DeLone, 2000; Crank, 1998). Some argue that this perception is based in reality. However, it should be strongly emphasized that the charge of racism is not limited to law enforcement, but rather, has been leveled against the whole legal system. The system of laws and punishment, the courts that administer the laws, and the corrections system that makes decisions regarding the liberties of those convicted have all been described as agencies that systematically and pervasively discriminate against minority groups. Police, in this view, are just one element in systematic, even institutional, racism.

Most studies indicate that blacks express more distrust of police than whites or Hispanics. In a Pew Hispanic Center study conducted in 2008, it was found that while 74 percent of whites felt that police would "treat them fairly," only 46 percent of Hispanics and 37 percent of black citizens thought so. About 78 percent of whites said they had a great deal or fair amount of confidence that police would do a good job, but only 60 percent of Hispanics and 55 percent of black respondents expressed the same view. Almost three-fourths (73 percent) of whites believed police would not use excessive force, compared to only 46 percent of Hispanics and 38 percent of black respondents (Yen, 2009).

Studies show that civil rights complaints against police are correlated positively to the percentage of minorities in the population, as well as the income differential of the jurisdiction (Holmes, 2000). Some studies report that lower-class African Americans have significantly more negative interactions with police. More than twice as many report disrespectful language or swearing by police officers (Weitzer, 1999). Interestingly, some studies indicate that middle-class African Americans express more negative attitudes than do lower-class African Americans. One speculation for this finding is that those who live in bad neighborhoods and experience the danger and inconvenience of prevalent criminality allow police more latitude to control those who "have it coming to them" (Weitzer, 1999: 838). Age, income, sex, and education, living in metropolitan areas, and experiences with police all have been shown as influencing attitudes toward police (Weitzer and Tuch, 2002, 2004). It appears that race remains a key variable even after controlling for other factors, arguably because blacks report having more negative interactions with police, are more likely to be exposed to negative media portrayals of police misconduct, and are more likely to live in high crime areas where police employ a more combative style (Weitzer and Tuch, 2004). Reisig and Parks (2000) found that areas of concentrated disadvantage showed the least satisfaction with police, but that race was still a predictor, even when controlling for neighborhood.

The Project on Policing studies utilized 240 hours of observations of encounters with 3,130 suspects in Indianapolis and St. Petersburg, Florida, in 1996–1997. In this study, trained observers noted characteristics of these encounters, and the results were used to examine things such as police officers' use of force and disrespect. The authors provide a careful review of prior studies and note that police behavior toward citizens is influenced by disrespectful or resistant behavior, intoxication, or mental illness. In other words, the results tend to point to aspects of demeanor rather than race or class (Mastrofski, Reisig, and McCluskey, 2002, citing Wesley Skogan; but see also Weitzer, 1999). Researchers noted that suspects were disrespectful toward police in 15 percent of encounters, while police were *initially* disrespectful toward suspects in only 5 percent of encounters. The elements that were related to suspect disrespect toward police included heightened emotion, number of bystanders, presence of intoxicants, being mentally impaired, and being in a disadvantaged neighborhood (Reisig et al., 2004; Mastrofski, Reisig, and McCluskey, 2002: 534).

Contrary to other studies and popular opinion, these researchers found that minority suspects experienced less "disrespect" than white citizens. The difference was more pronounced in St. Petersburg, arguably because a new police chief made race relations a priority in his administration. This research controlled for other factors, such as resistance. Only in the presence of large crowds when the minority suspects were disrespectful did they have a higher risk than whites of being shown disrespect. Other findings indicated that age, sex, and wealth influenced whether or not the citizen would experience disrespect, controlling for their behavior (Mastrofski, Reisig, and McCluskey, 2002). The authors pointed out that although the presence of researcher-observers may have affected the officers' treatment of citizens, it seems unlikely because the observers saw extreme cases where officers used excessive force. Further, race did seem to be a predictor in the use of verbal and physical coercion by officers observed in the encounters (Terrill, 2001; Terrill, Paoline, and Manning, 2003).

Mastrofski, Reisig, and McCluskey also suggest the possibility that minority members may experience more disrespect than whites if the frequency of encounters for them is greater than for whites. That is what actually happened, because blacks in both cities appeared in the pool of encounters at roughly 1.5 times their percentage in the general population. In other words, even though when stopped, blacks were no more likely than whites to receive disrespect, they were stopped 1.5 times as often as their population percentage would have predicted. Thus, the rate of blacks receiving disrespect was higher than that of whites (Mastrofski, Reisig, and McCluskey, 2002: 543).

African Americans are not the only minorities who suffer from differential enforcement patterns. Perhaps some of the most egregious cases of discriminatory law enforcement occur on this nation's southern borders (Crank, 2003; Huspek, Martinez, and Jiminez, 2001). In one sample of 204 persons, 43 percent reported seeing physical brutality and 12 percent reported being victimized by sexual or physical abuse (Huspek, Martinez, and Jiminez, 2001: 187). Many of those reporting incidents were legal residents of the United States, though of Mexican origin. Their passports were thrown away and official documents torn up, and they were told that they should go back to Mexico. They then had to wait in Mexico until family members could replace the documents and help them get back across the border. Huspek, Martinez, and Jiminez (2001: 185) argue that border agents act this way because they are encouraged by the "rhetoric of fear" and tacit acceptance of any means necessary to reduce or discourage illegal immigration.

It is possible that as illegal immigration becomes a more central political issue, local law enforcement agencies will be pressured to use "any means" to help enforce immigration laws, and that this will lead to discriminatory treatment of Latinos. In May 2010, Arizona passed a law requiring police officers in the state to ask for proof of citizenship or residency if there was reasonable suspicion that the person was an illegal immigrant. The passage of the law has generated a storm of controversy. One side argues that the law only requires police to enforce existing immigration laws and Arizona is defending its borders since the federal government seems unable to do so. The other side, joined by some police groups, argues that it would result in racial profiling and make the job of policing more difficult because victims and witnesses who are here illegally will not come forward to talk to police. "Your papers please!" is the stock line of old WWII movies of Nazi Germany, but many argue that it is time that the United States followed suit to stem the tide of illegal aliens. The immigration problem is a huge social, economic, and public policy debate in the United States; however, police officers, especially in Arizona now, are the ones who have to do more than debate the issue—they must make daily decisions that affect the lives of those they come across.

RACIAL PROFILING

Racial profiling occurs when a police officer uses a "profile" as reasonable suspicion to stop a driver (although it can also be used to refer to stops of pedestrians), primarily to request a consent search of the automobile. The so-called profile is based on race. When a young, black man is seen, for instance, driving a newer-model, expensive car, police officers suspect that the vehicle is stolen and/or that the man is holding drugs. A "pretext stop" refers to the practice of police officers to use some minor traffic offense to stop the individual and, in the course of the traffic stop, look for other evidence of wrongdoing, specifically by a search, usually a consent search. In general, minorities are targeted because of a belief that they are more likely to be criminal.

Racial profiling began when federal agents developed a profile of drug smugglers to assist border patrol and custom agents in airports. The list of indicators included behavior as well as demographic indices, including race. The concept was expanded to highway drivers by state patrol officers who were attempting to stem the flow of drugs up through the interstates in Florida, Georgia, Texas, and other southern states. (Harris, 2004; Crank, 2003).

Studies on racial profiling show that minorities may be stopped in numbers far greater than their proportion of the population would indicate. For instance, one study showed that although blacks represent only about 26 percent of the New York City population, 51 percent of all stops by NYPD officers are of blacks (as represented by "field interrogation cards" (Smith and Alpert, 2002: 675). However, the methodology of some racial profiling studies is problematic (Smith and Alpert, 2002; Engel, Calnon, and Bernard, 2002). Determining the base rate of minorities is difficult because one might use the percentage of nonwhites in the population, the percentage of nonwhite drivers, the percentage of nonwhite drivers who engage in traffic offenses, or some other denominator. Most of the earlier studies used percentage-of-population figures, but other researchers are highly critical of this rough approximation of the base rate. Interpreting the data is also mentioned as a problem. Numbers are typically collected without any theoretical framework, and they are often collected by the agencies themselves. Typically, no exploration of the connection between attitudes and behavior accompanies most racial profiling studies; in other words, there is no proof that the stops are due to prejudicial views toward those stopped. Racial profiling studies typically do not include measures of the suspects' demeanor even though another body of research concerning police–citizen stops and interactions (including use of force) has identified the important role of a suspect's demeanor in police decision making. Finally, few studies examine the reward structures and training in law enforcement agencies. Most studies place the decision making solely within the purview of the individual officer, but it is important to note organizational influences on such behavior, especially because studies show that black officers are just as likely as white officers to stop blacks in disproportionate numbers (Engel, Calnon, and Bernard, 2002).

Some charge that Arizona's new law, passed in the spring of 2010, requiring officers to inquire about citizenship if there is a reasonable suspicion that the person is an illegal immigrant will lead to racial profiling. Others argue that the law specifically states that race or ethnicity cannot be used as the sole criteria for stopping a person.

DILEMMA: Should you stop a late model car driven by two young Latino men because you suspect they cannot afford it and may have evidence of criminal activity in the car? You believe it's possible they may be illegal immigrants as well. The driver then makes a right turn without signaling as you watch. Should you stop the car (even though you wouldn't bother in other circumstances)? Should you ask for evidence that the men are legal residents of the United States?

LAW What does the law say about racial profiling? In cases such as *United States v. Martinez-Fuerte* (425 U.S. 931 [1976]), the U.S. Supreme Court has basically legitimated the use of race as a criterion in profiles (although lower courts are not in agreement when race seems to be the sole or primary reason for the stop). Further, pretext stops (where police stop a driver because of some minor traffic violation but the real reason is to investigate suspected criminal activity) have been accepted by the court in *Wren v. United States* (517 U.S. 806 [1996]), in effect allowing the police to use their discretion to enforce minor laws as a tool to implement race-based stops. Generally, the law allows the use of race as one element in the decision to stop, but does not allow it to be used as the sole element in the decision to stop or for profiling purposes.

In Arizona, the officer may be legally obligated to ask for proof of citizenship if there is a reasonable suspicion that the individual is here illegally. Legal challenges are underway by civil rights lawyers in Arizona as well as the Department of Justice, but unless it is overturned, police officers in Arizona have a legal obligation not present in other states.

POLICY Police policies have definitely undergone dramatic change in the last 20 years regarding racial profiling, largely as a result of public concern. In 1999, President Bill Clinton condemned the practice, and congressional hearings were held to investigate how widespread the practice was. Most people objected to racial profiling as used in the "war on drugs" in the 1980s and 1990s. In their telephone attitude survey of 2,006 respondents in 1999, Weitzer and Tuch (2002: 441) discovered that only 6 percent of blacks and only 16 percent of whites were in favor of stops based on race. The result of public scrutiny was that many states passed legislation requiring police departments to collect demographic information on police stops to determine whether racial profiling was an issue, and many departments instituted these collection procedures and training to sensitize officers to the possibility that their discretion was being used in a racially discriminatory manner.

As for profiling based on suspicion of being an illegal immigrant, some police departments have a policy that does not allow officers to pursue immigration-related queries because of a belief that it will hamper police–community communications (victims and witnesses will be afraid to come forward). Other departments encourage officers to contact federal officials if there is a suspicion of immigration violations. However, many departments provide no formal policy at all to assist officers in decision making in incidents where Latinos are involved.

ETHICS Do ethical rationales help us determine whether or not racial profiling, if legal, is ethical? A utilitarian argument for racial profiling would be that the "end" of drug interdiction justifies the "means" of harassing and inconveniencing the group. However, it appears that the end is not well served. The "hit rate" for finding drugs is lower for African Americans than it is for other racial groups (Cole and Lamberth, 2001). Harris (2004) proposes the idea that when officers use race in decision making, they become less effective, not more effective, because they do not concentrate on what is important for investigation—behavior, not demographics.

An ethical formalist system would probably not support profile searches because this approach is treating those individuals as a means, and it is probably contrary to the universalism principle unless everyone would agree that they should be stopped in the same manner. Because most of us would object to numerous stops every week by police who have no reason to be suspicious other than the color of our skin, it violates the first part of the categorical imperative.

After 9/11, those who looked like they were Middle Eastern were subject to increased scrutiny before they boarded airliners. In some cases, individuals were denied entry to airplanes when other passengers complained that they would not fly with men who looked like they might be suicide bombers. Interestingly, many people who are opposed to racial profiling as applied to blacks for drug interdiction agree that it is a necessary and ethical response to terrorism. Arguably, the reason is that the "end" of protecting us from a terrorist attack is greater than the "end" of protecting us from drug smuggling or other crime. Deontological ethical systems would not arrive at a different answer based on the "end" because they are not consequentialist.

Perhaps another reason some people have changed their minds about the value of racial profiling is that they are affected by a non-profiling approach to security. While traffic stops that infringed on blacks had little effect on whites, airline security now conducts random searches (along with more targeted searches) of everyone. Many people object that it is wasteful to search "a little old lady from Kansas" in an effort to be politically correct, and that such searches should be targeted to those who pose the most risk (Middle Eastern–looking men). Others argue that everyone should be subject to the same scrutiny because the risk is so high and people might have something slipped into their luggage without their knowledge. This argument gained greater traction recently with the exposure in early 2010 of "Jihad Jane," a white woman who was evidently preparing for her role in history by some type of terrorist action. As a middle-class white woman, she would have escaped any race/ethnicity based profiling in airport security (CNN.com, 2010). Then, a few months later, a white man flew a plane into the IRS building in Austin, Texas, another tragic case that illustrates profiling based on race or ethnicity is not a panacea to the threat of terrorist acts.

Ultimately, there are three questions concerning racial profiling that must be considered separately. There is a question of fact: What is the most efficient and effective method to identify criminals and terrorists? This is different from the question of law: What is the legal duty of an officer and what are the civil rights of an individual in any interaction between them? Both of these questions are different from the question of ethics: Should an officer act upon a belief and suspicion created by nothing more than an individual's membership in a minority or ethnic group?

Discretion and Criminal Investigations

Recall that Klockars identified persuasion as a type of control that allowed police officers to utilize verbal argument and even deception, if necessary, in order to gain compliance. In this section, we return to the use of deception as an integral element of undercover investigations. First, however, we should note that different issues are involved in proactive investigations versus reactive investigations.

PROACTIVE INVESTIGATIONS

In proactive police investigations, police officers initiate investigations rather than simply respond to crimes. Drug distribution networks, pornography rings, and fences of stolen property all tend to be investigated using methods that involve undercover work and informants. This is because such crimes often do not result in victims coming forward or crimes being reported. It may be that deception is a necessary element in this type of investigation. In fact, deception is recognized as an integral part of police work.

According to one author, "Deception is considered by police—and courts as well—to be as natural to detecting as pouncing is to a cat" (Skolnick, 1982: 40). Offenses involving drugs, vice, and stolen property are covert activities that are not easily detected. Klockars (1984) discussed "blue lies and police placebos." In his description of the types of lies that police routinely use, he differentiated *placebos* as being in the best interest of those being lied to—for example, lying to the mentally ill that police will take care of laser beams from Mars, lying to people that police will keep an eye out for them, or not telling a person how a loved one was killed. The motive is benign, and the effect relatively harmless. *Blue lies* are those used to control the person or to make the job easier in situations where force could be used. For example, to make an arrest easier, an officer will lie about where the suspect is being taken, or to get someone out on the street to be arrested, the officer will say that she only wants to talk.

Barker and Carter (1991, 1994) proposed a typology of lies differentiating accepted lies, tolerated lies, and deviant lies. *Accepted lies* are those used during undercover investigations, sting operations, and so on. Accepted lies must meet the following standards:

- They must be in furtherance of a legitimate organizational purpose.

- There must be a clear relationship between the need to deceive and the accomplishment of an organizational purpose.

- The nature of the deception must be one wherein officers and the management structure acknowledge that deception will better serve the public interest than the truth.

Tolerated lies, according to Barker and Carter, are those that are "necessary evils," such as lying about selective enforcement. Police may routinely profess to enforce certain laws (such as prostitution) while, in reality, they use a selective manner of enforcement.

in the **NEWS**

TELL THE TRUTH, THE WHOLE TRUTH?

William Bailey was the public safety director of North Myrtle Beach until he lied about the theft of his police-issued gun. In the investigation of his missing gun, he said his truck was unlocked, but the glove compartment, where he kept the gun, was locked. However, a newspaper investigator uncovered evidence that showed that his model of truck did not have a locking mechanism on the glove compartment. Some states, such as Washington, mandate that police officers can be terminated for lying. Such laws are based on the fact that prosecutors must produce and hand over to the defense any evidence that casts doubt on a police officer's testimony. Therefore, if an officer has been disciplined for lying, it can be used by a defense attorney to challenge his or her credibility.

AND ELSEWHERE...

An officer in a small town was terminated for lying to the chief of police about a use-of-force incident. He appealed the decision, and an independent arbitrator ordered that his job be reinstated. Then the district attorney wrote a letter advising that she would not prosecute any case that required the testimony of this officer since his credibility had been compromised. The chief then faced the problem of where to assign this officer where he would not damage the successful investigation and prosecution of criminal cases.

SOURCES: Wren, 2010; personal communication, 2010.

Lies during interrogation or threats to troublemakers that they will be arrested if they don't cease their troublemaking are also tolerated lies.

Deviant lies are those used in the courtroom to make a case or to cover up wrongdoing. However, one might argue with Barker and Carter that, in a few documented instances, the lies of rogue divisions to make a case seemed to become prevalent enough to be categorized as tolerated lies rather than deviant lies. It is definitely true that a police officer, once identified publicly as a liar, is unable to perform his duties as effectively, as is made clear in the In the News box.

Undercover investigations are based on accepted lies; but there are issues as to how such lies are employed. In proactive investigations, the central question is who the police target and why. Selection of targets on any basis other than reasonable suspicion is a questionable use of discretion. Louisiana State Representative William Jefferson was targeted by an FBI sting in 2005. As part of that sting, he was offered and accepted money to bribe the Nigerian president to give lucrative contracts to a technology company that he was connected with. When an FBI team searched his home, they found $90,000 wrapped in tinfoil and hidden in his freezer. Jefferson maintains that he was entrapped and that he was conducting his own investigation. Voters in Louisiana reelected him in 2007 even though he was under federal indictment for bribery and a range of other crimes (Foxnews.com, 2007). In November 2009, he was sentenced to 14 years in prison (Tilove, 2009). It is important to note, though, that his defense and supporters utilized a suspicion that threads though many people's minds that the choice of target in undercover investigations is based on factors other than probable cause or reasonable suspicion.

White Collar Crime: Whistleblower or Target?

In the last several years, we have seen a number of highly visible white collar crime investigations and prosecutions. Bernie Madoff was convicted of perhaps one of the biggest Ponzi schemes in history. Jeffrey Skilling of Enron remains in prison for his role in the defrauding of Enron investors. Allen Stanford in Texas will be tried sometime in 2010, accused of running a Ponzi scheme almost as large as Madoff's. In many of these cases, it is through the actions of a whistleblower that authorities are alerted, not through targeting a suspect and undercover police work. Generally, schemes such as insider trading, Ponzi schemes, corporate fiduciary malfeasance, and other criminal operations do not attract the attention of the authorities until they begin to unravel and victims come forward or until an insider tells authorities about the crime. One such case is Bradley Birkenfeld, a banker who approached the FBI and federal authorities with an offer to expose tax fraud schemes by Americans who hid their money in Swiss banks. Birkenfeld's information led to UBS, one of the largest banks in Switzerland, agreeing to pay the U.S. government $780 million for helping Americans dodge taxes. Birkenfeld came forward because of a new whistleblower law that awards up to 30 percent of the tax revenue retrieved based on the information to the whistleblower and immunity from criminal prosecution. Unfortunately for him, his information implicated him, and he was prosecuted and is now in prison despite pleas from his lawyers and whistleblower organizations that punishing the person who comes forward will discourage others. His case is on appeal. It does seem to be true that no undercover officer could have obtained the information that Birkenfeld brought to authorities.

Source: Hilzenrath, 2010.

How targets are selected is a serious question. Arguably, the selection should be based on reasonable suspicion. However, Sherman (1985b) reported that "tips" are notoriously inaccurate as a reason to focus on a certain person. To the targets of an FBI sting, it may appear that they have been unfairly targeted and, especially when targets are political figures, the charge of improper target selection is easy to make. In financial crimes, often there must be a whistleblower before financial crimes are discovered at all. When the whistleblower himself has committed crimes, it becomes problematic.

Police operations that provide opportunities for crime change the police role from one of discovering who has committed a crime to one of discovering who might commit a crime if given a chance. For instance:

- A fake deer placed by the side of the road is used to entice overly eager hunters, who are then arrested for violating hunting laws.

- Police officer decoys dress as drunks and pretend to pass out on sidewalks with money sticking out of their pockets.

- Undercover officers, posing as criminals, entice doctors to prescribe unneeded medications that are controlled substances, such as Percoset and Oxycontin.

- Police undertake various stings in which they set up fencing operations to buy stolen goods.

Are only bad people tempted? If taken too far, this role expansion is arguably dangerous, undesirable, and inconsistent with the social-contract basis of policing because police are, in effect, creating crime. The opposing argument is that crimes would occur regardless of whether police set up the opportunity and that the good of catching criminals outweighs the negative possibility that some people might not have committed that particular crime at that time if the police had not presented the opportunity. Both of these arguments exist under a utilitarian framework. So even when using the same ethical system, a particular action may be judged as ethical or unethical depending on how one perceives the facts.

Other types of stings are designed to catch those who have already committed crimes, and thus are, arguably, less problematic. Creative scams include sending party invitations or prize announcements to those with outstanding warrants to get them to come to a certain location, or staging a murder in a high-crime neighborhood and then arresting those (with outstanding warrants) who come out to see what is happening. The utility of such stings is undeniable. The only argument against them is that the government deception appears unseemly. It is also possible that such actions may undermine public confidence in the police when they are telling the truth.

informants
Civilians who are used to obtain information about criminal activity and/or participate in it so evidence can be obtained for an arrest.

THE USE OF INFORMANTS **Informants** are individuals who are not police officers but assist police by providing information about criminal activity, acting as buyers in drug sales or otherwise "setting up" a criminal act so police may gather evidence against the target. Informants perform such services for a reward: for money, to get charges dropped or reduced, or—in some documented cases—for drugs supplied by an officer. They may inform on former associates to get back at them for real or perceived wrongs, or they may cooperate with police to get rid of criminal rivals. Informants typically are not middle-class, upstanding citizens. South (2001) lists reasons why informants cooperate: money, revenge, dementia, kicks, attention, repentance, and coercion.

Informants have been or are probably engaged in criminal activities themselves. Police use informants who often continue to commit crime while helping police. In some instances, the police handlers protect the informant from prosecution (Scheingold, 1984: 122). In one case that is reputed to be the basis for the 2006 movie *The Departed*, it came to light that the FBI protected two mob informers even after they had committed murders. John Connolly, an FBI agent, was convicted of obstruction of justice, and is serving a 10-year prison sentence for protecting two organized-crime figures who were implicated in 18 murders during the time they worked for the FBI. Connolly was also indicted and tried for second-degree murder. Allegedly, he tipped off the criminals about a man who was informing on them and about to give testimony to a grand jury. They had this man killed as a result (Lush, 2007). Connolly received a 40-year sentence in that murder trial, which is to begin after he completes his 10-year federal prison sentence, but an appeal seems likely since the state may have missed the statute of limitations on the second-degree murder charge (Anderson, 2010). The government lost a civil lawsuit from the widow of the slain victim and recently paid $3.1 million. In a related case, two other murdered men were linked to the same informant, James "Whitey" Bulger, and Connolly has been implicated in those killings as well. The government was ordered to pay the victims' families $8.4 million, although the case may be appealed (Murphy, 2009a).

Other agents have admitted that they bend the rules in order to keep information sources. The In the News box shows that some FBI agents evidently believed that the "end" of convicting some criminals justified the "means" of letting four innocent men languish in prison. Critics argue that FBI agents should not make decisions regarding which crimes are more or less important (Donn, 2003: A16).

The federal witness protection program has provided new identities for some witnesses after they have accumulated bad debts or otherwise victimized an unwary public. The rationale for informant protection is that greater benefit is derived from using them to catch other criminals than their punishment would bring. This also extends to overlooking any minor crime they engage in during the period of time they provide information or afterward if that is part of the deal (Marx, 1985a: 109). However, the ethical soundness of this judgment may be seriously questioned.

One of the problems in using informants is that it presents temptations for police to slide into unethical acts as a result of the relationship with them. Officers may develop

in the NEWS

RELEASED AFTER 30 YEARS

For 30 years, Peter Limone and Joe Salvati were imprisoned for murder. Limone ended up on death row for the murder; Salvati got a life sentence. Two other men convicted of the same murder died in prison. For 30 years, the wives of Limone and Salvati waited for them and raised their children. The men's pleas of innocence were disbelieved until evidence came to light that they were framed by the mob hitmen who had committed the murder. They were finally exonerated when secret FBI files were released showing that FBI agents knew that one of the witnesses had lied in order to protect the real killer. Since this witness and the real killer were informants for the FBI, the agents kept the truth from the prosecutors, and the framed men ended up spending decades—and for two of them, the rest of their lives—in prison for crimes they didn't commit.

In a lawsuit, the federal government presented an incredible argument that the FBI agents had no duty to share the truth with the prosecutors, even if innocent men would go to the electric chair. The judge did not agree and awarded the largest settlement on record to the four families. They will split a $100 million settlement.

SOURCES: Lavoie, 2007: A19, 21; Belluck, 2007: A13.

friendships with professional criminals that compromise their judgment; officers may pay informants with tips or drugs and violate the law themselves; officers may protect informants when other law enforcement officials pursue them for other crimes; and officers may unknowingly allow the informant to use them by directing law-enforcement investigations to criminal rivals. In a Baltimore case, it came to light that Officer Mark Lundsford, who was part of a DEA task force, was putting his informant's name on drug cases he was not involved in, recommending the informant be paid bonuses for the arrests, and then splitting the money with the informant. It also was discovered that their relationship was so close that the informant had installed flooring and an air conditioner in the officer's house (Hermann, 2009).

One of the biggest problems with informants is that their reliability is highly questionable. In the Baltimore case described above, the informant had been rejected by the FBI as unreliable, but evidently this fact was unknown to the DEA and Baltimore police department (Hermann, 2009). Their rewards, whatever those might be, are contingent upon delivering some evidence of crime to law enforcement. In some cases, this evidence may be purely manufactured. In Dallas, an informant was used to buy drugs from suspected drug dealers, who were then arrested and convicted using his testimony. When the supposed cocaine that he allegedly bought from those arrested was finally tested, it turned out to be powdered plasterboard. In several cases involving the same informant, there was no evidence at all that the drug buy had taken place. Defendants, in the meantime, had spent months in jail protesting their innocence before charges were dropped. Police and prosecutors concluded that this informant had lied and used the cocaine substitute to get innocent men arrested. Why? He had been paid for every buy and had earned $200,000 before his lies were finally discovered (Curry, 2002).

Sometimes officers are tempted to manufacture informants. When writing affidavits for search warrants, officers may use information supplied by a "confidential informant" without having to name the informant. All the officer has to do is to state that the informant has given good information in the past and that it would be dangerous to reveal his or her identity. This boilerplate language is routinely accepted, so information is used to establish probable cause that cannot be verified or challenged. Barker and Carter (1991) argue that some officers are tempted to use imaginary confidential informants to allow the use of otherwise illegally obtained or simply manufactured evidence. They report on a tragic case in which an officer made up evidence from a so-called informant in order to get a search warrant. In the search, an officer was killed and the lie was exposed.

Some officers openly admit that they could not do their job without informants. However, there are other arguments that the perceived value of informants is overstated. In a British study, the Home Office concluded that informants were cost-effective. But other analysts argued that the study did not factor in issues such as tolerating continued crime (by informants) and informants who create crime in order to report it (Dunningham and Norris, 1999).

South (2001) summarizes the ethical issues with using informants as follows:

- Getting too close and/or engaging in love affairs with informants
- Overestimating the veracity of the information
- Being a pawn of the informant who is taking advantage of the system for money or other reasons
- Creating crimes by letting the informant entrap people who would not otherwise have committed the crime
- Engaging in unethical or illegal behaviors for the informant, such as providing drugs
- Letting the informant invade one's personal life
- Using coercion and intimidation to get the informant to cooperate

There are disturbing questions that one might ask about using informants. It may be true that narcotics investigations are difficult, if not impossible, without them; however, guidelines and standards exist to govern the use of informants. The Commission on Accreditation for Law Enforcement Agencies (CALEA) has developed such standards. There is also a manual from the U.S. Attorney General's office on how informants should be legally and ethically used, including how to properly register them (Hermann, 2009).

THE USE OF UNDERCOVER OFFICERS Undercover officers, such as Joseph Pistone (Donnie Brasco), described at the beginning of the chapter, may pretend to be drug dealers, prostitutes, johns, crime bosses, friends, and—perhaps—lovers in order to collect evidence of crime. They have to observe or even participate in illegal activities to protect their cover. Undercover work is said to be a difficult role for individual officers, who may play the part so well that they lose their previous identity. Marx (1985a: 109) cited examples of officers who became addicted to drugs or alcohol and destroyed their marriages or careers because of undercover assignments. He noted a disturbing belief system among undercover officers that laws don't apply to them or that they are exempt from the law because of their assignment. It has been found that undercover officers possess high levels of neuroticism and low levels of impulse control, and that there are adverse psychological effects from the experience of being undercover (Mieczkowski, 2002: 162).

Conlon (2004), a Harvard-educated New York City police officer, described how undercover officers entered a no-man's land in the department, where they were treated almost more like informants than fellow cops. Those who were successful at setting up buys were treated like "star performers," and some developed "prima donna" attitudes. In general, they were treated and they behaved in a way that made it hard for them to maintain relationships with other police, not to mention probable issues with their families.

Policemen routinely pretend they are johns, and policewomen impersonate prostitutes. Community members who live in neighborhoods plagued with street prostitution may applaud any police efforts to clean up their streets. But do we want our police officers to engage in this type of activity? An important element of this debate is the type of relationship involved in the police deception. On a continuum of intimacy, at one end is a brief buy-bust incident wherein the officer pretends to be a drug addict and buys from a street dealer, and moments later an arrest is made. At the other end of the continuum is a situation in which an undercover officer pretends to be romantically involved with a target of an investigation to maintain his or her cover.

The second situation violates our sense of privacy to a much greater extent. In one case, a private detective (not a police detective) engaged in this type of relationship over a period of months and even agreed to an engagement of marriage with the suspect in order to get a confession on tape (Schoeman, 1986: 21). In another case, a police officer acted as a friend to a target of an investigation, to the extent of looking after his child and living in his house for six months. The purpose of the investigation was to get evidence on the man so the topless bar he owned could be shut down. Eventually the officer found some white powder on a desk in the home that tested positive for cocaine, and a conviction was secured. The Supreme Court denied a writ of certiorari in this case (*United States v. Baldwin*, 621 F.2d 251 [1980]), letting the decision stand.

It was reported that New York City undercover officers, a year before the 2004 Republican convention, began to infiltrate activist groups that they believed might be a problem during the convention. Officers attended meetings, made friends, signed petitions, and then reported on the activities to supervisors. In the records of the NYPD's "Intelligence Squad" are hundreds of reports on people who had no clear criminal plan, including church groups, antiwar organizations, and anti-Bush groups. Reports were evidently shared with police departments in other cities. Whether the prior undercover investigations had any relationships to the mass arrests that occurred during the convention is not clear (Dwyer, 2007).

Undercover operations during the antiwar activist era of the 1960s and early 1970s led to strict controls on police powers to engage in undercover investigations absent probable cause that a group was planning to commit a crime. Covert government surveillance of groups antagonistic to government policy is considered to be a threat to democracy by civil liberty experts. Obviously, there is a proper role for law enforcement in preventing threats to public safety, but the need to investigate threats while at the same time respecting the privacy rights of citizens who, in a democracy, are free to oppose governmental policies must be carefully balanced.

entrapment
When an otherwise innocent person commits an illegal act because of police encouragement or enticement.

More generally, the use of undercover officers who pretend to be someone they are not in order to catch criminals is a power that should be used with caution and with a sensitivity to the damage it does to individual relationships and public trust.

DILEMMA: Should you, an undercover officer, pose as a client in a methadone clinic and pretend to befriend other clients, and then ask them to "hook you up" with a drug dealer? Should you continue to ask someone, even beg them, over the course of several months when they initially refuse?

LAW In legal terms, **entrapment** occurs when an otherwise innocent person commits an illegal act because of police encouragement or enticement. Two approaches have been used to determine whether entrapment has occurred. The *objective approach* examines the government's participation and whether it has exceeded accepted legal standards. For instance, if the state provided an "essential element" that made the crime possible, or if there was extensive and coercive pressure on the defendant to engage in the actions, a court might rule that entrapment had occurred. The *subjective approach* looks at the defendant's background, character, and predisposition toward crime. Currently, the Supreme Court has endorsed the subjective test and will allow a wide range of police officer behavior if they can show the subject showed a predisposition to commit the crime (*United States v. Russell*, 411 U.S. 423 [1973]). In the dilemma above, one might argue that the fact the target was going to a methadone clinic showed a predisposition to drug use and dealing; therefore, such actions would probably be legal.

POLICY Departmental policies may provide some guidance as to how long an operation can continue when there is no criminal activity. Arguably, a "fishing expedition" where there is no particular target and the undercover officer is simply seeing who might respond to the offer may be less consistent with departmental policy than when there is a specific target of someone who there is reason to believe is engaged in continued illegal activity. It should also be noted that sometimes narcotics task forces have very little departmental oversight or policies that guide their actions. Such task forces have been the subject of several scandals nationwide, and one of the defining features of each incident was the absence of formal policies to guide officers' behaviors.

ETHICS What about ethical rationales? One might disagree with legal standards as being too restrictive if one believes that police should be able to do anything necessary to trap criminals. Alternatively, legal guidelines may not be sufficient to eliminate what some consider unethical behavior. What if the undercover officer targeted someone for 11 months, continually begging and pleading with the target to sell him drugs, until finally, simply to get rid of him, the target did so and was promptly arrested? While this would probably not violate the subjective test of entrapment, it does raise ethical questions. Utilitarian ethics might consider it a waste of resources without enough utility for the community to justify the harm to the individual. Deontological ethics may not support such an action either, as it does not seem to conform to the categorical imperative (treat each person as an end and act in a way that you would will it to be a universal law).

It is helpful, first, to consider the deception on a continuum of trust. In the dilemma above, it makes a difference whether the relationship is between simple acquaintances or if the undercover officer created a friendship with the target. The reason that we are concerned with the type of relationship is that intimate relationships form the fabric of social support in our society and should be protected. Note we are not talking necessarily about sexual intimacy, but, rather, a relationship that crosses from acquaintance into friend. There are greater moral duties present in intimate relationships than in public ones. There is damage to all when personal relationships are used deceptively; in fact, some argue that an intimate relationship may take precedence over a concern for social well-being generally (Schoeman, 1985: 144). This comes from an ethics-of-care position. In this ethical system, the relationship of two people is more important than rights, duties, or laws. There is no forfeiture of rights in the ethics-of-care position; thus, one can't say that the suspect deserves to be deceived. The harm to the relationship goes in both directions. In cases where a personal relationship has developed, if the target is hurt by the deception, so, too, is the deceiver.

Generally, undercover actions are analyzed under utilitarian ethics. If the relationship is an intimate one, there should be a greater utility at stake before that relationship is used. If the operation is a simple buy-bust relationship, then there is less damage to trust and, therefore, the utility derived can be less in order to justify such deception.

Marx (1985a: 106–107) proposed a set of questions to ask before engaging in any undercover operation, that are consistent with utilitarianism:

- How serious is the crime being investigated?

- How clear is the definition of the crime—that is, would the target know that what he or she is doing is clearly illegal?

- Are there any alternatives to deceptive practices?

- Is the undercover operation consistent with the spirit as well as the letter of the law?

- Is it public knowledge that the police may engage in such practices, and is the decision to do so a result of democratic decision making?

- Is the goal prosecution, as opposed to general intelligence gathering or harassment?

- Is there a likelihood that the crime would occur regardless of the government's involvement?

- Are there reasonable grounds to suspect the target?

- Will the practice prevent a serious crime from occurring?

Marx (1985b, 1991) argues that undercover operations might actually create more crime. They may also lead to unintended crime and danger. For instance, Marx mentions situations where decoys have been attacked, undercover officers have been robbed, undercover officers have been killed by other officers who mistook them for criminals, and policewomen acting as prostitutes have been attacked.

Thus, utilitarianism may justify undercover operations or condemn them depending on the utility derived and the harm done to all parties involved. Act utilitarianism would probably support deceptive practices, but rule utilitarianism might not, because the actions, although beneficial under certain circumstances, might in the long run undermine and threaten our system of law. Under act utilitarianism, one would measure the harm of the criminal activity against the methods used to control it. Deceptive practices, then, might be justified in the case of drug offenses but not for business misdeeds, or for finding a murderer but not for trapping a prostitute, and so on.

The difficulty of this line of reasoning, of course, is to agree on a standard of seriousness. I might decide that drugs are serious enough to justify otherwise unethical practices, but you might not. Pornography and prostitution may be serious enough to some to justify unethical practices, but to others only murder or violent crime would justify the practices.

Cohen (1991) also proposed a test to determine the ethical justification for police practices. His focus is the use of coercive power to stop and search, but we might apply the same test to analyze undercover or other deceptive practices:

- The end must be justified as a good—for instance, conviction of a serious criminal rather than general intelligence gathering.

- The means must be a plausible way to achieve the end—for example, choosing a target with no reasonable suspicion is not a plausible way to reduce any type of crime.

- There must be no better alternative means to achieve the same end—no less intrusive means or methods of collecting evidence exist.

- The means must not undermine some other equal or greater end—if the method results in loss of trust or faith in the legal system, it fails the test.

Religious ethics would probably condemn many kinds of police actions because of the deceptions involved. Ethical formalism would probably also condemn undercover operations where innocent people are deceived because the actions could not be justified under the categorical imperative. Recall that you cannot use people as a means to an end, therefore, if innocent people would be used, it would violate the categorical imperative. Egoism might or might not justify such actions, depending on the officer involved and what his or her maximum gain and loss were determined to be.

Many people see nothing wrong—certainly nothing illegal—in using any methods necessary to catch criminals. But we are concerned with methods in use before individuals are found guilty. Can an innocent person, such as you, be entrapped into crime? Perhaps not, but are we comfortable in a society where the person who offers you drugs or sex or a cheap way to hook into cable television turns out to be an undercover police officer? Are we content to assume that our telephone may be tapped or our best friend could be reporting our conversations to someone else? When we encounter police behavior in these areas, the practices often have been used to catch a person who, we realize after the fact, had engaged in wrongdoing, so we believe that police officers are justified in performing in slightly unethical ways. What protectors of due process and critics of police investigation practices help us to remember is that those practices, if not curbed, may be used just as easily on the innocent as on the guilty.

These investigative techniques are unlikely to be eliminated. Perhaps they should not be, as they are effective in catching a number of people who should be punished. Even if one has doubts about the ethics of these practices, it is entirely possible that there is no other way to accomplish the goal of crime control. However one decides these difficult questions, there are no easy answers. Also, we must realize that for us these questions are academic, but for thousands of police officers they are very real.

REACTIVE INVESTIGATIONS

In reactive investigations, a crime has already occurred and the police sift through clues to determine the perpetrator. When police and other investigators develop an early prejudice concerning who they believe is the guilty party, they look at evidence less objectively and are tempted to engage in noble-cause corruption in order to convict. This can take the form of ignoring witnesses or evidence or even manufacturing evidence to shore up a case against an individual.

Rossmo (2008) brings together descriptions of several investigations that failed because of the human tendency to ignore evidence that does not fit preconceived notions. In these cases, the true criminal was not discovered and others were suspected, and sometimes charged and convicted, because police officers did not follow proper protocol in the collection and interpretation of evidence. Protocol is necessary to avoid errors in judgment when a criminal investigator who "knows" someone is guilty happens to be wrong. Good investigators do not let their assumptions influence their investigations, because assumptions jeopardize effectiveness. Unfortunately, Rossmo's examples show that proper investigative methods are sometimes discarded when police officers think they know who committed the crime.

This tendency to slant the evidence is not limited to police investigators. FBI lab examiners have compromised cases by completing shoddy work and misrepresenting their findings, evidently to support police theories regarding the guilty party. In effect, they were not objective scientists, but rather, co-conspirators with police. This led to overstating their findings on the witness stand and covering up tests that were done improperly. A whistle-blower exposed these practices and was suspended for his efforts. His story is presented in the Walking the Walk box. Ultimately, 13 examiners were implicated, although only two were ever formally censured (Sniffen, 1997; Serrano and Ostrow, 2000).

The Houston crime lab has also been a target of investigation. Lab practices and possible perjury by examiners forced the district attorney's office to initially re-examine more than 100 cases (Axtman, 2003). The Houston police lab was eventually shut down in 2002 because of shoddy practices, although it has since reopened. An independent investigation by the Justice Department discovered that untrained workers were conducting DNA analysis, there was evidence of contamination from a leaky roof, "drylabbing" (making up scientific results) was being done, and there was no quality control. Eventually, more than 2,000 cases required review because of potentially tainted testimony from the police lab. Two men had their sentences overturned or were granted new trials because of the findings concerning the lab (Hays, 2005).

Other labs across the country have also been the subject of news reports. Joyce Gilchrist was the supervisor of the forensic lab for the Oklahoma City police department. She came under scrutiny for shoddy practices and alleged misstatement of the evidence while testifying. After several convicted individuals were exonerated, the Oklahoma attorney general suspended executions while her cases were reexamined (Luscombe, 2001). Sometimes the criticism has been simple incompetence and shoddy work practices, but in other allegations it appears that the lab examiners are engaged in noble-cause corruption by working with police departments to arrive at desired results.

The problem is that once investigators decide who the guilty party is, they may ignore evidence that doesn't fit with their idea of who did it and how it was done. It is human nature to complete the puzzle—to see things that conform to one's way of looking at the world. Good police work doesn't close the door to contrary evidence, but human nature does. Utilitarian ends-oriented thinkers may be more likely to ignore contrary evidence or overstate existing evidence if they believe they have the guilty party. Ethical formalism, however, emphasizes duties, not the end result, so those whose ethical values lean toward ethical formalism may be less likely to slide into the types of behavior that have put these forensic professionals under scrutiny.

INTERROGATION Interrogating a person one believes to be guilty of a crime is probably an extremely frustrating experience. How do you get someone to confess? In past eras, the infamous "third degree" was used—in other words, physical force in the form of beatings or threats of force were used to get a confession. The third degree is no longer used, so officers have resorted to persuasion, including the use of deception. The classic father confessor approach (a sympathetic paternal figure for the defendant to confide to) or "good cop/bad cop" (a nice guy and a seemingly brutal, threatening officer) are ways to induce confessions and/or obtain information without using force (Kamisar, LeFave, and Israel, 1980: 54).

It may be that some officers have continued to use physical coercion to obtain confessions. LaPeter (2004) discusses how Jon Burge, a former Chicago cop, ended up

WALKING THE WALK

Dr. Frederic Whitehurst joined the FBI in 1982 after earning a Ph.D. in chemistry. He was also a decorated war veteran, serving three tours in Vietnam, earning four Bronze Stars and being offered (but not accepting) the Purple Heart. Between 1986 and 1998, he was associated with the FBI's highly acclaimed crime lab, becoming an international expert in explosives. During his association with the FBI, he became increasingly troubled by the practices of lab personnel. His concerns involved both shoddy procedures as well as a tendency to take a pro-prosecution stance when examining evidence rather than maintaining scientific objectivity. He complained to the FBI Office of Professional Responsibility and the director of the FBI, but nothing happened. Eventually he took his concerns to the Department of Justice and the Office of the Inspector General, and his criticisms led to a 517-page Inspector General's report after an 18-month investigation, the first time ever that the highly esteemed lab had received any external review.

The report was damning, indicating that FBI examiners had given inaccurate testimony or overstated scientific findings, altered lab reports, failed to document procedures, and had hidden exculpatory evidence from defense attorneys. Further, there was evidence of shoddy management and record keeping and a failure to investigate allegations of incompetence. The report, however, examined only three of the seven units that comprised the FBI lab and only investigated Whitehurst's specific allegations. Still, it led to congressional hearings, a dramatic overhaul of the lab, and, more recently, independent accreditation.

It also derailed Whitehurst's career. Shortly before the report was released in 1997, he was put on administrative leave and criticized for violating policy. In response, he argued that he was following Executive Order 12731, which required federal employees to report fraud, waste, abuse, or corruption to the proper authorities. He was eventually demoted and sanctioned, but ultimately

won a whistleblower lawsuit against the FBI. His whistleblowing led to a review by the Department of Justice of hundreds of cases where FBI examiners gave testimony. It seemed clear that there were people in prison who were there based on flawed evidence, but these individuals were never told their convictions could be challenged.

In 2007, the FBI was criticized in investigative reports by the television show *60 Minutes* and by the *Washington Post* for continuing to withhold the names of about 2,500 defendants who were convicted partially based on the results of examiners' testimony. In response, FBI officials stated that the public announcements of the faulty tests should have been notice enough to these individuals and their lawyers to pursue any appropriate appeals. In November 2007, the FBI spokesperson finally agreed that the FBI would send letters to the prosecutors in these cases to notify them that the testimony was based on faulty science. Unfortunately for many of these defendants, it may have come too late to file an appeal.

Since leaving the FBI, Whitehurst earned a law degree and is now the executive director of an independent organization called the Forensic Justice Project, which collects and disseminates information about controversial forensic science (Post, 2005). He continues to investigate some of the cases from his days in the FBI to try and identify any innocent people that might have been affected by inaccurate scientific testimony. He is largely forgotten even though his actions led to a seismic shift in the faith placed in the FBI lab and forensic science more generally. As news stories about shoddy practices in labs continue to chronicle problems, he prefers the focus stay on the topic rather than about him. In response to a reporter's queries recently about yet another crime lab scandal and his role in improving the field, he said, "We have made the justice system question itself and that is what is important. Let the …[attention] remain about injustice … not about Frederic Whitehurst."

Sources: Kohn, 1997; Solomon, 2007b; Kelly and Wearne, 1998; Stein, 2010.

having four chapters devoted to him in a book about torture (*Unspeakable Acts, Ordinary People*, by John Conroy). Burge came from a blue collar family and earned a Bronze Star, a Purple Heart, the Vietnam Gallantry Cross, and two army commendations for valor in Vietnam. He was 22 years old when he joined the Chicago police department. In 20 years, he worked his way up to commander of the detective division, and received 13 commendations and a letter of praise from the Department of Justice. But his career also had a dark side. Burge was a lieutenant and supervisor of detectives in the Area 2 Violent Crimes Unit from about 1981 to 1986. Later, he was commander of the Bomb and Arson Unit and then commander of Area 3 detectives. He was suspended by the police department in 1991 and fired in 1993. Since then, he has been investigated and indicted for his actions. In 1982, two Chicago police officers were shot and killed. Five days later, Andrew Wilson was questioned, and 13 hours later, he confessed to the killing, but emerged from the interrogation room with severe bruising and cuts on his head, a torn retina, burns on his chest and thighs, and U-shaped marks on his body. He was evidently injured so badly that jail staff refused to accept the booking, fearing that they would be held responsible. He was convicted and sentenced to death, but the Illinois Supreme Court threw out his confession, finding that he had been injured by police officers during the interrogation. He was convicted again during a retrial, but was sentenced to life without parole instead of capital punishment. In his lawsuit against the city and police department, Wilson testified that Burge and another officer used two electroshock devices on his ears, nose, fingers, and groin area, and he was burned by being handcuffed to a radiator. Police have denied the torture, but other prisoners have alleged they saw the device Wilson described and suffered similar torture. A judge awarded Wilson $1 million.

Burge was subpoenaed to give depositions in suits filed by former death row inmates and others who allege they were tortured during interrogations. A special prosecutor was appointed in 2002 to investigate the allegations of torture, and he and his staff investigated cases going back to 1973. Four death row inmates who were subsequently released by Illinois Governor George Ryan were interrogated under Burge's command.

The U.S. Attorney's Office obtained an indictment against Burge for perjury and obstruction of justice in relation to the string of wrongful convictions associated with his interrogations. He and his lawyers asked for a change of venue because of all the negative publicity he received in the Chicago area: 1,300 news stories appeared with his name between 1986 and March 2009, including one story with the caption "Worst Chicago Cop." A judge in another case was even quoted as saying that it was "common knowledge" that Jon Burge and officers working under him engaged in physical abuse to get confessions. Burge's trial began in May 2010. On June 28, 2010, he was convicted on all counts (Main, 2009; LaPeter, 2004).

Despite what might have occurred in Chicago, the use of physical coercion is an aberration today, and evidence exists that deception and skill work more effectively at getting suspects to confess. Skolnick and Leo (1992) have presented a typology of deceptive interrogation techniques. The following is a brief summary of their descriptions of these practices:

- Calling the questioning an interview rather than an interrogation by questioning in a noncustodial setting and telling the suspect that he [or she] is free to leave, thus eliminating the need for *Miranda* warnings
- Presenting *Miranda* warnings in a way designed to negate their effect, by mumbling or by using a tone suggesting that the offender had better not exercise the rights delineated or that they are unnecessary
- Misrepresenting the nature or seriousness of the offense—for instance, by not telling the suspect that the victim has died
- Using manipulative appeals to conscience through role playing or other means
- Misrepresenting the moral seriousness of the offense—for instance, by pretending that the rape victim "deserved" to be raped—in order to get a confession

- Using promises of lesser sentences or non-prosecution beyond the power of the police to offer
- Misrepresenting identity by pretending to be lawyers or priests
- Using fabricated evidence such as polygraph results or fingerprint findings that don't really exist

Interrogative techniques can be very effective. In fact, they have resulted in false confessions. Trainum (2008) notes how he never would have believed that an innocent person would confess to a crime they didn't commit until he reviewed a videotaped interrogation that he had conducted on a female suspect accused of murder. After a long interrogation, the woman confessed to the crime, even describing how she dumped the body. There was some evidence to tie her to it as well, including an ATM video of a person who resembled her using the victim's ATM card and a handwriting analyst who said it was her signature. However, she had an alibi and officers found she was telling the truth about being somewhere else when the crime occurred. Trainum writes how he reviewed the interrogation videotape and realized that he had unconsciously fed her information about the crime. This officer believes that videotaping interrogations is essential for improving the accuracy of confessions despite opponents who argue it is too expensive or too burdensome for departments. Today, only 10 states mandate that interrogations be videotaped.

Some researchers estimate that about 5 percent of confessions are false (Kassin et al., 2010: 5). They are one of the leading causes of false convictions (along with faulty eyewitness identification and mishandling of evidence). Research indicates that suspects don't always understand their *Miranda* rights, and juveniles are especially prone to psychological manipulation. There are attempts to reduce false confessions by requiring corroborating evidence before the confession can be used in court and requiring confessions to be videotaped (Kassin et al., 2010).

?

DILEMMA: Should you use physical coercion to induce a confession? Should you lie about finding physical evidence (i.e., DNA or a fingerprint) and tell the suspect that you have enough to convince a jury to give him the death penalty if he doesn't confess to a lesser crime?

LAW   The use of physical force to obtain a conviction is illegal (*Brown v. Mississippi*, 297 U.S. 278 [1936]). Most countries have eliminated torture and formally condemn the practice. Unfortunately, some countries still endorse physical coercion as acceptable police practice. Amnesty International has documented abuses in Chile, Argentina, and many other countries around the world.

Legal proscriptions against torture are based on the belief that torture renders a confession unreliable. Tortured victims might confess to stop their suffering; thus, the court would not get truthful information. Many would argue that whatever information is gained from an individual who is physically coerced into confessing or giving information is not worth the sacrifice of moral standards even if the information is truthful. Human rights treaties signed by the majority of free countries condemn such practices, regardless of the reason for the interrogation.

Legal proscriptions against deception are more nuanced. Lower court holdings have endorsed the use of some forms of deception, while rejecting others. Challenges to convictions based on confessions obtained when police interrogators deceive the defendant are based on voluntariness—in other words, the fact that the person did not voluntarily offer a confession because a necessary element of voluntariness is "knowing," which is absent when being deceived.

Another argument is that deception by police may result in unreliable results. Similar to the legal argument against torture, this stance holds that when a lie is too powerful, it will induce an innocent to confess, thereby creating verdicts that are not based on facts. An example of such a case occurred in 1989 when 17-year-old Marty Tankleff confessed to killing his parents. Even though there was no physical evidence to link him to the crime, interrogators told the teenager that hairs found on his mother pointed to him, that they had obtained a spot of blood from his shoulder that was matched to his mother, and that his father had emerged from a coma long enough to tell them that Marty had attacked them. All of this was untrue, but it convinced the teen to confess. He served 19 years in prison before having the conviction dismissed and charges vacated (Kassin et al., 2010: 18). Courts may employ a "shock the conscience" standard. If what the officers do seems to be too egregious, any evidence obtained will be excluded (*Moran v. Burbine*, 474 U.S. 412 [1986]). Of course, this begs the question as to what shocks one's conscience. In practice, the lower courts have interpreted the Supreme Court's reluctance to place any restrictions on deception during interrogation as a green light to allow most forms of deception (Magid, 2001), although some state courts will rule as inadmissible confessions obtained by using faked physical evidence, such as fake lab reports or fingerprint analysis results (Kassin et al., 2010: 13).

POLICY Policies in any police department should provide guidance to the individual officer regarding the use of acceptable techniques in interrogation. Some departments routinely videotape interrogations in order to forestall any allegations of improper conduct. Such videotapes are powerful tools when used in the prosecution of guilty parties, but they also can be harmful to those officers who violate law and/or policy in their zeal to obtain a confession.

Dirty Harry problem
The question of whether police should use immoral means to reach a desired moral end (taken from a Clint Eastwood movie).

ETHICS What about ethical rationales for the use of physical coercion or deception during interrogation? Klockars's (1983) **Dirty Harry problem**, described in the last chapter, originated in a situation from the movie where a captured criminal refuses to tell the location of a kidnapped victim. Because the victim is sure to die without help, the police officer (played by Clint Eastwood) tortures the criminal by stepping on his injured leg until he admits the location. The problem represents the situation where one believes the dirty act will result in a good end, there are no other means to achieve the good end, and the dirty act will not be in vain.

Most people (but not all!) would agree that to torture the suspect in that scene was immoral, but Klockars's point is that the situation has no good solution. If the police officer behaves in a professional manner, the victim would be sure to die. If the officer behaves in an immoral manner, there is a chance he could save a life. This is a dominant theme in detective and police fiction. Klockars's conclusion is that by engaging in dirty means for good ends, the officer has tainted his innocence and must be punished, for there is always a danger that dirty means will be redefined as neutral or even good by those who use them. Police may lose their sense of moral proportion if such actions are not punished, even though the individual police officers involved may have no other way out of their moral dilemmas.

Delattre (1989a) also discussed the use of coercive power. He disagreed with Klockars that the officer must inevitably be tainted in the Dirty Harry situation. Delattre pointed out that choosing physical coercion, regardless of temptation, leads to perjury and lying about the activity and perhaps other tactics to ensure that the offender does not go free because of the illegal behavior of the police officer. However, Delattre (1989a: 211) also excused the actions of those who succumb to temptation in extreme situations and perform an illegal act:

> Such an act may be unjustifiable by an unconditional principle, but it also may be excusable.... Still less does it follow that those who commit such acts are bad, that their character is besmirched, or that their honor is tainted.

However, one might argue that if officers commit an illegal and unethical act, it is hard for their character not to be affected or their honor tainted. To understand an action (in this case an act that results from anger or frustration) is not to excuse it. Delattre presents a virtue-based ethical system and evidently believes that an officer can have all the virtues of a good officer and still commit a bad action—in this case, the illegal application of punishment or what some would call torture. His point that one act of violence does not necessarily mean that the officer is unethical in other ways is well taken. Indeed, we usually reserve the terms *ethical* and *unethical* for actions rather than persons. The reaction of the officer to his or her mistake is the true test of character. Does the officer cover up and/or ask his or her partner to cover up the action? Does the officer lie to protect himself or herself? Or does the officer admit wrongdoing and accept the consequences?

Klockars's underlying point is more subtle: we all are guilty in a sense by expecting certain ones among us to do the dirty work and then condemning them for their actions. In effect, police (and other law enforcement) become our *sin eaters* of early folklore; they are the shady characters on the fringe of society who absorb evil so the rest of us may remain pure. These persons are depended upon to protect us, but shunned and avoided when their actions see the light of day. In times of war or other threats, the populace often wants results without wanting to know tactics. What percentage of the population cared that the CIA attempted to assassinate Fidel Castro or that the attorney general's office during the Kennedy years used questionable tactics and violated the due-process rights of Cosa Nostra members targeted in the campaign against organized crime? Today, we continue to discuss whether or not CIA agents and others should have inflicted "extreme interrogative techniques" (to some, torture) on detainees in Guantanamo and Bagram Prison. It should be remembered that these are not new questions; the justification for such actions is always utilitarianism, and only the particular threat changes.

Setting aside physical coercion, what about deception during interrogation? Is it ethical and, if so, what are the limits to such deception? It is certainly much easier to justify deception than physical coercion and intimidation, but their justifications are the same: they are an effective and perhaps necessary means to get needed information from a resisting subject. The criticism against them is also the same. Under utilitarianism, there may not be any utility in such actions because they may result in false confessions. Several convictions have been overturned because new evidence proves that those convicted were innocent, yet they confessed. Why would someone confess to a crime he or she didn't commit?

A suspect might confess because he is a 14-year-old juvenile who was mentally overpowered by police who fed him information from the crime and exerted intense psychological pressure until he confessed to the crime. This is alleged to have happened in the Central Park jogger "wilding" case. In 1990, five black and Hispanic youths were convicted of the beating and rape of a female stockbroker. Years later, Matias Reyes confessed, stating that he acted alone in the crime. DNA evidence supports his contention that he raped the victim (Tanner, 2002; Getlin, 2002). Evidently, the youths were intimidated by police interrogators into confessing to the crime.

Allegedly, a similar scenario occurred in an Austin, Texas, case where two men were found guilty and sentenced to death for a robbery/murder. One of them confessed and implicated the other. Then, 12 years later, another man wrote to the district attorney offering his confession. DNA evidence confirmed his guilt. The innocent man who confessed alleges that he did so because the police officer who interrogated him threatened that if he did not confess, Mexican police would arrest his mother and they could not guarantee her safety. They also told him that he would receive the death penalty if he didn't confess (Hafetz, 2002).

In another case, Keith Longtin was held by Prince George County, Maryland, police detectives for 38 hours after his wife was raped and stabbed to death. He alleges that during this time, police officers accompanied him to the bathroom, would not let him call an attorney, and continually questioned him (employing different teams of interrogators). Finally, they said that he told them what happened, but he remembers it as them telling him what happened to his wife and asking him to speculate about how the murder occurred.

Detectives allege that he confessed. Longtin alleged that he never did. A sex crimes investigator noticed the similarity between the attack and other rapes in the area, and after the rape suspect was arrested, a DNA test proved that this man killed Longtin's wife. Longtin was freed after eight months in jail, and all charges were dropped. Longtin's case and four other homicide confessions that were thrown out because other evidence proved they were false confessions led to a federal monitor for this law enforcement agency (Witt, 2001).

Although such events sound like something from television drama rather than reality, they do happen. In 2001, Illinois Governor Ryan commuted the death sentences of everyone on death row because of suspicion that more innocent men may be in danger of being executed. Thirteen death penalty cases were overturned when evidence indicated that the convicted might be innocent or, at the very least, did not receive due process. Five of those thirteen were from Chicago, and evidence indicated that the convictions were obtained through coerced confessions and manufactured evidence by the Chicago police investigators, including Jon Burge, as described earlier in this chapter (Babwin, 2001). Thus, even utilitarianism may not provide justification for the use of deception in interrogations if it is so extreme that it leads to false confessions.

Deontological ethics would focus on the duty of the officer. Although he or she has a duty to protect society, there is also the duty to follow the law, thus, any form of physical coercion or deception that has been ruled illegal would not be ethically justified. Do the actions conform to the categorical imperative? If the officer had a brother or mother who was accused of a crime, or was accused themselves, would they believe their actions justified? If not, then they cannot be supported by ethical formalism.

Discretion and the Use of Force

Police have an uncontested right to use force when necessary to apprehend and/or subdue a suspect of a crime. When their use of force exceeds that which is necessary to accomplish their lawful purpose, or when their purpose is not lawful apprehension or self-defense, but rather, personal retaliation or coercion, it is defined as excessive force and is unethical and illegal.

How do victims of force come to the attention of police? Often it is by challenging police authority—passing a patrol car, asking questions, challenging the stop, or intervening in the arrest of another (Kappeler, Sluder, and Alpert, 1994: 159). In Klockars's (1984) description of types of police power (authority, power, persuasion, and force) described in Chapter 5, force is brought into play when one's authority is challenged and/or persuasion is ineffective. Thus, individuals who question or refuse to recognize police authority become vulnerable to the use of force. Such use of force may be perfectly legal. Officers have the right to tackle a fleeing suspect or hit back when they are defending themselves. Illegal or excessive force occurs when the officer goes beyond what is necessary to effect a lawful arrest.

First, it is important to note that force seems to be present in a very small percentage of the total encounters between police and citizens. Second, research indicates that a small percentage of officers seem to be responsible for a disproportionate percentage of the force incidents. Finally, some studies do find an association between force and race or socioeconomic status, but other factors, such as demeanor, seem to be even more influential.

Worden and Catlin (2002) offer studies showing that use of force is present in between 1.3 and 2.5 percent of all encounters. A BJS study reported that force was used in about 1.6 percent of all police–citizen interactions (Ducrose, Langan, and Smith, 2007). However, use of force seems to vary depending on the city. Garner, Maxwell, and Heraux (2002) found in their study that use of force ranged from 12.7 percent of encounters in one city to 22.9 percent of encounters in another city. In addition, a national survey of law enforcement agencies that found that the rate of use-of-force events varied by region, with the highest in the South (90 incidents per 100,000), followed by the Northeast (72), the Midwest (68), and the West (50) (Terrill, 2005). In a study based on participant observations of police–citizen encounters, Alpert and Dunham (2004: 47) reported that officers did not use the level of force that they were legally and (by policy) entitled to use in the majority of encounters, based on the resistance of the suspect.

Some types of police–citizen interactions seem to generate the most frequent use of force reports. In one study, officers used force in an estimated 53 percent of vehicle pursuits. Further, 47 percent of the surveyed suspects who fled from police reported that force was used (in contrast to the official number of 17 percent) (Alpert and Dunham, 2004). Some officers seem to get involved in use-of-force situations repeatedly, whereas others, even in similar patrol neighborhoods, rarely get involved in such altercations. According to Souryal (1992: 242), the report by the Independent Commission of the Los Angeles Police Department in 1991 revealed that the top 5 percent of officers ranked by number of reports of the use of force accounted for more than 20 percent of all reports, and that of approximately 1,800 officers who had been reported for excessive use of force between 1986 and 1990, most had only one or two allegations, but 44 had six or more, 16 had eight or more, and one had 16 allegations.

Studies exploring use of force date back to Friedrich's (1980) now classic study that examined how individual, situational, and organizational factors have been offered as explanations to the decision to use force. In his study, however, he identified only the behavior of the offender and the visibility of the encounter as predictive of the decision to use force. Worden and Catlin (2002) reported on a number of studies documenting the presence of differential use of force by officers in police departments. A small number of officers seem to be disproportionately involved in use-of-force incidents and, arguably, are more likely to also engage in excessive force. Further, some evidence seems to indicate that these officers may be identifiable by certain psychological traits:

- Lack of empathy
- Antisocial and paranoid tendencies
- Proclivity toward abusive behavior
- Inability to learn from experience

- Tendency not to take responsibility for their actions
- Cynicism
- Strong identification with the police subculture

Other risk factors include age of the officer (being young and impressionable may increase the risk of using improper force) and being involved in a traumatic event (thus, use of force would be a type of post-traumatic stress behavior) (reported in Worden and Catlin, 2002: 101). Terrill, Paoline, and Manning (2003) found that officers who identified more strongly with the police culture were more likely to use force and that differences between individuals were more predictive than differences in departments' management strategies or formal cultures of departments.

Other researchers (Garner, Maxwell, and Heraux, 2002; Alpert and MacDonald, 2001; Terrill and Mastrofsky, 2002; Alpert and Dunham, 2004) have identified the following factors as associated with the use of force:

- Suspect's race
- Suspect's manner toward police (disrespectful demeanor)
- General agitation or emotionality of suspect
- Suspect's mental illness
- Intoxication of suspect
- Number of citizens present (positive association)
- Number of police officers present (positive association)
- Possession of a weapon by the suspect (or belief that there is a weapon)
- Knowledge that suspect had committed other crimes (especially, violent crimes)
- Suspect's use of force
- Gang involvement
- Suspect being male
- Officer being male
- Age of officer (younger)
- Officer having prior injuries
- Encounter involving a car chase
- Race of officer (but the association is for Hispanics, not African Americans)
- Socioeconomic status of suspect

Alpert and Dunham (2004) found that female officers used significantly less force in response to resistance, and the longer an officer was employed, the more force was used in relation to the suspect's resistance. As to race, there were few significant relationships, but the highest force factors occurred with Hispanic officers to Hispanic suspects. Black and Hispanic officers who arrested black suspects also employed higher levels of force. Alpert and Dunham found that black and Anglo officers arresting Anglo suspects used lower levels of force in relation to level of resistance than other ethnic matches (2004: 159). Alpert and MacDonald (2001) found that agencies that required supervisors to fill out use-of-force forms had lower levels of use of force than did agencies that allowed officers to fill out their own forms. It should be emphasized that these studies and the factors identified are associated with the use of force, not necessarily *excessive* force.

Probably the most well-known use of force was that by Los Angeles police against Rodney King, revealed by the amateur video taken by a bystander. This can still be seen on YouTube.com even though the event occurred in 1991. In the Rodney King incident, an initial act of passing a police vehicle and leading officers in a high-speed chase (although the actual speed of the chase was subject to dispute) led to the involvement of 12 police cars, one helicopter, and up to 27 officers. The incident resulted in King being struck at least 56 times, with 11 skull fractures, a broken cheekbone, a fractured eye socket, a broken ankle, missing teeth, kidney damage, external burns, and permanent brain damage (Kappeler, Sluder, and Alpert, 1994: 146).

After the incident, officers justified their actions by the explanation that King was on the drug PCP (he was not, and, in fact, his alcohol level was .075), impervious to pain, and wild. These claims were repeated in the newspapers and can be interpreted as the attempt to fit the use of force into a pattern that the public could understand and accept. This use of force probably was prosecuted (unsuccessfully) in this case only because of the existence and widespread dissemination of the videotape. In other circumstances it would hardly have rated a small newspaper article. The media typically become interested in police use of force when the victim cannot be fit into the stereotype of the "dangerous criminal"—when he is a middle-class insurance agent (as in a Miami case that sparked riots), Andrew Young's son (in an incident involving the Washington, D.C., police), or a high school athlete who would have been on his way to Yale on an academic/athletic scholarship.

The King incident is an example of lawful force or excessive force, depending on one's perception. In the video, King clearly continued to try to rise and the officers continued to use their tasers, kick, and hit him with their batons. Some argue that the officers continued to hit him because he continued to resist; others argue that he continued to resist because he was disoriented and was trying to escape the injuries being inflicted upon him.

This case represents a situation in which law, policy, and ethics present different answers to this question: "Did the officers do anything wrong?" The legal question of unlawful use of force is contingent on whether the Los Angeles Police Department's use-of-force policy was legal and whether the officers conformed to departmental policy. The policy stated that the officers could use escalating and proportional force to a suspect's "offensive" behavior. The reason that two use-of-force experts—one for the prosecution and one for the defense—disagreed was that the policy, like many other policies in policing, depends on the ethical use of discretion. The defense's use-of-force expert analyzed the video and identified offensive movements in King's every attempt to rise and in every arm movement. The prosecution expert (who wrote the departmental policy) testified that a suspect lying on the ground is not in a position to present offensive movements to officers; therefore, any use of force once the suspect is down is excessive. The point is that if an officer perceives offensiveness in any movement of a suspect, the policy justifies his or her use of force.

Although use-of-force policies have reduced the incidence of improper use of force by officers, these policies still leave a great deal of discretion. In many cases, an officer's ethics will become as powerful as his or her training and understanding of the policy itself. If an officer gets shot at, the policy obviously would justify use of force, but if the officer decides that he or she is safe enough behind his or her patrol car to talk the suspect out of shooting again and into giving up the weapon, the use-of-force policy would support that nonviolent response as well. If an officer is hit in the face by a drunk, the policy would support use of force because the drunk obviously performed an offensive action; however, the officer who accepts that the drunk is irrational, allows for it, and simply puts the person in the back of the patrol car (in effect, giving him a "free punch") is also supported by the policy. In other words, the policy can be used to justify all but the most blatant abuse of police power, or not, depending on the interpretation of the individual officer.

In a 2005 case in Austin, Texas, an event that was similar to the Rodney King case occurred with similar results. Ramon Hernandez was involved in a minor car accident and ran from the scene. After being tackled and brought to the ground, three police officers surrounded him and, when he continued to try to get up, one held his foot to Hernandez's neck and another administered many blows to his back. Hernandez argued that his face was being pressed into an anthill and that he was only struggling to move away from that. The officers argued that he had earlier tried to wrest one's gun away and Hernandez was, and continued to be, physically combative. The officers were acquitted of official oppression charges, and they also won a federal civil lawsuit against them by Hernandez (Kreytak, 2008). Similar to the Rodney King case, individuals can view this incident and see either a legitimate use of force that conforms to the continuum-of-force policy (meeting resistance with force) or a gratuitous application of force that was not necessary to subdue the suspect. Legally, it appears that the officers did nothing wrong, at least according to the juries who decided the criminal and federal civil cases. As for policy, one officer was fired, one resigned, and one received a 70-day suspension, so it seems that their superiors did find that they violated the department's policy on the use of force.

In a similar incident in Minneapolis in February 2009, a single officer stopped a driver and, after the driver got out of his car after being told not to, the officer wrestled the man to the ground. The video camera on the car shows a number of other officers arriving who then proceed to kick, hit, and use a taser on the man. The videotape of the incident (available on YouTube.com) was reviewed by command staff, but no concerns emerged about the police officer actions until the chief saw the tape. He disciplined the officer and used the tape as a training tool. The man filed suit against the police department and the case was referred to the FBI for potential charges against the officer (Olson and Chanen, 2009).

What is interesting about these cases is that some people see the tapes as clear evidence of police brutality and others see them as appropriate use of force against noncomplying suspects. If we can assume that both sides are reasonable, this shows that officers involved in use-of-force incidents face a dilemma regarding not only what is legal, but also what is ethical. Clearly, the crux of the issue is the policy whereby police officers are empowered to use force against resistance. No one would argue that police officers have a dangerous job and must protect themselves against individuals who may do them harm. The incidents that are brought to light, however, show situations where, perhaps, the use of force might have been legally justified, but not necessary if the officer had made different choices leading up to the use of force. Just because you *can* do something doesn't mean you *should*.

USE OF TASERS (CEDS)

The TASER©, produced by Taser International, is similar to Xerox© in that Xerox is a particular brand of copying machine, but, because of its popularity, the name has become almost a synonym for copying. The TASER is one type of CED (conducted energy device), but the word *taser* has come to be used in common language to refer to any CED. The devices use electrical stimuli to interfere with the body's nervous system, impairing the muscular control of the target. While the use of the CED has become popular among law enforcement agencies, it has also created controversy over how it is used, and its role in the deaths of individuals who have been subdued by police.

It was reported that in 2008, 12,000 law enforcement agencies employed CEDs (Chermak, 2009: 861). In one study of newspaper articles, it was found that reports of CEDs increased from 24 news stories in 2002 to 338 in 2006 (White and Ready, 2009: 875), and one can assume the number of stories have increased again in the last several years. Proponents argue that the use of these devices has resulted in less injury to officers and combatants and reduced the need for lethal force (Williams, 2010). An NIJ-funded research panel examined mortality reviews of CED-related deaths and other evidence to conclude that there was not a high risk of injury or death, although tasers may produce secondary effects that could result in death (NIJ, 2008). Generally, research indicates that CEDs seem to be associated with a decrease in the number of deaths of suspects, a decrease in the number of injuries to suspects, and a decrease in the number of injuries to officers (Dart, 2004: A14; White and Ready, 2009). Supporters allege that CEDs are safe in the vast majority of cases and are potentially dangerous only when there is some underlying medical condition. One study found that death was more likely in cases where the target was under the influence of drugs or mentally ill and when the device was used more than once; however, the methodology of the study was to collect data through newspaper articles, so it was not clear whether this association was direct, indirect, or spurious (White and Ready, 2009: 883).

On the other side, Amnesty International (2007) alleges that police use CED or stun guns in hundreds of cases in which their use is unjustified and "routinely" inflict injury, pain, and death. Its investigation uncovered the fact that the CEDs were used on unarmed suspects 80 percent of the time and for verbal noncompliance in 36 percent of the cases. CEDs allegedly have been used on "unruly schoolchildren," the "mentally disturbed or intoxicated," and those who do not comply immediately with police commands. Amnesty International's report indicates that there have been at least 300 CED-related deaths (Amnesty International, 2007).

After police used a CED on a confused and out-of-control man in the Vancouver (British Columbia) airport, he died, creating a firestorm of controversy. The Canadian government initiated a wide-ranging review and study of conducted energy devices and their risk of injury or death. After reviewing numerous medical studies and technology reports, the Braidwood Commission concluded that, although research indicated there was little risk, there was enough risk to justify limiting the use of the device to only situations where the subject posed an immediate risk of harm and no lesser means of force were effective (Williams, 2010). There are those, however, who argue that the Braidwood Commission ignored the volumes of medical and scientific evidence that indicated that the electrical charge carried by the devices was not sufficient to affect the heart and that their conclusion was based more on public policy (and responding to the public's reaction to the incident) than medical science (Williams, 2010).

Evidence does seem to indicate that the CED is unlikely to stop the heart or cause harm based on the electrical charge; however, there is no doubt that injury can occur when the person falls and/or where the probes enter the body. There is concern when police departments and other law enforcement agencies do not provide proper guidance or control over the use of CEDs. Englewood, California, was the subject of a Department of Justice report concerning its use of force, including the use of the taser. The Department of Justice study found that a taser was used on handcuffed suspects and those in custody, and that the department offered little direction to officers over how it should be used (Kim and Leonard, 2010).

Amnesty International (2007) proposes that the standard for force should be only as a "last resort," and in proportion to the resistant force met. The legal standard in this country, however, is reasonableness (*Graham v. Connor*, 490 U.S. 386 [1989]). Legally, officers have a right to use "reasonable" force in any interaction with the public, as determined by the facts and circumstances. They are not obligated to use the least possible force as long

in the NEWS

TASER USED IN TRAFFIC STOPS

Two taser incidents in Austin, Texas, illustrate problematic uses of the weapon. In 2007, a police officer used a CED on a black motorist on his way to a Thanksgiving dinner with his mother because the driver did not produce his license when requested. The incident was caught on the officer's patrol camera, and the police chief made an unprecedented decision to release the tape and use it for training purposes. The officer was suspended, and, in an unusual move, members of the police officer union apologized to the public at large for the actions of this one officer.

In 2009, a sheriff's deputy used his CED on a 72-year-old woman who refused to sign a ticket, and pushed the deputy toward traffic in an attempt to get back into her car and drive away. The county settled a lawsuit with the woman for $40,000, but the deputy's supervisor said he did nothing wrong and followed procedure. (Both of these incidents can be seen on Youtube.com.)

SOURCES: Plohetski, 2007; Gonzales, 2009.

as the force used is objectively reasonable given the circumstances. However, in December 2009, the Ninth Circuit Court of Appeals ruled that a police officer could be held liable when the taser is used on a person that poses no immediate threat (*Bryan v. McPherson*, 590 F.3d 767 [2009]). In the case, Carl Bryan was stopped for speeding and stepped out of his car visibly angry. There is dispute between the officer involved and Bryan as to whether he stepped toward the officer, but there is no question that he was unarmed and the officer used the taser within seconds of approaching him. Bryan fell to the ground and fractured four teeth, and a doctor had to remove one of the CED probes with a scalpel. Bryan sued for assault and battery and intentional infliction of emotional distress, and the lower court refused the motion for summary judgment from the officer. The Ninth Circuit affirmed the lower court's holding, indicating that the taser was an unreasonable use of force for a traffic stop, opening the door for lawsuits by individuals who are the targets of tasers used by officers. (See the accompanying In the News box for more on the use of tasers during traffic stops.)

It is probably the case that officers could use more training over the use of tasers; however, little is known about the extent or content of CED training across the country. Morrison (2009) notes that training for CEDs is more expensive than firearms training (because the cartridges are more expensive than bullets). Consequently, officers may get much less training with CEDs than with guns, even though it is harder to hit a subject with a CED than it is with a firearm. Studies indicate that CED training is often not a part of the state-mandated training required of all officers (Morrison, 2009).

CULTURE OF FORCE

The use of force in response to perceived challenges to police authority is highly resistant to change, even in the presence of public scrutiny and management pressure. Even with the notoriety of the Rodney King episode and the extreme public reaction to the spectacle of police use of force, several incidents involving other officers' abusive behavior toward motorists occurred shortly thereafter. This pattern might be so ingrained in some police department cultures that it remains relatively unaffected. Research indicates that the "culture of force" is international in scope and this may be due to similarities experienced by all police officers (Coady et al., 2000).

The Christopher Commission described a culture of force at the Los Angeles Police Department; at the time that included an apparent failure to punish or control those who had repeated citizen complaints of violence (Rothlein, 1999). Skolnick and Fyfe (1993), too, have discussed the culture of LAPD in the 1980s and 1990s as one where the use of violence was tolerated, even encouraged. Breaking up departments into elite units seems to encourage "swashbuckling behavior." Skolnick and Fyfe (1993: 191) described how one squad (the infamous Ramparts Division, discussed more fully in the next chapter) acting on a tip totally destroyed a citizen's home, including breaking toilets, ripping sofas, and spray-painting "LAPD Rules!" on the wall of the house. These specialized units evidently create their own culture, even within the subculture of the larger department, and sometimes this subculture promotes violence.

The fact that the prevalence of use of force varies among cities or in one city between two time periods indicates that there is more than individual factors at play. Certain cities seem to have a problematic reputation as using force in a manner that creates controversy. Human Rights Watch (1998) identified serious problems in the use of force in Atlanta, Boston, Chicago, Detroit, Indianapolis, Los Angeles, Minneapolis, New Orleans, New York, Philadelphia, Portland, Providence, San Francisco, and Washington, D.C. The report cited police leadership and the "blue wall of secrecy" as serious barriers to reducing police violence. According to this report, the mechanisms for handling complaints can ensure that violence will continue. In most cases where a citizen alleges excessive force, there is no discipline and the case is closed as unfounded. If there is a civil suit and the plaintiff wins, the city pays, and, again, the officer may not even be disciplined. One study is cited concerning the fate of police officers named in 100 civil lawsuits between 1986 and 1991 in 22 states in which juries awarded payments of $100,000 or more. It was found that only eight of these officers were disciplined (Human Rights Watch, 1998: 82; see also Payne, 2002). More recently, Detroit reportedly paid out in excess of $45 million for police officer misconduct between 2002 and 2005 (Associated Press, 2005). The problem is that by ignoring such actions, the department may be encouraging the continued existence of improper uses of force.

EXCESSIVE FORCE

One might argue there is a fine line between the lawful use of force in subduing a suspect and a gratuitous punch at the end of the scuffle because he tore your new uniform. In an adrenalin-fired foot chase and wrestling match to get the handcuffs on, it is impractical to hold police officers to some ideal of being able to calibrate exactly the amount of force necessary and not a whit more. That is why the legal standard of reasonableness is usually given a generous interpretation by juries and civilian review boards. However, there are examples where officers engage in what is clearly excessive force, such as a situation where the suspect is on the ground in handcuffs and is kicked in the head. It should also be noted that it is estimated that officers use excessive force in a miniscule portion of total encounters with the public—estimated at one-third of 1 percent (Micucci and Gomme, 2005: 487).

The most common explanations for excessive force is that force is the only thing "these people" understand or that "officers are only human" and consequently get mad or frightened or angry, just like anyone else would in that situation. Another comment that seems to be fairly prevalent among individuals who respond to these events is that the person "deserved it" because of his or her commission of a crime or because he or she ran away from police. The weakness of such arguments is obvious. Even if the only thing "these people" understand is force, it removes the differences that we like to think exist between us and "them." If other people get angry and use force, it is called assault and battery, and they are arrested and prosecuted. Finally, punishment comes after a finding of guilt in a court of law, not by law enforcement officers, and does not ever involve the infliction of corporal punishment, which has been ruled as violating the Eighth Amendment.

Although reasonable people may disagree about the Hernandez case, or even the Rodney King case, the Abner Louima case involved, without question, clearly illegal force. NYPD officer Justin Volpe's assault on Abner Louima shocked the nation and led to a prison sentence for Volpe. The truly amazing thing about this criminal act is that it occurred in a police station with at least one officer reportedly assisting but with a whole squad room just outside the door. Volpe brutally sodomized Louima with a broken broom handle, requiring several operations to repair the damage. According to Volpe's testimony, Louima was brought up to the squad room and taken into the bathroom for the purpose of beating him, and the broken handle was put in the bathroom for that purpose. This evidently didn't raise any red flags to officers at the booking desk or other officers. How could this have happened in a police station? The fact that Louima was a minority, the fact that Volpe believed he had been hit in the head by Louima, and the fact that the blue curtain of secrecy is still intact in many police departments seem to be insufficient to answer this question. Eventually four officers were convicted. Justin Volpe received 30 years; Charles Schwarz, 15 years; Thomas Weise and Thomas Bruder received 5 years each. A civil rights suit against the police department and the city was settled for $7.125 million and, in a rare event, the Police Benevolent Association also paid out $1.625 million for its role in assisting the officers in the cover-up after the assault. The case also resulted in policy changes, including initiating a civilian review panel for excessive force complaints and phasing out the so-called 48-hour rule where police officers didn't have to talk to internal affairs about any use of force for 48 hours and after they had conferred with union lawyers (Skolnick, 2001: 17).

Another case where a suspect alleged he was sodomized by New York City police officers occurred in 2009. Michael Mineo was arrested in the subway and alleges that in the scuffle and search for drugs officers sodomized him with a police baton. The officers were prosecuted, and witnesses, including another police officer, supported Mineo's story. The officers testified that Mineo was lying and the motivation was a $400 million lawsuit against the NYPD and city. The jury acquitted the officers in March 2010; however, they still face the civil lawsuit (Marzulli, 2010).

Although use-of-force figures exist, it is difficult to determine the true number of incidents of excessive force because they often do not find their way into official statistics. Researchers address the question in four ways:

1. They use official documents, such as police incident reports.

2. They ask police officers about their actions or the actions of their peers regarding excessive force.

3. They use civil rights complaints or public opinion surveys to ask people what their experiences have been.

4. They use observers in police cars to record interactions between police and citizens, including instances of excessive force.

In documenting the perceptions of the use of excessive or unnecessary force, Alpert and Dunham (2004) reported on research where officers estimated that 13 percent of vehicle pursuits ended in excessive use of force. In addition, Weisburd and Greenspan (2000) asked officers about use of force, and 22 percent of the respondents said that police officers in their department "sometimes," "often," or "always" used *more force than necessary* when making an arrest. Further, 15 percent of the respondents indicated that their fellow officers "sometimes," "often," or "always" responded to verbal abuse with physical force. However, 97 percent thought that extreme uses of unnecessary force were extremely rare.

Recall that in Barker and Carter's (1994) study, officers reported that 39 percent of their peers engaged in brutality. A Gallup Poll finding indicated that 20 percent of respondents said they knew someone who had been abused by police, but the percentage increased to 30 percent of minority respondents (reported in Alpert and Dunham, 2004: 36).

Nelson (2000) chronicled a long list of personal stories of harassment, brutality, illegal arrests, and coerced confessions by police toward minority members, especially African Americans. Her conclusion was that in the minority community, at least, there are reasons to fear police. Holmes (2000) found that the number of civil rights complaints filed (which were mostly claims of excessive force) was only weakly affected by the percentage of blacks in the population in small cities. However, other studies have shown a significant association between race and number of civil rights complaints in cities with a population exceeding 150,000, and a strong association between the number of complaints filed and the percentage of Hispanics in the city's population (Garner, Maxwell, and Heraux, 2002; Smith and Holmes, 2003). In conclusion, it can be said that excessive force is extremely rare, but there are factors that seem to be associated with its existence, both individually and organizationally.

DEADLY FORCE

Nothing is more divisive in a minority community than a police shooting that appears to be unjustified. Cities are quite different in their shooting policies and in their rates of civilian deaths. There can also be quite a change within one city. The District of Columbia, for instance, went from 32 police shootings (with 12 deaths) in 1998 to only 17 in 2001 (with three deaths) (C. Murphy, 2002). The D.C. police department was under a court monitor, which might have had something to do with the fairly dramatic decline in shootings.

Skolnick and Fyfe (1993: 235) and Chevigny (1995) argued that New York City's shooting policy encouraged a low shooting rate. In New York and many other cities now, there is an automatic investigation every time shots are fired, with multiple layers of report writing and investigation before the officer is cleared. The authors also noted that NYPD officers showed a lower rate of being shot than in other cities, so the stringent policy did not seem to affect their safety.

Even New York, however, has had its share of deaths that have raised tensions. Amadou Diallo allegedly resembled a known serial rapist, and when he ignored police orders to show his hands and continued to unlock an apartment building door to go inside, he was shot at 41 times by officers in the NYPD Special Crimes Unit. The case threatened to spark riots in the city, especially when the police officers' trial was moved to Albany and the officers were acquitted.

There are periodic scandals in cities when officers shoot suspects, especially minority suspects, and the media present the case as possibly unjustified. The shooting of Fong Lee continues to be a flashpoint in police–community relations in Minneapolis. In 2008, a Minneapolis police officer shot and killed Fong Lee in a chase. He testified that he saw the youth with a gun, and there was one at the scene near the body, but in an investigation, there was some question as to whether the gun had previously been in the police evidence room as stolen property. The jury exonerated Officer Lawrence, but he later was arrested for domestic violence, was fired, and then rehired after an appeal (Hanners, 2009; Carlyle, 2009). In Austin, the Nathanial Sanders case continues to bedevil the police department's relationship with the minority community. In 2009, Sanders was sleeping in the back seat of a car when police approached. The officers detained the driver and an officer was lifting Sanders's shirt to see if he had a weapon when he awoke and began struggling with the officer. The video camera of the backup officer's car showed the officer backing away and shooting into the car. Sanders died from the shots fired. A gun was later found in the back seat. The officer was sanctioned for not turning on his video camera, but the shooting was ruled justified and a grand jury refused to return an indictment in the case. However, an independent consultant firm described the use of force as reckless and excessive, and the controversy continues even though the officer involved has since been fired based on a DWI charge (Plohetski, 2010). The lesson drawn from these cases is that lethal force will always be subject to the most intense scrutiny imaginable by the public and department alike, as it should be. Officers deserve a careful review of the evidence, free from political and inappropriate considerations, and with an understanding of the factors that are involved in human perception and decision making. The Quote and Query box indicates the legal implications of officer's decisions in these situations.

QUOTE & QUERY

Reckless conduct can be criminal if it involves taking actions knowing that they are likely to yield a particular result but the actor does so despite the risk. (Independent report describing police officer's actions)

[The actions were] objectively reasonable based on the totality of the circumstances…. (Police chief describing same actions after internal investigation and review)

—SOURCE: CITED IN PLOHETSKI, 2010.

These quotes refer to the actions taken by the officer in the Sanders case. How can two objective reviews of an officer's actions come to such different conclusions? Is it "just politics" or do use-of-force policies create the possibility that reasonable people will disagree over what was reasonable?

Whether it be lethal force, a taser, or physical blows, officers have been given the discretion to employ force that, if performed by citizens, would be illegal. We expect them to use such power wisely, and they have a legal duty to do so—that is, they must make reasonable decisions based on the facts and circumstances of each case. Officers are trained in the law and departmental policies, but both by necessity require the application of individual discretion to determine reasonableness. Further, as we have discussed, sometimes what officers have a legal right to do may not be wise or ethical, given certain situations.

DILEMMA: You have stopped a 72-year-old woman for speeding. She is argumentative and refuses to sign the ticket. She ignores your command to move away from the highway and tries to get back into her vehicle. You attempt to push her to the side of the road away from traffic, but she continues toward her car. Should you use your taser?

LAW The Supreme Court has defined legal force as that force which is objectively reasonable (*Graham v. Connor*, 490 U.S. 386 [1989]). What is reasonable, however, is still subject to controversy. The use of a taser has been determined by the Ninth Circuit Court to be unreasonable in a traffic stop when there is no threat of assault—therefore, this officer would be clearly in the wrong applying the Ninth Circuit's standard. We do not have any indication, however, that other circuit courts would agree with the conclusion that tasers are de facto unreasonable uses of force in traffic stops. Further, even applying a reasonableness standard, courts may disagree.

POLICY Police departments' use-of-force policies specify when force may be used, when it may not be used, and the proper level of force to be used given certain circumstances. Most departments utilize a continuum-of-force approach that allows proportional force to the suspect's resistance, with increasing levels of force by the officer in direct response to escalating resistance of the suspect (Walker, 2007). Policies regarding tasers have been suggested by the International Association of Chiefs of Police. Such policies recommend that the taser not be used on juveniles, the elderly, or pregnant women, and should not be used repeatedly or by multiple officers. According to one county's policy, the taser should be used only for "aggressively assaultive acts." One city's policy specifies that the taser not be used on individuals who are clearly under the influence of drugs (Bunker, 2009). Such policies often have been put in place because of scandals regarding their use. In fact, it seems safe to say that most of the restrictions on taser use have come about because of notorious cases of misuse and the public's concern. The problem, according to some observers and law enforcement officials, is that the individual officer may now second-guess the use of the taser and end up using more lethal force because of departmental policies restricting taser use (Bunker, 2009).

ETHICS Note that the discussion of tasers or any CED involves issues of facts, law, and policy. There is still disagreement regarding whether or not the taser causes deaths. Without this fundamental knowledge, it is hard to apply an ethical system like utilitarianism, which would weigh the benefit against the harm of tasers. Generally, one might say that if the choice was between a gun and a taser, the suspect would benefit, but the officer may not (because tasers don't always stop people and the officer may be injured). If the choice was between being shocked and being subdued physically, generally the suspect would still benefit except in certain situations that are still being determined (elderly, intoxicated, and young are possible groups that are put at greater risk even though there is little evidence to indicate this is so).

Deontological ethics would be focused on duty. If the officer has a legal right to use the taser and does so, then resulting injury is not a reason to not use it. However, as with most duties, there are complicating factors. Officers also have a duty of protection, so if they can accomplish their purpose without hurting the individual, then that duty would require the lesser degree of force. It is unfortunate that most people's opposition to tasers seems to be fueled by a few instances of clear abuses.

CONCLUSION

In this chapter, we explored some of the ways that police use of authority, power, persuasion, and force have created ethical dilemmas and sparked controversy. Some of us remember images from the 1960s, wherein law enforcement officers appeared on newscasts beating and using attack dogs against peaceful civil rights demonstrators. One might argue that those negative images of the 1960s led to greater professionalism, better training, and racial and sexual integration of police departments in the 1970s and 1980s.

The Rodney King incident in 1991 and the resulting scrutiny led to a groundswell of attention to "police ethics," including a national outcry against racial profiling and discriminatory enforcement, and better accountability measures to guide the use of force. The 9/11 attack was another major effect on policing and created new challenges. Racial profiling, the use of undercover operations, and other tactics are being re-evaluated in the wake of the threat of terrorism, and many now argue they are justified as necessary.

In this chapter, we showed how, for most of us, controversial issues regarding police methods are abstract, but for individual officers who are faced with dilemmas regarding what they should do in certain situations, the questions are much more immediate. To resolve them, the individual should look to legal holdings, departmental policies, and, finally, ethical rationales. Utilitarian reasoning is used to justify many actions, but the question remains whether it is ever ethical to achieve a good end through bad acts. It seems clear that how one resolves the dilemmas involved in policing has everything to do with whether law enforcement officers are seen fundamentally as crime fighters or as public servants.

CHAPTER REVIEW

1. Provide any evidence that exists that law enforcement officers perform their role in a discriminatory manner.

Minorities express less satisfaction with police than do whites and report they experience more disrespect. Studies show that minorities are not more likely to experience disrespect per incident, but they are stopped 1.5 times as often as whites. Racial profiling studies indicate that blacks are stopped more often than their percentage of the population; however, the early studies suffer from methodological problems.

2. Present the ethical issues involved in proactive investigations.

Ethical issues concern how the targets of undercover investigations are chosen, whether the use of informants leads to them making up stories, whether informants are protected from sanctions for their own criminal behavior, whether such operations create crime or entrap individuals, and whether undercover operations violate the privacy rights of individuals who are deceived.

3. Present the ethical issues involved in reactive investigation.

Ethical issues concern the tendency of police investigators to not remain objective in their interpretation and collection of evidence if they believe they know a suspect is guilty. Also, the use of physical coercion during interrogation is clearly illegal, but deception is not and is perhaps just as powerful. There is a possibility that such tactics may lead to false confessions.

4. Present information concerning the prevalence of and factors associated with the use of force by police officers.

The use of force seems to be present in only about 1.6 percent of all encounters with the public; however, it takes place more often in certain cities and during certain types of encounters. It is also true that some officers seem to be involved in uses of force more than others and characteristics of these officers have been identified as including: lack of empathy, antisocial and paranoid tendencies, proclivity toward abusive behavior, inability to learn from experience, tendency not to take responsibility for their actions, cynicism, and a strong identification with the police subculture.

5. Enumerate predictors associated with the use of excessive force.

The use of excessive form is miniscule but extremely problematic when it occurs. There seems to be evidence that excessive force occurs in certain types of calls (pursuits) and with certain groups (minorities). Female officers are less likely to use excessive force; however, any correlations should be viewed with caution since the sample size is so small.

The legal standard for what is appropriate force is reasonableness, but it is somewhat problematic to review an officer's behavior after the fact and without knowing or perceiving the circumstances in the same way as the officer on the scene.

KEY TERMS

Dirty Harry problem   entrapment   informants

STUDY QUESTIONS

1. What factors were associated with citizens' experiences of "disrespect" from police officers in the Project on Policing study?
2. What are some of the methods of interrogation according to Skolnick and Leo?
3. Describe Barker and Carter's typology of lies.
4. List the questions posed by Marx that police should use before engaging in undercover operations.
5. What factors are associated with the use of force?

WRITING/DISCUSSION EXERCISES

1. Write an essay on (or discuss) whether you think it is ever right for a police officer to make a decision to stop someone based on race or ethnicity. Do you think that it is ethical for police to enforce immigration laws by asking whether suspects, witnesses, and/or victims are legal residents?
2. Write an essay on (or discuss) appropriate tools in interrogation. For this essay you should review important court cases and research typical police practices. Should interrogations be videotaped? Should attorneys always be present? Should juveniles ever be interrogated without their parents? Should deception be used? If so, what kinds?
3. Write an essay on (or discuss) the best explanation for excessive force. If you could be a change agent in a police department, describe the changes or procedures you would institute that you believe would reduce the incidence of excessive force.

ETHICAL DILEMMAS

Situation 1

You are a rookie on traffic patrol. You watch as a young black man drives past you in a brand new silver Porsche. You estimate the car's value at around $50,000, yet the neighborhood you are patrolling in is characterized by low-income housing, cheap apartments, and tiny houses on the lowest end of the housing spectrum. You follow him and observe that he forgets to signal when he changes lanes. Ordinarily you wouldn't waste your time on something so minor. What would you do?

Situation 2

You are a homicide investigator and are interrogating someone you believe picked up a 9-year-old in a shopping mall, and then molested and murdered the girl. He is a registered sex offender, was in the area, and, although he doesn't have any violence in his record, you believe he must have done it because there is no other suspect who had the means, opportunity, and motive. You have some circumstantial evidence (he was seen in a video following the child), but very little good physical evidence. You really need a confession in order to make the case. You want to send this guy away for a long time. After several hours of getting nowhere, you have a colleague come in with a file folder and pretend that the medical examiner had obtained fingerprints on the body that matched the suspect's. You tell him that he lost his chance to confess to a lesser crime because now he is facing the death penalty. He says that he will confess to whatever you want him to if the death penalty is taken off the table. Do you tell him what you did? Do you tell the prosecutor?

Situation 3

You are a federal agent and have been investigating a major drug ring for a long time. One of your informants is fairly highly placed within this ring and has been providing you with good information. You were able to "turn" him because he faces a murder charge: there is probable cause that he shot and killed a coworker during an argument about five years ago, before he became involved in the drug ring. You have been holding the murder charge over his head to get him to cooperate and have been able, with the help of the U.S. District Attorney's office, to keep the local prosecutor from filing charges and arresting him. The local prosecutor is upset because the family wants some resolution in the case. You believe that the information he is able to provide you will result in charges of major drug sales and racketeering against several of the top smugglers, putting a dent in the drug trade for your region. At the same time, you understand that you are constantly risking the possibility that he may escape prosecution by leaving the country and that you are blocking the justice that the family of the murdered victim deserves. What would you do?

Situation 4

You are a rookie police officer who responds to a call for officer assistance. Arriving at the scene, you see a ring of officers surrounding a suspect who is down on his knees. You don't know what happened before you arrived, but you see a sergeant use a taser on the suspect, and you see two or three officers step in and take turns hitting the suspect with their nightsticks about the head and shoulders. This goes on for several minutes as you stand in the back of the circle. No one says anything that would indicate that this is not appropriate behavior. What would you do? What would you do later when asked to testify that you observed the suspect make "threatening" gestures to the officers involved?

Situation 5

You are a male suspect in a murder case. You were drunk the night of the homicide and did meet and dance with the victim, a young college girl. You admit that you had a lot to drink, but are 99 percent sure that you didn't see her except in the bar. The trouble is that you drank way too much and passed out in someone's apartment close to the bar rather than drive home. The girl was found in an apartment in the same complex. Police are telling you that they have forensic evidence that ties you to the murder. They say that they have her blood on your clothes and that it is your DNA in the sperm found in her body. They have been interrogating you now for several hours, and you are beginning to doubt your memory. You are also told that if you plead guilty, you would probably get voluntary manslaughter and might get probation, but if you insist on your innocence, you will be charged with first-degree murder and face the death penalty. What would you do?

[Obviously, this situation shifts our focus from the criminal justice professional's dilemma. If you decided earlier that the police tactic of lying about forensic evidence is ethical, this hypothetical illustrates what might happen when innocent suspects are lied to—assuming you are innocent!]

7

Fred W. McDarrah/Premium Archive/Getty Images

Police Corruption and Misconduct

Chapter Objectives

1. Describe the types of police corruption.
2. Describe the ethical arguments for and against gratuities.
3. Explain and give examples of graft and other forms of police corruption.
4. Provide the three types of explanations of police misconduct, with examples of each.
5. Describe the ways to reduce corruption and misconduct.

Frank Serpico is arguably the most famous police officer in the United States, even though he hasn't worked in law enforcement since 1972. After serving in Korea, he became a New York City police officer in 1959. His pride in wearing the uniform quickly dissipated when he realized that his partner was picking up "pad" money—payments by store owners to ensure that the cops would be there in case of trouble but also ignore minor violations of store owners and their customers. The "pad" was widespread in the department at the time, and Serpico quickly became known as the cop who didn't want the money, earning him the distrust of those who did.

Eventually, over 12 years, he rose to the rank of detective. When he discovered that corruption was rampant in the divisions he worked in, he began talking to police supervisors about the wrongdoing, but to no avail. It seemed that no matter whom he talked to, nothing was done and he continued to get the runaround. Finally, in 1970–1971, he and David Durk, a fellow officer, went to the *New York Times* and participated in an exposé of police corruption.

The series of stories led to the Knapp Commission, which conducted a wide-ranging investigation of police corruption. Serpico and Durk continued to work even though rumors that they were the "rats" were widespread and there was a real danger that corrupt police officers would retaliate against them. Before he had a chance to testify, Serpico was shot in the face at point-blank range in a drug bust while his fellow officers stood behind him. The shooting was suspected of being a setup, especially since the "officer down" call never was issued. However, no officer was investigated or charged with any wrongdoing in relation to the shooting.

173

Serpico survived and went on to testify before the Knapp Commission. He received a Medal of Honor from the police department, but retired and left the United States for 10 years. He returned in the early 1980s and continues to speak out against police corruption and supports whistleblowers, calling them "lamplighters" (referring to Paul Revere's famous ride). "Doing the right thing" evidently continues to be his life's work. (See his official website, at www.frankserpico.com.)

One of the sad facts is that the name Serpico continues to elicit two different reactions. For some, it represents the epitome of an honest and brave man who stood against corruption at great risk to self. For others, it represents a "rat," a man who turned his back on his friends, and, for some officers, to be called a "Serpico" is an insult.

There is no doubt that most police officers are honest and strive to be ethical in all they do; however, examples of corruption and graft in law enforcement agencies are not difficult to find. We have discussed police misconduct, such as excessive force, in previous chapters. In this chapter, we provide a more detailed discussion of misconduct and corruption. First we discuss its prevalence, including some attention to police corruption in other countries. Then we examine in detail certain categories of corruption. We also offer explanations for corruption and suggested methods to reduce it.

Since the very beginning of organized police departments, various investigative bodies have documented cases of corruption. Fyfe and Kane (2006), for instance, provide a long list of commissions and task forces that investigated police corruption scandals in a number of cities, including the Chicago Police Committee (in 1931), the Knapp Commission (New York City in 1972–1973), the Kolts Commission (Los Angeles County in 1992), the Mollen Commission (New York City in 1993), the Philadelphia Police Study Task Force (in 1987), the Christopher Commission (Los Angeles in 1996), the New Orleans Mayor's Advisory Committee (in 1993), the Royal Commission (Sydney, Australia, in 1997), and the St. Clair Commission (Boston in 1992), to name only a few. Cities also pay out large sums of money for settlements when police officers and their departments are sued for excessive force and other forms of misconduct.

Even though there is a large body of literature on police corruption, few studies have been able to measure its extent and prevalence. An obvious barrier to discovery is getting police officers to admit to wrongdoing. One early study reported that, by officers' own accounts, 39 percent of their number engaged in brutality, 22 percent perjured themselves, 31 percent had sex on duty, 8 percent drank on duty, and 39 percent slept on duty (Barker and Carter, 1994). Barker (1983) reported that between 9 and 31 percent of officers who had been employed for 11 months or less reported observing corrupt practices.

In a sample of narcotics officers, Stevens (1999) reported that 63 percent said they had very often heard of narcotics officers using more force than necessary to make an arrest, 26 percent had often heard of other officers personally consuming and/or selling drugs, and 82 percent had very often heard of other narcotics officers violating the civil rights of suspects. These numbers must be interpreted carefully in that they do not mean that large numbers of officers were corrupt, only that a fairly large number of officers had heard of some case of corruption "very often."

Fyfe and Kane (2006; also see Kane and White, 2009) studied police officers in New York City who were terminated for cause and found that only 2 percent of officers in the 22 years under study (1975–1996) were terminated for misconduct. We will review this study in detail in the coming paragraphs, as it is helpful to understand the factors associated with officers who are investigated and found to have committed misconduct serious enough to warrant termination. The number of officers who come to the attention of supervisors and are officially sanctioned by termination is probably quite a bit lower than the numbers who commit corrupt acts. Further, an officer might be terminated for rule-breaking that does not exactly fit into any category of corruption; thus, the study is not perfect, but it does provide data that is hard to obtain.

Unfortunately, the perception that police are corrupt is widespread in some cities. In one older New York City poll, 93 percent of those polled believed that police were corrupt (Kraus, 1994). Moore (1997) reported, interestingly, that the public still has a high opinion of police even though the majority also believes that police are dishonest. National opinion polls show that more people have a high respect for police officers' integrity and ethics today than in decades past. In 1977, 37 percent of the public rated police integrity and ethics as high or very high, and 12 percent rated police integrity as low or very low. By 1997, the percentage of those who rated police high or very high went up to 49 percent and those who rated police low or very low was 10 percent. By 2007, 53 percent of the public rated police integrity as high or very high and only 9 percent of the population rated this factor as low or very low (Sourcebook of Criminal Justice, 2007).

Most misdeeds of police officers are only marginally different from the unethical behaviors of other professions. For instance, some doctors prescribe unneeded surgery or experiment with unknown drugs, some businesspeople cheat on their expense accounts, lawyers sometimes overcharge clients, and contract bidders and purchase agents offer and accept bribes. It is an unfortunate fact of life that people in any profession or occupation will find ways to exploit their position for personal gain. This is not to excuse these actions, but rather, to show that police are no more deviant than other professional groups. In all of these occupational areas, most people attempt to uphold the profession's code of ethics and their own personal moral code. However, a few exploit their position and exhibit extremely unethical behaviors.

A Worldwide Problem

Police corruption does not occur just in the United States. Around the world there are instances of many different types of corruption. *Baksheesh*, a euphemism for graft, is endemic in many developing countries. Officials, including law enforcement officers, expect *baksheesh* to do the job they are supposed to do; alternatively, they extort money in exchange for not doing their job. "It's just the way it is" is the explanation for why such corruption exists. In all countries, corruption includes: corruption of authority, kickbacks, opportunistic theft, shakedowns, protection of illegal activity, internal payoffs, and excessive force.

In Queensland, Australia, the Fitzgerald (1989) Inquiry found a network of vertical corruption reaching to the commissioner, and widespread misconduct, including fabrication of evidence, assaults on suspects, and bribery related to gambling and prostitution. The scandal eventually resulted in legislation pertaining to freedom of information and whistleblower protection. In addition, an independent watchdog agency—the Criminal Justice Commission—was created (Prenzler, Harrison, and Ede, 1996: 5; Prenzler and Ransley, 2002; Fitzgerald, 1989). The so-called Queensland model has become the most well-known integrity model, promulgated by Transparency International (ABC News, 2009). Elsewhere, the Wood Commission Report exposed corruption in the New South Wales Police Department in 1997 (Wood, 1997), including instances of fabrication of evidence, theft, armed robberies, sale of drug evidence, sale of information, and a protection racket (Prenzler, Harrison, and Ede, 1996; Coady et al., 2000). A later scandal in 2007 occurred when evidence emerged that New Zealand police may have been involved in sexual assaults of teenage girls followed by obstruction of justice by officers seeking to cover up the events (Rowe, 2009).

in the NEWS

CORRUPTION IN MEXICO

It was reported that 284 police commanders in Mexico were purged from the top ranks of the federal police force in 2007 in an effort to combat the influence of drug cartel leaders on law enforcement. The commanders were replaced with members of an elite squad that had been trained and tested. In 2007, more than 1,000 civilians, 178 police officers, and 19 soldiers were killed in drug-related shootings. Traffickers often employ police officers as the shooters.

SOURCE: McKinley, 2007.

Other countries have also had notable scandals. Police scandals have emerged when suspects die or are severely injured in police custody (Austria, Canada, Great Britain, Pakistan, South Africa), when police use illegal means to catch suspects (Canada, Great Britain, Ireland), or when investigations seem to be compromised by police relationships with the suspect (Belgium). Often police are implicated in bribery scandals (France, Pakistan, Russia) and having "slush funds" (Japan). Drug scandals also have arisen where police are accused of accepting bribes and conspire with smugglers or dealers (Netherlands, Mexico) (Edelbacher and Ivkovic, 2004; Neyroud and Beckley, 2001; Alain, 2004; Mores, 2002; Barker, 2002; Westmarland, 2005; Fielding, 2003; D. Johnson, 2004; Chattha and Ivkovic, 2004; Associated Press, 2008a). In 2009, the Metropolitan police in London were accused of using a type of waterboarding by forcing one suspect's head into a toilet repeatedly and beating another. Evidently, the internal affairs unit had been investigating theft from the evidence room with a hidden camera and tape recorder and caught officers talking about the incident, unaware that they were being recorded. Their conversation corroborated what the suspect alleged. Several officers resigned or were terminated (Rawstorne and Wright, 2009; Edwards, 2009).

Mexico presents a dramatic example of corruption and its effects on the citizenry. Police officers are threatened or persuaded by rewards to work for the drug cartels, and there have been instances where local police (acting as protectors for drug cartel members) have engaged in tense showdowns with soldiers brought in to do the work of the police. Citizens in some locales do not trust the police at all and do not bother to seek their assistance when suffering crime victimization. The In the News box describes drug-related corruption in Mexico several years ago. News reports indicate the problem has, if anything, grown worse. In July 2010, prisoners were let out of a prison, given guns and cars, and ordered to go kill rival cartel members. They killed 17 people and are suspected of three more mass killings. After the killings, they returned to prison. Top prison officials were implicated, and the incident is an illustration of how much control the drug cartels have over the police and criminal justice system in Mexico.

INTERNATIONAL MEASURES OF CORRUPTION

Transparency International charts corruption worldwide, ranking more than 90 countries. This agency defines corruption as abuse of public office (including police) for private gain (e.g., bribe taking). The countries with the highest scores for honesty have included Finland, Denmark, New Zealand, and Sweden. Some of the poorest countries, including

Azerbaijan, Bolivia, Kenya, Uganda, and Bangladesh, produced very low scores. The United States, to many people's surprise perhaps, does not rate as highly as a number of other countries (Transparency International, 2008).

Finland is a country that evidently has a very low level of police corruption (Puonti, Vuorinen, and Ivkovic, 2004). It has received the highest or one of the highest rankings by Transparency International for the last several years. According to official records, the country had only 23 cases of official corruption in the 1990s, and only one of these cases involved a police officer (Laitinen, 2004). Only about 10 percent of all citizen complaints about officials are about law enforcement officers (Laitinen, 2002).

Surveys indicate that Finnish people trust their police more than any other professional group, including court officials and church officials (Laitinen, 2004). This phenomenon may be attributed to the culture of open and accountable government. Finland's police force is highly educated as well and can be described as endorsing a public service model of policing. There are strong proscriptions against most of the types of corruption that will be described in this chapter, even gratuities. Laitinen (2004) illustrates with a joke how gratuities, in general, are frowned on—"a cold sandwich and a warm beer" is acceptable, but "a warm sandwich and a cold beer" is a gratuity. Although there certainly are cases of corrupt police officers in Finland, the police there do seem to have a strong ethical code that minimizes the level of corruption.

In the latest rankings available from Transparency International, which used polls to rank 180 countries, New Zealand was ranked first in the public's trust in the honesty of their public officials, followed by Denmark, Singapore, Sweden, Switzerland, and then Finland in the sixth position on the list. The United States followed the United Kingdom in rankings of 18 and 17, respectively. At the bottom of the current rankings were countries such as Iraq, Sudan, Myanmar, Afghanistan, and Somalia, which was ranked last in perceptions of honesty (Transparency International, 2009). It would be instructive to examine countries that seem to have minimal levels of corruption to see what elements of these societies might contribute to the perceived higher levels of ethics. One interesting study that compared the police of different countries was conducted by Klockars, Ivkovic, and Haberfeld (2004). In this study, samples of police officers from 14 countries rated the seriousness of 11 hypothetical situations ranging from gratuities to "shopping" at a crime scene (taking items and then attributing their loss to the burglary). They also indicated what level of discipline would be administered to the transgressions. This second measure reflected the officers' perception of the degree of seriousness that management staff would assign to the incidents.

There were great differences in the rankings of some of the hypotheticals. For instance, the excessive-force situation was ranked as the third most serious in Hungary, but the least serious in Pakistan, and ranked seventh in seriousness by police in the United States. Although most countries ranked bribery very high, Croatia and Hungary did not. Theft from a found wallet was ranked high in all countries except South Africa.

Countries also differed in their pattern of rankings. Some countries ranked all situations relatively high, whereas other countries ranked all or almost all situations relatively low. For instance, Finland ranked all but three situations in the 4+ range (the scores went up to 5), but South African police ranked only one situation in the 4+ range. However, Pakistani police also ranked all but two situations highly, indicating perhaps that they answered the survey in the way they thought they were supposed to. An important finding of the research was that the officers' beliefs seemed to be influenced by what discipline they perceived would be forthcoming for each incident (Klockars, Ivkovic, and Haberfeld, 2004). Thus, management has an opportunity to shape officers' beliefs by its responses to deviant behavior. Whether beliefs, in turn, influence behavior is another question. Now we will look at some types of corruption.

Types of Corruption

Corruption has been described as "acting on opportunities, created by virtue of one's authority, for personal gain at the expense of the public one is authorized to serve" (Cohen, 1986: 23). There is a huge body of literature on police corruption, only some of which is touched on in this chapter. As we said, trying to establish the prevalence of corruption is exceedingly difficult, but so, too, is trying to agree upon a definitive description of what constitutes corruption.

In 1973, the Knapp Commission detailed its findings of corruption in the New York City Police Department. The terms *grass eaters* and *meat eaters* were used to describe New York City police officers who took advantage of their position to engage in corrupt practices. Accepting bribes, gratuities, and unsolicited protection money was the extent of the corruption engaged in by grass eaters, who were fairly passive in their deviant practices. Meat eaters participated in shakedowns, "shopped" at burglary scenes, and engaged in more active deviant practices. The Mollen Commission, which investigated New York City Police Department corruption 20 years later (1993), concluded that meat eaters were engaged in a qualitatively different kind of corruption in more recent times. Beyond just cooperating with criminals, the corrupt cops were active criminals themselves, selling drugs, robbing drug dealers, and operating burglary rings.

The distinction between passive and active corruption is a helpful one. Another way to identify and categorize police corruption is offered by Barker and Carter (1994), who propose that police abuse of authority comes in three different areas:

- Physical abuse—excessive force, physical harassment
- Psychological abuse—disrespect, harassment, ridicule, excessive stops, intimidation
- Legal abuse—unlawful searches or seizures, manufacturing evidence

In another source, Barker (2002) lists the types of police corruption as including corruption of authority (gratuities), kickbacks, opportunistic theft, shakedowns, protection of illegal activities, fixes (quashing tickets), direct criminal activities, and internal payoffs.

Fyfe and Kane (2006) also provide a detailed discussion of the types of police corruption. They argue that it is important to note that in some situations when police officers commit crimes, it is not truly police corruption in that the crimes are committed off-duty and have no relationship to their job. In effect, they are criminals who happen to be cops, but being cops has no relationship to their criminality. However, they might have learned how to commit the crime, obtained criminal contacts, or developed criminal values through their job, so, in a sense, it might be considered job-related corruption. The point is that it is difficult to draw a line between police corruption (acts intrinsically tied to the job) and criminals who happen to be police officers. Fyfe and Kane provide a detailed explanation of the types of police misconduct discussed in the literature, summarized in the following paragraphs.

Police crime involves situations where police officers violate criminal statutes. Police might engage in crimes that have nothing to do with their position (e.g., commit burglaries or insurance fraud while off-duty), however, it may be that their ability to commit the crime might be entirely related to their position (e.g., stealing drugs from an evidence locker or identity theft using information obtained by writing tickets).

Police corruption involves offenses where the officer uses his or her position, by act or omission, to obtain improper financial benefit. For instance, officers may take bribes either to not do their job (write a ticket) or to do their job (provide police protection). Note that these acts may overlap with police crime because some police corruption violates criminal statutes as well (e.g., extortion and bribery). Police officers may commit acts for personal profit of either a non-criminal or a criminal nature related to their employment. An example of a non-criminal form of police corruption would be to violate the department's extra-job policy or to take gratuities. An example of criminal corruption would be to take a bribe.

The key element of this type of corruption is personal gain. Examples offered by Fyfe and Kane of "unambiguous" police corruption would be an officer who steals from a drug seizure (an individual "event") or a group of officers who repeatedly extort or accept money from criminals (an "arrangement"). However, it is not clear why Fyfe and Kane distinguish these activities as distinct from police crimes as defined above.

Abuse of power involves actions where officers physically injure or offend a citizen's sense of dignity. Physical abuse can be divided into brutality, which occurs when officers inflict physical abuse on persons to teach them a lesson, and unnecessary force, which occurs when police officers make mistakes that lead them to have to resort to force that would not have been necessary had they followed proper procedures. Psychological abuse ranges from deception in interrogation to intimidation on the street. Legal abuse involves various forms of wrongdoing designed to convict suspects, including perjury, planting evidence, and hiding exculpatory evidence. Another type of abuse of power involves off-duty misconduct (e.g., driving while intoxicated or physical assaults), with the expectation that the wrongdoing will be covered up by fellow officers.

In their own classification of police misconduct, Fyfe and Kane (2006: 37–38) offer the following typology:

- Profit-motivated crimes (all offenses except those that are drug-related with the goal of profit)
- Off-duty crimes against persons (all assaultive, non-profit-related crimes off-duty)
- Off-duty public-order crimes (not including drugs, and most commonly DWI [driving while intoxicated] and disorderly conduct)
- Drugs (all crimes related to possession, sale, conspiracy, and failing departmental drug tests)
- On-duty abuse (use of excessive force, psychological abuse, or discrimination)
- Obstruction of justice (conspiracy, perjury, official misconduct, and all other offenses with the goal of obstructing justice)
- Administrative/failure to perform (violating one or more departmental rules, policies, and procedures)
- Conduct-related probationary failures (simple failure to meet expectations)

An important distinction that should be made is between crimes and ethical transgressions. It is an insult to law enforcement officers when certain actions, such as stealing from a burglary scene or taking money from a drug dealer to guard a shipment of drugs, are discussed as if they were ethical dilemmas in the same category as whether to avoid responding to a minor traffic accident or whether an officer should call in sick so he can go fishing. Stealing, robbing, and conspiring to sell drugs are crimes. The officers who engage in such acts are criminals who are quite distinct from officers who commit ethical lapses akin to other workers who do so within the parameters of their particular professions or jobs.

GRATUITIES

gratuities Items of value received by an individual because of his or her role or position rather than because of a personal relationship with the giver.

We will begin our discussion of specific types of misconduct with gratuities, which also will receive the longest discussion since gratuities are so ubiquitous. **Gratuities** are items of value received by an individual because of his or her role or position rather than because of a personal relationship with the giver. The widespread practices of free coffee in convenience stores, half-price or free meals in restaurants, and half-price dry cleaning are examples of gratuities. Frequently, businesspeople offer gratuities, such as half-price meals, as a token of sincere appreciation for the police officers' work. Although the formal code of ethics prohibits accepting gratuities, many officers believe there is nothing wrong with businesses giving "freebies" to police officers. They see these as small rewards indeed for the difficulties they endure in police work.

Prenzler (1995: 21) found that people generally did not support gratuities (only 4 percent), but that two-thirds of respondents agreed that it was acceptable for police to take coffee, and about one-quarter approved of Christmas gifts. The majority were still opposed to large gifts and regular gifts, and 76 percent were opposed to *regular* free coffee, cold drinks, or discounted meals when on duty. Few of Prenzler's respondents agreed with the commonly used arguments for acceptance of gratuities:

- That they build community relations (15 percent)
- That they give businesses police protection (8 percent)
- That every occupation has its perks (6 percent)
- That they compensate police for poor pay (6 percent)

In criminal justice classrooms in the United States, it is common to find fairly strong support for minor gratuities, but this may not be true if one were to poll other groups. Lord and Bjerregaard (2003) found that students initially ranked gratuities as a minor ethical issue, but after taking a criminal justice ethics class, ranked accepting gratuities as a more serious ethical transgression.

One author writes that gratuities "erode public confidence in law enforcement and undermine our quest for professionalism" (Stefanic, 1981: 63). How do gratuities undermine public confidence? Cohen (1986: 26) believes that gratuities are dangerous because what might start without intent on the part of the officer may become a patterned expectation; it is the taking in an official capacity that is wrong, for the social contract is violated when citizens give up their liberty to exploit only to be exploited, in turn, by the enforcement agency that prevents them from engaging in similar behavior. To push this argument to the extreme, some might argue that there are similarities between someone coming into an inner-city store and demanding "protection money" (to avoid torching and vandalism) and a police officer coming into the store expecting liquor or other goods (if the store owner believes that he will receive a lower level of protection if he doesn't provide them). How does the store owner know that his silent alarm will receive the same speed of response if he is not grateful and generous to police officers?

Offering a different view, Kania (1988: 37) writes that police "should be encouraged to accept freely offered minor gratuities and ... such gratuities should be perceived as the building blocks of positive social relationships between our police and the public." He rejects the two major arguments against gratuities:

- The slippery slope argument—that taking gratuities leads to future, more serious, deviance
- The unjust enrichment argument—that the only honest remuneration for police officers is the paycheck

Kania proposes that gratuities actually help cement relations between the police department and the public. Officers who stay and drink coffee with store owners and businesspeople are better informed than officers who don't, according to Kania. A gift, freely given, ties the giver and receiver together in a bond of social reciprocity. This should not be viewed negatively, but rather, as part of a community-oriented policing concept. Kania also points out that those who offer gratuities tend to be more frequent users of police services, which justifies more payment than the average citizen.

The only problem, according to Kania, is when either or both the giver and taker (officer) have impure intent. For instance, it would be an unethical exchange if the intent of the giver was to give in exchange for some future service, not as reward for past services rendered. Another unethical exchange would be when the intent of the police officer taking the gratuity was not to receive unsolicited but appreciated gifts, but rather, to use the position of police officer to extort goods from business owners. A third type of unethical exchange would be if both the giver and the police officer's motives were unethical: if the giver expected special treatment *and* the officer's intent was to take the gratuity in exchange for performing the special service. In Kania's scheme, ethical exchanges are when they are true rewards or gifts with no expectation of future acts. Unethical exchanges are when either the giver or receiver expects something in return, such as understandings, bribes, arrangements, and shakedowns.

Another issue that Kania alludes to but doesn't clearly articulate is that a pattern of gratuities changes what would have been a formal relationship into a personal, informal one. This moves the storekeeper-giver into a role that is more similar to a friend, relative, or fellow officer, in which case personal loyalty issues are involved when the law has to be administered. In the same way that an officer encounters an ethical dilemma when a best friend is stopped for speeding, the officer who stops a store owner who has been providing him or her with free coffee for the past year may also experience divided loyalties. They have become, if not friends, at least personally involved with each other to the extent that formal duty becomes complicated by the personal relationship.

Critics (Ruiz and Bono, 2004; Coleman, 2004a, 2004b) argue against gratuities for the following reasons:

- Police are professionals, and professionals don't take gratuities.
- Gratuities are incipient corruptors because people expect different treatment.
- Gratuities are an abuse of authority and create a sense of entitlement.
- Gratuities add up to substantial amounts of money and can constitute as high as 30 percent of an officer's income.
- Gratuities can be the beginning of more serious forms of corruption.
- Gratuities are contrary to democratic ideals because they are a type of fee-for-service for public functions that are already paid for through taxes, such as police protection.
- Gratuities create a public perception that police are corrupt.

Kania (2004) counter-argues:

- Other professionals accept gratuities.
- There is nothing wrong with more frequent users of police services "paying" extra.
- "No gratuity" rules are tools of playing "gotcha" by administrators who enforce them only against individuals that they target for some other reason. This differential use of discipline erodes morale.
- Educators and academics tend to distort the seriousness of gratuities.

Where should one draw the line between harmless rewards and inappropriate gifts? Is a discount on a meal okay, but not a free meal? Is a meal okay, but not any other item, such as groceries or tires or car stereos? Do the store or restaurant owners expect anything for their money, such as more frequent patrols or overlooking sales of alcohol to underage juveniles? Should they expect different treatment from officers than the treatment given to those who do not offer gratuities? Suppose that an officer is told by a convenience store owner that she can help herself to anything in the store—free coffee, candy, cigarettes, chips, magazines, and such. In the same conversation, the store owner asks the officer for her personal pager number "in case something happens and I need to get in contact with you." Is this a gift, or is it an exchange? Should the officer accept the free merchandise?

Many merchants give free or discount food to officers because they like to have police around, especially late at night. The question then becomes the one asked frequently by citizens: Why are two or three police cars always at a certain restaurant? Police argue that they deserve to take their breaks wherever they want within their patrol area. If it happens that they choose the same place, that shouldn't be a concern of the public. However, an impression of unequal protection occurs when officers make a habit of eating at certain restaurants or congregating at certain convenience stores. Free meals or even coffee may influence the pattern of police patrol and, thus, may be wrong because some citizens are not receiving equal protection.

What happens when all surrounding businesses give gratuities to officers and a new business moves in? Do officers come to expect special favors? Do merchants feel pressured to offer them? Many nightclubs allow off-duty officers to enter without paying cover charges. Does this lead to resentment and a feeling of discrimination by paying customers? Does it lead to the officers thinking that they are special and different from everyone else? Other examples of gratuities are when police accept movie tickets, tickets to ball games and other events, and free or discounted merchandise.

The extent of gratuities varies from city to city. In cities where rules against gratuities are loosely enforced, "dragging the sack" may be developed to an art form by some police officers, who go out of their way to collect free meals and other gifts. One story is told of a large Midwestern city where officers from various divisions were upset because the merchants in some areas provided Christmas gifts, such as liquor, food, cigarettes, and other merchandise, whereas merchants in other divisions either gave nothing or gave less attractive gifts. The commander, finally tired of the bickering, ordered that no individual officer could receive any gifts and instead sent a patrol car to all the merchants in every district. Laden with all the things the merchants would have given to individual officers, the patrol car returned, and the commander parceled out the gifts to the whole department based on rank and seniority.

Ruiz and Bono (2004) presented other instances of gratuities. In a southern city, a restaurant owner who had been giving free meals to officers stopped doing so. Officers then engaged in a ticket-writing campaign, targeting his customers who double-parked. After several weeks of this, the restaurant owner changed his mind and began giving free meals to officers again. Those authors also mentioned a type of contest whereby officers competed to see how many free bottles of liquor they could collect; the winning team collected 50 bottles from the bars and businesses in one district on a single shift. "The blue discount suit," according to the authors, was a term that indicated how officers felt about gratuities. Some other terms described businesses that offered free or discounted goods; these establishments were said to "show love" or give "pop"—hence the saying, "If you got no pop, you got no cop."

Officers in some departments are known for their skill in soliciting free food and liquor for after-hours parties. In the same vein, officers also solicit merchants for free food

in the

POLICE FREEBIES AND ETHICS

A technical advisor in charge of ethics training for the Canadian Association of Chiefs of Police resigned over the decision of the association to continue to accept sponsorship from Taser International for their annual conference. The company, which manufactures and markets tasers to law enforcement agencies, contributed $75,000 to the event over the last three years. The president of the association said there is no reason not to accept sponsorship since they do not endorse tasers; however, they did join the Canadian Police Association in a "position document" that backed the use of the weapon. The ethics advisor resigned, arguing it was hypocritical when the rank and file officer is punished for accepted gratuities.

SOURCE: Javed, 2009.

and beverages for charity events sponsored by police, such as youth softball leagues. The first situation is similar to individual officers receiving gratuities, but the second situation is harder to criticize. Officers bring up the seeming hypocrisy of a departmental prohibition against individual officers accepting gratuities, yet at the same time there may be an administrative policy of actively soliciting and receiving donations from merchants for departmental events, such as pastries, coffee, or more expensive catering items. The In the News box illustrates an example of how such gratuities can lead to a conflict of interest.

Professional ethics discourages gifts or gratuities when the profession involves discretionary judgments about a clientele (i.e., judges, professors, appraisers, inspectors). While bribery laws punish taking or receiving something of value in return for a specific act of omission or commission related to one's office, conflict-of-interest laws punish merely taking something of value prohibited by the law when one holds a public office, with no necessity to show that a specific vote or decision was directly influenced by receipt of the valued items or services. Conflict-of-interest laws recognize the reality that one's discretion is compromised after receiving things of value; however, it does not seem unusual or particularly unethical for a doctor, a lawyer, a mechanic, or a mail carrier to receive gifts from grateful clients. Whether gifts are unethical relates to whether one's occupation or profession involves judgments that affect the gift givers. The police obviously have discretionary authority and make judgments that affect store owners and other gift givers. This may explain why some think it is wrong for police to accept gifts or favors. It also explains why so many other people do not see anything wrong with some types of gratuities, for police officers in most situations are not making decisions that affect the giver and, instead, are simply providing a service, such as responding to a burglary or disturbance call.

An important distinction that might aid the discussion is the difference between a *gift* and a *gratuity*. A gift is something that is clearly given with no strings attached. An example might be when a citizen pays for a police officer's meal without telling the officer; when the officer gets ready to pay, the bill is already taken care of. Many officers have had this experience. In this case, because the police officer did not know of the reward (because the gift giver did not make the gift known), no judgment can be affected.

Ethical formalism would indicate that we must be comfortable with a universal law allowing all businesses to give all police officers certain favors or gratuities, such as free meals, free merchandise, or special consideration. However, such a blanket endorsement of this behavior would probably not be desirable. The second principle of ethical formalism indicates that each should treat every other with respect as an individual and not as a means to an end. In this regard, we would have to condemn gratuities in cases where the giver or receiver had improper motives according to Kania's typology. This also explains why some gifts seem acceptable. When something is given freely and accepted without strings, there is no "using" of others; therefore, it might be considered an innocent, honorable act by both parties.

If utilitarian ethics were used, one would have to weigh the relative good or utility of the interaction. On one hand, harmless gratuities may create good feelings in the community toward the officers and among the officers toward the community (Kania's "cementing the bonds" argument). On the other hand, gratuities often lead to perceptions of unfairness by shopkeepers who feel discriminated against, by police who think they deserve rewards and don't get them, and so on. Thus, the overall negative results of gratuities, even "harmless" ones, might lead a utilitarian to conclude that gratuities are unethical.

Macintyre and Prenzler (1999) conducted a survey of officers to see if they would be influenced by gratuities. They asked officers what they would do if a café owner who gave them free coffee and meals was stopped for a traffic violation. The researchers found that supervisory officers were more likely than rookies to give a ticket. Although only 15 percent would not write the ticket and would continue to go back for meals, an additional 41 percent would also not write the ticket but would give the owner a warning and not go back for free meals. The remaining officers would write the owner a ticket. Another study evaluated police coverage in a medium-sized U.S. city, taking into account whether or not the businesses gave gratuities, food quality, cost, convenience, and location and found that gratuities increased coverage (Deleon-Granados and Wells, 1998). These studies indicate that gratuities do influence officers' decisions both in how they patrol and what they might do when they have to make a decision about a giver of gratuities. More research is needed to see if these findings would be replicated.

The ethics of virtue would be concerned with the individual qualities or virtues of the officer. A virtuous officer could take free coffee and not let it affect his or her judgment. According to this perspective, no gift or gratuity would affect the judgment of the virtuous officer. However, if the officer does not possess those qualities of virtue, such as honesty, integrity, and fairness, even free coffee may lead to special treatment. Further, these officers would seek out gifts and gratuities and abuse their authority by pursuing them.

PROFESSIONAL COURTESY

The practice of not ticketing an officer who is stopped for speeding or for other driving violations is called "professional courtesy." Obviously officers do not ticket everyone they stop. They often give warnings instead, and that is a legitimate use of their discretion. Whether to ticket or give a warning should depend on objective criteria, such as the seriousness of the violation. If the officer would let another person go with a warning in the same situation, there is no ethical issue in giving a warning to a fellow officer. However, if *every other person* would have received a ticket, but the officer did not issue one *only because* the motorist was a fellow officer, that is a violation of the code of ethics ("enforce the law ... without fear or favor"). It is a violation of deontological universalism as well as utilitarianism. Under deontological ethics, it is the officer's duty to enforce the law against everyone, including officers. Under utilitarianism, the fact that the speeding officer can cause an accident means that the utility for society is greater if the ticket is issued, for it might make the officer slow down, and by doing that, accidents can be avoided.

in the NEWS

PROFESSIONAL COURTESY?

The San Jose, California, police chief fired a popular sergeant for conduct unbecoming to an officer for a cover-up involving Sandra Woodall, an investigator for the district attorney's office. Her husband is a San Jose sergeant, and her father-in-law is a former lieutenant and current D.A. investigator. She was involved in an accident while speeding, crashed into several cars, and injured a teenager. Officers on the scene did not do a breath test even though EMTs said she was disoriented and didn't know the year and smelled like alcohol. The officers also noted in their report no signs of intoxication and, at the hospital, told the injured teenager's mother that it was too late to do a blood alcohol test. The mother, unsatisfied with the police investigation, went to the D.A.'s office; that office passed the case to the state attorney general's office. Woodall later pleaded guilty to drunken driving and received a sentence of 45 days in jail. Both officers were no-billed by grand jury, but were fired by the chief, who also fired their sergeant. All said they would appeal the firing.

SOURCE: Webby, 2009.

Justifications for not ticketing other officers are diverse and creative. For instance, some honest justifications are purely egoistic: "If I do it for him, he will do it for me one day." Other justifications are under the guise of utilitarianism: "It's best for all of us not to get tickets, and the public isn't hurt because we're trained to drive faster." On websites where police officers post comments about a variety of issues, professional courtesy (for officers and their family members) is a hot-button topic that generates strong emotions on both sides. While many officers maintain they treat other officers the same as anyone else, some officers seem to think of professional courtesy as a job "perk" similar to medical professionals who receive free medical care from colleagues or cooks and restaurant workers who receive free dinners from other restaurants. One might argue, however, that they do not understand the difference between being a private professional and a public servant, nor do they fully understand their extremely important role in the administration of law and justice.

One troubling aspect of professional courtesy for traffic offenses is that the practice has a tendency to bleed over into other forms of misconduct. Officers who are stopped for driving while intoxicated are sometimes driven home rather than arrested, but this application of discretion is highly unlikely to be afforded to any other citizen. In some cases of domestic violence, victims of police officer husbands or boyfriends describe how the responding officers do nothing or take their complaints more lightly than they would if the alleged perpetrator were not a police officer. The In the News box describes a situation that might have started out as extending professional courtesy to a wife of a fellow officer.

The idea that officers are above the law is insidious. Officers who believe that they should not have to follow the same laws they enforce against others may be more prone to other forms of abuse of authority as well. It should also be noted that many officers think that they are held to a higher standard of behavior than the public. Officers point out that a domestic violence, DUI, or any other arrest may cost them their job, which may not be the case for others. The argument against this position is that perhaps one who is tasked with enforcing the law, but is engaged in unlawful behavior should not have the job.

ON-DUTY USE OF DRUGS AND ALCOHOL

Carter (1999) discussed the extent of on-duty drug use, citing previous research that found up to 20 percent of officers in one city used marijuana and other drugs while on duty. That seems to be a high figure; in other surveys, about 8 percent of employees reported drug use and only 3 percent of all workers in a "protective services" category reported drug use. In a more recent survey, protective service employees were the least likely to report any drug use (Mieczkowski, 2002: 168).

It could also be that the decrease seen in the use of drugs by the general population is reflected in police officer samples. As well, the sources are not exactly comparable. Thus, it is impossible to determine which source is more accurate. However, certain circumstances are present in law enforcement that, perhaps, create more opportunities for drug use. Elements of police work (especially undercover work) that can lead to drug use include the following:

- Exposure to a criminal element
- Relative freedom from supervision
- Uncontrolled availability of contraband

Carter (1999: 316) also discussed the phenomenon of police officers who go undercover and become socialized to the drug culture. They may adopt norms conducive to drug taking. Further, they may think they need to use drugs to maintain their cover. They are also able to rationalize stealing drugs from sellers: "It should not be a crime to steal something that is contraband in the first place." Drug use by officers creates the potential for even more serious misbehavior, such as stealing evidence, being blackmailed to perform other unethical or illegal actions, and being tempted to steal from drug users instead of arresting them. This, of course, is in addition to the obvious problem of compromising one's decision-making abilities by being under the influence of any drug while on duty.

The use of drug tests during the hiring process is long-standing, but periodic and/ or random drug testing of employed officers is a more recent policy. Many police officers, as is true of many other types of employees, are now subject to drug testing. Employees in the protective services sector are the most likely to undergo drug testing in the workplace. While about 60 percent of protective service workers say that their workplace engages in random drug testing, only 14 percent of other professionals have the same experience (reported in Mieczkowski, 2002: 172). Generally, courts have upheld the right of law enforcement agencies to employ drug testing, applying the balancing test between a compelling governmental interest and individual privacy rights. The list of compelling-interest elements served by drug testing includes the following, as reported by Mieczkowski (2002: 179):

- Public safety
- Public trust
- Potential for official corruption
- Official credibility
- Worker morale
- Worker safety

Officers have some due process rights, however, and they must be notified of the policies and procedures involved in the agency's drug testing, have access to the findings, and have available some sort of appeal process before sanctions are taken

(Mieczkowski, 2002: 179). In Fyfe and Kane's (2006) study of police officers terminated for cause in New York City, the most common reason for termination was a failed drug test.

Alcohol use is more socially acceptable than drug use, and it has also been cited as a problem. In one survey, it was found that about 8 percent of those in protective services occupations (which include police officers) reported heavy alcohol use. This compared to 12 percent of construction workers and 4 percent of sales workers (Mieczkowski, 2002: 179). Barker and Carter (1994) indicated that 8 percent of officers reported drinking alcohol on duty. The problem of drinking on duty does not involve the vulnerability to blackmail that drug use does, but there are obvious problems, and officers who are aware of another's on-duty intoxication are faced with an ethical dilemma of whether or not to take official action. Officers may choose to informally isolate themselves from drinking officers by refusing to partner with them or avoid working calls with them. As the Quote and Query box indicates, however, reporting fellow officers is not the thing to do.

> ### QUOTE & QUERY
>
> When I showed up for work the next night, nobody would talk to me. I was treated like an invisible stinking turd for the whole month. My new shoes and leather gloves disappeared from my locker. Even officers on the other shifts shunned me.
>
> —SOURCE: QUINN, 2005: 34.
> This officer reported another officer for drinking on duty.
>
> *Why would officers protect a drunken officer who might endanger his partner or others by being intoxicated on the job?*

GRAFT

graft Any exploitation of one's role, such as accepting bribes, protection money, or kickbacks.

Graft is the exploitation of one's role by accepting bribes or protection money. Graft also occurs when officers receive kickbacks from tow truck drivers, defense attorneys, or bail bond companies for recommending them.

In Klockars, Ivkovic, and Haberfeld's (2004) international comparison of officers' views regarding hypotheticals drawn to illustrate various forms of corruption, officers in the United States rated bribery as the second most serious offense. Only theft from a crime scene was rated as more serious. Officers in Austria, Finland, Japan, the Netherlands, Sweden, and the United Kingdom rated bribery as even more serious than did U.S. officers.

While police officers in small and medium-sized departments might argue that most of the misconduct described in this chapter does not happen in their department, examples of graft do appear in smaller communities (Bloom, 2008a, 2008b, 2008c). A small-town police chief or county sheriff has a great deal of power that is largely unnoticed and unquestioned until a blatant misuse of power brings it to the public's attention.

SEXUAL MISCONDUCT

It is a sad reality that a few police officers use their position of authority to extort sex from female citizens (there doesn't seem to be the parallel situation of female police officers extorting sex from male victims). Sexual harassment of female police officers is also a problem in some departments. Finally, officers may engage in other types of sexual misconduct for which they may be sanctioned.

Amnesty International has documented widespread mistreatment of women by police around the world. Egregious cases in the United States include rapes by officers on duty and by jailers in police lockups, and a few instances where the sexual misconduct of police officers was widespread and protected by departmental supervisors, such as in Wallkill, New York. In that town, the 25-member police department evidently engaged in numerous instances of sexual intimidation of citizens before being investigated by the state police and sued in a federal civil rights lawsuit (reported in McGurrin and Kappeler, 2002: 133).

Kraska and Kappeler (1995) looked at a sample of 124 cases of police sexual misconduct, including 37 sexual assaults by on-duty officers. These authors challenged earlier studies indicating that sexual misconduct of officers occurred most often when women traded sexual favors for lenient treatment and that it was the victim who initiated the trade. This study's authors concluded that norms in a police department that ignored or condoned the exchange of sex for favored treatment opened the door to officers who used more aggressive tactics to coerce sex from citizens. Kraska and Kappeler (1995: 93) propose a continuum of sexual invasion that ranges from some type of invasion of privacy to sexual assault. This range of behavior includes the following:

- Viewing a victim's photos or videos for prurient purposes
- Field strip searches
- Custodial strip searches
- Illegal detentions
- Deception to gain sex
- Provision of services for sex
- Sexual harassment
- Sexual contact
- Sexual assault
- Rape

Sapp's (1994) inventory of sexual misconduct includes the following:

- Nonsexual contacts that are sexually motivated (non-valid traffic stops)
- Voyeurism (e.g., patrolling lovers' lanes to watch sexual activity)
- Contact with crime victims (excessive call-backs that are not necessary for investigative purposes)
- Contact with offenders (sexual demands or inappropriate frisks)
- Contacts with juvenile offenders (sexual harassment and sexual contact)
- Sexual shakedowns (demanding sex from prostitutes or the homeless)
- Citizen-initiated sexual contact (an officer is approached by a citizen because of his officer status)

Even the most innocuous of contacts between female citizens and officers—whereby an officer might ask a woman he has stopped for a date—involve issues of power and coercion. In a study by Kraska and Kappeler, police described how they routinely went "bimbo hunting," which involved sexual harassment of women out drinking (1995: 104). Prostitutes and homeless women are extremely vulnerable populations to sexual extortion by police officers, but studies indicate that middle-class citizens have also been subject to intimidation and outright assault. Most victims are under age 30 (McGurrin and

in the NEWS

SEXUAL MISCONDUCT

Craig Nash was fired from the San Antonio Police Department and indicted for charges related to picking up a transgender prostitute, driving her to a deserted location, handcuffing her, and forcing her to perform sexual acts. Another victim also came forward alleging similar victimization by the officer. In a second case, an officer was fired for allegedly having sex in his patrol car, along with other violations. In 2009, San Antonio fired 18 officers over various forms of misconduct, including sexual assaults and indecent exposure.

In New York, an officer was convicted of sexual abuse in one case for extorting sex from an 18-year-old girl and will be tried for sexual abuse for using his position as a police officer to coerce two other women to have sex with him. In another case, a Brooklyn officer faces federal charges for threatening to arrest a woman if she didn't perform oral sex on him in a precinct bathroom. Then, when he was under investigation for that charge, he ordered a prisoner in custody to lift up her shirt so he could see her breasts. This officer is also facing rape charges in a separate case.

SOURCES: Holley, 2010; Sulzberger and Eligon, 2010

Kappeler, 2002). The defense of officers is usually that, if sex occurred, it was consensual. The problem is that when officers acting in their official capacity meet women (as victims, witnesses, defendants, or suspects), the power differential makes consent extremely problematic, as the following In the News box illustrates.

McGurrin and Kappeler (2002) reported on a study of official records of sexual misconduct by police officers that uncovered hundreds of instances of sexual assault, rape, and even murder by police officers in and out of uniform. Rape charges commonly are downgraded to a conviction of "official oppression" in a plea agreement. Also, these researchers found that some officers who had criminal records for sexual offenses simply moved and obtained law enforcement positions in other jurisdictions.

In their own study of newspaper articles concerning sexual misconduct, McGurrin and Kappeler (2002: 134) uncovered more than two dozen cases where the officers had been disciplined for sexual misconduct prior to the case that was reported in the news article. They also found that of the cases taken up by the justice system, about half of the alleged offenders did not receive any punishment. Only a third received jail or prison time. A department may be aware of an officer's pattern of sexual harassment and do nothing about it. This obvious lapse of supervision is unfair to the public and also costs money. Kraska and Kappeler (1995) reported that police lost 69 percent of the civil rights suits brought by the victim of sexual misconduct.

Two newspaper reports of sexual abuse by a police officer in 2007 illustrate two different types of sexual abuse. In the first case, a police officer was arrested and charged with indecency with a child; he was accused of fondling the child after consuming large quantities of alcohol at a party. In the second case, a sheriff's deputy was found guilty and sentenced to two years of probation and fined for "improper sexual activity with a person in custody" based on an incident in which he ordered a college co-ed to expose herself and groped her breasts, threatening her with a DWI arrest. In this case, the county settled a civil lawsuit by the victim (Bloom, 2007).

In the first case, the fact that the alleged perpetrator was a police officer is immaterial and unrelated to the offense, but in the second case, the deputy used his position to victimize a citizen that he was entrusted to "protect and serve." Because police officers are in a position to stop women late at night, events like this are incredible blows to a department's reputation. Unfortunately, the relatively few cases of sexual abuse by police officers have led to the popular advice for women who drive late at night to "drive slowly with parking lights on to a well-illuminated location with people around" before stopping for flashing lights. Ethical officers should understand and accept this response from motorists who have come to fear potential victimization by officers.

Sexual harassment of fellow officers is also a problem. In one research study, 70 percent of female officers reported being sexually harassed by other police officers (Kraska and Kappeler, 1995: 92). It may be that the culture of policing is particularly conducive to sexual harassment. It has been described as a "macho" or "locker room" culture even though women have been integrated into patrol since the early 1970s. Female officers today do not encounter the virulent harassment and hostility that was present in the 1970s when patrol forces were first integrated, but some remnants of that culture remain. More research is needed to update older studies of the prevalence of sexual harassment.

Sexual harassment is a violation of policy and against the law, and it is also unethical. None of the ethical systems from Chapter 2 would support coercing coworkers for sex or creating a hostile work environment. Perpetrators' defense may be that it is innocent "kidding" or honest infatuation, but universalism provides a good check on this type of behavior. Would the perpetrator want his daughter or sister to be subjected to the behavior?

There have been other cases where officers may receive administrative punishments for "conduct unbecoming to an officer" related to their sexual activity or other off-duty conduct. For instance, in a few cases officers have posed nude, participated in sexually explicit videos, or, in one case, an officer posted nude pictures of his wife on the Internet. In the cases where these officers have been fired, courts have generally upheld the department's right to fire, although the First Amendment rights of officers is still an unsettled area of law.

In other cases, officers who have affairs with supervisors, coworkers, or wives of co-workers sometimes get sanctioned for "conduct unbecoming" (Martinelli, 2007). The fact of the matter is that officers are held to a higher standard of behavior, and even when no laws are broken, the behavior may be unethical in that it brings discredit or embarrassment to the department and makes it harder for fellow officers to keep the respect of the citizenry. For instance, in the case of the officer who posted nude pictures of his wife, a female officer in that town testified at the disciplinary hearing that citizens familiar with the website urged her to take off her clothes when she entered a bar to break up a fight (Egelko, 2007).

CRIMINAL COPS

There are instances where the transgressions that officers engage in go beyond ethics and enter the realm of crime and criminal conspiracies. Every year there are news stories of police officers who cross over into criminal activity.

FLORIDA In the 1980s, the "Miami River Rats" committed armed robberies of drug deals, collecting cash and drugs. These robberies by a small group of police officers eventually led to at least one homicide (Dorschner, 1989; see also Rothlein, 1999; Crank and Caldero, 2000: 162). More recently, the Hollywood, Florida, Police Department has been identified as having problems with officer misconduct. Aaronson (2005) reports that there were a number of officers hired in the early 1990s who were rejected by other police departments, and these and other officers have been responsible for the city paying out over $1 million in lawsuits that involve excessive force and other abuses.

ILLINOIS In 1996, seven Chicago cops were indicted for conspiracy to commit robbery and extortion for shaking down undercover agents they thought were drug dealers (Crank and Caldero, 2000). In 2001, a former chief of detectives pleaded guilty to running a jewel-theft ring for more than a decade. William Hanhardt, 80, is now sitting in a federal prison with a 12-year sentence, but continues to receive his police pension (Fountain, 2001; Novak, 2009).

Anthony Abbate, an ex-Chicago police officer, became infamous in 2007 when a video of him savagely beating a female bartender for not serving him more alcohol went viral on YouTube. Then he and other police officers evidently attempted to intimidate the woman and the bar manager to prevent them from pursuing charges against him. He was convicted of felony aggravated assault for the attack and sentenced to probation and 130 hours of community service. In January 2010, he failed a drug test and will most probably serve the original five-year sentence. The bartender and manager have also filed a civil rights lawsuit against Abbate and the department in federal court, seeking $1 million (ChicagoTribune.com., 2008; CBS Chicago, 2010).

In 2009, officers in a Chicago Special Operations Unit were indicted for shaking down drug dealers for money. Seven officers pleaded guilty to felony theft or official misconduct, and most have received probation or only several months in prison for cooperating. The alleged ringleader, ex-cop Jerome Finnigan, has been charged in a murder-for-hire plot aimed at a fellow officer who was thought to be cooperating with investigators. Reports indicate that the federal investigation is continuing and may reach management, involving supervisors who either participated in the shakedowns or knew about them and did nothing (Meincke, 2009).

In another case, a deputy U.S. Marshal was convicted and sentenced for exposing the location of a witness against a mob figure. Deputy U.S. Marshal John Ambrose told a family friend who was linked to the mob-defendant that he was guarding the federal witness in the witness protection program, possibly in an attempt to set up a hit, although his defense was that he was just bragging. He was sentenced to four years in prison. Ambrose's father was a Chicago cop convicted of corruption in the 1980s in the infamous Marquette Ten case (Mitchum, 2009; Mack, 2009).

INDIANA Indianapolis police officers were recently indicted and convicted for a theft ring. Robert Long, the leader of the officers, was convicted when another officer testified against him. Six incidents involving thefts of drugs and money formed the case against the officers, who were under surveillance by the FBI from March to June 2008. Long was sentenced to 25 years, which was five years higher than federal guidelines, reportedly because he expressed no remorse during sentencing. He plans to appeal. The prosecutor had to dismiss 26 pending cases where the involved officers were witnesses (Murray, 2009).

LOUISIANA New Orleans police officers in the past have been linked to drugs, robberies, and even attempted murder (Human Rights Watch, 1998). More recently, the Danziger Bridge incident occurred in the aftermath of Hurricane Katrina. Officers shot unarmed citizens who were attempted to cross the bridge to escape the devastation of the city. Then they covered up the incident by inventing a fictitious witness and planting a gun supposedly used by the victim. Evidently, their supervisor helped the officers set up their stories to make sure they were all consistent. McCarthy (2010: 1) argues that "The extent of the alleged cover-up, the sheer number of cops involved or implicated, and the nonchalance with which officers carried out these crimes could point to systemic problems in the police force." Four officers and one civilian have pleaded guilty to the shooting and cover-up, but an equal number have been implicated and additional charges are expected.

A *Times-Picayune* investigative report indicates that other police shootings in the days following Katrina were not investigated properly and a re-examination of what evidence exists raises red flags in some of them. Police argue that conditions existed that were almost "apocalyptic," and there was no way to gather and preserve evidence or conduct thorough investigations of any event (nola.com, 2009). Recently, Mayor Mitch Landrieu has asked the Department of Justice to conduct an external investigation of the NOPD, leading possibly to a consent decree to address widespread allegations of corruption and transform the department. It was noted that the Department of Justice already has eight open civil rights investigations concerning the actions of NOPD officers, several of them over the events after Katrina (nola.com, 2010).

MARYLAND Prince George's County, Maryland, had just been released from a federal consent decree that it had been under for seven years for civil rights violations, but a new investigation led to evidence that police officers had provided security and assistance to drug dealers. One officer allegedly stood guard during a bank robbery as well. The cases are pending (Valentine, 2009).

MASSACHUSETTS A trio of Boston police officers was prosecuted and convicted in 2008 of conspiracy and other crimes associated with drug trafficking. The ringleader, Roberto Pulido, evidently recruited the others to help him provide counter-surveillance and protection to undercover FBI agents posing as drug dealers. Pulido was also implicated in an identity theft scam where he sold the identities of individuals he stopped for traffic violations to be used for fraud, and he also sold illegal steroids. He evidently framed a former business partner by planting guns and drugs in his car and then having him arrested (Vaznis, 2008; WBZtv.com, 2007; United States Attorney's Office, 2008).

In Stoughton, former police officers have pleaded guilty to federal obstruction charges and to making false statements in an investigation of corruption. The officers were accused of trading information obtained through official police computers for stolen goods, such as large screen televisions, and gift cards from Home Depot. It turned out to be an FBI sting operation, though, and the officers were caught on tape and video making the arrangements and accepting the goods (Guilfoil, 2010; Saltzman, 2010).

MINNESOTA In 2009, a narcotics strike force involving 34 officers from 13 agencies was the target of suspicion. Ten officers are alleged to have taken cash from suspects without filing criminal charges, and seized large screen televisions and computers for their personal use. Other items that were stolen goods were sold for extremely low prices at police auctions instead of being returned to the victims or kept as evidence. Officers are also accused of conducting warrantless searches, and taking valuable items and then falsely reporting they were destroyed (Pioneer Press, 2009). One of the officers has filed a whistle-blower lawsuit against the city and police department. He alleges that he was removed from the strike force after expressing concerns to superiors of unprofessional handling of evidence. He said that a leak to the press that he was the one who took property was to deflect blame and ruin his reputation and that he had suffered a campaign of retaliation (Chanen, 2009b).

In another case, a 14-month corruption investigation that started with an informant who said that he paid officers for information ended with an indictment against only one officer, who said he was entrapped. He was found guilty of using his patrol car's computer to look up and give driver's license information to a known drug dealer. He was also charged with income tax violations for not reporting his income from extra jobs (Chanen, 2009a).

MISSOURI Leo Liston, a St. Louis, Missouri, police officer (more accurately, ex-officer) was sentenced to three months in prison after admitting to the theft of cash found in a drug search. Three officers split $8,000 in cash, turning in only $4,000 of the total amount of cash found. Ironically, the officer was first approached to give information about other officers suspected of corruption, but confessed to the theft himself. The other officers who split the cash faced federal charges and pleaded guilty to theft of government property, two counts of conspiracy to commit wire fraud, two counts of false statements, misapplication of government funds, and theft. They also confessed to planting evidence and false arrest (Patrick, 2009).

NORTH CAROLINA Two officers were indicted for embezzlement, obtaining property by false pretenses, breaking and entering, second degree kidnapping, and obstruction of justice. Since 2006, four sheriffs have been convicted. In Robeson County, 23 people pleaded guilty to money laundering, racketeering, and theft of federal money, among other crimes. The other sheriffs were convicted of accepting money to protect illegal poker games, embezzlement, obstruction of justice, and sexual battery (Futch, 2009).

NEW YORK In the early 1980s, the "Buddy Boys" in New York were able to operate almost openly in a precinct rife with lesser forms of corruption. Ultimately, 13 officers in a precinct of only a little over 200 were indicted for crimes ranging from drug use to drug sales and armed robbery (Kappeler, Sluder, and Alpert, 1984/1994). In the early 1990s, Michael Dowd testified to the Mollen Commission that he and other officers accepted money for protecting illegal drug operations, used drugs and alcohol while on duty, robbed crime victims and drug dealers of money and drugs, and even robbed corpses of their valuables (Kappeler, Sluder, and Alpert, 1994: 201–202).

New York police officers have even been linked to the mafia. Ex-officers Louis Eppolito and Stephen Caracappa were on the payroll of the Luchese crime family. They were indicted in September 2005 for a range of crimes, including murder, and convicted of a wide range of racketeering and other charges in federal court in 2006, but the judge threw out most of the convictions, saying that the statute of limitations on the racketeering charges had expired.

OKLAHOMA Tulsa police officers and an ATF agent have been the subject of an intensive state and federal probe of alleged crimes and misconduct. Six officers and the former ATF agent were indicted on charges ranging from theft of U.S. property to civil rights violations. They evidently planted evidence on individuals and/or used faked informant testimony to engineer false arrests and convictions, stole drugs seized as evidence, and lied in court proceedings against individuals they wrongfully accused. The former ATF agent and a Tulsa officer have pleaded guilty to conspiracy, civil rights violations, and theft and are cooperating with authorities. Ex-officer Jeff Henderson faces 58 charges of perjury, witness tampering, civil rights violations, drug-related crimes, and bribery. Several individuals have been released from prison as a result of the probe. The city has been sued by two individuals who were wrongfully convicted, and they expect many more lawsuits to

in the **NEWS**

SHOW ME THE MONEY!

The LAPD, in response to a federal consent decree, instituted a policy in 2009 that requires gang and narcotics officers to disclose details of their personal finances. It is intended to help catch corrupt cops or those who might be tempted because of financial problems. Officers must disclose outside income, real estate, stocks, and other assets. They also have to report the size of bank accounts and debts, including mortgages and credit cards; all the information includes finances shared with family or partners. The policy has been challenged by the police union, which has also encouraged officers not to transfer to the affected units. It has affected the ability of the department to attract officers to the gang unit, despite the status of the unit as elite. The roughly 600 officers already assigned to the affected units when the policy went into effect in April were granted a two-year grace period, but getting new officers to transfer into the units seems to have become the problem. The problem is compounded because there is another policy that limits gang unit assignments to five years, increasing the number of new transfers necessary to keep a full complement of officers. Reportedly some units are down from 18 to 13 officers and another from 35 to 24, without the empty slots being filled. Officers say they fear that the financial information may be used against them or that their privacy may be compromised. Others argue it isn't fair for only certain officers to have to comply and LAPD's policy is more stringent than even the federal policy for its law enforcement officers. Supervisors say that the problem will escalate in 2011 when the grace period is over and all officers are required to fill the disclosure forms. Others hope that officers will relent and sign. One officer said it's the right thing to do: "They gave me an opportunity to do something with my life," he said. "There comes a time when it is time to give something back to the department."

SOURCE: Gold and Rubin, 2009.

follow. The district attorney has indicated that he will need to review hundreds of convictions that were obtained through one or more of these officers' testimony. The civil suits, along with an earlier lawsuit by Arvin McGee—who received a settlement of $12 million for being wrongfully accused and convicted of kidnapping and rape based on false testimony and manufactured evidence—have prompted the mayor of Tulsa to suggest that newly hired police officers be required to purchase insurance or post a bond that protects the city against their misconduct (Barber and Lassek, 2010).

PENNSYLVANIA A Philadelphia narcotics squad became the subject of an internal investigation and FBI probe when Latino bodega owners complained to city and police department officials about a pattern of raids where officers targeted Latino stores for narcotics raids, turned off the security cameras, and then (allegedly) stole money and goods from the stores (Moran, 2009). The same narcotics squad, including two brothers, Officers Cujdik, is also under investigation for lying to obtain search warrants. There are 15 civil rights lawsuits pending against officers from the unit, including one where a woman has accused one of the officers of fondling her breasts after she was arrested and handcuffed (Laker and Ruderman, 2010).

Observers note that the pattern of misconduct seems to be a problem with narcotics squads. In the early 1980s, there was the "One Squad" scandal where a small squad of officers were prosecuted and convicted of selling the drugs they stole from dealers. Later in the 1980s, the "Five Squad" scandal erupted and several officers were convicted in federal court of racketeering and stealing drugs and cash from dealers between 1980 and 1989. In the early 1990s, five narcotics officers were prosecuted in federal court for preying on drug suspects, robbing and falsely prosecuting them. This case ultimately led to 500 charges being dismissed and $4 million in federal civil rights suits by those who alleged were wrongly arrested. In 2000, yet another narcotics squad was the target of an FBI investigation. Those officers were accused of using false information to get search warrants, planting evidence and committing perjury, and stealing drugs, cash, and valuables from drug dealers (Slobodzian, 2009). The vulnerability of narcotics squads to temptation has led at least one city to require special scrutiny of officers' finances, as described in the In the News box.

Financial disclosure rules seem to be a method of investigating and preventing corruption that is gaining traction. The CIA and FBI require them. As the In the News box indicates, LAPD has instituted them in response to the court monitor appointed after the Ramparts scandal. Michael Cherkasky, the court monitor for LAPD, said that financial disclosure is both a prophylactic and an investigative tool. Prince George's County, Maryland, near Washington, D.C., has faced a recent scandal involving five of its officers who are suspected of receiving protection money from illegal gambling operations. In response to queries, the police chief said he is not opposed to considering the idea of financial disclosure policies, after they discovered that the officers targeted in the corruption probe had unusual finances, such as one officer who owned a Dodge Viper and other luxury cars (Zapotosky, 2009).

We have examined a range of corruption, from the arguably trivial (gratuities) to criminal acts that include murder. There is a legitimate argument that the officers who engage in minor rule breaking or some types of unethical behaviors that are not criminal should not be in the same discussion as "criminal cops" whose pattern of wrongdoing and criminality is much more serious. The opposing argument is that the minor transgressions lead to an environment in which the truly rogue cops feel free to engage in criminality because of the minor transgressions of everyone, leading to a situation where all officers engage in a conspiracy of silence. The Walking the Walk box illustrates how difficult it is to come forward in an atmosphere where even criminal cops are sometimes protected.

Explanations of Deviance

Explanations of corruption can be described as

- Individual
- Institutional (or organizational)
- Systemic (or societal)

Individual explanations, such as the *rotten apple* argument (discussed below), assume that the individual officer has deviant inclinations before he or she even enters the police department and merely exploits the position. Sloppy recruiting and the development of a police personality are other individual explanations of deviance. Institutional (or organizational) explanations point to organizational problems (low managerial visibility, low public visibility, and peer-group secrecy, among others). Institutional

WALKING THE WALK

In the movie *Training Day*, a new recruit is "schooled" in the methods of a veteran, decorated cop that included brutalizing suspects, planting drugs, and generally committing crimes to catch the criminals. In a real-life version of *Training Day*, Keith Batt earned a criminal justice degree at California State University at Sacramento and fulfilled his life's dream by being hired by the Oakland Police Department. He graduated at the top of his recruit class and became an Oakland police officer in 1999.

Batt was assigned to Clarence Mabanag as his field training officer. Almost from the first day, Batt says, he was told to falsify offense reports and to use force on suspects. Batt did as he was told for two and a half weeks, including hitting a suspect and lying on an offense report, because he knew that he would be retaliated against if he did not. Then he decided that he could not continue to be a police officer if it meant violating the law he was sworn to uphold. He quit the Oakland force and turned in his FTO and the other officers to internal affairs.

Mabanag and other officers, including Matt Hornung, Jude Siapno, and Frank (Choker) Vazquez, were known as the "Riders." According to testimony, they patrolled their western, poverty-stricken district of Oakland with an iron fist and used excessive force, planted drugs, and intimidated witnesses as the means to keep the peace. Partly as a result of Keith Batt's report, all four officers were fired and charged with a range of offenses including obstruction of justice, conspiracy to obstruct justice, filing false police reports, assault and battery, kidnapping, and false imprisonment. Even before these charges, the four had records of misconduct. The department had paid $200,000 to settle suits involving Siapno and Mabanag, and other lawsuits existed against Vazquez and Hornung.

Not everyone believes the foursome's culpability or applauds Keith Batt's decision to testify against them. According to one fellow officer at the time, "These guys are awesome cops, they never did anything to anybody who was innocent, just pukes, criminals, see? They just got a little too intense and went over the line." Even residents had mixed feelings, with some arguing that it took a tough cop to police a tough street. As one resident said, "The only thing the bad people understand is force...." Sometimes, however, their activities evidently were not limited to just drug dealers and other criminals. One witness testified that he called police to report a stolen stereo, and when his dog wouldn't stop barking and Mabanag threatened to shoot the dog, his angry response resulted in Mabanag's choking him and ordering Batt to lie on the offense report to cover the use of force.

In the course of the ensuing scandal, Oakland paid out $11 million to settle civil suits from 119 victims of police officers (including the Riders) and ended up under a court-ordered federal consent decree. Hornung, Mabanag, and Siapno were prosecuted in two lengthy trials between 2000 and 2005. Vazquez is a fugitive of justice, believed to be in Mexico. Perhaps he should have waited to have his day in court, too, as all three escaped guilty verdicts. Hornung was acquitted of all charges, and the jury deadlocked in two trials on Mabanag and Siapno. The police chief has refused to reinstate them, and they have sued for back pay and reinstatement.

The fired officers and their attorneys say that the deadlocked jurors exonerated them. The prosecutor is convinced of their guilt, but decided not to seek a third trial because he believed that he could not get a jury to convict them. Batt has been honored as a courageous whistleblower who stood up to the "blue curtain of secrecy," but also has been vilified as a "liar" who feared a negative evaluation. Today, he is a respected police officer in Pleasanton, California, and received an award for "Ethical Courage." But Clarence Mabanag is also a police officer in a different department in southern California, which hired him after the deadlocked jury verdict. In February 2009, in response to their appeal, an independent arbitrator ruled that the city was justified in dismissing Mabanag and Siapno.

Sources: Institute for Law Enforcement Administration, 2008; Lee, 2004; Zamora, Lee, and van Derbeke, 2003; Bay City News, 2007.

explanations also include looking at the police role in the criminal justice system (as the front-line interface with criminals), the tension between the use of discretion and bureaucracy, and the role of commanders in spreading corruption. A systemic (or societal) explanation of police deviance focuses on the relationship between the police and the public (Johnston, 1995).

INDIVIDUAL EXPLANATIONS

rotten-apple argument The proposition that the officer alone is deviant and that it was simply a mistake to hire him or her.

The most common explanation of police officer corruption is the **rotten-apple argument**—that the officer alone is deviant and that it was simply a mistake to hire him or her. This argument has been extended to describe *rotten bushels*—groups of officers banding together to commit deviant acts. The point of this argument is that nothing is wrong with the barrel, that deviance is individual, not endemic.

Sherman explained that deviant officers go through what he called a "moral career" as they pass through various stages of rationalization to more serious misdeeds in a graduated and systematic way. Once an individual is able to get past the first "moral crisis," it becomes less difficult to rationalize new and more unethical behaviors. The previous behaviors serve as an underpinning to a different ethical standard, for one must explain and justify one's own behaviors to preserve psychological well-being (Sherman, 1982).

When one accepts gradations of behavior, the line between right and wrong can more easily be moved farther and farther away from an absolute standard of morality. Many believe, for instance, that gratuities are only the first step in a spiral downward, as the Quote and Query box illustrates.

QUOTE & QUERY

For police, the passage from free coffee at the all-night diner and Christmas gifts to participation in drug-dealing and organized burglary is normally a slow if steady one.

—SOURCE: MALLOY, 1982: 33.

Do you believe that free coffee inevitably leads to committing crimes for officers? Why or why not?

Others dispute the view that after the first cup of coffee, every police officer inevitably ends up performing more serious ethical violations. Many police officers have clear personal guidelines on what is acceptable and not acceptable. Whereas many, perhaps even the majority of, police see nothing wrong with accepting minor gratuities, few police would accept outright cash, and fewer still would condone thefts and bribes. The problematic element is that the gradations between what is acceptable and what is not can vary from officer to officer and department to department.

Sherman also believes in the importance of a signification factor, or labeling an individual action that is acceptable under a personal rationale (Sherman, 1985a: 253). Police routinely deal with the seamier side of society—not only drug addicts and muggers but also middle-class people who are involved in dishonesty and corruption. The constant displays of lying, hiding, cheating, and theft create cynicism, and this, in turn, may develop into a vulnerability to temptation because officers may redefine them as acceptable behaviors.

Following are some rationales that police might easily use to justify unethical behavior (Murphy and Moran, 1981: 93):

- The public thinks every cop is a crook, so why try to be honest?

- The money is out there; if I don't take it, someone else will.

- I'm only taking what's rightfully mine; if the city paid me a decent wage, I wouldn't have to get it on my own.

- I can use it because it's for a good cause—my son needs an operation, or dental work, or tuition for medical school, or a new bicycle....

Greene et al. (2004) examined predictive variables related to those who received citizen complaints or departmental discipline in the Philadelphia police department. In their study, they utilized background and file information on about 2,000 officers and obtained attitudinal survey results from a random sample of 500 officers. They collected data on citizen complaints, internal investigations, departmental discipline incidents, and police shootings. About a third of the sample had received departmental discipline (2004: iii). They found that 15 characteristics were significantly related to receiving departmental discipline, including being younger, being previously rejected for hire, experiencing military discipline, scoring low on some sections of academy training, and receiving academy discipline. Officers having six or more of these risk factors were 2.5 times more likely to receive departmental discipline (2004: iv). The research found that 22 factors were significantly related to receiving a citizen complaint of physical abuse, including being younger, receiving military discipline, having one's driver's license suspended, having ever been placed under arrest, and having had one or more deceptive polygraph results (2004: v). They found, using a cynicism scale, that higher levels of cynicism predicted disciplinary actions, shootings, and other misconduct. They also found that officers who worked in districts with lower ethics scores were more likely to be involved in shootings, but no other relationships were found (2004: 65). Note that this study did not collect the data in a way that would allow them to match the actions and attitudes of individual officers; instead they had to aggregate ethics scores by district level.

Greene and his colleagues also utilized hypotheticals, finding that officers expressed a fair amount of "ethical ambiguity." Findings also indicated that where an officer was assigned was associated with the likelihood of receiving discipline, complaints, or becoming involved in police shootings. The authors indicated that there seemed to be a district culture that affected officer behavior, and the better way to look at risk factors is to see individual factors interacting with organizational elements. This is an important finding and is related to the "bad barrel" research reviewed below. The researchers emphasized that it seemed to be both individual and environmental factors that led to the likelihood of misconduct (2004: 48).

Other research has looked at correlates of police misconduct; in other words, are some individuals more likely to succumb to the temptations of police work? In their study of New York City police officers who were terminated for misconduct, Fyfe and Kane (2006; also see Kane and White, 2009) analyzed correlates that might influence misconduct. In the discussion below, their review of the literature and their findings are used to discuss possible predictors.

GENDER In journalistic accounts of police corruption and in common thought, there is a perception that female police officers are less likely to be involved in corrupt activities. No women have been involved in the largest scandals in recent memory. Some academic research has indicated that women engage in less aggressive policing and receive fewer citizen complaints. Also, some studies on misconduct find that women are less likely to commit unethical acts (Pogarsky and Piquero, 2004). However, measurements of police-culture attitudes by other researchers indicate that women are not significantly different from male officers in their values and beliefs. Fyfe and Kane found that women in their sample were more likely than male officers to be terminated during their probation. They also found that, although male officers were more likely to be terminated for bribery, there was no difference in all other profit-oriented misconduct. Male officers were more likely than female officers to be terminated for brutality and other forms of non-profit-oriented abuses, but women were more likely to be terminated for non-line-of-duty criminal conduct (e.g., drug crimes) and administrative rule breaking. Thus women may be just as prone to certain types of corruption as male officers, although the researchers were cautious in this finding because of the small numbers and because the relationship seemed to wash out when conducting multivariate analysis.

AGE Prior research on age indicates that, although younger officers (younger than 22) have fewer instances of prior bad behavior, they are more likely to be terminated during probationary periods than officers who were older when they were hired. Other research indicates that age has no relationship to use of force. In Fyfe and Kane's New York City study, those under 22 years of age when appointed were more likely to be terminated during probation but no more likely than older officers to be terminated for any form of misconduct after probation.

EDUCATION College-educated officers receive fewer citizen complaints; however, researchers wonder if this finding isn't confounded by assignments because educated officers are also more likely to be promoted off the street into supervisory or detective positions. Although some research indicates that there is a relationship between higher education and less misconduct, other research finds no relationship. In the New York City study, those with more years of education upon hire were less likely to be terminated for misconduct.

RACE Prior research indicates that black officers were more likely than whites to be disciplined for misconduct. A possible explanation might be differential rule enforcement or differential assignments and vulnerability to situations where use of force, for instance, was necessary. Research seems to support the notion that differential assignments have something to do with black officers' greater use of force. Fyfe and Kane's study found that blacks, but not other minorities, were more likely to be terminated during probation, and terminated for misconduct, including non-line-of-duty criminal conduct, drug test failures, and administrative rule breaking.

MILITARY EXPERIENCE, PERFORMANCE IN THE ACADEMY, AND BACK-GROUND CHARACTERISTICS Research indicates that prior bad conduct predicts future bad conduct. If someone has received unfavorable job evaluations or been dishonorably discharged from the military, they are more likely to commit police misconduct as well. Other indicators of misconduct seem to be poor performance in the academy and other forms of misconduct, such as misdemeanors or other arrest histories. In Fyfe and Kane's study, those who had prior negative employment histories, dishonorable discharges, and/or did poorly in the academy were more likely to be terminated for misconduct.

In sum, according to this one study of terminations for misconduct, factors associated with high risk include: being black or (to a lesser extent) Latino, prior citizen complaints, prior criminal history, history of a public-order offense, and prior employment disciplinary history. Non-individual factors included being assigned to posts with low supervision and high citizen contact. Length of service, higher education, and older age at appointment were negatively related to misconduct (Fyfe and Kane, 2006: xxvi–xxviii). These findings must be viewed with caution, however, as they are only from one department, they utilize only official reports of misconduct, and they do not control for other variables. Manning (2009) criticizes Kane and White's (2009) description of the study's findings as complicating the variables of misconducts like administrative rule-breaking with much more serious deviance such as lawbreaking, not providing ethnographic data to enrich the quantitative findings, and not taking into account in their analysis of factors such as race the changes over time in the size and composition of the department. These are valid concerns, indeed, but arguably there is nothing in their findings regarding individual characteristics that seem to contradict earlier studies. What is more problematic is the relative weight of individual factors as compared to organizational factors that influence the presence and degree of deviance.

It should also be noted that identifying correlates of misconduct is atheoretical. It is interesting to note that, with a few exceptions, researchers have not attempted to test traditional criminological theories to see if they explain police deviance, or develop original theories. One example of applying a criminological theory to police deviance is Hickman and colleagues' (2001) use of the data from the Philadelphia study to test Tittle's control balance theory and social learning theory. These researchers found that officers with a control deficit were more likely to report fellow officers for misconduct. The Philadelphia data was also used to test social learning theory to see if it was helpful in understanding police deviance, and researchers concluded that the data did support the social learning theory (Chappell and Piquero, 2004).

Deterrence theory has also been applied to police misconduct. Pogarsky and Piquero (2004) tested the theory using a sample of 210 officers from the Philadelphia study. They found that the threat of extra-legal and legal sanctions did potentially deter misconduct and that the trait of impulsivity tended to reduce the effect of such threats.

Harris (2010) adds to this discussion by offering a life-course perspective to officer misconduct. He first explains that criminological theory may be helpful to understand more serious forms of misconduct (as distinguished from minor rule violations). Then he explains life-course theory and how it may be applied to law enforcement; for instance, while some officers may engage in misconduct early in their career, they may mature out of these acts as they become more skilled, while others would be similar to the "life-course persistent" offender and engage in misconduct relatively early and consistently throughout their career. Harris tests his theory using citizen complaints as a measure of misconduct, acknowledging that this is a somewhat problematic measure. His data supports findings that gender, education, and race are related to misconduct (being female, having a higher education, and not being a minority are related to lower levels of misconduct). He found that, indeed, officers tend to receive citizen complaints early in their career and there is a desistance over the course of the career; however, he also found that most officers had fewer than three complaints over their entire career. There was a group of officers who received a higher level of citizen complaints, and the number did not decline as dramatically as all other officers after the sixth year. Harris suggests that this group should be targeted for further study and intervention.

Most researchers who identify correlates and/or who apply criminological theories to police misconduct believe that individual explanations present only part of the picture. In addition to individual factors, it is important to look at organizational factors as well.

ORGANIZATIONAL EXPLANATIONS

Some argue that the Miami River scandal, involving officers committing armed robberies of drug dealers, was caused by the rapid hiring of minorities during an affirmative action drive without proper background checks; disaffection by white, mid-level supervisors who basically did not do their job of supervision—who were, instead, merely counting the days to retirement; ethnic divisions in the department; and the pervasive influence of politics in the department, which disrupted internal discipline mechanisms (Dorschner, 1989). These concepts are largely organizational explanations of police corruption. Another example of the effects of rapid hiring is the finding that of the 1,000 new officers hired in Washington, D.C., in the early 1990s as a result of political pressure, nearly a quarter have been fired because of their involvement in various acts of misconduct or crime (reported in Lersch, 2002b: 77).

Murphy and Caplan (1989) argue that there are situational elements that "breed corruption," including lax community standards over certain types of behavior (gambling, prostitution), hesitation of the chief to enforce rules and discipline officers, tolerance by fellow officers, unguided police discretion and incompetence, and lack of support from prosecutors and the courts (or corruption at that stage of the system). Most of these explanations fall into an organizational category as well.

Crank and Caldero's (2000/2005) "noble-cause" explanation of some types of deviance (described more fully in Chapter 5), whereby officers lie or commit other unethical acts to catch criminals, is an organizational explanation, as is any description of deviance that includes the aspect of subcultural support. Whenever deviance is explained as being supported by the organizational culture—whether that be the formal culture or the informal culture—falls into this category.

Gilmartin and Harris (1998) also have discussed why some officers become compromised and argue that it is because the law enforcement organization does not adequately train them to understand and respond to the ethical dilemmas they will face. They coined the term *continuum of compromise* to illustrate what happens to the officer. The first element is a "perceived sense of victimization," which refers to what happens when officers enter the profession with naïve ideas about what the job will be like. Citizen disrespect, bureaucratic barriers, and the justice system's realities sometimes makes officers cynical, feeling that no one cares and that they are needlessly exposed to danger. Cynicism leads to distrust of the administration and the citizenry. At that point, the officer is alienated and more prone to corruption.

Gilmartin and Harris also talk about the officers' sense of entitlement and how that can lead to corruption. There is a sense that the rules don't apply to them because they are different from the citizenry they police. This leads to the "blue curtain of secrecy," discussed more fully in Chapter 5, when officers believe it is more ethical to cover up for other cops than it is to tell the truth.

Trautman (2008) has also discussed how organizational leaders contribute to the unethical actions of their employees. In his "corruption continuum," he argues that organizations create unethical employees through the following steps:

1. *An atmosphere of administrative indifference toward integrity.* There is no ethics training, and internal politics, hidden agendas, and unfairness are elements of the organizational culture. Indifference is also apparent in the quality of recruitment and hiring, unfair promotions, or discipline, allowing disgruntled field officers to influence recruits, and supervisors treating employees with a lack of respect.

2. *Ignoring obvious ethical problems.* Supervisors ignore problem employees and, in the worst cases, engage in active cover-ups rather than trying to rectify the problem.

3. *Hypocrisy and fear-dominated culture.* After years of indifference and ignoring problem individuals, employees come to fear saying anything. They believe that there are always hidden agendas and it is better to be a survivor than a whistleblower. Morale is low because no one wants to work in such an environment.

4. *Survival of the fittest.* Employees will do whatever it takes to survive in the organization. Honest employees fear the dishonest, cover-ups are the standard method of response when scandals threaten, and there is no hope of things getting better.

Huberts, Kaptein, and Lasthuizen (2007) obtained measures of corruption (or what they called integrity violations) by asking officers to report what they knew was happening.

The independent variable was leadership style. They were able to collect surveys from 3,125 police officers in the Netherlands with a response rate of about 51 percent within police agencies. Their survey covered 20 different integrity violations and questions on leadership characteristics. Instead of asking about personal integrity violations, they asked officers to estimate violations by others as a measure of the corruption in the organization. Their findings gave them confidence that the respondents reported truthfully with fairly substantial percentages reporting various types of ethical infractions. They found that leadership styles differentially affect (perceived) levels of ethical violations. Specifically, role modeling leadership seems to reduce all measures of integrity violations; strictness has an effect on the level of financial types of ethical violations (i.e., falsely calling in sick, misusing work time for private purposes); and openness seems to reduce other types of ethical violations, such as favoritism and discriminatory remarks.

SOCIETAL EXPLANATIONS

Rationalizations used by some police when they take bribes or protection money from prostitutes or drug dealers are made easier by the public's tolerant stance toward certain areas of vice; for example, to accept protection money from a prostitute may be rationalized by the relative lack of concern that the public shows for this type of lawbreaking. The same argument could be made about gambling or even drugs. We often formally expect the police to enforce laws while we informally encourage them to ignore the same laws.

Signification occurs here as well. Although gambling carries connotations of the mob and organized crime, we typically don't think of church bingo or the friendly football pool down at Joe's Bar. If police were to enforce gambling laws against the stereotypical criminal, the public would support the action, but if the enforcement were to take place against "upstanding citizens," there would be an outraged response. "Police Arrest Grandma Bingo Players!" would be the headline.

Fyfe and Kane (2006) present an interesting societal explanation of why profit-motivated corruption seems to occur more often in large Northeastern cities, and abuse of authority (specifically in the use of force) occurs more often in Western "newer" cities. They argue that the older cities are characterized by the "watchman" style of policing that performs differential policing depending on the sector of the community. Police enforce laws that are perceived as inapplicable and undesirable to ethnic enclaves (such as gambling). Members of these ethnic communities do not trust government, and thriving underground economies are present. The community is not invested in the laws, which leads to kickbacks, protection rackets, bribery, and other forms of graft by the police who do not care if the "gray area" laws are enforced or not. Western cities, by contrast, were settled by homogeneous groups that all arrived around the same time. Policing was perceived to be about keeping undesirables under control; therefore, use of force was tolerated and even expected, while profit-oriented corruption was harshly punished. The "legalistic" style of policing characterized, until recently, cities such as Los Angeles, Denver, and Seattle.

If police are expected to make a distinction between good people and bad people, and good people should be excused, ignored, or, at worst, scolded for their involvement, but bad people should be investigated, caught, and punished, it should come as no surprise that they sometimes take extra-legal liberties with those they think are bad people. It should also come as no surprise that if the public doesn't want full enforcement of the laws, especially if it impacts them, some officers may decide that a hypocritical public won't mind a few gambling operations, or a certain number of prostitutes plying their trade, or even a few drug dealers, so they might as well accept protection money.

As long as the public supports certain types of illegal activities by patronage, it is no surprise that some police officers are able to rationalize non-enforcement. Also, as long as the public relays a message that crime control, especially against "bad" people, is more important than individual liberties and rights, we should not be surprised when police act on that message.

Reducing Police Corruption

There are several authors who have proposed comprehensive lists of tactics to reduce police misconduct and corruption, including Malloy (1982: 37–40), who suggested increasing the salary of police, eliminating unenforceable laws, establishing civilian review boards, and improving training.

Metz (1990) also suggested several ways in which police administrators can encourage ethical conduct among officers:

- Set realistic goals and objectives for the department
- Provide ethical leadership
- Provide a written code of ethics
- Provide a whistleblowing procedure that ensures fair treatment of all parties
- Provide training in law enforcement ethics

Carter (1999: 321) offers some specific ways to control drug corruption: leadership by the chief, management and supervision, supervisory training, organizational control and information management, internal auditing of the use of informants, internal affairs units, drug enforcement units having audit controls, periodic turnover of staff, better evidence handling, early warning systems, and better training and discipline. Prenzler and Ransley (2002) presented the most exhaustive list, also found in the 1997 Wood Report, written after an investigation of widespread corruption in the New South Wales (Australia) police department. They suggest: internal affairs units, independent civilian oversight agencies, asset and financial reviews, video cameras in patrol cars, covert high technology surveillance, targeted and randomized integrity testing, surveys of police and the public, personnel diversification, comprehensive ethics training, complaint resolution methods, monitoring and regulation of informants, decriminalizing vice, and risk analysis (Wood, 1997). Note that the majority of these suggestions target administrative changes rather than identifying the individual officer as the problem.

In the next sections, we take a closer look at some of these means to reduce corruption and improve the ethical climate of police agencies. Generally, "accountability reforms" have emerged and grown in the last 20 years in an effort to control misconduct (Harris, 2005) even while researchers note that their effectiveness has not been established (Walker, 2007). The mechanisms discussed below can be considered as responses to the explanations above; specifically, some mechanisms address the "rotten apple" idea that misconduct is due to the wrong individuals being hired. These suggestions would include: improve testing and screening, increase the qualifications to be an officer, and improve training. They would also include suggestions that attempt to identify the problem officer sooner, such as early warning systems and integrity testing. Organizational explanations address elements of the police organization, including such things as improving investigation and disciplinary procedures, addressing subcultural elements, and improving leadership. Societal explanations of deviance are beyond the power of police departments to address. However, one might argue that community policing itself is a type of societal re-engineering by having community members take responsibility for their neighborhood and the problems within it and become partners with police.

"ROTTEN APPLE" RESPONSES

IMPROVING SCREENING Background checks, interviews, credit checks, polygraphs, drug tests, and other screening tools are used to eliminate inappropriate individuals from the pool of potential hires. The extent of screening varies from department to department, but generally has become more sophisticated, especially in the use of psychological testing and interviews. Sanders (2008) argues that the process is more "weeding out" than selecting in those candidates best suited to policing and points out that it is hard to develop tools to identify traits that are associated with successful police performance when, in fact, there is no consensus on what makes a good police officer. Most research on the effectiveness of screening tools utilizes academy test scores or firings as the measure of good (or failed) performance.

The most common pre-employment screening tool that is used by law enforcement agencies is the Minnesota Multiphasic Personality Inventory (MMPI or its subsequent versions) (Arrigo and Claussen, 2003; Dantzker and McCoy, 2006). The Inwald Personality Inventory (IPI) was developed to measure personality characteristics and behavioral patterns specific to fitness for law enforcement. Researchers have found that the IPI more accurately identifies individuals who are unsuccessful in law enforcement (terminated) (cited in Arrigo and Claussen, 2003). The so-called "Big Five" (extroversion, neuroticism, agreeableness, conscientiousness, and openness) have been the target of enough studies to indicate that they are reliable measures of personality and, of those, conscientiousness seems to be the most relevant to job performance. Conscientiousness is related to the degree of organization, control, and motivation one has and has been related to being organized, reliable, hard working, self-governing, and persevering. There has been very little research done to determine if the trait accurately measures police performance success, and research has produced mixed results (Arrigo and Claussen, 2003; Claussen-Rogers and Arrigo, 2005; Sanders, 2008).

EDUCATION AND TRAINING Education has been promoted as a necessary element to improve the ethics of policing; however, education itself is certainly not a panacea. Many of the unethical officers described in this book have been college graduates. Fyfe and Kane (2006) did find a correlation between education and reduced risk of terminations for cause in the New York Police Department; however, it is by no means clear that education by itself increases the ethics of police officers.

Ethics training in the academy, and in in-service courses, is common and is recommended for all police departments today. Reuss-Ianni (1983) described how, after the Knapp Commission uncovered wide-ranging corruption in the New York Police Department, ethical awareness workshops were begun. Unfortunately, they have not stopped the periodic corruption scandals that have occurred since that time.

The International Association of Chiefs of Police (2008) found that about 80 percent of responding agencies said they committed resources to ethics instruction. Most of the courses were lecture (78 percent), followed by readings and discussion (67 percent), videotapes (53 percent), and video scenarios (49 percent). Other methods (role playing, computers, or games) were used less often. Most (70 percent) reported that the course was four hours or less. In terms of content, 81 percent discussed gratuities, 76 percent discussed conflicts of interest, 90 percent discussed abuse of force, 80 percent discussed abuse of authority, 69 percent discussed corruption, and 71 percent discussed off-duty ethics. The IACP found that the amount of time devoted to ethics topics did not match how important respondents indicated the topics were. Interestingly, only about a third of the agencies utilized an ethics criterion for probationary officer evaluations.

The major recommendations of the IACP based on this study were to provide job-specific training on ethics and to differentiate training for recruits, in-service, and management, as well as other units. Another recommendation was that ethics training begin with recruits and be an integral part of the departments' structure and policies. The IACP also recommended enhancing content, and using appropriate learning styles. A final recommendation was that departments concentrate more on ethics training for field training officers (IACP, 2008).

Moran (2005) described several models of police ethics training, including a view of ethics as a "shield" to protect officers from trouble, as a programmed element in the officer's training "hardwire," as a mission or crusade, or as a "command from on high," along with the sanctions for disobeying. He explained most ethical training as presenting the "slippery slope" argument—i.e., don't do the little stuff, because you may slide into doing more serious acts of misconduct. The second most common approach in training is to warn recruits against the elements of the police culture that lead to transgressions. Conti and Nolan (2005: 167) found that ethics training typically is structured in such a way to encourage conformity to the "traditional image and identity of police officers."

Delattre (1989a) and Delaney (1990) have emphasized the importance of character. This approach would seem to negate the relevance of any attempts to improve the ethics of officers, for character is fairly well formed by adulthood. Yet, we might say that ethics training at this point serves to delineate those situations that might not be recognized as questions of ethics. Also, discussions of such dilemmas point out egoistic rationalizations for unethical behavior, making them harder to use by those who would try. Other training options may concentrate on only one ethical system, such as utilitarianism, or involve a more balanced treatment of other ethical systems. All must resolve the issues of relativism versus absolutism, duty versus personal needs, and minor transgressions versus major transgressions.

Martinelli (2000) offers a different training model. He proposes a course that is grounded in the actual discipline cases of each law enforcement agency. He argues that some of the law enforcement code provisions are ambiguous to officers and require explanations—such as keeping one's private life "unsullied." Officers may not realize that they can receive departmental sanctions for their behavior in their private life. Further, case law indicates that if some attempts are not made to instruct officers in appropriate behaviors, and if agencies and city councils continue to rubber-stamp the violations of civil rights that some officers commit, the agencies themselves will be held responsible. For instance, if there is a pattern of abuse in a discipline record and the officer then commits another violation, the city and police department will probably lose a resulting civil suit.

integrity testing
"Sting" operations to test whether or not police officers will make honest choices.

INTEGRITY TESTING **Integrity testing** occurs when a police officer is placed in a position where he or she might be tempted to break a rule or a law and monitored to see what he or she will do. New York City has used integrity testing since the late 1970s, after the Knapp Commission exposed widespread corruption. Field associates were recruited straight from academies to investigate suspected officers (Reuss-Ianni, 1983: 80). Integrity testing is like undercover work in that officers are tempted with an opportunity to commit an illegal or corrupt act, such as keeping a found wallet or being offered a bribe (Marx, 1991). It is reported that almost 30 percent of officers have failed this type of honesty test (Prenzler and Ronken, 2001a: 322). After the Mollen Commission in the mid-1990s, the integrity testing program in New York City was expanded. In one report, in 355 tests involving 762 officers, no criminal failures were reported, and only 45 procedural failures were reported (Prenzler and Ronken, 2001a: 322).

Prenzler and Ronken (2001a) discuss integrity testing in police departments in Australia and around the world. They point out that the London Metropolitan Police instituted random integrity testing in 1998. In their study of Australia, they discovered that only two reporting police agencies used *targeted* integrity testing and none used *random* integrity testing. In New South Wales, integrity testing resulted in 37 percent failing; only 27 percent passed, and the rest were referred for further investigation or discontinued (2001a: 327).

Needless to say, most police officers have highly negative attitudes about integrity testing. Spokesmen argue that "testing raises serious issues regarding privacy, deception, entrapment, provocation, and the legal rights of individuals" (Prenzler and Ronken, 2001a: 323–324). There is a widespread belief that such testing is unfair, overly intrusive, wasteful of resources, and detrimental to morale. One study of opinions of police managers found that the majority agreed that targeted integrity testing had a place in the investigation of wrongdoing, but that random testing was ill-advised (Prenzler, 2006).

It is interesting to compare integrity testing with undercover operations. The planted wallet is similar to the buy-bust operation, and the use of field associates is similar to undercover operations. Officers despise the idea that an officer who pretends to be a friend may instead be someone who is trying to obtain evidence that they are doing wrong. The argument for undercover work is that if officers aren't doing anything wrong, they have nothing to fear. However, field associates create a sense of betrayal and lack of trust, regardless of whether someone is involved in wrongdoing. This same argument, of course, is used to criticize undercover operations. Specifically, critics argue that the use of undercover operations may undermine the fabric of social relations by reducing the level of trust.

EARLY WARNING OR AUDIT SYSTEMS Barker (2002) describes the evidence indicating that a small percentage of officers often accounts for a disproportionate number of abuse or corruption complaints. This problem was first recognized as far back as the 1970s (Walker and Alpert, 2002). Therefore, the practice of identifying these officers through some form of early warning system seems logical. The officers who were prone to use force were the first targets of early warning systems. It seemed clear that a small number of officers were responsible for a disproportionate share of excessive-force complaints. Then the practice spread to officers who garnered a disproportionate share of any type of citizen complaint.

Early warning systems have been used in New Orleans, Portland (Oregon), and Pittsburgh (Barker, 2002). The early warning systems look at number of complaints, use-of-force reports, use-of-weapon reports, reprimands, or other indicators to identify officers. Intervention may include more supervision, additional training, and/or counseling. In one city's program, the officer's supervisor is alerted that the system has tagged the officer; then the supervisor may counsel the officer, engage in other responses, or do nothing (Walker and Alpert, 2002: 225). In Miami's early warning system, officers identified by the early warning system may be subject to the following: reassignment, retraining, transfer, referral to an employee assistance program, fitness for duty evaluation, and/or dismissal (Walker and Alpert, 2002: 224).

These programs have been endorsed by the National Institute of Justice and have been incorporated into several consent decrees between cities and federal courts to avert civil rights litigation. By 1999, about 27 percent of all police agencies had early warning systems in place (reported in Walker and Alpert, 2002: 220).

Walker (2007) reports that early warning systems vary in the elements they count and where they set the threshold of concern. The systems also have various objectives: some departments use them to provide assistance and additional training, others utilize them for punishment, and still others use them to target high achievers. The In the News box describes a computer-assisted early warning system.

One cannot simply count the number of incidents or complaints, because the officer's shift and duty, length of service, types of calls responded to, and other factors affect the number of complaints (Walker and Alpert, 2002: 223). Further, the programs are only as effective as the interventions that are triggered by the identification of a problem. Walker and Alpert note that such systems are as much of a reflection of management as of individual officers. Supervisors are put on notice that they may have a problem officer and, thus, are more responsible if nothing is done and the officer engages in serious forms of misconduct.

"ROTTEN BARREL" RESPONSES

internal affairs model A review procedure in which police investigators receive and investigate complaints and resolve the investigations internally.

INTERNAL AFFAIRS MODEL In one sense, the internal affairs model is also a rotten apple approach to reducing corruption since the model provides the mechanism whereby the department investigates and punishes the miscreant officer. One could also, however, see the internal affairs model as a rotten barrel approach in that if a department did not have an internal affairs function or it was widely seen as toothless, then the message to individual officers would be that the department did not care about wrongdoing. Unfortunately, the internal affairs model has been widely seen as ineffective. In one Toronto study, 70 percent of those who filed complaints were not confident with the process, and only 14 percent thought their complaint was handled fairly (Prenzler and Ronken, 2001b: 180). There is no research that evaluates the actual effectiveness of internal affair models (Walker, 2007), only news reports of citizen dissatisfaction.

The New York Police Department Internal Affairs Bureau was completely revamped in 1993 after a scandal prompted then-Commissioner Raymond Kelly to overhaul the department. Since then, internal affairs has generated an annual report, albeit going from 81 pages in 1993 to only 15 pages in 2007 and 2008. The annual reports, released via a Freedom of Information request by the ACLU, chronicle the changes that have taken place over the last 17 years. Critics contend that the bureau has drastically reduced the number of cases it investigates, even though tips have tripled since 1992, and has become more secretive about corruption, as contrasted with the years following 1993. NYPD officials point out that the budget for IA has increased from $43 million in 2000 to $61.8 million in 2010 and there are 650 officers who investigate wrongdoing (Baker and McGinty, 2010).

Some departments have enlarged the mission of internal anti-corruption units. These units, especially in other countries, now undertake a mission of not only investigation and punishment but also deterrence and prevention. Such units may undertake integrity testing, promote awareness, improve selection and screening procedures, develop performance standards, and in other ways "police" the police to minimize corruption (Moran, 2005). This may represent the future of internal anti-corruption models.

CIVILIAN REVIEW/COMPLAINT BOARDS There is a continuing belief that some police departments have proven they are incapable of internal policing and that what is needed is some outside oversight. Civilian review boards have been created in several cities to monitor and review the investigation and discipline of officers who have complaints filed against them. Many models exist under the name of civilian review, and no one model has been reported to be more effective or better than any other. Prenzler and Ronken (2001b) argue that it is difficult to analyze the success of such bodies because a high level of complaints may mean that there is greater trust in the process, not necessarily an increase in misconduct.

civilian review/ complaint model
The use of an outside agency or board that includes citizens and monitors and investigates misconduct complaints against police.

In the **civilian review/complaint model**, an independent civilian agency audits complaints and investigations. The board may also respond to appeals and act in an advisory role in investigations. Police still investigate and conduct the discipline proceeding. The Police Complaints Authority in the United Kingdom is one example of this model. Other models may involve an external board, but without any powers of subpoena or oversight (Prenzler and Ronken, 2001b).

Walker (2001) reviewed the range of civilian review models, but did not find that any one model seemed to be better than any other. Worrall (2002) found that cities with civilian review procedures received more citizen complaints. This was a consequence of having a process that made it easier for citizens to complain rather than more incidents of police misconduct. Prenzler and Ronken (2001b) reported that external review models have about the same substantiation rate as do internal affairs models—about 10 percent of all complaints filed. The major criticism of such models centers on the idea that they are not truly independent, for police still conduct the investigations and sometimes even sit on the board. Prenzler (2000) argues that the "capture" theory is operative in civilian review models. This occurs when the regulatory or investigative body is "co-opted" by the investigated agency through informal relationships.

CHANGING THE CULTURE If the police culture influences the level of police misconduct, it is important to change it. Harris (2005) discusses the difficulty of changing an entrenched negative police culture, but offers examples of how it can be done. He argues that in successful change efforts, the department has reconceptualized its mission, developed measurements of what matters most, improved recruiting, changed training to emphasize human rights at least as much as crime fighting, and changed the incentive and reward structure to encourage service-oriented policing as much as crime control. He argues that change occurs as generations of new police officers take over who have been socialized to the new mission.

in the **NEWS**

NEW YORK'S CIVILIAN COMPLAINT REVIEW BOARD

Recent articles indicate that many believe that New York's civilian review board is in need of reform. The board was established in 1992 in response to a widespread belief that the police department could not adequately respond to civilian complaints. In 2009, there were about 8,200 complaints, but the number of complaints acted upon by the police has declined. In 2005, the police department declined to prosecute 2 percent of the cases referred by the civilian review board, but in 2008, 33 percent were declined, and in 2009, about 40 percent were declined. In response, the department points out that the conviction rate has increased from 30 to 60 percent, indicating that the decision to prosecute is based on which cases will lead to success. The ability of the board to respond to civilian complaints is further compromised by budget shortfalls. In the last two years, 26 investigators have been let go and the board's director projects that they will have to drop more than half their cases because of missing the 18-month deadline for investigation.

SOURCE: Hauser, 2009.

ETHICAL LEADERSHIP Hunter (1999) surveyed police officers in Florida and found that officers believed that strict and fair discipline was the best response and deterrent to misconduct. The officers also identified clear policies and peer review boards. It was clear that, according to officers, leadership had everything to do with an ethical police force; 95 percent believed that supervisors should be moral examples, and 70 percent that unethical supervisors contributed to the problem. However, less than half (42 percent) agreed with the idea of a citizen review board.

Crank (1998: 187) and others have noted that there is a pervasive sense among rank-and-file police that administrators are not to be trusted: "Officers protect each other, not only against the public, but against police administrators frequently seen to be capricious and out of touch." The classic work in this regard is Reuss-Ianni's (1983) study of a New York City precinct in the late 1970s. She described the "two cultures" of policing—street cops and management cops. She observed that law enforcement managers were classic bureaucrats who made decisions based on modern management principles. This contrasted with the street-cop subculture, which still had remnants of quasi-familial relationships in which "loyalties and commitments took precedence over the rule book" (1983: 4). The result of this conflict between the two value systems was alienation of the street cop.

Despite the gulf between management and line staff, most people agree that employee behavior is influenced more directly by the behavior of superiors than by the stated directives or ethics of the organization. Executives engaged in price fixing and overcharging should not be surprised that their employees steal company supplies or time. Managers cannot espouse ethical ideals, act unethically, and then expect employees to act ethically. Thus, regardless of formal ethical codes, police are influenced by the standards of behavior they observe in their superiors. One might note that most large-scale police corruption that has been exposed has implicated very high level officials. Alternatively, police departments that have remained relatively free of corruption have administrators who practice ethical behavior on a day-to-day basis.

Research reveals that close supervision, especially by mid-level managers such as sergeants, reduces the use of force and incidents of misconduct by officers (Walker, 2007). Other research indicates that role modeling seems to be significant in limiting unethical conduct of an interpersonal nature (sexual harassment, discrimination, bullying), while strictness in supervision seems to be more important in controlling the misuse of resources, fraud, and other forms of financial corruption. A third component of leadership was described as openness and refers to leaders encouraging subordinates to talk to them about ethical dilemmas. This was associated with fewer violations in a number of areas, especially in favoritism and discrimination. Interestingly, this study of more than 6,000 police officers found that strictness had no effect on reducing the gratuitous use of violence, but that role modeling and openness did (Huberts, Kaptein, and Lasthuizen, 2007).

Administrators face their own unique ethical dilemmas. Budget allocations, the use of drug testing, affirmative action, sexual harassment, and decisions about corrupt officers all present ethical dilemmas for administrators and supervisors. For instance, some supervisors face problems when they are promoted from the ranks and have friends who become their subordinates. Such friends may expect special consideration, leaving the supervisor to decide how to respond. Supervisors also report ethical dilemmas about how they should allocate resources, such as a new patrol car or overtime. Should seniority take precedence over competence? Should friendship take precedence over seniority?

Another issue is what should be done with officers who have drug or alcohol problems. If the administrator decides to counsel or suggest treatment without any change in duty status, and the officer endangers the life of someone or actually harms a citizen or other officer because of the problem, is the administrator to blame? In many situations where police leaders must make decisions, lives, property, or liberty can be at stake.

It is extremely important for supervisors and administrators to understand the impact that their decisions and their behavior have on everyone in the organization.

Even if leaders are not directly involved in corruption, encouraging or participating in the harassment and ostracism directed at those who expose wrongdoers supports an organizational culture that punishes whistleblowers. In some departments, there is a perception that favored cliques are not punished for behaviors for which others would receive punishment. This climate destroys the trust in police leadership that is essential to ensure good communication from the rank and file.

It seems that in some departments management is just as likely as peer officers to cover up wrongdoing of officers. Only when the scandal cannot be contained does management "throw officers to the wolves." Unless there is a scandal, corruption is swept under the rug and individual offending officers may receive little or no discipline. For instance, Crank and Caldero (2000: 114) reported that in 100 civil lawsuits in 22 states between 1986 and 1991, the awards paid out by cities and police departments totaled $92 million, but of the 185 officers involved, only 8 were disciplined. In fact, 17 were promoted.

Two case studies, one in New York and another in Los Angeles, illustrate the problem when administrators attempt to cover up wrongdoing by individual officers. In both of these cases, the investigator who attempted to identify and expose corruption was met with resistance from the administration (Rothlein, 1999; Glover and Lait, 2000; Lait and Glover, 2000; Jablon, 2000; Sterngold, 2000; Deutsch, 2001; Golab, 2000).

NEW YORK

THE INVESTIGATOR Sgt. John Tromboli was stymied in his attempt to investigate and expose the actions of Michael Dowd, an obviously crooked cop whose lifestyle far exceeded a cop's pay. For five years, Tromboli had been trying to get enough evidence on Dowd to file charges, but was routinely turned down by his superiors for extra resources and for permission for wiretaps and other means of investigation. Tromboli believed that his superiors were trying to shut down his investigation. Dowd was finally arrested by Suffolk County police when he was videotaped conducting narcotics transactions in uniform and in a police car. Internal affairs routinely did not share information with the prosecutor's office on crooked cops. Instead, information on corrupt officers would be hidden in a "tickler file" that was never made public.

THE SCANDAL The Mollen Commission in New York was formed in 1992 by Mayor David Dinkins to investigate allegations of corruption. The practices of Dowd and a number of other officers were exposed, including drug dealing, theft from corpses, robberies of drug dealers, setting up rival drug dealers for arrest and prosecution, protection rackets, and other misconduct. In the highly publicized hearings, officers were pressured to testify against others, and indictments and punishments were handed down. The hearings prompted Judge Milton Mollen to comment that the Knapp Commission found that officers were in league with criminals, but that, today, officers have become the criminals themselves.

LOS ANGELES

THE INVESTIGATOR Detective Russell Poole, a Robbery-Homicide Division investigator, uncovered a pattern of complaints of violence by the anti-gang task force in the Ramparts Division when investigating an alleged beating of a gang member in a police squad room (his story was also described in Chapter 2). He concluded that a number of the officers in the division were "vigilante cops" and requested that the investigation proceed further, but Chief Bernard Parks ordered him to limit his investigation solely to the Jimenez beating.

His superiors replaced a 40-page report he had prepared for the prosecutor's office with a 2-page report that did not give any information about the possibility that there might be a pattern of corruption on the part of Ramparts officers. A year later, the Ramparts scandal exploded. Poole quit the force.

THE SCANDAL

The Ramparts scandal refers to the public disclosure of a wide range of corrupt activities by an anti-gang unit task force in the Ramparts Division of the LAPD (CRASH, Community Resources Against Street Hoodlums). Investigators from the prosecutor's office discovered the pattern of corruption when they made a deal with Rafael Perez, a Ramparts officer who had stolen cocaine from the evidence room. The scandal eventually led to dozens of criminal cases being voided because the prosecutor's office could not depend on the truthfulness of officers' testimony. Evidence indicated that between 1995 and 1998 the officers lied, planted evidence, beat suspects, and shot unarmed suspects. Officers also evidently held parties to celebrate shootings, gave out plaques when one killed a gang member, and spread ketchup at a crime scene to imitate blood.

Hundreds of cases had to be reviewed by the staff in the prosecutor's office to evaluate whether there was a possibility of manufactured evidence. At least one gang member's conviction was overturned when Rafael Perez, the officer who implicated all the others, confessed under oath that they had shot the man and then planted a gun on him and testified that he had shot at them first. The suspect has been released from prison, but is paralyzed and in a wheelchair.

Some evidence indicates at least 99 people were framed by Ramparts officers. Prosecutors were also quoted in the paper as saying, "You can't trust the LAPD anymore." Mayor Richard Riordan reported to the press that the city would have to use $100 million from tobacco settlements to cover anticipated lawsuits. Eleven officers were fired, and 40 convictions were overturned.

The LAPD responded with an internal management audit that admitted to a lapse of supervision and oversight. The report concluded that the corruption was caused by a few individuals whose wrongdoing had a "contagion effect." This report (conducted just eight years after the Christopher Commission presented a scathing commentary concerning the management and ethos of the LAPD) recommended an outside civilian oversight committee. The LAPD came under a federal court monitor because of the scandal, although it has since been released from the consent decree. Lawsuits against the city and the officers involved are still going on. In 2009, there were still over 50 federal lawsuits pending (Associated Press, 2009d).

These case studies provide an interesting lesson in that evidently the attempts to cover up scandals are often unsuccessful and, arguably, only make the situation worse when the corruption is inevitably exposed. In order to combat police corruption, it seems clear that the key is to have leadership that is not afraid to expose the "skeletons in the closet" and deal with problems openly without attempting to hide them from the public.

CONCLUSION

In this chapter, we reviewed the range of deviant behaviors in law enforcement. It was also noted that police scandals have occurred in all countries around the world, but that there are apparent differences in the relative levels of corruption among police in different countries. Reasons for law enforcement deviance can be categorized into individual explanations, organizational explanations, and societal explanations. We also examined a wide range of suggestions for combating police corruption, including education and training, early warning systems, integrity testing, and other methods.

CHAPTER REVIEW

1. Describe the types of police corruption.

The Knapp Commission identified grass eaters (police who passively take advantage of opportunities) and meat eaters (police who actively commit crimes). Fyfe and Kane identified the following: *police crimes*, where officers use their position to commit crimes, or commit crimes in their off-duty time; *police corruption*, where the officer uses his or her position, by act or omission, to obtain improper financial benefit; and *abuse of power*, actions where officers physically injure a citizen or offend a citizen's sense of dignity.

2. Describe the ethical arguments for and against gratuities.

Arguments for gratuities are that they are harmless or honest rewards, they build community relations, they give businesses police protection, they are no different from the perks of other occupations, and they compensate police for poor pay. Arguments against gratuities are that they demean the status of police as professionals, are incipient corruptors because people expect different treatment and create a sense of entitlement, can be the beginning of more serious forms of corruption, are contrary to democratic ideals because they require taxpayers to pay again for services that should be free, and create a public perception that police are corrupt.

3. Explain and give examples of graft and other forms of police corruption.

Graft is any type of abuse of one's position for personal gain. Corruption involves using the position for financial benefit, such as bribes, protection rackets, or accepting kickbacks (these can also be crimes).

4. Provide the three types of explanations of police misconduct, with examples of each.

Individual explanations target the individual officer, such as identifying personality characteristics that predict either misconduct or successful performance of the job. Organizational explanations look at factors that encourage or support misconduct, such as the police subculture or an ineffective discipline system. Societal explanations focus on what messages society sends to their police department that might encourage lawlessness.

5. Describe the ways to reduce corruption and misconduct.

Suggestions to reduce corruption either target the individual: improved screening and psychological testing, training, integrity testing, or early warning systems; or they target the organization: internal affairs units, civilian review boards, changing the culture, or improving the leadership.

KEY TERMS

civilian review/complaint
  model
graft

gratuities
integrity testing
internal affairs model

rotten-apple argument

STUDY QUESTIONS

1. What countries score high in integrity according to Transparency International? Provide some examples of worldwide police corruption.
2. List and describe Kane and Fyfe's types of police corruption.
3. What are the arguments for and against the acceptance of gratuities?
4. List and describe the three types of explanations for police deviance.
5. List the methods suggested by the Wood Commission for reducing police corruption.

WRITING/DISCUSSION EXERCISES

1. Write an essay on (or discuss) gratuities. Prove a persuasive argument as to whether or not gratuities should be acceptable. If you are arguing that they are ethical and should be acceptable, discuss what limits, if any, should be placed upon them.
2. Write an essay on (or discuss) the potential disciplinary sanctions that should be taken against officers who commit legal, policy, and/ or ethical transgressions. What is the rationale for the administration of punishment? Which acts warrant more severe sanctions? What should be done with an officer who has a drinking or drug problem? Taking a bribe? Stealing from a crime scene? Hitting a handcuffed suspect? Having checks bounce? Being disrespectful to a member of a minority group? Sexually harassing a co-worker?
3. Write an essay on (or discuss) the best methods to reduce noble-cause corruption among officers. Are they the same methods as those that should be used to reduce egoistic corruption for pecuniary gain? Explain why or why not. Also explain why you think the selected methods would work.

ETHICAL DILEMMAS

Situation 1

You are a rookie police officer on your first patrol. The older, experienced officer tells you that the restaurant on the corner likes to have you guys around, so it gives free meals. Your partner orders steak, potatoes, and all the trimmings. What are you going to do? What if it were just coffee at a convenience store? What if the owner refused to take your money at the cash register?

Situation 2

There is an officer in your division known as a "rat" because he testified against his partner in a criminal trial and a civil suit. The partner evidently hit a handcuffed suspect in the head several times in anger, and the man sustained brain injuries and is now a paraplegic. Although none of the officers you know supports the excessive use of force, they are also appalled that this officer did not back up his partner's testimony that the suspect continued to struggle, in an attempt to justify his use of force. After all, punishing the officer wasn't going to make the victim any better. Now no one will ride with this guy, and no one responds to his calls for backup. There have been incidents such as a dead rat being placed in his locker, and the extra uniform in his locker was set on fire.

One day you are parking your car and see your buddies in the employee parking lot moving away from his car; they admit they just slashed his tires. Each officer is being called into the captain's office to state whether he or she knows anything about this latest incident. Your turn is coming. What are you going to do?

Situation 3

You are a waitress (or waiter) in an all-night diner and are not too happy about pulling the midnight shift. Every evening, luckily, police officers drift in for their coffee breaks. You have been told that the diner does not offer gratuities and that you are not to give free coffee or meals to anyone, including police officers. But it's 2:00 a.m., and there are a lot of scary people out there. You figure that the pot of coffee might cost only a couple of bucks, so it's worth it to keep officers coming in. You suspect that the owner of the diner wouldn't be happy (because he doesn't like police), but he's not here, so you fall into the habit of giving all the officers free coffee. Then it escalates to free pie (it was going to be thrown out anyway), and now when no one is around, you'll let the officers go without paying for their meal. Do you see a problem with your actions? Who should make the decision—the owner or the employee who is on site? If you were to stop giving free coffee and pie, do you think the officers would stop coming in?

Situation 4

You are a police officer testifying in a drug case. You have already testified that you engaged in a buy-bust operation, and the defendant was identified by an undercover officer as the one who sold him a small quantity of drugs. You testified that you chased the suspect down an alley and apprehended him. Immediately before you caught up with him, he threw down a number of glassine envelopes filled with what turned out to be cocaine. The prosecutor finished his direct examination, and now the defense attorney has begun cross-examining you. He asked if you had the suspect in your sight the entire time between when you identified him as the one who sold to the undercover officer and when you put the handcuffs on him. Your arrest report didn't mention it, but for a couple of seconds you slipped as you went around the corner of the alley and fell down. During that short time, the suspect had proceeded a considerable distance down the alley.

You do not think there was anyone else around, and you are as sure as you possibly can be that it was your suspect who dropped the bags, but you know that if you testify to this incident truthfully, the defense attorney might be able to argue successfully that the bags were not dropped by the suspect and get him acquitted of the much more serious charge of possession with intent to distribute. What should you do?

Situation 5

You (a female police officer) have been working in a small-town police department for about six months. During that time you have been dealing with a fellow police officer who persists in making comments about how pretty you are, how you don't look like a police officer, how you shouldn't be dealing with the "garbage" out on the streets, and so on. He has asked you out more than a dozen times even though you have told him every time that you are not interested and that you want him to stop asking you out and to stop making comments. Although he hasn't made any derogatory or offensive comments, his constant attention is beginning to make you not want to go to work. You have a romantic partner, and you are definitely not interested in your fellow officer. You have mentioned it to your FTO, who is a sort of father figure, but he likes the guy and tells you that you should be flattered. You want to file a sexual harassment charge against him but hesitate because, although you do feel harassed, you don't feel especially threatened; further, you know that you would encounter negative reactions from the other officers in the department. What should you do?

PART III

Law

8

Mark Wilson/Getty Images

Law and Legal Professionals

Chapter Objectives

1. Understand the justifications for law, including protections against harm to others, offensive conduct, harm to self, and harm to societal morals.

2. Explain the role of law in society and the paradigms that have developed to understand how law is formed and enforced.

3. Compare the idea of our criminal law system as an adversarial system to other descriptions of how the courtroom works and the relationships between the legal professionals.

4. Present the controversy concerning the role of advocate as legal agent or moral agent.

5. Describe the history and source of legal ethics for attorneys and judges. Explain the types of ethical rules that exist and compare them to the subculture of winning.

In the Walking the Walk selection for this chapter, Charles Swift's commitment to the law and to his professional obligations as an attorney in the Navy is described. Swift was the JAG officer who defended Salim Ahmed Hamdan and won a Supreme Court case against the federal government, which took the position that Guantanamo detainees could be held indefinitely with no due process.

"We are a nation of laws, not of men" is a phrase meaning that once a law is duly enacted, it applies to all of us. Once a legal right is recognized, it cannot be denied to anyone. As we discussed in Chapter 3, law can be considered the administration of justice. Civil law is the administration of commutative (or rectifactory) justice, and criminal law is the administration of corrective justice. Law recognizes and enforces the rights of the individual against the state, and the rights of each party in conflicts between individuals. It also controls the behavior of the individual in all aspects of life, from driving to how to raise one's child.

In this chapter and the next two chapters, we will discuss the ethics of legal professionals. Even though all professionals in the criminal justice system adhere to the law and the law defines their duties, this is even truer for defense lawyers, prosecutors, judges, and other legal professionals. These three chapters on legal professionals are set up in a similar

WALKING THE WALK

Charles Swift is from a small town in North Carolina. He entered the United States Naval Academy in 1980 and served seven years as a surface-warfare officer. He graduated from Seattle University School of Law in 1994 and returned to active duty as a member of the Judge Advocate General's Corps (JAG). In March 2003, he was assigned to the defense counsel's team for the Office of Military Commissions, set up to provide a unique form of due process for Guantanamo detainees. Lt. Commander Swift was assigned to defend Salim Ahmed Hamdan, a Yemeni who at one time had been Osama Bin Laden's driver.

One of the first things Swift was told in the case was that he could have access to his client only on the condition that he attempt to negotiate a guilty plea from him. When Swift decided that it was clear that there was no real due process in the so-called military commissions process, as it did not follow the Uniform Code of Military Justice, the Geneva Conventions, or any rule of law recognized in 250 years of United States jurisprudence, he sued his chain of command, including the commander in chief, President George W. Bush. Swift says:

> [In most countries] ... when a military officer openly opposes the president, it is called a coup. In the United States, it is called *Hamdan v. Rumsfeld*. After the Supreme Court's decision ..., the world was rightly in awe of our system. ... [W]e proved once again that we are a nation of laws and not of men.

Swift's exhaustive and fearless defense of Hamdan, a defense that basically challenged the military commissions as constructed by the Bush administration, resulted in the Supreme Court ruling 5–3 that the president had exceeded his power in ignoring the Geneva Conventions, the Uniform Code of Military Justice, and Congress in creating the tribunals. In an irony that was not lost on any observer, Swift was passed over for promotion and was forced to retire from his beloved Navy shortly after the Supreme Court decision was handed down. His superiors said they had submitted exemplary reports on his performance, but that promotions are granted for "breadth," not just "depth," and therefore, even though he was a brilliant lawyer, he would not be rewarded with a promotion.

Because of the Navy's up-or-out promotional policies, Swift had to leave the Navy at the age of 44 and was not around for further developments, such as the Military Commissions Act of 2006, when Congress put the military commissions back in play by providing the legal imprimatur for them. In June 2007, the Supreme Court refused to hear two court challenges to the congressional act's military commissions, but then reversed its decision and heard *Boumediene v. Bush* (553 US 723 [2008]). Their final ruling was that the military commissions, without any habeas corpus protection, did not meet minimum due process requirements and were therefore unconstitutional. Since then, however, President Obama has indicated that military commissions will be revised to remedy the due process concerns of the Court.

Would Swift do it differently if he had it to do over? He says, "If we are to be a great nation, then we must be willing to be a nation bound by the rule of law in our treatment of all people." He isn't finished defending the laws of this country. He continues to oppose the military commissions, arguing that there was no reason for their creation other than to be able to use evidence obtained by the use of torture in Guantanamo and other locations. He argues that officials knew that information obtained through the use of torture would be ruled unacceptable in a military or civilian court.

Today, Swift is a visiting associate professor and acting director of the International Humanitarian Law Clinic at Emory University, providing legal assistance to those involved in humanitarian law, including military tribunals. He was honored with the Medal of Liberty by the American Civil Liberties Union and named by the *National Law Journal* as one of the most influential lawyers in the country.

Sources: Swift, 2007; Shukovsky, 2006.

way as the three chapters on law enforcement. In this first chapter, we will examine some basic issues concerning the role of the law in society and the relationships between legal professionals. We also will present the ethical codes that guide legal professionals' actions and subcultural elements that may be contrary to formal ethics. Then, in Chapter 9, we will examine the discretion of legal professionals and how such discretion creates ethical dilemmas. Finally, in Chapter 10, we will examine cases of misconduct and corruption and discuss measures that may improve the integrity of the legal field.

The Role of Law

laws Formal, written rules of society.

natural law The idea that principles of morals and rights are inherent in nature and not human-made; such laws are discovered by reason but exist apart from humankind.

positivist law Human-made law.

Our **laws** serve as the written embodiment of society's ethics and morals. Laws are said to be declarative as well as active; they declare correct behavior and serve as a tool for enforcement. While **natural law** refers to the belief that some law is inherent in the natural world and can be discovered by reason, **positivist law** refers to those laws written and enforced by society. This type of law is of human construction and, therefore, fallible (Mackie, 1977: 232).

We can trace the history of law back to very early codes, such as the Code of Hammurabi (ca. 2000 BCE), which mixed secular and religious proscriptions of behavior. These codes also standardized punishments and atonements for wrongdoing. Early codes of law did not differentiate between what we might call public wrongs and private wrongs. As mentioned, two different areas of law can be distinguished today: criminal law, which is punitive, and, civil law, which is reparative (or restitutive). The first punishes, whereas the second seeks to redress wrong or loss. Of the two, criminal law is more closely associated with enforcing the moral standards of society, yet it is by no means comprehensive in its coverage of behavior.

Laws, in the form of statutes and ordinances, tell us how to drive, how to operate our business, and what we can and cannot do in public and even in private. They are the formal, written rules of society. Yet, they are not comprehensive in defining moral behavior. There is a law against hitting one's mother (assault) but no law against financially abandoning her, yet both are considered morally wrong. We have laws against bad behavior, such as burglarizing a house or embezzling from our employer, but we have few laws prescribing good behavior, such as helping a victim or contributing to a charity. The exception to this consists of **Good Samaritan laws**, which are common in Europe. These laws

Good Samaritan laws Legislation that prohibits passing by an accident scene or witnessing a crime without rendering assistance.

make it a crime to pass by an accident scene or witness a crime without rendering assistance. Some states do have laws called Good Samaritan laws, but they are civil and protect medical professionals who stop at an accident scene and administer aid to the victims and then are sued for their actions under negligence or some other cause of action. These laws provide some level of immunity to those who stop and render aid, but they do not require helping as the Good Samaritan laws in Europe do.

Law can be seen as a tool of social engineering and a way of changing behavior to a desired state (Hornum and Stavish, 1978: 148). Law may influence behavior directly by prohibiting or mandating certain behavior, or indirectly by affecting social institutions such as family or education that, in turn, influence behavior (Dror, 1969: 93). Thus, law controls behavior by providing sanctions but also, perhaps even more important, by teaching people which behaviors are acceptable and which behaviors are not. Thus, academics argue whether, for instance, *Brown v. Board of Education* (347 U.S. 483 [1954]) came after a shift in people's values and attitudes toward segregation, or whether the legal holding that ruled segregation as illegal was the change agent in transforming values and attitudes. Probably both statements are true. There is no doubt that there is a dynamic between the law and public opinion and the power of law is most noticeable "at the margins" where it heralds social change or, to the contrary, acts as a resistant force to evolving belief systems. Consider the issue of immigration law—today, there is much controversy over whether states should pass and enforce their own immigration laws or leave the issue to the federal government. The Policy Box illustrates that law is often controversial and that law and policy are not necessarily consistent.

POLICY ISSUES · Are You a Citizen?

There is controversy across the nation regarding the proper role of local law enforcement in enforcing immigration law and the role of state versus federal law. Some police departments argue that it is not their role to enforce federal immigration law, and they do not ask witnesses, victims, or even suspects their immigration status. Other departments follow a policy that their role is to enforce the law—federal as well as state and local. Critics argue that if police officers become enforcers for Immigration and Customs Enforcement (ICE), witnesses to crimes will not come forward, victims will not receive help, and illegal immigrants will become easy prey for predators. Arizona has recently intensified this debate by passing a state law that requires officers to ask individuals suspected of a wide range of infractions about their immigration status if there is reasonable cause to believe that they are illegal aliens. Those with some form of immigration status are required to carry their papers.

Law

Immigration laws have, until recently, been solely federal laws since protection of the border is a federal role. As mentioned above, in the spring of 2010, Arizona passed an immigration law that received a huge amount of attention since it was the first time that a state has mandated that individuals carry their papers with them. Polls taken show that a majority of the public support such a law, but critics argue that it will lead to racial profiling and is a violation of constitutional rights since those of Hispanic heritage may be asked to prove their citizenship if they have an interaction with a police officer. In July 2010, a U.S. federal district judge issued a preliminary injunction blocking the portions of the Arizona law that were most controversial, including the requirement that police officers check the immigration status of those they reasonably suspected of being illegal aliens, the provision that required individuals to carry their

immigration papers with them, and the warrantless arrest of those who could not prove their immigration status satisfactorily. This ruling was based on the finding that legal residents would have their liberty unreasonably curtailed while their status was checked and that the state law usurped federal jurisdiction. The ruling blocked enforcement of these portions of the Arizona law until an appeal is completed. Observers believe the case will end up in the Supreme Court before a final ruling.

Policy

Policy considerations can be examined at the state and local level. Some cities declare openly that they will not be agents for ICE, and federal officials have threatened to cut off federal funds for law enforcement. A compromise policy used by some agencies is to check the immigration status of those who are arrested but not those with whom they come into contact as witnesses or victims. In Arizona, proponents of the law argue that it is not going to create an "open season" on citizens or legal residents and the policy will be strictly enforced so that racial profiling will not occur. Critics argue that racial profiling will be inevitable since whites' citizenship status will not be questioned.

Individual Ethics

Legislators struggle over whether to vote in favor of immigration laws. City officials ponder how to respond to opposing constituencies. Laws and policies may be put in place after due consideration, but the individual officer is still left with the decision to ask the person who reports a crime or the assault victim, "Are you a citizen?" The problem of illegal immigration is extremely controversial, and both sides have legitimate arguments, however, most of us will never be faced with an ethical dilemma concerning the topic—unless we happen to be a police officer, judge, or legislator.

Just as important as a tool of behavior control and change, the law provides a blanket of protection for individuals against the awesome power of the state. We cherish our Constitution and the Bill of Rights because we understand that in those countries that do not have our legal traditions, citizens have no protection against tyranny and oppression. We know that our bedrock of rights set down by our founding fathers ensures, to some extent, that even if government officials wanted to do us harm or treat us in a way that offends the concept of due process, they could not do so without violating the law. Thus, the law is our social contract. It dictates limits on our own behavior, but also provides protection against governmental violations. Legal professionals ensure that this contract is enforced.

Justifications for Law

social contract theory The concept developed by Hobbes, Rousseau, and Locke in which the state of nature is a "war of all against all" and, thus, individuals give up their liberty to aggress against others in return for safety. The contract is between society, which promises protection, and the individual, who promises to abide by laws.

The major justification for corrective (criminal) law is prevention of harm. Under the **social contract theory**, law is a contract; each individual gives up some liberties and, in return, is protected from others who have their liberties restricted as well. Thomas Hobbes's (1588–1679) claim that self-preservation (the law of the jungle) is paramount, and John Locke's (1632–1704) view that property is a natural right created the foundation for the social contract theory. According to this theory, members of society were originally engaged in a "war of all against all" where

> ... every man is an enemy to every man ... [there is] continual fear and danger of violent death; and the life of man, solitary, poor, nasty, brutish, and short (Hobbes, 1651).

In this "contract," individuals give up the freedom to aggress against others in return for their own safety. According to Hobbes, each individual has chosen to "lay down this right to all things; and be contented with so much liberty against other men, as he would allow other men against himself" (1651). Hobbes said that in order to avoid this war of all against all, people needed to be assured that people will not harm one another and that they will keep their agreements. But how much liberty should be restricted, and what behaviors should be prohibited? Rough formulas or guidelines indicate that the law should interfere as little as possible in natural liberties and should step in only when the liberty in question injures or impinges on the interests of another.

PREVENTING HARM TO OTHERS

John Stuart Mill (1806–1873), proposed the "harm principle," which basically is the idea that every individual should have the utmost freedom over their own actions unless they harm others. In this view, the law would restrict only those actions that can or do cause harm to others, such as assault, attempted murder, or theft. Most of our criminal laws are created to punish individual harms. However, preventing harm to others is not the only justification for law. Others include preventing offense to others, preventing harm to self (paternalistic laws), and preventing harm to societal morals.

PREVENTING OFFENSIVE BEHAVIOR

There are some actions that do not exactly harm others, but give rise to disgust or offense. Such actions as public lewdness, disturbing public behavior, noise, or other actions that infringe on the quality of life of others can be the subject of laws, and individuals who flaunt such laws may be fined or punished in some way. These laws are sometimes controversial because there is an argument that no law should restrict an individual's behavior that may create inconvenience or disgust, but that does not damage others' interests. For instance, many cities control the population of homeless people and beggars by a variety of laws because their presence and their actions upset and frighten tourists and downtown workers. Some of these laws, such as vagrancy laws, have been overturned by the Supreme Court for unduly infringing on personal liberties (*Pappachristou v. Jacksonville*, 405 U.S. 157 [1972]), but others have been upheld, such as "no camping" ordinances to dissuade the homeless from congregating in a downtown area.

PREVENTING HARM TO SELF (LEGAL PATERNALISM)

legal paternalism
Refers to laws that protect individuals from hurting themselves.

Many laws can be described as examples of **legal paternalism**—laws in which the state tries to protect people from their own behavior. Examples include seat belt laws, motorcycle helmet laws, speed limits, drug laws, licensing laws, alcohol consumption and sale laws, smoking prohibitions, and laws limiting certain types of sexual behavior. The strict libertarian view would hold that the government has no business interfering in a person's decisions about these behaviors as long as they don't negatively affect others. The opposing view is that as long as a person is a member of society (and everyone is), he or she has a value to that society, and society is therefore compelled to protect the person with or without his or her cooperation.

It may also be true that there are no harmful or potentially harmful behaviors to oneself that do not also hurt others, however indirectly, so society is protecting others when it controls each individual. Speeding drivers may crash into someone else, drug addicts may commit crimes to support their habit, gamblers may neglect their families and cause expense to the state, and so on. You may remember that in Chapter 1 we limited moral judgments to behavior that influences another. The justification for paternalistic laws depends on the view that almost everything we do affects others.

Some believe that government can justify paternalism only with certain restrictions. These rules try to create a balance between an individual's liberty and government control (Thompson, 1980):

- The decision-making ability of the person may be somehow impaired, by lack of knowledge or competency. Examples are child labor laws and laws that restrict the sale of alcohol to children. In both cases, there is a presumption that children do not understand the dangers of such behavior and therefore need protection.

- The restriction should be as limited as possible. For example, driving-under-the-influence (DUI) laws define the point of legal intoxication as when one's ability to drive safely is impaired, not simply after any alcohol consumption at all. Laws exist that ban the sale of cigarettes to minors, but cigarettes are still available to adults—who supposedly have reached a level of maturity to understand the dangers associated with smoking.

- The laws should seek only to prevent a serious and irreversible error—DUI laws help to prevent fatal accidents, as do all other traffic laws, and so on.

Paternalistic laws can be supported by an ethics of care. Remember that in this framework, morality is viewed as integral to a system of relationships. The individual is seen as having ties to society and to every other member of society. Relationships involve responsibilities as well as rights. We can expect the minimum level of care necessary for survival from society under the ethics of care. However, the corollary is that society can also care for us by restricting harmful behaviors. Rights are less important in this framework; therefore, to ask whether society has a right to intervene or an individual has a right to a liberty is not relevant to the discussion. Utilitarianism would also support paternalistic laws because of the net utility to society that results from protecting each of its members.

Other ethical systems may not so clearly support paternalistic laws. Individual rights are perhaps more important under ethical formalism than the other ethical systems; individuals must be treated with respect and as ends in themselves. This view results in recognizing the rights of individuals to engage in careless or even harmful behavior as long as it is consistent with the universalism principle of the categorical imperative. In other words,

in the NEWS

SAME-SEX MARRIAGE BAN BLOCKED

In August 2010, a U.S. district judge ruled that the California ban of same-sex marriage as passed by voters in Proposition 8 was violative of the Fourteenth Amendment. Specifically, the federal judge ruled that the ban unfairly withheld basic rights of citizenship from a certain group (homosexuals) with no rational relationship to some important governmental interest. The ruling included a stay so that supporters of the ban could appeal the decision to the Ninth Circuit Court of Appeals. The case will, no doubt, eventually be heard by the Supreme Court.

people may have the moral right to engage in self-destructive or careless behavior as long as they do not hurt others. Of course, the opposing argument would be that all behaviors prohibited by paternalistic laws have the potential to affect others indirectly.

PREVENTING HARM TO SOCIETAL MORALS (LEGAL MORALISM)

legal moralism
A justification for law that allows for protection and enforcement of societal morals.

The law also acts as the moral agent of society, some say in areas where there is no moral agreement. This rationale is called **legal moralism**. Some sexual behaviors, gambling, drug use, pornography, and even suicide and euthanasia are defined as wrong and are prohibited. The laws against these behaviors may be based on principles of harm or paternalism, but they also exist to reinforce society's definitions of moral behavior. For example, consensual sexual behavior between adults arguably harms no one, yet the Georgia state law prohibiting sodomy was upheld by the U.S. Supreme Court in *Bowers v. Hardwick* (106 S.Ct. 2841 [1986]), although later effectively overturned in *Lawrence v. Texas* (539 U.S. 558 [2003]). More recently, there has been a great debate over whether the law ought to recognize and legitimize same-sex marriages, as the In the News box illustrates. The underlying justification that both sides employ is legal moralism.

Pornography (at least that involving consenting adults) that is defined as obscene is prohibited arguably because of moral standards, not harmful effect. Under the legal moralism rationale, obscenity is prohibited simply because it is wrong. The issue has become even more complicated with the increasing use of the Internet and the ease with which individuals may obtain pornographic materials from anywhere in the world. Privacy rights conflict with the government's right to enforce morality.

It should also be noted that whether an action is moral or immoral is a different question than whether there should be laws and governmental sanctions regarding the behavior. In some cases, individuals may agree that a particular action is immoral, but at the same time may not believe that the government should have any power to restrict an individual's choice. Some proponents of choice regarding abortion take great care to distinguish between pro-choice and pro-abortion. To them, one does not have to approve of abortion to believe that it is wrong for government to interfere in the private decision of the individual to use the procedure. Similarly, some who advocate decriminalization of drugs do so because of cost-effectiveness or libertarian reasons, not because they approve of drug use. We do not have a legal system that completely overlaps our moral code, and some would argue that it would be impossible in a society as heterogeneous as ours for this to occur.

Hate-crime legislation gives us another example of a law that might be rationalized under legal moralism, although it could also be supported by a harm principle. In challenges to hate-crime legislation, appellate courts have typically drawn a line between action and speech. That is, if a person commits an act that is already a crime, such as vandalism, assault, stalking, or harassment, and does so because of an expressed hatred for the victim's membership in a protected class, then the act can be punished as a hate crime. However, if the only act prohibited by the hate-crime legislation is speech, then the law violates the First Amendment's protection of free speech. Even though we abhor the message, we must protect the right of the person to express it, unless he or she also engages in a legal harm. The interesting question is why we think it necessary to create a new law instead of using the existing act-based law (such as vandalism). The reason might be that the true rationale for hate crime is legal moralism: we believe it is important to enforce our moral code that hating others because of their race or sexual orientation is wrong.

Some propose that only those actions that violate some universal standard of morality, as opposed to merely a conventional standard, should be criminalized. This "limited legal moralism" would prevent the situation of some groups forcing their moral code on others. Of course, this begs the question of what behaviors would meet this universal standard. Even child pornographers argue that their behavior is unfairly condemned by a conventional, rather than a universal, morality. The vast profits that are made by producing and distributing child pornography indicate that many people buy such products. Does this mean that it is simply a matter of choice and not some universal moral sense that should influence whether children should be seen as objects of sexual gratification? What would Immanuel Kant say about child pornography? What would Jeremy Bentham say about it?

In conclusion, we must allow for the possibility that some laws that are justified under legal moralism may not necessarily conform to our personal views of good and bad. Many criminal justice professionals also believe that some of the so-called gray areas of crime are not very serious, so it is not surprising that law enforcement professionals employ their discretion in enforcement. Police will ignore prostitution, for instance, until the public complains, and police may routinely let petty drug offenders go rather than take the trouble to arrest. Prosecutors may let gamblers go with a warning if no publicity is attached to the arrest. Decision makers in criminal justice use discretion in this way partly because these behaviors are not universally condemned. Consider, for instance, the argument that organized crime grew tremendously during Prohibition and that an unknown number of law enforcement officers, prosecutors, and judges accepted bribes or were involved in protection rackets. Some argue that the same scenario has occurred during the war on drugs. The rationalization of authorities who are inclined to accept protection money or bribes is that the offenders are engaged in providing a commodity that the public desires. Also, one might add that the state loses its moral authority to condemn when it engages in the same activity; for instance, it is hard to defend laws against gambling when there is a state lottery.

Paradigms of Law

Our understanding of the law's function in society is informed by more fundamental views of the world around us, called paradigms. Basically, paradigms are models of how ideas relate to one another, forming a conceptual model of the world around us. A paradigm helps us organize the vast array of knowledge that we absorb every day. We see the world and interpret facts in a way that is influenced by our paradigms—for example, if we have a paradigm that government is corrupt—everything we read and hear will be scanned for facts that fit our paradigm, and inconsistent or contrary facts will be ignored and/or forgotten. Paradigms aren't bad or good; they are simply a function of how the human mind works. Our paradigms can shift, of course, when we are confronted with overwhelming facts that come from trusted sources or personal experiences that are contrary to our paradigm.

The three paradigms that might affect our view of the law are:

consensus paradigm
The idea that most people have similar beliefs, values, and goals and that societal laws reflect the majority view.

conflict paradigm
The idea that groups in society have fundamental differences and that those in power control societal elements, including law.

- The **consensus paradigm**, which views society as a community consisting of like-minded individuals who agree on goals important for ultimate survival. This view is functionalist because it sees law as an aid to the growth and/or survival of society.

- The **conflict paradigm**, which views society as being made up of competing and conflicting interests. According to this view, governance is based on power; if some win, others lose, and those who hold power in society promote self-interest, not a greater good.

- The **pluralist paradigm** shares the perception that society is made up of competing interests; however, pluralism describes more than two basic interest groups and also recognizes that the power balance may shift when interest groups form or coalitions emerge. These power shifts occur as part of the dynamics of societal change.

THE CONSENSUS PARADIGM

pluralist paradigm
The concept that there are many groups in society and that they form allegiances and coalitions in a dynamic exchange of power.

mechanical solidarity
Durkheim's concept of societal solidarity as arising from similarities among society's members.

repressive law
Durkheim's view that law controls behavior that is different from the norm (related to mechanical solidarity).

organic solidarity
Durkheim's concept of societal solidarity as arising from differences among people, as exemplified by the division of labor

restitutive law
Durkheim's view that law resolves conflicts between equals, as in commutative justice (related to organic solidarity).

According to the consensus paradigm, law serves as a tool of unification. Emile Durkheim (1858–1917) wrote that there are two types of law: the *repressive*, criminal law, which enforces universal norms, and the *restitutive*, civil law, which developed because of the division of labor in society and resulting social interests. In Durkheim's view, criminal law exists as a manifestation of consensual norms: "We must not say that an action shocks the common conscience because it is criminal, but rather that it is criminal because it shocks the common conscience" (1969: 21). What this statement means is that we define an action as criminal because the majority of the populace holds the opinion that it is wrong. This common or collective conscience is referred to as **mechanical solidarity**. Each individual's moral beliefs are indistinguishable from the whole. The function of **repressive law** is the maintenance of social cohesion. Law contributes to the collective conscience by providing an example of deviance.

Although Durkheim recognized individual differences, he believed that these differences, resulting from the division of labor in society, only made the individual more dependent on society as a part of a whole. His concept of **organic solidarity** draws the analogy of individuals in society as parts of an organism—all doing different things, but as parts of a whole. Individuals exist, but they are tied inextricably to society and its common conscience. **Restitutive law** is said to mediate those differences that may come about because of the division of labor. Even here the law serves an integrative function.

The consensus view would point to evidence that people agree on, for the most part, what behaviors are wrong and the relative seriousness of different types of wrongful behavior. In criminology, the consensus view is represented by classical thinkers such as Jeremy Bentham and Cesare Beccaria, who relied on the accepted definitions of crime in their day without questioning the validity of these definitions, only their implementation. While the positivist school of criminology, which looked for the cause of crime in the individual, virtually ignored societal definitions of crime, Raffaele Garofalo (1852–1932), a legal anthropologist, believed in natural law. As defined earlier, natural law holds that certain behaviors are so inherently heinous that they go against nature; therefore, there are natural proscriptions against such behavior that transcend individual societies or time periods (Kramer, 1982: 36).

We have evidence that there is at least some consensus in people's definitions of what constitutes criminal behavior. Studies have shown that not only do individuals in Western culture tend to agree on the relative seriousness of different kinds of crime, but there is substantial agreement cross-culturally as well (Nettler, 1978: 215). In the consensus paradigm:

- *Law is representative.* It is a compilation of the do's and don'ts that we all agree on.
- *Law reinforces social cohesion.* It emphasizes our "we-ness" by illustrating deviance.
- *Law is value-neutral.* It resolves conflicts in an objective and neutral manner.

THE CONFLICT PARADIGM

A second paradigm of law and society is the conflict paradigm. Rather than perceiving law as representative, this perspective sees law as a tool of power holders that they use for their own purposes—to maintain and control the status quo. In the conflict paradigm, law is perceived as restrictive or repressive, rather than representative, and as an instrument of special interests.

Basically, the conflict paradigm has three parts (Sheley, 1985: 1):

1. Criminal definitions are relative.
2. Those who control major social institutions determine how crime is defined.
3. The definition of crime is fundamentally a tool of power.

Quinney (1974: 15–16) also discussed the conflict paradigm. He explained that in a capitalist society, the state is organized to serve the interests of the dominant economic power-holders, and criminal law is a tool of the state to do that.

Advocates of the conflict paradigm would point to laws against only certain types of gambling or against the use of only certain types of drugs as evidence that the ruling class punishes the activities of other classes more severely than their own activities. In other words, cultural differences in behavior exist, but only the activities of certain groups (the powerless) are labeled deviant. For instance, numbers running is always illegal, yet some states have legalized horseracing, dog racing, and/or casinos. Heroin and cocaine are illegal; Valium and alcohol are not. The Quote and Query box illustrates that the belief that law is used by the powerful against those without power is long-standing.

QUOTE & QUERY

Laws are just like spider's webs, they will hold the weak and delicate who might be caught in their meshes, but will be torn to pieces by the rich and powerful.

—SOURCE: ANACHARSIS, 600 BCE.

The more mandates and laws which are enacted, the more there will be thieves and robbers.

—SOURCE: LAO-TZE, 600 BCE.

What do these statements mean? Is it true that laws are manipulated by the powerful and oppress the weak?

The conflict theorist notes instances of how the law has been written differentially to serve the interests of the power holders. The definition of what is criminal often excludes corporate behavior, such as price fixing, toxic waste dumping, and monopolistic trade practices, because these behaviors, although just as harmful to the public as street crime, are engaged in by those who have the power to define criminality. The *regulation* of business, instead of the *criminalization* of harmful business practices, is seen as arising from the ability of those in powerful positions to redefine their activities to their own advantage.

The Quote and Query box presents a statement made by Jeffrey Reiman in 2004 in his radical critique of the criminal justice system. In the latest edition of his book *The Rich Get Richer and the Poor Get Prison*, he repeats the charge that safety violations are punished less severely than street crime even though they result in deaths (Reiman and Leighton, 2010: 59). Unfortunately, the statement continues to be true. In the spring of 2010, a deadly mine explosion resulted in the deaths of 29 men. In 2006, the same company, Massey Coal, was found to be negligent in an explosion that killed two men, and in the 18 months before the most recent explosion, there were 600 cited violations against the company. Federal prosecutors are investigating whether criminal negligence charges can be brought against the mining company officials (Yost, 2010). Conflict theorists would predict no charges or minimal sanctions, and in some future year we will still be reading about mining explosions or other tragedies because of corporate decisions that ignore safety regulations in the interest of expediency and profit.

QUOTE & QUERY

Why do 26 dead miners amount to a "disaster" and six dead suburbanites a "mass murder"? "Murder" suggests a murderer, and "disaster" suggests the work of impersonal forces. But if over 1,000 safety violations had been found in the mine—three the day before the first explosion—was no one responsible for failing to eliminate those hazards? And if someone could have prevented the hazards and did not, does that person not bear responsibility for the deaths of 26 men? Is he less evil because he did not want them to die, although he chose to leave them in jeopardy? Is he not a murderer, perhaps even a mass murderer?

—SOURCE: REIMAN, 1984: 23.

Do you think that employers who put their employees in harm's way should be prosecuted for manslaughter?

The Occupational Health and Safety Administration, the Food and Drug Administration, the Federal Aviation Administration, and other similar governmental agencies are charged with the task of enforcing regulations governing business activities in their respective areas; however, regulatory sanctions are not as stigmatizing or painful as criminal convictions. Critics also argue that the relationships between the watchdog agencies and those they watch are frequently incestuous: heads of business are often named to watchdog agencies, and employees of these agencies may move to the business sector they previously regulated. The latest example of this is the tragedy of the oil spill in the Gulf of Mexico. It is the worst oil spill in history, and some allege that it occurred because of oil company BP's focus on profit over safety. There are also allegations that the federal agency employees responsible for overseeing deep sea drilling and monitoring safety procedures accepted expensive trips and engaged in personal relationships with oil executives. No doubt the investigation will continue long after the total costs of the spill are computed. Conflict theorists will predict, however, that business will go on as usual after the public loses interest in the case.

In criminology, the conflict view was represented by early theorists such as Willem Bonger (1876–1940), a Marxist sociologist who explained that crime was caused by the economic power differential and that power holders labeled only others' behavior as criminal. During the 1970s, a small number of criminologists attempted to redefine criminals as political prisoners, based on their views that the state used criminal definitions to control minority groups (Reasons, 1973). Labeling theorists also questioned the criminal justice system's definitions by pointing out that only some offenders are formally labeled and treated as deviant.

Conflict theory is represented by theorists such as Anthony Platt, Julia and Herman Schwendinger, Barry Krisberg, Richard Quinney, Ian Taylor, Paul Walton, Jock Young, Walter Chambliss, and Jeffrey Reiman. Conflict theorists explain that the myth of justice and equality under the law serves to protect the interests of the ruling class, because as long as there is a perception of fairness, fundamental questions about the distribution of goods will not be raised (Krisberg, 1975). Law functions to depoliticize even the most obviously political actions of the oppressed by defining these actions as crime, but its greatest power is to hide the basic injustice of society itself. Reiman and Leighton (2010) present the conflict theorist's view that the definitions of law, as well as its enforcement, are fundamentally affected by power.

It is important to understand that our paradigms of law shape our interpretation of current events. The Los Angeles riots of 1992 were sparked by the acquittal of four police officers who were videotaped beating Rodney King, a motorist who had outstanding arrest warrants for traffic violations. The riots were described by some as political action by minorities who were frustrated by economic hopelessness and angered by the criminal justice system's oppressive and brutal treatment. Alternatively, others described the same actions as blatant and simple criminality. Conflict theorists would support the first definition, and consensus theorists would support the second. The looting and general lawlessness in New Orleans after Hurricane Katrina would be explained by conflict theorists through the prism of economic hopelessness and desperation. Further, they would point to other forms of lawlessness, such as price gouging, and no-bid contracts with large profits for the contractor, as just as heinous as looting and assault. Consensus theorists, on the other hand, would see the crimes as examples of individual deviance. Generally, in the conflict paradigm:

- *Law is repressive.* It oppresses the poor and powerless by differential definitions and/or enforcement.

- *Law is a tool of the powerful.* Those who write the laws do so in a way to promote their economic and political interests.

- *Law is not value-neutral.* It is biased and bent toward the interests of the powerful.

What is a just sentence for someone who engages in price fixing, insider trading, gouging, or other forms of corporate crime? What is a fair punishment for someone who dumps toxic waste because it is too expensive to dispose of properly and a community suffers high rates of cancer because of it? The White Collar Crime box reminds us of some past and recent white collar crime offenders.

THE PLURALIST PARADIGM

Distinct from the conflict paradigm is the pluralist paradigm. In this view, law is seen as arising from interest groups, but power is more complicated than the bifurcated system described by the Marxist tradition. Power is exercised in the political order, the economic

White Collar Crime: Crime or Bad Business?

Conflict theorists argue that those with economic power also have political and social power. They write the laws to benefit themselves, and, if caught and prosecuted, inevitably end up spending much less time in prison for their crimes. Some of the white collar crime examples below lend weight to these assertions.

Ford Firestorm

In 2001, the public discovered that the Firestone tires installed on the Ford Explorer were vulnerable to blowing out in high temperatures at a high rate of speed, causing rollovers. More than 100 fatal accidents were tied to tire blowouts. When this fact came to light, the media also reported that both the tire company and Ford Motor Company knew about the tires' weakness and continued to use the tires on new Explorers. Angry consumers were even more enraged when they discovered that Ford had voluntarily replaced the tires and stopped using them on Ford vehicles sold overseas, but not in the United States. Ford eventually replaced 13 million tires at a reputed cost of $3 billion. A costly lesson, surely. But the financial loss was less costly than going to prison for knowingly exposing an unsuspecting public to a preventable risk. The case was similar to the infamous Ford Pinto case back in the 1970s, when it was discovered that there had been corporate knowledge that the gas tank was vulnerable to explosions, but a decision been made that it was less costly to defend wrongful death suits than it would be to reengineer the automobile. Ford executives were charged with negligent manslaughter, but they were ultimately acquitted of criminal wrongdoing.

Toyota Troubles

In 2009–2010, Toyota was in the news and became the topic of stand-up comedy routines when it became known that there were design flaws that led to unacceptable numbers of vehicles that had uncontrolled acceleration and/or lack of braking. Some accidents, and even deaths, have been attributed to the mechanical problems of many models of the Toyota brand. What is even more troubling is that it became clear that Toyota officials knew of the problem from complaints and their own engineers. As of spring 2010, there were no indications that any Toyota executives would face any type of prosecution for their actions.

Enron Exits

Enron is no more, but at one time the company was a giant in the energy field. The Enron executives who knew that their accounting practices were fraudulent and engaged in them to hide corporate losses and to obtain high bonuses for themselves have largely been forgotten now in the wake of newer white collar crime, and it should be pointed out that the top executives, Jeffrey Skilling and Andrew Fastow, did end up in prison.

Other Offenders

Other white collar criminals have also been prosecuted, and some have received long sentences, as cited by Farrell (2005):

- *WorldCom:* CEO Bernie Ebbers, convicted of masterminding an $11 billion accounting fraud scheme, received a 25-year sentence.
- *Adelphia Communications:* CEOs Jon Rigas and Tim Rigas, convicted of theft, received, respectively, 15 and 20 years.
- *Tyco:* CEO Dennis Kozlowski and CFO Mark Swartz were convicted of grand larceny.
- *ImClone Systems:* CEO Sam Waksal, convicted of insider trading, received an 87-month sentence.
- *Martha Stewart:* Convicted of obstruction and perjury and received a five-month prison sentence and two years of supervised release (including five months of house arrest).

In other cases, white collar defendants were either acquitted or the prosecution was dropped (Farrell, 2005):

- *HealthSouth:* CEO Richard Scrushy was acquitted of a $2.7 billion fraud even though the government had already received 15 guilty pleas in the same case.
- *Kmart:* Two indictments against company executives for accounting fraud were withdrawn.
- *Arthur Andersen:* A judge threw out the conviction against the company, holding that the jury instructions were faulty.
- *Qwest:* Two mid-level executives were acquitted of criminal charges in relation to accounting fraud even though the government had already secured guilty pleas from two other executives.

order, the religious order, the kinship order, the educational order, and the public order. Law and social control constitute the public order, and powerful interests affect the law by influencing the writing of laws and the enforcement of written laws (Quinney, 1974).

Pluralism views law as influenced by interest groups that are in flux. Some interests may be at odds with other interests, or certainly the interpretation of them may be. For instance, conservation of natural resources is a basic interest necessary to the survival of society, but it may be interpreted by lumber companies as allowing them to harvest trees in national forests as long as they replant trees or, alternatively, interpreted by conservation groups as mandating more wilderness areas. According to the pluralist paradigm, laws are written by the group whose voice is more powerful at any particular time.

Interest groups hold power, but their power may shrink or grow depending on various factors. Coalitions and shared interests may shift the balance of power. The definition of crime may change, depending on which interest groups have the power to define criminal behavior and what is currently perceived to be in the best interests of the most powerful groups. For example, Federal Sentencing Guidelines used to assess punishment for crack cocaine versus powder as about 100:1, even though they were chemically the same substance. Conflict theory would have explained such a discrepancy by noting that poor people use crack and rich people use powder cocaine; however, it cannot explain why the 100:1 ratio has been addressed with judicial efforts to reduce the disparity, and why, in the summer of 2010, Congress eliminated the disparity entirely with new legislation. A pluralist paradigm would point to the growing public sentiment that the sentencing guidelines were unfair. Diverse groups such as the ACLU, Families Against Mandatory Minimums, and other interest groups do have power to affect law when they attain a certain level of public support. Under this view, law is dynamic and changes to reflect public sentiment. It is also true that law is given its form and effect by legal professionals who create the reality of law for all of us.

Law and the Legal Professional

We began this chapter with the story of Charles Swift, the lieutenant commander who may have ended his career in the Navy by his decision to adhere to the ethical duty to zealously defend his client, even if it happened to be an individual deemed to be an enemy combatant and dangerous to the interests of the United States. Thus far in our discussion, we have been discussing the law as an abstraction, however, it should be understood that the law is a reality created by legal professionals—legislators who pass new laws, prosecutors who decide who and how to prosecute, defense attorneys who do their duty, and judges who protect the sanctity of the process are all important actors in creating this reality.

The ideal of the justice system is that two advocates of equal ability will engage in a pursuit of truth, guided by a neutral judge. The truth is supposed to emerge from the contest. Actual practices in our justice system may be quite different. Various descriptions profess to offer a more realistic picture of the system.

Does the "best" opponent always win? If a powerful and rich defendant is able to hire the best criminal lawyer in the country, complete with several assistants and investigators, the prosecutor (who is typically overworked and understaffed) may be overwhelmed. Of course, this is the exception. More commonly a defendant must rely on an overworked and probably inexperienced public defender or an attorney who can make criminal law profitable only by high caseloads and quick turnover. In these instances, the defense is outmatched by a prosecutor in a public office with greater access to evidence and investigative assistance. Heffernan and Kleinig (2000) discuss how poverty affects a wide range of judicial processing decisions. It is hard to refute the notion that one's socioeconomic status affects one's experience in the justice system.

Blumberg (1969) refers to the practice of law as a *confidence game* because the prosecutor and the defense attorney conspire to appear as something they are not—adversaries in a do-or-die situation. What is more commonly the case is that the prosecutor and the defense attorney will still be working together when the client is gone. Attorneys may display adversarial performances in the courtroom, but the "show" lasts only as long as the jury is in the room, and sometimes not even then. Defense attorneys, prosecutors, and judges work together every day and often socialize together; they may even be married to each other. Many defense attorneys are ex-prosecutors. In some respects, this is helpful to their clients because the defense attorneys know how the prosecutor's office works and what a reasonable plea offer would be. But one must also assume that the prosecutorial experience of these attorneys has shaped their perceptions of clients and what would be considered fair punishment. Judges also have social relationships with defense attorneys and prosecutors. The courtroom actually is often a network of social and personal relationships, all of which are a subtext to the formal interactions seen in a trial or courtroom proceeding.

Other authors, too, have used the analogy of a confidence game to describe the interaction among prosecutors, defense attorneys, and clients. For example, Scheingold (1984: 155) refers to defense attorneys as "double agents" whose true loyalty is to the court itself and their own relationship with prosecutors and judges.

bureaucratic justice
The approach in which each case is treated as one of many; the actors merely follow the rules and walk through the steps, and the goal is efficiency.

Another perspective describes our courts as administering **bureaucratic justice**. Each case is seen as only one of many for the professionals who work in the system, and the actors merely follow the rules and walk through the steps. The goal of the system—namely, bureaucratic efficiency—becomes more important than the original goal of justice. Also, because each case is part of a workload, decision making takes on more complications. For instance, a defense lawyer may be less inclined to fight hard for a "loser" client if the lawyer wants a favor for another client later in the week. The prosecutor may decide not to charge a guilty person in order to get him or her to testify against someone else. In this sense, each case is not tried and judged separately, but is linked to other cases and processed as part of a workload.

The bureaucratic system of justice is seen as developing procedures and policies that, although not intentionally discriminatory, may contribute to a perception of unfairness. For instance, a major element in bureaucratic justice is the presumption of guilt, whereas the ideal of our justice system is a presumption of innocence. District attorneys, judges, and even defense attorneys approach each case presuming guilt and place a priority on achieving the most expeditious resolution of the case. This is the basic rationale behind plea bargaining, whether it is recognized or not: the defendant is presumed to be guilty, and the negotiation is to achieve a guilty plea while bargaining for the best possible sentence. The lowest possible sentence is the goal of the defense, whereas the highest possible sentence is the goal of the prosecutor. Plea bargaining is consistent with the bureaucratic justice system because it is the most efficient way of getting maximum punishment with minimum work.

Judges, prosecutors, and defense attorneys operate to maintain their personal standards of justice (Scheingold, 1984). This is exemplified by a judge who determines that an individual offender is a threat to society and so overlooks procedural errors during trial to make sure that he or she ends up in prison. Or a person who is legally guilty might get a break from the prosecutor because it is determined that he is a decent guy who made a mistake. Moreover, in almost all cases there may be general consensus on both sides about what is fair punishment for any given offender. Defense attorneys who argue for unrealistically low sentences do so in a desultory and uncommitted fashion, knowing that the prosecutor would not and could not offer such a sentence. Prosecutors put up little argument when defense attorneys ask for sentences that fit office guidelines.

Instead of describing the justice system as one that practices the presumption of innocence and takes careful steps to determine guilt, what may be more realistic is to view it as a system wherein all participants assume guilt, take standard, routine steps to arrive at the punishment phase, and operate under a value system that allocates punishment and mercy to offenders according to an informal consensus of fairness. It should be noted that there has been increased influence from victims in this process so that today what is "fair" may also be determined by the victim's wishes. Prosecutors may not agree to a plea bargain if the victim actively opposes it. Only in cases where the victim does not take an active part does the bureaucratic system operate unfettered (Stickels, 2003).

One other perception of the criminal justice system is that of Samuel Walker's (1985) **wedding-cake illustration**, based on a model proposed by Lawrence Friedman and Robert Percival. In this scheme, the largest portion of criminal cases forms the bottom layers of the cake and the few "serious" cases form the top layer. The top layer is represented most dramatically by cases such as the murder trial of O. J. Simpson. In this highly publicized case, the defendant had an extremely skilled (and highly paid) team of attorneys as well as trial consultants, investigators, and public relations specialists. Los Angeles County paid millions to keep up with its own team of attorneys, experts, and investigators. The criminal processing and trial proceeded with admirable speed. Each side worked incredibly hard and used an arsenal of tactics (which were then critiqued by armchair experts each evening). The case has been used in law school evidence classes because of the wealth of material present in pretrial discovery, exclusionary motions, jury selection, and the like. The bottom of the cake is represented by the tens of thousands of cases that are processed every year in which defendants may meet with an attorney only once or twice for a few minutes immediately before agreeing to a plea arrangement.

Because the public is exposed only to the top of the wedding cake, people develop a highly distorted perception of the system. The U.S. public may be disgusted with the multitude of evidentiary rules and the Byzantine process of the trial itself. However, these concerns are valid for only a very small portion of criminal cases. In the vast majority of cases, there is no trial at all and the process is more of an assembly line. What happens to individuals is largely determined by the courtroom work group (composed of all the actors in the court process, including defense attorneys, prosecutors, and judges).

According to Walker's wedding-cake analysis, the courtroom work group is believed to share definitions of seriousness and operate as a unit to keep the dynamics of the courtroom static despite changes that are forced upon it. Changes in the justice system that have occurred over time, such as the exclusionary rule and determinate sentencing, have had surprisingly little impact on court outcomes because of a shared perception of serious crime and appropriate punishment. The vast majority of crime is considered trivial, and the processing of these cases involves little energy or attention from system actors (Walker, 1985).

Dershowitz's view of the criminal justice system, as displayed in the Quote and Query box, is obviously (as Dershowitz admits) an exaggeration, but he does touch on some aspects of the system that many people agree with, such as a widespread perception of guilt and a general view that case processing is routine for everyone except the individual at risk of conviction. The major ethical problem with this view (if it does represent reality) is that innocence, truth, and due process are perceived as inconvenient and expendable.

wedding-cake illustration The model of justice in which the largest portion of criminal cases forms the bottom layers of the cake and the few "serious" cases form the top layer; the bottom-layer cases get minimal due process.

QUOTE & QUERY

Alan Dershowitz, a well-known defense attorney and law professor, presents the "rules" of the courtroom.

Rule I: Almost all criminal defendants are, in fact, guilty.

Rule II: All criminal defense lawyers, prosecutors, and judges understand and believe Rule I.

Rule III: It is easier to convict guilty defendants by violating the Constitution than by complying with it, and in some cases it is impossible to convict guilty defendants without violating the Constitution.

Rule IV: Almost all police lie about whether they violated the Constitution in order to convict guilty defendants.

Rule V: All prosecutors, judges, and defense attorneys are aware of Rule IV.

Rule VI: Many prosecutors implicitly encourage police to lie about whether they violated the Constitution in order to convict guilty defendants.

Rule VII: All judges are aware of Rule VI.

Rule VIII: Most trial judges pretend to believe police officers whom they know are lying.

Rule IX: All appellate judges are aware of Rule VIII, yet many pretend to believe the trial judges who pretend to believe the lying police officers.

Rule X: Most judges disbelieve defendants about whether their constitutional rights have been violated, even if they are telling the truth.

Rule XI: Most judges and prosecutors would not knowingly convict a defendant whom they believe to be innocent of the crime charged (or a closely related crime).

Rule XII: Rule XI does not apply to members of organized crime, drug dealers, career criminals, or potential informers.

Rule XIII: Nobody really wants justice.

—SOURCE: DERSHOWITZ, 1982: XXI.

Do you believe this is more accurate than the idealized vision of the adversarial system of justice?

Legal Agent or Moral Agent?

Many lawyers believe that loyalty to the client is paramount to their duties as a professional. This loyalty surpasses and eclipses individual and private decision making, and the special relationship said to exist between lawyer and client justifies decisions that otherwise might be deemed morally unacceptable. Others argue that an attorney must never abandon his or her own moral compass and if the client desires some action that the attorney would not countenance, ethics demand that he or she convince the client not to do so or withdraw. Historians indicate that this dilemma has been problematic for lawyers since the first ethics codes were written. In writings in the 1800s, lawyers were admonished not to "plate sin with gold," but others wrote that "a lawyer is not accountable for the moral character of the cause he prosecutes, but only for the manner in which he conduct it" (reported in Ariens, 2008: 364, 367).

The conundrum of what to do when a client wants you to commit some act contrary to good conscience occurs in both civil and criminal law. The following are the types of positions described and defended.

- *Legal agent.* One position is that the attorney is no more than the legal agent of the client. The lawyer is neither immoral nor moral, but merely a legal tool. This position is represented by the statement, "I am a lawyer, first and foremost."

- *Special relationship.* A more moderate position is that the loyalty to the client presents a special relationship between client and lawyer, similar to that between mother and child or with a trusted friend. This protected relationship justifies fewer actions than the legal agent relationship. The lawyer is expected to dissuade the client from taking unethical or immoral actions, but loyalty would preclude absolutely going against the client's wishes.

- *Moral agent.* The third position is that the lawyer is a moral agent who has to adhere to his or her own moral code. The client's interests come first only as long as they do not conflict with the lawyer's morality and ethical code. If there is a conflict, the lawyer follows his or her conscience.

Shaffer and Cochran (2007) offer a slightly different typology, describing the *godfather* (promotes clients' interests above all others), the *hired gun* (does whatever the client wants), the *guru* (controls the client with his own moral compass as guide), and the *friend* (engages the client in moral dialogue and tries to convince the client of a proper course of action and refuses only after the client insists). The hired gun and guru are similar to the legal agent and moral agent roles described above.

Some critics of the legal agent approach reject perspectives that discount the lawyer's responsibility as an individual to make his or her own moral decisions. In this view, lawyers should be the legal *and* moral agents of their clients rather than merely legal agents. Their personal responsibility to avoid wrongdoing precludes involving themselves in their clients' wrongdoing (Postema, 1986: 168). This position is represented by the statement, "I am a person first, a lawyer second."

Elliot Cohen (1991), an advocate of the moral agent position, believes that being a purely legal advocate is inconsistent in several ways with being a morally good person. For instance, the virtue of justice would be inconsistent with a zealous advocate who would maximize the chance of his or her client's winning, regardless of the fairness of the outcome.

A pure legal agent would sacrifice values of truthfulness, moral courage, benevolence, trustworthiness, and moral autonomy in furtherance of his or her client's interests. Only if the attorney is a moral agent as well as a legal advocate can there be any possibility of the attorney maintaining individual morality. Cohen (1991: 135–136) suggests some principles for attorneys to follow to be considered moral:

1. Treat others as ends in themselves and not as mere means to winning cases.

2. Treat clients and other professional relations who are relatively similar in a similar fashion.

3. Do not deliberately engage in behavior that is apt to deceive the court as to the truth.

4. Be willing, if necessary, to make reasonable personal sacrifices—of time, money, popularity, and so on—for what you justifiably believe to be a morally good cause.

5. Do not give money to, or accept money from, clients for wrongful purposes or in wrongful amounts.

6. Avoid harming others in the process of representing your client.

7. Be loyal to your clients, and do not betray their confidences.

8. Make your own moral decisions to the best of your ability, and act consistently upon them.

The rationale for these principles seems to be an amalgamation of ethical formalism, utilitarianism, and other ethical frameworks. Some of the principles may seem impossible to uphold and may be subject to bitter criticism on the part of practicing attorneys. For instance, how does one avoid harming others when one is an advocate for one side in a contest? There are losers and winners in civil contests as well as in criminal law, and lawyers must recognize their responsibility when the loser is harmed in financial or emotional ways.

Cohen's position has been attacked as naïve and wrong on several counts. Memory and Rose (2002: 29) argued against Cohen's proposed principle that a lawyer "may refuse to aid or participate in conduct that he sincerely believes, after careful reflection on the relevant facts, to be unjust or otherwise morally wrong notwithstanding his obligation to seek the lawful objectives of his client." They believe that lawyers can be effective and morally good at the same time and argue that rules in place already prevent unscrupulous acts. For instance, a code of ethics for attorneys (described in a later section of this chapter) is offered in the Model Rules of Professional Conduct, and Model Rule 3.3 prohibits lying. It states that lawyers may not make false statements of material facts or law, cannot fail to disclose a material fact to a tribunal when disclosure is necessary to avoid assisting a criminal or fraudulent act by the client, cannot fail to disclose legal authority that is directly adverse to one's client's interest, or cannot offer evidence that one knows to be false. According to the authors, this rule and others prevent attorneys from sacrificing truth even when zealously pursuing clients' interests.

Further, Memory and Rose (2002) argue that decisions regarding justice and morality are so subjective that it is impossible for them to be judged after the fact. They argue that if lawyers were to act as moral agents, the result would be the loss of the clients' trust in lawyers, for the lawyer would be able to substitute his or her individual morality for the clients.

In a rebuttal article, Elliot Cohen (2002: 39) used the ethics of care as the rationale for his continued defense of the moral agent idea:

[M]orality concerns concrete interpersonal relationships that can be understood only by people who have compassion and empathy for the predicaments of other people.... Morally virtuous lawyers (moral agents) possess such affective aspects of emotional development, but it is precisely such a dimension that must be lacking from the pure legal advocate who must get used to working injury upon others without having any strong feelings of guilt, sorrow, or regret.

In general, Cohen (1991) and Memory and Rose (2002) seem to be in agreement that the Model Rules should prevent the most egregious misconduct of lawyers. Their disagreement comes from the value they place on rules versus individual responsibility for more ambiguous moral judgments.

Cohen's argument is essentially that training and socialization into the culture of law create the legal agent role and encourage a type of noble-cause corruption similar to what we discussed in Chapter 5 for police officers. In the legal profession, the noble cause is winning a case (at all costs). In a culture that supports "ends" thinking (winning) over "means," rules are no more likely to control misconduct by lawyers than they do some police officers. The Quote and Query box gives examples of legal agent and moral agent statements.

QUOTE & QUERY

About half the practice of a decent lawyer consists in telling would-be clients that they are damned fools and should stop.

—SOURCE: REPORTED IN GLENDON, 1994: 76.

You're an attorney. It's your duty to lie, conceal and distort everything, and slander everybody.

—SOURCE: GIRADEAUX, 1949: ACT TWO

Which of these statements represents a legal agent statement? Which represents a moral agent statement?

Research indicates that the position taken by attorneys depends partially on whom they represent. On the one hand, public defenders take a more authoritarian role and seem to support the attorney as a "guru" or moral agent who tells the client what to do; attorneys for corporations, on the other hand, are apt to follow a more client-centered approach (Mather, 2003).

In an interesting application of Carol Gilligan's ethics-of-care approach, Vogelstein (2003) argues that attorneys' rules are concerned with rights, not care. Thus, attorneys must sacrifice third parties if they are to follow the rules and protect their clients' interests. This, she argues, contributes to the negative perception of attorneys. She proposes a type of moral agent approach in which the attorney must take into consideration the needs of others, as well as of the clients. Of course, others, such as Memory and Rose, who argued against Cohen's propositions, would strongly disagree. It should be noted that the rules do show glimmers of the moral agent idea. For instance, Model Rule 2.1 states that "a lawyer may refer not only to law but to other considerations such as moral, economic, social, and political factors. ..." in making decisions. This indicates that the rules do encourage attorneys to look to the ethical systems to resolve problems. Again, though, the rules are not much help when the client and the attorney strongly disagree over what is the right thing to do.

Ethics for Legal Professionals

Formal ethical standards for lawyers and judges were originally promulgated by the American Bar Association in the Model Code of Professional Responsibility. The original canons, adapted from the Alabama Bar Association Code of 1887, were adopted by the ABA in 1908 and have been revised frequently since then. In 1983, the ABA switched its endorsement of the Model Code as the general guide for ethical behavior to the Model Rules of Professional Conduct. The Model Rules continue to be revised periodically, responding to changing sensibilities and emerging issues. Today's Model Rules cover many aspects of the lawyer's profession, including areas such as client–lawyer relationships, the lawyer as counselor, the lawyer as advocate, transactions with others, public service, and maintaining the integrity of the profession (see www.abanet.org/cpr/mrpc/mrpc_toc.html.).

The rules require that attorneys zealously protect and pursue a client's interest within the boundaries of the rules while maintaining a professional and civil demeanor toward everyone involved in the legal process. Critics charge that the rules have replaced earlier ethical codes that expressed ethical norms based on a moral tradition with regulatory, some might say, picayune prohibitions (Ariens, 2008). Others argue that by placing pure client interest ahead of a transcendent professional ethos, lawyers have lost the meaning and value that used to be associated with the practice of law, and this lack of professional purpose undercuts public confidence and is the cause of a "cycle of cynicism" (Kreiger, 2009). Note that this "cycle of cynicism," where a loss of moral direction leads to cynicism, unethical behavior, and, therefore, more cynicism, is very similar to the description presented in Chapter 7 of police departments that have lost their moral grounding, leading to ethical misconduct by officers.

Section 1 of the rules is titled "Client–Lawyer Relationship." This section offers rules that require the attorney maintain a level of competence in his or her field and not take cases that are beyond his or her expertise. Rules in this section also govern the relative power between the attorney and client—in other words, who should make decisions regarding the legal strategy to pursue the client's interest. The rules mandate that attorneys, once they take a case, practice due diligence, communicate with their client, and assess appropriate fees. A controversial rule demands attorneys maintain confidentiality regarding information obtained in their representation of a client. We will discuss client confidentiality as a dilemma in Chapter 9. There are also rules that guide the attorney when there are conflicts of interest, such as the attorney should not have two clients who have competing interests or take on clients whose interests may conflict with the attorney's interests. These protections extend to former clients as well.

Section 2 offers rules concerning the lawyer's role as counselor, and Section 3 covers those situations where the attorney is pursuing the client's interest as an advocate. The Model Rules require that the attorney only pursue legitimate claims (Rule 3.1), and not engage in needless delays (Rule 3.2). Further, the attorney has an ethical obligation of "Candor Toward the Tribunal" (Rule 3.3), which means, for instance, that when presenting a legal argument, the attorney must present opposing case law as well. There are additional rules that cover fairness, decorum, trial publicity, and when the lawyer is a witness.

Rule 3.8, "Special Responsibilities of a Prosecutor," requires the prosecutor to pursue justice rather than simply a conviction. In recent years, the ABA has voted to add the following provisions (Saltzburg, 2008):

> (g) When a prosecutor knows of new, credible, and material evidence creating a reasonable likelihood that a convicted defendant did not commit an offense of which the defendant was convicted, the prosecutor shall: (1) promptly disclose that evidence to an appropriate court or authority, and (2) if the conviction was obtained in the prosecutor's jurisdiction, (a) promptly disclose that evidence to the defendant unless a court authorizes delay, and (b) undertake further investigation, or make reasonable efforts to cause an investigation, to determine whether the defendant was convicted of an offense that the defendant did not commit.

> (h) When a prosecutor knows of clear and convincing evidence establishing that a defendant in the prosecutor's jurisdiction was convicted of an offense that the defendant did not commit, the prosecutor shall seek to remedy the conviction.

These new provisions were in response to the growing number of cases where innocent people have been released from prison after being exonerated, often by DNA evidence. New York was the first state to revise its state ethics rules to assign these duties to prosecutors, and the ABA began discussing such a rule in 2000. While critics argued that prosecutors are too overworked already to consider post-conviction claims of innocence and that the rules may serve as a bar to the finality of criminal convictions, proponents successfully argued that the number of exonerations and the fact that the duty of a prosecutor is to seek justice, not secure convictions, supported the inclusion of the new provisions. As of 2010, however, only Wisconsin has adopted amendments (g) and (h) (Mulhausen, 2010).

Another section of the Model Rules is titled "Transactions with Persons Other than Clients." In this section, rules require the lawyer to maintain truthfulness in statements to others, and not communicate with opposing parties except through their attorneys. Other rules cover practices concerning unrepresented persons and the rights of third persons. In a section that covers how law firms should operate, there are many rules concerning the relationships between attorneys in firms, between firms, and with other non-lawyer associates. One rule, for instance, bars attorneys from using "runners," which are non-attorneys who find cases by following up on accidents or finding victims of torts or defective merchandise.

The section on public service mandates that lawyers provide some *pro bono* (free) legal service, and otherwise contribute to the legal community and society in general. It also cautions against acting against clients' interests in one's activities in public service. Another section covers how the attorney may advertise and communicate with prospective clients. There are also rules about how to advertise specialties or being board certified (passing a special examination in a particular area of law). Section 8 is titled "Maintaining the Integrity of the Profession" and covers bar admission and discipline. Rule 8.2 is directed specifically to "Judicial and Legal Officials." Rule 8.3 dictates that attorneys have an ethical obligation to reporting professional misconduct. Rule 8.4 more specifically details misconduct, and the final rule covers the authority to enact discipline (Martyn, Fox, and Wendel, 2008).

In addition to the Model Rules, there is also the American Law Institute's Restatement of the Law Governing Lawyers (Martyn, Fox, and Wendel, 2008). Developed in 2000, the Restatement provides guidelines and commentary covering most of the same issues that the Model Rules cover. Some of the sections of the Restatement are:

- Admission to Practice Law
- A Lawyer's Duty of Supervision
- A Lawyer's Duties to a Prospective Client
- Client–Lawyer Contracts
- Duty of Care to a Client
- A Lawyer's Duty to Safeguard Confidential Client Information
- Using or Disclosing Information to Prevent Death or Serious Bodily Harm
- Client Crime or Fraud
- Falsifying or Destroying Evidence

The Restatement has eight chapters and 135 different sections. Note that the ABA and American Legal Institute (ALI) promulgate these ethical codes, but state bar associations must adopt them or adapt them to have any effect. It is the state bars (and the federal bar) that have the power to discipline attorneys, the most serious punishment being disbarment. Finally, it should be noted that the Model Rules and the Restatement cover the practice of law generally; thus, most of the commentary and elements relate to civil practice. Because our discussion focuses exclusively on criminal defense attorneys, prosecutors, and criminal court judges, we will be referring to the ABA Criminal Justice Standards, as developed by the American Bar Association in 1991–1992. These standards offer guidelines and commentary directed specifically to the practice of criminal law. Ethical issues in criminal law may involve courtroom behavior, perjury, conflicts of interest, use of the media, investigation efforts, use of immunity, discovery and the sharing of evidence, relationships with opposing attorneys, and plea bargaining.

Standards relating to ethical obligations of defense attorneys appear in Chapter 4, "The Defense Function" and cover a multitude of issues, such as these:

- Function of defense counsel
- Punctuality
- Public statements
- Duty to the administration of justice
- Access and the lawyer–client relationship
- Duty to investigate
- Control and direction of litigation
- Plea bargaining
- Trial conduct
- Appeal

Chapter 3 of the ABA Criminal Justice Standards covers the prosecution function. There are also National Prosecution Standards promulgated by the National District Attorneys Association. Model Rule 3.8, described in preceding paragraphs, also covers the duties of a prosecutor. Ethical guidelines for prosecutors make special note of the unique role of the prosecutor as a representative of the court system and the state. Some of the sections of the ABA Standards for Prosecutors cover:

- Working with police and other law enforcement agents
- Working with victims, potential witnesses, and targets during the investigative process
- Contact with the public
- The decision to initiate or to continue an investigation
- Selecting investigative techniques
- Use of undercover law enforcement agents and undercover operations
- Use of confidential informants
- Cooperation agreements
- Use of subpoenas
- Use of the investigative powers of the grand jury
- Special prosecutors, independent counsel, and special prosecution units
- Prosecutor's role in addressing suspected law enforcement misconduct
- Prosecutor's role in addressing suspected judicial misconduct
- Prosecutor's role in addressing suspected misconduct by defense counsel
- Prosecutor's role in addressing suspected misconduct by witnesses, informants, or jurors
- Illegally obtained evidence
- Responding to political pressure and consideration of the impact of criminal investigations on the political process

These standards for legal professionals in the criminal justice system are much more specific than the Law Enforcement Code of Ethics. Instead of being aspirational, the standards are specific guidelines for behavior. (The Criminal Justice Standards from the American Bar Association's website can be accessed at http://new.abanet.org/sections/criminaljustice/Pages/Standards.aspx.)

ETHICAL GUIDELINES FOR JUDGES

To help guide judges in their duties, the Model Code of Judicial Conduct was developed by the American Bar Association. The latest revision was undertaken beginning in 2003, with the final document submitted to the membership in 2007. This code identifies the ethical considerations unique to judges. It is organized into four canons, which are overriding principles of ethical behavior, and under each canon there are more specific rules. The four canons of the code are as follows (ABA, 2007):

1. A judge shall uphold and promote the independence, integrity, and impartiality of the judiciary, and shall avoid impropriety and the appearance of impropriety.
2. A judge shall perform the duties of judicial office impartially, competently, and diligently.
3. A judge shall conduct the judge's personal and extrajudicial activities to minimize the risk of conflict with the obligations of judicial office.
4. A judge or candidate for judicial office shall not engage in political or campaign activity that is inconsistent with the independence, integrity, or impartiality of the judiciary.

The primary theme of judicial ethics is impartiality. We must be confident that the judge's objectivity isn't marred by any type of bias. Judges should not let their personal prejudices influence their decisions. To avoid this possibility, the ABA's code specifies that each judge should try to avoid all appearance of bias as well as actual bias. To this end, the rules prohibit a judge from engaging in speeches or activities that indicate a particular bias. Such ethical rules, however, cannot impinge on the right of free speech. In *Minnesota v. White* (536 U.S. 765 [2002]), the Supreme Court held that Minnesota's rule prohibiting judges from making speeches violated the First Amendment.

Judges must be careful to avoid financial involvements or personal relationships that may threaten their objectivity. We expect judges, like police officers and prosecutors, to conform to higher standards of behavior than the rest of us. Therefore, any hint of scandal in their private lives also calls into question their professional ethics. The obvious rationale is that judges who have less than admirable personal values cannot judge others objectively, and that judges who are less than honest in their financial dealings do not have a right to sit in judgment of others.

Culture and Ethics

The Model Code of Professional Responsibility dictated that lawyers should be "temperate and dignified" and "refrain from all illegal and morally reprehensible conduct." The Model Rules expect that "a lawyer's conduct should conform to the requirements of the law, both in professional service to clients and in the lawyer's business and personal affairs." These prescriptions are similar to those found in the Law Enforcement Code of Ethics. Both groups of professionals are expected to uphold a higher standard of behavior

in the **NEWS**

A LEWD LAWYER

A trial judge held a lawyer in contempt and sentenced him to 90 days in jail for making gestures simulating masturbation during a plea-taking in the courtroom. Evidently, the lawyer made the gestures while looking at the female judge and rolling his eyes. It wasn't clear exactly what message he was trying to convey, but he was frustrated with the plea process going on and angry at the prosecutor. The lawyer said the gesture was directed at the prosecutor, not the judge. The appellate judge held that he "tarnished the dignity of the judicial process" and upheld the original judge's order of 90 days. The sentence was appealed, and the lawyer ended up serving 10 days in jail, the remainder of the contempt sentence at home, and received a three-year probation of his law license.

SOURCES: Kreytak, 2008: Bl, B6; Kreytak, 2010.

than the general public. These professionals have chosen to work within the legal system and help to enforce the law; thus, it is not unreasonable, perhaps, to expect that they provide a model of behavior for the rest of us. However, similar to our discussion of law enforcement officials, it seems to be true that the real world of lawyers is sometimes quite different from the vaunted ideals of the Model Rules. The In the News box describes one attorney who evidently did not subscribe to the view that there exists a higher standard of behavior for legal professionals.

Law schools have been criticized for being singularly uninterested in fostering any type of moral conscience in graduating students. Law schools purport to be in the practice of reshaping law students so that when they emerge "thinking like a lawyer," they have mastered a type of thinking that is concerned with detail and logical analysis. Others argue this is done at the expense of being sensitive to morality and larger social issues (Spence, 1989). Stover (1989) writes how public interest values decline during law school. The reason for this decline seemingly has to do with the low value placed on public interest issues by the law school curriculum, which also treats ethical and normative concerns as irrelevant or trivial compared to the "bar courses" such as contract law and torts.

Even though all law schools today require professional-responsibility courses, sometimes these courses do not promote morality and ethics. Instead, instructors relate stories (humorous and otherwise) of how to get around ethical and legal mandates. For instance, law students are taught that in the discovery phase of a lawsuit, the legal rule that requires an attorney to turn over documents requested by the other side (that are not otherwise privileged) can be circumvented by burying important documents in 600 boxes of paperwork. Rather than being taught to abide by the spirit and principle of the ethical guidelines, sometimes these are presented as obstacles to be overcome.

Ethical issues have received more attention in recent years, and most law schools now have a variety of public service clinics where students help the poor, elderly, immigrants, and/or criminal clients. Bar exams now have a special section devoted to the Model Rules and the state's own professional responsibility code, but these tests are often hyper-technical, testing the minutiae of the rules rather than the spirit of practicing law ethically and honestly. Most states also require continuing legal education credit hours in the area of ethics. However, similar to our earlier discussion of police officers, classroom ethics training that encourages one set of behaviors is often contradicted and disparaged by the professional subculture. If this is the case, such training might not be very effective.

Patrick Fitzgerald (2009), a well-known and highly respected U.S. attorney, in an essay concerning ethics in the prosecutor's office, identified office culture as an important component to ensure that prosecutors acted ethically. He also identified a "good" office as one that hires not just smart people, but individuals who express values conducive to public service and integrity. It seems to be probable that just as police departments each have their own culture that supports or discourages ethical decision making, prosecutors' offices also have different cultures.

In a highly critical overview of the legal profession, Glendon (1994) proposed that the legal profession has changed in dramatic ways, not all of which have been for the better. Although the practice of law was once governed by rules of ethics and etiquette, and lawyers acted like gentlemen (literally, because the profession was for the most part closed to women, minorities, and the lower class), since the 1950s, it has become increasingly open to those excluded groups. Although the inclusion of these groups is a step forward, at the same time, law practice has become less of a "gentlemen's club" where the majority followed written and unwritten rules of conduct, and more of a world of "no rules" or, more accurately, only one rule: "Winning is everything."

CONCLUSION

In this chapter, we have explored the role and justification for law, and, also how our paradigms affect how we see it function in society. While some view law as enforcing the will of the majority, others see law as a tool of oppression by those in power. The justification for law is primarily prevention of harm, including paternalistic laws that seek to protect individuals from themselves, and laws that enforce society's morals. The attorney and judge are the human embodiments of the law. They create the reality of how law operates. Rules defining ethical conduct for legal professionals come from their state bar, but the ABA has promulgated Model Rules that most state bar associations either adopt completely or adapt. Similar to our discussion concerning law enforcement professionals' noble-cause corruption, we note that there is a subculture of winning that competes with, and sometimes eclipses, the ethical standards that attorneys learn in law school.

CHAPTER REVIEW

1. Understand the justifications for law, including protections against harm to others, offensive conduct, harm to self, and harm to societal morals.

The primary justification for law is the social contract—we each give up the right to do whatever we want in return for protection. John Stuart Mill advocated the "harm principle," which justified laws only when they prevented harm (i.e., assault, murder). Other justifications include preventing offensive conduct (i.e., lewd behavior, public disturbance). Another justification is to prevent harm to self. Legal paternalism refers to laws in which the state tries to protect people from their own behavior (i.e., seat belt laws, motorcycle helmet laws). Finally, laws prevent harm to societal morals (legal moralism), but these laws are often controversial because we don't all agree on right and wrong behaviors (i.e., pornography, gambling).

2. Explain the role of law in society and the paradigms that have developed to understand how law is formed and enforced.

Basically, paradigms are models of how ideas relate to one another, forming a conceptual model of the world around us. In the consensus paradigm, law is seen as enforcing the will of the majority, and most people agree on what should be illegal. In the conflict paradigm, law is seen as a tool of the power holders to control the powerless. In the pluralist paradigm, law is seen as dynamic and changeable depending on coalitions of various interest groups.

3. Compare the idea of our criminal law system as an adversarial system to other descriptions of how the courtroom works and the relationships between the legal professionals.

The ideal of the justice system is that two advocates of equal ability will engage in a pursuit of truth, guided by a neutral judge. The truth is supposed to emerge from the contest. The system has also been described as a "confidence game" where the prosecutor and the defense attorney conspire to appear as adversaries when, in fact, they will still be working together when the client is gone. Another view is that of bureaucratic justice, where the goal is efficiency, not truth or justice. One other view is that of a wedding cake model, where a few celebrated cases receive the vast majority of attention and resources, a middle group of cases receive a moderate amount of resources, but the vast majority of cases are processed through the system with minimal energy and minimal due process.

4. Present the controversy concerning the role of advocate as legal agent or moral agent.

The legal agent is a position where the attorney is no more than the legal tool of the client and does his or her bidding as long as it is not illegal. The moral agent approach is that the lawyer has to adhere to his or her own moral code. The client's interests come first only as long as they do not conflict with the lawyer's morality and ethical code. A third position is that of a "special relationship" where the attorney attempts to convince the client to do what is right, but the position is not clear on what the course of action would be if the client refuses.

5. Describe the history and source of legal ethics for attorneys and judges. Explain the types of ethical rules that exist and compare them to the subculture of winning.

The Model Code of Professional Responsibility was adapted from the Alabama Bar Association Code of 1887 and adopted by the American Bar Association in 1908. In 1983, the ABA switched its endorsement of the Model Code as the general guide for ethical behavior to the Model Rules of Professional Conduct. The Model Code of Judicial Conduct was adopted by the American Bar Association in 2007 to provide ethical standards for judges. Each state, however, must have its own model rules or ethical code to use as a vehicle of discipline. The ethical code has the force of law in each state, and lawyers may face a range of sanctions up to disbarment for violating the rules. On the other hand, disciplinary proceedings are fairly rare, and there is a subculture in the law that promotes putting the client's interests ahead of everything, and winning is valued over all else. This leads to the possibility of behavior that violates the formal Model Rules.

KEY TERMS

bureaucratic justice
conflict paradigm
consensus paradigm
Good Samaritan laws
laws
legal moralism

legal paternalism
mechanical solidarity
natural law
organic solidarity
pluralist paradigm
positivist law

repressive law
restitutive law
social contract theory
wedding-cake illustration

STUDY QUESTIONS

1. List some laws justified by legal paternalism. Provide the rationale for such laws, as well as opposing arguments. Discuss some types of laws that are justified by legal moralism. What are the major arguments for and against such laws?

2. Discuss how pluralism differs from the conflict paradigm and provide examples to support the view.

3. Describe in detail the evidence for and against the bureaucratic justice model of the system.

4. Describe the recent additions to Rule 3.8 for prosecutors and why they were adopted.

5. Provide some examples of the types of issues covered in Chapter 3 (for prosecutors) and Chapter 4 (for defense attorneys) of the ABA Criminal Justice Standards.

WRITING/DISCUSSION EXERCISES

1. Write an essay on (or discuss) how the conflict and consensus paradigms would interpret the following: decriminalization of marijuana for medical purposes, stem-cell research, passage of hate-crime legislation, prohibiting the use of race in admissions procedures in universities and in competitions for state scholarships, and laws prohibiting racial profiling in police stops.

2. Write an essay on (or discuss) the legitimate functions of law in society. Do you agree with laws that prohibit gambling? Drinking while driving? Underage drinking? Prostitution? Liquor violations? Drugs? Helmet laws for bicycles or motorcycles? Leash laws? Seat belts? Smoking in public places? Can you think of any paternalistic laws not mentioned above? Analyze pornography, gambling, homosexuality, and drug use under the ethical systems discussed in Chapter 2. What other laws have limited Americans' (or certain groups') freedoms? Can they be justified under any ethical rationale?

3. Write an essay on (or discuss) whether or not the justice system is simply a bureaucratic assembly line that does not promote justice as much as it simply ensures its own survival, with an emphasis on production. What should be the professional goals of the various actors in the system (judges, prosecutors, defense attorneys)?

ETHICAL DILEMMAS

Situation 1

You ride a motorcycle, and you think it is much more enjoyable to ride without a helmet. You also believe that your vision and hearing are better without a helmet. Your state has just passed a helmet law, and you have already received two warnings. What will you do?

What if your child were riding on the motorcycle? Do you think your position would be any different if you had any previous accidents and had been hurt?

Situation 2

You are a legislator who believes absolutely and strongly that abortion is a sin. You have polled your constituents and are surprised to find that the majority do not believe that the government should legislate the private decision of a woman to have an abortion. Should you vote your conscience or the will of the majority of your constituents?

Situation 3

You are a district attorney prosecuting a burglary case. The defendant is willing to plead guilty in return for a sentence of probation, and you believe that this is a fair punishment because your evidence may not support a conviction. However, the victims are upset and want to see the offender receive prison time. They insist that you try the case. What should you do?

Situation 4

You are a prosecutor with the unwelcome task of prosecuting a 12-year-old for a particularly brutal assault. You personally believe that the child basically went along with his older brother in the assault, and you think that he should have been left in the juvenile system. However, the juvenile court judge waived him to the adult system, and the media and the victim's family are demanding that he be tried as an adult. You have to decide whether to try him for attempted murder, assault, or some lesser crime. You could deny the waiver and send the case back to juvenile court. What will you do? How do you determine your duty? Is it to the victims, to society, or to your own conscience?

Situation 5

You are a judge who believes that individuals should be allowed to choose when to die. You personally had to watch both your parents die long and agonizing deaths because your state does not have a right-to-die statute. Before you is a doctor who is being prosecuted for giving a lethal dose of morphine to a patient dying of terminal cancer. The family of the patient did not want the prosecution, the majority of the public is not in favor of the prosecution, but the prosecutor believes that if there is a law in place, it should be enforced. The doctor has opted for a bench trial. What would you do?

9

Foto24 / Alamy

Discretion and Dilemmas in the Legal Profession

Chapter Objectives

1. Describe the ethical issues faced by defense attorneys.
2. Describe the ethical issues faced by prosecutors.
3. Describe some of the areas of forensic science that have been challenged by opponents.
4. Describe the ethical issues faced by judges.
5. Explain why electing judges leads to a perception of unfairness.

Cameron Todd Willingham was not someone who was ever going to be very successful in life. Raised in foster care, he drank and smoked too much, used drugs more than occasionally, and never had much of a plan about how to get ahead. Still, most people said he was a fairly decent father to his three daughters. Living with his wife in Corsicana, Texas, in 1991, the 23-year-old struggled to make ends meet. On the morning of December 23, his wife left the house to go buy Christmas presents. Todd was sleeping when his 2-year-old daughter woke him up and said the house was on fire. Describing the events later, Todd said he told her to leave the house and he tried to get to his 1-year-old twins, but couldn't find them in the smoke and the fire forced him to run outside. Neighbors reported that he was extremely distraught, and firemen had to hold him back from trying to break through the window and crawl into the house even though it was fully engulfed by that time. However, later, when investigators began to focus on Willingham himself as a suspect of arson, they also remembered that he wanted to move his car from the driveway, which they thought was strange for a distraught father.

Willingham was arrested for arson, and the prosecutor sought and obtained the death penalty because of the tragic deaths of the three little girls. The case theory was that Willingham was tired of the responsibilities of fatherhood and was a sociopath whose actions during the fire were mere acting. The main evidence came from two senior fire investigators who testified that the fire was definitely arson. They reported that they discovered pour marks indicating an accelerant, and the heat of the fire, as measured by the spidery cracks in the glass, could only be from a fuel source. Further, they found a pour mark immediately outside the front door, indicating that he had poured an accelerant there to block escape.

Willingham steadfastly maintained his innocence and would accept no plea deal. His wife remained convinced of his innocence through the first trial and first appeal, but eventually came to be persuaded that he indeed had killed their daughters. Still, not everyone was convinced. Dr. Gerald Hurst, who was asked to review the case file, immediately found statements from the fire investigator that had no basis in fact and had been discounted in the early 1990s when Willingham was on trial. A well-respected scientist, Hurst had conducted experiments in other arson cases that proved that "flashovers" can cause scorch patterns that look like pour marks. He discovered that the positive trace of mineral spirits at the front door was probably due to a small grill and bottle of lighter fluid that had been on the front porch, seen in a photograph from the first pictures taken of the fire, but removed in the cleanup. Hurst had been instrumental in freeing Ernest Willis, who had also been on death row in Texas for a fire that killed his children, but had been exonerated by Hurst's evidence that the fire was not arson.

The report Hurst wrote detailing his findings was finished quickly because Willingham's execution date was rapidly approaching. The Texas Board of Pardons and Paroles reviews death sentences and can recommend clemency to the governor. They had Hurst's report indicating that the most likely explanation was that the fire was set by candles or a space heater in the girls' room. It is unknown how much weight was placed on the report by the board, or if they read it at all, because they did not recommend the execution be stayed. In the state of Texas, the final decision is up to the governor and Governor Rick Perry ordered that the execution proceed (Mills, 2005). Cameron Todd Willingham was executed on February 17, 2004 (Mills, 2005; Grann, 2009).

The story doesn't end there. In 2005, Texas established a government commission to investigate cases where forensic science might have led to the convictions of innocent people. One of the first cases reviewed by the Texas Forensic Science Commission was the Willingham case. A fire scientist, Craig Beyler, completed his investigation in 2009 and issued a scathing report concluding that the arson investigators' testimony had no basis in fact and they should have known it at the time. Before the commission had a chance to hear the testimony of Dr. Beyler, however, Governor Rick Perry dismissed the chairman and another member and reorganized the board under the chairmanship of John Bradley, a "law-and-order district attorney" from Williamson County. Bradley cancelled the meeting. Finally, in the summer of 2010, they issued a preliminary finding that the state deputy fire marshal and assistant fire chief based their testimony on flawed science, but they also found that the men were not negligent or guilty of misconduct in any way (Lindell and Embrey, 2009; Lindell, 2009; Turner, 2010).

In Chapter 6, we described ethical dilemmas for police officers as inevitable because of the discretion inherent in the role. The same is true of legal professionals. Although the roles and duties of a defense attorney, prosecutor, and judge are very different, what they do have in common is a great deal of discretion. Similar to all other criminal justice professionals, the power of discretion inherent in each of these roles affects individuals' lives in dramatic ways. As the Willingham case above illustrates, it is entirely possible that the actions of the defense attorneys, prosecutors, and judges in a criminal case can set in motion events that can take the life of an innocent man.

Ethical Issues for Defense Attorneys

Due process, including notice, neutral fact finders, cross-examination, and presentation of evidence and witnesses, is supposed to minimize mistakes in judicial proceedings that might result in the deprivation of life, liberty, or property. The defense attorney is there

in the **NEWS**

A LACK OF ADVOCACY

"I decided that Mr. Tucker deserved to die, and I would not do anything to prevent his execution."

This statement was made by defense attorney David Smith of Greensboro, North Carolina, who accepted a capital appeal case and then admitted that he "sabotaged" the appeal of his client because he believed the man deserved execution. The attorney went through a moral crisis afterward and confessed to the state bar what he did.

SOURCE: Rimer, 2000.

during the important steps of the process to ensure that these rights are protected. For instance, defense attorneys are present during interrogation to make sure no coercion is used, at lineup to make sure it is fair and unbiased, and during trial to ensure adequate cross-examination and presentation of evidence. This pure role of advocate is contradictory to the reality that the defense attorney must, if he or she is to work with the other actors in the court system, accommodate their needs as well as those of clients.

Many defense attorneys started out as prosecutors. This sometimes causes problems when they have trouble making the transition from "good guy battling evil" to the more subtle role of defender of due process. If the attorney cannot make the transition from prosecution to defense and feel comfortable in the role, it is difficult to offer a zealous defense (R. Cohen, 2001). Some argue that the system tends to operate under a presumption of guilt. Indeed, defense attorneys are often in the position of defending clients they know are guilty. The rationale for defending a guilty person is that everyone deserves due process before a finding of guilt and punishment. If defense attorneys are doing their job, we can be more confident that justice has been served. If they are not doing their job, we have no system of justice, and none of us is safe from wrongful prosecution and the awesome power of the state to investigate, prosecute, and punish. In the In the News box, one lawyer decided that justice demanded that he subvert the role of the defense attorney. What is the attorney's responsibility to the client when he or she knows the client is guilty of a horrible crime?

RESPONSIBILITY TO THE CLIENT

[A defense attorney's duty is] to serve as the accused's counselor and advocate with courage and devotion (Standard 4-1.2[b]).

The ABA Criminal Justice Standards will be used to highlight selected ethical issues for defense attorneys and prosecutors. In the first standard we will discuss, defense attorneys are exhorted to serve as counselor and advocate; however, they are always in the position of balancing the rights of the individual client against their overall effectiveness for all their clients. Extreme attempts to protect the rights of one person will reduce the defense attorney's ability to advocate effectively for other clients. Furthermore, defense attorneys must balance the needs and problems of the client against their ethical responsibilities to the system and the profession.

A lawyer is supposed to provide legal assistance to clients without regard for personal preference or interest. Once he or she takes a case, a lawyer is not allowed to withdraw except:

- if the legal action is for harassment or malicious purposes,
- if continued employment will result in violation of a disciplinary rule,
- if discharged by a client, or
- if a mental or physical condition renders effective counsel impossible.

In other cases, a judge *may* grant permission to withdraw when the client insists on illegal or unethical actions, is uncooperative and does not follow the attorney's advice, or otherwise makes effective counsel difficult. In general, judges are loath to allow a defendant to proceed with a *pro se* defense (defending oneself) because of the risk that the conviction will be overturned on appeal. Nor are judges likely to allow withdrawal if it will delay ongoing proceedings. Legal ethics mandate that people with unpopular causes and individuals who are obviously guilty still deserve counsel, and that it is the ethical duty of an attorney to provide such counsel.

Many people are firmly convinced that the quality of legal representation is directly related to how much money the defendant can pay. When people can make bail and hire private attorneys, do they receive a better defense? Research, unfortunately, supports the proposition that those who can afford private attorneys receive "better" representation (Martinez and Pollock, 2008). However, a private attorney, appointed by the court and paid with state funds, may not be better than a public defender. A Harvard study found, in reviewing federal criminal cases between 1997 and 2001, that lawyers who were appointed to represent indigent clients were less qualified than federal public defenders, took longer to resolve cases, with worse results for clients, including sentences that were, on average, eight months longer (Liptak, 2007). The private-appointed attorneys also cost the public $61 million more than the public defenders. Evidently, these findings were due to inexperience, as public defenders practiced federal criminal law full time. In the federal system, roughly three-fourths of all defendants are represented by publicly funded attorneys; about half are public defenders and the other half are appointed (Liptak, 2007).

Do defense attorneys exert more effort for clients who pay well than they do for court-appointed clients? Obviously, professional ethics would dictate equal consideration, but individual values also affect behavior. If an attorney was confident that his or her court-appointed clients would receive at least adequate representation, could one not justify a more zealous defense for a paying client? Where adequate representation is vaguely and poorly defined, this question is problematic.

A more recent issue has emerged with the rise of specialty courts, the most common being drug courts. In such courts, defense attorneys, prosecutors, and judges take on quite different roles from the more typical adversary approach in regular criminal courts. There is an emphasis placed on the actors as a team, and the judge plays a much more active role, interacting with the defendant and monitoring progress. In these courts, the defense attorney appears almost redundant since the court's goal is to do what is best for the client/defendant.

In fact, Meekins (2007) argues that defense attorneys face sensitive and serious ethical challenges in such courts because they should not forget that their primary responsibility is to the client, just as in a criminal trial, even if it means objecting to and arguing against treatment options. There is a tendency for defense attorneys in such courts to influence clients to accept treatment, even in post-adjudicative systems, where the client has to plead guilty in order to obtain treatment. Then the defense attorney faces issues involving communication with clients and confidentiality, because of the monitoring that such courts undertake while the client is in treatment and under supervision. Even though drug courts are set up to promote the best interest of the client, the defense attorney's role as advocate should not be sacrificed, and the individual lawyer should not forget his or her role in the desire for such courts to be successful.

CONFLICTS OF INTEREST

[A defense attorney] should not permit his or her professional judgment or obligations to be affected by his or her own political, business, property, or personal interests (Standard 4-3.5[a]).

This standard, along with Model Rules 1.7, 1.8, 1.10, and 1.11, cover conflicts of interest. Attorneys are supposed to avoid any conflicts of interest when defending clients. For instance, an attorney may not represent a client who owns a company that is a rival to one in which the attorney has an interest. The attorney also must not represent two clients who have opposing interests—for instance, co-defendants in a criminal case—for one often will testify against the other. The attorney would find it impossible in such a situation to represent each individual fairly. Disciplinary rules even prohibit two lawyers in a single firm from representing clients with conflicting interests.

Although attorneys may not ethically accept clients with conflicting interests, there is no guidance on the more abstract problem that all criminal clients in a caseload have conflicting interests if their cases are looked upon as part of a workload rather than considered separately. Many defense attorneys make a living by taking cases from people with very modest means or taking court-appointed cases with the fee set by the court. The defense attorney then becomes a "fast-food lawyer," depending on volume and speed to make a profit. However, quality may get sacrificed along the way. When lawyers pick up clients in the hallways of courtrooms and from bail company referrals, the goal is to arrange bail, get a plea bargain, and move on to the next case. Rarely do these cases even come to trial.

plea bargain
Exchange of a guilty plea for a reduced charge or sentence.

The vast majority of cases in the criminal justice system are settled by a **plea bargain**, an exchange of a guilty plea for a reduced charge or sentence. The defense attorney's goal in plea bargaining is to get the best possible deal for the client—probation or the shortest prison sentence that the prosecutor is willing to give for a guilty plea. The defense attorney is aware that he or she cannot aggressively push every case without endangering an ongoing relationship with the prosecutor. A courtroom appearance may be an isolated event for the client, but for the defense attorney and prosecutor it is an ongoing, weekly ritual; only the names of the defendants change. Because of the nature of the continuing relationship, the defense attorney must weigh present needs against future gains. If the defense becomes known as unwilling to "play ball," reduced effectiveness may hurt future clients.

Another conflict of interest may arise if the attorney desires to represent the client's interests in selling literary or media rights. Standard 4-3.4 specifically forbids entering into such an agreement before the case is complete. The temptations are obvious: if the attorney hopes to acquire financial rewards from a share of profits, his or her professional judgment on how best to defend the client may be clouded. It is debatable whether putting off signing such an agreement until the case is complete removes the possibility of unethical decisions. One wonders if trial tactics and speeches aren't evaluated, at least subconsciously, on how they will appear in a later first-person narrative or movie screenplay. The potential for biased judgments is obvious. For instance, if an attorney has a client who has committed a particularly spectacular crime, there is the potential for celebrity status only if the case comes to trial, so a plea bargain—even if it is in the best interest of the client—may be considered less carefully by the attorney.

ZEALOUS DEFENSE

[The defense attorney] has no duty to execute any directive of the accused which does not comport with law or such standards (Standard 4-1.2[e]).

Few would challenge the idea that all people deserve to have their due-process rights protected. However, what many people find unsettling is the zeal with which some defense attorneys approach the courtroom contest. How diligent should the defense be in protecting the defendant's rights? A conflict may arise between providing an effective defense and maintaining professional ethics and individual morality. Lawyers should represent clients zealously within the bounds of the law, but the law is sometimes vague and difficult to determine.

Ethical standards and rules forbid some actions. The lawyer may not:

- Engage in motions or actions to intentionally and maliciously harm others
- Knowingly advance unwarranted claims or defenses
- Conceal or fail to disclose that which he or she is required by law to reveal
- Knowingly use perjured testimony or false evidence
- Knowingly make a false statement of law or fact
- Participate in the creation or preservation of evidence when he or she knows or it is obvious that the evidence is false
- Counsel the client in conduct that is illegal
- Engage in other illegal conduct

The attorney is also expected to maintain a professional and courteous relationship with the opposing attorneys, litigants, and witnesses and to refrain from disparaging statements or badgering conduct. The defense attorney must not intimidate or otherwise influence the jury or trier of fact or use the media for these same purposes.

Despite these ethical rules, practices such as withholding evidence, manufacturing evidence, witness badgering, and defamation of victims' characters are sometimes used as tactics in the defense arsenal. For instance, the practice of bringing out the sexual history of rape victims is done purely to paint her as a victim who deserved or asked for her rape. Even though rape-shield laws prohibit exposés of sexual history solely to discredit the reputation of the victim-witness, attorneys still attempt to bring in such evidence. Destroying the credibility of honest witnesses is considered good advocacy, at least for defense attorneys. For instance, if a witness accurately testifies to what he or she saw, a good attorney may still cast doubt in the jurors' minds by bringing out evidence of the use of eyeglasses, mistakes of judgment, and other facts that tend to obfuscate and undercut the credibility of the witness. Attorneys will do this even when they know that the witness is telling the truth. A zealous defense may include questioning the credibility of all prosecution witnesses.

Most ethical conflicts arise over subtle questions of how far one should go to provide a zealous defense. It is sometimes difficult to determine when a defense attorney's treatment of a witness is badgering as opposed to energetic cross-examination, or when exploring a witness's background is character assassination as opposed to a careful examination of credibility. Some attorneys focus attacks on opposing counsel. For example, female attorneys report that opposing male attorneys attempt to infantilize, patronize, or sexualize them in front of the judge and jury, as a tactic to destroy their credibility. Young attorneys encounter condescending treatment by opposing counsel, with comments such as, "What my young colleague here has evidently not learned yet…" designed to persuade the jury that the older attorney is wiser, more honest, or more mature than the younger attorney. Whispering during opposing counsel's opening or closing, rolling one's eyes in response to a statement or question, or making other verbal or physical gestures indicating disbelief, amusement, or disdain are part of the arsenal of the trial attorney. They are considered by some to be fair and within the rules of the "game."

JURY CONSULTANTS A recent innovation in trial tactics is the development of "scientific" jury selection. Attorneys often contend that a trial has already been won or lost once they have selected the jury. Whether or not this is true, attorneys are becoming increasingly sophisticated in their methods of choosing which members of a jury panel would make good jurors. A good juror for a defense attorney (or prosecutor) is not someone who is unbiased and fair, but rather, someone who is predisposed to be sympathetic to that attorney's case. Jury experts are psychologists, communication specialists, or other professionals who sit with the attorney and, through a combination of nonverbal and verbal clues, identify those jury panel members who are predisposed to believe the case presented by the attorney. Some allege that jury consultants can help to stack juries with the least sophisticated or most educated group, or any other type of group desired by the attorney.

Some lawyers, such as the famed Richard "Racehorse" Haynes of Houston, have used methods such as surveying a large sample of the population in the community where the case is to be tried to discover what certain demographic groups think about issues relevant to the case so these findings can be used when the jury is selected. Another method uses a **shadow jury**—a panel of people selected by the defense attorney to represent the actual jury. This shadow jury sits through the trial and provides feedback to the attorney on the evidence being presented during the trial. This allows the attorney to adjust his or her trial tactics in response.

Attorneys have always used intuition and less sophisticated means to decide which jury members to exclude, but the more modern tactics are questioned by some as too contrary to the basic idea that a trial is supposed to start with an unbiased jury (Smith and Meyer, 1987). Consultants also provide services such as

shadow jury A panel of people selected by the defense attorney to represent the actual jury; sits through the trial and provides feedback to the attorney on the evidence presented during the trial.

- Preparing witnesses
- Assisting with mock trials
- Developing desirable juror profiles
- Conducting phone surveys on public attitudes about a case
- Analyzing shadow juries
- Giving advice on effective posture, clothing choice, and tone of voice

Can our ethical systems help to determine what actions are ethically justified in defending a client zealously? Utilitarianism and egoism would probably allow a wider range of actions, depending on the particular interests or rewards represented by the case. Ethical formalism and religion might restrict the actions of a defense attorney to those allowed by a strict interpretation of the Model Rules.

CONFIDENTIALITY

Defense counsel should not reveal information relating to representation of a client unless ... counsel believes [it] is likely to result in imminent death or substantial bodily harm (Standard 4-3.7[d]).

attorney–client privilege The legal rule by which an attorney cannot disclose confidential information regarding his or her client except in a very few specified circumstances.

The **attorney–client privilege** refers to the inability of authorities to compel an attorney (through subpoena or threat of contempt) to disclose confidential information regarding his or her client. The ethical duty of confidentiality prohibits an attorney from disclosing to any person, or using for one's own gain, information about one's client obtained through the attorney–client relationship. Any attorney who breaches confidentiality may face disbarment.

Confidentiality is inherent in the fiduciary relationship between the client and the attorney, but more important is that the client must be able to expect and receive the full and complete assistance of his or her lawyer. If a client feels compelled to withhold negative and incriminatory information, he or she will not be able to receive the best defense; thus, the lawyer must be perceived as a completely confidential agent of the client. Parallels to the attorney–client relationship are relationships between husband and wife and between priest and penitent. In these cases, the relationship creates a legal entity that approximates a single interest rather than two interests, so a break in confidentiality would violate the Fifth Amendment protection against self-incrimination (Schoeman, 1982: 260).

According to Model Rule 1.6, the only situations wherein a lawyer can ethically reveal confidences of a client are these:

- When the client consents
- When disclosure is required by law or court order
- When one needs to defend oneself or employees against an accusation of wrongful conduct
- To prevent reasonably certain death or substantial bodily harm
- To prevent the client from committing a crime or fraud that is reasonably certain to result in substantial injury to the financial interests or property of another and the lawyer's services have been used to accomplish that end
- To prevent, mitigate, or rectify substantial injury to the financial interest or property of another that is reasonably certain to result or has resulted from the client's commission of a crime or fraud when the lawyer's services have been used

One of the most debated portions has been the part of this rule that specifies what type of crime justifies divulging the confidences of a client. The Model Code (used before the Model Rules) allowed disclosure to prevent *any* crime. An earlier version of the Model Rules dictated that an attorney could ethically violate a client's confidence only to prevent a future crime involving imminent death or grievous bodily harm. Many state bar associations refused to adopt the restrictive rule or enlarged it to include any crime. The current version requires disclosure of financial crimes if there is substantial injury, but it also allows disclosure to mitigate or rectify a financial crime. The Enron and WorldCom cases no doubt influenced the committee that updated this rule. Proponents of enlarging the scope of the rule argued that such a rule would have prevented Enron lawyers from participating in the scheme to defraud stockholders by hiding the true level of debt (Ariens, 2009).

Neither the restrictive rule nor the inclusive rule regarding disclosing a client's future crime applied to the Garrow incident (described in the Walking the Walk box), so the lawyers felt ethically bound to withhold the location of two bodies from the family of the victims. Do the ethical systems support keeping the client's confidences in a situation such as the one faced by Frank Armani when defending Robert Garrow?

It should be noted that the rule of confidentiality does not apply to physical evidence. Anything that is discoverable in the possession of a client is equally discoverable if in the possession of an attorney. Therefore, an attorney must hand over files or other incriminating evidence subject to a valid search warrant, motion, or subpoena. If the attorney is

WALKING THE WALK

Frank Armani may be one of the most revered and, also, hated lawyers in the past century. In 1973, Armani was asked to represent Robert Garrow, accused of murder and attempted murder. Garrow, who had already served eight years in prison for rape, was identified as the man who tied up four college students and brutally stabbed one to death, although luckily the other three got away. Because of the similarity of the attacks, Garrow was also suspected of being responsible for another murder of a young man. The man's companion was missing, and authorities were desperate to either find her alive or find her body. One other young woman was also missing, and Garrow was suspected of being responsible for her disappearance as well.

Armani took the case because he had previously represented Garrow on a minor charge. Armani brought in Francis Belge, a criminal defense attorney. During their questioning of Garrow, he confessed to the murders of the two missing women and told the lawyers where the bodies were hidden. The two lawyers confirmed that the bodies were where Garrow said they were, and they even took pictures. In one location, the girl's head was 10 feet away from her torso, and Belge moved the head closer to the body before he took the picture. In the other case, the body was in an abandoned mine shaft, and the lawyers lowered each other down to take pictures.

The lawyers believed that attorney–client confidentiality prevented them from revealing the location of the bodies or even that Garrow had confessed to being involved. They did, however, imply to the district attorney that Garrow might reveal the location in a plea agreement. They were trying to get the prosecutor to agree to an insanity plea with commitment to a mental hospital.

The prosecutor refused the deal, and before the case could come to trial for the first murder, the two girls' bodies were found. Garrow was the prime suspect.

In the small town where the trial was held, the two attorneys were shunned, vilified, and threatened. Both of the missing girls' families had pleaded with the attorneys to tell them if their daughters were alive or dead, and the families had no doubt that the attorneys knew more than they would reveal. Their suspicions became clear because after Garrow was convicted, Armani and Belge admitted in a press interview that they had known about the bodies all along.

The enraged prosecutor charged Belge with the crime of "failure to give a proper burial" and threatened both with obstruction of justice. The criminal charges were dropped, as were the state ethics charges, but both attorneys endured threats and the virtual loss of their law practices. One newspaper editorial at the time called Armani "a malignant cancer on the society that fostered him" and "less than useless to the human race." Belge left the practice of law entirely, and Armani was forced to build up his practice again after most of his clients left him. His marriage almost failed, and he flirted with alcoholism and suffered two heart attacks during the long ordeal.

When asked why he kept the murderer's secrets, Armani explained that civil rights are for the worst of us because, only then, are they there for the best of us. Eventually he was recognized for his ethical courage, but many still disagree on his stand that the client's confidentiality rights are more important than "common decency." One thing that no one can dispute, however, is that he paid a high price for his ethical principles.

Sources: Zitrin and Langford, 1999; Hansen, 2007: 28–29.

merely told where these items may be found, he or she is not obliged to tell the authorities where they are. For instance, if a client tells an attorney that a murder weapon is in a certain location, the attorney cannot divulge that information to authorities. However, if the client drops a murder weapon in the attorney's lap, the lawyer runs the risk of being charged with a felony if it is hidden or withheld from the police. If the attorney is told where a murder weapon is and goes to check, that information is still protected; however, if the attorney takes the weapon back to his or her office or moves it in any way, then the attorney may be subjected to felony charges of obstruction of justice or evidence tampering. Belge was charged in the Garrow case because he moved the body, although he was never convicted.

A defense attorney's ethics may also be compromised when a client insists on taking the stand to commit perjury. Model Rule 3.3 specifically forbids the lawyer from allowing perjury to take place; if it happens before the attorney realizes the intent of the client, the defense must not use or refer to the perjured testimony (Freedman, 1986; Kleinig, 1986). The quandary is that if the attorney shows his or her disbelief or discredits the client, this behavior violates the ethical mandate of a zealous defense, and to inform the court of the perjury violates the ethical rule of confidentiality.

Pellicotti (1990) explains that an attorney should first try to dissuade the client from committing perjury. If the client persists in plans to lie, the attorney then has an ethical duty to withdraw from the case, and there is some authority that the attorney should disclose the client's plan to the court. Withdrawal is problematic because it will usually jeopardize a case, and disclosure is even more problematic because, arguably, it will affect the judgment of the hearing judge.

In *Nix v. Whiteside* (475 U.S. 157, 89 L.Ed.2d 123 [1986]), the Supreme Court held that it did not violate the defendant's Sixth Amendment right to counsel for the attorney to refuse to help the defendant commit perjury. In this murder case, the defendant told his lawyer that he had not seen a gun in the victim's hand. At a later point, he told his attorney that if he didn't testify that he saw a gun, he would be "dead" (lose the case). The attorney told him that if he were to testify falsely, he would have to impeach him and would seek to withdraw from the case. The defendant testified truthfully, was found guilty, and then appealed based on ineffective counsel. The court found that the right to effective counsel did not include the right to an attorney who would suborn perjury.

Pellicotti (1990) describes the *passive* role and the *active* role of an attorney with a client who commits perjury. In the passive role, the attorney asks no questions during direct examination that would elicit untruthful answers and may make a statement that the client is taking the stand against the advice of an attorney. The attorney does not refer to perjured testimony during summation or any arguments. The active role allows for the attorney to disclose to the court the fact of the perjured testimony. There is no great weight of authority to commend either approach, leaving attorneys with a difficult ethical dilemma. The best defense of some attorneys is not to know about the lie in the first place.

If the attorney is not sure that the client would be committing perjury, there is no legal duty to disclose. The weight of authority indicates that the attorney with doubts should proceed with the testimony; any disclosure of such doubts is improper and unethical. Thus, some attorneys tell a client, "Before you say anything, I need to tell you that I cannot participate in perjury, and if I know for a fact that you plan to lie, I cannot put you on the stand," or they ask the client, "What do I need to know that is damaging to this case?" rather than ask if the client is guilty of the crime. Further, many attorneys argue that all defendants lie about everything and they can't be believed anyway. If this is true, some attorneys may conclude that since they don't know with certainty that the defendant is lying, they can allow the defendant to say anything they want on the stand.

While the attorney–client privilege is sacrosanct, some argue that there should be some exceptions when keeping quiet harms third parties. It is quite troubling, for instance, to ponder how many people are in prison for crimes they did not commit and somewhere an attorney for the real criminal knows, but cannot do anything about it.

DILEMMA: You are defending a client whom you believe is guilty of the brutal rape and murder of a young girl. He has not admitted the crime to you, but he hasn't denied it either, and the physical and circumstantial evidence is overwhelming. One day he tells you that another man is in prison for a similar rape and murder that he committed 10 years earlier. You check and find out that, indeed, there is a person by that name who was convicted and is, in fact, facing execution in the next month for the crime. What do you do? What do you do if the other man is not facing execution but a 40-year prison sentence?

LAW Recall that the Model Rules carry the weight of law in that if a lawyer violates a client's confidentiality, any evidence may be excluded by the court. Further, the attorney would face sanctions, including being disbarred from the practice of law. The Model Rules seem clear that since this situation does not involve a new crime, it is not covered by the "new crime" exception; however, an execution does seem to fall under the exception to prevent a "reasonably certain death or substantial bodily harm." Lately, some states have debated adding an exception that would allow attorneys to come forward to prevent wrongful imprisonment, but there is resistance because it may create a situation where attorneys will have to frequently go against the best interests of their client.

POLICY Unlike law enforcement, policy analysis seems less relevant in many of the ethical issues facing defense attorneys. Of course, public defenders have office policies that may affect some of their decision making, but very often defense attorneys are sole practitioners who have no office policy considerations to guide their behavior.

ETHICS The rule seems to be justified by utilitarianism because society benefits in the long run from the presence of attorney–client confidence. Therefore, this confidence should be sacrificed only when it endangers a life (which would be a greater loss than the benefit of client–attorney trust) (Harris, 1986). Religious ethics might condemn the attorney's actions because withholding information—for instance, the location of the bodies in the Garrow case described in the Walking the Walk box—was a form of deception. In the Roman Catholic religion, however, a similar ethical dilemma might arise if someone were to confess to a priest. In that case, the priest could not betray that confession no matter what the circumstances.

No easy answers to the dilemma are forthcoming using ethical formalism. First of all, under the categorical imperative, the lawyer's actions must be such that we would be willing for all others to engage in similar behavior under like circumstances. Could one will that it become universal law for attorneys to keep such information secret? What if you were the parents in the Garrow case who did not know the whereabouts of their daughter, or even if she was alive or dead? Or what if you were the loved one of someone who was wrongfully convicted and imprisoned? It is hard to imagine that you would be willing to agree with this universal law. If you were the criminal, however, you would not want a lawyer to betray confidences that would hurt your case. If you were a lawyer, you would want a rule encouraging a client to be truthful so you would be able to provide an adequate defense. Ethical formalism is also concerned with duty; it is obvious that the duty of an attorney is always to protect the interests of his or her client. However, there are also larger duties of every attorney to protect the integrity of the justice system.

The ethics of care would be concerned with the needs of both the client and the parents in the Garrow case, and in the dilemma of the person wrongfully convicted. This ethical system might support a resolution in a less absolutist fashion than the other rationales. For instance, when discussing the Garrow case in a college classroom, many students immediately decide that they would call in the location of the bodies anonymously, thereby relieving the parents' anxiety and also protecting, to some extent, the confidential communication. One could make the same type of phone call in the case of the wrongfully convicted if an attorney had evidence that could help the person prove his or her innocence. However, this compromise is unsupported by an absolute view of confidentiality because it endangers the client, but it does protect the relationship of the attorney and the client and still meets the needs of others concerned.

situational model A conceptualization in which lawyers weigh the priorities in each case and decide each case on the particular factors present.

systems model An absolute or legalistic model in that an attorney's behavior would always be considered wrong or right depending on the ethical rule guiding the definition.

Aronson (1977: 59–63) discusses two methods for resolving ethical dilemmas. The first is called the **situational model**, wherein lawyers weigh the priorities and decide each case on the specific factors present. This is similar to our explanation of situational ethics. In some cases, client confidentiality may be sacrificed when others' interests are at stake, but confidentiality may be paramount in other cases. The **systems model** utilizes a more absolute or legalistic model in that behavior would always be considered wrong or right depending on the ethical rule guiding the definition. Obviously, these two systems of decision making bear a great deal of resemblance to the situational and absolutist ethical models discussed in Chapter 2. As a pure advocate, the defense attorney's duty is to pursue a client's interest. As long as the attorney does not run afoul of the law or ethical mandates, the client's defense is the sole objective.

Ethical Issues for Prosecutors

Prosecutors do not serve an individual client; rather, their client is the system or society itself, and their mission is justice. As the second line of decision makers in the system, prosecutors have extremely broad powers of discretion. The prosecutor acts like a strainer; he or she collects some cases for formal prosecution while eliminating a great many others. Prosecuting every case is impossible. Resources are limited, and some cases' evidence is weak, making it unlikely to win a conviction. Early diversion of such cases saves taxpayers money and saves individuals trouble and expense.

USE OF DISCRETION

> A prosecutor should not institute ... criminal charges ... not supported by probable cause (Standard 3-3.9[a]).

The prosecutor must seek justice, not merely a conviction. Toward this end, prosecutors must share evidence, exercise restraint in the use of their power, represent the public interest, and give the accused the benefit of reasonable doubt. Disciplinary rules are more specific. They forbid the prosecutor from pursuing charges when there is no probable cause and mandate timely disclosure to defense counsel of evidence, especially exculpatory evidence or evidence that might mitigate guilt or reduce the punishment. Despite these ideals of prosecutorial duty, an unstated influence over prosecutorial discretion is that prosecutors want to and must (to be considered successful) win. A decision to prosecute is influenced by political and public pressures, the chance for conviction, the severity of the crime, a "gut" feeling of guilt or innocence, prison overcrowding, and the weight of evidence. The prosecutorial role is to seek justice, but justice doesn't mean the same thing to everyone and certainly does not mean prosecuting everyone to the fullest extent of the law. Whether to charge is one of the most important decisions of the criminal justice process. The decision should be fair, neutral, and accomplished with due process, but this is an ideal that is sometimes supplanted by other considerations. Prosecutors don't usually use their charging power for intimidation or harassment, but other factors may be involved in the decision to charge. For instance, a prosecutor might have a particular interest in a type of crime such as child abuse or drugs and pursue these cases more intensely. How sure should a prosecutor be that a suspect is guilty before prosecuting? Can a prosecutor ethically prosecute one individual of a crime, obtain a conviction, and then prosecute another individual for the same crime? It has been known to happen (Zachiaras and Green, 2009).

The Genarlow Wilson case presents a difficult issue of how prosecutorial discretion is sometimes used (McCaffrey, 2007; ESPN News Service, 2007). Wilson was a 17-year-old high school athlete on his way to a college scholarship. Instead, he ended up in prison because of a party in which several teenagers, including Wilson, engaged in consensual sex. One of the girls involved was 15. The evidence was incontrovertible—a videotape clearly showing Wilson with the underage girl. The prosecutor charged him with rape, and a jury convicted him, which meant a mandatory 10-year prison sentence. The uproar resulted in the legislature changing the law to make sex between teenagers a misdemeanor, but the law could not be retroactively applied to Wilson. He spent two years in prison before the Georgia Supreme Court released him on the grounds that the punishment was cruel and unusual. The prosecutor decided to charge Wilson rather than use his discretion and decide not to charge, and he also filed an appeal against the first appellate decision to reduce Wilson's sentence to 12 months. In cases such as these, the prosecutor's beliefs dramatically affect what happens in a case.

Other considerations that affect the decision to charge include pressure from law enforcement—for instance, when a bargain is struck for a lesser charge in return for testimony or information that could lead to further convictions. There is also the pressure of public opinion. Prosecutors might pursue cases that they otherwise would have dropped if there is a great deal of public interest in the case. The victim also affects the decision to prosecute. Victims who have mental impairments may not make the best witnesses and there may be less chance of getting a conviction. In one such case, five women with developmental disabilities had been raped and terrorized by the owner of a licensed home where they lived. The prosecutor declined to pursue charges under the rationale that "any woman with a developmental disability would have zero credibility in court." Only when the licensing authority secured additional testimony, revoked the license of the owner, and publicly exposed the situation did the prosecutor press charges (Hook, 2001).

Prosecutors in state capitals often have "public integrity" units that prosecute wrongdoing on the part of public officials. Some prosecutors might file charges against political opponents at election time, but other prosecutors might be falsely accused of such political considerations when they do charge politicians with public-integrity violations.

A special case of discretion and charging is the decision to pursue a capital homicide conviction. Prosecutors have the power to decide whether to seek the death penalty or a prison term. Clearly, the decision to seek the death penalty is not made uniformly across jurisdictions. One of the biggest considerations is cost. Because capital trials are extremely expensive, counties that have bigger budgets are more likely to seek the death penalty; they have the resources and staff to handle the cases (Hall, 2002). Obviously, these considerations have nothing to do with justice, and it should cause concern that a criterion other than severity of the crime or future risk affects whether an offender ultimately receives the death penalty.

Various studies have attempted to describe prosecutors' decision making; one cites office policy as an important influence (Jacoby, Mellon, and Smith, 1980):

- *Legal sufficiency* is an office policy that weeds out those cases in which the evidence is not strong enough to support further action.
- *System efficiency* is an office policy with goals of efficiency and accountability; all decisions are made with these goals in mind, so many cases result in dismissals.
- *Defendant rehabilitation* emphasizes diversion and other rehabilitation tools rather than punitive goals.
- *Trial sufficiency* is an office policy that encourages a charge that can be sustained through trial.

Another study looked at the prosecutor as operating in an exchange system. The relationship between the prosecutor and the police was described as one of give-and-take. Prosecutors balance police needs or wishes against their own vulnerability. The prosecutor makes personal judgments about which police officers can be trusted. Exchange also takes place between the prosecutor's office and the courts. When the jails become overcrowded, prosecutors recommend deferred adjudication and probation; when dockets back up, prosecutors drop charges. Finally, exchange takes place between defense attorneys and prosecutors, especially because many defense attorneys have previously served as prosecutors and may be personally familiar with the procedures and even personalities in the prosecutor's office (Cole, 1970).

On the one hand, discretion is considered essential to the prosecutorial function of promoting individualized justice and softening the impersonal effects of the law. On the other hand, the presence of discretion is the reason that the legal system is considered unfair and biased toward certain groups of people or individuals. Even though we would not want to eliminate prosecutorial discretion, it could be guided by regulations or internal guidelines. For instance, an office policy might include a procedure for providing written reasons for dropping charges, and this procedure would respond to charges of unbridled discretion.

One writer argues that the ethics of virtue can help determine ethical decisions for prosecutors. Cassidy (2006) presents three ethical issues:

- When is it proper for a prosecutor to offer charging or sentencing concessions to an accomplice in order to secure the accomplice's testimony against a co-defendant?

- When, if ever, may a prosecutor impeach a defense witness whom the prosecutor believes has testified truthfully?

- How should a prosecutor react at trial when opposing counsel appears to be advocating ineffectively on behalf of his client?

Then Cassidy describes Aristotle's ethics of virtue, as well as the thinking of St. Thomas Aquinas and Alasdair MacIntyre, a modern virtue theorist. Basically, as we learned in Chapter 2, the ethics of virtue proposes that the ethical person is the virtuous person, and the virtuous person is the person who behaves in a way consistent with the virtues. Aristotle classified virtues into moral virtues and intellectual virtues. His moral virtues include temperance, courage, industriousness, generosity, pride, good temper, truthfulness, friendliness, modesty, justice, and pleasantness; and the intellectual virtues include understanding, science, theoretical wisdom (philosophy), craft, and practical wisdom. St. Thomas Aquinas added theological virtues of faith, hope, and charity. Alasdair MacIntyre defined the most important virtues as justice, courage, honesty, and prudence. Cassidy argues that virtue ethics are different from absolute rule-based ethics and that each person must have sensitivity to the "salient features of [particular] situations" (2006: 637).

Turning to the ethical dilemmas, Cassidy explains that neither Model Rule 3.8 nor the Standards gives prosecutors much guidance in any of the cases, and so they must apply the virtues. In the situation of offering a deal to a co-conspirator, he argues that the virtue of courage would require the prosecutor to have the courage to refuse to deal if justice demanded it. The virtue of honesty would mean that the prosecutor must make sure that the suspect was not lying and also make sure that he or she was not more culpable than the person he or she was testifying against. The prosecutor must disclose the agreement to the defense and the court so the veracity of the testimony can be challenged. The virtue of justice or fairness would mean that the prosecutor should not give the most punishment to those who are least involved.

In the second ethical dilemma, the prosecutor must decide whether to try to impeach a witness who is telling the truth. Cassidy argues that the Model Rules allow defense attorneys the right to impeach prosecution witnesses even if they are telling the truth, but there is no mandate that prosecutors should do so, as they are supposed to be seeking justice, not pursuing the best interest of their client. He offers Standard 3-5.7(b), which states:

> A prosecutor should not use the power of cross-examination to discredit or undermine a witness if the prosecutor knows the witness is testifying truthfully.

Cassidy argues that the virtues of honesty and courage require a prosecutor to forgo cross-examination if he or she knows that the truth has been told. Regarding the last ethical dilemma involving an incompetent defense attorney, he points to Model Rule 8.3, which requires that attorneys report incompetent colleagues to bar authorities, but also admits that the "snitch" rule is widely ignored by all attorneys. Further, it would be difficult to distinguish incompetence from trial tactics in some cases. The virtues that apply are justice and honesty, and if the attorney's actions seem to be offending the system of justice, it is the prosecutor's duty to bring it to the attention of the judge.

Admitting that the virtues of courage, honesty, and prudence are only slightly more abstract than the concept of justice, Cassidy urges prosecutors' offices to seek employees who already exhibit character that displays virtue. Qualifications for hiring should include evidence that the individual is honest and sensitive to others. Further, those working in a prosecutor's office should be rewarded for virtuous behavior over and above simply winning cases.

CONFLICTS OF INTEREST

> A prosecutor should avoid a conflict of interest with respect to his or her official duties (Standard 3.1-3[a]).

About a quarter of chief prosecutors are part time, compared to about half in the early 1990s (Dawson, 1992: 1; Perry, 2006: 2). Obviously, this poses the possibility of a conflict of interest. It may happen that a part-time prosecutor has a private practice, and there may be situations where the duty to a private client runs counter to the duty of the prosecutor to the public. In some cases, a client may become a defendant, necessitating the prosecutor to hire a special prosecutor. Even when there are no direct conflicts of interest, the pressure of time inevitably poses a conflict. The division of time between the private practice, where income is generated by the number of cases and hours billed, and prosecuting cases, where income is fixed no matter how many hours are spent, may result in a less energetic prosecutorial function than one might wish.

It is well known that the prosecutor's job is a good stepping-stone to politics, and many use it as such. In these situations, one has to wonder whether cases are taken on the basis of merit or on their ability to place the prosecutor in the public eye and help his or her career. Populous counties have many assistant district attorneys (ADAs), perhaps hundreds, and only the district attorney is elected. Many ADAs work in the prosecutor's office for a number of years and then move into the private sector. The reason has largely to do with money. Assistant district attorneys make an average of $40,000 to $60,000 a year, but in private practice they could make much more than that (R. Cohen, 2001). The question then becomes: does the career plan to enter private practice as a litigator affect their prosecutorial decision to take a case to trial?

ASSET FORFEITURE The Racketeer Influenced and Corrupt Organizations Act (RICO) was passed as a tool to help combat organized crime. Among its provisions is

asset forfeiture
A legal tool used to confiscate property and money associated with organized criminal activity.

asset forfeiture, a legal procedure to confiscate property and money associated with organized criminal activity. Once this tactic was approved by the courts, a veritable flood of prosecutions began that were designed, it seems, primarily to obtain cash, boats, houses, and other property of drug dealers. Making decisions based on the potential for what can be confiscated rather than the culpability of offenders is a real and dangerous development in this type of prosecution.

The origins of civil forfeiture were in the Comprehensive Drug Abuse and Control Act of 1970 and the Organized Crime Control Act of 1970. Both of these laws allowed mechanisms for the government to seize assets gained through illegal means. Eventually the types of assets vulnerable to seizure were expanded, including assets *intended* to be used as well as those gained by or used in illegal activities. All of the states have passed similar asset forfeiture laws. The "take" from asset forfeiture increased from $27.2 million in 1985 to $874 million in 1992 (Jenson and Gerber, 1996). Between the early 1990s and the early 2000s, the total amount of federal forfeiture proceeds shared with state and local law enforcement was $2.5 billion! (Hartman, 2001) According to one recent source, the U.S. Department of Justice's Assets Forfeiture Fund held more than $1 billion in net assets in 2008 (Williams et al., 2010).

There are a number of problematic issues with asset forfeiture. The exclusionary rule does not apply to civil forfeiture proceedings, so some allege that police are now pursuing assets instead of criminals, because in a civil proceeding the defendant does not receive legal aid. A civil forfeiture hearing can take place without any criminal prosecution and without the alleged criminal being present. Unlike a criminal trial, in asset forfeiture it had been the case that the government had only to show probable cause, and then the burden of proof shifted to the individual to prove his or her innocence. This changed when President Bill Clinton signed into law the Civil Asset Forfeiture Reform Act, which shifted the burden of proof from the claimant to the government (Worral, 2001). Now at least the presumption of innocence has been put back into place.

YOUR MONEY OR YOUR CHILDREN?

The small town of Tenaha, Texas, received the wrong kind of publicity in 2009 when an investigative report revealed that black and Hispanic motorists passing through the town were stopped and threatened with jail or the loss of their children if they did not hand over large amounts of money. One man was carrying $8,500 to buy a new car and was pulled over for going a couple miles per hour over the speed limit. He was taken to jail and told that he would be charged with money-laundering, but he could leave with no charges if he would sign over the cash to the city. The district attorney in the town denied any impropriety, arguing that Texas law allows the confiscation of money and personal property used in a crime. It was this same prosecutor who threatened another couple passing through town that their children would be taken away by social services if they did not sign over $6,000 they were carrying. CNN reporters discovered that the prosecutor's office wrote a $10,000 check from the asset forfeiture account to a police officer who stopped many of the people, for "investigative costs." The scandal has spurred the Texas legislature to look at tightening the asset forfeiture law to prohibit the type of property waivers in return for no charges filed that were used in Tenaha.

SOURCE: Tuchman and Wojleck, 2009.

Perhaps one of the most troubling aspects of civil forfeiture is that third parties are often those most hurt by the loss. For example, the spouse or parents of a suspected drug dealer may lose their home. In one of the most widely publicized forfeiture cases, a man solicited a prostitute; the state instituted proceedings and was successful in seizing the car he was driving when he solicited the prostitute—which was, in fact, his wife's car! This case received so much press because the Supreme Court ruled that no constitutional violation occurred with the forfeiture, even though his wife had nothing to do with the criminal activity. Another case that received a great deal of media attention was that of a man who lost his expensive motorboat when one marijuana cigarette was found on it. These and other uses of asset forfeiture have spurred reforms and court decisions that are curtailing its use to some extent. However, asset forfeiture clearly has become an almost indispensable source of revenue for law enforcement and the courts (Worral, 2001). The In the News box presents a conflict where prosecutors in one small town were evidently acting as revenue agents for the town.

PLEA BARGAINING

> A prosecutor should not knowingly make false statements or representations as to fact or law in the course of plea discussions (Standard 3.41[c])

As discussed earlier, there are serious ethical concerns over the practice of plea bargaining. In jurisdictions that have determinate sentencing, plea bargaining has become "charge bargaining" instead of sentence bargaining. Most conclude that plea bargaining, even if not exactly "right," is certainly efficient and probably inevitable. Should we measure the morality of an action by its efficiency? This efficiency argument is similar to the argument used to defend some deceptive investigative practices of police. If the goals of the system are crime control or bureaucratic efficiency, plea bargaining makes sense. If the goals of the system are the protection of individual rights and the protection of due process, plea bargaining is much harder to justify. Obviously, plea bargaining would fail under the categorical imperative, for the individual is treated as a means in the argument that plea bargaining is good for the system.

Arguments given in defense of plea bargaining include the heavy caseloads, limited resources, legislative over-criminalization, individualized justice, and legal problems of cases (legal errors that would result in mistrials or dropped charges if the client didn't plead) (Knudten, 1978: 275). If we concede that plea bargaining can be justified, there are remaining ethical problems concerning specific practices relating to it. Only 36 percent of chief prosecutors reported that explicit criteria for plea bargains were in place in 1990 (Bureau of Justice Statistics, 1992). Guidelines providing a range of years for certain types of charges would help individual prosecutors maintain some level of consistency in a particular jurisdiction. Plea bargaining continues to be prevalent across the United States; felony defendants are 20 times more likely to plead than go to trial, and 86 percent of federal cases are resolved with a plea bargain (Hashimoto, 2008: 950). See the Policy Box for a critique of plea bargaining.

Should prosecutors overcharge—that is, charge at a higher degree of severity or press more charges than could possibly be sustained by evidence—so they can bargain down? Should prosecutors mislead defense attorneys about the amount of evidence or the kind of evidence they have or about the sentence they can offer to obtain a guilty plea? Gershman (1991) documents instances of prosecutors engaged in false promises, fraud, misrepresentation of conditions, deals without benefit of counsel, package deals, and threats during plea bargaining. Critics contend that prosecutors hold all the cards in plea bargaining.

POLICY ISSUES   Plea Bargaining

The practice of exchanging a reduced charge or a reduced sentence for a guilty plea is widespread. Although some disagree with the practice and say it leads to innocent people pleading guilty and a reduction in the integrity of the system, most argue that the system couldn't work without the practice. Also, proponents argue that it is ethical to give the offender something in exchange for not putting the state to the expense of a trial.

Law

U.S. Supreme Court opinions have legitimated the use of plea bargaining. They have held that prosecutors and judges must abide by the agreements made and that defendants cannot turn around and claim afterward that the exchange was unfair. The Supreme Court has also allowed prosecutors to threaten harsher sentences if the defendant does not plead.

Policy

Different prosecutors' offices handle plea bargaining differently. Some have guidelines, and others leave it to the prosecutor's discretion. In general, there are informal office policies so that some offices give more generous offers than other jurisdictions do. Plea bargaining is something that is covered in the training of new prosecutors.

Ethics

Prosecutors' ethical issues with plea bargaining include whether to overcharge to get someone to plead or to lie about how much evidence there is. Defense attorneys' ethical issues include the extent to which they will try to convince individuals to plead if they swear they are innocent. Judges have ethical issues as well, in that they do not have to accept a plea in a case where they do not believe evidence is sufficient to uphold the verdict.

Another discussion is whether the prosecution should have to share exculpatory evidence (facts that support innocence) with the defense before a plea. In *Brady v. Maryland* (373 U.S. 83[1963]), the Supreme Court held that the prosecution must share any exculpatory information with the defense that is material to the case (which means if it would affect the outcome of the trial) when they ask for it, but it is unclear whether such a requirement applies pre-plea or only before trial. Legal observers predict that the Court would not apply *Brady* to pre-plea negotiations because the legal rationale is fairness of trial, not voluntariness of plea. In fact, U.S. attorneys and some state prosecutors routinely require the defendant to waive *Brady* rights as part of a plea arrangement. Obviously such information is important in order to make the decision to plead guilty or not. Prosecutors resist the interpretation of *Brady* that requires them to provide the defense with exculpatory evidence before a plea because they lose bargaining power. Proponents of pre-plea discovery argue that it violates due process to allow a defendant to think there is no exculpatory evidence when, in fact, there is (Hashimoto, 2008).

MEDIA RELATIONS

The prosecutor has an important relationship with the press. The media can be enemy or friend, depending on how charismatic or forthcoming the prosecutor is in interviews. Sometimes cases are said to be "tried in the media," with the defense attorney and the prosecutor staging verbal sparring matches for public consumption. Prosecutors may react to cases and judges' decisions in the media, criticizing the decision or the sentence and, in the process, denigrating the dignity of the system. More often, the defense attempts to sway the press to a sympathetic view of the offense, which is easier to accomplish during prosecutorial silence.

In many of the celebrated criminal cases of the past and today, the prosecutor and defense utilized the media to promote their version of events. The Sam Sheppard case (supposedly the case that spurred the idea for *The Fugitive* television series and movie) was the first one to illustrate the power of the media and related misconduct by the prosecution, such as discussing evidence with reporters that could not be admitted at trial. The media storm was actively encouraged by the prosecutor and, ultimately, led to the Supreme Court ruling that due process had been violated (Kirchmeier et al., 2009).

ABA Model Rule 3.6(b) is a prohibition against out-of-court statements that a reasonable person should expect would have a substantial likelihood of materially prejudicing a proceeding. Defense attorneys might be expected to make statements to exonerate their client and disparage the state's case, but prosecutors' statements have a greater ring of authority. The rule specifies that no statements should be given involving any of the following topics:

- The character, credibility, reputation, or criminal record of a party, suspect, or witness
- The identity of a witness
- The expected testimony of a party or witness
- The performance or results of any test or examination
- The refusal of any party to submit to such tests or examinations
- The identity or nature of physical evidence
- Inadmissible information
- The possibility of a guilty plea
- The existence or contents of a confession or an admission
- The defendant's refusal to make a statement
- An opinion about the guilt or innocence of the defendant or suspect
- A statement that the defendant has been charged with a crime unless it is in the context that a charge does not mean the party is guilty

The following facts may be disclosed:

- The general nature of the claim or charge
- Any information in a public record
- The fact that the matter is being investigated and the scope of the investigation
- The schedule of litigation
- A request for assistance in obtaining information
- A warning of danger
- The identity, residence, occupation, and family status of the accused
- Information to enable the accused's capture (if at large)
- The fact, time, and place of arrest
- The identity of investigating and arresting officers

The case of the Duke University lacrosse players accused of rape resulted in the prosecutor (Mike Nifong) being disbarred. In this high profile 2007 case, a stripper alleged that she was raped by members of the lacrosse team after she was hired to perform at a party for them. Very early in the case, the district attorney made several public statements indicating that the athletes were guilty, that just because they were white and rich and the alleged victim was black and poor, they weren't going to get away with the crime, and so on. No doubt the fact that the district attorney was in a hotly contested election had something to do with his decision to make such public statements so early in the case.

As the investigation progressed, the victim's story changed in substantive ways about who raped her and when it took place. Furthermore, no physical evidence substantiated her story. Despite this, the district attorney continued to make comments to the media that the players were guilty. Later, the alibi of one defendant was substantiated by an ATM camera showing that he was somewhere else when the rape was supposed to have taken place. Still Nifong did not drop the charges and in fact instructed a lab technician to drop a sentence from his report indicating that the semen found on the alleged victim contained the DNA of several unknown males, but not the accused men's.

Eventually, the state attorney general sent in a special prosecutor to handle the case, and this prosecutor promptly dropped the charges against the accused college athletes. Nifong was publicly sanctioned and, in an unusually harsh punishment, was disbarred from the practice of law. Ethical experts argue that Nifong's actions were egregious. The case is a good example of why public expressions of guilt are strictly prohibited: the prosecutor gets locked into a position that is difficult to back out of. After Nifong had committed himself to the conclusion that the college men were guilty, he found himself under intense pressure to pursue the case, even in the face of contradictory evidence (Jeffrey, 2007).

Another prosecutor in the news was U.S. Attorney Johnny Sutton, in the Western District of Texas, when he pursued charges against two border agents after they shot a suspected drug smuggler. The agents, José Compeán and Ignacio Ramos, were sent to prison for more than 10 years for shooting the unarmed man, violating their use-of-force policies, and trying to cover up the shooting. During the trial and after the conviction, there was an outpouring of anger that the prosecutor was "supporting the enemy" rather than our own agents, especially for pursuing the charge of "use of a firearm in the course of another crime," which was the basis for the mandatory 10-year sentence under federal sentencing law. Sutton's position in pursuing charges was that the agents had broken the law, and no one is above the law.

During Michael Mukasey's confirmation hearings as U.S. attorney general in October 2007, several legislators urged him to commit to an investigation of the case and Sutton's decision to prosecute (Moscoso, 2007). Although it might have been more politically popular to drop or reduce the charges against the border agents in the face of extreme public and political pressure, the prosecutor in this case chose to endure public antipathy in his decision to pursue prosecution. Most decisions do not generate this degree of public controversy, but each decision to prosecute begins with a prosecutor choosing whether and how to pursue charges against suspected offenders. In a final note, one of President George W. Bush's last acts in office was to commute the sentences of the two men.

EXPERT WITNESSES

> A prosecutor who engages an expert for an opinion should respect the independence of the expert and should not seek to dictate the formation of the expert's opinion on the subject (Standard 3-3.3[a]).

The use of expert witnesses has risen in recent years. Psychiatrists often testify as to the mental competency or legal insanity of an accused. Criminologists and other social scientists may be asked to testify on topics such as victimization in prison, statistical evidence of sentencing discrimination, the effectiveness of predictive instruments for prison riots and other disturbances, risk assessment for individual offenders, mental health services in prison, patterns of criminality, battered-woman syndrome, and so on (see Anderson and Winfree, 1987). A whole range of experts in the field of criminalistics also have emerged as important players in criminal prosecutions. Expert testimony is allowed as evidence in trials when it is based on sound scientific method (the *Daubert* standard; this replaced the *Frye* standard, which required acceptance in the scientific community). Judges apply this standard, and they can accept or bar such evidence from being offered to the jury (Giannelli and McMunigal, 2007). When experts are honest in their presentation as to the limitations and potential bias of the material, no ethical issues arise. However, expert witnesses may testify in a realm beyond fact or make testimony appear factual when some questions are not clearly answerable. Because of the **halo effect**—essentially, when a person with expertise or status in one area is given deference in all areas—an expert witness may endow a statement or conclusion with more legitimacy than it warrants. Those who always appear on one side or the other may also lose their credibility. For instance, a doctor who was often used by prosecutors in one jurisdiction during capital-sentencing hearings became known as "Dr. Death" because he always determined that the defendant posed a future risk to society—one of the necessary elements for the death penalty. Although this doctor was well known by reputation to prosecutors and defense attorneys alike, juries could not be expected to know of his predilection for finding future risk and would take his testimony at face value unless the defense attorney brought out this information during cross-examination (Raeder, 2007).

> **halo effect** The phenomenon in which a person with expertise or status in one area is given deference in all areas.

The use of expert witnesses can present ethical problems when the witness is used in a dishonest fashion. Obviously, to pay an expert for his or her time is not unethical, but to shop for experts until finding one who benefits the case is unethical, for the credibility of the witness is suspect. Another difficulty arises when the prosecutor obtains an expert who develops a conclusion or a set of findings that would help the defense. Ethical rules do not prohibit an attorney in a civil matter or criminal defense attorneys from merely disregarding the information and not giving notice to the opponent that there is information that could benefit his or her case. However, prosecutors operate under a special set of ethics because their goal is justice, not pure advocacy. Any exculpatory information is supposed to be shared with the defense; this obviously includes test results and may also include expert witness findings (Giannelli and McMunigal, 2007). Because much of expert testimony concerns scientific principles that are incomprehensible to laypeople, the potential for being misled by an expert witness is magnified.

CSI *AND THE COURTS* For many years, forensic experts have testified regarding factual issues of evidence ranging from ballistics to blood spatter. Television shows such as *CSI* contribute to the mystique of the crime-scene investigator as a scientific Sherlock Holmes who uses physics, chemistry, and biology to catch criminals. However, the reality is that some of this "expert" testimony has been called *junk science* (McRoberts, Mills, and Possley, 2004). Also, lab examiners who work for police laboratories may exhibit a heavy prosecution bias that colors their analysis and testimony.

As mentioned in Chapter 6, the FBI and several police departments have had their labs come under fire for shoddy practices or biased analyses. The Houston police crime lab has been investigated and was even closed down for a period of time, and several defendants have been exonerated by retests of the DNA evidence that convicted them. Criticism of the lab included poorly trained technicians, lax procedures, shoddy records, overstated testimony, and the inability to do certain tasks such as separate DNA from mixed samples. Thousands of cases were eventually reviewed, but because Harris County has sent more defendants to death row than any other county in Texas, some of those convicted through tainted evidence may have been executed (Liptak, 2003; Axtman, 2003). One of the cases is that of Gary Alvin Richard. He was convicted in 1987 of rape and robbery, partially due to the testimony of a lab examiner who did not reveal evidence that could have exonerated him. Richard was released in 2009, after serving 22 years, when a court threw out his conviction based on the evidence that the forensic evidence was hidden from the defense. Pat Lykos, the Harris County district attorney, was quoted as supporting an independent crime laboratory separate from the police department to guard against any bias that might occur with a police-run lab (KTRK, 2009).

The highly respected Virginia state crime lab has also been investigated after outside experts hired by the defense called into question the DNA analysis that sent a man to death row. This case is one of several dozen death row cases around the country that are being reviewed because of potentially faulty, biased, or perjured lab analyst testimony (Possley, Mills, and McRoberts, 2004). Two other lab scandals—in Oklahoma and in West Virginia—have led to millions of dollars in settlements for those falsely incarcerated, and forced reviews of hundreds of cases. Joyce Gilchrist, a forensic chemist from Oklahoma, was implicated in several DNA exonerations for her hair analysis. In one case, it was proven she knew her testimony was false because she hid the true results from the defense (Raeder, 2007). In Montana, there was a petition to the state supreme court to undertake independent testing of hundreds of cases handled by a lab examiner who was responsible for three false convictions based on faulty hair analysis (Possley, Mills, and McRoberts, 2004). It strains belief to assume that prosecutors in these cases did not know that the testimony of these examiners was questionable.

criminalistics The profession involved in the application of science to recognize, identify, and evaluate physical evidence in court proceedings.

Even when mismanagement, shoddy practices, and untrained staff aren't the issue, many areas of the science of **criminalistics** seem to be more in the nature of art than science. Criminalists have been defined as professionals who are involved in the "scientific discipline directed to the recognition, identification, individualization, and evaluation of physical evidence by the application of the natural sciences to law-science matters" (Lindquist, 1994: 59). Questions have been raised about the reliability of virtually all areas of this science:

- *Hair analysis.* A Justice Department study of 240 crime labs found hair-comparison error rates ranging from 28 to 68 percent. Hair-comparison testimony is so suspect that it is outlawed in Michigan and Illinois (Hall, 2002). In Montana, a chief lab analyst collected more than 5,000 hair samples and claimed a statistical analysis that could identify a person's hair from the sample with an error rate of 1 in 1,000. A panel of experts disagreed, and convictions based on this analyst's testimony have been overturned (Possley, Mills, and McRoberts, 2004).

- *Arson investigation.* Arson "science" started when arson investigators used their experience with thousands of fires, confessions of suspects, and crude experiments to identify burn patterns and accelerants. "Facts" such as "fires started with accelerants burn hotter" have been disproved. So-called "pour patterns" that have been used as proof of arson have now been associated with a natural phenomenon called "flashover," which occurs when smoke and gas in a room build to a point where the entire room explodes in flames, consuming everything. The flashover effect also calls into question the traditional belief that if the floor showed burning, it was arson, because heat rises and the floor shouldn't show burning unless an accelerant is used (Posseley, 2004).

  In the Cameron Todd Willingham case that opened this chapter, the Innocence Project commissioned a panel to study some of the arson "facts" that were presented in the trial, and the study proved that many were not supported. For instance, glass cracking in a spidery fashion may not be because the fire was started with an accelerant; it is just as likely to be caused by water sprayed by firefighters. There also was no way to prove that the fire has multiple origins. However, fire investigators are still testifying in court based on science that is called by some "a hodgepodge of old wives' tales" (Tanner, 2006).

- *Ballistics testing.* Recently there have been questions as to the accuracy of the chemical composition tests the FBI labs use to match bullets. This method has been used in thousands of cases to tie suspects to the bullet retrieved at the crime scene. The theory is that the chemical composition of bullets in a single production batch is similar and that bullets from a single batch are different from those from other batches. Bullets owned by the suspect are compared to the crime-scene bullet, and the expert testifies as to whether the crime-scene bullet came from the suspect's box of remaining bullets.

  Independent scientific studies by the National Research Council challenged the method because tests indicated a large margin of error; chemical compositions between batches are more similar than believed, and the chemical composition within a batch can vary quite a bit depending on a number of factors. These findings indicated that ballistics experts from the FBI lab and other labs have testified in a way that greatly overstated the importance of the chemical matches (Piller and Mejia, 2003; Piller, 2003). Although the FBI stopped comparative bullet lead analysis in 2004 in response to these findings, FBI lab experts were allowed to testify in cases that had already been analyzed through 2005. Also, the FBI has been criticized for not releasing a list of cases in which the testimony of lab examiners was given on the faulty science so the case could be reviewed to see if an innocent person was convicted on the basis of the results (Post, 2005).

  In one New Jersey case, the state supreme court threw out a murder conviction that had been based on the testimony of an FBI ballistics expert using the faulty testing method (Post, 2005). In a North Carolina case, a former state supreme court chief justice took up the case of Lee Wayne Hunt, who has been in prison for 22 years for a shooting based on FBI testimony on comparative lead analysis and the testimony of a co-defendant. Recently the co-defendant's attorney came forward and said the man confessed to him that he had lied about Hunt's involvement in return for a plea deal. The attorney came forward only because his former client had died (J. Solomon, 2007a). Arguably, Hunt may not have been convicted but for the ballistics testimony that supported the co-defendant's perjury.

- *DNA testing.* The use of DNA evidence has risen dramatically in recent years. Based on the scientific principle that no two individuals possess the same DNA (deoxyribonucleic acid), a DNA "fingerprint" is analyzed from organic matter such as semen, blood, hair, or skin. Whereas a blood test can identify an individual only as being a member of a group (e.g., all those with blood type A positive), DNA testing can determine, with a small margin of error, whether two samples come from the same individual. This has been described as the greatest breakthrough in scientific evidence since fingerprinting, but there are problems with its use. Careless laboratory procedures render results useless, and there are no enforced guidelines or criteria for forensic laboratories conducting DNA tests.

  Labs often have only a small amount of organic matter to extract DNA. They use a procedure whereby the incomplete DNA strand is replicated using computer-simulation models. This procedure allows a DNA analysis of the tiniest speck of blood or skin, but critics argue that it opens a door to a margin of error that is unacceptable. Without vigorous investigation and examination of lab results from the opposing counsel, incorrect DNA test results or poorly interpreted results may be entered as evidence and used to determine guilt or innocence.

  A different problem has emerged when DNA testing is done and the results help the defense by excluding the defendant from possible suspects. In these cases, prosecutors have an ethical duty to provide test results to the defense; however, there are cases where this is not done.

- *Fingerprint analysis.* Most citizens assume that fingerprint analysis is infallible, that all criminals' fingerprints are accessible through computer matching technology, and that fingerprint technicians can retrieve fingerprints from almost any surface and can use partials to make a match. Unfortunately, the reality is far from what is seen on television. There have been attempts to undertake a comprehensive analysis of how much of a partial print is necessary to have a reliable match—an objective that is resisted by professional fingerprint examiners. Most fingerprints are partials and smudged. Some studies show that about a quarter of matches are false positives.

  In 2006, the federal government settled a suit for $2 million after three FBI fingerprint examiners mistakenly identified the fingerprint related to a terrorist bombing in Madrid, Spain, as belonging to an Oregon lawyer. European fingerprint analysts discovered the error (CBS/AP, 2006). Standards do not exist for determining how many points of comparison are necessary to declare a match (Mills and McRoberts, 2004).

- *Bite mark comparison.* There is no accurate way to measure the reliability of bite mark comparisons, yet forensic dentists have given testimony that resulted in convictions of several innocent defendants, and several individuals exonerated through DNA evidence were convicted largely on evidence of bite mark identification. Evidently, the experts sometimes can't even agree if an injury is a bite mark at all. One study indicated that identifications were flawed in two-thirds of the cases. Even their own organization cautions that analysts should not use the term "match," because the technique is not exact enough, but many do. Contrary to popular belief, a bite mark is not just like a fingerprint. Teeth change over time, and the condition of the skin or other substance holding the bite mark changes the indentation patterns of teeth (McRoberts and Mills, 2004). So-called experts have confused juries by confabulating dentition and bite marks since there is general agreement that identity can be established within reasonable parameters of error by comparing dental records to a full set of teeth (i.e., comparing dental records to a corpse). However, bite marks only typically involve the front teeth, and there is no evidence to indicate that bite marks are similar every time; furthermore, there are no standards to guide agreement that there is a match. Critics argue that bite mark testimony does not meet the *Daubert* standard (evidence must be from a reliable scientific methodology), but courts let the evidence in because it is presented as merely identification, not science (Beecher-Monas, 2009).

- *Scent identification.* Also not a science is scent identification. A Texas deputy has been both lauded and reviled for using his dogs to track criminals and identify them through their smell. Keith Pikett, now retired from the Fort Bend County Sheriff's Department, was in demand along with his dogs for finding and identifying criminals through "scent lineups." The dogs evidently could identify criminals through scents left at the scene or on property. In some cases, the dogs led the police from the crime scene to the home of the alleged offender, even though the house was miles away. Critics contend that Pikett gave the dogs unconscious clues to tag the correct suspect, and, in other cases, there was no way the dogs could do what Pikett says they did. There are several lawsuits pending, both for civil damages and appeals from convictions (Lindell, 2010).

In 2009, the National Academy of Sciences issued a 225-page report on forensics and crime labs across the country. It was a highly critical report, incorporating the descriptions of many cases of innocent people convicted because of faulty scientific evidence. The authors concluded that crime labs lacked certification and standards, and that many forensic disciplines, including most of those described above, were not grounded in classic scientific methods; DNA analysis was the exception. Much of the problem is in pattern recognition (of fingerprints, bite marks, tool marks, etc.). There is no agreed upon scientific standard for when to conclude a match, and there are human errors introduced when the examiner knows the evidence is obtained from a suspect. The report calls on Congress to establish a national institute of forensic science to accredit crime labs and require that analysts be certified (Fountain, 2009).

Yet the scandals continue. In New York, the inspector general released a report in December 2009 that detailed the shoddy management and protocols in the state police crime lab. One examiner had been working there for 15 years with no training; he didn't even know how to use the microscope he supposedly used to conduct trace evidence and hair analysis. He evidently made up reports using a "cheat sheet" left by a former supervisor. This examiner committed suicide, but before his death implicated many others in the lab and accused supervisors of countenancing widespread malfeasance and report-fudging to aid prosecution efforts. Critics argue that the only way crime labs can be objective is to remove them from police departments or state police and use private, independent laboratories (Balko, 2009; Bauman, 2009).

A slightly different issue is when prosecutors use high-tech aids to present their case. Computer simulations, animations, and other devices can bring the alleged crime to life for the jury, and such technology is extremely powerful. It is also true that because it is so powerful and persuasive, its use should be strictly controlled with the requirements of accuracy, relevance, and avoidance of unfair prejudice (Aronson and McMurtrie, 2007).

ZEALOUS PROSECUTION

> The duty of the prosecutor is to seek justice, not merely to convict (Standard 3-1.2[c]).

Just as the defense attorney is at times overly zealous in defense of clients, prosecutors may be overly ambitious in order to attain a conviction. The prosecutor, in preparing a case, is putting together a puzzle, and each fact or bit of evidence is a piece of that puzzle. Evidence that doesn't fit the puzzle is sometimes conveniently ignored. The problem is that this type of evidence may be exculpatory, and the prosecutor has a duty to provide it to the defense.

Both defense attorneys and prosecutors sometimes engage in tactics such as using witnesses with less than credible reasons for testifying, preparing witnesses (both in appearance and testimony), and "shopping" for experts. Witnesses are not supposed to be paid, but their expenses can be reimbursed, and often this is incentive enough for some people to say what they think the prosecutor wants to hear. A tool in the prosecutor's arsenal that the defense attorney does not have is that prosecutors can make deals to reduce charges in return for favorable testimony. The use of jailhouse informants is a particularly problematic issue. Jailhouse informants are those individuals who come forward to testify that a defendant confessed to them or said something that was incriminating. Often the "pay" for such testimony is a reduction in charges, but it could be reduced sentencing or being sent to a particular prison, or any other thing of value to the informant. It could even be money. In some cases, such payment is not revealed to the defense, which is problematic because the defense could use such payment to call into question the credibility of the testimony. In fact, jailhouse informants' credibility should always be questioned. It is frequently implicated in wrongful convictions, especially when prosecutors withhold the fact that they have made a deal with the person for a reduced sentence (Kirchmeier et al., 2009). Raeder (2007) points out that jailhouse informants not only respond to solicitations from police and prosecutors, sometimes they are entrepreneurs who ply their trade against any cellmate or casual conversationalist they meet in the jail yard. She argues for ethical standards whereby prosecutors should use such informants only when they can point to specific factors that support the truthfulness of the testimony. She also points out that Los Angeles instituted such a policy and dramatically cut down the use of jailhouse informants with no deterioration of its conviction rate (Raeder, 2007).

DILEMMA: You are a prosecutor who is preparing a case against a defendant accused of a brutal rape and murder of a young child. The suspect lived in the same neighborhood as the child and is a registered sex offender. He says he didn't do it, of course, but has no alibi for the time in question, and you know in your gut that he did the crime. Unfortunately, you have no scientific evidence that incriminates him. You do have one witness who thinks she saw his car close to the playground where the child was taken, and you can prove he didn't show up for work the afternoon of the abduction. You are hoping that someone in the playground will be able to make a positive ID. One day you receive a call from the detective on the case. He tells you that there is a man in the jail cell with the defendant who says that the defendant confessed to him. The informant is willing to testify to it, but he wants a reduction in his own sentence. You meet with the man, who is a drug offender, and sure enough, he says that the defendant "spilled his guts" and told him that he took the little girl and killed her when she wouldn't stop screaming. You feel you've got the conviction sewn up. You proceed to trial. The second morning of the trial, you find out that your star witness had made a similar deal in his last drug case in a different jurisdiction and received probation for a substantial amount of meth. Since the trial has begun, double jeopardy applies. Do you reveal the information to the defense? Do you put him on the stand and let the jury decide whether to believe him or not?

LAW There is no law prohibiting the use of jailhouse informants. The Model Rules, which have the force of law, dictate that prosecutors cannot put false information on the stand, but if you were the prosecutor, would you tell yourself that you don't "know" the informant is lying and, therefore, you are not violating the rule? On the other hand, the Model Rules and *Brady* motions do indicate that the information about the prior case be given to the defense since it could be considered exculpatory. It certainly calls into question the credibility of the informant.

POLICY As mentioned above, Los Angeles has an office policy that discourages the use of jailhouse informants. Most jurisdictions do not, however, although they may have an office policy of not taking a case to trial that hinges on such testimony. All offices have policies that dictate responding to *Brady* motions, but some offices also have an "open file" policy that allows the defense to have access to any information the prosecutor has except the identity of confidential informants or other information that needs to be kept secret.

ETHICS Utilitarian ethics tolerate actions that lead to a good end, but, in this case, there is not much evidence to indicate that the defendant is guilty so it is questionable that conviction is even a good end. Therefore, any "bad means" (such as keeping the information from the defense) may result in a bad end as well. The more difficult ethical issue is whether to continue with the trial at all. Juries are loath to let a murdering sex offender go free and are likely to believe that if someone is prosecuted, they are more than likely guilty. Therefore, even if you provide the information to the defense, it is possible that they will be unable to undercut the credibility of the informant and the defendant will be found guilty. Utilitarian ethics may support such an action if it results in the greatest benefit for the majority. Ethical formalism may not, however, if one interprets a prosecutor's duty as pursuing justice, since a case dependent on a witness who is probably lying is contrary to due process. This explains why jurisdictions are moving away from using jailhouse informant testimony unless it can be corroborated.

Prosecutors want to win, and there are few checks or monitors on their behavior (Elliott and Weiser, 2004). Noble-cause corruption is when prosecutors do "anything it takes" to win a case. This can take the form of persistent references to illegal evidence, leading witnesses, nondisclosure of evidence to the defense, appeals to emotions, games and tricks, and so on. One prosecutor admitted that early in his career he sometimes made faces at the defendant while his back was to the jury and the defense attorney wasn't looking. The jury saw the defendant glowering and looking angry for no discernible reason, which led to a negative perception of his sanity, temper, or both. Of course, the defense attorney may engage in the same type of actions, so the contest becomes who has better tricks rather than who has the better case.

QUOTE & QUERY

There are a couple of golden rules that I have picked up over the years….

First, never say anything to a witness that you would not want to see on the front page of the New York Times….

The second rule … is to never do anything if you would not feel comfortable explaining to a Second Circuit judge why you did it.

—SOURCE: PATRICK FITZGERALD, U.S. ATTORNEY, 2009.

Do you think that defense attorneys also have a similar set of rules? Explain why or why not.

Ethical Issues for Judges

Perhaps the best-known symbol of justice is the judge in a black robe. Judges are expected to be impartial, knowledgeable, and authoritative. They guide the prosecutor, defense attorney, and all the other actors in the trial process from beginning to end, helping to maintain the integrity of the proceeding. This is the ideal, but judges are human, with human failings.

There are a number of problematic issues in the perceived objectivity of judges. For instance, 87 percent of judges are elected, and when they have to win elections, judges must solicit campaign contributions. These monies are obtained most often from attorneys, and it is not at all unusual for judges to accept money from attorneys who practice before them. In fact, quite often the judge's campaign manager is a practicing attorney. Does this not provide at least the appearance of impropriety? This situation is exacerbated in jurisdictions that use court appointments as the method for indigent representation. In these jurisdictions judges hand out appointments to the same attorneys who give money back in the form of campaign contributions or have other ties to the judge. Obviously, the appearance, if not the actuality, of bias is present in these situations.

In some cases, large corporations and special interest groups fund judicial campaigns. One might expect that judges would recuse themselves when these corporations have cases before the judge, but this does not always happen, as with Brent Benjamin, who ran for the supreme court in West Virginia funded by $3 million from Massey Energy, a coal company. The amount far exceeded the total of other contributions in his campaign. When an appeal of a case came before the court involving the company, he did not recuse himself, and he, along with the majority of the court, overturned a $50 million judgment against the company. In an appeal to the U.S. Supreme Court concerning the refusal of the judge to recuse himself, the Court held that the facts of the case violated a proportionality standard to be used to determine when a single contribution to a campaign might give rise to a conflict of interest. The Supreme Court sent the case back to the West Virginia courts for rehearing and, with only one original judge sitting, the West Virginia court ruled 4 to 1 again in favor of the coal company (*Caperton v. Massey*, 129 S. Ct. 2252 [2009]). The Massey Coal Company was in the news again in the spring of 2010 when 29 miners died in an explosion. Investigations over safety violations are underway.

The practice of awarding indigent cases to one's friends or for reasons other than qualifications may not only be unethical but also may have serious consequences for the defendant. The Texas Bar Association (2002) reported major problems in the system of appointing attorneys for indigent defendants. The bar association's investigation found that some lawyers who received appointments had been disciplined by the state bar and there was no system for monitoring the quality of the representation. In 2006, a major newspaper ran a series of reports after an investigation of the system of appointing lawyers for capital habeas corpus appeals for death row inmates. The investigation found that some lawyers turned in ridiculously short appeals that did not cover even the most obvious points and/or were poorly written (Lindell, 2006a, 2006b, 2006c).

In one egregious case, an attorney turned in a brief in 2003 that was basically copied from one letter from the inmate, complete with nonsensical arguments, grammatical lapses, and misspelled words. For this, the attorney billed the state for about $23,000, claiming 220 hours of work. In another writ, the attorney copied facts that were from another case and didn't apply to the case under appeal (Lindell, 2006a, 2006b). There was no system to evaluate the competence of the attorneys seeking appointments concerning the habeas corpus petitions (Lindell, 2007c). When habeas corpus appellate attorneys are competent, they may literally save the lives of innocent men and women; thus, who the judge appoints is an extremely important decision.

USE OF DISCRETION

As we have learned in several previous chapters, discretion refers to the authority to make a choice between two or more actions. Judges' discretion occurs in two major areas: interpretation of the law and sentencing.

INTERPRETATION OF LAW AND RULES Judges are like the umpire in an athletic contest; they apply the rules and interpret them. Although rules of law are established in Rules of Criminal Procedure and case law, there is still a great deal of discretion in the interpretation of a rule—what is reasonable, what is probative, what is prejudicial, and so on. A judge assesses the legality of evidence and makes rulings on the various objections raised by both the prosecutors and the defense attorneys. A judge also writes the extremely important instructions to the jury. These are crucial because they set up the legal questions and definitions of the case.

One of the clearest examples of judicial discretion is in the application of the exclusionary rule, which basically states that when the evidence has been obtained illegally, it must be excluded from use at trial. The exclusionary rule has generated a storm of controversy because it can result in a guilty party avoiding punishment because of an error committed by the police. The basis for the exclusionary rule is the right to due process. The ideals of justice reject a conviction based on tainted evidence even if obtained against a guilty party. A more practical argument for the exclusionary rule is that if we want police officers to behave in a legal manner, we must have heavy sanctions against illegalities. Arguably, if convictions are lost because of illegal collection of evidence, police will reform their behavior. Actual practice provides little support for this argument, though. Cases lost on appeal are so far removed from the day-to-day decision making of the police that they have little effect on police behavior. In the succeeding years since the cases that recognized the rule, such as *Mapp v. Ohio*, 367 U.S. 643 (1961), several exceptions to the exclusionary rule have been recognized. Judges can now rule that the illegally obtained evidence be allowed because of public safety (*New York v. Quarles*, 467 U.S. 649 [1984]), good faith (*U.S. v. Leon*, 468 U.S. 897 [1984]), or inevitable-discovery exceptions (*Nix v. Williams* 467 U.S. 431 [1984]).

In addition to applying the exclusionary rule, the judge is called upon to decide various questions of evidence and procedure throughout a trial. Of course, the judge is guided by the law and legal precedent, but in most cases each decision involves a substantial element of subjectivity. For instance, a defendant may file a pretrial petition for a change of venue. This means that the defendant is arguing that public notoriety and a biased jury pool would make it impossible to have a fair trial in the location where the charges were filed. It is up to the judge, however, to decide if that indeed is true or whether, despite pretrial publicity, the defendant will be assured of a fair trial. If judges are biased either toward or against the prosecution or defense, they have the power to make it difficult for either side through their pattern of rulings on objections and evidence admitted. Even a personal dislike of either lawyer may be picked up by jury members, and it does affect their attitude toward that side's case.

Despite the belief that simply applying the rules will lead to the right conclusion or decision, the reality is that judges and justices are simply human, and real biases influence their decision making. The suspicion that some appellate court judges decide where they want to end up and make up the argument to get there is one that is hard to deny after a careful reading of some case decisions. At other times, appellate decision making seems to reflect a complete absence of "equity" thinking (basic fairness) in place of hyper-technical application of rules. Petitions that are denied because a deadline was missed or appeals denied because they were not drawn up in the correct fashion are examples of this application of discretion.

In one case in Texas, the chief justice of the court of criminal appeals refused to accept an appeal on a death row case because the lawyers could not file it before 5 p.m. This was despite the fact that several justices were working late that night in case of late filings, and the attorneys had asked for permission to file it late because they were having computer problems. Sharon Keller, the chief justice, instructed her clerk via telephone to deny the request and close the office, and the prisoner was executed. The basis of the appeal was that the method of execution (lethal injection) was cruel and unusual, and the Supreme Court of the United States, only a week later, accepted a writ of certiorari on this very issue, indicating there was a good chance that the appeal would have resulted in at least a hearing on the merits. In fact, two days later, a second appeal by a different inmate was granted, while in the case where the appeal was denied for being late, the man was executed. This hyper-technical application of rules was considered so wrong that 19 attorneys filed an ethics complaint against Keller for her actions, alleging that she violated the bar association rules that judges preserve the integrity of the judiciary and act in ways that promote public confidence, and a rule that requires judges to allow interested parties to be heard according to law. The State Commission on Judicial Conduct issued a ruling that resulted in no sanctions for Keller, although she was admonished. In 2010, she received a $100,000 fine in an unrelated case for not reporting $3.8 million in income and property on her filing papers for election. She is appealing both decisions (Lindell, 2007c, 2010b).

An attorney's ethical lapse in performing his or her duties is sometimes compounded by judges' adhering to the "letter" rather than the spirit of the law. An example is the case of Johnny Conner, who was convicted of robbery. His trial attorney neglected to bring forward evidence in which the witnesses described the robber as "sprinting" away from the scene, but Conner had nerve damage in his leg and could only limp. The appellate attorney brought up the issue on appeal, but he neglected to attach any medical evidence, so the appellate judges refused to consider it as new evidence. The attorney general of Texas later argued that, *regardless of the factuality of the evidence*, it should not be allowed in the federal appeal because it was not admitted in the state appeal (Lindell, 2006c). Johnny Connor was executed in August 2007.

In another case, a federal appeals court refused to hear the appeal of a condemned man based on his mental retardation because his lawyer filed the appeal one day late. The Supreme Court had already ruled that executing someone with mental retardation was cruel and unusual, but in an appeal to the Fifth Circuit Court of Appeals, the justices ruled that the appeal did not have to be heard because of the late filing. A huge outpouring of criticism of the court focused on the distinct possibility that a man would be executed even though the Supreme Court had ruled that it would be unconstitutional because of his mental retardation. In an unusual about-face, the Fifth Circuit conducted a re-hearing and changed its opinion (Liptak, 2005b).

Judges may simply apply black-and-white rules, or they may attempt to enact the "spirit of justice." In June 2010, the majority of the Supreme Court decided that basic fairness and the spirit of justice should trump black-and-white rules. An inmate missed the deadline for an appeal because his attorney did not communicate with him for years despite the inmate's numerous and increasingly frantic written pleas to file the appeal. He even provided the attorney with the information necessary to file it. He also asked the Florida court to replace the attorney, but they refused, and when he filed a *pro se* brief five weeks late, they rejected it. The federal circuit court agreed that the circumstances were not "extraordinary"; therefore, the missed deadline must result in rejecting the appeal regardless of the merit of the appeal. The Supreme Court disagreed, arguing that due process is more important than what Justice Breyer described as "the evils of archaic rigidity" (*Holland v. Florida*, No. 09-5327, June 14, 2010). When should judges ignore the rules, and when should they follow them?

SENTENCING The second area of judicial discretion is in sentencing. Judges have an awesome responsibility in sentencing offenders and, yet, receive little training to guide their discretion. It is also true that judges' decisions are scrutinized by public watchdog groups and appellate-level courts. One wonders if judges actually aren't overly influenced in their sentencing by the current clamor for strict punishments, but if judges are supposed to enact community sentiment, perhaps it is proper for them to reflect its influence. Does justice dictate a certain punishment for a certain type of offender, or does the definition of what is just depend on community opinion of the crime, the criminal, and the time?

Evidence indicates that judges' decisions are actually based on personal standards, for no consistency seems to appear between the decisions of individual judges in the same community. Hofer, Blackwell, and Ruback (1999) point out that most of the disparity in sentencing in the federal system before the advent of the sentencing guidelines occurred because of different patterns exhibited by individual judges. They cite studies that found, for instance, that judges' sentences were influenced by whether they had been prosecutors and by their religion.

Federal Sentencing Guidelines Mandated sentences created by Congress for use by judges when imposing sentence (recent Supreme Court decisions have overturned the mandatory nature of the guidelines).

The other extreme is when judges have *no* discretion in sentencing. **Federal Sentencing Guidelines** were written by Congress requiring the judge to impose a specific sentence unless there was a proven mitigating or aggravating factor in the case. The Sentencing Guidelines did reduce disparity among federal judges (Hofer, Blackwell, and Ruback, 1999); however, the guidelines received a great deal of criticism because of the draconian sentences applied to drug crimes. Racial bias was alleged in that the sentence for crack cocaine crimes was 100 times longer than sentences for powder cocaine crimes, even though these two drugs are chemically exactly the same. The argument supporting this disparity was that crack cocaine was more associated with other crimes and more addictive; however, there was a widespread belief that the disparity was simply racist. African Americans are much more likely to be convicted of crack crimes, and white Americans are more likely to be convicted for powder cocaine (Hofer et al., 1999).

Some federal judges, such as J. Lawrence Irving in 1991 and others, were so appalled by the length of drug sentences as required by the Sentencing Guidelines that they refused to sentence offenders. Some even quit, refusing to impose the mandated sentences, which they considered to be ridiculously long and overly punitive in certain cases (Tonry, 2005: 43). In a series of cases, the U.S. Supreme Court has basically invalidated the mandatory nature of federal sentencing guidelines. First, they ruled that the defendant's Sixth Amendment rights were violated if the judges used elements to increase the sentence without first proving such elements in a court of law (*United States v. Booker*, 125 S.Ct. 1006 [2005]). Then, they ruled that judges could adjust the sentences downward if it was reasonable to do so (*Kimbrough v. United States*, 552 U.S. 85 [2007]). Finally, they extended that ruling to all federal cases, not just drug cases (*Gall v. United States*, 552 U.S. 38 [2007]). The standard to be used to evaluate any legal error in sentencing is an abuse of discretion test rather than if the sentence was required because of extraordinary circumstances (Barnes, 2007). Finally, in August 2010, President Obama signed into law legislation that reduced the disparity to 18:1 from 100:1. The new law also eliminated the five-year mandatory minimum sentence for crimes involving five grams of cocaine or more.

?

DILEMMA: You are a judge who is trying a case against a serial killer, accused of killing three people. The prosecution has put on a good case thus far, linking the killer with the victims through carpet fibers found on one victim that are consistent with the trunk of the suspect's car, eyewitness testimony that links the suspect with two of the victims shortly before they went missing, and the suspect's possession of a ring that was owned by one of the victims. Then the prosecutor attempts to introduce testimony of a police officer who arrested the suspect. He is willing to testify that the suspect ran and was chased down by the two officers. After he was handcuffed but before he was read his *Miranda* rights, in response to the officer saying, "You killed those people?" the suspect said, "I didn't want to." The defense attorney objected to the testimony and asked that the confession be excluded because of the violation of the Fifth Amendment. The prosecutor argues that what the officer said was not actually a question and, therefore, the outburst was spontaneous, or, alternatively, asks you to apply the good faith exception in that the officer's question "slipped out," and he didn't know that the suspect would answer him, or, finally, as a third alternative, he asked you to apply a voluntariness interpretation to Fifth Amendment cases and replace an absolute rule about the *Miranda* warnings to one where the absence of *Miranda* can be excused if the statement is otherwise considered voluntary.

LAW The Supreme Court seems to be less committed to the exclusionary rule than in earlier years and has made case decisions that dramatically reduce the scope of the rule, especially as it affects the Fifth Amendment. As mentioned above, the law is not absolute in many areas, and lower court judges often "make law" in developing new interpretations that become the law when appellate courts agree. It is possible that, given the facts of the case, an appellate court would allow the statement in as evidence, although it is also possible that they would not.

POLICY Similar to the defense attorney, there are no office or departmental policies that should influence the judge's decision, but there are policy considerations to consider. What would happen to police interrogations if judges routinely ignored violations of the *Miranda* warning?

ETHICS Utilitarian ethics supports the exclusionary rule and also its exceptions. The public safety exception, for instance, basically recognizes that if the police officer questioned the suspect for information to protect public safety, not for the gathering of evidence, the absence of the *Miranda* warning should not bar the use of any incriminating confession of the suspect. The "end" of public safety is more important than the "end" of ensuring that the suspects know their rights by giving them the *Miranda* warning before questioning them. Excluding tainted evidence disregards short-term effects for more abstract principles—specifically, the protection of due process.

Religious ethics doesn't give us much help unless we decide that this ethical system would support vengeance and thus would permit the judge to ignore the exclusionary rule in order to punish a criminal. However, religious ethics might also support letting the criminal go free to answer to an ultimate higher authority, for human judgment might be imperfect in this case. Egoism would support the decision to let a criminal go free or not, depending on the effect it would have on the judge's well-being and future interests.

Ethical formalism's emphasis on duty over "ends" would dictate that judges must apply the law even in difficult cases. The rule itself seems to be supported by the categorical imperative, because one would probably not want a universal rule accepting tainted evidence, despite the possibility of further crime or harm to individuals.

Act utilitarianism would support ignoring the exclusionary rule if the crime was especially serious as in this case or if there was a good chance the offender would not be ultimately punished. The utility derived from ignoring the rule would outweigh the good. However, rule utilitarianism probably does not support the exclusionary rule, for the long-term effect of undercutting the *Miranda* warning would be more serious than letting one criminal go free.

CONCLUSION

In this chapter, we examined how the discretion of defense attorneys, prosecutors, and judges leads to ethical dilemmas. There are crucial differences in the duties and ethical responsibilities of defense attorneys and prosecutors. The prosecutor's goal is justice, which should imply an objective pursuit of the truth; however, we know that sometimes the only goal seems to be winning. Judges have their own unique ethical dilemmas, and their discretion can be understood in the two areas of court rulings and sentencing.

CHAPTER REVIEW

1. Describe the ethical issues faced by defense attorneys.

Defense attorneys have ethical issues that arise in the areas of responsibility to the client (they must defend clients even if they believe they are guilty and whether or not the client can pay once appointed), conflicts of interest (balancing an individual client against overall effectiveness as an attorney with a caseload of many), zealous defense (determining the limits of what should be done to defend clients), and confidentiality (keeping clients' confidences even if it harms third parties).

2. Describe the ethical issues faced by prosecutors.

The prosecutor must seek justice, not merely a conviction. Ethical issues may arise in the areas of use of discretion (determining whom to charge), conflicts of interest (and how they affect decision making), plea bargaining (specifically, whether to overcharge and/or hide exculpatory evidence), media relations (and how much to reveal about the case), expert witnesses (including the halo effect, discovery, and the use of forensic evidence), and zealous prosecution (what is acceptable in zealous prosecution).

3. Describe some of the areas of forensic science that have been challenged by opponents.

Only DNA evidence has not received a barrage of criticism regarding the lack of scientific method involved in analysis. Hair analysis, arson investigation, ballistics, fingerprint analysis, bite mark identification, and scent identification have been criticized.

4. Describe the ethical issues faced by judges.

Ethical issues for judges occur in the areas of how to interpret the law or rules (letting biases affect their judgments) and sentencing. While judges have the ability to use their discretion to sentence, they should be guided by reasonableness, not any personal or public bias.

5. Explain why electing judges leads to a perception of unfairness.

Many criticize the practice of electing judges because it gives the appearance, if not the reality, of bias introduced when benefactors have cases in front of the judge. Most judges in this country are elected.

KEY TERMS

asset forfeiture
attorney–client privilege
criminalistics
Federal Sentencing
    Guidelines

halo effect
plea bargain
shadow jury

situational model
systems model

STUDY QUESTIONS

1. Explain the confidentiality rules of defense attorneys, and some situations where they may be able to disclose confidential information.
2. Compare the potential conflicts of interest of defense attorneys and those of prosecutors.
3. List and describe the functions of jury consultants and why they are criticized.
4. Describe asset forfeiture and why it has been criticized.
5. List the types of information that can be disclosed to the media and the information that should not be revealed to the media.

WRITING/DISCUSSION EXERCISES

1. Write an essay on (or discuss) the proper role of defense attorneys regarding their clients. Should attorneys pursue the wishes of their clients even if they think it is not in the clients' best interest? What if it would hurt a third party (but not be illegal)? Do you think that attorneys should maintain confidentiality if their clients are involved in ongoing criminal activity that is not inherently dangerous?

2. Write an essay on (or discuss) what your decision would be if you were on a disciplinary committee evaluating the following case: A prosecutor was working with police in a standoff between a triple murderer and police. When the murderer demanded to talk to a public defender, the police did not want to have a public defender get involved, so the prosecutor pretended to be one. He spoke with the suspect on the telephone and lied about his name and being a public defender. The man then surrendered to police. The prosecutor was sanctioned by the state bar for misrepresentation and was put on probation and required to take 20 hours of continuing legal education in ethics, pass the Multistate Professional Responsibility Examination, and be supervised by another attorney (Tarnoff, 2001). In your essay, describe what you think should have occurred, and why.

3. Write an essay on (or discuss) the legality/ethics of the following actions of a prosecutor:

   • Announcing a suspect of a drive-by shooting to the media so the offender was in danger from rival gang members, and then offering protective custody only if the man would plead guilty.
   • Authorizing the arrest of a 10-year-old boy who confessed to a crime, even though there was no serious possibility that he was guilty, in order to pressure a relative to confess.
   • Authorizing the arrest of one brother for drugs, even though the prosecutor knew the charge would be thrown out (but the young man would lose a scholarship to college), in order to have leverage so that he would give evidence against his brother.

ETHICAL DILEMMAS

Situation 1

Your first big case is a multiple murder. As defense attorney for Sy Kopath, you have come to the realization that he really did break into a couple's home and torture and kill them in the course of robbing them of jewelry and other valuables. He has even confessed to you that he did it. However, you are also aware that the police did not read him his *Miranda* warning and that he was coerced into giving a confession without your presence. What should you do? Would your answer be different if you believed that he was innocent or didn't know for sure?

Situation 2

You are completing an internship at a defense attorney's office during your senior year in college. After graduation you plan to enter law school and pursue a career as an attorney, although you have not yet decided what type of law to practice. Your duties as an intern are to assist the private practitioner you work for in a variety of tasks, including interviewing clients and witnesses, organizing case files, running errands, and photocopying. A case that you are helping with involves a defendant charged with armed robbery. One day while you are at the office, the defendant comes in and gives you a package for the attorney. In it you find a gun. You believe, but do not know for a fact, that the gun is the one used in the armed robbery. When the attorney returns, he instructs you to return the package to the defendant. What should you do? What should the attorney do?

Situation 3

You are an attorney and are aware of a colleague who could be considered grossly incompetent. He drinks and often appears in court intoxicated. He ignores his cases and does not file appropriate motions before deadlines expire. Any person who is unlucky enough to have him as a court-appointed attorney usually ends up with a conviction and a heavy sentence because he does not seem to care what happens to his clients and rarely advises going to trial. When he does take a case to trial, he is unprepared and unprofessional in the courtroom. You hear many complaints from defendants about his demeanor, competence, and ethics. Everyone—defense attorneys, prosecutors, and judges alike—knows this person and his failings, yet nothing is done. Should you do something? If so, what?

Situation 4

You are a prosecutor in a jurisdiction that does not use the grand jury system. An elderly man has administered a lethal dose of sleeping tablets to his wife, who was suffering from Alzheimer's disease. He calmly turned himself in to the police department, and the case is on the front page of the paper. It is entirely up to you whether to charge him with murder. What would you do? What criteria did you use to arrive at your decision?

Situation 5

You are a deputy prosecutor and have to decide whether to charge a defendant with possession and sale of a controlled substance. You know you have a good case because the guy sold drugs to students at the local junior high school, and many of the kids are willing to testify. The police are pressuring you to make a deal because the defendant has promised to inform on other dealers in the area if you don't prosecute. What should you do?

10

moodboard RF/PhotoLibrary

Ethical Misconduct in the Courts and Responses

Chapter Objectives

1. Detail the types of misconduct that have been associated with defense attorneys, prosecutors, and judges.
2. Explain the reasons why such misconduct occurs.
3. Describe the Innocence Projects, how many individuals have been found to be wrongly imprisoned, and why.
4. Discuss some proposals to improve the justice system and reduce ethical misconduct.
5. Describe the concepts associated with judicial activism or constructionism and how this issue relates to ethical misconduct.

Clarence Brandley was a high school janitor in a small Texas town near Houston. In 1980, a young woman on a visiting girls' volleyball team disappeared while her team was practicing. The school was empty except for five janitors and the volleyball team. A search uncovered the girl's body in the school auditorium; it was later determined that she had been raped and strangled. Clarence Brandley and another janitor found the body and were the first to be interrogated by police. Brandley was black; the other janitor was white. The police officer who interrogated them reportedly said, "One of you two is going to hang for this." Then he said to Brandley, "Since you're the nigger, you're elected." Police and prosecutors then evidently began a concerted effort to get Brandley convicted, in the following ways:

- Evidence that might have been helpful to the defense was "lost." (Caucasian hairs near the girl's vagina were never tested and compared to those of the other janitors.)
- Witnesses were coerced into sticking to stories that implicated Brandley. (One of the janitors reported that he had been threatened with jail if he didn't promote the story supporting Brandley's guilt.)
- Witnesses who came forward with contrary evidence were ignored and sent away. (The father-in-law of one of the janitors who later became a prime suspect told the prosecutor that this man had told him where the girl's clothes would be found two days before police actually found them.)

283

- Defense attorneys were not told of witnesses. (A woman came to the prosecutor after the second trial and stated that her common-law husband had confessed a murder to her and ran away the same night the girl's body had been found. This woman's husband had worked as a janitor at the school, had been fired a month previous to the murder, but had also been seen at the school the day of the murder.)

What defense attorneys eventually discovered was that in all probability this man and another janitor had abducted and murdered the girl. The other janitors had seen the girl with these two men (not Brandley), but had lied during the two trials. Here are the words of an appellate judge who ruled on the motion for a new trial:

> In the thirty years that this court has presided over matters in the judicial system, no case has presented a more shocking scenario of the effects of racial prejudice ... and public officials who for whatever motives lost sight of what is right and just.... The court unequivocally concludes that the color of Clarence Brandley's skin was a substantial factor which pervaded all aspects of the State's capital prosecution against him. (Radelet, Bedau, and Putnam, 1992: 134)

Even after this finding, it took another *two years* for the Texas Court of Criminal Appeals to rule that Brandley deserved a new trial. He served nine years on death row before his defense attorneys finally obtained his freedom. At one point, he was just six days away from execution (Davies, 1991).

Do people end up in prison for crimes they did not commit? The fact is that they do. Joyce Ann Brown and James Curtis Giles are two more examples. Both of these individuals were accused of crimes that were committed by someone with the same name. James Curtis Giles was finally exonerated of a gang rape after spending 10 years in prison and 14 years as a registered sex offender. DNA analysis showed that there was no physical evidence linking him to rape, and there was evidence of another perpetrator. In 1982, a man who pleaded guilty to the rape said he did the crime along with men named James Giles and Michael Brown. James Curtis Giles lived 15 miles away from the victim and did not match her description of the attacker. He also had an alibi. Investigators ignored another man with same name who lived across the street from the victim and had been arrested with Brown on other charges. Despite this information, the wrong Giles was convicted (Garay, 2007).

A similar pattern of mistaken identity occurred when Joyce Ann Brown was arrested and convicted for a murder she did not commit. The real perpetrator shared the same name as Brown, who was imprisoned for nine years before she was exonerated (Brown and Gaines, 1990). Each of these cases represents a grievous mistake that should have been corrected by the due-process protections provided in the criminal justice system but was not. While ethical misconduct on the part of legal professionals is not always the reason innocent people end up in prison, unfortunately in many cases it is. In fact, on the grading scale of ethics, lawyers don't fare too well, at least measured by public opinion.

First, Let's Kill All the Lawyers

Public perceptions of lawyers indicate that the public has little confidence in their ability to live up to ideals of equity, fairness, and justice. In 2006, respondents in a Gallup Poll rated their level of trust in the integrity of attorneys. Only about 18 percent rated attorneys as "high" or "very" high. Only a few professions were rated lower than lawyers, including stockbrokers, senators, congressmen, HMO managers, car salesmen, and advertising executives (Gallup Poll, 2006).

In the 1980s, the law scandal was the savings and loan fiasco, in which the greed and corruption of those in the banking industry were ably assisted by the industry's attorneys, and the taxpayers picked up the bill for the bankrupt institutions and outstanding loans. The scandal of the 1990s was the Bill Clinton–Monica Lewinsky investigation, with opinions mixed as to which set of lawyers was more embarrassing—those who could coach the president that oral sex wasn't technically "sexual relations" or the special prosecutor, Kenneth Starr, and his assistants, who spent millions of dollars in an investigation that centered on semen stains and the definition of sex. The new century brought us the debacle of WorldCom and Enron, and, again, lawyers played a central role, along with business executives and accountants.

After 9/11 and the War on Terror, we had the situation of the White House counsel parsing the definition of torture in secret memoranda. There have also been growing numbers of individuals released from prison by Innocence Projects nationwide, reportedly because of egregious errors and/or unethical behaviors on the part of police, prosecutors, defense attorneys, and judges. News stories described how innocent people were released after serving years in prison for crimes they did not commit.

Finally, most recently, we have had a virtual meltdown of our national economy fueled largely by Wall Street, again aided ably by their highly paid attorneys. After the Enron bankruptcy and other blatant acts of crime by CEOs and CFOs in the early 2000s, Congress passed the Sarbanes-Oxley Act, which created culpability for CEOs who could no longer plead ignorance when a pattern of blatant criminality was within the scope of their responsibility. The act also required standards for attorneys appearing and practicing before the SEC that allowed for permissive disclosure of client's confidences to prevent fraud or other financial crimes. This response still did not stop the lending frenzy, the derivatives market, and the subsequent dissolution of AIG and the need to bail out the big banks in 2008–2009. For many, it seemed a virtual replay of the savings and loan scandal of the 1980s, and many wondered how it could have happened again. For every CEO and bank official who skirted the finer points of law and ethics, there was an attorney by his or her side.

Apparently, even lawyers don't think much of their profession. A *National Law Journal* study found that over 50 percent of lawyers described their colleagues as "obnoxious" (reported in Krieger, 2009: 882). In a 2006 poll, about 60 percent of those in the practice of law for six to nine years were dissatisfied with their career, although the percentage went down to 40 percent for those practicing more than 10 years. Overall, only about 55 percent of attorneys were satisfied with their career. Only about a third of lawyers practicing six to nine years would recommend law as a profession to young people, and only 44 percent of all lawyers would recommend it as a career (S. Ward, 2007).

The perception of the lawyer as an amoral "hired gun" is in sharp contrast to the ideal of the lawyer as an officer of the court, sworn to uphold the ideals of justice declared sacrosanct under our system of law. Interestingly, but perhaps not surprisingly, our government is made up predominantly of lawyers: A large percentage of elected officials are lawyers, and 25 of 44 presidents have been lawyers. Our nation's leaders and historical heroes have just as likely been lawyers (Abraham Lincoln, for example) as military generals, and our nation's consciousness is permeated with the belief in law and legal vindication.

On the one hand, the public tends to agree with a stereotype of lawyers as amoral, motivated by money, and with no conscience or concern for morality. On the other hand, the first response to any perception of wrong is to find a legal advocate and sue, with the belief that a lawyer will right any wrong and solve any problem. From ancient times, the ethics of those associated with the legal process has been suspect. Plato and

Aristotle condemned advocates because of their ability to make the truth appear false and the guilty appear innocent. This early distrust continued throughout history. Early colonial lawyers were distrusted and even punished for practicing law. For many years, lawyers could not charge a fee for their services because the mercenary aspect of the profession was condemned (Papke, 1986: 32). Gradually, lawyers and the profession itself were accepted, but suspicion and controversy continued in the area of fees and qualifications. Partly to counteract public antipathy, lawyers formed their own organization, the American Bar Association (ABA), in 1878. Shortly afterward, this professional organization established the first ethical guidelines for lawyers; these became the Model Code of Professional Responsibility reviewed in Chapter 8. The Quote and Query box puts the problem in a humorous light.

QUOTE & QUERY

Lawyers are upset. They have discovered what they believe to be an alarming new trend: People don't like them. The American Bar Association recently appointed a special panel to investigate the legal profession's bad image. The California State Bar has commissioned a survey to find out why so many people dislike lawyers.... We wish to reassure lawyers. This wave of anti-lawyer feeling is nothing new. People have always hated you.

—SOURCE: ROTH AND ROTH, 1989: I.

This passage is humorous, but the underlying problem is not. Why do people have such low opinions of lawyers?

Perhaps the best explanation for the long-standing distrust of lawyers is that they typically represent trouble. People don't require a lawyer unless they believe that a wrong has been done to them or that they need to be defended. In fact, let us not forget the full context of the quote, "The first thing we do, let's kill all the lawyers," widely used as a stab at attorneys. In Shakespeare's *Henry VI, Part 2*, the scene involves a despot who, before making a grab for power, argues that the first thing he must do is kill all the lawyers, for it is lawyers who are the guardians of law. However, the reason the existing power holders in the play were vulnerable to an overthrow in the first place was that they were using the law to oppress the powerless. And so it is today. The law can be either a tool of oppression or a sword of justice, with lawyers and judges as the ones who wield its power. Unfortunately, there are all too many examples of attorneys and judges who do not uphold the standards of their profession.

Ethical Misconduct

In the sections to follow, it is true that more attention is given to the misconduct of prosecutors and judges than defense attorneys. This is not to say that defense attorneys are more ethical than the other two groups—one might argue, in fact, the opposite. However, except for public defenders, defense attorneys are not public servants as are the other two groups of legal professionals. It is a legitimate argument that prosecutors and judges have higher duties than defense attorneys because they represent the body politic. They are the public servants referred to in Chapter 4 who have immense powers of discretion but also are held to higher standards of behavior in their public and private life.

DEFENSE ATTORNEY MISCONDUCT

The major complaint about attorneys is that they do not communicate regularly with clients. This is true for civil as well as criminal attorneys. Complaints received by bar associations generally involve clients who believe that they are not getting what they paid for, in that attorneys don't return their calls, don't keep them informed about what is being done on their case, and don't seem to be putting any effort in the case after they have been paid. Criminal defendants particularly are helpless since they may be in jail. Some attorneys meet with their client only before hearings or other court appearances. Such neglect occurs because attorneys make money by volume—the more cases, the more income. Criminal cases, especially, do not pay very well, and so attorneys have large caseloads. Many attorneys operate under a crisis management approach whereby the to-do list every week can only accommodate those tasks that are at deadline or after a deadline has passed. The consequence is that some cases do not get the attention they should—witnesses are not contacted, legal research is not conducted, and exculpatory evidence is not asked for.

One of the most often cited reasons for false convictions (in addition to eyewitness testimony) is ineffective assistance of counsel. The legal standard for what constitutes ineffective counsel is set quite high—so high that in the case of Calvin Burdine, whose lawyer slept through parts of his trial, the appellate court said that if a lawyer wasn't sleeping during a *crucial* part of the trial, it wasn't ineffective counsel. Other behaviors reported of lawyers in capital and other cases include the following (Schehr and Sears, 2005):

- Attorneys' use of heroin and cocaine during trial
- Attorneys letting the defendant wear the same clothes described by the victim
- Attorneys admitting that they didn't know the law or facts of the case
- Attorneys not being able to name a single death penalty case holding
- Attorneys drinking heavily each day of the trial and being arrested for a 0.27 blood alcohol level

There are also cases where the attorney has crossed the line from zealous defense to breaking the law. In a very few cases, defense attorneys go to extreme lengths to change the course of testimony, such as bribing witnesses, allowing their client to intimidate a witness, or instructing their client to destroy physical evidence or manufacture an alibi and

CRIMINAL LAWYER

Robert Simels, a criminal defense attorney in New York, was sentenced in federal court in December 2009 for witness tampering and bribery, but could have been guilty of much more. He was recorded talking to a person he thought was a confederate of his client, a drug lord from Guyana, but who was really a government agent. In the conversation, he discussed how to "silence" and "eliminate" a witness, in effect, ordering a hit on the person to stop him from testifying against the client. In his sentencing, Simels said, "Whatever self-esteem I had, whatever self-worth I had has been destroyed by this process." It was unclear if he was talking about his prosecution or the process of turning from criminal defense attorney to criminal attorney.

SOURCE: Fahim, 2009.

then commit perjury. Chapter 5 addressed noble-cause corruption on the part of law enforcement officers. This type of motivation may also affect the behavior of attorneys when they believe that their client is innocent or for other reasons believe obtaining an acquittal is more important than the rules of their profession. The In the News box presents one egregious case of a defense attorney who became a criminal. Most misconduct by defense attorneys probably falls into the realm of negligence, not criminal behavior.

PROSECUTORIAL MISCONDUCT

When prosecutors forget that their mission is to protect due process, not obtain a conviction at all costs, misconduct can occur. The types of misconduct range from minor lapses of ethical rules to commission of criminal acts (such as hiding evidence). It is reported that there were instances of prosecutorial misconduct in about a quarter of a sample of 2,100 cases in California, as identified by a panel of judges (reported in Aronson and McMurtrie, 2007: 1455). This could be an undercounting since the sample was only of trial cases. and most cases do not go to trial. Kirchmeier et al. (2009) discuss four types of prosecutorial misconduct: withholding exculpatory evidence; misusing pretrial publicity; using preemptory challenges to exclude jurors despite *Batson v. Kentucky* (476 U.S. 79 [1986]), which prohibited race discrimination in jury selection; and using false evidence in court.

Most prosecutorial misconduct occurs in the furtherance of the case; however, there are some examples where it appeared that the prosecutors involved did not take their duty as public servants seriously. For instance, the Two-Ton Contest in Illinois has been written about by several authors. It occurred when prosecutors participated in a contest to see who could convict 4,000 pounds of flesh. In the attempt to win, they vied to handle cases of the most overweight defendants and, one assumes, let their prosecutorial judgment be affected by the size of the defendant (Medwed, 2009).

Prosecutors and judges work together daily. There is a prohibition on attorneys and judges discussing a case outside the presence of the other attorney, but because of working conditions, this is much more likely between prosecutors and judges than with defense attorneys. The reason for the rule is fairness. It is not fair for the judge to hear one side without the other side there to defend its point of view. This rule applies to casual conversations as well as more formal interchanges or offerings of information. When there is a close relationship between a judge and attorney, it is generally the practice for the judge to recuse himself or herself from any cases involving that attorney. The capital murder conviction of Charles Dean Hood in 1990 was questioned when it was discovered that the judge in the case was having a secret affair with the prosecutor during the trial. This fact was unknown to the defense attorney at the time, and appellate attorneys could not verify the relationship until 18 years after the original trial. Hood's appellate attorneys alleged a violation of due process because the judge did not recuse herself, but the Texas Court of Criminal Appeals ruled the undisclosed relationship and the judge's lack of recusal was "harmless error" (Lindell, 2008).

Similar to a defense attorney's quandary when a witness commits perjury, a prosecutor must also take steps to avoid allowing false testimony to stand. The prosecutor's role is the easier one because there are no conflicting duties to protect a client; therefore, when a prosecution witness perjures himself or herself, the prosecutor has an affirmative duty to bring it to the attention of the court. In a Tulia, Texas, case, a large number of black defendants were convicted based on the perjured testimony of one investigator. The prosecutor knew that the police officer on the stand had lied about his past, yet he did not disclose that information and allowed the perjury to stand. It was also revealed that the investigator lied about the defendants as well. After the intervention of the ACLU and, eventually, the governor of Texas commuting the sentences, the dozens of people convicted were finally released. The prosecutor was sanctioned by the Texas bar and almost lost his law license. Many believe he should have, considering his role in the convictions (Herbert, 2002, 2003).

Model Rule 3.3(a) forbids an attorney from knowingly allowing false evidence to be admitted; some argue that "knowingly" is too strict a standard because prosecutors have argued that they did not "know" that the evidence was false. Some argue that an objective negligent standard should be used instead (Zacharias and Green, 2009). In Florida, James Brown came close to being executed before his conviction was reversed by the Court of Appeals for the Eleventh Circuit. The prosecutor in that case allowed false testimony to be introduced. Once the appellate court overturned the conviction, the state declined to retry the case (reported in Kirchmeier et al., 2009: 1339). Recall from Chapters 5 and 7 that the prevalence of "testilying" by police officers is unknown, but many believe that it is fairly widespread. Researchers, observers, and especially defense attorneys believe that testilying would not occur as much if not for the active or passive acceptance of the practice by prosecutors (Cunningham, 1999).

Many of the cases where an innocent person eventually is exonerated involve jailhouse informants. In one case, the convicted man alleged that the informant was promised a favorable sentence in which he would be sent to a federal prison instead of state prison in return for his testimony that the convicted man confessed to him while they were cellmates in jail. During the trial, when asked by the defense attorney if anything had been promised to him for his testimony, the informant committed perjury by answering that he had not been promised anything, and the prosecutor allowed the perjury to take place, knowing that he was lying (Lindell, 2007).

Misconduct also occurs when prosecutors intentionally use scientific evidence that they know to be false. There are proven instances where prosecutors put on the stand so-called experts that they knew were unqualified and/or their expertise was without merit (Gershman, 2003). Prosecutors may bolster a witness's credentials or allow him or her to make gratuitous and unsupported claims on the witness stand, such as to state "unequivocally" that the fingerprint, hair, or lip print was the defendant's. Giannelli and McMunigal (2007) describe a long list of expert witnesses who became well known for their pro-prosecution bias and outlandish testimony in the area of bite marks and other areas. So-called experts include Louise Robbins (who testified in one notorious case that a boot mark matched the defendant's even though no other forensic examiner agreed), Joyce Gilchrest (whose testimony was discounted in several exonerations), Fred Zain (from the West Virginia state crime lab whose test results could not be replicated by others), and Michael West (who supposedly invented a way to use light to identify bite marks on murder victims and always seemed to find a match to the suspect). These experts continued to be used by prosecutors even after appellate courts had excoriated their testimony and they were widely criticized by peers.

Prosecutors have had experts suppress information that was favorable to the defense and not put it in their report or not conduct tests that might be helpful to the defense. Sometimes expert reports are provided to the defense, but delay is used to undercut the ability of the defense to use the information. In other cases, experts are asked not to write a report at all if their findings do not help the prosecution, or prosecutors have the report filed as inconclusive so that they do not have to provide it to the defense (Giannelli and McMunigal, 2007). In their closing arguments, prosecutors may overstate the expert's testimony so "is consistent with" becomes "matched" (Gershman, 2003: 36). In some egregious cases, prosecutors have simply lied about physical evidence, such as stating that the red substance on a victim's underpants was blood when, in fact, it was paint (Gershman, 2003: 36).

The most common charge leveled against prosecutors, failure to disclose evidence, stems from a duty to reveal exculpatory evidence to the defense. The right was established in *Brady v. Maryland* (373 U.S. 83[1963]). A "*Brady* motion" requests all evidence that is "likely to lead to a different outcome." However, some prosecutors who withhold evidence argue that "It wasn't important" or "I didn't believe it." These rationalizations ignore a basic difference between the role of the prosecutor and the role of the defense attorney. Whereas the defense attorney's only mission is the defense of his or her client, the prosecutor's role is to seek justice. This means that all evidence should be brought forward and shared so "truth shall prevail." In fact, the ABA's Standing Committee on Ethics and Professional Responsibility has concluded that a prosecutor's ethical duty to share exculpatory information exceeds even the requirements of the *Brady* holding; however, there are numerous cases where prosecutors withhold important information from the defense (Kirchmeier et al., 2009). In the Ted Stevens case described in the In the News box, the prosecutors' misconduct led to their public chastisement and loss of a conviction.

When prosecutors are too zealous in their attempts to obtain a conviction, their role as officer of the court is ignored and they become judge and jury. A *Chicago Tribune*

in the NEWS

PROSECUTOR MISCONDUCT

Ted Stevens was a veteran Republican lawmaker, suspected of padding his pockets with the fruits of his long tenure in Congress while serving the citizens of Alaska. Before he died in an airplane crash in August 2010, a federal investigation (labeled "Operation Polar Pen") regarding his reported acceptance of improper benefits led to charges of conflict of interest and bribery. The prosecutors, however, were scolded repeatedly throughout the trial for withholding evidence from the defense. Arguably, they felt outgunned by the expensive legal team assembled by Stevens and sought to maximize any advantage. Whatever the reason, their ethical lapses ended up costing them the case. Stevens was convicted in 2008, but after an FBI special agent filed a whistleblower complaint, the judge threw out the conviction in April 2009 and Stevens was set free. The FBI agent complained that prosecutors tried to hide a witness and did not share transcripts where Bill Allen, their star witness, made contradictory statements during interviews, and prior statements contradicted what he said on the stand. The prosecutors face investigation and possible sanction from the Office of Professional Responsibility of the Justice Department. William Welch II, the lead prosecutor, stepped down as head of the Justice Department's public integrity section.

The case led to demands for retrials from other Alaska defendants tried by the same team and using the testimony of Bill Allen, the witness. It came to light that he had been accused of having sex with underage girls and the Justice Department prosecutors used those pending charges as leverage for his testimony, a fact not shared with defense attorneys in these other cases. Justice Department officials have announced new training initiatives to educate prosecutors on discovery duties and created an official to review discovery decisions.

SOURCES: Perksy, 2009; Johnson, 2009.

investigation found that between 1963 and 2002, 381 defendants across the country had a homicide conviction thrown out because prosecutors concealed exculpatory evidence or presented evidence they knew to be false. Of the 381 defendants, 67 had been sentenced to death and were exonerated by DNA evidence or independent investigations. Nearly 30 of the 67 on death row were freed, but they served between 5 and 26 years before their convictions were reversed. The prosecutorial misconduct included the following (Armstrong and Possley, 2002):

- Concealed evidence that discredited their star witnesses, pointed to other suspects, or supported defendants' claim of self-defense
- Suppressed evidence that the murder occurred during a time when the defendant had an alibi
- Depicted red paint as blood
- Portrayed hog blood as human
- Suppressed statements of eyewitnesses that offenders were white when prosecuting two black men
- Received a knife from a crime scene from police but hid it, and when defendant argued that he killed after he had been stabbed with the knife, the prosecutor challenged the defense because of the absence of a knife
- Hid a victim's gun when the defendant argued self-defense
- Hid an iron pipe the victim had used to attack the defendant
- Hid a blood-spatter expert's report that supported the defendant's version of events
- Withheld evidence suggesting that a police informant had framed the defendant
- Concealed evidence indicating that their chief witness was the killer, not the defendant

News reports of prosecutorial misconduct occur periodically. In Georgia, the prosecutor in the Genarlow Wilson case released a videotape of teenagers having sex in response to an open-records request without blurring the faces of the alleged victims or suspects. The prosecutor said that the law required him to release the tape; critics argue that he released the tape to discredit Wilson's case that he should not have been charged because it was consensual sex between teenagers. Some argue that the prosecutor's action in releasing the tape could even be defined as distributing child pornography (McCaffrey, 2007).

A former federal prosecutor and a State Department security officer were indicted on charges that they lied during the trial of a suspected terrorist. The two were charged with conspiracy, obstruction of justice, and making false statements in connection with the 2003 prosecution of Karim Koubriti and others who were suspected of being members of a sleeper cell. The convictions were overturned because of gross prosecutorial misconduct. It was alleged that Richard Convertino, the prosecutor charged, presented false information at a sentencing hearing in order to get a favorable sentence for an informant and failed to turn over exculpatory evidence to the defense. Convertino alleged that he was the target of a smear campaign because of his whistleblower lawsuit against the government. In the subsequent trial, both men were acquitted of all charges (Eggen, 2006; Hsu, 2007).

A government aviation lawyer working with the prosecutors of the Zacarias Moussaoui trial was admonished by the trial judge for improperly coaching witnesses. Moussaoui was alleged to have been involved in the 9/11 attack, and government officials sought to try him for the World Trade Center deaths, arguing that his knowledge could have prevented the attack from happening. The prosecution was seriously damaged when the judge refused to allow testimony of aviation officials after it was discovered that the lawyer Carla Martin had shared trial transcripts with the witnesses and tried to shape their testimony to help the prosecution's case (Markon and Dwyer, 2006).

Prosecutors who engage in acts such as those described above not only risk losing the immediate case, but they also lose their credibility and undercut the trust and faith we place in the justice system.

JUDICIAL MISCONDUCT

Public exposes of judicial misconduct are fairly rare. Operation Greylord, in Chicago, took place in the 1980s. As a result of an FBI investigation, 92 people were indicted, including 17 judges, 48 lawyers, 10 deputy sheriffs, 8 police officers, 8 court officials, and a member of the Illinois legislature; and 31 attorneys and 8 judges were convicted of bribery. Judges accepted bribes to "fix" cases—to rule in favor of the attorney offering the bribe. Not unlike law enforcement's "blue curtain of secrecy," not one attorney came forward to expose this system of corruption, even though what was occurring was fairly well known (Weber, 1987: 60). The In the News box describes a judicial scandal in Pennsylvania where judges almost literally "sold" the youthful offenders to a private correctional facility.

in the NEWS

JUDICIAL MISCONDUCT

Former Luzerne County, Pennsylvania, judges Michael Conahan and Mark Ciavarella were charged with racketeering, money laundering, fraud, bribery, and federal tax violations for accepting millions of dollars in return for sending juveniles who appeared before them to a private correctional facility. Conahan had earlier shut down the county-run youth corrections center so they would have to send the kids to the private facilities. The judges conducted hearings without appointing lawyers for the juveniles and then sent them to the private facilities for minor offenses.

The scandal has led to overturning hundreds of juvenile convictions and releasing many of the juvenile offenders sent to the facility. No one can explain why the scheme was not exposed years ago and continued without prosecutors, probation officers, or defense attorneys questioning what was happening. But red flags were raised. A newspaper had done an exposé on harsh juvenile sentencing in 2004; and a defense attorney had filed a complaint with the state judicial disciplinary board in 2006, but it failed to act until after the two judges had been indicted by the federal grand jury. The investigation began after another judge in the jurisdiction went to the FBI with his suspicions. The judges are also being investigated for possibly "fixing" criminal cases where serious offenders received light sentences. Both judges pleaded guilty in a plea bargain in February 2009, but retracted their guilty pleas when the sentencing judge required that they admit their sentencing of juvenile delinquents was directly affected by kickbacks. In July 2010, Conahan pleaded guilty to a racketeering conspiracy charge; he will be sentenced sometime in the fall of 2010. As of August 2010, there was no plea agreement with Ciavarella and the case is scheduled for trial in February 2011.

SOURCES: Rubinkam, 2009; Grezlak and Strupczewski, 2009; *Philadelphia Inquirer*, 2010.

Thankfully, such cases are extremely rare. Judges, for the most part, are like police officers and prosecutors. They strive to fulfill their role with integrity and honesty, taking care to protect the appearance and reality of justice. In some cases, however, neutrality is questioned when judges voice strong opinions on issues or cases. Talking to the media used to be rare, but now some judges have apparently decided it is acceptable to express their views, take a stand, and act as advocate. Many question this role for judges. In some cases, judges have been asked to recuse themselves—to step down and allow another judge to take over the trial—because they have indicated to news media that they already had opinions on a case before it was concluded.

Even Justice Antonin Scalia of the Supreme Court has been the target of such a request. In 2006, Justice Scalia, in a public speech, opined that giving full due-process rights to detainees in Guantanamo was "crazy" and also made remarks referring to his son, who was serving in Iraq at the time. Several groups demanded that the Justice recuse himself from the case of *Hamdan v. Rumsfeld* (126 S. Ct. 2749 [2006]) because the case was about that very subject (what, if any, due-process rights in American courts the detainees deserved). Justice Scalia did not recuse himself, and Hamdan did win his case, with the Supreme Court holding that detainees deserved some due process and that the military commissions that were created at the time were not sufficient. Scalia was in the dissent, however, so arguably one might conclude that he had already made up his mind before the case was decided (Lane, 2006).

In the 2007 Model Code of Judicial Conduct, one of the most debated areas was how judges should comport themselves in terms of public speaking and political engagement. The ideal, of course, is that judges should not have any preconceived ideas of who is right or wrong in any controversy they will rule on, but the reality is that judges do not live in a vacuum and, of course, have opinions, values, and beliefs regarding the issues of our times. As mentioned in Chapter 8, the rules have been changed to accommodate First Amendment challenges that were upheld in *Minnesota v. White* (536 U.S. 765 [2002]) (McKoski, 2008).

Some question judges' motives in allowing cameras in the courtroom. Some argue that judges, as well as defense attorneys, prosecutors, and witnesses, become too interested in their appearance in the media rather than the interests of justice. There seems to be real concern that judges and lawyers play to the camera, perhaps to the detriment of swift resolution of the case. In general, judges who are more concerned with their public image than maintaining the judicial integrity of their office may make biased decisions. Judges who must be reelected to maintain their positions may be more vulnerable to worrying about their public image.

Courtroom decorum is established by the judge, and if judges display an irreverent or self-aggrandizing attitude or flaunt the law, their behavior degrades the entire judicial process. Some judges seem to be overly influenced by their power—as was the case of one district court judge who instructed courtroom workers to address him as "God." Most courtroom gossip includes the idiosyncrasies of some judges, such as the judge who was reputed to keep a gun under his robes and point it at tardy attorneys; the judge who arrested citizens in the hallway outside his courtroom for "creating a public disturbance" because they were talking too loud while he was holding court; the judge who ordered a woman arrested for contempt when she wrote a scathing letter to a newspaper regarding his competence; the judge who sentenced a man to probation for killing his wife (excusing such behavior in open court with a statement indicating that the nagging victim deserved it); and the judge who signed an order of execution with a smiley face. These individuals illustrate that putting on a black robe doesn't necessarily give one the wisdom of Solomon.

Swisher (2009) lists and discusses various forms of judicial misconduct, including failing to inform defendants of their rights, coercing guilty pleas, exceeding sentencing authority, exceeding bail authority, denying full and fair hearings or trials, abusing the criminal contempt power, ignoring probable cause requirements, denying defendants' rights, and penalizing defendants for exercising their rights. Other forms of unethical behavior are less blatant. Judges have a duty to conclude judicial processing with reasonable punctuality. However, there are widespread delays in processing, partly because of the lack of energy with which some judges pursue their dockets. In the same jurisdiction, and with a balanced assignment of cases, one judge may have only a couple dozen pending cases and another judge may have literally hundreds. Some judges routinely allow numerous continuances, set trial dates far into the future, start the docket call at 10:00 a.m., conclude the day's work at 3:00 p.m., and in other ways take a desultory approach to swift justice.

There are continual news examples of judges who evidently do not uphold the high standards of behavior that should be associated with the black robes. In Boston, an immigration judge was suspended for a year because he referred to himself as Tarzan when hearing a case involving a Ugandan woman named Jane. Another judge deported a man without bothering to check to see that his tax records and birth certificate were authentic (they were). Attorney General Alberto Gonzales wrote a strongly worded memo to all federal immigration judges at the time insisting that they abide by rules of professional decorum (Simmons, 2006).

It was reported that 128 complaints were filed to the Judicial Conduct Commission against Utah judges in 2005. Two high-profile cases involved a judge who was arrested on drug charges and another who was charged with violating the law for not deciding juvenile cases by deadlines set by law. Members of the Utah Judicial Conduct Commission argue that Utah judges have fewer misconduct charges than other states, where judges have been disciplined for DUI, sexual harassment, and "using a sexual device while on the bench" (Fattah, 2005). Pimental (2009) notes that while egregious cases of judicial misconduct appear in the news (i.e., sexual misconduct or bribery), the more prevalent forms of misconduct may only be known to the attorneys who practice before the judge (i.e., favoritism, racial or gender bias, arbitrary decision making). However, it is extremely rare for attorneys to file complaints against judges. In fact, Pimental notes one case in which an attorney reported that his client bribed a judge, and, as a result, the attorney was sanctioned by the bar association for revealing client confidences. Nothing happened to the judge (2009: 938).

In other news, a state district judge in El Paso has been indicted for mail fraud, wire fraud, and lying to a federal agent for allegedly taking cash bribes and sex from defendants in his court. Judge Thomas Porteous, a federal judge based in New Orleans, was finally impeached by the House of Representatives in the winter of 2010 for bribery, perjury, and improper conduct even though he had been suspended from hearing cases back in 2008 (but continued to receive his salary of $174,000). The Senate must also vote on his impeachment and is expected to complete hearings sometime in 2010. Another federal judge, Samuel Kent of Texas, resigned before his impeachment process was completed in 2009. His misconduct involved sexual harassment and assault of female employees and obstruction of justice in the investigation that ensued when one of his victims filed complaints against him (Alpert, 2010). A New York state judge, Thomas Spargo, was found guilty of bribery and sentenced to prison. Mississippi judge Bobby DeLaughter pleaded guilty to obstruction of justice in 2009. DeLaughter was accused of giving a favorable ruling in a case in return for consideration for a federal judgeship. The case involved Richard Scruggs, an extremely powerful attorney who was being sued by a colleague for fees from the multi-billion dollar tobacco suit he won. The fall from grace for DeLaughter was uniquely sad in that he had obtained fame as the courageous district attorney who

WALKING THE WALK

Judge Justice. In a perfect marriage of name and career, William Wayne Justice became part of the fabric of Texas history, beloved and reviled for his definition of justice, but always standing firm for what he believed was right. Justice's father was a criminal defense attorney in Athens, Texas. His career in law was inevitable; his father added the boy's name to the door of his criminal defense firm when he was only seven. He obtained his law degree in 1942 and served four years in the army during World War II before joining his father's practice. In 1961, he was appointed U.S. attorney for the Eastern District of Texas. In 1968, President Lyndon Johnson appointed him to the federal bench. Almost immediately, he was presented with a case that created controversy and enemies. He held that a junior college's policy of requiring men to have short hair was unconstitutional—a holding that did not sit well with the conservative small town of Tyler, where he lived. In 1970, in *United States v. Texas*, he held that Texas was violating the law by continuing to racially segregate schools. He held for the plaintiffs in class action suits against the juvenile corrections system and ruled that the children of illegal aliens should be able to attend public schools free of charge just as citizens did. In one of his most famous cases, *Ruiz v. Estelle*, Justice agreed with Texas prisoners that using building

tenders (inmates who guarded other inmates) and a host of other policies and conditions violated their constitutional rights, and he put the prison system under a federal monitor for over 20 years.

During the course of the 41 years he was a federal judge, Justice experienced a steady stream of death threats, hate mail, and shunning from neighbors, acquaintances, and colleagues for his unpopular holdings and unabashedly activist approach to legal interpretation. A bumper sticker at one time referred to him as "the most hated man in Texas," and he faced threats of impeachment. Through it all, however, he kept his name in the phone book, regularly worked out at the YMCA, and reported that he never lost sleep over his decisions. His biographer claims that Judge Justice single-handedly changed the legal landscape, not just for Texas, but for the nation. Others note that he dragged Texas "kicking and screaming" into the 20th century. Indeed, his early rulings seem obvious to us today, but at the time, he stood against a tide of widespread resistance and anger. His decisions for the rights of illegal immigrant children, the poor, prisoners, and minorities did not make him a hero of the majority. However, as he has remarked, "Sometimes the majority are wrong." Judge Justice died in 2009 at the age of 89.

Source: Gamino, 2009.

prosecuted the killer of civil rights leader Medgar Evers (this case was the basis for the movie *Ghosts of Mississippi*).

We must be careful not to paint with too broad a brush. Only a few judges are involved in the most egregious examples of unethical behavior, such as taking bribes or trampling the due-process rights of defendants, just as only a small percentage of police officers, defense attorneys, and prosecutors commit extreme behaviors. Most judges are ethical and take great care to live up to the obligations of their role. However, as with the other criminal justice professionals, sometimes there are systemic biases and subtle ways in which the principles of justice and due process are subverted. It cannot be ignored that the justice system is assailed as violative of the rights of defendants, especially minorities. There are also judges who exhibit the very best of judicial neutrality, courage, and fairness, as the Walking the Walk box illustrates.

Justice on Trial?

One of the reasons that many people distrust our justice system is that there seems to be a small—but steady—stream of cases in which prosecutors, along with police, deliberately ignore evidence, destroy exculpatory evidence, lie about evidence, or do not share exculpatory evidence with the defense. Radelet, Bedau, and Putnam (1992) gathered together dozens of capital cases where innocent defendants were convicted of crimes they did not commit. Some were sentenced to death. False convictions occurred because of incompetent defense counsel and unethical and illegal practices on the part of prosecutors and police, but also because judges, who are supposed to ensure that the process is fair, evidently did not do their job.

Scott Christianson (2004) described 42 cases where innocent people were convicted. The errors occurred largely through the actions of police, prosecutors, and judges who neglected their duty to be objective officers of the court and traded neutrality for an individual ends-based approach to their duties. Eyewitness perjury (sanctioned by the prosecutor), ineffective counsel, the use of false confessions, police misconduct, fabrication of evidence, and misuse of forensics were the reasons that these innocent people were convicted. Their stories are chilling reminders that innocent people can end up in prison.

The Delma Banks case illustrates the problem. Banks was convicted based on the testimony of a police informant and a long-time drug offender who was promised a shorter sentence and coached to provide details of the crime scene. Neither of these facts was brought out at trial. Further, the jury pool was race-coded by prosecutors, and all African American jurors were excluded. Reanalysis of forensics indicated that the victim was killed when Banks was out of town. Lawyers for Banks were denied a clemency hearing from the State Board of Pardons and Paroles despite the new evidence and the fact that the transcript of the coaching was deliberately withheld from the defense for close to 19 years and finally surrendered only when ordered by a federal district judge. The reason the board denied the petition? It was filed one week late (Pasztor, 2003a, 2003b). The U.S. Supreme Court issued a writ of certiorari and granted a stay of execution, and, evidently refusing to ignore the distinct possibility that an innocent man was to be executed, overturned the verdict and remanded the case for a new trial (Pasztor, 2003b; *Banks v. Dretke*, 540 U.S. 668 [2004]). Others have been executed, and only afterward did evidence or perpetrators' confessions exonerate the accused and expose the prosecution's misconduct that led to the miscarriage of justice (Radelet, Bedau, and Putnam, 1992).

Whereas some of the cases described by Radelet, Bedau, and Putnam involved pure and extreme racial prejudice, probably a more prevalent factor in false convictions is a more subtle form of racism. Many in the criminal justice system tend to prejudge the guilt of the accused, especially if they are black men. There is a pervasive stereotypical belief that all defendants are guilty, and most defendants are black. This thought pattern shapes and distorts decision making on the part of prosecutors who sift and use evidence in a way that will support their predetermined beliefs.

Racial bias in wrongful convictions has been attributed to individual factors and structural factors. Structural factors include systemic bias against minorities in all institutions of society (political, economic, and social) that leads to different opportunities and treatment. Individual factors include: (Schehr and Sears, 2005):

- Racism
- Higher error rate in cross-racial identification
- Stereotyping
- Lack of resources of the defendant

There is a divergence in the perceptions of blacks and whites regarding the fairness of the system. For instance, in a Gallup Poll, 71 percent of whites said murder charges against O. J. Simpson were probably or definitely true, but only 28 percent of blacks agreed (reported in Mitchell and Banks, 1996: Bl). Is this a reflection of a different way of measuring evidence or a different perception of trust in law enforcement and legal professionals' ability to collect and interpret evidence? Is the lack of trust warranted? Unfortunately, the answer to that question is probably yes.

In 2000, the *Cincinnati Inquirer* published the results of an investigation where they found 14 cases where prosecutors had used various forms of misconduct in capital cases (reported in Kirchmeier et al., 2009). In a study conducted by the Columbia Law School, 68 percent of all death verdicts handed down between 1973 and 1995 were reversed because of serious errors. Between 1993 and 2002, 90 death row inmates were exonerated of the crimes of which they were accused. The errors involved defense lawyers' incompetence, and also police and prosecutors suppressing exculpatory evidence or engaging in other types of professional misconduct. Almost 10 percent of the cases sent back for retrial resulted in not-guilty verdicts. The study concluded that the high rate of errors occurred because of the indiscriminate use of the death penalty and factors such as race, politics, and poorly performing law enforcement systems (Columbia Law School, 2002). In this study, 328 cases over the last 15 years in which the individuals were exonerated (usually by DNA) were examined. The study authors allege that there may be thousands of innocent people in prison. Most of the cases that reach national attention are homicide (199 cases) and rape (120 cases), so less serious cases—which may also suffer from the errors of mistaken eyewitness testimony, evidence withholding, and other misconduct—go undiscovered. In 125 cases, a mistaken verdict depended upon false confessions, usually of the mentally ill, the mentally retarded, and juveniles.

Prosecutors have objected to the study's methodology, arguing that the study counted cases where the evidence was weak but the defendant might still be guilty. Further, they argue that the number of exonerations is quite small compared to the number of convictions. (Liptak, 2004; Columbia Law School, 2002).

As of August 2010, the national Innocence Project website states that more than 250 people have been exonerated by DNA evidence as a result of their efforts. The **Innocence Project** consists of an affiliation of groups of lawyers in many states that identify cases where people may have been falsely convicted and there is DNA evidence still on file that could be used to prove or disprove their protestations of innocence. This organization has been pivotal in getting the wrongly accused off death row and freed from prison. (To read more about the project, you can visit their website, www.innocenceproject.org, which lists some of the Innocence Project affiliates around the country.)

A typical case is one from Dallas County, Texas, in which a man was sentenced to life in prison in 1981 for rape. After the Innocence Project tested the DNA evidence, the man was cleared of the rape. He was the 15th inmate from Dallas County to be freed by DNA evidence since 2001, and the 30th wrongfully convicted inmate exonerated in Texas, the highest number of any state. The man had been convicted partially based on an eyewitness who picked him from a photo lineup, but experts report that eyewitness testimony is notoriously unreliable. Partially as a response to this case, the district attorney in Dallas County began a program where law students, supervised by Innocence Project lawyers, reviewed about 450 cases in which convicts had requested DNA testing (Associated Press, 2008c).

Another DNA case, involved four sailors, the "Norfolk Four," who were convicted of rape and murder in 1997. They allege that they falsely confessed to the crime because of the coercive interrogation tactics of a police investigator. There was no other evidence to link them to the crime. Before they were brought to trial, another man, who knew the victim, confessed, admitting he did it alone, and his DNA was found at the crime scene, yet

Innocence Project
An organization staffed by lawyers and law students who reexamine cases and provide legal assistance to convicts when there is a probability that serious errors occurred in their prosecution.

the prosecutors continued with their case against the Norfolk Four. One of the Norfolk Four served eight years before being released, but the other three were still in prison until being pardoned by Virginia's governor in August 2009. The pardon was conditional, however; the men were released on parole and had to register as sex offenders. The case may become a movie; it is reported that John Grisham has expressed his intent to write a screenplay (Jackman and Kumar, 2009).

Another study reviewed different sources to estimate wrongful convictions and concluded that the range was 1 percent to 15 percent, depending on which sources were used (inmate reports illustrated the higher figure) (Poveda, 2001). Even at the lower range, however, the number of innocent people imprisoned is substantial, given that close to 2 million are incarcerated in prisons and jails. In one study using a sample of 798 criminal justice professionals in Ohio, respondents perceived system errors resulting in wrongful convictions occurred at a rate of 0.5 to 1 percent of all felony cases in their own jurisdiction and in 1 to 3 percent of all felony cases across the country. They also indicated that an acceptable rate was less than 0.5 percent (Ramsey, 2007). The Quote and Query box presents two questions. How one might answer them depends on one's perceptions of the costs involved in wrongful convictions.

QUOTE & QUERY

Is it better for 100,000 guilty men to walk free rather than have one innocent man convicted? The cost-benefit policy answer is no.

—SOURCE: (PROSECUTOR) QUOTED IN LIPTAK, 2004: 3.

No rate of preventable errors that destroy people's lives and destroy the lives of those close to them is acceptable.

—SOURCE: (LAW PROFESSOR) QUOTED IN LIPTAK, 2004: 3.

Do either of these statements represent ethical formalism? Which statement represents utilitarian thinking? Why does it have to be a choice between letting guilty people go free and punishing innocents?

In an interesting study that compared a group of those who were released from prison based on exonerations and those who were executed, the authors found that there may have been at least a dozen possible executions of innocents (Harmon and Lofquist, 2005: 592). In the cases where the defendant was executed, they found that it was more likely that there were no allegations of perjury, there were multiple types of evidence, the defendant had prior felony records, and the attorneys were public defenders. The study revealed, for instance, that inmates were 9 times more likely to be released if they had a private attorney at trial (although there was no difference in the type of attorney at the appellate level). Inmates were 27 times more likely to be released when there were allegations of perjury (Harmon and Lofquist, 2005: 511).

Some of the reasons for false convictions include the following (Schehr and Sears, 2005):

- Mistaken eyewitness testimony
- Perjury by informants
- Police and prosecutorial misconduct
- False confessions
- "Junk science"
- Ineffective assistance of counsel

in the NEWS

PARDON US

In February 2010, Charles Baird, a criminal district court judge in Austin, Texas, took the case of Tim Cole, who was convicted of a rape and murder. Later DNA evidence was matched to the real killer, who also had written letters to prosecutors about a decade earlier confessing to the crime and explaining that Cole was not involved and was innocent. Judge Baird issued an order detailing his findings that evidence proved Cole was innocent. The next month, Governor Rick Perry pardoned Cole. This was welcome news to Cole's family, even though Tim Cole was dead. He had died nine years earlier in prison from asthma. The pardon was the first posthumous pardon ever issued as far as anyone can remember.

SOURCE: Janey, 2010.

confirmatory bias Fixating on a preconceived notion and ignoring other possibilities, such as in regard to a specific suspect during a police investigation.

- Racial bias

- **Confirmatory bias** (when a specific suspect has been fixated upon and other possibilities are ignored)

The state of Texas executes the most people and also has freed the most offenders. The In the News box describes a case where the exonerated inmate could not be released because he died in prison. Cases such as Clarence Brandley, James Curtis Giles, and Joyce Ann Brown, discussed previously, create real doubt that only guilty parties are executed. Randall Dale Adams, another freed inmate, was the subject of the documentary *The Thin Blue Line*. He was convicted in 1976 of killing a Dallas police officer who stopped a car driven by David Harris. Harris said Adams was the gunman. Adams said he wasn't even in the car. The state relied on an eyewitness who had picked someone else out of a lineup, and the testimony of Harris, a 16-year-old with a long juvenile record. Harris eventually confessed that he killed the officer alone. The prosecutor withheld the fact that he had made a deal with Harris to testify and hid his lengthy criminal record. Adams spent years in prison and on death row before finally being released (Hall, 2002; Kirchmeier et al., 2009).

Ordinarily, state courts that lean too far in either a liberal or conservative direction would be adjusted by appellate decisions. It is also true, however, that the federal circuit courts have their own reputations for being either too conservative or too liberal, or in the case of the Fifth Circuit, "insolent." The Fifth Circuit court has been admonished by the U.S. Supreme Court because of what some call its "insolence" in ignoring the holdings of Supreme Court decisions in rehearings. In the case of Thomas Miller-El, the Supreme Court ruled in favor of the defendant's appeal based on systematic exclusion of black jurors and remanded the case to the Fifth Circuit. The judges on the Fifth Circuit then used a dissent by Clarence Thomas to deny relief. The case was appealed to the Supreme Court again, and it once again granted relief and rebuked the court, ordering the Fifth Circuit to apply its legal reasoning (Liptak and Blumenthal, 2004; *Miller-El v. Dretke*, 125 St. Ct. 2317 [2005]).

The ideal, or vision, of our justice system is that it is fair, unbiased, and, through the application of due process, arrives at the truth before finding guilt and assessing punishment. The reality is that the law is administered by humans with human failings and that errors and misconduct result in innocent people being convicted, incarcerated, and sometimes executed. There is also a pervasive theme of racism in these miscarriages of justice. This indicates that something else is at work besides individuals not performing their duties and that what is wrong is more fundamental than simply bad or unethical decision making. Even more pervasive than racism, perhaps, is the confirmatory bias that is endemic in the system. When everyone believes that defendants are always guilty, due process is an empty promise.

Explanations for Misconduct

In response to a question about why prosecutors commit the various forms of misconduct described above and in Chapter 9, one commentator explained succinctly, "Because they can." The office of the prosecutor is one of the least scrutinized in the criminal justice system and has not experienced the intense analysis directed to law enforcement or the courts. Hidden from public view are the decisions as to whom to prosecute and what charges to file.

The Supreme Court has ruled that prosecutors cannot be subject to civil suits against them even in cases of egregious rule breaking, if it concerns their adversarial function or prosecutorial decisions. They have limited immunity for actions taken during the investigative phase of a case and for administrative activities. Thus, lying for a warrant, coercing confessions, or making false statements to the press could expose them to liability (Kirchmeier et al., 2009; Zacharias and Green, 2009). However, when Thomas Lee Goldstein was wrongfully convicted in Los Angeles County partially due to the prosecutor's misconduct, he was barred from suing because the prosecutor's action fell under his immunity protections. In this case, the prosecutor used a jailhouse informant who testified that Goldstein confessed, but the informant lied on the stand that he had never been an informant in the past. In fact, he had and had received money for previous testimony in another case. The prosecutor allowed the perjury to stand. Goldstein had his case overturned and was exonerated and is now suing on a theory of misconduct during the administrative functions of the prosecutor role (Zacharias and Green, 2009). It is unlikely that such a legal theory will result in success, however, since the Supreme Court expressed resistance to reducing immunity for prosecutors in the recent case of *Pottawattamie County v. McGhee and Harrington* (129 S. Ct. 2002 [2009]). Although the case was dismissed when the parties settled, during oral arguments, the justices seemed concerned that reducing the immunity of prosecutors would make them more hesitant to aggressively prosecute crime and subject them to frivolous lawsuits. The case involved two men who were wrongfully convicted when they were teens and served almost 30 years in prison because a prosecutor helped assemble and present false testimony against them and hid evidence that implicated the relative of a city official. They settled for $12 million with the county before the Supreme Court made any decision whether or not the immunity of prosecutors extends to the acts of preparing false testimony to be used in court.

Raeder (2007) argues that one of the reasons for prosecutorial misconduct is that the Model Rules and Standards do not cover many of the activities described as misconduct, or they refer to them obliquely with no clear guidance. Furthermore, there are few complaints against prosecutors, except in high profile cases. Gershman (1991) writes that prosecutors misbehave because it works and they can get away with it. Because misconduct is scrutinized only when the defense attorney makes an objection and then files an appeal (and even then the appellate court may rule that it was a harmless error), there is a great deal of incentive to use improper tactics in the courtroom. The most important fact uncovered in the *Chicago Tribune* investigation was that not one of the prosecutors was convicted of a crime, and none was even disbarred. Some became judges or district attorneys, and one became a congressman! (Armstrong and Possley, 2002)

Aronson and McMurtrie (2007), in their discussion of prosecutorial misconduct, describe noble-cause corruption, only with different terminology. They identify the issue as "tunnel vision," arguing that prosecutors work under a bias that defendants are guilty, therefore they ignore exculpatory evidence. Similar to the problems this causes with police investigators, these authors discuss the presence of confirmatory bias (human tendency to seek to confirm rather than disconfirm), selective information processing (only recognizing evidence to fit one's theory), belief perseverance (believing one's original theory of the case despite evidence to the contrary), and avoidance of cognitive dissonance (adjusting beliefs to maintain existing self perceptions). Medwed (2009) also discusses the prosecutor's "conviction psychology" and noted the fact that prosecutors work closely with police officers and victims and their families, and the emotional connections make it difficult to maintain professional objectivity in cases.

Another possible issue is that immunity of judges insulates them from the effects of their decisions, although their decisions are public and can create storms of controversy. Their case holdings can be scrutinized and their courtroom behavior may be grounds for an appeal. Even so, it is difficult for attorneys to challenge judges' actions or testify against them in disciplinary proceedings (Swisher, 2009). Thus, some judges evidently believe they are invulnerable and use the office as a personal throne. In the Pennsylvania case where two judges received kickbacks for sending kids to a private prison, employees and lawyers explained that anyone who criticized the judges, even slightly, found themselves facing retaliation. Judges have immense powers and, as the saying goes, "power corrupts."

Responding to Misconduct

To enforce rules of ethics, the ABA has a standing committee on ethical responsibility to offer formal and informal opinions when charges of impropriety have been made. Also, each state bar association has the power to sanction offending attorneys by private or public censure or to recommend a court suspend their privilege to practice law. Thus, the rules enforced by the state bar have essentially the power of law behind them. The bar associations also have the power to grant entry into the profession because one must ordinarily belong to the bar association of a particular state to practice law there. Bar associations judge competence by testing the applicant's knowledge, and they also judge moral worthiness by background checks of individuals. The purpose of these restrictive admission procedures is to protect the public image of the legal profession by rejecting unscrupulous or dishonest individuals or those unfit to practice for other reasons. However, many believe that if bar associations were serious about protecting the profession, they would also continue to monitor the behavior and moral standing of current members with the same care they seem to take in the initial decision regarding entry (Elliston, 1986).

Disciplinary committees investigate a practicing attorney only when a complaint is lodged against him or her. The investigative bodies have been described as decentralized, informal, and secret. They do little for dissatisfied clients because most client complaints involve incompetence and/or lack of attention; these charges are vague and ill-defined (Marks, Raymond, and Cathcart, 1986: 72). Many bar disciplinary committees are hopelessly understaffed and overburdened with complaints. Complaints may take years to investigate, and in the meantime, if prospective clients call, they will be told only that the

in the **NEWS**

A Lawyer Disbarred

A lawyer in New York was disbarred for incompetent defense and other actions. Among the charges was a case where he accepted $20,000 to conduct an immigration deportation appeal, but then did nothing and did not file the appeal. The client was deported, and the lawyer refused requests from the family to give back any of the money. The lawyer also refused to return clients' bail money after it was returned by the court.

In another case, this lawyer had a criminal client sign a deposit fee agreement stating that the $10,000 deposit was nonrefundable regardless of how much time was spent on the case. The defendant signed the deposit agreement, and immediately afterward the attorney was disqualified from representing the client because he was also representing a co-conspirator. He refused to return any of the deposit money.

Source: Lin, 2006.

attorney is in good standing and has no substantiated complaints. A study of attorney discipline by an organization for legal reform reported that only 3 percent of investigations by state disciplinary committees result in public sanctions and only 1 percent end in disbarment (*San Antonio Express News*, 2002).

While individuals with complaints against their lawyers in the civil arena receive little satisfaction, criminal defendants are arguably even less likely to have anyone care or rectify incompetence or unethical behavior on the part of their attorney. "You get what you pay for" may be true to an extent, but even that phrase does not truly represent the possibility of a family mortgaging its home, signing over cars, and emptying its bank account for an attorney who promises to represent a family member against a criminal charge and then finding that the attorney will not answer calls, doesn't appear in court, or is unprepared and forgets to file necessary motions. One of the most common complaints against attorneys is that they do not diligently work on a case and allow deadlines to pass or miss court dates. Criminal defense attorneys could face civil suits for their incompetence or poor work performance, sanctions from their bar association, and even be cited by courts for contempt, but events such as those described in the In the News box are fairly rare.

As mentioned earlier, it is extremely rare for prosecutors to be censured for misconduct; however, it has happened in a few cases. In Arizona, Kenneth Peasley, a prosecutor who was once named Prosecutor of the Year by the Arizona Bar Association, was disbarred for soliciting and using false testimony (Kirchmeier et al., 2009). Mike Nifong, in the Duke University lacrosse case, endured a highly publicized disbarment in 2007 because of his actions (described in Chapter 9). However, there are generally few controls on the behavior of prosecutors in the courtroom. Voters have some control over who becomes a prosecutor, but once in office, most prosecutors stay in the good graces of a voting public unless there is a major scandal or an energetic competitor. In cities, most of the work is conducted by assistant prosecutors, who are hired rather than elected. Misconduct in the courtroom is sometimes orally sanctioned by trial judges. Perhaps an appellate decision may overturn a conviction, but prosecutors are rarely punished even when cases are overturned. Many times, when there is clear misconduct in the prosecutor not turning over exculpatory evidence or other forms of misconduct, the court rules it is harmless error and does not even overturn the conviction. Some states have created more stringent responses to prosecutorial misconduct and will overturn cases even if there is no way to prove that such misconduct affected the outcome of the case (Kirchmeier et al., 2009). When a prosecutor violates the *Batson* ruling to not use peremptory challenges in a racially discriminatory manner, there should be some sanction; however, the prosecutor must show only that he or she had some other reason for exclusion and the legal standard is whether there is any explanation for the exclusion, even if implausible (*Purkett v. Elem*, 514 U.S. 765 [1995]). Statistics from the Equal Justice Initiative, a legal advocacy group, indicate that black jurors are dismissed at a blatantly disproportionate rate compared to white jurors. In some jurisdictions, blacks were removed three times as often as whites and, in another jurisdiction, 80 percent of blacks were struck from capital cases by prosecutors (*New York Times*, 2010c).

There is little reason for the prosecutor who sees injustice occur in the office to come forward. In *Garcetti v. Ceballos* (547 U.S. 410[2006]), the Supreme Court ruled against a prosecutor who objected to misconduct occurring in the office where he worked. In this case, Richard Ceballos was an attorney for the Los Angeles County District Attorney's office. He submitted a memorandum to his superiors detailing his findings that a search warrant obtained by law enforcement officers had serious flaws and recommended the case be dismissed. Instead, his supervisor continued the prosecution. Ceballos, against orders, provided the defense with a copy of his memorandum and was called as a defense witness. He was subsequently passed over for promotions and sanctioned in other ways, and filed a Section 1983 claim arguing that his First Amendment rights were violated. The Supreme Court, in a 5–4 decision, held that the First Amendment did not apply to public servants in the course of their public duties. Sadly, this decision may act as a barrier to public officials who attempt to challenge what they believe to be miscarriages of justice.

Some have argued that the seemingly widespread evidence of prosecutorial misconduct supports rethinking prosecutorial immunity, and perhaps employing criminal sanctions against prosecutors, and establishing independent commissions to investigate innocence (Raeder, 2007). Zacharias and Green (2009) proposed that Model Rule 1.1 requiring all attorneys to display a level of competency could be used against prosecutors who use evidence that they should know is false or withhold evidence from the prosecution. The advantage of using the competency rule rather than the rule prohibiting the use of false testimony is that the "knowing" standard is difficult to meet (the prosecutor has to "know" the evidence is false), but competency would be an easier standard to meet when prosecutors engage in acts that result in innocent people being convicted. Others argue that training is necessary, with perhaps requiring prosecutors to work with Innocence Commissions, to counteract the psychology of conviction at all costs. It has also been suggested that prosecutors' offices should have ethics officers and sanction employees who cross over the line. There should also be clear and public policies in each prosecutor's office concerning the use of jailhouse informants and turning over exculpatory material (Kirchmeier et al., 2009).

While the number of Innocence Project affiliates is growing and the groups have been successful in identifying cases and prevailing in court, they can't be the only solution to the problem of false convictions. Unfortunately, most of these projects are under-resourced and overwhelmed. Some argue that what is needed is a model such as Great Britain's Criminal Cases Review Commission, which is a governmental agency rather than a volunteer and/or private organization. Others (Schehr and Weathered, 2004) question the efficacy of Britain's model, arguing that

in the **NEWS**

SHOW ME YOUR GRADES!

The Northwestern University Journalism School's Innocence Project has been instrumental in overturning 11 convictions, embarrassing the Cook County prosecutor's office in the process. In early 2010, they faced a legal challenge of their own when the chief prosecutor in Chicago filed motions to demand students turn over grades, e-mails, notes, and course evaluations. She believes that their discovery of evidence was influenced by grades received—specifically, that they manufactured evidence to obtain good grades. The director of the Innocence Project alleges harassment and retaliation, and pledges to fight the order.

SOURCE: Folkenflik, 2010.

- It is subordinate to the Court of Appeal and thus deferential to it.
- It relies on untrained caseworkers to review cases.
- It relies on petitioners to raise claims.
- It is understaffed and pays too little attention to each case.

Others argue that the Innocence Project affiliates can serve an important purpose, but that they must be better funded and not left to the vagaries of budget cuts. Medved (2009) argues for innocence divisions in prosecutors' offices. Craig Watkins, the district attorney of Dallas County, instituted such a division when he was elected in 2007. The unit reviews DNA cases that have been identified by the Innocence Project of Texas and all cases where DNA evidence has identified unknown suspects in addition to the defendant. As of August 2010, the unit has thus far exonerated 40 people and is reviewing hundreds of other cases (Raeder, 2007; Medved, 2009: 63). Also, recall from Chapter 8 that the ABA added two sections to Rule 3.8 for prosecutors that concerned their ethical duty to investigate and remedy when there is a chance that an innocent person has been convicted. In contrast, some prosecutors actively resist post-conviction DNA testing, and, as the In the News box illustrates, there are other examples that indicate that prosecutors' offices may be more concerned with protecting their convictions than discovering if innocent people have been convicted.

As mentioned above, DNA has been the vehicle by which many innocent prisoners have obtained their release from prison. Even after many years, a small amount of preserved DNA evidence could exclude someone or help to identify the real perpetrator of a crime. Some states have mandated DNA testing of old cases when the inmate requests it. Some locales have instituted prosecution divisions that review cases where DNA still exists. Still other offices, however, actively oppose retesting of DNA. In *District Attorney v. Osborne* (129 S. Ct. 2308 [2009]), the Supreme Court, in a 5–4 decision led by the conservative majority, ruled that defendants had no constitutional right to DNA evidence, even if it was still held by the state and even if they were willing to pay for its testing. In this case, the prisoner argued that the testing done in his trial matched him only to 1 in 6 black men and more advanced tests available today could determine more accurately that he was not the rapist. The state, in this Alaska case, argued that such a right would jeopardize the finality of case decisions when the trial was otherwise fair. One wonders, however, how a trial could be thought of as fair if an innocent person was convicted. One also wonders why the Supreme

Court would not consider access to such evidence a part of due process. The last section in this chapter returns again to the theme that justice is created or thwarted by the actors in the system.

Judicial Independence and the Constitution

Recall that discretion is the ability to make a decision and that discretion exists at each stage of the criminal justice system. Professionals at each stage have the opportunity to use their discretion wisely and ethically, or, alternatively, they may use their discretion unethically. In the courts, prosecutors have discretion to pursue prosecution or not, defense attorneys have discretion to accept or refuse cases and choose trial tactics, and judges have discretion to make rulings on evidence and other trial procedures, as well as decide on convictions and sentences.

One view of law is that it is neutral and objective and that formal and absolute rules of law are used in decision making (Pinkele and Louthan, 1985: 9). However, the reality is that lawmakers, law enforcers, and lawgivers are invested with a great deal of discretion in making and interpreting the law. Far from being absolute or objective, the law is a dynamic, ever-changing symbol of political will. If we accept that discretion is an operating reality in the justice system, we must ask in what ways legal professionals use this discretion. If individual value systems replace absolute rules or laws, the resulting decisions may be ethical or unethical. For instance, a judge may base a decision on fairness or on prejudicial beliefs (e.g., that blacks are more criminal and deserve longer sentences, or that women are not dangerous and should get probation).

There are many other situations where one's biases and prejudices may not be so easily identified. Judges' rulings on evidentiary matters are supposed to be based on rules of evidence, but sometimes there is room for interpretation and individual discretion. While most judges use this discretion appropriately and make decisions in a best effort to conform to the spirit of the evidentiary rule, other judges use arbitrary or unfair criteria, such as personal dislike of an attorney, disagreement with a rule, or a desire for one side or the other to win the case.

In this text, we address the ethical issues in the *implementation*, rather than the *creation*, of law. As you learned in political science or government classes, the creation of law is political. Laws are written by federal and state representatives who supposedly enact the public will. One might think that once a law is created, its implementation would be fairly straightforward, but it should be clear by now that this is not the case. An appellate court can change over time and be influenced by political shifts in power. Far from being static, the implementation of law reflects political realities, in direct contrast to the ideal of judicial independence that is the cornerstone of our system of government.

If the judiciary is not independent of political powers, this calls into question the very existence of the checks and balances upon which this country's government is constructed. For instance, many Democrats suspected that the political composition of the Supreme Court had a great deal to do with its decision in the case challenging the Florida vote after the Bush–Gore presidential election in 2000. Whether or not the allegations are true, it should be obvious that the strength of the justice system rests on the independence of its judiciary.

In 2005, several leaders in Congress publicly chastised the federal judiciary because they did not like the decisions that the federal judges had been handing down, and then, in turn, were criticized by others who argued that the essence of separation of powers is that federal judges are not influenced, intimidated, or ordered by legislative leaders to enact anyone's political agenda. The Quote and Query box illustrates the controversy.

QUOTE & QUERY

[T]he time will come for the men responsible for this to answer for their behavior... [I want to] look at an arrogant, out-of-control, unaccountable judiciary that thumbed their nose at Congress and the president.

—SOURCE: TOM DELAY, U.S. HOUSE OF REPRESENTATIVES MAJORITY LEADER, SPEAKING IN RESPONSE TO THE TERRI SCHIAVO CASE, MAY 2005, AS QUOTED IN ALLEN, 2005.

Attempts to intimidate judges into deciding pending cases in a particular way with threats of impeachment or investigation, as has been the recent practice of some members of Congress, have no place in a functioning democracy.

—SOURCE: *AMERICAN JUDICATURE*, 2005.

Do you think that members of Congress should be sanctioned for threatening impeachment when they don't like the decisions of federal judges? If not, who does serve as oversight for judges who are appointed for life?

The political uproar over the firings of eight federal prosecutors in 2007 by the Bush administration may have seemed overblown to some people. After all, why shouldn't a president be able to hire and fire at will? However, what was at stake was the very essence of the separation of powers that is the greatest strength of our system of government. Traditionally, when a new president comes into office, he engages in a process whereby those affiliated with the old administration are removed and new employees are placed into those positions. That has been done in all sectors of executive government, including the Justice Department, by Democrat and Republican administrations alike, with very little criticism. What happened in 2007, however, was that, apparently, in the middle of the term of office, there was a "hit list" of federal prosecutors who were removed not for incompetence or poor performance, but rather, because White House aides relayed a message to Justice Department officials that these individuals should be replaced with others who were more loyal to the Bush administration.

Observers noted that the prosecutors targeted for firing were those who either pursued prosecutions against Republicans or were too slow to respond to pressure to pursue prosecutions against Democrats. In effect, the firings were politically motivated, not a "house cleaning" at the beginning of a term of office. When Attorney General Alberto Gonzales responded to the congressional inquiry in an unsatisfactory way (saying more than 70 times that he couldn't remember), he ultimately had to resign because of the scandal (Carr and Herman, 2007). In 2008, the Justice Department released a scathing 400-page report charging ethical violations in the firing of U.S. attorneys such as David Iglesias in New Mexico; however, it received very little press since Wall Street's financial crisis eclipsed all other news stories at the time (Johanek, 2008).

If the justice system, including prosecutors and judges, is a pawn or an agent of political power, due process is a sham and the very essence of democracy is threatened. The importance of due process is that even criminals and enemies of the state are given due-process rights that protect them from errors in the deprivation of life, liberty, and property. If due process is reserved only for those who are not enemies of the state, all are threatened because anyone may become an enemy. If for some reason state power would become despotic, it would be likely to label as enemies anyone favoring open government and democracy. What this illustrates is that the law (and the nature of its protections) is more important than the state and, indeed, is even more important than threats to the state. Those who are more influenced by political allegiance than allegiance to due process and civil liberties create a weak link in the mantle of protection against despotic state power.

The U.S. Supreme Court, as the ultimate authority of law in this country, decides constitutionality, and these interpretations are far from neutral, despite the myth of objective decision making. This is the reason that the selection of Supreme Court justices (as well as all federal judges) is such a hard-fought political contest. Ideological positions do make a difference, and no one is fooled that a black robe removes bias. The latest confirmations of John Roberts as Chief Justice (during the Bush administration) and Sonia Sotomayor and Elena Kagan (during the Obama administration) illustrate this. The most recent confirmation hearing, of Elena Kagan in 2010, was a replay of past hearings with opponents and proponents lined up predictably on ideological sides.

JUDICIAL ACTIVISM

strict constructionist
The view that an individual has no rights unless these rights are specified in the Constitution or have been created by some other legal source.

Our law derives from the Constitution. Two basic philosophies regarding how to apply constitutional principles are at work in the legal arena. The first group might be called **strict constructionists** because they argue that the Constitution should be implemented as written, and if any changes are to take place in rights, responsibilities, or liberties, the changes should take place through the political system (Congress).

The extreme view of this position is that if a right isn't in the Constitution, it doesn't exist. So, for instance, the right to be free from state interference in the decision to abort one's fetus does not exist in the Constitution; therefore, it doesn't exist and cannot be created except through the actions of duly elected representatives. Strict constructionists argue that just because something *should* be a right doesn't mean that one can decide the framers meant for it to be a right. Judges should not create law.

interpretationist An approach to the Constitution that uses a looser reading of the document and reads into it rights that the framers might have recognized or that should be recognized as a result of "evolving standards."

Interpretationists (or activists) have a looser reading of the Constitution and read into it rights that the framers might have recognized or that should be recognized because of "evolving standards." They argue that the Constitution is meant to be a living document and that the language of the framers was intentionally written as to accommodate interpretation based on changing times and circumstances. Concepts such as due process, for instance, from the Fifth and Fourteenth Amendments, are flexible so they can be used to address new questions and new concerns. Interpretationists place less emphasis on precedent, minimize procedural obstacles (such as standing, ripeness, and federalism), and offer less deference to other political decision makers (e.g., they use the strict scrutiny test rather than the rational relationship test when evaluating governmental actions). When the Court was in its most activist phase during the Warren Court (1953–1969), it delivered broad opinions that have had dramatic effects on the political and legal landscape (Wolfe, 1991). The debate as to whether the Constitution should be strictly construed or liberally interpreted is an old one, as the Quote and Query box indicates.

QUOTE & QUERY

When we are dealing with words that also are a constituent act, like the Constitution of the United States, we must realize that they have called into life a being the development of which could not have been foreseen completely by the most gifted of its begetters.

—SOURCE: OLIVER WENDELL HOLMES, JR., SUPREME COURT JUSTICE, 1902–1932, AS QUOTED IN WOLFE, 1991: 36.

Does this quote by Holmes indicate he was a strict constructionist or an interpretationist?

Critics of judicial activism point out that just because judicial activists have been promoters of civil liberties and socially progressive causes, such as integration and free speech, there is no absolute necessity that activism could or would always champion such individual rights. Activism could, for instance, be just as likely to recognize greater rights of the state to restrict individual liberties (Wolfe, 1991).

Proponents of activism argue that the federal government itself has not been content to stay within the boundaries of its enumerated powers as specified in the Constitution, and that proliferation of the federal government's reach into all areas of criminal and civil law through the expansive interpretation of the Commerce Clause requires greater judicial checks. Furthermore, there are limits to judicial power, including impeachment, confirmation, congressional definition of appellate powers, and the power to override a Supreme Court opinion through a constitutional amendment (Wolfe, 1991). The Warren Court was called activist or liberal because it recognized a whole range of civil liberties and due-process rights for groups that had been historically disenfranchised. The source of such rights was found in an expansive reading of the Constitution and based on the idea of "fundamental liberties"—those freedoms and protections that the framers would have recognized if they had been asked. Central to this view is the idea of **natural rights**. Recall that the natural law ethical system holds that there are natural laws of ethics that humans may or may not discover. Several of the authors of the Bill of Rights were natural law theorists; thus, taken out of the context of their time, they would probably recognize that humans have the following rights:

natural rights The concept that one has certain rights just by virtue of being born, and these rights are not created by humans, although they can be ignored.

- To be free
- To be treated equal to other groups
- To be able to make decisions about personal matters without governmental interference
- To be free from torture and punishments that degrade the human spirit
- To have some protections against state power

In addition, there may be recognition that humans also have rights

- To basic necessities to survive
- To avail themselves of opportunities to better themselves

The first set of rights leads to less government; the second set leads to more government. That is why the political terms *conservative* and *liberal* are not strictly comparable to "strict constructionist" and "interpretationist" and why there is such confusion when these terms are being used to describe judicial and political appointees and elected officials. "Liberals" argue that if the Warren Court hadn't interpreted the Constitution to recognize civil rights, blacks would still be eating at separate lunch counters. Constructionists argue that if interpretationists had their way, government and the courts would be involved in every decision from birth to death.

The Supreme Court's "activism" has been intimately tied to who has been on the bench. Observers note that it has moved back to a constructionist stance, because of the confirmations of John Roberts, Samuel Alito, Clarence Thomas, and Antonin Scalia. In recent holdings, the Court has restricted the coverage of the *Miranda* warnings, upheld federal anti-abortion laws, cut back on free-speech rights of public school students, strictly enforced procedural requirements for bringing and appealing cases, and limited the ability to use racially conscious measures to achieve or preserve integration.

One can predict case decisions based on the justices' ideological positions, with Scalia, Alito, Thomas, and Roberts almost always voting in a block and usually winning in 5–4 decisions when Justice Anthony Kennedy provides the swing vote. What is interesting is that so-called "liberal" justices were appointed by Republican presidents: Justices John Paul Stevens (appointed by Gerald Ford), Justice David Souter (appointed by George H.W. Bush), and Sandra Day O'Connor (appointed by Ronald Reagan) were not considered activist or liberal when they were appointed but moved in that direction compared to the justices that have been appointed since then (Greenhouse, 2007). It is expected that Sonia Sotomayor and Elena Kagan will not change this formula since they replace justices who voted with the liberal block (Souter and Stevens).

Judges' political leanings shouldn't influence their decisions, but it is hard to argue that there is no correlation. Even an analysis by the Justice Department determined that immigration judges (also called hearing examiners) who were hired by the George W. Bush White House based on a political affiliation requirement and their views on immigration and abortion were less likely to grant asylum than judges hired with politically neutral criteria. Using such criteria was determined to be illegal and abandoned, but the immigration hearing examiners continue to remain in place (Savage, 2008).

One thing is clear: a judge is human and carries baggage of personal, political, and social bias. Judges no doubt strive for objectivity, and we attempt to protect their independence, but individual ethics clearly are important considerations in any discussion of judicial discretion. The law is subject to interpretation; thus, individual ethics play a part in the use of the powers given to the judiciary.

CONCLUSION

One might expect that the public's respect and trust for legal professionals, as guardians of the justice system, would be high, but that is not the case. Part of the reason is the ability to take either side in a controversy. We should not forget that attorneys and judges protect the bedrock of our structure of laws.

In criminal justice, it is crucial that legal professionals remember and believe in the basic tenets of due process and be ever vigilant against the influence of prejudice or bias in the application of law toward the pursuit of justice. Unfortunately, there are cases where defense attorneys, prosecutors, and judges do not uphold the ethical standards of their profession and instead engage in various forms of misconduct. Although the types of misconduct vary depending on one's role in the system, each can be explained by individual enrichment (money, status, or time), or by ends/means thinking due to confirmatory bias (similar to noble-cause corruption for police officers).

There is a need to improve the ethics of the system, as evidenced by the Innocence Project's exonerations of hundreds of people who ended up in prison because of the failings of the system and system actors. It is important to remember that the law, despite those who advocate strict constructionism, can never be truly objective or formulistic. Every decision is made through a reasoned and, one hopes, ethical application of the law rather than by a robotic question and answer. The law must be seen as a living entity, and legal professionals are its life's blood.

CHAPTER REVIEW

1. Detail the types of misconduct that have been associated with defense attorneys, prosecutors, and judges.

Misconduct by defense attorneys includes ignoring cases, incompetence, and going over the line when defending clients, including presenting false evidence. The types of prosecutorial misconduct include withholding exculpatory evidence, misusing pretrial publicity, using preemptory challenges to exclude jurors, and using false evidence in court. Misconduct by judges includes allowing bias (including bribery) to influence their decision making and acting arbitrarily and otherwise abusing their power.

2. Explain the reasons why such misconduct occurs.

The reason why misconduct occurs is that the disciplinary functions carried out by the state bar associations rarely result in serious sanctions. Prosecutors experience very little oversight and seldom suffer from sanctions when violating the ethical rules in their zeal to obtain a conviction. Court often rule such misconduct as harmless error. Judges are feared by employees and lawyers who hesitate to file complaints against them.

3. Describe the Innocence Projects, how many individuals have been found to be wrongly imprisoned, and why.

These are loose associations of lawyers who identify cases where the prisoner may be innocent and investigate, often resulting in a new trial and exoneration. Thus far, Innocence Projects across the country have succeeding in obtaining exonerations for more than 250 individuals.

4. Discuss some proposals to improve the justice system and reduce ethical misconduct.

Suggestions to improve the system have been to institute official Innocence Projects or fund them with public money. Some prosecutors have established divisions to investigate wrongful convictions. Suggestions also include more training and ethics officers. Also, some have suggested re-evaluating prosecutorial immunity and using civil and criminal sanctions against prosecutors who create and use false evidence and engage in other forms of misconduct to obtain convictions.

5. Understand the concepts associated with judicial activism or constructionism and how this issue relates to ethical misconduct.

An activist judge is one who believes such concepts as due process and liberty rights are evolving and the founding fathers did not mean for the rights enumerated in the Constitution to remain static throughout time. Constructionists argue that legislators should make law, not judges. One's opinion regarding this—and one's values, opinions, and biases in general—affect decision making, so judges' opinions on cases can be predicted ahead of time in many cases. This calls into question judicial neutrality and reminds us that, in the end, our system of laws is a system of people who enforce the law, and thus it is only as good or bad as the people in the system.

KEY TERMS

confirmatory bias	interpretationist	strict constructionist
Innocence Project	natural rights	

STUDY QUESTIONS

1. What is the evidence that shows the public mistrusts attorneys?
2. What are the four types of ethical violations that have been associated with prosecutors?
3. Discuss the number of innocents who may be imprisoned. What are the sources for the estimates? What are the criticisms of the sources?
4. What factors have been identified as contributing to false convictions?
5. What is the evidence to indicate a pervasive pattern of racial bias in the system?

WRITING/DISCUSSION EXERCISES

1. Using ethical and moral criteria, write an essay on (or discuss) courtroom practices: the use of videotaped testimony, allowing television cameras into the courtroom and jury room, victim statements during sentencing, preventive detention, neighborhood justice centers, the use of a waiver to adult court for violent juvenile offenders, and any others that have been in the news recently.
2. After watching a movie that presents a legal dilemma (e.g., *Presumed Innocent, 12 Angry Men, Philadelphia,* or *Michael Clayton*), write an essay on (or discuss) the ethical dilemmas of the characters. Use one or more of the ethical frameworks provided in Chapter 2.
3. Write an essay on (or discuss) judicial activism. Present the arguments on both sides of the question as to whether judges should interpret or simply apply the Constitution. Provide more current examples (the current Supreme Court docket) and predict how justices will decide. If one can predict the decisions of the justices on the Supreme Court, where does that leave the idea that no case is prejudged?

ETHICAL DILEMMAS

Situation 1

You are a defense attorney who is defending a man against a charge of burglary. He tells you that he was drunk on the night in question and doesn't remember what he did. He asks you to put him on the stand, and when you do, he responds to your questions by stating unequivocally that he was home watching a television show, describing the show and plotline. You understand that you cannot participate in perjury, but to call attention to his inconsistent stories would violate other rules, such as confidentiality and zealous defense. What do you do?

Situation 2

You are a member of a jury. The jury is hearing a child molestation case in which the defendant is accused of a series of molestations in his neighborhood. You have been advised by the judge not to discuss the case with anyone outside the courtroom, and especially not with anyone on either side of the case. Going down in the elevator after the fourth day of the trial, you happen to ride with the prosecutor in the case. He tells you that the man has a previous arrest for child molestation, but that it has not been allowed in by the judge, as being too prejudicial for the jury. You were fairly sure that the guy was guilty before, but now you definitely believe he is guilty. You also know that if you tell the judge what you have heard, it will probably result in a mistrial. What would you do? What should happen to the prosecutor?

Situation 3

You are a court administrator and really like Judge Sonyer, your boss. He is pleasant, punctual, and hardworking. One day, you hear him talking to the prosecutor in chambers. He is talking about the defendant in a trial that is about to start, and you hear him say that "the son-of-a-bitch is as guilty as sin." You happen to be in law school and know that, first, the prosecutor and judge should not be talking about the case without the presence of the defense attorney, and, second, the judge has expressed a pre-existing bias. The judge's statement is even more problematic because this is a bench trial and he is the sole determiner of guilt or innocence. What would you do?

Situation 4

You are a federal judge and are about to start a federal racketeering trial that is quite complicated. Prosecutors allege that certain lobbyists funneled money into political campaigns by "washing" it through individual employees of a couple of large corporations. Still, the evidence seems equivocal—at least what you've seen so far. You get a call from one of your state's U.S. senators (who is not implicated in the case, although members of his party are), and the conversation is innocuous and pleasant enough until the senator brings up the case and jocularly pressures you to agree with him that it is a "tempest in a teapot." Then he mentions that a higher, appellate-level judgeship will be opening soon and that he is sure you would like his support on it. The message is not subtle. What would you do?

Situation 5

You are a defense attorney who sees a judge in your jurisdiction having dinner with a prosecutor. Both are married to other people. You happen to have a case in front of this judge and the prosecutor is your opponent. You consider that you could request the judge recuse himself from the case, but this may create animosity, and if he refuses, it could be detrimental to your client. Alternatively, you could keep quiet and use the information on appeal, but this may mean your client spends years in prison. Finally, you could do nothing and hope that the judge is not biased toward the prosecution in his rulings. What would you do?

PART IV

Corrections

11

PAT GREENHOUSE/Boston Globe /Landov

The Ethics of Punishment and Corrections

Chapter Objectives

1. Provide the definitions of punishment and treatment and their rationales.
2. Describe how the ethical frameworks justify punishment.
3. Describe the ethical rationales for and against capital punishment.
4. Describe the ethical codes for correctional officers, treatment professionals, and probation and parole officers.
5. Explain how occupational subcultures affect adherence to professional ethics codes.

Imagine that you are arrested and convicted of a drug crime. Because of harsh drug laws in your state, you are sent to prison for three years. Nothing in your background prepares you for the experience. Your family and friends are horrified; you are terrified. Jail was bad enough, but this is a small county and only six other women were housed there who, despite constant verbal taunting, were relatively harmless. Now, however, you arrive at the state women's facility. The whole process, from the long bus ride to the prison, to the humiliating public shower and delousing, to the body-cavity search, to the yelling of the correctional officer in charge that "all you crack ho's better get moving" has been confusing, overwhelming, and soul-destroying.

Once you finally are settled in your cell, your cellmate tells you that a woman can do certain things for the guards in this prison to make the time pass easier. Further, she says, if you catch the eye of a certain guard, you won't have any choice in the matter because he doesn't like to be refused. You think she is exaggerating. After all, things like that don't happen in real life, only in the movies. You are wrong. By the end of your first six months in prison, the person you used to be and why you are being punished are distant memories.

Two famous quotes resonate throughout the discussion of ethics in corrections. The first is from Dante's *Divine Comedy*: "Abandon all hope, ye who enter here." This inscription at the portal to hell, often scrawled as graffiti in prisons, unfortunately encapsulates what some prisons mean to those who are sent there. The second quote, by Fyodor Dostoyevsky, who was reputed to have said, "The degree of civilization in a society can be judged by entering its prisons," cautions that the best of us still have certain duties of respect and care toward the worst of us.

Once someone has been found guilty of a criminal offense, the type of punishment must be determined. Punishments range from a suspended sentence to death. Sometimes punishment includes treatment, at least in name. During incarceration, the wrongdoer may be required to participate in treatment programs or self-help groups such as Alcoholics Anonymous. Probationers may be required to go to drug-treatment programs; they may even be required to get their GED or obtain some type of job training. In addition to formal, legal punishments, there are informal, extra-legal punishments that should not exist, but unfortunately do exist. Inmates are raped and beaten, more often by other inmates, but sometimes by guards. Their personal property is destroyed. They get sick or injured and receive no treatment. Prisoner advocates maintain that these events should never be part of the formal punishment of prison, but others believe that the prisoner "shouldn't do the crime if he (or she) can't do the time."

According to one author (Leiser, 1986: 198), five elements are essential to the definition of **punishment**:

punishment
Unpleasantness or pain administered by one in lawful authority in response to another's transgression of law or rules.

1. There are at least two persons—one who inflicts the punishment and one who is punished.

2. The person who inflicts the punishment causes a certain harm to the person who is being punished.

3. The person who inflicts the punishment has been authorized, under a system of rules or laws, to harm the person who is punished in this particular way.

4. The person who is being punished has been judged by a representative of that authority to have done what he or she is forbidden to do or failed to do what he or she is required to do by some relevant rule or law.

5. The harm that is inflicted upon the person who is being punished is specifically for the act or omission mentioned in condition 4.

treatment Anything used to induce behavioral change with the goal of eliminating dysfunctional or deviant behavior and encouraging productive and normal behavior patterns.

We also need to define **treatment**. According to correctional terminology, treatment may be anything used to induce behavioral change. The goal is to eliminate dysfunctional or deviant behavior and to encourage productive and normal behavior patterns. In prison, treatment includes diagnosis, classification, therapy, education, religious activity, vocational training, and self-help groups.

The infliction of punishment and even treatment is usually limited by some rationale or guideline. For instance, von Hirsch (1976: 5) presents the following restrictive guidelines:

- The liberty of each individual is to be protected as long as it is consistent with the liberty of others.

- The state is obligated to observe strict parsimony in intervening in criminals' lives.

- The state must justify each intrusion.

- The requirements of justice ought to constrain the pursuit of crime prevention (that is, deterrence and rehabilitation).

This chapter and the next two follow the format we have established in the previous sections on law enforcement and legal professionals. In this chapter, we will first explore relevant issues such as the various rationales for punishment and capital punishment in particular, present the formal codes of ethics for correctional professionals and describe occupational subcultures that sometimes conflict with the formal code of ethics.

In Chapter 12, we will discuss some ethical dilemmas for correctional professionals that arise because of the discretion inherent in these roles. In Chapter 13, we will review past and current instances of misconduct by correctional professionals, explanations proposed for such behavior, and suggestions for improving the ethical climate in corrections.

Rationales for Punishment and Corrections

Does society have the right to punish or correct miscreants? If it does, where does that right come from? The rationale for punishment and corrections comes from the social contract. In the same way that the social contract forms the basis for police power, it also provides a rationale for further control in the form of punishment and corrections. Recall that according to this theory, we avoid social chaos by giving the state the power to control us. In this way we protect ourselves from being victimized by others by giving up our liberty to aggress against others. If we do step outside the bounds of this agreement, the state has the right to control and punish us for our transgressions. Concurrently, the state is limited in the amount of control it can exert over individuals. To be consistent with the social contract, the state should exert its power only to accomplish the purpose of protection; any further interventions in civil liberties are unwarranted.

Corrections pursues a mixture of goals, including retribution, reform, incapacitation, deterrence, and rehabilitation. The long-standing argument between proponents of punishment and proponents of treatment reveals a system without a clear mandate or rationale for action. Garland (1990) writes that the state's goal of punishment is problematic because it is marked with inconsistencies between the intent and the implementation. The moral contradictions are that it seeks to uphold freedom by means of its deprivation, and it punishes private violence by inflicting state violence. Can treatment and punishment occur at the same time? Some argue that because punishment has the goal of inflicting pain on an individual, it is fundamentally incompatible with the goal of treatment. Others argue that there is no reason that positive change cannot occur in a correctional setting.

One of the most problematic issues in justifying what we do in the name of punishment is that what we do to offenders changes over time (and place). If what is considered to be appropriate punishment changes, how can any particular punishment be considered to be just under some form of universalism or natural law theory? In other words, in earlier centuries we might have hanged a pickpocket. Was that just, or is it just today to incarcerate the person? Is it just to incarcerate drug users today when in times past (or, perhaps, in future times) they would not be imprisoned at all? Prisoners in different prisons have vastly different sentences. How can the worst prison be fair if it is just chance whether a prisoner ends up there or in a prison with better living conditions?

An important question to ask is: "Whom are we punishing?" Studies show that only a small minority of individuals who commit crimes end up in prison; furthermore, we may assume that those individuals are not representative of the larger population. Those in our jails and prisons are there not only because they committed crimes, but also because they are poor, members of a minority group, or powerless. Certain types of criminals tend to avoid the more punitive sanctions of the corrections system. For instance, businesses routinely bilk consumers out of billions of dollars annually and chalk up the punitive fines imposed to operating expenses; property offenders in prison cost us far less, but we punish them more severely. Streams and land are routinely polluted by industrial waste, but, again, punitive fines are the typical sanctions, and these cannot begin to restore what has been taken away in the flagrant pursuit of financial profit. Such costs are typically passed on to the consumers, so taxpayers suffer the crime and then also pay the fine.

White Collar Crime: Fair Punishment?

Many people think that white collar ("suite") criminals do not get punished as severely as "street" criminals. There is some truth to that. Even though Tyco International's Dennis Kozlowski, WorldCom's Bernie Ebbers, and, of course, Bernie Madoff received long prison sentences, many do not. Michael Milken was the king of junk bonds and insider trading in the early 1990s and his "cost" of two years in prison gained him $500 million to spend when he was released. Enron's Jeffrey Skilling and Andrew Fastow will serve several years in prison, but HealthSouth's Richard Scrushy was acquitted, as was Global Crossing's Gary Winnick. Observers note that white collar criminals face harsher sentences today than they did in the early 1990s. The wide-scale fraud and illegalities that resulted in many investors losing their retirement holdings in the early 2000s led to calls for serious punishments, such as the 15-year sentence received by Adelphia's John Rigas. In the late 2000s, we experienced an even bigger financial scandal, but the names of the players behind the derivatives market and stock market crash are not as clearly identified. In fact, it is unlikely that the largest financial crisis in modern history will result in anyone serving prison time. More to the point, it is not even clear if their activities broke any laws.

Long ago, criminals were viewed as sinners with no ability to change their behavior, so punishment and incapacitation were seen as the only logical ways to respond to crime. Jeremy Bentham (1748–1832) and Cesare Beccaria (1738–1794) viewed the criminal as rational and as having free will and, therefore, saw the threat of punishment as a deterrent. Neoclassicists such as Adolphe Quetelet (1796–1874) and André-Michel Guerry (1802–1866) recognized that insane persons and juveniles could not be held entirely responsible for their actions and, therefore, believed that they should not be punished. The insane and the young were treated differently because they were considered to be moral infants, not possessing the sense to refrain from wrongdoing.

treatment ethic The idea that all criminal acts are symptoms of an underlying pathology.

retribution A rationale for punishment that states that punishment is an end in itself and should be balanced to the harm caused.

prevention A rationale for punishment that views it as a means rather than an end and embraces any method that can avoid crime, painful or not (includes deterrence, rehabilitation, and incapacitation).

In the 1800s, the positivist school looked for differences between criminals and noncriminals. The search for differences eventually, in the 1960s and 1970s, led to the short-lived rehabilitative era and the **treatment ethic**—the idea that all criminal acts were symptoms of an underlying pathology. The treatment programs created in the last hundred years or so operate under the assumption that we can do something to offenders to reduce their criminal activity. That "something" may involve

- Treating a psychological problem, such as a sociopathic or paranoid personality
- Addressing social problems, such as alcoholism or addiction
- Resolving more pragmatic problems, such as chronic unemployment, with vocational training and job placement

Obviously, the perception of the criminal influences the rationale for correction and punishment. The two major justifications for punishment and treatment are **retribution** and **prevention**. The retributive rationale postulates that punishment is an end in itself, whereas the prevention approach views punishment as a means rather than an end and embraces other responses to crime. The retributive rationale is probably more consistent with a view of the criminal as rational, and the prevention rationale, with certain exceptions, is more consistent with the view of the criminal as somehow less responsible for his or her behavior, both morally and legally.

RETRIBUTION

As mentioned before, the social contract provides the rationale for punishment. The retributive rationale for punishment is consistent with the social contract theory. Simply stated, the retributive rationale is that the individual offender must be punished because he or she deserves it. Mackie (1982: 4) describes three specific types of retribution:

- *Negative retribution* dictates that one who is not guilty must not be punished for a crime.
- *Positive retribution* demands that one who is guilty ought to be punished.
- *Permissive retribution* allows that one who is guilty *may* be punished.

This formulation states that retribution may support punishment, but may also limit it. There are limits as to who may be punished (only those who commit crimes) and restrictions on the amount of punishment (only that sufficient to balance the wrong). Further, this formulation implies that punishment need not be administered in all cases. The exceptions, although not discussed by Mackie, may involve the concepts of mercy or diminished responsibility.

expiation Atonement for a wrong to achieve a state of grace.

Another retributivist justification for punishment is that it is the only way the individual can achieve salvation. Thus, we owe the offender punishment because only through suffering can atonement occur, and only through atonement or **expiation** can the offender achieve a state of grace. Some would strongly object to this interpretation of religious ethics and argue that Christianity, while supportive of just punishment, does not necessarily support suffering as the only way to achieve a state of grace: There must be repentance, and there is also room for forgiveness.

One other view consistent with retribution is that punishment balances the advantage gained by a wrongdoer. The criminal act distorts the balance and parity of social relationships, and only a punishment or similar deprivation can restore the natural balance that existed before the criminal act.

What is an appropriate amount of punishment? This is a difficult question even for the retributivist. The difference between a year in prison and two years in prison is measurable only by the number of days on the calendar, not by how it is experienced by different people. Should this be considered during sentencing? Punishment of any kind affects individuals differently. For instance, a whipping may be worse than death for someone with a low tolerance for pain, better than prison for someone with a great need for freedom, and perhaps even pleasurable for someone who enjoys physical pain. Prison may be experienced as an inconvenience for some, and such a traumatic experience for others that it may induce suicide. Our current system of justice seldom recognizes these individual vulnerabilities or sensitivities to various punishments.

Sentencing studies routinely show little or no agreement regarding the type or amount of punishment appropriate for a wrongdoer. Disparity in sentencing is such a problem that many reforms have been aimed at reducing or even eliminating judges' discretion, such as determinate sentencing and sentencing guidelines. Yet, when legislators take on the task themselves by setting determinate sentences, their decisions are arrived at by obscure methods, probably more influenced by political pressure and compromise than by the application of fair and equitable standards.

justice model Fogel's conceptualization that the punishment of the individual should be purely retributive and balanced to the seriousness of the crime.

The justice model and the just deserts model, developed in the late 1970s and early 1980s, came about partly as a backlash to the abuses of discretion that characterized the rehabilitative era of the 1970s, and led the way to the current punitive era. Basically, the **justice model** holds that individuals are rational and that, even though free will may not exist perfectly, the concept must serve as a basis for the criminal law. Punishment is to be used for retribution, not deterrence, treatment, or any other purpose. This model promoted a degree of predictability and equality in sentencing by reverting to earlier retributive goals of punishment and restricted the state's right to use treatment as a criterion for

just deserts model Fogel's conceptualization that the punishment of an individual should be limited by the seriousness of the crime, although treatment could be offered.

new rehabilitationists Theorists and researchers who believe that evidence shows that rehabilitative programs do result in lower recidivism.

penal harm The idea that the system intentionally inflicts pain on offenders during their imprisonment or punishment, because merely depriving them of liberty is not considered sufficiently painful.

release. Finally, prisoners should be seen as volitional, responsible humans, not as patients (Fogel, 1975).

The **just deserts model**, appearing about the same time as the justice model, was also retributive and based punishment on "commensurate deserts" (von Hirsch, 1976: xxvi). As the spokesperson for this view, von Hirsch (1985: 138) disagreed with combining retributive and deterrent or incapacitative goals. According to von Hirsch, crimes should be weighed in seriousness based on their recidivism potential. Offenders who commit similar crimes should be punished equally, but the rank ordering of crimes is determined by recidivistic potential. This system—categorical incapacitation—combines deserts and prevention, but in a way that, according to von Hirsch, is not unjust to the individual offender. Von Hirsch continued to champion the retributive rationale for punishment well into the 1990s, in opposition to those he called the **new rehabilitationists**, who advocate treatment (von Hirsch, 1985: 150; von Hirsch and Maher, 1992).

Garland (1990) offered a different view, proposing that the emphasis of society should be on socializing and educating citizens. The punishment that was still necessary for those who broke the law should be viewed as morally expressive rather than instrumental and should be retributive rather than attempt prevention goals. Feeney (2005) continues this idea that sentencing should be purely retributive, and be "morally significant" in that it expresses condemnation of the behavior. Both of these writers are similar to the earlier just deserts theorists in that they believe punishment should be retributive rather than serve the goals of deterrence.

Our current time has been described as the era of **penal harm**; this refers to the idea that the system intentionally inflicts pain on offenders during their imprisonment, because merely depriving them of liberty is not considered sufficiently painful (Clear, 1996; Cullen, 1995). No one doubts that we have become more punitive in sentencing and that offenders are serving more time in prison. The interested reader can also go to government sources, such as the Bureau of Justice Statistics, to see how imprisonment patterns have changed over the years. The national incarceration rate of 150 per 100,000 in the 1980s has increased to 952 for men and 68 for women in 2008, with minorities having even higher rates of imprisonment. There are now about 1.7 million people under federal and state jurisdiction (Sabol, West, and Cooper, 2009).

PREVENTION

Three common justifications or rationales for punishment can all be subsumed under a general heading of "prevention." Prevention assumes that something should be done to the offender to prevent future criminal activity. There are three possible methods of prevention: deterrence, incapacitation, and treatment. Each of these goals is based on certain assumptions that must be considered in addition to the relevant moral questions. For instance, it is a factual question as to whether people can be deterred from crime, but it is a moral question as to what we should do to an individual to ensure deterrence.

DETERRENCE There are two types of deterrence. Specific deterrence is what is done to offenders to prevent them from deciding to commit another offense. General deterrence is what is done to an offender to prevent others from deciding to engage in wrongful behavior. The first teaches through punishment; the second teaches by example.

Our right to deter an individual offender is rooted in the same rationale used to support retribution. By virtue of membership in society, individuals submit themselves to society's controls. If we think that someone's actions are damaging, we will try various means to persuade him or her to cease that activity. The implicit assumption of a deterrence philosophy is that in the absence of controls, society would revert to a jungle-like, dangerous "war of all against all"; we need the police and official punishments to keep us in line. Under this rationale, the true nature of humankind is perceived to be predatory and held in check only by external controls. Deterrence advocates support deterrence as a justification of punishment. The Quote and Query box enumerates the key points of view in this justification for punishment.

QUOTE & QUERY

1. Those who violate others' rights deserve punishment.
2. However, there is a countervailing moral obligation not to deliberately add to the amount of human suffering, and punishment creates suffering.
3. Deterrence results in preventing more misery than it creates, thereby justifying punishment.

—SOURCE: ADAPTED FROM VON HIRSCH, 1976: 54.

Is this utilitarian thinking or ethical formalism? Explain your answer.

The rationale of specific deterrence depends on the effectiveness of punishment in deterring future bad acts by the individual being punished. The support for general deterrence is even more problematic. First, it becomes much harder to justify even if there is evidence of effectiveness. If we know that a term of imprisonment will not deter an offender but can deter others, can it still be justified? A clear example of this situation is the so-called passion murderer who probably does not need specific deterrence because the chance of killing again is slim. However, he or she is usually given a long sentence to make it clear that killing will not be tolerated. (There is, of course, also a good retributive rationale for the long sentence.) Under general deterrence, the offender is only a tool to teach a lesson to the rest of us. The sociologist Emile Durkheim believed that the value of criminals is in establishing the parameters of acceptable behavior. Their punishment helps the rest of us define what is "good."

If one's goal is purely general deterrence, there does not necessarily have to be an original crime. Consider a futuristic society wherein the evening news routinely shows or describes the punishments received by a variety of criminals. The crime—or the punishment, for that matter—does not have to be real to be effective. If punishing innocent people for crimes they *might* do were just as effective as punishing criminal offenders, this action might satisfy the ends of deterrence, but would obviously not be acceptable under any system of ethics—except perhaps act utilitarianism. The movie *Minority Report* presented a somewhat related ethical issue in that it portrayed a future where the government knew ahead of time when individuals would commit a crime and punished them for what they were going to do. The idea of punishing an individual for reasons other than their own acts seems wrong because it violates the retributive justification of punishment, but it certainly might be more effective to prevent crime than punish it after the fact.

INCAPACITATION Another purpose of punishment is to prevent further crime through incapacitation. Strictly speaking, incapacitation does not fit the classical definition of punishment, for the purpose is not to inflict pain but only to hold an offender until there is no risk of further crime. The major issue concerning incapacitation is prediction. Unfortunately, our ability to predict is no better for incapacitative purposes than it is for deterrence purposes. Two possible mistakes are releasing an offender who then commits further crimes and not releasing an offender who would not commit further crimes.

Carrying the goal of incapacitation to its logical conclusion, one would not have to commit a crime at all to be declared potentially dangerous and subject to incapacitation. We now incarcerate career criminals for life—not for their last offense, but for what they might do if released. These "habitual-felon laws" are justified by the prediction that these criminals will continue to commit crimes. Some argue that a small group of offenders commit a disproportionate share of crime and that those individuals can be identified by predictive elements such as prior convictions, prior incarcerations, juvenile convictions and detentions, use of heroin or barbiturates, and lack of employment (Greenwood, 1982). Selective incapacitation is a policy of incarcerating these individuals for longer periods of time than other criminals. Other studies, however, have indicated that our ability to predict who would commit further crime is actually poor, with an error rate of 48 percent (Auerhahn, 1999). Obviously, there are grave ethical issues in using these predictive devices to increase sentences when the error rate is so high.

three-strikes laws Sentencing legislation that imposes extremely long sentences for repeat offenders—in this case, after three prior felonies.

Three-strikes laws are defended under an incapacitative rationale because it is argued that repeat offenders are more likely to commit future crimes, so they should be held for long periods of time. More than half of all states now have some type of three-strikes or habitual-offender laws, but only a few states, such as California, have laws that impact a large number of offenders (King and Mauer, 2001).

Critics argue that for both practical and ethical reasons, the California three-strikes sentence is bad policy. It incarcerates those who are past their crime-prone-age years; it incarcerates nonviolent offenders for long periods of time; and it is so expensive that it draws resources away from other social needs, such as schools. Further, it is unfairly disproportionate to the crime. Some offenders convicted of fairly minor third felonies have received 25 years to life in prison (King and Mauer, 2001; Zimring, Hawkins, and Kamin, 2001). Another troubling aspect of three-strikes laws is that African Americans tend to be disproportionately affected (Cole, 1999).

The U.S. Supreme Court ruled in March 2003 that California's three-strikes law was not grossly disproportionate and deferred to the state's authority in setting punishments (*Lockyer v. Andrade*, 538 U.S. 63 [2003] and *Ewing v. California*, 538 U.S. 11 [2003]). Clearly, if three-strikes laws are changed, it will be through state courts ruling that the long sentences violate state constitutional rights or state legislatures changing the law. In the Policy Box, the law, policy, and ethics of the three-strikes movement are untangled.

TREATMENT If we can find justification for the right to punish, can we also find justification for treatment? Treatment is considered to be beneficial to the individual offender as well as to society. This is a very different approach from the moral rejection implicit in retributive punishment. Treatment implies acceptance rather than rejection, support rather than hatred. However, the control over the individual is just as great as with punishment; some people would say it is even greater.

What is treatment? We sometimes consider anything experienced after the point of sentencing to be treatment, including education, prison discipline, and religious services. A court was obliged to define treatment in *Knecht v. Gillman* (488 F.2d 1136 [1973]). Inmates challenged the state's right to use apomorphine, a drug that induces extreme nausea and a feeling of imminent death, as a form of aversive conditioning. In its holding, the court stated that calling something "treatment" did not remove it from Eighth Amendment scrutiny. In other words, merely labeling some infliction of pain as treatment would not necessarily render it immune from legal challenge as cruel and unusual punishment.

POLICY ISSUES | **Three Strikes**

Many states have three-strikes legislation, and this type of sentencing has been around for a long time (also called habitual-felon laws). The basic assumption is that the second or third felony is more serious than the first felony and/or that punishment must be made harsher because it did not deter the first time. The first is a deontological rationale; the second is a utilitarian rationale. Opponents argue that these sentences are contrary to our justice system in that they punish the offenders twice for the same offense.

Law

With the rulings by the Supreme Court, it is clear that no federal constitutional right is violated by a state habitual-criminal sentencing law. State courts could interpret state constitutional rights to be broader, and legislatures, of course, can change the law if the public pressures them to do so. In California, for instance, there are still attempts to change the law at least to exclude minor property offenders from its reach and to reduce the 25-year sentence for second-strike offenders.

Policy

There is great disparity among jurisdictions in how prosecutors apply habitual sentencing laws. Some jurisdictions

account for the majority of three-strikes offenders in the system, while others use it hardly at all. Thus, whether or not an offender receives a life sentence may depend, partially, on the county or state in which the crime was committed. As long as prosecutors have discretion in whether to charge under three-strikes statutes, such disparity will continue. Some argue also that three-strikes and habitual-offender laws are used disproportionately against minorities.

Ethics

Although prosecutors have discretion in whether to charge offenders under three-strikes statutes, there are ethical and unethical criteria for such decisions. Ethical criteria would be the danger posed to the public based on the felonies the offender has committed, whereas unethical criteria would include political pressure or the race of the offender. More problematic are other criterion, such as using three strikes when an offender insists on a trial and won't plead guilty, or when an offender will not cooperate and testify against a crime partner.

Treatment was further defined as that which constitutes accepted and standard practice and which could reasonably result in a "cure."

The Supreme Court has also ruled on whether prison officials can administer antipsychotic drugs against the will of the prisoner. Despite arguments that even prisoners have an inherent right to be free from such intrusive control, the Court held, in *Washington v. Harper* (494 U.S. 210 [1990]), that an inmate's right to refuse such medication did not outweigh the state's need to administer it if there was a showing that the inmate posed a security risk.

What we think needs to be cured is another issue. Recall the discussion of whether our society could be characterized by consensus or conflict. Treating a deviant may be justifiable if one believes that society is basically homogeneous in its values and beliefs, but viewed from a conflict perspective, treatment may look more like brainwashing and a coercive use of power. Civil libertarians would point out that it is no accident that political dissidents in totalitarian states are often handled as if they have mental problems and are treated with mind-altering drugs and other brainwashing regimens. The greater intrusiveness inherent in treating the mind is sometimes considered worse than punishment.

According to some experts, treatment can be effective only if it is voluntary; others disagree. It is true that much of the treatment that inmates and other correctional clients participate in is either implicitly or directly coerced. Providing treatment for those who want it is one thing; requiring those who are resistant to participate in psychotherapy, group therapy, or religious activities is quite another. It is not justifiable under a retributivist ethical system. Is it consistent with a prevention perspective? The answer is yes, as long as the results support the intervention.

The evaluation literature on rehabilitative treatment programs could fill a room. We now have more than 40 years of evaluations, as well as dozens of meta-analyses and exhaustive reviews of the literature on rehabilitation. It is simply not true that "nothing works," as was widely believed through the 1980s and 1990s. However, what works is more complicated than one program for all offenders. One interesting finding that comes from evaluation research is that, evidently, sometimes a program works because of the staff characteristics, not the modality of the program. Thus, we can see again that the individual ethics and performance of public servants (treatment professionals in corrections) have a great deal to do with how well the system (in this case, treatment) works.

Ethical Frameworks for Corrections

The various rationales for punishment just described are well established and can be found in corrections textbooks. The ethical systems that were introduced in Chapter 2 are discussed less commonly in corrections texts, but they form the underlying philosophical rationale for the goals or missions of retribution and prevention (including deterrence, incapacitation, and treatment).

UTILITARIANISM

The principle of utilitarianism is often used to support the last three rationales of punishment: deterrence, incapacitation, and treatment. According to utilitarianism, punishing or treating the criminal offender benefits society, and this benefit outweighs the negative effect on the individual offender. It is a teleological argument because the morality of the punishment is determined by the consequences derived—reduced crime. Jeremy Bentham was the major proponent of the utilitarian theory of punishment and established basic guidelines for its use.

Bentham believed that punishment works when it is applied rationally to rational people, but is not acceptable when the person did not make a rational decision to commit the crime, such as when the law forbidding the action was passed after the act occurred, the law was unknown, the person was acting under compulsion, or the person was an infant, insane, or intoxicated (Bentham, 1843; also see Beccaria, 1977). The utility of the punishment would be lost in these cases; therefore, punishment could not be justified (Borchert and Stewart, 1986: 317). Bentham's basic formula for punishment provides that the utility of punishment to society (by deterring crime) outweighs the negative of the punishment itself (it is negative because it is painful). Utilitarian theory also supports treatment and incapacitation if these can be shown to benefit society. If, for instance, treatment and punishment were to have equal amounts of utility for society, treatment would be the more ethical choice because it has a less negative effect on the individual. Likewise, if incapacitation and punishment would be equally effective in protecting and providing utility to society, the choice with the least negative utility would be the ethical one.

Some argue that the harms inherent in imprisonment in either jail or prison are so extreme that they must be counterbalanced by rehabilitative programs in order to result in a greater good (Kleinig, 2001b). It is certainly true that minor offenders should not be incarcerated, because the harm caused by incarceration far exceeds the harm they caused to a victim or society. It is also problematic when drug users are incarcerated because it is hard to identify the harm caused to others by their actions, especially as weighed against

in the **NEWS**

FAIR PUNISHMENT?

Bernie Madoff is arguably the biggest swindler in history, being the architect of a Ponzi scheme that was reputed to have defrauded investors in the neighborhood of $65 billion. Caught and convicted, he is serving a 150-year sentence. The 71-year-old was evidently beaten by a fellow inmate in March 2010 and suffered a broken nose, fractured ribs, and cuts to his face and head. He was moved to a medium security prison that has a lower level of inmate disturbances.

SOURCE: Bone, 2010.

the harms that they may endure in this nation's jails and prisons, such as beatings, economic exploitation, rape, and gratuitous abuse by correctional officers. The In the News box illustrates the type of extra-legal punishments that are meted out in prison.

ETHICAL FORMALISM

While utilitarianism supports the prevention goals above, ethical formalism clearly supports a retributive view of punishment. It is deontological because it is not concerned with the consequences of the punishment or treatment, only its inherent morality. It would support the idea that a criminal is owed punishment because to do otherwise would not be according him or her equal respect as a human. However, the punishment should not be used as a means to any other end but retribution. Treatment is not supported by ethical formalism because it uses the offender as a means to protect society. The Quote and Query box presents Immanuel Kant's views.

QUOTE & QUERY

Juridical punishment ... can be inflicted on a criminal, never just as instrumental to the achievement of some other good for the criminal himself or for the civil society, but only because he has committed a crime; for a man may never be used just as a means to the end of another person.... Penal law is a categorical imperative, and woe to him who crawls through the serpentine maze of utilitarian theory in order to find an excuse, in some advantage to someone, for releasing the criminal from punishment or any degree of it, in line with the Pharisaical proverb "it is better that one man die than that a whole people perish"; for if justice perishes, there is no more value in man living on the earth...

—SOURCE: IMMANUEL KANT, THE SCIENCE OF RIGHT, 1790

Do you understand what Kant was trying to say? Rephrase the passage to make it more simple and current.

Several arguments support this retributive rationale. First, Mackie (1982) discusses the universal aspects of punishment: the urge to react in a hostile manner to harm is an element inherent in human nature; therefore, one might say that punishment is a natural law. Another supporting argument is found in the principle of forfeiture, which postulates that when one intrudes on an innocent person's rights, one forfeits a proportional amount of one's own rights. By restraining or hurting a victim in some way, the aggressor forfeits his or her own liberty; in other words, he or she forfeits the right to be free from punishment (Bedau, 1982). The major point to remember about ethical formalism as an ethical rationale for punishment is that it does not need to result in any good end, such as deterrence. The offender should receive punishment because he deserves it, not because it will result in something useful for him or society.

ETHICS OF CARE

The ethics of care would probably not support punishment unless it was essential to help the offender become a better person. This ethical system defines good as that which meets everyone's needs—victims and offenders alike. Several authors have discussed the ethics of care in relation to the justice and corrections system. For instance, Heidensohn (1986) and Daly (1989) discuss differences in the perception of justice from a care perspective versus a retributive perspective—as female and male perceptions, respectively. The female care perspective emphasizes needs, motives, and relationships, while the male retributive perspective emphasizes rights, responsibilities, and punishments.

The corrections system, ideally, is supported by a caring ethic because it takes into account offender needs. Community corrections, especially, emphasizes the relationship of the offender to the community. From this perspective, one should help the offender to become a better person because that is what a caring and committed relationship would entail. Retributive punishment and deterrence are not consistent with the ethics of care. However, some say that retribution and a care ethic are not, nor should they be considered, in opposition to each other. Restorative justice, which is discussed in more detail in Chapter 13, might be considered the merger of the two in that this approach views the offender as responsible for the wrong committed, but the responsibility is satisfied by reparation to the victim rather than by punishment and pain.

RAWLSIAN ETHICS

John Rawls presents an alternative to utilitarianism and retributivism. Rawls's defense of punishment starts with Kant's proposition that no one should be treated as a means, and with the idea that each should have an "equal right to the most extensive basic liberty compatible with a similar liberty to others." According to Rawls, a loss of rights should take place only when it is consistent with the best interests of the least advantaged. Rules regarding punishment would be as follows (cited in Hickey and Scharf, 1980: 169):

1. We must punish only to the extent that the loss of liberty would be agreeable were one not to know whether one were to be the criminal, the victim, or a member of the general public [the veil of ignorance].

2. The loss of liberty must be justified as the minimum loss consistent with maintenance of the same liberty among others.

Furthermore, when the advantage shifts—when the offender instead of the victim or society becomes the one with the least advantage—punishment must cease. This theory leaves a lot of unanswered questions. For instance, if victims were chosen carefully (e.g., only those who would not suffer financially or emotionally) and the criminal were from an impoverished background, the criminal would still be at a disadvantage and, thus, not morally accountable for his or her actions. This rationale for punishment promotes the idea that the criminal act creates an imbalance between offender and victim, and that punishment should be concerned with regaining that balance. The utilitarian thread in this proposition is that by having this check-and-balance system in determining punishment, all of society benefits.

Punishments

We have discarded many punishments that were acceptable in earlier times, such as flogging, hanging, banishment, branding, cutting off limbs, drawing and quartering, and pillories and stocks. Although we still believe that society has the right to punish, what we do in the name of punishment has changed substantially. As a society, we became gradually uncomfortable with inflicting physically painful punishments on offenders, and as these punishments were discarded, imprisonment was used as the substitute.

Inside prison, we have only relatively recently abandoned physical punishments as a method of control (at least formally), but that is not to say that prisons are not injurious. In addition to the informal corporal punishments that are inflicted by officers and fellow inmates, prison is painful because it consists of banishment and condemnation; it means separation from loved ones and involves the total loss of freedom. More subtly, it is an assault on one's self-esteem and prevents the individual from almost all forms of self-definition, such as father, mother, professional, and so on. About the only self-definition left is as a prison "tough guy" (or woman)—a stance that destroys the spirit and reduces the individual to a baser form of humanity.

cruel and unusual punishment
Punishment proscribed by the Eighth Amendment.

The Eighth Amendment protects all Americans from **cruel and unusual punishment**. Although what is "cruel and unusual" is vague, several tests have been used to define the terms, such as the following, discussed in *Furman v. Georgia* (408 U.S. 238, 92 S.Ct. 2726, 33 L.Ed.2d 346 [1972]):

- *Unusual* (by frequency). Punishments that are rarely, if ever, used thus become unusual if used against one individual or a group. They become arbitrary punishments because the decision to use them is so infrequent.

- *Evolving standards of decency.* Civilization is evolving, and punishments considered acceptable in the past century are no longer acceptable in this century.

- *Shock the conscience.* A yardstick for all punishment is to test it against the public conscience. If people are naturally repelled by the punishment, it must be cruel and unusual by definition.

- *Excessive or disproportionate.* Any punishment that is excessive to its purpose or disproportionately administered is considered wrong.

- *Unnecessary.* Again, we are looking at the purpose of the punishment in relation to what is done. If the purpose of punishment is to deter crime, we should administer only an amount necessary to do so. If the purpose is to protect and the offender presents no danger, prison should not be used.

These tests have eliminated the use of the whip and the branding iron, yet some say that we may have done nothing to move toward humane punishment and that, instead, we may have moved away from it. It may be that corporal punishment, at least the less drastic kinds such as whipping, is actually less harmful than a prison sentence. After all, a whipping takes perhaps days or weeks to get over, but a prison sentence may last years and affect all future earnings.

Some sentences given to offenders, especially some conditions attached to a probation sentence, have been criticized as being inhumane. Although typical probation conditions include performing community service, paying court costs and/or restitution, finding em ployment, and submitting to drug tests, other conditions are more problematic. Someone convicted of driving while intoxicated (DWI) may be required to donate blood to a blood bank, but if he or she has a phobia about needles or is a Jehovah's Witness, this punishment may be worse than jail.

So-called "shaming" conditions include DWI offenders having special license plates that indicate to other drivers that the driver has been convicted of DWI; probation officers putting up signs in the yard or nailing them to the door of convicted sex offenders' homes, warning people that a sex offender lives there; announcing to one's church congregation one's criminal conviction and asking for forgiveness; and taking out an advertisement in the town newspaper for the same purpose. These types of shaming punishments hark back to the days of the stocks and pillory, when punishment was arguably effective more because of the community scorn received than the physical pain involved. Some believe that this is not a useful or helpful trend. For instance, one American Civil Liberties Union (ACLU) spokesperson called such punishments "gratuitous humiliation that serves no social purpose" (cited in Book, 1999: 653). Whitman (1998) argued that the use of such penalties is contrary to a sense of dignity and creates an "ugly complicity" between the state and the community by setting the scene for "lynch justice." There is even a question as to whether such punishments are legal, because some state laws typically demand that probation conditions have a "rehabilitative function." In general, however, judges have imposed these punishments without much serious challenge. Legally, they seem to be acceptable, but what about ethically?

We could also examine these conditions in light of the ethical systems discussed earlier. One issue is the effect that "shaming" conditions have on family members of offenders and whether these conditions constitute a type of extra-legal punishment for them without any due-process procedures of trial and conviction. Punishments such as house signs and other public disclosures subject family members to stigma along with the offender. Braithwaite (2000), Karp (1998), and others distinguish between **stigmatizing shaming** and **reintegrative shaming**. The first is a rejection of the individual and has negative effects; the second is only a rejection of the person's behavior and creates a healthier relationship between the individual and his or her community. Braithwaite (2000) is the best-known spokesperson for reintegrative shaming. He argues that shame is different from guilt because it comes from one's beliefs about how one's community feels about the crime. He argues that societies that don't have shame attached to certain crimes have a lot of that type of crime. Thus, what is necessary to reduce crime is a return to the concept of shame, but not stigmatizing shame.

All states now have sex offender registries. These are listings of those convicted of sex crimes, and the offender must report his or her address to the registry. Some states' sex offender registries are made public so anyone can find out if any convicted sex offenders live in their neighborhood. The stated purpose of such registries has been to help parents protect their children, but there have been troubling reports of sex offenders being the target of vigilante justice. Many offenders have been harassed and threatened, the house of one was set on fire, and garbage was thrown all over the lawn of another. A sex offender in New Hampshire was stabbed, two were killed in the state of Washington by the same man and, in 2006, a man in Maine evidently targeted sex offenders and killed two before killing himself. This case also illustrates that sex offender registries are inclusive of individuals that may not fit the typical stereotype of a sex offender. One of the victims in the Maine case was a young man who had been convicted of statutory rape because of consensual sex with his teenage girlfriend. Even though no sex offender deserves to die at the hand of a gunman, certainly the death of this young man, who was clearly not the predator that most people think of when they hear the term "sex offender," is a tragedy (Fahrenthold, 2006).

stigmatizing shaming The effect of punishment whereby the offender feels cast aside and abandoned by the community.

reintegrative shaming Braithwaite's idea that certain types of punishment can lead to a reduction of recidivism as long as they do not involve banishment and they induce healthy shame in the individual.

SUPERMAX PRISONS

So-called "supermax" prisons hark back to the days of the Eastern State Penitentiary, with 24-hour isolation and no programs of self-improvement to salvage the waste and pain of time served (Pollock, 2004). The criticism of these prisons has been directed both to the conditions and to the criteria and procedures used for transferring prisoners to them. Pelican Island in California, the most notorious supermax facility, was the target of a court case, *Madrid v. Gomez* (889 F.Supp 1146 [N.D. Cal. 1995]), in which the courts held the state responsible for brutality and lack of medical care. The case also exposed the practice of guards covering up for each other and the power of union officials in squelching official investigations (Martin, 2003).

The other problem with the supermax prisons has been who is sent there. There are allegations that the prisons are being used for troublemakers who are not especially dangerous. Some report that mentally ill offenders who cannot control their behavior are sent to supermax prisons and become even more ill because of the isolation and lack of medical services. Haney (2008) reports other research that indicates that 45 percent of supermax prisoners suffer from some psychological impairment—either diagnosed mental illness, severe psychiatric symptoms, psychotic or self-injurious episodes, or brain damage. Haney himself reports that he found up to two-thirds of supermax prisoners suffer psychological problems (2008: 964).

After a supermax had been built in Ohio, it was found that only half the beds could be filled with those in the prison system who met the original criteria for transfer, so officials moved death row inmates to the supermax (*Wilkinson v. Austin*, et al., 125 S.Ct. 2384 [2005]). The supermax in this case was similar to all the other supermaxes in having the following characteristics:

- Human contact was strictly prohibited.
- Cell lights were on 24 hours a day.
- Inmate exercise was for only one hour a day and in a small room indoors.
- The transfer was of indefinite duration and reviewed only annually.
- Transfer to supermax disqualified the inmate from parole consideration.

These prisons have been described as soul-destroying. They involve horrific deprivations of some of the most basic elements of what most people take for granted, including social support, self-esteem, and hope. Haney (2008) describes the supermax as having an "ideological toxicity," an "ecology of cruelty," and a "dynamic of desperation." He explains that the ideology of the supermax is toxic in that it is purely punishment with no redeeming elements of rehabilitation or hope. It is the "penal harm" ideology magnified. "Ecology of cruelty" refers to the architecture and policies of supermaxes that are structured to employ more and more punishment to the inmates inside. Because there are no available rewards to encourage positive behavior, the cycle of punishment spirals to levels that become normal to those working within the institution but are objectively horrific. Haney describes the "dynamics of desperation" as the inevitable tension that exists between the guards and guarded and the tendency for relationships between them to escalate into cruelty. Inmates react in seemingly irrational violence and/or unruliness because of the powerlessness of their environment, and officers react with greater and greater force, going through a cycle where each side's hatred of the other is reinforced. In this sense, Haney argues, the prison affects not only the inmates, but also the guards who become desensitized to its violence and become cruel enforcers because the environment reinforces the notion that the inmates do not deserve to be treated as human (2008: 960). Officers are faced with moral crises when their behavior is normalized to a level of cruelty that would seem abnormal to anyone not inured to the environment of a supermax.

Haney portrays the supermax as incapable of coexisting with treatment or counseling. Treatment professionals must wear bulletproof vests and sit outside the bars of an inmate's cell with an officer standing by. In some units, he describes "programming cages" set up in a semicircle in a surreal parody of group therapy. If the inmates require such Hannibal Lector–like security, one wonders how they could ever benefit from therapy. How do treatment professionals in such environments reconcile their codes of ethics with the elements of the supermax? If supermax prisons must be used at all, they should be used with the greatest of care and with the greatest attention to how the environment affects the individuals housed there.

PRIVATE PRISONS

In much of the foregoing discussion, we described punishment as a state function. However, the state may delegate the authority to punish. Private prisons are built and then leased to the state or, in some cases, actually run by the private corporation, which bills the state for the service. Many have objected to the profit motive being introduced into corrections and point to a number of ethical issues raised by private "profiteers" (Pollock, 2004). First, there are potential abuses of the bidding process, as in any situation where the government contracts with a company for services or products. Money may change hands to ensure that one organization receives the contract; companies may make informal agreements to "rig" the bids; and other potentially corrupt practices may go on. Legal as well as ethical issues abound when private and public motives are mixed.

In the building phase, private corporations may cut corners and construct buildings without meeting proper standards for safety. Managing the institution also raises the possibility that a private contractor will attempt to maximize profits by ignoring minimum standards of health and safety and will, if necessary to this end, bribe inspectors or monitors to overlook the deficiencies. It has certainly happened in other areas, such as nursing homes, that those who contract with the state government and receive state monies reap large profits by subjecting clients to inhumane conditions. Some believe that punishment and profit are never compatible and that linking the two has led to a variety of historical abuses (such as the contract labor system in the South).

Private corporations argue that some state systems subject them to endless and picayune rules and continually audit them to the point where it appears that state prison officials are trying to find noncompliance in order to cancel contracts. There is probably some truth that some corrections department officials are not happy to have legislators approve the use of private contractors and would like to see them fail.

Private prisons hold about 7.2 percent of all prisoners in the country (Bureau of Justice Statistics, 2006: 3). Corrections Corporation of America and the GEO Group (formerly Wackenhut Corrections Corporation) are the largest players in the private prison industry, holding a little more than half of all private prison beds (more than 60,000 beds in the United States alone). In late 1998, Corrections Corporation of America (CCA) merged into the Prison Realty Trust (PRT), an accounting move that allowed the entity to be exempt from tax liability as long as it distributed 95 percent of its earnings to its stockholders (Geis, Mobley, and Shichor, 1999). The company was affected by a rash of scandals, including escapes, violence, under-trained officers, and understaffing (Parenti, 1999: 219).

The GEO Group is considered number two among the private prison providers. It also runs mental health facilities and addiction treatment centers. In the late 1990s, the company had a number of incidents that affected its reputation and financial standing (Greene, 2001). Lawsuits in states concerned the use of tear gas (Louisiana), failing to prevent sexual abuse (Texas), paying $3 million to a member of the state's prison policy panel (Florida), and a murder rate higher than that of the state-run institutions (New Mexico) (Solomon, 1999; Fecteau, 1999). In addition to the "big two," more than a dozen smaller companies across the nation are competing for the private prison bids put out by the states.

Proponents argue that private corrections can save the state money. In California, for instance, Governor Schwarzenegger is promoting the use of private prisons, which are supposedly $3,200 to $7,800 less per year per inmate than state-run institutions. Corrections Corporation's contract with California was around $632 million in 2008 for housing 10,000 inmates, which isn't a large portion of the more than 140,000 inmates in California prisons (Morain, 2010). Private corporations are said to be more efficient; they can build faster with less cost and less red tape, and they have economies of scale (they can obtain savings because of their size). States and local governments are bound by a myriad of bidding and siting restrictions, unlike private corporations.

Some studies have concluded that private prisons produce results equal to those of state institutions for less cost. Bourge (2002) describes a study by Segal and Moore that examined 28 governmental and institutional studies, comparing public and private facilities, and found that 22 of the private prisons had cost savings of 5 to 15 percent. They concluded that there is "significant evidence" that private facilities can provide quality comparable to that of state institutions. However, critics argue that studies that look only at costs and ignore higher assault rates in private prisons and other indices of quality of service are flawed. Also, a General Accounting Office (now the Government Accountability Office) meta-analysis concluded that private and public institutions cost about the same (General Accounting Office, 1996). Any profits realized by a private entity being "leaner and meaner" are offset by the profit margin that private companies maintain and a regulatory system that the state must put in place to make sure that contract specifications are adhered to.

In an example of what can go wrong with private prisons, a Texas contract was pulled from the GEO Group when it was discovered that a juvenile facility did not meet basic standards. It was reported that three of the state monitors who were supposed to be checking to make sure that the facility met state standards had worked for the GEO Group and reported no violations. Six state employees were fired and one resigned (M. Ward, 2007a).

There have been issues concerning the evaluators as well. The evaluation by Segal and Moore, for instance, was funded by a libertarian think tank that arguably would be inclined to promote private enterprise over government involvement (Bourge, 2002). The biggest scandal in private prison evaluation research concerned Charles Thomas, a University of Florida professor who published many articles and books as "objective" evaluations of private prisons. Thomas testified before Congress and state legislatures considering private prison contracts. He consistently promoted the effectiveness and efficiency of private prisons, presumably as an independent, objective evaluator. However, his objectivity was called into question when it was discovered that he was a highly paid consultant of Corrections Corporation of America and owned more than $500,000 in CCA stock. He was sanctioned by the state of Florida in 1999 for violating its conflict of interest laws (Geis, Mobley, and Shichor, 1999; Mobley and Geis, 2002).

Ogle (1999) argues that private correctional facilities operate in a Catch-22, where organizational imperatives are contradictory. On the one hand is the corporate imperative of profit; on the other hand is the public service imperative of legitimacy. The two clash when the most profitable way to run a prison conflicts with the perceived just or humane way to run a prison. When the private corporation is pursuing profit, it uses adaptations such as compromise and avoidance techniques or defiance and manipulation techniques to circumvent governmental mandates for services and contract fulfillment. A more abstract and subtle criticism of private corrections is that if people are making money from incarcerating offenders, where is the incentive to correct them?

CAPITAL PUNISHMENT

What sets capital punishment apart from all other punishments is its quality of irrevocability. This type of punishment leaves no way to correct a mistake. For this reason, some believe that no mortal should have the power to inflict capital punishment because there is no way to guarantee that mistakes won't be made. The growing number of innocent men and women who came perilously close to being executed indicates that we have an imperfect system (Radelet, Bedau, and Putnam, 1992; Christianson, 2004; Associated Press, 2008b).

Public support for capital punishment has swung up and down. Public opinion polls reveal that public support for the death penalty declined gradually through the 1960s, reaching a low of 44 percent in 1966, but has increased over the past 30 years. In the late 1990s, 75 to 80 percent supported the death penalty (Britt, 1998). Public support seems to be declining in more recent years. In a poll in 2008, only 63 percent of Americans supported capital punishment (Harris Poll, 2008).

Research indicates that certain groups are more likely to favor the use of capital punishment; for instance, support is higher by 20 to 25 percentage points among whites as compared to blacks. Membership in fundamentalist Protestant churches predicts higher support for the death penalty as well. Political conservativism also predicts support. Interestingly, church activity negatively predicts support (the more active one is in one's church, the less likely one is to support the death penalty). Women are also less likely than men to support the death penalty. In one study, researchers found that black Protestant fundamentalists showed the least support for the death penalty, while white fundamentalists showed the most support (Britt, 1998).

Retentionists (who believe that we should continue to utilize capital punishment) and abolitionists (who believe that we should not execute anyone) both use utilitarianism, ethical formalism, and religion as moral justifications. Retentionists argue that capital punishment is just because it deters others from committing murder and it definitely deters the individual who is executed. This is a utilitarian argument. They also argue that capital punishment is just because murder deserves a proportional punishment. This argument is more consistent with ethical formalism. Finally, they argue that the Bible dictates an "eye for an eye." This is, of course, a (Judeo-Christian) religious justification for capital punishment.

Abolitionists argue that capital punishment has never been shown to be effective in deterring others from committing murder, and, therefore, the evil of capital punishment far outweighs any potential benefits for society because there is no proof that it actually deters. This is a utilitarian argument. Abolitionists might also utilize the categorical imperative under ethical formalism to argue that deterrence is using the individual as a means to an end. Finally, abolitionists would point to the religious command to "turn the other cheek," an argument against any Christian justification for capital punishment.

The reason why utilitarianism can be used to justify or oppose capital punishment is that the research on deterrence is mixed. Those who have summarized the evidence marshaled on both sides of the deterrence question found little support for the proposition that executions are useful deterrents, although there are contrary findings by other researchers (Walker, 1985: 79; Kronenwerter, 1993; Land, Teske, and Zheng, 2009). However, despite the lack of research for general deterrence, many are still convinced that it does deter, at least the individual offender. Ethical formalism supports capital punishment; however, the imperfect nature of the system is problematic. Recall that under the categorical imperative, you should act in a way that you can will it to be a universal law. In this case, knowing that innocent people may be sentenced to death, could you agree that murderers should be executed if you did not know whether you were the victim, the murderer, the judge, or any citizen?

Religion, also, can be and has been used to support and condemn capital punishment. As with other issues, Christians have pointed to various verses in the Bible to justify their position. Kania (1999), for instance, presents a comprehensive religious justification for capital punishment, along with a social contract justification.

Questions also arise about the methods and procedures of capital punishment. Should all murderers be subject to capital punishment, or are some murders less serious than others? Should we allow defenses of age, mental state, or reason? If we do apply capital punishment differentially, doesn't this open the door to bias and misuse? Evidence indicates that capital punishment has been used arbitrarily and discriminatorily in this country. One study, cited by the Supreme Court, indicated that minorities are more likely to be executed when their victims are white; in Georgia, black offenders charged with killing a white person were 4.3 times more likely to be sentenced to death than those charged with killing a black person. Yet the Supreme Court stated that this evidence of statistically disproportional administration is not enough to invalidate the death penalty (*McClesky v. Kemp*, 481 U.S. 279 [1987]).

Because our justice system is based on rationality, executions of persons with mental illness and mental retardation have been vehemently criticized. The Supreme Court has ruled that executing the mentally ill is cruel and unusual (*Ford v. Wainwright*, 411 U.S. 399 [1986]). Miller and Radelet (1993) present a detailed account of the *Ford* case, describing the mental deterioration of Ford and the long ordeal of appeals before the Supreme Court finally ruled. They also point out the ethical issues involved when psychiatrists, other medical professionals, and psychologists participate in procedures that involve certifying someone as *death ready* and then assist in the administration of the chosen method of execution. These professions have deep and divisive arguments regarding the seeming inconsistency between identifying oneself as a helping professional and then helping someone be put to death.

In *Atkins v. Virginia* (536 U.S. 304 [2002]), the Supreme Court held that a man with an IQ of 59 could not be put to death, finding that the evolution of decency and public opinion supported such a decision. The holding does not answer all the questions that it raises, however, in how serious mental retardation must be to serve as a bar to capital punishment.

In *Roper v. Simmons* (125 S.Ct. 1183 [2005]), the Court, in a narrow ruling (5–4), held that juvenile offenders could not be classified as the "worst" offenders; therefore, death sentences of juveniles would be cruel and unusual and violate the Eighth Amendment. In *Kennedy v. Louisiana* (554 U.S. 407 [2008]), the Supreme Court held that the death penalty was not proportional to the crime of rape and thus would be a violation of the Eighth Amendment. Note that the question of culpability and whether or not the death sentence is a just sentence for mentally ill, retarded, or juvenile offenders, and the type of crime for which it is a just punishment, are both legal and moral questions.

The 2006 renewal of the Patriot Act added a provision that changed federal habeas corpus procedures to speed up death penalty appeals for states that are qualified. To be qualified, a state has to show that it has competent legal representation; however, it is completely up to the discretion of the U.S. attorney general as to whether or not a state is qualified. Once qualified, states can "fast track" a death penalty appeal, which means that prisoners have less time to file appeals and federal appellate judges can consider fewer issues (Copp, 2006). Critics argue that, given the woefully inadequate representation of some on death row, such a procedure is certain to result in innocent people being executed.

More recently, the Supreme Court ruled on a challenge to the method of execution. Opponents argued that lethal injection is cruel and unusual because the drugs administered do not prevent the sensation of pain, but they do paralyze; therefore, the individual suffers but is unable to scream or otherwise indicate distress. In *Baze v. Rees* (553 U.S. 35 [2008]), the Court held that there was no evidence of substantial or an objectively intolerable risk of serious harm (pain). The arguments supporting the current "cocktail" of drugs used to execute prisoners fall into two camps. The first is that offenders should experience pain because, after all, they killed somebody. The second argument is that offenders do not experience pain under these drugs. The first argument is a philosophical one; the second is a factual one.

Unless the Supreme Court revises its current position, which seems unlikely, the legality of executions is not in question. However, the procedures used to arrive at the decision to execute may continue to be challenged. Recently the influential American Law Institute announced its lack of support for the death penalty. The institute created the Model Penal Code in 1962, and its legal discussion of the death penalty was used by the Supreme Court to support their decision to uphold it. Now, however, the group has concluded that capital punishment in this country is "irretrievably broken" and has withdrawn their intellectual rationale for it (Liptak, 2010). The morality of capital punishment is still very much a topic of debate, and it elicits strong feelings on the part of many people.

COMMUNITY CORRECTIONS

community corrections A term that encompasses halfway houses, work release centers, probation, parole, and any other intermediate sanctions, such as electronic monitoring, either as a condition of probation or as a sentence in itself that takes place in the community rather than prison.

Community corrections encompass probation, parole, work release, educational release, halfway houses, and other forms of supervision in the community. The concept of community corrections is supported by the ethics of care; it promotes meeting the needs of the offender and the victim (through restitution). A prison sentence is basically a rejection or banishment; however, community supervision represents the concepts of acceptance and integration with the community. Even parole, coming after a prison sentence, originally operated with the philosophy of reintegration. Utilitarianism also supports community corrections because the benefit to the community by not banishing the offender to prison is both financial and emotional.

QUOTE & QUERY

[Community corrections] signifies moral concern for the individual, one that is consistent with the natural law ethics of "dignity of man," the constitutional ethics of individualized treatment and perhaps the religious ethics of redemption.

—SOURCE: SOURYAL, 1992: 356.

Explain how community corrections are either consistent or inconsistent with the various ethical systems.

Even a retributive philosophy can support community corrections because some crimes are simply not serious enough to justify a prison sentence. Probation and parole sentences involve supervision but also usually require meeting some other conditions. Some of these conditions pose special issues of privacy, liberty, and impact on others. For instance, should conditions specify whom the offender can associate with? Mandate that the offender go to church? Dictate to the offender where he or she can live or what type of job he or she can have? Require the use of contraception?

Electronic monitoring programs, usually using ankle bracelets and a telephone, raise issues of privacy. Such sanctions are said to blur the line between the offender and his or her family. Electronic monitoring sometimes involves a camera connected to the telephone. When the offender calls into a monitoring station, the monitor can see past the offender into the home. Is this a violation of family members' privacy, or do we consider it a consent entry? In general, probation and parole require consent for warrantless searches, but is it really consent when the option is prison? And even if the offender gives consent, can he or she give consent for other family members who are also affected?

net widening The concept that some intermediate sanctions are used for those who would not have received any formal correctional sanction before, so instead of diverting those who would have been sentenced to harsher sanctions, the program increases the total number under correctional supervision.

Some contend that we are needlessly "widening the net" (**net widening**) of corrections by putting more and more people on some form of correctional supervision. Further, the use of surveillance techniques against offender populations is spilling over into other contexts. For instance, drug testing started with probationers and now seems to be common in the workplace. Other forms of surveillance started with correctional populations but then became accepted practices in other applications. Metal detectors are used now in a number of settings, and some workplaces use a polygraph, monitor employees' calls, use video cameras, track e-mails, and in other ways apply the surveillance practices created for lawbreakers to the rest of us (Staples, 1997). Some worry that we have become so used to these incursions on privacy that basic freedoms are being infringed upon without much opposition from the population; in fact, one often hears, "If you're not doing anything wrong, you shouldn't have anything to worry about." Some argue that this accepting attitude toward "big brother" would be an anathema to previous generations.

The danger of intermediate sanctions is that because they are typically so innocuous, they are used more frequently for offenders who may not have received any formal system response in years past. Unfortunately, what sometimes happens is that the offender, once in the system, fails because of technical violations (rule violations, not new crimes) and becomes more and more immersed in the system. Can we foresee a time when a large portion of the population is on some type of governmental monitoring status? Some say it is already here. We may be happy to note that tax monies may not be burdened by such monitoring because offenders are usually charged supervision fees to pay for the technology.

Other than providing employment for the legions of criminal justice students who are graduating from colleges and universities, are there good reasons for the dramatic expansion of the net of corrections? Perhaps the dramatic increase of those under correctional supervision has led to the substantial drop in crime? Researchers continue to debate this question, but even if it were possible to assess the relationship, the ethical issue would not be resolved.

Formal Ethics for Correctional Professionals

The American Correctional Association's (ACA) Code of Ethics outlines formal ethics for correctional officers and other correctional personnel. This code has many similarities to the Law Enforcement Code of Ethics presented in Chapter 5. For instance, integrity, respect for and protection of individual rights, and service to the public are emphasized in both codes, as are the importance and sanctity of the law. Also, the prohibition against exploiting professional authority for personal gain is stressed in both codes.

The ACA code indicates that members should exhibit honesty, respect for the dignity and individuality of human beings, and a commitment to professional and compassionate service. The following principles are identified: protect legal rights; show concern for the welfare of individuals; promote mutual respect with colleagues and criticize only when warranted; respect and cooperate with all disciplines in the system; provide public information as consistent with law and privacy rights; protect public safety; refrain from using one's position to secure personal privileges or advantage or let these impair objectivity; avoid conflicts of interest; refrain from accepting gifts or services that appear improper; differentiate one's personal views from professional duties; report any corrupt or unethical behaviors; refrain from discriminating because of race, gender, creed, national origin, religious affiliation, age, disability, or other prohibited categories; preserve the integrity of private information; abide by civil service rules; and promote a safe, healthy, and harassment-free workplace (ACA Code, available at www.aca.org/pastpresentfuture/ethics.asp.)

In an interesting discussion of implementing an ethics program for correctional officers, Barrier et al. (1999) described how officers presented elements of what they thought were important in an ethics code:

- Acting professionally
- Showing respect for inmates and workers
- Maintaining honesty and integrity
- Being consistent
- Acting impartially
- Being assertive but not aggressive
- Confronting bad behavior but reinforcing good behavior
- Standardizing rule enforcement
- Respecting others
- Practicing the Golden Rule
- Encouraging teamwork
- Using professional language
- Not abusing sick leave
- Telling inmates the truth
- Admitting mistakes

The American Jail Association has a similar code of ethics for jail officers. The preamble states that the jail officer should avoid questionable behavior that will bring disrepute to the agency. The code mandates that officers keep the institution secure, work with everyone fairly, maintain a positive demeanor, report what should be reported, manage inmates even-handedly without becoming personally involved, take advantage of training opportunities, communicate with individuals outside the agency in a way that does not bring discredit, contribute to a positive environment, and support professional activities (American Jail Association, available at www.aja.org/ethics.aspx).

Formal ethical guidelines for probation and parole officers are provided by the American Correctional Association Code of Ethics, and possibly by their own state ethics codes.

Federal probation officers subscribe to the Federal Probation and Pretrial Officers Association's ethical code. The formal ethics of the profession is summarized by the ideal of service—to the community and to the offender. As with other codes, the federal probation officer is exhorted to maintain "decorum" in one's private life, avoid granting or receiving favors or benefits that are connected to the position, uphold the law with dignity, strife for objectivity in performance of duties, "appreciate the inherent worth of the individual," cooperate with fellow workers and related agencies, improve professional standards and recognize the office as "a symbol of public faith" (Federal Probation and Pretrial Officers Association, available at www.fppoa.org/fppoa_codeofethics.asp.)

Ethical codes exist for other correctional professionals as well. Treatment professionals typically belong to a professional organization and this organization will have a code of ethics, such as the National Association of Social Workers Code of Ethics or, for psychiatrists, the Principles of Medical Ethics with Annotations Especially Applicable to Psychiatry. Mental health counselors adhere to the code of ethics of the American Mental Health Counselors Association, and psychologists follow the Ethical Principles of Psychologists and Code of Conduct. There are also organizations or separate divisions of professional organizations specifically for correctional workers in that profession, such as the Criminal Justice Section of the American Psychological Association. Finally, the American Correctional Health Services Association and the American Association for Correctional and Forensic Psychology also have their own ethical codes to guide their members. The American Association for Correctional and Forensic Psychology's code includes the following sections: Offender's Right to Dignity and Respect, Avoid or Minimize Harm, Maintain and Advocate for Competent Mental Health Services and Rights, and Social Responsibility. The Ethical Principles of Psychologists promote five aspirational principles: beneficence (do no harm), fidelity and responsibility (create relationships of trust), integrity (honesty and truthfulness in science and practice), justice (fairness), respect for rights and dignity (protect privacy and self-determination) (cited and described in Bonner and Vandecreek, 2006; Ward, Gannon, and Vess, 2009).

The American Correctional Health Services Association is an affiliate of the American Correctional Association and has developed a code of ethics for health care providers in correctional facilities, including medical care workers as well as mental health professionals. In developing this code, they surveyed their members and consensus emerged as to the leading principles that should guide professionals in providing health care in corrections: respect for human dignity, beneficence, trustworthiness, autonomy, prevention of harm, and promotion of a safe environment. The code includes "should" statements such as "Respect the law and also recognize a responsibility to seek changes in those requirements that are contrary to the best interest of the patient." And "Honor custody functions but not participate in such activities as escorting inmates, forced transfers, security supervision, strip searches, or witnessing use of force" (described in Bonner and Vandecreek, 2006). All of these codes in general or specific language attempt to provide guidance to members who strive for ethical performance of their duties.

Occupational Subcultures in Corrections

Another similarity between the corrections field and law enforcement is that sometimes the ideal behavior described in the ethical codes is different from the subcultural norms. Although the ethical codes clearly call for fair and objective treatment, integrity, and high standards of performance, the actual practices found in some agencies and institutions may be quite different.

THE CORRECTIONAL OFFICER SUBCULTURE

The correctional officer subculture has not been described as extensively as the police subculture, but some elements are similar. First of all, the inmate may be considered the enemy, along with superiors and society in general. Moreover, the acceptance of the use of force, the preference toward redefining job roles to meet only minimum requirements, and the willingness to use deceit to cover up wrongdoing seem to have support in both subcultures (R. Johnson, 2002; Crouch, 1980; Grossi and Berg, 1991).

In an excellent study of the officers' world, Kauffman (1988: 85–112) notes the following norms of the correctional officer subculture:

- *Always go to the aid of another officer.* Similar to law enforcement, the necessity of interdependence ensures that this is a strong and pervasive norm in the correctional officer subculture. Kauffman describes a "slam" in Walpole Prison as when the officer slams a heavy cell door, which reverberates throughout the prison building, bringing a dozen officers to his or her aid in minutes—an obvious parallel to the "officer down" call in law enforcement.

- *Don't lug drugs.* This prohibition is to ensure the safety of other officers, as is the even stronger prohibition against bringing in weapons for inmates. The following norm against "ratting" on a fellow officer may exclude informing on an officer who is a known offender of this lugging norm.

- *Don't rat.* In ways similar to the law enforcement subcultural code and, ironically, the inmate code, correctional officers also hate those who inform on their peers. Kauffman notes two subordinate norms: Never rat out an officer to an inmate, and never cooperate in an investigation or, worse yet, testify against a fellow officer in regard to that officer's treatment of inmates.

- *Never make a fellow officer look bad in front of inmates.* This applies regardless of what the officer did, for it jeopardizes the officer's effectiveness and undercuts the appearance of officer solidarity.

- *Always support an officer in a dispute with an inmate.* Similar to the previous provision, this prescribes behavior. Not only should one not criticize a fellow officer, but one should support him or her against any inmate.

- *Always support officer sanctions against inmates.* This is a specific version of the previous provision, which includes the use of illegal physical force as well as legal sanctions.

- *Don't be a white hat.* This prohibition is directed at any behavior, attitude, or expressed opinion that could be interpreted as sympathetic toward inmates. Kauffman also notes that this prohibition is often violated and does not have the strong subcultural sanctions that accompany some of the other norms.

- *Maintain officer solidarity against all outside groups.* Similar to police officers, correctional officers feel denigrated and despised by society at large. This norm reinforces officer solidarity by making any other group, including the media, administration, or the public, the out-group.

- *Show positive concern for fellow officers.* This norm promotes good will toward other officers. Two examples are (1) never leave another officer a problem, which means don't leave unfinished business at the end of your shift for the next officer to handle, and (2) help your fellow officers with problems outside the institution, which means lending money to injured or sick officers or helping in other ways.

If a correctional officer violates the subcultural code, the sanctions are felt perhaps even more acutely than by police officers, because one must work closely with other correctional officers all day long. Whereas police officers cite the importance of being able to trust other officers as backups in violent situations, one could make the argument that correctional officers have to trust each other more completely, more implicitly, and more frequently, given that violence in some institutions is pervasive and unprovoked, and that the correctional officer carries no weapon. An officer described to Kauffman (1988: 207) the result of violating peer trust:

> If an incident went down, there was no one to cover my back. That's a very important lesson to learn. You need your back covered and my back wasn't covered there at all. And at one point I was in fear of being set up by guards. I was put in dangerous situations purposely. That really happened to me.

Fear of violating the code of silence is one reason that officers do not report wrongdoing. Loyalty is another reason. Correctional officers feel a strong esprit de corps similar to the previously discussed loyalty among police. This positive loyalty also results in covering for other officers and not testifying or reporting offenses. McCarthy (1991) discusses how theft, trafficking in contraband, embezzlement, and misuse of authority went unreported by other correctional officers because of loyalty and subcultural prohibitions against "ratting." The In the News box describes a rare case where officers were found guilty, despite support from their union.

A pattern of complicity also prevents reporting. New officers cannot possibly follow all the many rules and regulations that exist in a prison and still adequately deal with inmates on a day-to-day basis. Before long they find themselves involved in activity that could result in disciplinary action. Because others are usually aware of this activity and do not inform supervisors, an implicit conspiracy of silence develops so no one is turned in for anything because each of the others who might witness this wrongdoing has engaged in behavior that could also be sanctioned (Lombardo, 1981: 79).

Hamm (1989) discussed what happened when correctional professionals did come forward. He pointed out that whistleblowers sometimes are pursuing self-interest or personal goals by informing. Sometimes there are minimal costs; however, in instances where the individual goes against the subculture, there may be serious consequences. In the

in the NEWS

"THE PROGRAM"

A rogue disciplinary system enacted by a group of guards at Riker's Island used beatings and extortion by other inmates to keep order in a facility where young offenders aged 16 to 18 were housed with adults. One of the guards was sentenced to six years for his part in the group's activities. The Correction Officers' Benevolent Association argued that it was simply a scheme by the inmates to get money from the state, but the judge ruled the officer's testimony "unbelievable and contrived." At least three other guards have been charged and may be tried and, if found guilty, could spend up to 25 years in prison for what is considered to be organized crime activity.

SOURCE: Raftery, 2010.

WALKING THE WALK

Tom Murton found his career dramatically altered when he was hired by the Arkansas Department of Correction as its director of corrections. He had been instrumental in setting up the prison system for the state of Alaska in the late 1950s and was teaching at Southern Illinois University when he was hired by Governor Winthrop Rockefeller, who wanted to modernize the Arkansas prison system. Upon arriving in 1967 to head the Tucker prison farms, he discovered abuses and inhumane conditions, described later in several writings by Murton and immortalized in the movie *Brubaker*. The U.S. Supreme Court case of *Holt v. Sarver* (442 F.2d 304 [8th Cir. 1971]) also documented the abuses, which included subjecting prisoners to electric shocks, staff taking food meant for prisoners and feeding them a disgusting gruel, forcing inmates into a metal box for long periods of time as a punishment, allowing prisoners to guard and inflict brutal discipline on other prisoners, and other inhumane treatments. Murton began to address these issues and received information that more than 200 inmates had disappeared and were listed as escapees. Acting on the information of one informant, he dug up (on the grounds of the prison) two bodies that had injuries exactly as the inmate had described. One had been decapitated, and one had a crushed skull. Even though one of the bodies was eventually positively identified as a missing inmate, opposing testimony at the legislative hearing called in response to his investigation proposed that the bodies were from an old church cemetery. Instead of pursuing the matter further and digging up more bodies or testing them in any way for age and other identifying marks, state officials fired Murton and threatened him with prosecution as a grave robber if he didn't leave the state. He never worked in corrections again.

Sources: Murton and Hayams, 1969; Murton, 1976.

Walking the Walk box, one correctional administrator went against the pattern of cover-ups in a state system, and his actions eventually cost him his career.

The correctional officer code, and sanctions against whistleblowers, varies from institution to institution, depending on factors such as permeability, the administration, the level of violence from inmates, architecture, and the demographic profile of officers. Distrust of outsiders, dissatisfaction, and alienation are elements of both the police subculture and the correctional officer subculture. In both professions, individuals must work with sometimes unpleasant people who make it clear that the practitioner is not liked or appreciated. Further, there is public antipathy (either real or perceived) toward the profession, which increases the social distance between criminal justice professionals and all others outside the profession. The working hours, the nature of the job, and the unwillingness to talk about the job to others outside the profession intensify the isolation that workers feel.

One additional point to be made about the occupational subculture is that both law enforcement and corrections have experienced an influx of minorities, the college-educated, and women. These demographic changes no doubt have altered the dynamics of the subculture in both fields.

It should also be pointed out that some researchers believe that some of the values embedded in the correctional officer subculture may not be shared by most officers—a concept referred to as **pluralistic ignorance**. This refers to the idea that a few outspoken and visible members do not reflect the silent majority's views. In a prison, this may mean that a few officers endorse and publicize subcultural values, whereas the majority of officers, who are silent, privately believe in different values (R. Johnson, 1996: 130). Kauffman (1988: 179) found this to be true in attitudes toward the use of force (where the silent majority did not endorse it to the extent of the verbal minority) and toward the value of treatment (which was silently supported).

pluralistic ignorance
The prevalent misperception of the popularity of a belief among a group because of the influence of a vocal minority.

TREATMENT PROFESSIONALS

While there may be subcultural elements from correctional officers that migrate to those who work in treatment roles in correctional facilities, there doesn't seem to be much research documenting it. Thus, we can only assume that when treatment professionals such as psychologists and counselors work in a prison or other correctional facility, they are not a part of the correctional officer subculture, but they may have a different, albeit weaker subculture of their own. Similarly, correctional medical care professionals may be influenced in greater or lesser ways by the "penal harm" atmosphere that pervades some correctional institutions where inmates are seen as not deserving of the care associated with medical services outside the prison. The profession's ethical code responds to this tendency. Ethical issues exist for treatment professionals that are different from those of correctional officers, and these will be described in the next chapter.

THE PROBATION/PAROLE OFFICER SUBCULTURE

The subculture of probation and parole officers has never been documented as extensively as that of police and correctional officers. Because of differences between these professions, the subculture of the former is not as pervasive or strong as that of the latter. Probation and parole officers do not feel as isolated as police or correctional officers do. They experience no stigmatization; they have normal working hours; they do not wear a depersonalizing uniform; and they have a less obviously coercive relationship with their clients. These factors reduce the need for a subculture. Still, one can probably identify some norms that might be found in any probation or parole office:

cynicism A trait of those who work in corrections, characterized by a pessimistic view of human nature and their ability to change.

- *Cynicism.* They have a norm of **cynicism** toward clients. The subculture promotes the idea that clients are inept, deviant, and irredeemable. Probation and parole professionals who express positive attitudes toward clients' capacity for change are seen as naïve and guileless.
- *Lethargy.* At least in some offices, there is a pervasive subcultural norm of lethargy or minimal work output. This norm is supported by the view that officers are underpaid and overworked.
- *Individualism.* A norm of individualism can be identified. Although parole and probation officers may seek opinions from other professionals in the office, there is an unspoken rule that each runs his or her own caseload. To offer unsolicited opinions about decisions another person makes regarding his or her client violates this norm of autonomy.

Even though there does not seem to be the "blue curtain of secrecy" to the same extent as is found in policing, there no doubt is a norm against informing on colleagues for unethical or illegal behaviors. This relates somewhat to the norm of individualism, but is also part of the pervasive occupational subculture against informing on colleagues. Probation and parole officers may see and hear unethical behaviors and not feel comfortable coming forward with such information. If they work in an office where the norm against exposing such wrongdoing is strong, they may indeed suffer sanctions similar to those of police and correctional officers for exposing others' wrongdoing.

Some offices develop norms that accept unethical practices and lethargy. Once this occurs, it becomes a difficult pattern to change. If it is already present, a single officer will have a hard time not falling into the pattern. If all officers feel overwhelmed by their caseloads and their relative lack of power to do anything about failure, the result may be that they throw up their hands and adopt a "who cares?" attitude. If the supervisor does not exhibit a commitment to the goal of the organization, does not encourage workers, treats certain officers with favoritism, or seems more concerned with his or her personal career than with the needs of the office, there is an inevitable deterioration of morale. If the organization does not encourage and support good workers, it is no wonder that what develops is an informal subculture that encourages minimum effort and treats organizational goals with sarcasm and cynicism.

CONCLUSION

In this chapter, we have looked at some of the ethical rationales for punishment. What we do to offenders is influenced by our views on things such as free will and determinism, the capacity for individual change, and the basic nature of humankind. Punishment has always been used against those who hurt other members of society and thus might be considered consistent with natural law. However, the limits of punishment have been subject to the laws and mores of each historical era. Today, our punishments primarily consist of imprisonment or some form of restricted liberty, such as probation or parole. The death penalty continues to be used; however, the controversy surrounding it continues as well.

Formal ethics for those who work in corrections come from their professional organizations, such as the American Correctional Association. Common to all the codes is adherence to the law, respect for persons, and maintaining objectivity and professional standards of competence. Similar to police officers, there are elements in occupational subcultures that sometimes conflict with and subvert formal ethics.

CHAPTER REVIEW

1. Provide the definitions of punishment and treatment and their rationales.

According to Leiser, punishment is defined as follows: There are at least two persons—one who inflicts the punishment and one who is punished; a certain harm is inflicted; the punisher has been authorized, under a system of rules or laws; the punished has been judged by a representative of that authority by some relevant rule or law; and the harm that is inflicted upon the person who is being punished is specifically for the act or omission relevant to such law. The definition of treatment is that which may create behavioral change. The rationale for punishment and treatment is the social contract. Further, specific rationales for punishment include retribution, deterrence, incapacitation, and treatment.

2. Describe how the ethical frameworks justify punishment.

Utilitarianism is often used to support the three rationales of punishment: deterrence, incapacitation, and treatment. According to utilitarianism, punishing or treating the criminal offender benefits society, and this benefit outweighs the negative effect on the individual offender. Ethical formalism clearly supports a retributive view of punishment. It is deontological because it is concerned not with the consequences of the punishment or treatment, only its inherent morality. The punishment should not be used as a means to any other end but retribution. The ethics of care would probably not support punishment unless it was essential to help the offender become a better person.

3. Describe the ethical rationales for and against capital punishment.

Retentionists (who believe that we should continue to utilize capital punishment) and abolitionists (who believe that we should not execute anyone) both use utilitarianism, ethical formalism, and religion as moral justifications. Retentionists argue that capital punishment is just because it deters others from committing murder and it definitely deters the individual who is executed. This is a utilitarian argument. They also argue that capital punishment is just because murder deserves a proportional punishment. This argument is more consistent with ethical formalism. Finally, they argue that the Bible dictates an "eye for an eye." This is, of course, a (Judeo-Christian) religious justification for capital punishment. Abolitionists argue that capital punishment has never been shown to be effective in deterring others from committing murder, and, therefore, the evil of capital punishment far outweighs any potential benefits for society because there is no proof that it actually deters. This is a utilitarian argument. Abolitionists might also utilize the categorical imperative under ethical formalism to argue that deterrence is using the individual as a means to an end. Finally, abolitionists would point to the religious command to "turn the other cheek" an argument against any religious (Christian) justification for capital punishment.

4. Describe the ethical codes for correctional officers, treatment professionals, and probation and parole officers.

Codes come from professional organizations such as the American Psychological Association, or more specific organizations for correctional personnel such as the American Correctional Association. Elements of codes for correctional officers, treatment personnel, and those who work in community corrections all seem to include the following elements: integrity, respect for and protection of individual rights and autonomy, service to the public, sanctity of the law, and prohibitions against exploiting professional authority for personal gain.

5. Explain how occupational subcultures affect adherence to professional ethics codes.

Subcultural elements are, in some ways, similar to those of law enforcement—the inmate is the "enemy" along with superiors and the public, acceptance of the use of force, the preference toward redefining job roles to meet only minimum requirements, and the willingness to use deceit to cover up wrongdoing for fellow officers. Treatment and probation/parole subcultures are not strong, probably because they do not share the same characteristics of the job as law enforcement and correctional officers. Generally, the major issue of these subcultures seems to be an attitude toward the client/offender that is pessimistic and cynical, and, in some offices, a culture of lethargy that promotes doing the least work possible.

KEY TERMS

community corrections
cruel and unusual
  punishment
cynicism
expiation
just deserts model
justice model

net widening
new rehabilitationists
penal harm
pluralistic ignorance
prevention
punishment
reintegrative shaming

retribution
stigmatizing shaming
three-strikes laws
treatment
treatment ethic

STUDY QUESTIONS

1. Define punishment using the elements provided by Leiser.

2. What are the three different objectives or approaches to prevention? Explain some issues with each.

3. How would Bentham defend punishment? Contrast that position with Kant's position.

4. What are the criticisms of the supermax prison? Compare them to the Supreme Court's definition of cruel and unusual punishment.

5. What are the arguments for and against private prisons?

WRITING/DISCUSSION EXERCISES

1. Write an essay on (or discuss) the "pains" of different types of punishment for different people, including yourself. Would you rather spend a year in prison or receive a severe whipping? Would you rather spend a year in prison or receive five years of probation with stringent restrictions? Would you rather spend a year in prison or pay a $30,000 fine?

2. Write an essay on (or discuss) your views on the justification for punishment. If you knew for certain that prison did not deter, would you still be in favor of its use? Why? If we could predict future criminals, would you be willing to incapacitate them before they commit a crime in order to protect society? Explain.

3. Write an essay on (or discuss) your views on the use of capital punishment and the reasons for your position. Now take the opposite side, and give the reasons for this view.

ETHICAL DILEMMAS

Situation 1

A legislator has proposed a sweeping new crime and punishment bill with the following provisions for punishment. Decide each issue as if you were being asked to vote on it:

- Mandatory life term with no parole for any crime involving a weapon
- Corporal punishment (using an electrical apparatus that inflicts a shock) for all personal violent crimes
- Mandatory five-year prison sentences for those convicted of DWI
- Public executions
- Abolition of probation, to be replaced with fines and prison sentences for those who are not able to pay or are unwilling to do so

Situation 2

Another legislator has suggested an alternative plan with the following provisions. Vote on these:

- Decriminalization of all drug crimes
- Mandated treatment programs for all offenders who were intoxicated by alcohol or other drugs at the time of the crime

- Restructuring the sentencing statutes to make no sentence longer than five years, except homicide, attempted homicide, robbery, and rape
- Implementation of a restitution program for all victims whereby offenders stay in the community, work, and pay back the victims for the losses and/or injuries they received

Situation 3

Your state is one of the few that allows relatives of homicide victims to witness the execution of the perpetrator. Your brother was killed in a robbery, and the murderer is about to be executed. You receive a letter advising you of the execution date and your right to be present. Would you go? Would you volunteer to be the executioner?

Situation 4

Your house has been burglarized. Your community has a new sentencing program, and the program's directors have asked you to participate along with the offender who burglarized your house. As you understand it, this means that you would be sitting down with representatives from the police department and court system and the offender and his family. The group would discuss and come to an agreement on the appropriate punishment for the crime. Would you do it? Why or why not?

Situation 5

You are a legislator who is the chairman of a committee that is making decisions about whether to build a new prison or contract with a private prison provider. You are visited by a lobbyist for one of the companies that is being considered and he explains that the company is sponsoring a "fact finding" trip to Scandinavia and other parts of Europe to tour several prisons and meet with correctional officials. He invites you and your spouse to go with the group. You would stay in very nice hotels and have social and entertainment events as well as the official activities—everything would be paid for by the company. He explains that because it is a fact finding or educational trip for you, it does not violate your state's laws or ethics code. Would you go?

12

Thinkstock/Comstock/Jupiter Images

Discretion and Dilemmas in Corrections

Chapter Objectives

1. Describe the role conflict of correctional officers.
2. List and describe some ethical issues for correctional officers.
3. Describe the different challenges that face jail officers as compared to correctional officers in prisons.
4. Explain the role conflict of treatment professionals and provide examples.
5. Describe the ethical issues of probation and parole officers.

Institutional correctional personnel can be divided into two groups: (1) correctional officers and their supervisors, and (2) treatment professionals, a group that includes educators, counselors, psychologists, and all others connected with programming and services. These groups have different jobs and different ethical issues. There are also community correctional professionals, including probation and parole officers and staff in work release and halfway houses. All correctional professionals share the two goals of protecting society and assisting in the reform of the criminal offender.

Throughout this text, discretion has been shown as pivotal in each phase of the criminal justice system. In corrections, discretion is involved when a correctional officer chooses whether to write a disciplinary ticket or merely delivers a verbal reprimand; this is similar to the discretion that police have in traffic stops. Discretion is also involved when the disciplinary committee makes a decision to punish an inmate for an infraction: the punishment can be as serious as increasing the length of a sentence through loss of good time or as minor as a temporary loss of privileges. This type of discretion is similar to the discretion of the prosecutor and judge in a criminal trial. Officers make daily decisions regarding granting inmates' passes, providing supplies, and even answering questions. Probation and parole officers have discretion in when to file a violation report or what to recommend if a client violates one or more conditions of their supervision.

As always, when the power of discretion is present, the potential for abuse is also present. Sometimes correctional professionals have the *power* to do things that they don't have the *legal authority* to do. That is, some officers can deny an inmate a pass to go to the doctor even though, according to the prison rules, the inmate has a right to go. When

347

in the **NEWS**

COs on the Take

In 2008, seven correctional officers were caught in Riker's Island, New York, in a scheme where they accepted money to smuggle contraband into the jail. They had agreed to deliver drugs, cigarettes, and cash to inmates who paid them up to $2,700 for each delivery. The corrections system had fired three of the officers on "unrelated reasons" after they were arrested by undercover officers who posed as associates of the prisoners.

Source: NY1 News, 2008.

officers exceed their authority, inmates' only recourse is to write a grievance. Professional ethics, as provided in a code of ethics, should guide officers and other staff members in their use of discretion and power, but, as with law enforcement and legal professionals, adhering to a code of ethics is influenced by the occupational subculture and institutional values. There are also examples where correctional officers become as criminal as the inmates they are supposed to be supervising, as the In the News box indicates.

Correctional Officers

Correctional officers (COs) are similar to police officers in that their uniform represents the authority of the institution quite apart from any personal power of the person wearing it. Some COs are uncomfortable with this authority and do not know how to handle it. Other COs revel in it and misperceive the bounds of authority given to them as a representative of the state. The following statement is a perceptive observation of how some COs misuse the authority they have:

> [Some officers] don't understand what authority is and what bounds you have within that authority. . . . I think everyone interprets it to meet their own image of themself. "I'm a corrections officer! [slams table] You sit here! [slam] You sit there!" rather than, "I'm a person who has limited authority. So, you know, I'm sorry, gentlemen, but you can't sit there. You are going to have to sit over there. That's just the rules," and explaining or something like that the reason why. (Kauffman, 1988: 50)

This observer obviously recognizes that the uniform bestows the authority of rational and reasonable control, not unbridled domination. The power of the CO is limited. In actuality, it is impossible to depend on the authority of the uniform to get tasks accomplished, and one must find personal resources—respect and authority stemming from one's personal reputation—in order to gain cooperation from inmates. Some officers who perceive themselves as powerless in relation to the administration, the courts, and society in general may react to this perceived powerlessness by misusing their little bit of power over inmates. They may abuse their position by humiliating or abusing those in their control. As discussed in the Walking the Walk box, Chaplain James Yee stood up to what he believed were abuses of power in the Guantanamo detainment facility and paid a heavy price for it.

Thus, in ways somewhat similar to those of police officers, correctional officers have power over offenders. They have the full range of coercive control, including loss of liberty through physical force if necessary. Their power may be misused. Blatant examples are an

WALKING THE WALK

James Yee was raised as a Lutheran in a Chinese American family in New Jersey. He converted to the Muslim faith after graduating from West Point in 1990. Yee left the army for a short time, but then came back into the army as a chaplain. In 2002, he was sent to Guantanamo to minister to the prisoners. For 10 months, from November 2002 to September 2003, he witnessed hostile acts toward the prisoners, including beating and humiliation by military police and interrogators. He saw religion used as a weapon. Prisoners were made to bow down in the middle of a satanic circle and profess that Satan was their god, not Allah. Detainees were mocked during prayer and teased sexually by female soldiers. Detainees begged Yee to take away their copies of the Quran because, allegedly, the military police would deface the holy books.

Chaplain Yee began to be known as a prisoner advocate. He ministered to the detainees and tried to intervene to stop the abuse they endured. As he explained, "I was not willing to silently stand by and watch U.S. soldiers abuse the Quran, mock people's religion, and strip men of their dignity—even if those men were prisoners." He advocated openly for the prisoners, especially against actions that were taken against the religious practices of the Muslim prisoners. His advocacy brought him into conflict with his superiors. "I believed that the hostile environment and animosity toward Islam were so ingrained in the operation that Major General Miller and the other camp leaders lost sight of the moral harm we were doing."

He became concerned especially about the young detainees. Boys as young as 12 to 14 years old, who had been seized as they engaged in hostilities against American soldiers in Afghanistan, were detained at Guantanamo. Once there, they were held with no idea as to when they would be released, or even if they would be. They may have been interrogated with coercive measures, and they experienced day-to-day treatment by guards that is typical of the worst prisons. Yee asked himself how these young men would turn out and what they would think of America. Despite the pervasive attitudes that he experienced that discouraged any attempt to advocate for prisoners, he continued to do so.

On his first leave from Guantanamo, in September 2003, Yee was arrested at the airport coming back into the United States, and accused of being a spy. He was imprisoned for 76 days under conditions of sensory deprivation and interrogated. Yee's wife and daughter were subjected to interrogation as well.

Eventually the treason and spying charges were dropped. Because Yee was carrying names of detainees and interrogators, he was charged with mishandling classified information. He was also charged with pornography because of pictures on his computer, and with adultery for an affair he had had with another officer. Even those charges were dropped in 2004. General Miller (the superior officer he had criticized at Guantanamo) was quoted as saying that the reason charges were dropped was that national security would be compromised in any prosecution; however, nothing in the record indicated that Yee was, in any way, a spy. He was never formally exonerated nor was he ever issued an apology, even though his life had been torn apart by the accusations and he ended up with $260,000 in legal bills.

Yee believes that there was a plan to discredit him (by accusing him of being a spy) in case he exposed the treatment of the Guantanamo detainees. He left the military in 2005, with an honorable discharge, and today continues to speak out against what the United States has done in Guantanamo.

Sources: Buchholz, 2008: Gl, G4; Lewis, 2005; Yee and Molloy, 2005.

officer who beats an inmate or coerces sex from an inmate. The possibility for these abuses of power exists because of the powerlessness of the offender relative to the officer. Inmates have even less power against officer abuses than do citizens on the street against police officers' abuses of power. Sensitivity to ethical issues in corrections involves recognition and respect for the inherent powers and concurrent responsibilities of the profession.

correctional officer
The term that replaced the old label of *guard*, indicating a new role.

During the rehabilitative era of the 1970s, professional security staff in corrections exchanged the old label of *guard* for a new one—**correctional officer**. Crouch (1986) examined how changing goals (from custody to rehabilitation) in the 1970s and 1980s created role conflict and ambiguity for the correctional officer. Also in the 1970s, federal courts recognized an expanding number of prisoner rights, including the rights to exercise religious beliefs, obtain medical care, and enjoy some due process. The disruption in the "old way" of doing things created real chaos, and the 1970s and 1980s brought danger, loss of control, and stress for officers. In addition to increasing prisoner rights, the advent of unionization, professionalism, and bureaucratization changed the guard's world (Crouch, 1980, 1986; Silberman, 1995; R. Johnson, 2002).

The prisoners' rights era of the 1970s gave way to the "due deference" era of today, where courts are more apt to defer to prison officials. Now, when responding to prisoner challenges, prison officials only have to prove a "rational relationship" between prison policies or procedures and the correctional goal of safety and security (Pollock, 2004). The Prison Litigation Reform Act of 1996 (PLRA) drastically curtailed the ability of inmates to file lawsuits and made it nearly impossible for federal courts to order consent decrees or order injunctive relief. It also limited attorney's fees.

Today, the prison is not the same as it was before the rights and rehabilitation era of the 1960s and 1970s, and correctional officers probably think that inmates still have too many rights. However, the courts' retreat into due deference has arguably led to a new era of penal harm. When legal rights are limited, professional ethics must step into the breach to guide what is appropriate treatment of those in custody.

RELATIONSHIPS WITH INMATES

One would assume that the general relationship between officers and inmates is one of hatred. That is not necessarily the case. As Martin (1993), a prisoner writer, points out, the posturing and vocalization from either side come from a small number, with the majority of inmates and officers living in an uneasy state of truce, hoping that no one goes over the line on either side. The Quote and Query box points out the extremes in relationships between convicts and guards.

QUOTE & QUERY

Some convicts hate all prison guards. They perceive them as the physical manifestation of their own misery and misfortune. The uniform becomes the man, and they no longer see an individual behind it. . . . Many guards react in kind. The hatred is returned with the full force of authority. These two factions become the real movers and shakers in the prison world. They aren't a majority in either camp, but the strength of their hatred makes its presence known to all.

—SOURCE: MARTIN, 1993: 94–95.

How would one reduce the level of hate between these small numbers of prisoners toward guards and guards toward prisoners?

The majority of guards and inmates prefer to live in peace and understand that they have to treat each other with some modicum of respect in order to get along. Unfortunately, both believe they must take sides when conflict arises. Even though prisoners have come to the aid of officers in physical confrontations, in general, inmates support their fellow inmates and guards support their fellow guards, regardless of how little support the individual deserves. Thus, a brutal guard may be protected by his fellows, and a racist guard will not be informally or formally sanctioned. Likewise, an assaultive inmate will not be kept in check by his peer group unless his actions are perceived to hurt their interests.

reciprocity Sykes's term denoting the situation in which officers become indebted to inmates and return favors.

An officer's ethics and professionalism are seriously threatened when relationships with inmates become personal. Gresham Sykes (cited in Crouch, 1980) discussed the issue of **reciprocity** in supervision: officers become dependent on inmates for task completion and smooth management of the housing unit; in return, COs may overlook inmate infractions and allow some favoritism to enter their supervision style. An example of a type of reciprocal relationship that may lead to unethical actions is that between an officer and an informant. Several authors have described how rewarding informants sometimes creates tension and trouble in a prison environment even though management often depends on the information (Hassine, 1996; Marquart and Roebuck, 1986).

COs who become personally involved with inmates compromise their professional judgment. Involvement is possible because of proximity and close contact over time, combined with shared feelings of victimization by the administration. Officers may start to think they have more in common with inmates than with the administration, especially now that officers are more likely to come from urban areas, come from minority groups, and be more demographically similar to the inmates they supervise. Identification and friendship may lead to unethical conduct, such as ignoring infractions or doing illegal favors for an inmate. McCarthy (1991) writes of this exchange relationship as an incentive for further corruption. He also points out that lack of training, low visibility, and unfettered discretion contribute to a variety of corrupt behaviors.

An extremely problematic situation arises when the officer becomes sexually involved with an inmate (or inmates). Sexual relationships run a continuum of coercion from "true love" to rape. Coercion is more likely to be present with a female inmate and a male officer (Pollock, 2004). Some research indicates that just as many female officers become involved with male inmates as male officers with female inmates, and there are instances of homosexual relationships between officers and inmates as well (Marquart, Barnhill, and Balshaw-Biddle, 2001). In Dial and Worley's (2008) research, out of a sample of 367 male inmates, 63 percent reported no boundary violations with officers, but 14 percent reported that they had a sexual relationship with an officer. In most cases, this was with a female officer. Correctional officers go down a "slippery slope" of developing a personal relationship with an inmate by talking about their private life, then sharing pictures, then perhaps talking with the inmate's family outside of the prison. Even if the officer wanted to retreat from such a relationship, they cannot because they fear exposure. Many times the inmate "grooms" the officer to be a "mule" (carrying in illegal contraband) by developing the sexual relationship; in these cases, it is the officer who ends up being coerced instead of the other way around. Regardless of how benign the relationship, these relationships

TOO CLOSE!

The U.S. Attorney's Office for the Eastern District of Virginia announced in a news release that a female correctional officer for the Federal Bureau of Prisons had pleaded guilty to bribery and carnal knowledge with an inmate. She faces up to 15 years in prison, a $250,000 fine, and supervised release for the bribery charge and five years for carnal knowledge. She admitted to a sexual relationship with an inmate and also admitted that she would bring in contraband to him such as cell phones, cigarettes, and alcohol, in return for cash and gifts.

SOURCE: U.S. Attorney's Office, 2008b.

are unethical and, in many states, illegal. The In the News box describes a situation where love may have led to an officer experiencing prison from the other side of the bars.

The subcultural norms against sympathizing with or becoming too friendly with inmates may be seen as a tool to prevent officers from becoming personally involved with inmates and compromising their professional integrity. An officer who is too close to inmates is seen by other officers as untrustworthy. The officer subculture minimizes this possibility with a view of inmates as animalistic and not worth human sympathy. The negative effect of this is that positive elements of relationships between officers and inmates are lost. How they are treated by COs is sometimes described by inmates as more painful than any physical deprivations. Kauffman (1988) notes that inmates themselves make it difficult for COs to continue to hold sympathetic or friendly views because of their negative behaviors.

Just as officers may act in unethical ways when they like an inmate, they also may abuse their authority with inmates they do not like. These extra-legal harassments and punishments may include "forgetting" to send an inmate to an appointment, making an inmate stay in "keeplock" longer than necessary, or pretending not to hear someone locked in a cell asking for toilet paper or other necessary items. Lombardo (1981, 1989) noted the practices of putting an inmate in "keeplock" on a Friday even without a supportable charge because the disciplinary committee would not meet until the following Monday to release the inmate; the use of profanity toward inmates even in front of families; not notifying an inmate of a visitor; and losing passes. During the time period she studied, Kauffman (1988) noted that officers sometimes flushed cell toilets to aggravate inmates, dumped good food into the garbage, withheld toilet paper or matches, made up "tips" reporting contraband in a cell that resulted in a shakedown, scratched artwork, and in other innumerable informal ways made the targeted inmate's life miserable.

Because prisoners are in a position of need, having to ask for things as simple as permission to go to the bathroom, officers have the power to make inmates feel even more dependent than necessary and humiliated because of their dependency. The relative powerlessness of officers in relation to their superiors, the administration, and society in general creates a situation where some take advantage of their only power—that over the inmate. The gulf between the status of guard and guarded is the theme of the Quote and Query box.

QUOTE & QUERY

I never shake hands with an inmate.... They neither are nor ought to be viewed as equals.

—SOURCE: GEORGE BETO, ADMINISTRATOR OF TEXAS PRISON SYSTEM, 1962–1972, QUOTED IN DILULIO, 1987: 177.

[T]he sergeant had succeeded in making me feel even more isolated from the world that existed outside the prison walls. I was no longer so proud to be an American. I was just a convict without rights....

—SOURCE: VICTOR HASSINE, INMATE, 1996: 52.

Because legitimate power is so unevenly distributed between the keepers and the kept, left to its own inertia abuses of that power will inevitably creep into any prison without diligent and sensitive oversight.

—SOURCE: PATRICK MCMANUS, STATE CORRECTIONAL OFFICIAL, REPORTED IN MARTIN, 1993: 333.

Should the attitude of correctional professionals be that inmates are not worthy of a handshake, or does that isolation from the "community of man" create the potential for abuse?

For officers, the potential of injury or being taken hostage is never far from their mind, and may affect to a certain extent their supervision of inmates, for it is potentially dangerous to be personally disliked. Also, on a day-to-day basis, inmates are not that much different from anyone else. Some are friendly, some are funny, and some are good conversationalists. This strange combination of familiarity and fear results in a pervasive feeling of distrust. Officers insist that "you can be friendly with inmates, but you can never trust them." Mature officers learn to live with this basic inconsistency and are able to differentiate situations in which rules must be followed from those in which rules can be relaxed. Younger and less perceptive officers either take on a defensive attitude of extreme distrust or are manipulated by inmates because they are not able to tell the difference between good will and gaming.

Officers, of course, are individuals, and they respond differently to the demands and job pressures of corrections. However, certain types have been identified by R. Johnson (2002):

- *The violence-prone*, who use the role of correctional officer to act out an authoritarian role.

- *Time-servers*, who serve time in prison much the same way as the inmates do, avoiding trouble and hoping that nothing goes wrong on their shift.

- *Counselors*, who seek to enlarge their job description and perceive their role as including counseling and helping the inmate rather than merely locking doors and signing passes. This type of officer has been called the **human service officer** and incorporates the tasks of providing goods and services, acting as a referral agent or advocate, and helping with institutional adjustment problems.

human service officer The corrections officer who perceives the role to include influencing and interacting with the offender.

Changes over time have taken away many of the service functions that COs used to perform. In his update of an older study, Lombardo (1997) found that in the 10 years following his first study, much of the ability of COs to grant favors had been taken away. For instance, telephones in the yard eliminated the need for COs to run interference for inmates and get them a pass to make a phone call. This situation increased the autonomy of inmates, but it reduced the ability of the COs to develop helping relationships with inmates, or, to put a more negative interpretation on their loss, it reduced their ability to create debts from the inmate—favors owed in return for favors given.

"tune-ups" "Lessons" taught to inmates by Texas prison guards that involved verbal humiliation, profanity, shoves, kicks, and head and body slaps.

COs have much less discretion today, and practically every decision that in the past had been made by a CO is now made by sergeants and specialized officers. COs think they have much less power today to grant favors and, thus, have less control over inmates. One type of control they do have is the use of force, albeit one that is and should be restrained by legal and ethical norms.

USE OF FORCE

Tucker telephone An electrical device attached to the genitals of inmates that delivered severe shocks as a form of torture; formerly used at an Arkansas prison farm.

The use of force is a legal and sometimes necessary element of correctional supervision, and most observers say that the serious abuse that occurred in prisons in the past simply does not take place today. For instance, "**tune-ups**" in the Texas prisons involved "verbal humiliation, profanity, shoves, kicks, and head and body slaps," "ass-whipping," and using blackjacks and batons to inflict injury (Crouch and Marquart, 1989: 78). Murton (1976) described a litany of abuses that occurred in Arkansas prison farms, including the **Tucker telephone**, an electrical device that was attached to the genitals of inmates to deliver severe shocks as a form of torture.

One prison warden described hanging inmates on cell bars so their feet did not touch the floor and leaving them overnight, or making them stand on a 2-by-4 or a barrel for hours; if they fell off, the time would start again (Glenn, 2001: 25–26). This same warden described a situation in which an inmate tried to escape, was shot, and then was hung on the front gate, bleeding, for the field hoe squads to see as they came back from the fields. This was described by Glenn as an "effective … object lesson" rather than brutality (2001: 44). Glenn also described a prison captain who played a "game" with inmates whom he believed weren't working hard enough on the hoe squad. The captain had them tied and stripped, and then lowered his pants and threatened to sodomize them (2001: 69).

Ironically, as violence by officers decreased in the late 1970s and 1980s, it opened the door to the violence of inmate gangs and cliques. Inmates in the 1980s had less to fear from guards but more to fear from one another as racial gangs and other powerful cliques or individuals solidified their control over prison black markets. There was a time in the 1970s and 1980s when officers described some prisons as "out of control." There were prisons where guards were afraid to walk into living units and inmates literally controlled some parts of the prison (Carroll, 1998; Taylor, 1993).

Bowker (1980) and other authors who described the victimization of inmates by correctional officers explained the violence by the officers' pervasive sense of fear and a CO subculture that tolerated, if not encouraged, such victimization. Crouch and Marquart (1989) and Crouch (1986) also discussed the use of violence as a rite of passage for the correctional officer, a way to prove oneself as competent. Today, illegal uses of force are not pervasive, but they do still exist (Pollock, 2004; Prendergast, 2003). Evidence that beatings still occur can be found in court cases. For instance, in *Hudson v. McMillian* (503 U.S. 1 [1992]), the U.S. Supreme Court dealt with a case involving an inmate who had been forced to sit in a chair while two officers hit him in the head and chest area, with a lieutenant looking on. The state argued that because there was no "serious injury," there was no constitutional violation, because cruel and unusual punishment had to involve serious injury. Although some justices agreed with this logic, the majority held that injuries need not be serious to constitute a constitutional violation if the injury was gratuitous.

As with the use of force in law enforcement, policy definitions of *necessary force* are vague. This may mean that the resort to violence is absolutely the last alternative available, or it may mean that force is used when it is the most convenient way to get something accomplished (Morris and Morris, cited in Crouch, 1980: 253).

In 1999, nine Florida guards were indicted for the murder of an inmate. The inmate died from his injuries, which included broken ribs, swollen testicles, and innumerable cuts and bruises. He was on death row for killing a prison guard in a botched escape attempt in 1983. Prosecutors alleged that he was killed because he was planning to go to the media with allegations of widespread abuse in the prison. The accused guards insisted that he killed himself by flinging himself against the concrete wall of his cell or, alternatively, that he was killed by other inmates (Cox, 2000). Three officers were acquitted in the case in February 2002 (*New York Times*, 2002). This case and others illustrate the tendency for jurors to believe officers, especially when the inmate is particularly unsympathetic as this man was.

If the guards did beat the inmate in the Florida case, the officers involved probably viewed the beating as utilitarian in that beatings serve as warnings to all inmates that they will receive similar treatment if they attack COs. Thus, the action protects all officers from inmate aggression to some extent. Officers might also defend the action on retributive grounds because the inmate would probably not be punished for the attack through legal channels. However, these retaliations always represent the most brutal and inhumane aspects of incarceration and damage the integrity of all correctional professionals.

MAINTAINING MORALITY IN PRISON

Correctional officers report that they experience a great deal of stress, and stress-related illnesses such as hypertension are common among officers, as well as social problems such as alcoholism and divorce. Some reports indicate that these problems exist in higher numbers with correctional officers than with police officers. Correctional officers feel criticized and even scorned by many, so it is little wonder that they adapt to their role by sometimes unethical and egoistic patterns of behavior. Yet, it is important to understand the consequences of such a position. Kauffman (1988: 222) talked to officers who reported that they had lost their morality in the prison:

> These officers experienced anguish at the change that was wrought in them by the prison environment: Initially, many attempted to avoid engaging in behavior injurious to inmates.... As their involvement in the prison world grew and their ability to abstain from morally questionable actions within the prison declined, they attempted to neutralize their own feelings of guilt by regarding prisons as separate moral realms with their own distinct set of moral standards or by viewing inmates as individuals outside the protection of moral laws. When such efforts failed, they shut their minds to what others were doing and to what they were doing themselves.

Without a strong moral and ethical code, correctional officers may find themselves drifting into relativistic egoism: Behavior that benefits the individual is considered to be acceptable, despite long-term effects or inconsistencies with their duty and their personal value system. The result is a feeling of disillusionment and anomie, and the side effects can be serious dissatisfaction and depression. To maintain a sense of morality in an inherently coercive environment is no easy task, yet a strong set of individual ethics is probably the best defense against being changed by the negative environment of the prison.

Not surprisingly, COs and inmates tend to agree on a description of a good officer as one who treats all inmates fairly with no favoritism but who does not always follow rules to the letter. Discretion is used judicially; when a good officer makes a decision to bypass rules, all involved tend to agree that it is the right decision. A good officer is not quick to use force, or afraid of force if it becomes necessary. A good officer treats inmates in a professional manner and gives them the respect they deserve as human beings. A good officer treats inmates in the way anyone would like to be treated. If an inmate abuses the officer, that inmate will be punished, but through formal, not informal, channels. In some cases, the officer will go far outside regular duties to aid an inmate who is sincerely in need; however, he or she can detect game playing and cannot be manipulated. These traits—consistency, fairness, and flexibility—are confirmed as valuable by research (Johnson, 2002).

JAIL OFFICERS

Little has been written about jail officers, who may be sheriff deputies who must complete their assignment at the jail before they can be "promoted" to street patrol. Sometimes jail officers are street deputies who are transferred back to the jail as punishment. In other situations, jail officers are not deputies and have a separate title and lower pay scale. In all these situations, the tasks and skills associated with managing jail inmates are discounted or ignored. There is a need for greater recognition of the profession of jail officer; the position should not merely be a dreaded rite-of-passage assignment, a punishment, or a stepping-stone to deputy status, because the body of knowledge required to perform the job well is different from that which a street deputy needs. Recently there has been an attempt to professionalize the image of jail officers, starting again with a code of ethics (discussed in the last chapter).

Arguably, the job of jail officer is even more difficult than that of correctional officer because jail officers must deal with a transitory population rather than a fairly stable one. Inmates include truant children, violent criminals, misdemeanants, mentally ill, and mentally challenged. Offenders may come into jail intoxicated, have undiagnosed epilepsy or other diseases, suffer overdoses, or be suicidal. Visitation is more frequent, and family issues are more problematic in jails than prisons. The constant activity and chaotic environment of a jail often create unique ethical dilemmas.

Many jail inmates, especially those with mental illness, cannot or will not follow rules. Prisoners and guards alike do not tolerate their irrational behavior very well. Jail officers tend to deal with all troublesome behavior as a discipline issue. Is throwing feces a behavioral problem or an indication of mental illness? Sometimes it is both. When the person is placed in isolation (as in segregation), the situation may bring on hallucinations, anxiety attacks, and distorted thinking (Turner, 2007). Mentally ill inmates are more likely to be charged with rule violations, including physical or verbal assaults on staff members, and more likely to be injured, yet jail officers are not trained to be mental health specialists.

Unfortunately, in jails one can find the same type of unethical behavior that one finds with police and correctional officers. Jail officers can be uncaring and insensitive to human needs. Then again, some jail officers may be described as human service officers who seek to enrich their job by taking on more of a counseling role with inmates.

???

DILEMMA: An inmate asks you to mail a letter for him because he's on daylock with no privileges. He tells you that you can open the envelope and look at it in order to make sure it is okay; it is only a birthday card for his daughter. If it doesn't get in the mail today, she will not get it in time. He is a good inmate, never gives you any trouble, and has actually helped you out a few times with more troublesome inmates. You believe that there is nothing wrong with the card, think the guy got a bad deal with the discipline anyway because he was only out of place and that usually gets only a warning, not daylock. You also know that if you do the favor for him, he will continue to be a help to you on the tier. What should you do?

LAW Some acts committed by correctional officers are crimes. Having sex with an inmate is a felony in some states; obviously, smuggling drugs is a crime and an officer who smuggled would probably end up with a prison sentence himself. Taking items out of the prison is against the rules, and could be considered bribery if the officer received money or anything of value for transporting the contraband. In this case, while taking the letter out is obviously against the rules, since the officer is not receiving anything of value from the inmate to do so, there may be no law involved.

POLICY Policies against taking letters out of the institution for inmates exist because such activities bypass censorship and intelligence-gathering procedures. While in this case, it could be that it is only an innocent birthday card, it could also be a code for something else that gang intelligence officers would flag. It could also be a situation where the inmate was under a judicial order to not make contact with his daughter. Another consideration is that the inmate may be testing the officer to see if he may be willing to do more serious acts in the future. If he does take the letter out against the rules, the inmate has gained a little control over him because he can report the officer and get him in trouble. Next time, he may ask the officer to do something a little more serious and, then the next time, something more serious, so that the officer becomes entirely controlled by the inmate. Policies exist for a reason, even if they may not make sense in one particular case.

ETHICS An egoistic rationalization would be that a favor done for the inmate may result in benefit to the officer because the inmate owes him; however, as noted above, it may backfire because the officer will also "owe" the inmate in order for him to keep quiet about the rule violation. A utilitarian rationale would weigh up the costs and benefits to all concerned, but, as usual with utilitarian reasoning, there is no way to know all of the possible ramifications of the act ahead of time, or even what the true nature of the act is (innocent card or something else). An ethical formalist would abide by the duties of the role, which, in this case, is to obey the policies about not carrying out letters. Ethics of care reasoning would attempt to solve the problem so the officer may take the card and talk to his sergeant or lieutenant to see if an exception to the suspension of mail privileges could be granted. This way would meet the needs of the inmate, protect the officer from any negative effect of breaking the rule, and protect the institution since the superior officers would presume to know more about the circumstances of the inmate and whether the card was innocent or not.

Treatment Staff

A number of ethical issues that correctional treatment personnel may be faced with are similar to those experienced in a more general way by all treatment professionals, so available sources dealing with ethics in the helping professions would also be applicable to those who work in the corrections field (see, for instance, Corey, Corey, and Callanan, 1988; Braswell, Miller, and Cabana, 2006). However, the unique issues facing correctional treatment professionals derive from their dual goals of treating the individual and being an employee (or contractor) of the state with a corresponding duty to maintain safety and security (whether in an institution or community setting).

The professional goal of all treatment specialists is to help the client, but sometimes helping the client is at odds with the safety and security of the institution. For instance, prison psychologists may be privy to information or confessions that they feel bound to hold in confidence, even though this may jeopardize the security of the prison. Assessing risk also involves mixed loyalties. Any treatment necessarily involves risk. How much risk one is willing to take depends on whether the public should be protected at all costs, in which case few people would ever be released, or whether one thinks the public must risk possible victimization in order to give offenders a chance to prove themselves.

Another dilemma is the administration of treatment programs. If a program has potential, someone must make decisions on who is accepted into the program. Ideally, one would want similar people in the treatment program and in a control group, but it is hard sometimes to justify withholding the program from some people who may sincerely wish to participate. Laypersons have difficulty understanding the concepts of random sampling and control groups. There sometimes is pressure to admit anyone who sincerely wants a chance to participate, despite what this might do to experimental design.

Another, more basic issue is whether to provide treatment to people who do not want it. One of the elements of codes of ethics for treatment professionals is that one should respect the autonomy of individuals, and this generally is interpreted to mean no forced treatment. In corrections, however, treatment professionals are often involved in what may be considered coerced treatment. In particular, psychiatrists and psychologists have to reconcile their professional ethics in two fields—corrections and psychiatry—and at times this is hard to do. Psychiatrists in corrections, for instance, believe at times that they are being used for social control rather than treatment (Tanay, 1982). Disruptive inmates, although needing treatment, pose security risks to prison officials, so intervention, especially the use of antipsychotic drugs and barbiturates, often takes the form of control rather than treatment, as the Quote and Query box illustrates.

QUOTE & QUERY

As it was, John's illness needed to be controlled, not because he was unhappy with it, but because those around him found it objectionable. What can the psychiatrist do in cases like this?

—SOURCE: DISCUSSING AN INMATE WHO WAS NOT VIOLENT BUT WAS EXTREMELY TALKATIVE, LOUD, AND INCLINED TO DISCUSS HIS DELUSIONS, AS QUOTED IN ARBOLEDA-FLOREZ, 1983: 52.

Should psychiatrists use drugs to quiet an inmate who is not violent?

The practice of using antipsychotic drugs is especially problematic for treatment professionals. Although the Supreme Court determined in *Washington v. Harper* (494 U.S. 210 [1990]) that the administration of such drugs to unwilling inmates is not unconstitutional, the practice must be scrutinized and held to due-process protections in order to uphold professional ethical standards. Some allege that psychotropic drugs are used to control inmates, rather than used for legitimate treatment purposes. There are pervasive stories from ex-inmates of inmates being maintained on high dosages of drugs during their prison stay. Once released, they may go through withdrawal and have no assistance from community mental health facilities because of governmental cutbacks in services (Martin, 1993).

Psychologists in correctional settings have two ethical codes to follow: the American Psychological Association's Ethical Principles of Psychologists and Code of Conduct, and the code for the American Association for Correctional and Forensic Psychologists. Some principles of the Ethical Principles of Psychologists seem especially relevant to corrections. For instance, in Standard 3.11, psychologists who are providing services through other organizations are instructed to provide information beforehand to clients about (1) the nature and objectives of the services, (2) the intended recipients, (3) which of the individuals are clients, (4) the relationship the psychologist will have with each person and the organization, (5) the probable uses of services provided and information obtained, (6) who will have access to the information, and (7) the limits of confidentiality. This obviously affects institutional psychologists, who must make clear to inmates their responsibility to custody concerns.

Other principles also reflect the reality of correctional placements. For instance, in Standard 3.10, psychologists are mandated to obtain informed consent for treatment; however, the ethical code recognizes that some activities without consent may be mandated by law or governmental regulation. The standard does state that when treatment is court-ordered, the individual must be informed of the nature of the anticipated services and any limits of confidentiality.

Haag (2006) describes some ethical dilemmas of prison psychologists in Canada, which apply to the United States as well. In his discussion, he mentions issues of:

- *Confidentiality*: The inability to keep prisoners' secrets
- *Protection of psychological records*: Whether or not psychologists should create "shadow files" that are not subject to view by other staff
- *Informed consent*: Whether consent is possible from a coerced population
- *Assessment*: What the psychologist's role is when assessment is used for correctional purposes

- *Corroboration*: The importance of not accepting everything the inmate says, as the inmate may be engaged in "impression management"
- *Refusal of services*: Whether psychologists should honor an inmate's refusal of psychological services
- *Nondiscrimination*: Treating all inmates equally regardless of group membership or individual characteristics
- *Competence*: The importance of being aware of the boundaries of one's competence
- *Knowledge of legal structure*: Being aware of the rights of the parties involved
- *Accuracy and honesty*: Making clear the limits of predictive validity of psychological assessments
- *Misuses of psychological information*: Refusing to allow file information to be misused to damage an inmate's interests
- *Multiple relationships*: Avoiding dual roles (such as assessment and treatment), which is problematic and creates confusion for the client

Lichtenberg, Lune, and McManimon (2004) use the 1971 movie *A Clockwork Orange* to discuss issues of voluntariness and morality in treatment. The movie is a critical treatment of behavior modification and illustrates the fear that manipulating people's minds through aversive conditioning takes away, in some respects, the essence of what it means to be a free individual. Although the film is a satire and obviously an extremely drawn portrait of the power of aversive conditioning, the central idea—that when people have been conditioned, they are not rationally choosing good because they cannot freely choose evil—is relevant and important to our discussions of moral culpability, as well as the ethics of trying to change individuals who do not want to be changed.

As in the legal profession, confidentiality is an issue for psychologists. The ethical principles (Standard 4.01) address this issue. Psychologists have a primary obligation and take reasonable precautions to protect confidential information obtained through or stored in any medium, recognizing that the extent and limits of confidentiality may be regulated by law or established by institutional rules or professional or scientific relationship. Treatment professionals in corrections must inform their clients, whether they are prison inmates or on some form of supervised release in the community, of the extent or limitations of the confidentiality. It may be that there is no confidentiality at all when the counselor, psychologist, or other professional is employed by the court. In any environment, psychologists and counselors must be aware of the *Tarasoff* rule (*Tarosoff v. Regents of the University of California*, 17 Cal. 3d 425 [1975]), from a case that held a psychologist liable for not warning a victim of imminent harm from one of their clients. Treatment professionals do have legal duties to third persons if they have cause to reasonably believe that one of their clients is going to harm that person.

Treatment and security concerns clash in many instances. The treatment professional must choose between two value systems. To emphasize security concerns puts the psychiatrist or counselor in a role of a custodian with professional training used only to better control inmate behavior. To emphasize treatment concerns puts the professional in an antagonistic role *vis-à-vis* the security staff, and he or she may be in situations where these concerns directly conflict.

Glaser (2003) argues that these concerns are especially relevant to professionals in sex offender treatment programs. He argues that the values and mission of sex offender treatment is at odds with traditional ethical codes. He notes specifically: the protection of society overriding client interest, advocacy for involuntary treatment, breaches of confidentiality, no choices for the client regarding modality or therapist, treatment programs utilizing unqualified staff, and therapy that infringes on dignity and autonomy. The concern is that therapists who work in treatment programs with the foregoing elements are in an ethical vacuum. Traditional ethical codes don't apply, but they have no code that accommodates the unique elements of sex offender treatment.

Faith-based treatment programs, such as the Prison Fellowship Ministries, a Washington, D.C., group headed by former Watergate figure Charles "Chuck" Colson, can be found in many prisons. The program is Christ-centered, biblically rooted, and values-based, and it emphasizes family and community. Inmates volunteer for the program (M. Ward, 1996). The InnerChange Freedom Initiative, introduced in 1997 in the Texas prison system, has shown reduced recidivism. During a two-year study period, only 8 percent of program participants returned to prison, compared to 20 percent for the control group (Criminal Justice Policy Council, 2003). Having such programs in prison raises several issues. Some argue that the programs violate the separation of church and state and are an unconstitutional violation of freedom of religion. If a Christian program offers hope for early release or other advantages, Muslims or those following other religions may participate only if they also compromise their faith. Individuals associated with such programs must take care not to intrude upon the religious freedom of inmates and not use the benefits of the program to coerce religious conformity.

Probably the most prevalent issue for treatment professionals is how to maintain one's commitment to a helping profession while being in an environment that does not value the goals and mission of treatment. This dichotomy of treatment versus punishment creates a myriad of ethical issues for treatment professionals.

Another area that must be considered under the general heading of treatment is that of medical services. There have been a number of scandals concerning the level of medical care in prisons around the country (Associated Press, 2002). Court cases and exposés have documented the sometimes deadly consequences when the medical needs of inmates are ignored or not met. Vaughn and Smith (1999) described several different ways in which medical services—or more specifically, the lack of such services—created pain and suffering for inmates. Sometimes poor medical care is a result of neglect or lack of resources, but sometimes the medical staff simply did not care, believed that prisoners should suffer, and/or did not believe that inmates were sick or injured. The authors suggest that the medical staff itself sometimes furthers penal harm by withholding medical services and justifies such actions by a type of ethical relativism in which inmates aren't seen as deserving the same type of care as others.

One example of where custody and medical care conflict is in the case of shackling pregnant prisoners. In some states, female prisoners would be routinely shackled with leg chains even when they were in labor, and the chains would not be removed unless escort officers were ordered to do so by doctors. Opponents argued that there was no safety or security issue because when a woman was giving birth, she was unlikely to escape or assault someone. In a case before the Eighth Circuit, Shawanna Nelson experienced intense pain when she could not adjust her position during the late states of labor because she was shackled to the hospital bed. She may also have experienced injuries due to the shackling. The Eighth Circuit held that shackling in late stages of labor was cruel and unusual punishment (*Nelson v. Norris*, No. 07-2481, U.S. Court of Appeals, Eighth Circuit, July 18, 2008). Since escort officers have discretion to decide whether or not to keep a female offender under their supervision shackled during labor, this is an ethical issue as well as a legal one.

Others argue that medical professionals in American prisons have begun to fill roles that may be inconsistent with their allegiance to medical ethics—for instance, assisting in body-cavity searches and testing for drugs. These control activities are not a part of the helping profession of medicine and may interfere with the medical professional–client relationship (Kipnis, 2001).

DILEMMA: You are a correctional counselor with an MSW. Although you don't have time to "counsel" inmates since you have a caseload of 1,000 and barely have time to simply process classification paperwork, periodically an inmate is open to talking and you feel that you make a difference when you take the time to talk to them. One inmate, Jerome, has been talking to you sporadically for over a year. You feel some affinity for him since he is young, doesn't seem to have much of a criminal identity, and seems to be trying to make better decisions for himself. He is participating in the prison's Narcotics Anonymous program, is getting his GED, and works in the prison library. One day he's clearly troubled by something so you put your papers aside and invite him to sit down. It turns out that some gang members in his tier are pressuring him for sex. He's being taunted and harassed every day, and they either want him to "put out" or act as a mule for their drug business. Since he's obtained a lower security classification he is able to travel with more freedom in the facility, and they want him to deliver their drugs for them. If caught, he would face many years added to his sentence. If he doesn't do it, he may become a rape victim. You tell him that the only thing to do is report the threat and seek protective custody. He absolutely refuses to do so because it would mean that all the time he has spent in the GED program would be wasted (you can't participate in it in the protective custody wing) and he would lose his job in the prison library. Should you report what he told you?

LAW There is probably no law that requires you report what the inmate has told you nor any law that prevents you from doing so. You clearly have a responsibility to do something, and you have a legal obligation inherent in your job to protect the safety and security of the institution, but what that means in any given case is unclear.

POLICIES The policies of the institution would dictate that you report the threat to your supervisor, who would report it to custodial staff. The inmate may be pulled from general population for his own protection, or, in some facilities, he may be called to the lieutenant's office to have him directly report the threat. He either would deny he said anything and be sent back to the tier, or he would admit the threat and then the perpetrators would be interviewed. They would know who reported them. This ham-handed approach to reported threats sometimes gets victims seriously injured and ensures that few inmates come forward when threatened. Some institutions may have more effective responses to sexual threats, especially those which have instituted such procedures in response to the Prison Rape Elimination Act.

ETHICS This is a situation that has no clear right or wrong response. Ethical formalism would identify the duty to ensure the safety and security of the institution, but that might lead to different choices depending upon how you feel you could accomplish your duty. Utilitarianism also would not support a decision that would create more harm by setting up the inmate as a snitch. It may be that the inmate could be moved to a different tier or even transferred to a different prison without a reason given. This would remove him from the possibility of harm without the "snitch jacket." Still, prisons are small towns and gossip travels fast. If you told anyone, it is possible it would get back to the perpetrators. No ethical system (except perhaps egoism) would support doing nothing, but how exactly to protect the inmate depends on the personnel and procedures in any specific prison.

Probation and Parole Officers

Community corrections has a more positive and helpful image than does institutional corrections. However, even in this subsystem of the criminal justice system, the ideals of justice and care become diluted by bureaucratic mismanagement and personal agendas.

Professionals in community corrections do not have the same power as police or correctional officers to use physical force, but they do have a great deal of nonphysical power over the clients they control. Similarly to other treatment personnel, ethical dilemmas for probation and parole officials often revolve around the dual goals of promoting rehabilitation for the client and safety and security for the community.

Discretion in probation exists at the point of sentencing: probation officers make recommendations to judges concerning sentences. Discretion also exists during supervision in the following ways:

- Probation officers decide when to file violation reports.
- They decide what recommendation to make to the judge during revocation hearings.
- They make numerous decisions along the way regarding the people on their caseload.

Parole board members or their designees make decisions regarding release, and parole officers have the same discretion in managing their caseload that probation officers do. What criteria are used for these decisions? Usually, the risk to the public is the primary factor for decision making on the part of probation and parole officials, but other considerations also intrude. Some of these other considerations are ethical; some might not be, such as race, type of crime, family ties, crowding in institutions, who the victim was, what the judge wants, and publicity concerning the crime.

Probation officers write presentence reports to help judges decide sentences, but research has found that there may be errors in the information presented and that some officers are not as thorough as others in gathering information. This may not make much difference if it is true, as some have found, that probation officers' recommendations and judges' decisions are determined almost completely by the current offense and prior record (Whitehead, 1991).

Probation and parole officers have the authority and power to recommend revocation. This power is also limited because probation and parole officers' recommendations can be ignored by the judge or the parole hearing officer. Yet the implicit power an officer has over the individuals on his or her caseload must be recognized as an important element of the role, not to be taken lightly or misused.

Probation and parole officers have been described as adopting different roles on the job. Recall the typologies offered to describe how police officers approached their role and how their "type" might affect their decisions; the same discussion can be applied to probation and parole officers. They have also been described by their orientation to the job and individual adaptation to organizational goals. For instance, Souryal (1992) summarizes other literature in his description of the following types:

punitive law enforcer
The type of officer who perceives the role as one of enforcer, enforces every rule, and goes "by the book."

- The punitive law enforcer
- The welfare/therapeutic practitioner
- The passive time server
- The combined model

welfare/therapeutic worker The type of officer who perceives the role as one of counselor to the offender and who helps to effect rehabilitative change.

Different ethical issues can be discussed in relation to each of these types. For instance, the **punitive law enforcer** may need to examine his or her use of authority. This officer may have a tendency to use illegal threats and violate the due-process protections that each client deserves. The **welfare/therapeutic worker** may need to think about natural law rights of privacy and autonomy. These officers have a tendency to infringe on clients' privacy because of their mindset that they are helping the client (and, indeed, they

passive time server
The type of officer who does the bare minimum on the job to stay out of trouble.

might be), but the client may prefer less help and more privacy. The **passive time server** may violate professional ethics in not performing duties associated with the role.

All of us may have some tendency to be a time server in our respective professions. It is important to continue to take personal inventories and ask whether we are still putting in a "day's work for a day's pay." As is the case for many of the other criminal justice professionals we have discussed in this book, parole and probation officers often have a great deal of flexibility in their day. They leave the office to make field contacts, and they often trade weekdays for weekend days because weekends are more conducive to home visits. This flexibility is necessary if they are to do the job, but some abuse it and use the freedom to accomplish personal tasks or spend time at home. Some offices have attempted to prevent this behavior by instituting measures such as time clocks and strict controls on movements, but these controls are inconsistent with professionalism and not conducive to the nature of the task.

CASELOAD SUPERVISION

Discretion exists not only at the recommendation-to-release stage but also throughout supervision. Officers do not make the decision to revoke, but they do make the decision to file a violation report and make a recommendation to the judge or the parole hearing examiner to continue with supervision status (perhaps with new conditions), or recommend revocation and a prison sentence. Many do not submit violation reports automatically upon discovery of every offender infraction. In this way, they are like police officers, who practice selective enforcement of the laws. Like police officers, some of their criteria for decision making are ethical and some are not. Also like police officers, the individual officer may face ethical dilemmas when the law doesn't seem to take into account social realities, such as poverty.

The discretion to decide when to write a violation report is a powerful element in the control the officer has over the offender, but this can obviously be a difficult decision to make at times. If the officer excuses serious violations (e.g., possessing a firearm or continuing drug use) and the decision to do so is based on personal favoritism, fear, or bribery, that officer is putting the community at risk and is unethical in making the decision to do so. Situations in which the officer sincerely believes the offender made a mistake, has extraordinary excuses for such misbehavior, and is a good risk still present a danger to the community. Is the decision any more ethical because of the officer's belief in the offender? Would it be more ethical to conduct oneself "by the book" and always submit violation reports when the offender commits any violation, including a purely technical one?

Probation and parole officers are presented with other dilemmas in their supervision of offenders. For instance, the offender often acquires a job without the employer's knowledge of his or her previous criminality. Is it the duty of the officer to inform the employer and thereby imperil the continued employment of the offender? What about offenders' becoming personally involved with others and refusing to tell them about their past history? Does the probation or parole officer have a duty to the unwary party, especially if the offender is on probation or parole for an assaultive offense? If the probation or parole officer knows or suspects that the offender is HIV-positive and the offender begins an intimate relationship with someone, does the officer have a duty to warn the other party? Most states protect the confidentiality of victims of AIDS, and in these cases the officer has a legal duty *not* to disclose.

What is the probation or parole officer's responsibility to the offender's family? If family members are unwilling to help the offender and perhaps fear his or her presence, should the officer find a reason for revocation? Again, these questions revolve around competing loyalties to public and client. The correctional professional must balance these interests in every decision, and the decisions are often not easy to make.

Similar to the police officer, at times the probation officer's role as a family member or friend conflicts with the professional role. Family members and/or friends may expect special treatment or expect that the officer will use his or her powers for unethical purposes, such as using official records to find out information about someone. These are always difficult dilemmas because family and friends may not be sympathetic to the individual's ethical responsibilities to the organization and to society at large. Probation and parole officers are likely to have overlapping circles of acquaintances and family connections with those on their caseloads, especially in small towns. Confidentiality and favoritism are issues that come up frequently.

The officer also has to contend with the issue of gratuities. Again, similar to the police officer, probation or parole officers may be offered special treatment, material goods, or other items of value because of their profession. In most cases, the situation is even more clearly unethical for probation and parole officers because the gift is offered by a client over whom decisions are made, as opposed to police officers who may or may not ever be in a position to make a decision regarding a restaurant or convenience store manager.

Probation departments have clear rules against any "business relationships" with probationers, and this makes sense, but probation officers in small towns ask, "How can I avoid a business relationship with a client when the only coffee shop in town is run by one of my clients? Am I never to go there during the years he is on probation?" In the same manner as police, probation and parole officers may believe that some gifts offered are given in the spirit of gratitude or generosity and not to influence decision making.

Some probation or parole officers encounter ethical conflicts when they seek part-time employment at counseling centers. They may have counseling or drug treatment licenses that allow them to run groups and engage in individual counseling to earn extra income. This becomes an ethical issue when their part-time employment may involve working with correctional clients. Because their role as private counselor would conflict with their role as professional correctional supervisor, ethics boards have ruled that such employment is acceptable only when the counselor does not interact with their own clients.

Because probationers may appear to be similar to the probation or parole officer in socioeconomic status, family background, lifestyle, or personal value systems, they have a greater tendency to feel affinity and friendship for some clients. Some probation officers have been known to have clients babysit for them, to rent a room in their house, or to socialize with them and their families. Obviously, these personal relationships hinder the ability to perform one's official function as a protector of the community and enforcer for the legal system. Personal relationships of any type—romantic, platonic, or financial—are simply not appropriate or ethical for the probation and parole professional.

PAROLE

We have been discussing probation and parole officers simultaneously above, but there are some important distinctions between the two. First, parolees are perceived to be more of a threat to the community, so the supervision role of parole officers is emphasized much more strongly than in probation, where supervision is balanced with a service/counseling emphasis. Further, paroled offenders are usually older and have a longer criminal record, so the relationship between supervisor and client might be different. The problems faced by parolees are quite different from those faced by probationers.

The Bureau of Justice Statistics reports that 581,000 prisoners were released to parole in 2008. There are about 825,000 parolees, comprising about 17 percent of the community corrections population (probationers comprise the vast majority of community corrections clients) (Glaze and Bonczar, 2009: 6). Because of the drastic increase in the number of those incarcerated during the 1980s even though the use of parole decreased, the sheer number of those eligible has been swelling the ranks of parole caseloads. Most have the same low levels of education and vocational skills that they had going into prison and have not had access to many, if any, rehabilitative programs in prison. Further, many of those newly released will be those who *maxed out*—meaning that they completed their entire sentence with no requirements to be supervised (Talbot, 2003; Glaze and Bonczar, 2009).

Many of those released from prison return. According to a Justice Department study, 67 percent of released inmates were charged with at least one serious crime within three years. The study tracked 272,111 released inmates in 15 states (K. Murphy, 2002). Other study findings indicated that the recidivism rate of offenders is worse than 20 years ago, not better, despite the longer sentences imposed. Men were more likely than women to recidivate (68 percent compared to 57 percent); blacks were more likely to recidivate than whites (73 percent compared to 63 percent); and young people (under 18) were more likely to recidivate than older offenders (45 and above) (80 percent compared to 45 percent). Offenders with the highest recidivism rates included car thieves, those convicted of receipt of stolen property, burglars, and those convicted of robbery.

Our incarceration rates—currently some of the highest in the world—have had a tremendously negative impact on communities. Entire neighborhoods are affected when a large percentage of their population is sent away for years at a time. Generational effects are obvious; children of inmates are six times as likely to be delinquent (Mauer, Chesney-Lind, and Clear, 2002). More subtle effects exist as well. The economy and the social fabric of a community are also affected when large numbers of young people are removed. Community corrections professionals have some power in this scenario. They can make release recommendations and affect revocation rates. They can help offenders with reentry problems, or they can blindly enforce every bureaucratic rule.

Recall that under ethical formalism, to be an ethical professional, one must do one's duty. What is the parole officer's duty? Some officers believe that they have met their ethical duty by explaining the rules to a parolee and then catching the person if he or she "messes up." Others see a more expanded role wherein the officer has some duty to help the offender readjust to society. This may involve taking some responsibility for counseling the offender, referring him or her to services, acting as a troubleshooter or mediator in conflict with family or others, and acting as an advocate in obtaining help. In other words, this officer takes a proactive approach to the parolee's success. Is filing a violation report a success (because the offender was caught) or a failure (because the offender did not succeed)? How an officer feels about the answer to that question may indicate how they view their role.

AVOIDING BURNOUT AND DISILLUSIONMENT

Whitehead (1991) discusses probation and parole officers' frustration over incompetents being promoted, low wages, and high caseloads that lead to burnout. Souryal (1992) notes that low pay, a public view that probation and parole are ineffective, and the politicization of parole and probation are factors in professionals' feeling that their role is ambiguous, contradictory, and politically vulnerable. Disillusionment becomes almost inevitable.

Although these issues are present in many organizations, they are especially problematic in a profession that requires a great deal of emotional investment on the part of the practitioner. The problems of burnout and how to address it are beyond the scope of this discussion, but it does bear noting that burnout may lead to unethical acts. When officers "just don't care anymore," they may not take their duties seriously and/or use their discretion in inappropriate ways.

DILEMMA: You are a probation officer with a large caseload. One of your "clients" is a young woman who is a single mother. She is on probation for theft. She shoplifted food and baby formula from a grocery chain that had a no-tolerance policy for shoplifters. She has been doing okay on probation in terms of reporting and staying out of trouble (as far as you know). One day, you make a surprise home visit and find that she is at work, and her new boyfriend is watching her two toddlers. He sets off alarm bells and so you run a criminal background check on him when you return to the office. It turns out that he has been in prison for assault and has many arrests for drugs, assault, and other crimes. There are indications that he belongs to a criminal gang that controls a good portion of the drug market in your town and has also been implicated in armed robberies. You call her in and talk to her about the man, and she tells you that he is paying her rent and she can't get along without him. You insist that she avoid contact because one of her conditions is no association with known criminals. More importantly, you don't trust him with her young children and know that it is only a matter of time before she is drawn into criminal acts with him. She tells you that you might as well revoke her probation right now because she can't pay her rent without his help. What would you do?

LAW At this point, she has not broken any laws that you know of and there is no law that requires you to do anything. The enabling probation law in your state probably includes the provision that an offender can be revoked for technical violations—these are rules that are not new crimes. In her case, she is violating the general rule of no-association. You could write a violation report on her and a judge may revoke her probation and send her to prison, although, typically, mere technical violations do not warrant revocation.

POLICY There are formal policies and informal policies in every probation office. The formal policy is that an officer should write a violation report when he or she becomes aware of a violation. The informal policy varies from office to office in how serious and/or how many "technicals" deserve a violation report. Some offices are stricter than others. An officer may go to his or her supervisor with this issue, but that only transfers the dilemma from the officer to the supervisor; there is still an ethical decision to be made when law and policy do not absolutely dictate a response.

ETHICS Ethical formalism would apply the categorical imperative, and in this case it seems that universalism might dictate a different response from simply filing a violation report, but what response is best is still a problem. Utilitarianism also would probably not support revocation since the harm to her and her children outweigh the existing benefit (and you can't predict with certainty what might happen in the future, so that is hard to weigh against the certain harm of revocation). Ethics of care would attempt to satisfy all needs, so if her need was financial assistance, the best solution would be to try and help her find another way to pay her rent, such as subsidized housing, a halfway house that allows children, or some other solution. This would meet the need she expressed, so if she still chooses the man over her freedom and children, at least the officer can be satisfied that it was her decision and not economic necessity. Both utilitarianism and ethical formalism would also be consistent with this approach.

CONCLUSION

In this chapter, we touched on some of the ethical issues that correctional personnel face in institutional corrections and in the community. Discretion exists at each stage of the criminal justice system, and each of the correctional professionals we have introduced in these chapters has discretion in different ways. The difficult decisions for correctional officers arise from the personal relationships that develop with inmates, the trust that is sometimes betrayed, the favors that seem harmless, and the coercive environment that makes violence normal and caring abnormal. Correctional treatment personnel have their own problems in resolving conflicts between loyalty toward clients and toward the system. Community correctional professionals also must balance public safety with client interests. They often, especially in small towns, have difficulty in their supervisor role when it overlaps with other community relationships.

To be in a helping profession in a system geared for punishment is a difficult challenge for anyone, and the temptation to retreat into bureaucratic compliance or, worse, egoistic relativism is always present. Arguably, the criminal justice system operates as well as it does only because of the caring, committed, honest people who choose it as a career.

CHAPTER REVIEW

1. Describe the role conflict of correctional officers.

Prisons experienced changing goals (from custody to rehabilitation) in the 1970s and 1980s, and this created role conflict and ambiguity for the correctional officer. Also in the 1970s, federal courts recognized an expanding number of prisoner rights, including the rights to exercise religious beliefs, obtain medical care, and enjoy some due process. The disruption in the old way of doing things created real chaos, and the 1970s and 1980s brought danger, loss of control, and stress for officers.

2. List and describe some ethical issues for correctional officers.

Officers' uniforms bestow authority, not unbridled domination, and each officer learns how to utilize this authority. Most do so in ethical ways, although some officers abuse their position. Relationships with inmates present other ethical issues. Officers tend to support other officers against inmates, even when the officer is wrong. However, reciprocity and personal relationships with inmates also can be an issue and potential problem for officers; officers may like an inmate too much and compromise security, or utilize their position to coerce or harass an inmate. Correctional officers report that they sometimes experience a great deal of stress from their role. They are generally disliked by inmates and scorned by society. Some lose their morality in the negative environment of a prison.

3. Describe the different challenges that face jail officers as compared to correctional officers in prisons.

Jail officers have become more professional in recent years, but the position is still sometimes used as a dreaded rite-of-passage assignment, a punishment, or a stepping-stone to deputy status. The jail officer deals with a transient population that includes juveniles, the mentally ill or intoxicated, and those with other health problems. There is more interaction with relatives of offenders because the jail is in the community; this also means the jail officers may know or be neighbors of offenders or relatives of offenders. Contraband and other issues are a major problem in jails.

4. Explain the role conflict of treatment professionals and provide examples.

Correctional treatment professionals have dual goals of treating the individual and protecting the safety and security of the institution and/or the community. Sometimes this creates conflict—for instance, prison psychologists may be privy to information or confessions that they feel bound to hold in confidence, even though this may jeopardize the security of the prison. Treatment professionals must assess risk to the community in every decision to allocate more freedoms for clients. Allocating treatment resources is also an issue, specifically how to determine who should have access to treatment programs.

5. Describe the ethical issues of probation and parole officers.

Ethical issues arise in the probation or parole officers' ability to file violation reports or (for probation officers) recommend sentencing in that there are ethical and unethical criteria for such decisions. There is also discretion in managing the caseload, including issues of gratuities, relationships with clients, and when family or friends expect special favors or treatment.

KEY TERMS

correctional officer
human service officer
passive time server

punitive law enforcer
reciprocity
Tucker telephone

"tune-ups"
welfare/therapeutic worker

STUDY QUESTIONS

1. How do COs have discretion similar to police officers and court personnel?
2. Describe the role ambiguity that COs faced in the 1970s and 1980s. What are the role types of officers identified by R. Johnson?
3. What are the ethical issues identified by Haar for treatment professionals in corrections?
4. Explain the two areas where probation and parole officers have discretion.
5. What are the role types of probation and parole officers? Describe them.

WRITING/DISCUSSION EXERCISES

1. Write an essay on (or discuss) the range of legal rights that you believe prisoners should have. Look at international treaties on human rights, the ACA standards, and other sources before you write your essay.
2. Write an essay on (or discuss) how you would put together a policy manual for treatment professionals who work in a prison or jail. Evaluate the professional codes and identify problematic controversies, and then create a policy that can accommodate a conflict (such as confidentiality).
3. Write an essay on (or discuss) whether probation and parole officers should have the power to carry weapons (in some states they are required to, in others they are prohibited from doing so).

ETHICAL DILEMMAS

Situation 1

You are a prison guard supervising a tier. One of the inmates comes to you and asks a favor. He wants you to check to see why he hasn't been called down to the admin building to see a counselor, because he put in a slip to see his counselor that morning. You know that it is likely he won't be called out today, and you could tell him that, or you could make a call, or you could do neither. Which would you do? Why?

Situation 2

As a new CO, you soon realize that a great deal of corruption and graft are taking place in the prison. Guards routinely bring in contraband for inmates in return for money, food bought for the inmates' mess hall finds its way into the trunks of staff cars, and money is being siphoned from inmate accounts. You are not sure how far up the corruption goes. Would you keep your mouth shut? Would you go to your supervisors? What if, in exposing the corruption, you implicate yourself? What if you implicate a friend?

Situation 3

You are a prison psychologist, and during the course of your counseling session with one drug offender, he confesses that he has been using drugs. Obviously, this is a serious violation of prison rules. Should you report him? What if he tells you of an impending escape plan?

Situation 4

You are a parole officer whose caseload includes a single mother with three hyperactive, attention-deficit-disordered young children. She receives no support from her ex-husband. Her own mother wants nothing to do with her or the children, believing that "God is punishing her." The parolee works as a topless dancer but hates it. She continues dancing because it pays the bills so well. You know that she smokes marijuana on a fairly regular basis in an effort to deal with stress. Obviously, this is a violation of probation. However, if you file a violation report on her, she will go back to prison. You know she is doing the best she can with her kids, she is heavily involved with their school, and they are strongly bonded to her. You worry about what will happen to the kids. What would you do?

Situation 5

You are a prison counselor and have a good relationship with the other counselors. You all go out drinking after work sometimes, and in general you like and respect everyone. Recently you've noticed that something seems to be going on with one of the other counselors. Stella is usually outgoing and cheerful, but lately she seems distracted and upset. You see her in the parking lot one evening and ask her what is wrong. She confides to you that she is in love with an inmate. She knows it is wrong, but she says that they had an instant chemistry and that he is like no man she has ever known. She has been slipping him love notes, and he has also been writing her. You tell her that she has to stop it or else quit her job. She tearfully tells you that she can't let him go, she needs her job, and you've got to keep quiet or you'll get her fired. What would you do?

13

Jim West/Alamy

Correctional Professionals: Misconduct and Responses

Chapter Objectives

1. Describe types of misconduct by correctional officers, including the typologies of misconduct by Souryal and McCarthy.
2. Describe types of misconduct by community corrections professionals.
3. Explain the Zimbardo experiment and what it might imply for correctional professionals.
4. Provide other explanations for misconduct.
5. Present some suggestions to decrease misconduct by correctional professionals.

David Armstrong was feared by inmates in the Bureau of Prison's supermax prison in Florence, Colorado. He was a part of a group of correctional officers (COs) known as the Cowboys, who worked the Special Housing Unit (SHU), the segregation unit of the prison. Allegedly, Armstrong was one of the ringleaders of the group who, after several correctional officers had been injured in 1995, got the green light from their captain to "teach some inmates a lesson" by vicious beatings. At first the group selected defiant, violent inmates for "treatments." The COs would punch, kick, and choke the inmates, or drop them, handcuffed, headfirst on the concrete floor. They would then fabricate a story about why they had to use force, even to the point of inflicting injuries on themselves to justify the use of force. From 1995 through 1997, the group conducted these systematic beatings, eventually targeting not only violent inmates but gradually including mouthy and troublesome inmates as well. The Cowboys also threatened other officers, at one point promising that any officer who snitched would be taken out to the parking lot and beaten.

The group stuck together. Six of the seven were ex-military; several had gone through the Bureau of Prisons' training academy together and arrived at United States Penitentiary (USP) Florence together. The key phrases were "Lie 'til you die" and "What happens in SHU stays in SHU." A Catholic priest and other staff members heard complaints from inmates and tried to get the warden to listen, but most believed that the inmates were lying because, after all, inmates always lied. The Cowboys eventually broke up. Some, like Armstrong, were promoted and transferred. After he left Colorado and was working in a federal prison in Pennsylvania, he evidently had trouble breaking old habits and was disciplined repeatedly for his treatment of inmates. Then, in 1998, he was visited by an FBI agent who wanted to know what had happened in Colorado.

The ensuing FBI and Department of Justice investigation took five years and resulted in a grand jury indictment that listed more than 55 acts of beatings, intimidations, and lies. A nine-week trial with more than 60 witnesses ended with two weeks of jury deliberations. Armstrong was the government's star witness, and on the stand he described beating after beating, explaining that there were so many he couldn't remember them all. Why did he violate the "lie 'til you die" command? It may have been the plea bargain the government offered him in return for his testimony, or it may have been that he had terminal cancer and sought some type of redemption for what he had done before his death. On the witness stand, he could hardly talk and required an oxygen tank to breathe.

Armstrong might have been remorseful, or he might have been trying to make the best deal for himself, but the seven accused COs denied everything. Despite Armstrong's and other guards' testimony, the jury acquitted four officers of all charges and convicted three others of only some of the charges (Prendergast, 2003). The story of the Cowboys is not typical of correctional professionals today, but it does illustrate the difficulties of preventing, monitoring and investigating, and responding to correctional officer misconduct. The prison is a closed world, and outsiders may never know what happens inside the walls.

The vast majority of news items and academic attention in the area of ethics and misconduct has been directed to misconduct by correctional officers in prisons and jails, with very little attention given to probation and parole officers and even less to treatment professionals in corrections. Maybe the prevalence of misconduct is much lower with these other professional groups. That seems unlikely, but until more research is conducted, it is difficult to say.

Misconduct and Corruption

McCarthy (1991, 1995) and Souryal (1999a) discuss the major types of corruption by correctional officers and other officials in institutional corrections. Categories include theft, trafficking, embezzlement, and misuse of authority. Under misuse of authority, McCarthy (1991) details the following:

- Accepting gratuities for special consideration for legitimate purposes
- Accepting gratuities for protection of illicit activities
- Mistreatment/harassment or extortion of inmates
- Mismanagement (e.g., prison industries)
- Miscellaneous abuses

Souryal (1999a), in another typology, describes the types of corruption as falling into the following categories:

- Arbitrary use of power (treating workers or inmates preferentially or in a biased fashion)
- Oppression and failure to demonstrate compassion/caring
- Abusing authority for personal gain (extortion, smuggling, theft)

In a more recent typology, Souryal (2009: 28–29) describes corruption sociologically as the use of arbitrary power, legally as the use of oppression or extralegal methods, and ethically as the failure of officers to demonstrate compassion or keep a promise. He describes acts of misfeasance (illegitimate acts done for personal gain), acts of malfeasance (acts that violate authority), and acts of nonfeasance (acts of omission such as ignoring rule violations).

Bomse (2001) identifies different types of prisoner abuse as follows:

- *Malicious or purposeful abuse.* This is the type of abuse inflicted by individual officers intentionally, including excessive use of force; rape and sexual harassment; theft and destruction of personal property; false disciplinary charges; intentional denial of medical care; failure to protect; racial abuse and harassment; and excessive and humiliating strip searches.

- *Negligent abuse.* This type of abuse is also inflicted by individual officers, but not intentionally, and includes negligent denial of medical care; failure to protect; lack of responsiveness; and negligent loss of property or mail.

- *Systemic or budgetary abuse.* This type of abuse is system-wide and refers to policies, including overcrowding; inadequate medical care (systematic budget cutting); failure to protect; elimination of visits or other programs; co-payments and surcharges; and use of isolation units.

In the 1990s, investigations in several states uncovered abuses, including sexual abuse of inmates, brutality, bribery at the highest levels, and drug smuggling (Carroll, 1998; Houston, 1999). In Pennsylvania, an associate superintendent testified before an investigative committee of the state legislature of confirmed cases where officers had beaten a fellow officer; were caught smuggling contraband to inmates, including drugs; assisted an inmate in beating another inmate; raped an inmate; became sexually involved with an inmate; came to work under the influence of cocaine; embezzled inmates' funds; gambled with inmates; and conducted a "mock lynching" of a black inmate (cited in Hassine, 1996: 149–152).

Also in the 1990s, prison guards in Corcoran, California, were accused of setting up gladiator-type fights between inmates and encouraging or allowing prisoner rapes. One former guard testified that a "loudmouth" prisoner was placed with a prison rapist known as the "Booty Bandit" (Arax, 1999: A3). Other guards were accused of unlawful use of force by shooting an inmate during one of the gladiator fights. Eventually, several guards received federal indictments and were tried for the killing, as well as the other acts of oppression. Some argue that the officer union "tainted" the jury pool by running television ads before the jury selection, showing officers as tough, brave, and underappreciated. The television ads, with the tagline of "Corcoran officers: They walk the toughest beat in the state," aired only in the Fresno area, where the trial was held. The accused guards were acquitted even though former guards and other experts supported the inmates' allegations (Lewis, 1999).

California's Department of Corrections has been described as corrupt "from the top down" because investigations of wrongdoing seemed to be thwarted by powerful union leaders. There have been allegations that members of the independent Office of Inspector General were fired at the behest of the correctional officer union. During legislative hearings about a Folsom riot that was said by some to have originated through guards conspiring with one of the gangs, one legislator received death threats, and witnesses were put under protective custody (Thompson, 2004). The riot and its cover-up evidently led directly to the suicide of an officer who attempted to thwart the riot but was stopped by a supervisor. He left a message: "My job killed me" (Warren, 2004a). Several wardens and assistant wardens resigned, took early retirement, or were fired over the

WALKING THE WALK

D. J. Vodicka looks like someone you wouldn't want to anger. At six feet, six inches tall and 300 pounds, with a shaved head and an inscrutable look honed by a hitch in the military and 16 years as a correctional officer, he is definitely not the picture of a liberal do-gooder. Yet Vodicka gave up his career, and even some friends, and risked his safety when he broke rank with other correctional officers and exposed "the Green Wall" for their abuse of inmates. The phrase was adopted by a group of officers at the Salinas Valley State Prison in California after a prison disturbance on Thanksgiving Day in 1998; more than a dozen officers were injured in the melee. The prison suffered from the effects of understaffing and too many inexperienced officers combined with some of the worst offenders in the California prison system. The desire to teach the inmates a lesson and keep control of a dangerously unstable institution allegedly led to officers using illegal force, planting evidence on inmates, and utilizing a pattern of intimidation and threats upon inmates. Even other officers were threatened in order to keep their activities under the radar of prison officials.

When he was asked by his superior to write a report on the activities of the Green Wall, Vodicka followed orders, as he had always done in his military career and his years with the California Department of Corrections. He did not feign ignorance, as others did, but wrote a report that detailed the green armbands, lapel pins, and ink pens used by members, the incident where one member received an engraved green-handled knife upon his promotion, the graffiti scrawled on walls and desks proclaiming the group, and the evidence that indicated that Green Wall members were well known

in the institution and even tacitly supported by the warden. Instead of dealing with the situation through proper disciplinary channels, the lieutenant who asked for the report was summarily transferred and the report was leaked to other correctional officers, leading to a situation where Vodicka was transferred for his own safety. The news that he was a "rat" traveled with him to the new prison. He encountered hostile remarks and ostracism there until the day he ran to respond to an emergency alarm, turned around and found that the officers behind him had stopped behind a gate, leaving him alone in a yard full of brawling, violent inmates. Their excuse was that they were waiting for a sergeant. Realizing his vulnerability, Vodicka left the prison that day, never to return.

In 2004, he testified before a California state senate committee about the Green Wall and how prison administrators did little or nothing to stop the illegal activities, nor did they punish those who were retaliating against him for speaking out. The hearings led to the resignation of some officials and a broad effort by the Department of Corrections to "clean house" at Salinas Valley. Eventually Vodicka won a whistleblower lawsuit against the Department of Corrections, but he continues to live in an undisclosed location because his safety is still compromised by his decision to stand up against the Green Wall. He continues to be perceived by many correctional officers in the system as disloyal. Others argue that Vodicka displays the right kind of loyalty—loyalty to the law, to the truth, and to the citizens of the state who employed him, rather than the criminals in green uniforms who forgot what it meant to be public servants.

Sources: Vodicka, 2009; Arax, 2004.

Folsom Prison riot scandal, and dozens of correctional officers were fired for wrongdoing (Warren, 2004b).

Donald Vodicka, a 15-year correctional officer veteran in California, testified in a criminal case that the code of silence was pervasive, especially at the Corcoran and Pelican Bay prisons, and that a whistleblower would not be protected by the Department of Corrections against fellow guards. He described the activities of a group of officers at Salinas Valley State Prison, called "the Green Wall." His story is presented in the Walking the Walk box.

Advocates, journalists, and inmates have reported systematic abuses in another California prison in Susanville. Inmates have reportedly been strip searched and made to stand for hours in the snow, and guards allegedly tried to provoke attacks between inmates, spread feces on cell doors, and used excessive force. Inmates who filed grievances against

in the NEWS

INTEGRITY FOR SALE

Farhad "Fred" Monem was a purchasing officer for the state prison system in Oregon. Investigators allege that he worked with Doug Levene, a food broker who specialized in buying and selling food that had to be sold quickly because it was close to an expiration date or had minor imperfections. Monem allegedly began ordering from Levene in 1999 and saved Levene's company, which took a turn for the better after Monem began buying huge quantities of food from him. What also happened was that Monem asked for (according to Levene) and received a share of profits; the first payment was $1,500, and then regular payments began that were typically $4,000 or $5,000 each. Eventually the payments became $10,000 to $20,000, and the men took vacations together with their wives. But when Monem began making similar deals with other food vendors, Levene's profits fell off. Then a former employee reported the scheme to the FBI. Monem left Oregon and returned to his native Iran before he could be questioned, after allegedly pocketing more than $600,000 from Levene. Levene faces a federal prison sentence for bribery. Monem will probably not return to the United States to share with Levene this time.

SOURCE: Associated Press, 2009b.

officers were allegedly retaliated against and threatened. Reports indicate that the Department of Correction's own staff members sent to the prison in 2007 documented some abuses, but nothing was done with their report. These staff researchers, after visiting the facility, concluded that guards believed they could carry out extreme forms of punishment against inmates because it was a behavioral modification unit for inmates who had been identified as disruptive in other prisons. They urged state officials to begin a formal investigation, but instead, the lead author of the report, a 15-year employee, alleges he was retaliated against and has now filed a whistleblower lawsuit against the Department of Corrections. In response to a series of newspaper stories about the prison, the Department of Corrections indicated they would begin an internal investigation (Piller, 2010a, 2010b, 2010c).

Texas has also had its share of prison scandals. In the 1990s, James A. "Andy" Collins, an ex-director of the Department of Corrections, was investigated for his business association with a Canadian company that made VitaPro, a vegetable-based protein substance that evidently tasted bad and created digestive problems for some people. It was discovered that Collins had locked the state into a multiyear contract with the company and had received two payments of $10,000 from the company director. Collins resigned as director in 1996 and immediately became a $1,000-a-day consultant to VitaPro. In 2001, he and the director of that company were convicted by a federal jury on charges of bribery, conspiracy, and money laundering. Collins appealed, and in 2008 a federal judge overturned the guilty verdict. Despite the judge's decision to ignore the jury verdict, the scandal resulted in a new ethics code and a "housecleaning" of the top ranks (M. Ward, 2008). A more recent food scandal is described in the In the News box.

In recent years, the issue of prison rape has gained greater attention. The Prison Rape Elimination Act (PREA), passed by Congress in 2003, mandated that every state keep a record of prison rapes and allocated money to study the problem and develop solutions. No longer is prison rape seen as a joke; it is defined as an unacceptable risk of prison life, and the responsibility of prison staff and administrators. Ignoring the problem or telling prisoners to fight or submit is not an appropriate or ethical response. In the latest report offered by the Bureau of Justice Statistics, 4.5 percent of inmates reported some type of sexual victimization. In about 2.1 percent of these cases, the perpetrator was an inmate; in 2.9 percent, staff members were to blame. Also, the level of victimization varied widely from prison to prison; in one prison, for instance, fully 7.5 percent of inmates reported sexual assault with physical force used by staff assaulters (Beck and Harrison, 2007).

One of the results of this attention to prison rape has also been more attention to staff–inmate sexual relationships. Interestingly, with female inmates, we have come full circle in this issue. Until the mid-1800s, female prisoners were housed together with men in jails, with predictable results. Women were raped and sexually exploited, and they sold themselves for food and other goods. Various scandals and exposés of prostitution rings led to women's reform groups pressuring legislatures to build completely separate institutions for women in the late 1800s and early 1900s. These women's prisons were staffed by female matrons. This pattern continued until the mid-1970s, when female officers challenged the hiring patterns of state prison systems that barred them from working in institutions for men. They were successful in achieving the right to work in men's prisons, but the corollary was that men could also work in institutions for women.

In the early 1980s, fairly low percentages of male officers could be found in prisons for women, and the male officers were restricted to public places. Today, male officers are assigned to all posts inside prisons for women, including sleeping and shower areas. In some states, more than half of the officers in women's prisons are men. Thus, male officers again are in positions of power over women and, again, abuses are occurring (Amnesty International, 1999).

There are instances in women's prisons where male COs have committed rapes of female prisoners by force, and many more instances where they threatened and intimidated women to engage in sex (Henriques, 2001; Craig, 2003). In the most egregious case, one female inmate was raped in a federal prison when officials sent women to the

in the **NEWS**

ABSOLUTE POWER CORRUPTS ABSOLUTELY

Two administrators at a juvenile detention facility have been accused of sexually abusing the boys housed there. Witnesses reported that the men took the boys out of their dorms in the evenings, and various staff members saw them with the youths in darkened offices. Complaints from staff members went to the central state office, and one law enforcement investigation in 2005 concluded that there was abuse going on, but the internal investigator sent from the state youth corrections agency wrote a report stating that the charges were groundless. The county prosecutor had the same information and did nothing. Nothing was done until a volunteer went to the media and a newspaper series in 2007 exposed the charges. In the ensuing scandal, the director of the agency and the director of the facility resigned, several individuals were fired, the governor put a special monitor in charge of the agency, and a complete reorganization of the juvenile corrections agency was threatened by the legislature. The men still have not been tried, although one trial is set to begin in early 2011.

SOURCES: Associated Press, 2007d; Moreno, 2007; M. Ward, 2007a, 2007b.

segregation unit of a prison for men. Officers took money from male inmates in return for unlocking the women's cell doors so the male inmates could have sex (willing or unwilling) with them. When one female inmate fought back and reported her attempted rape, she was attacked again, and raped and viciously beaten by several men (Siegal, 2001). Periodically, news stories report that female inmates have been coerced to have sex with prison or jail guards. For instance, in Oklahoma, a sheriff was indicted on 35 counts of second-degree rape, forcible oral sodomy, and bribery by a public official for allegedly coercing and bribing female inmates to have sex with him from 2005 through 2007 (Juozapavicius, 2008). A case in Texas is described in the In the News box.

Some officers use their authority to search inmates as a license to grope; others unnecessarily view women in the showers and while they are using the toilet. Although only a few correctional officers would engage in or support these acts, more allow it to happen by setting the tone of the prison. Staying silent while other officers sexualize prisoners by ribald comments, allowing officers to demean and belittle inmates, and participating in conversations where women are referred to by their body parts allows the true predators to victimize. A prison culture that disparages and demeans inmates gives the green light to brutal individuals who wear a uniform. This situation is similar to the earlier discussion about rogue police officers who used the message that they could do anything in the name of controlling crime as encouragement to commit crimes against drug dealers.

It should be noted that female officers also engage in sexual relationships with inmates. Academic studies of one state indicate that the problem of officers having sexual relationships with inmates is about equally divided between female officers and male officers (Marquart, Barnhill, and Balshaw-Biddle, 2001; Dial and Worley, 2008). There are also homosexual relationships that occur between officers and inmates. The coercive sexual assaults that occur are obviously illegal, but even consensual relationships between inmates and officers are unethical and against prison rules. In some states, even consensual sex is a felony because inmates are presumed not able to give full consent, being in a dependent relationship to the officer. In any case, it is a violation of the officer (or employee) professional code and compromises prison security. Some states have considered going back to same-sex supervision because of the problem, but that is unrealistic because of EEOC and also because there are not enough female officers now to staff prisons for women in some states.

Other misconduct that is reported in the news includes felony bribery charges and money laundering (Associated Press, 2000: B3). Officers are often tempted by quite a bit of money offered to bring items into the prison (drugs, cash, cell phones) or out of the prison (notes or letters). Some officers are tempted and coerced; that is, they are offered money but also threatened by inmates who tell the officers they know where they live or where their kids go to school. In 2006, a review of disciplinary reports of the prison system in Texas by a newspaper found a wide range of misconduct: a prison official pleaded guilty to sexually harassing employees, a personnel chief of the prison school system was arrested for lewd conduct, a correctional officer was accused of raping a male convict, and another officer was accused of smuggling marijuana (Ward, 2006a).

Cameras in prisons recorded a range of unethical behaviors, including a female guard embracing an inmate, a sergeant hitting a guard in the face (to cover an unlawful use of force by the guard), and a guard leading an inmate into a closet to have sex (Ward, 2006a). In 2006, there were, in total, 761 arrests of 36,000 Texas correctional employees; these numbers compare to about 297 of 26,700 correctional employees in Florida. Not all of these arrests involved abuse or corruption related to the job; most (484) were for DWI (Ward, 2006b). Explanations for why arrest numbers are so high include the low salaries (Texas was 47th in correctional officers' salaries), a reduction in the number of Office of Inspector

General investigators (cut in half as a budget-reduction move), high turnover, and low standards for hiring (the state will accept applicants convicted of Class A or Class B misdemeanors as long as they were five years ago) (Ward, 2006b).

In a news investigation in 2009, it was found that from 2003 to 2008, 263 employees of the Texas prison system were reprimanded for possessing prohibited items, and most (75 percent) were put on a probationary status by the department of corrections. Only 35 lost their job, and only one was formally prosecuted. It should also be noted that the contraband was most often smokeless tobacco or cigarettes, not drugs, although cell phones and alcohol were also frequent examples of contraband. A cell phone scandal erupted shortly before this investigation when a death row inmate called and threatened a legislator. A shakedown resulted in the confiscation of more than 200 cell phones. Prison officials cite low pay and high turnover for guard misconduct and indicate that these issues are part of the reason why many officers who are caught are allowed to keep their job (Associated Press, 2009a).

A Florida news article reported that prison guards were more than twice as likely as police officers to violate state standards of conduct (Kleindienst, 1999). A review of recent news from Florida revealed that a female mental health counselor in the Lake Correctional Institution was arrested for possession of crack cocaine in September 2009. She had been investigated for drug smuggling into the prison after a tip from an inmate (Colarossi, 2009). A female corrections officer was sentenced to a year in jail for bringing in cash to a private prison in Florida run by the GEO Group. In a bizarre story, she was held hostage by a prisoner who alleged she kept $4,000 she had received from an inmate's relative to smuggle into the prison, which is how authorities found out about the scheme (Spencer-Wendel, 2010). In a case at the Palm Beach County jail, five corrections officers and one substance abuse counselor were arrested for smuggling and bribery. The affidavits to support the arrest from investigators report that the correctional employees took between $400 and $700 for every item smuggled into the prison, such as a cell phone or MP3 player. Allegedly one inmate informant told investigators that 85 percent of the guards were "crooked." Sheriff's investigators admitted that an inmate could get anything he wanted in the facility. The local investigation paralleled an FBI probe called "Operation Blind Justice," which resulted in indictments against 16 people on cocaine smuggling charges (LaForgia, 2010).

A federal prison in Florida also has had its share of corruption scandals. In 2008, nine employees were charged with smuggling. In October 2009, a female correctional officer at the federal prison in Coleman, Florida, was sentenced to life in prison for seeking revenge against an inmate who grabbed her arm. She placed him in a cell with a known violent inmate who beat him to death (Comas, 2010).

A prison scandal erupted in Maryland in 2009–2010 when widespread smuggling was exposed. Officers allegedly smuggled in cell phones and other contraband for prison gang members from the Black Guerrilla Family and had improper relationships with the inmates. Federal investigators received information about the prison activities from a gang member who was arrested outside the prison. Their investigation led to indictments of conspiracy, drugs, and weapons violations against 24 prisoners, guards, and other prison employees. The smuggling occurred in the Metropolitan Transition Center in Baltimore, the Maryland Correctional Institution in Jessup, and other state prisons. Federal investigators report that officers smuggled in vodka and champagne for prisoners, and, in one situation, couldn't get lobster as ordered to by the inmate so substituted salmon with shrimp and crab imperial instead, and the inmate complained. Fourteen cell phones were also confiscated; the phones were evidently used to manage criminal activities on the outside. In one recorded phone call, an inmate was heard complaining to a corrupt guard that there were too many guards smuggling in contraband, making it more competitive to sell drugs in prison. The guard agreed, saying that it used to be only one officer on a shift who might smuggle, but now it was "like seven, eight people." The director of corrections said the corruption was not widespread (Cauvin, 2009). In another related story, a female corrections officer's apartment was searched and authorities found a constitution for the Black Guerrilla Family, gang codes, and other paperwork related to the gang's leaders. Also found were inmate ID cards, debit cards, and other correspondence connected with known criminals and inmates. The officer has been accused of smuggling heroin and cell phones into the prison's laundry system and spying on federal agents as they met with gang members. In one incident, this officer allowed prison gang members to assault another inmate and did not report the assault until they were finished, but the response of prison officials was only to suspend her for five days. She was also disciplined for fraternizing with inmates on her Facebook page. Informants reported that her smuggling and association with inmates was known for years, but authorities allowed her to continue to work in the prison (Fenton, 2010).

Sometimes misconduct is more benign. A picture published in the *New York Post* in December 2009 drew chuckles but also dismay because it showed a female correctional officer sound asleep with her mouth open while an inmate posed next to her. The picture was taken by a fellow officer and sent to the paper. The female officer was transferred, and the officer who took the picture was disciplined. Even the union condemned the officer's actions in taking the picture (Associated Press, 2009c). One wonders if the officer, who had over a dozen years more service than the sleeping officer, took the picture in frustration over conduct that endangers other officers and should never have happened.

When the abuse in Iraq's Abu Ghraib prison was exposed, many made comparisons between the behaviors of military prison guards and those of correctional officers in U.S. prisons. The comparisons were hard to ignore because several of the worst abusers were correctional officers in civilian life, and the person who helped set up the Abu Ghraib prison was Lane McCotter, an ex-head of the Texas, New Mexico, and Utah prison systems (Ward, 2004).

Allegations of misconduct in prisons and jails in the United States include the following abuses, similar to what took place in Abu Ghraib (Butterfield, 2004):

- Male inmates being forced to wear pink underwear as punishment (Arizona)
- Inmates being stripped as punishment (Pennsylvania)
- Inmates being made to wear black hoods (Virginia)
- Using dogs to attack inmates (Texas)

A more recent issue concerns the tens of thousands of illegal aliens housed in immigration facilities run by private corporations. A Freedom of Information Act request filed by the ACLU obtained a list of deaths in such facilities that uncovered troubling issues where inmates did not receive medical care and the subsequent deaths were suppressed or attempts were made to avoid news exposure. The investigation showed that officials seemed to be more concerned with keeping the deaths out of the news and avoiding scandal than trying to improve medical conditions. The ACLU also learned that more than 10 percent of deaths in immigration facilities were omitted from official lists, and alleges that the approach where Immigration and Customs Enforcement (ICE) investigates itself over allegations of abuse and medical neglect is ineffective (Bernstein, 2010).

It cannot be denied that the very environment of an incarcerative facility sometimes brings out the worst in people. However, similar to the discussions concerning law enforcement and the courts, the fact that these incidents occur should not be taken as an indictment against the thousands of other correctional professionals who do their job competently and with integrity and professionalism. We focus on misconduct and how to prevent it partly to make their job better as well, because the type of activities described above lower morale and endanger everyone.

TREATMENT PROFESSIONALS

Most news items and academic articles describe misconduct in prisons in terms of correctional officers, but there are instances where counselors and other treatment professionals also engage in misconduct. Sometimes they smuggle in contraband, sometimes they coerce or engage in consensual sex with inmates. In the last chapter, we discussed the ethical dilemmas of treatment professionals when they have sincere conflicts about their competing goals of treatment and protection to society, but there are other acts taken by treatment personnel that are purely egoistic.

Probably the most common issue for treatment and medical personnel is not providing the services that inmates are legally entitled to. As discussed in the last chapter, medical personnel sometimes adopt the "penal harm" philosophy of corrections and deprive inmates of services because of a belief that they don't deserve treatment. It is very difficult to maintain a helping-profession orientation in a correctional environment. Inmates are often unpleasant individuals and sometimes violent as well. Similarly to law enforcement's attitude toward certain segments of society, personnel in corrections sometimes develop an attitude that all inmates are liars, crooks, and addicts and don't deserve what the rest of us do. The trouble with this line of reasoning is that once some are perceived as outside the bounds of professional duties, it is easier to ignore duties and respect for all.

CORRUPTION IN THE COMMUNITY

While most news items describe misconduct in prisons, there are also examples of ethical misconduct and criminal acts by community corrections professionals. Peter Maas's (1983) book *Marie* details a scheme in Tennessee that involved selling paroles to convicts. In the early 1990s, ex-parole board members in Texas were found to have sold their services as "parole consultants" to inmates and inmates' families in order to help them obtain a favorable release decision. The situation was brought to light when a serial killer was arrested for yet another murder while out on parole. When how he obtained parole was investigated, it was discovered that one of these "parole consultants" had been hired by the inmate. Whether that had anything to do with a favorable parole decision will never be known, and the practice was not against any state law at the time. In the wake of the investigation, rules were created that restricted such practices to attorneys (Ward, 2006c).

Today, parole decisions in Texas are criticized for being secretive and arbitrary. In one court case concerning the revocation of parole, a federal judge, exasperated with the state attorney for the parole board, blurted out that the attorney was misstating the law and then had to declare a mistrial because he had prejudiced the jury. Critics argue that the parole board operates in secrecy and makes parole decisions too quickly, on average of one every seven minutes. There are also troubling reports that the case summaries used for such decisions are often wrong, with some crimes inaccurately attributed to the wrong inmate or, in other cases, not enough detail is provided to indicate the true seriousness of the crime. Inmates and their lawyers do not have access to these case summaries, so they cannot correct any errors. Even legislators are frustrated, as the parole board releases so few prisoners that their low parole approval rates have added to the prison overcrowding problem. Inmates have, at present, no legal right to parole or due-process rights in the parole release decision, but some argue that they should. Until then, it is an issue of professionalism and ethics as to how parole board members make release decisions (Ward, 2009).

In other states, there have been scandals regarding probation departments. In Massachusetts, probation officials have been accused of giving jobs to relatives and friends of state legislators. Also, a legislator was accused of exerting pressure on the agency to promote an officer who gave campaign contributions to the legislator, and that same probation officer wrote a letter of recommendation on probation office stationery for a convicted racketeer (Levenson, 2010). In Georgia, three employees of a county-run department were arrested when an investigation uncovered a scheme whereby probationers would pay money to get out of performing community service sentences (Johnson, 2009). In Florida, a state probation officer was sentenced in federal court to four months' imprisonment and three years of supervised release for accepting bribes from a probationer in exchange for allowing the probationer to avoid mandatory drug testing and other restrictions (United States Department of Justice news release, 2005).

To run a safe and secure prison is consistent with running an ethical prison where officers and staff uphold and respect the rights of prisoners. The same reasoning can be extended to community corrections as well. All ethical systems support the need to respect basic rights and use appropriate and legal force and punishments to control offender populations. Under ethical formalism, violating rights and using illegal force against prisoners violate one's duty and are contrary to the categorical imperative. Under utilitarianism, it seems obvious that if one acts in illegal ways toward inmates or probation/parole clients, there is very little moral authority to influence them to become law-abiding. Research indicates that the system of punishment and retribution as implemented in our prison system does not engender remorse or guilt among prisoners, who feel that they themselves are the victims of an unethical and illegal system (Presser, 2003).

Many correctional professionals will complete their careers and retire without having heard about or been involved in any corrupt practices. However, the examples above illustrate that corruption can take place anywhere an ethical culture does not exist or where correctional workers are not monitored and encouraged to do the right thing.

Explanations for Misconduct

The Zimbardo experiment of the 1970s was one of the experiments that spurred the creation of human-subjects review boards in colleges and universities. In this experiment, college men were arbitrarily assigned to be guards or inmates, and a mock prison was set up in the basement of a building on the grounds of Stanford University. The changes in both groups were so profound that the experiment was canceled after six days. Zimbardo (1982) noted that about one-third of the guards became brutal and authoritarian, and prisoners became manipulative and exhibited signs of emotional distress and mental breakdown. If college men who knew the experiment was artificial succumbed to the temptation to inflict their will on the powerless, is it possible that the environment itself causes people to act in ways that they would not otherwise?

In all cases of abuse in prison, the reasons seem to be a failure of leadership and lack of discipline, training, and supervision (Ward, 2004). Certainly that seemed to be the case in Abu Ghraib. It can also be noted that the worst cases of abuse in civilian prisons occur when prison leaders ignore violations on the part of staff and do not clearly convey that the mission is to run a safe and secure prison without the corrupting presence of extra-legal force.

As in law enforcement, a few correctional officers will be "crooks" first and officers second. Many others probably slide into corruption because of a lack of organizational support for ethical behavior. Also as in law enforcement, officers who are stressed and burned out may be the most vulnerable to ethical relativism and bad decisions. Organizations experience corruption partly because they do not support and nurture ethical workers.

A prison is an interesting place in that individuals work together over long periods of time and, often, they live in small towns where acquaintances and family members also work at the prison. Male and female officers work together long hours and in close proximity; sometimes they engage in sexual relationships; sometimes they marry; sometimes they divorce; sometimes they have affairs with other staff members (or even inmates) while they are married. In some prison towns, everyone seems to be related to someone and/or has some type of relationship. While people's personal lives are their own, sometimes the personal lives of correctional officers, like police officers, influence their professional ethics. For instance, if a disciplinary sergeant is married to a CO who has written a ticket on an inmate, can that sergeant truly be objective when determining punishment? What happens when an inmate accuses an officer of sexual harassment and the grievance officer is the wife of the officer? Sometimes male and female COs allow a sexually charged atmosphere to develop where sexual joking and innuendos are rampant, and the atmosphere encourages officers to engage in the same type of behavior with inmates—obviously an inappropriate and unprofessional interaction.

Unions have been seen by researchers as a force resistant to rehabilitation, concerned only with individual benefits for members rather than the mission or goal of corrections. Unions provide legal assistance to officers when they become the subject of legal attacks and may support officers who, many would argue, have no business working in corrections. Because of their advocacy role toward officers, unions sometimes place individual officers' needs over what might be best for the system or society. This is similar to police unions that defend police officers who are guilty of using excessive force. Union representatives would argue that they only ensure that the accused receive their rightful due process after being accused.

There has been very little research done on correctional ethics, with a few exceptions noted below. Stohr et al. (2000) developed a survey instrument to measure the ethics of correctional workers. In their study, they could find few significant correlates between values or attitudes and behavior. For instance, only experience was correlated with use of force, with older and more experienced officers reporting less support for the use of force. They also found that the type of institution affected officers' attitudes. Mesloh, Wolf, and Henych (2003) conducted a study of one southern jail to measure the extent of corruption and correlates with ethical misconduct. They found that age was positively correlated with support for misconduct, and race and sex had no effect. Support and medical staff scored higher on the ethics scale than did custody staff. The authors attributed the findings to the existence of a deviant subculture among correctional officers. As mentioned earlier, correctional managers attribute misconduct to low pay and poor screening during hiring.

Responses to Corruption?

Correctional management has not developed in the way that law enforcement management has; there are fewer texts on correctional management, and those that can be found rarely mention ethics for supervisors and administrators (Wright, 2001). In Chapter 7, management efforts to respond to law enforcement misconduct and corruption were described. Surprisingly, parallel sources on correctional management efforts to respond to misconduct are fairly sparse.

The "trickle down" theory of ethical management is that officers will treat inmates the way they perceive they are being treated by management—with fairness, compassion, and respect, or with less than fairness, compassion, and respect. It becomes easier to justify unethical actions if one feels victimized. Obviously, if employees are expected to be responsible, loyal, and treat each other and inmates with respect, administrators should practice these same behaviors (Houston, 1999; Souryal, 1999a; Wright, 2001). Furthermore, staff members who are coerced by management to do unethical or illegal actions are more likely to behave in unethical and illegal ways by their own initiative.

Correctional managers can and should generate a strong anti-corruption policy (obviously, managers should not be engaging in corrupt practices themselves). Such a policy would include (McCarthy, 1991):

- Proactive measures such as mechanisms to investigate and detect wrongdoing
- Reduced opportunities for corruption
- Screening of employees using state-of-the-art psychological tools
- Improved working conditions
- Providing good role models in the form of supervisors and administrators who follow the appropriate code of ethics.

Souryal (2009: 33) discusses the "civility" of a correctional institution as being influenced by the level of education required for hire, the amount of in-service training officers receive, the policies regarding employees who act in unethical ways, and the presence of a professional association or union that can effectively monitor the agency's practices. He also discusses the importance of integrated thinking (use of reasoning and wisdom) and moral agility (distinguishing between shades of moral choice). To improve the ethical climate of an agency, he advocates upgrading the quality of personnel, establishing quality-based supervisory techniques, strengthening fiscal controls, and emphasizing true ethical training.

Wright (2001) offers seven principles as a guide for how administrators and supervisors should treat employees: safety, fair treatment, due process, freedom of expression, privacy, participation in decision making, and information. In regard to fair treatment, not penalizing staff members who do corrupt acts is not treating honest officers fairly. As to privacy, staff members have a right to a private life, but not when the use of drugs, alcohol, or inappropriate sexual partners interferes with their job performance.

Ironically, the scandal at Abu Ghraib led to a national commission to examine U.S. prison conditions, chaired by a former U.S. attorney general and a chief judge of the Third Circuit. The Commission on Safety and Abuse in America's Prisons spent several years holding hearings and obtaining testimony concerning the state of prisons in this country, and in 2006 issued its summary and recommendations. (The entire report or an executive summary can be accessed by going to www.prisoncommission.org/report.asp.) One of the findings was that this nation's prisons suffer from a culture of violence and a lack of positive treatment goals. The commission also found that better safety inside prisons and jails depends on changing institutional culture. This has to be done by enhancing the corrections profession at all levels, and promoting a culture of mutual respect, grounded in respectful behavior between staff and inmates.

Burrell (2000) directs attention to probation and proposes that in order to prevent stress and burnout, probation (and parole) organizations should provide clear direction, manage proactively, establish priorities if there are high workloads, ensure stability and constancy, be consistent in expectations, manage with fairness, enforce accountability, delegate authority, provide proper resources, maintain communication, and allow participative decision making.

Barrier and colleagues (1999) discussed an ethics training program with correctional officers, in which part of the training involved having the officers identify important elements of an ethics code. Many of the elements had to do with the practices of management rather than officers:

- Treating all staff fairly and impartially
- Promoting based on true merit
- Showing no prejudice
- Leading by example
- Developing a clear mission statement
- Creating a positive code of ethics (a list of dos, rather than don'ts)
- Creating a culture that promotes performance, not seniority
- Soliciting staff input on new policies
- Being respectful
- Getting the word out that upper management cares about ethics

As discussed earlier, correctional administrators in the 1970s and 1980s had to deal with court decisions that were decided in favor of prisoners. Implementation of court-ordered changes indicated that correctional administrators sometimes barely complied with the letter of a court ruling, much less the spirit of the ruling. The career path of an administrator, with its investment of time and energy and the mandate to be a "company man," often creates an immersion in bureaucratic thinking to the point that an individual loses sight of ethical issues. For instance, protecting the department or the director from scandal or litigation becomes more important than analyzing the behavior that created the potential for scandal in the first place. If decision making becomes influenced solely by short-term gains or by avoiding scandal, decisions may be unsupported by any ethical system.

Administrators are responsible for what happens in their facility, and training, supervision, and careful attention to assignments can avoid many problems. Obviously, administrators and managers should take pains to avoid illegal or unethical behavior themselves. Administrators should act as role models and never engage in behavior that may be misconstrued as sexual coercion or be perceived by their employees as offensive. Supervisors have a higher duty than coworkers to set a tone for an office free from sexual innuendo that may lead to a description of the workplace as a hostile work environment. Supervisors have an ethical and legal duty to stop sexual humor, inappropriate touching, and inappropriate behavior before there is a complaint.

It should be noted that in cases where there is a pattern of corruption, whether it be brutality or types of graft, it is hard to believe that administrators were not aware of what was going on. Prisons are smaller than small towns, and like a small town, they do not have secrets unless one is willfully ignorant of them. Top administrators often have an outward orientation because their role is to communicate with legislators, the central office, and the community; however, a good administrator does not ignore his or her own backyard. Management by walking around (MBWA) and having a good sense of what is happening in the institution have always been the marks of a good administrator and are also the best defense against having the institution ending up on the front page of the newspaper.

In community corrections, there seems to be the same management tendency to hide or ignore wrongdoing on the part of individual officers. This may be a misguided utilitarianism in managers who are attempting to protect the organization from public scandal, or it may be simply self-interested egoism from managers who fear that the blame will be directed at them. For whatever reason, there seems to be a tendency to ignore officers who are obviously unable or unwilling to do the job. Some officers even point out that those who are arrested for DWI or other crimes continue to work as probation and parole officers. If this is true, it's not surprising that some probation and parole officers seem to have little moral authority over the clients they supervise.

RESTORATIVE JUSTICE

Another way to respond to misconduct and corruption in corrections is to shift the orientation away from punishment and retribution. One out of every 31 Americans (7 million) are in prison, jail, or on some form of correctional supervision. The high incarceration rate in the United States has led to the prison-industrial complex, which has provided jobs and profits to legions of companies and people. The field of corrections is big business, but it might be time to consider new approaches. Senator Jim Webb from Virginia sponsored the National Criminal Justice Commission Act, which would examine every stage of the criminal justice system, including the use of prisons. As support for a major reexamination of the way this nation punishes its miscreants, he notes that the United States holds 5 percent of the world's population but 25 percent of its prisoners. The largest single portion of prison growth over the last 30 years has been in the area of drugs, and Webb reports that 47 percent of all drug arrests are for marijuana and the majority of prison sentences are for nonviolent offenses (Webb, 2009). Although the House version of the bill passed in July 2010, as of late summer 2010, it had not reached the Senate floor. Regardless of what happens with this act, it does appear that the time is ripe for rethinking our punishment system.

A major shift in the ideology of punishment may be spurred by the economic burden that the penal harm era has generated, but there is also a moral element in that many advocates consider that the pendulum has swung too far toward severe prison terms, especially

---

POLICY ISSUES | Restorative Justice

Restorative justice programs are used primarily with juvenile and nonviolent offenders. These programs have been financially supported by the federal government, and they have been widely hailed as a progressive advancement in the justice system. However, critics argue that they take away the victim's right to seek retribution, that they create a net-widening effect, and that there are problems when the formal due process of the justice system is bypassed.

Law

Typically, programs that use different sentences or different sentencing structures must have enabling legislation before they can be put into practice. In some cases, judges promote such programs and use their discretion by allowing some offenders to be diverted from the system into the programs.

Policy

Policies must be established regarding who is eligible for such programs and who will make the decision as to whether an offender is referred or not. Ordinarily, the offender and the victim must give consent for the case to be shifted to an alternative sentencing procedure. Policies must also be established for when an offender "fails" and what happens when he or she does not complete the program successfully. Typically, the case is then sent back for official processing. These policies do not carry the force of law, and they are often changed after the program has been in operation for some period of time. Inevitably, cases arise in which the policies do not seem to result in a fair outcome; then informal policies are often applied that do not carry the force of law or the sanction of formally approved policies.

Ethics

The decision makers (judge, probation officer, restorative justice staff, attorneys) must apply the law, policy, and their own individual ethics in the decision as to who goes into the program, what the offender is required to do, and what sanctions are given, keeping in mind the needs of the victim, the system, and the offender.

for drug offenders. There are alternative approaches that are not based on a punishment ideology. The restorative justice movement was mentioned briefly in Chapter 3 and also in Chapter 11. It is an approach that seeks to provide reparation rather than retribution (Reichel, 1997; Bazemore and Maloney, 1994). See the Policy Box for a discussion of the law, policy, and ethics of restorative justice.

The historical origins of and analogies to restorative justice can be found throughout recorded history. Early laws demanded victim compensation, and reparation has a much longer history than does penal servitude. Many advocates (see Umbreit, 1994; Umbreit and Carey, 1995; van Ness and Heetderks Strong, 1997; Perry, 2002) now believe that restorative justice appropriately places the emphasis back onto the victims and can be life-affirming and positive for the offender as well. The key is to find a method of restoration that is meaningful and somehow related to the offense instead of merely punitive labor—such as the infamous rock pile, which is devoid of worth to the victim, the offender, or society. The Quote and Query box is Braithwaite's summary of restorative justice.

QUOTE & QUERY

Key values of restorative justice are healing rather than hurting, respectful dialogue, making amends, caring and participatory community, taking responsibility, remorse, apology, and forgiveness.

—SOURCE: BRAITHWAITE, 2000: 300.

Do you think that restorative justice principles will ever be widely adopted by the criminal justice system? Why or why not?

peacemaking corrections An approach to corrections that depends on care and wholesight, or looking at what needs to be done with both the heart and the head.

Peacemaking corrections also offers an approach of care and of *wholesight*, or looking at what needs to be done with both the heart and the head (Braswell and Gold, 2002). Both restorative justice and peacemaking corrections are consistent with the ethics of care and might be considered "feminine" models of justice because of the emphasis on needs rather than retribution. It is said that a retributive, punitive orientation results in an offender's perception of unfairness (through denial of victim, denial of injury, or a belief that a more serious victimization was visited upon the offender). A different model may reduce those feelings and force the offender to squarely face his or her own responsibility. Arguably, a restorative justice program directs attention to the injuries of the victim and does not involve stigma, banishment, or exclusion, for the offender would not create the opportunity to generate rationalizations and excuses for the offender's behavior.

Programs under the rubric of restorative justice include sentencing circles, family group counseling, victim–offender mediation, community reparation boards, and victim education programs (Umbreit, Coates, and Vos, 2002; Monahan et al., 2004). Karp (1998) provides an interesting perspective on why restorative justice programs have received positive responses. The public may not believe that probation or other forms of alternative sanctions have the same moral condemnation that prison does; therefore, these punishments are seen as cheapening or lessening the moral blame of the offender. However, shaming penalties inherent in such programs as sentencing circles emphasize the individual's responsibility to the victim and society. Such programs instill a strong dose of morality and redemption, and the public seems to respond to that.

Forgiveness, like mercy, is an interesting concept. When a gunman killed five young girls in an Amish schoolhouse in 2006 before killing himself, the nation was appalled and grieved along with the Amish community. It was a truly horrific event, made all the more so by the gentle nature of the religious community, where violence was such a rarity. In a truly unusual and unique turn of events, the parents of the murdered children and the community immediately forgave the murderer and his family. In the Amish religion and tradition, forgiveness is said to be much more important than anger or revenge. This forgiveness was as newsworthy as the killings themselves and gave rise to many discussions about the nature of forgiveness and how it fits into religion and faith (Draybill, 2006).

Dzur and Wertheimer (2002) discuss how restorative justice can further forgiveness, but they ask the question: Is forgiveness a social good? They argue against the idea that what is good for the individual victim is also good for everyone else. They point out that forgiving offenders may be good for the individual victim but may not be good for the "class of victims" who have yet to be victimized. They argue that utilitarianism might support punishment even if the individual victim forgives the offender because the greater good will accrue to society from deterrence. Of course, there is no empirical approach that could determine (or has yet determined) whether punishment deters more offenders than forgiveness.

Restorative justice programs are looked upon with favor by some victims' rights groups because of the idea of restoration and restitution for victims. However, the approach is oriented to meeting the needs of both victims and offenders, and in some cases it may be that the offender is needier. Would a victim reject such an approach? Should the victim be able to veto this approach and demand traditional punishment? Is it possible for a victim to be too vindictive? Other victims' rights groups tend to be cautious about restorative justice programs in general because of the focus on offenders. The anger that victims feel toward offenders and the system that ignores their needs leaves little room for forgiveness. Most groups advocate harsher punishments, not restorative justice; they discuss "rights" rather than "needs" and thus draw their moral legitimacy from retribution rather than the ethics of care. However, other sources also argue that forgiveness and restorative justice are just as beneficial to the victim as the offender (Morris, 2000).

Restorative justice programs may lead to a greater sense of mission for correctional professionals and, therefore, decrease burnout and misconduct. However, there are ethical issues with such programs. First, because such interventions are seen as benign, they have the potential to create net widening, further enlarging the scope of corrections over the citizenry. There are also questions of due process and whether restorative justice meets the traditional goals of crime prevention (Dzur and Wertheimer, 2002). Another issue is the potential privacy issues of the offender and other members who are involved. One of the strengths of restorative justice interventions is the inclusion of a number of parties, including the offender's family, coworkers, and friends, as well as the victim and the victim's support group. But what if some individuals important to the process choose not to participate? If schools even have trouble getting some parents to involve themselves in their children's progress, it is entirely possible that a juvenile who is otherwise qualified for a program would not be able to participate because of unwillingness of family members. Even when the process is seen as a positive intervention, whenever state actors are involved, there is a potential for coercion, and some people react strongly to that idea.

Restorative justice programs would not be appropriate for all offenders; there will always be a need for incarceration facilities for the violent, recidivistic offenders who need to be incapacitated. It does, however, offer an approach that seems to be more positive for offenders and personnel alike. It provides a more optimistic vision and mission and, one assumes, creates better relationships between correctional professionals and offenders. Thus, it might be an approach where there is less burnout, cynicism, and unethical behavior. Even those mentioned above who must be incarcerated in prison deserve professional treatment without extra-legal punishments or coercion.

CONCLUSION

In this chapter, we examined various forms of misconduct by correctional professionals. Research has indicated that the very nature of a prison may encourage an abuse of power. It was also noted that much of the misconduct may occur because of burnout and a loss of a sense of mission by professionals, as well as poor management. Responses to ethical misconduct and corruption in corrections lag behind the efforts previously reported in law enforcement. Suggestions include ethics training and improving management. Restorative justice principles may help to improve the sense of mission and commitment to ethical behavior by correctional workers.

CHAPTER REVIEW

1. Describe types of misconduct by correctional officers, including the typology of misconduct by Souryal and McCarthy.

McCarthy's categories of misconduct include theft, trafficking, embezzlement, and misuse of authority. Under misuse of authority, he includes the following: gratuities (as bribes for legitimate or illegitimate activities), mistreatment/harassment or extortion, mismanagement, and miscellaneous abuses. Souryal's categories of corruption are arbitrary use of power, oppression and failure to demonstrate compassion/caring, and abusing authority for personal gain.

2. Describe types of misconduct by community corrections professionals.

There are not as many news stories of corruption, but there have been instances of inappropriate influences and errors in parole release decisions, nepotism in awarding jobs in probation departments, and accepting bribes from offenders to get out of community service obligations or drug testing.

3. Explain the Zimbardo experiment and what it might imply for correctional professionals.

The Zimbardo experiment of the 1970s put college men into an artificial prison as guards or inmates. The changes in both groups were so profound that the experiment was canceled after six days. About one-third of the guards became brutal and authoritarian, and prisoners became manipulative and exhibited signs of emotional distress and mental breakdown. It is widely used as evidence that placing people in absolute power over others is a corrupting situation.

4. Provide other explanations for misconduct.

Some reasons for misconduct seem to be a failure of leadership and lack of discipline, training, and supervision. Management practices that do not provide the direction, mission, oversight, and training needed contribute to misconduct. While there are a few correctional officers who would be deviant regardless of the environment, others probably slide into corruption because of a lack of organizational support for ethical behavior. As in law enforcement, officers who are stressed and burned out may be the most vulnerable to ethical relativism and bad decisions.

5. Present some suggestions to decrease misconduct by correctional professionals.

McCarthy's suggestions are largely directed to management practices, including proactive measures such as mechanisms to investigate and detect wrongdoing, reduced opportunities for corruption, screening of employees using state-of-the-art psychological tools, improved working conditions, and providing good role models in the form of supervisors and administrators. Ethics training is also suggested. Finally, restorative justice is offered as a different approach to respond to criminal offenders that is more positive and less conducive to the creation of a subculture that supports mistreatment.

KEY TERM

peacemaking corrections

STUDY QUESTIONS

1. Describe Bomse's categories of misconduct.
2. Describe some of the reported instances of misconduct and corruption in prisons.
3. What is PREA, and what has been discovered about the prevalence of prison rape?
4. What management practices were identified as contributing to an ethical workplace?
5. What are the principles of restorative justice? Contrast these with traditional models of justice.

WRITING/DISCUSSION EXERCISES

1. Write an essay on (or discuss) how you would implement an anti-corruption strategy in a prison known for brutality and other forms of corruption.
2. Write an essay on (or discuss) forgiveness. Would you want to meet with the murderer of a loved one? What would you want to ask him or her? Would you be able to forgive?
3. Write an essay on (or discuss) restorative justice. Find examples in your state. Do you agree or disagree with the philosophy of restorative justice? Why?

ETHICAL DILEMMAS

Situation 1

You are a probation officer and have a specialized sex-offender caseload. The judge disagrees with a recommendation for a prison sentence and places an offender on probation. This man was convicted of molesting his four-year-old niece. One of the conditions of his probation is that he notify you whenever he is around children. He becomes engaged to and moves in with a woman who has three children under the age of 12. You believe that the man is not repentant and that there is a good chance he will molest these children. Although the woman knows his criminal history, she does not seem to care and even allows him to babysit the young girls. The judge has indicated that he will not entertain new conditions or a revocation unless there is evidence of a crime, but you understand from the offender's counselor that the offender continues to be sexually aroused by children. What can you do? What should you do?

Situation 2

You are a probation officer with a DWI probationer who has not been reporting for any of the court-sanctioned programs, and a motion to revoke (MTR) was supposed to be filed. However, a high-ranking administrator in your office tells you not to file the MTR or take any other negative actions because the probationer is a personal friend and, anyway, he isn't a "serious criminal." What would you do?

Situation 3

You are the director of a restorative justice program in your community. It is set up for juvenile offenders and involves circle sentencing, in which the offender meets with family members, school officials, and the victim and the victim's relatives and friends. The circle comes up with what should be done, and often there is no punishment per se. Rather, the juvenile is connected with programs that can help him or her get back in school, get a job, or receive vocational training. In the case you are reviewing, you suspect that there are real questions as to whether or not the juvenile actually committed the burglary he is accused of. There is no evidence to link the juvenile with the crime, and he and his court-appointed attorney have claimed innocence. They then changed their plea and agreed to the restorative justice program, perhaps because if it is completed successfully, the juvenile will have no criminal record. Should you care whether the juvenile is innocent or not, given that the program is restorative, not punitive?

Situation 4

You are a prison warden, and a new CO comes to you and says she has been sexually harassed by the captain. You know that the captain has been with the prison for 20 years and has not had any negative reports in his record. On the one hand, you like him and think he is an excellent captain. On the other hand, this CO seems earnest and believable and is quite upset, so you believe something must have happened. What is the ethical course of action? What is the legal course of action?

Situation 5

You are a prison counselor in a co-ed prison and have some real concerns about your co-worker's treatment of offenders. You hear him screaming obscenities at them in his office, and one time you saw him pat a female prisoner on the rear end and say, "Be sweet to me and I'll get you out of here." No one else seems to notice that anything is wrong. Could you have misinterpreted the exchange with the prisoner? Might it have been simply bad taste rather than sexual harassment? Should you do anything?

14

Daniel Jones/Alamy

Making Ethical Choices

Chapter Objectives

1. Identify the basic themes of the book.
2. Describe the basic elements of the "just war" debate and the "just means" discussion.
3. Describe the responses to 9/11.
4. Compare the crime control approach to the human rights model of policing.
5. Present a method to resolve ethical dilemmas.

In this book, we have explored ethical issues in each of the subsystems of the criminal justice system. We have discovered certain themes that run through each of the subsystems:

- The presence of authority, power, force, and discretion
- Informal practices and value systems among criminal justice actors that are contrary to formal codes of ethics
- The importance of ethical leadership
- The tension between deontological ethical systems and teleological or "means–end" ethical analysis

In this final chapter, we will reiterate some of these themes and conclude with some last thoughts regarding how to behave in an ethical manner.

Just Wars and Just Means

On September 11, 2001, the United States was changed forever. The terrorist attack on the World Trade Center was the single most devastating terrorist attack in this country and, indeed, the world, with more than 3,000 deaths and the complete destruction of two buildings that stood as icons of Western capitalism. Although we had experienced earlier incidents—the 1993 bombing of the World Trade Center, the Oklahoma City bombing, and numerous attacks on U.S. targets worldwide—nothing prepared the country for the severity of the attack. The event traumatized a city, affected the American psyche, led to

U.S. military engagement on foreign soil in two countries, and spurred the dramatic restructuring of federal law enforcement. The long-term effects of this event are still unfolding, but we have already seen pervasive changes in law enforcement at both the federal and the local levels, and the country is still roiling with controversy over the responses taken in the "war on terror," from rendition to torture to wiretapping. This controversy is related to criminal justice ethics because the war on terror affects not only the military and federal agencies; every law enforcement and justice agency in the land may have occasion to be involved. Targets of terrorist activity include not only buildings and bridges in big cities, but also dams, power plants, schools, government buildings, and farms in the most remote areas. Further, it is possible that the enemy combatants who have been incarcerated in Guantanamo will be tried in civilian courts here in the United States. Finally, the issues that arose in Abu Ghraib led to a national investigation of our own prison system, and the reverberations of the scrutiny continue to be felt. The responses to the attack on the World Trade Center also illustrate the prevalence of means–end thinking: the idea that what would usually be wrong can be justified by a good end. We see this argument over and over again in the war on terror and, surprisingly, some people argue as if it is a new argument, or even as if terrorism is a new threat. It isn't.

terrorism The "deliberate, negligent, or reckless use of force against noncombatants, by state or non-state actors for ideological ends and in the absence of a substantively just legal process."

Terrorism has been defined as the "deliberate, negligent, or reckless use of force against noncombatants, by state or non-state actors for ideological ends and in the absence of a substantively just legal process" (Rodin, 2004: 755). Terrorism has led to questions about what is appropriate or ethical in law enforcement investigative techniques, individual rights vis-à-vis the government, and what is legal and ethical in the detention and treatment of prisoners. However, it is important to note that these are not new questions. From the very earliest philosophers, there has been a struggle to define and agree upon when it is right to wage war and what means are acceptable to secure victory. There is no coincidence in why we use the term *war* to denote a national challenge; by identifying the problem as such, the language of war creates the justification for methods. We can see the same argument played out whether we are talking about the war on terror, the war on drugs, the war on illegal immigrants, or the war against crime.

The traditional justification for war comes from natural law, and the second comes from positivist law. Classical "just war" theorists such as Hugo Grotius (1583–1645) have held that natural law gives sovereigns the right to use force to uphold the good of the community, when unjust injuries are inflicted on others, and to protect the state (Grotius, 2005; Bellamy, 2004). States are justified to engage in war when any of these events exist; otherwise, the war is unjust and immoral. However, natural law has been criticized as a justification for war because of the likelihood that leaders use moral arguments to justify wars that are, in reality, initiated for other means (e.g., when a sovereign engages in war against another state under the justification of self-defense or protecting a victim group, when the true motivation is a land grab or some other reason).

positivist law
Human-made law.

The second, more recent, justification for war comes from **positivist law,** which is man-made law. Increasingly, this is used as the only legitimate justification for war; legal incursions into the sovereignty of other nations are justified only under the auspices of international law as provided through the United Nations and other multilateral treaties and organizations. The problem with positivist law as the basis for justifying war is that no single authoritative legal body in international relations sits above all sovereigns, and international legal bodies do not include all countries and cover all circumstances (Bellamy, 2004).

Because of the lack of complete coverage of positivist law, natural law justifications for war still exist. The natural law justifications to engage in a war not sanctioned by the United Nations or other world body is either the defense of one's own state or humanitarian reasons—for instance, to protect the other country's citizens from serious victimization such as genocide. Intrusions in internal conflicts within states have been undertaken by other states when gross humanitarian violations have occurred (such as the ethnic cleansing campaigns in Rwanda and Bosnia). Again, however, the problem in using these natural law or moral imperative justifications to engage in war is that they can be abused and misused; therefore, limits on the moral justifications for war have been proposed, including the following (Bellamy, 2004):

- The violations must be knowable to all.
- The violations must be widespread and systematic.
- The force used must save more lives than it injures.

These are not too different from other justifications that have been offered by other writers. For instance, Crank and Gregor (2005: 230) and Hicks (2004) have offered the following justifications for war:

- The threat must be grave, lasting, and certain.
- There are no other means to avert the threat.
- There must be a good probability of success.
- The means must not create a greater evil than the threat responded to.

These justifications seem to be consistent with a utilitarian system of ethics and are not inconsistent with ethical formalism because of the principle of forfeiture, which states that someone who impinges on others' rights forfeits his or her rights to the same degree.

Even if a war can be justified by natural or positivist law, there is the second question as to what means are acceptable in fighting the war. Under utilitarianism, in determining "just means," the extent of the harm is weighed against the end or injury averted, just as when one asks if the war itself is justified. Ethical formalism does not look at the consequences of an action to justify it; however, the **principle of double effect** states that if one undertakes an action that is a good, but that also results in a negative end, as long as the negative end was not the intent of the actor, the good action and the good end can be considered a good. For instance, if one bombs a military target and innocents are harmed during the bombing, the act, if otherwise considered ethical, does not become unethical because of the death of civilians. The bombing of Dresden, the use of the atomic bomb on Hiroshima and Nagasaki, and not warning people in Coventry that the British had cracked the Nazi code and knew that the city was about to be bombed but didn't reveal that they knew the information—all have been discussed as ethical conundrums during World War II. Whether someone concludes that these were ethical actions or not, the analysis is usually an application of utilitarianism (the goal of ending the war—which saved lives—justified the means, even though the means included the death of many innocent civilians). We continue these same discussions today in debates about the war in Iraq and the means employed in Iraq, Afghanistan, and the more amorphous war on terror.

There has been a good deal of argument and analysis over whether traditional "just war" arguments can be applied to the fight against terrorists (Crank and Gregor, 2005; Zohar, 2004). Smilansky (2004) argues that terrorists have no moral justification, and they attack democracies partially because the ethos and values of such countries prohibit taking an "any means necessary" response. However, the fact is that democratic governments have resorted to a variety of means in response to terrorist attacks that are arguably inconsistent with democratic values.

In Chapter 6, the "Dirty Harry problem" was presented as a question of whether police should use any means necessary to obtain information from a criminal suspect in

principle of double effect The concept that a means taken for a good end results in the good end but also in an inevitable but unintended bad result.

order to save a life. A more recent Harry Callahan is Jack Bauer, the hero from the television show *24*. In this show, he was confronted with "the ticking bomb scenario," specifically, whether one should use torture to find the location of a bomb that is about to go off and kill many people. While the stakes may be higher, this is the same dilemma that faced the fictional Harry Callahan, and, one might add, the same analysis may be applied: Are bad means ever justified by a good end? Interestingly, the show was even used in discussions by White House spokespersons and pundits about what was ethical in responding to the war on terror. Whether Hollywood scriptwriters are the best judge of ethics, however, is debatable.

THE RESPONSE TO 9/11

Since 9/11, we have seen a fundamental shift in the goals and mission of law enforcement and public safety. This shift has included an expansion of the number of law enforcement agencies and personnel, a nationalization of law enforcement, a reduction of civil liberties, and a merging of immigration control and traditional law enforcement. We have seen federal money directed to training law enforcement officers to act as "first responders" to critical events such as terrorist attacks. There has also been more federal money available for hardware purchases. The trend of community or neighborhood policing that sought to forge links between law enforcement and the community it served has been eclipsed by these new initiatives, and federal financial support for community policing has been drastically reduced. Further, there are increasing links between local law enforcement and immigration and federal law enforcement. Since 9/11, the nation has been involved in moral debates over such responses as:

- Detainments and governmental secrecy
- Wiretapping and threats to privacy
- Renditions and secret prisons
- Guantanamo and the military commissions
- The use of torture

DETAINMENTS AND GOVERNMENTAL SECRECY Immediately after 9/11, hundreds of non-citizens were detained on either immigration charges or material witness warrants. The Patriot Act required that all individuals on visas report to immigration offices, and once there, many were detained for minor violations of their visa. Hundreds were held for months in federal facilities and county jails without hearings. Despite civil liberties groups pressing for the names of the detainees, it took months for the federal government to release even the numbers of individuals detained, much less their names.

The deportation hearings that were held were closed to the public and to the media, despite legal suits to open them. Individuals were deported for extremely minor immigration violations, some of whom had lived in the United States for 30 years or more. The detainment of individuals on material witness warrants seemed to be based on rumor, innuendo, and a level of proof that did not even meet reasonable suspicion, (Kreimer, 2007).

WIRETAPPING AND THREATS TO PRIVACY One of the effects of 9/11 has been the loss of some privacy rights that we enjoyed before the attack. In 1978, in response to perceived violations of privacy by our government, the Foreign Intelligence Surveillance Act (FISA) was passed, which created the Foreign Intelligence Surveillance Court (FISC), consisting of seven federal district court judges appointed by the Supreme Court's chief justice.

Federal agents who wanted to wiretap in this country had to go to this court and show that their target was an agent of a foreign power and that the information sought was in furtherance of counterintelligence. The FISA legislation originally approved only electronic eavesdropping and wiretapping, but was amended in 1994 to include covert physical entries and, in 1998, to permit pen/trap orders (which record telephone numbers) and business records. If the target is a U.S. citizen, there must be probable cause that his or her activities may involve espionage, and a warrant must be requested and obtained from the FISC; however, it is believed that the court has never denied a government request for a warrant.

The Patriot Act allowed expanded powers of federal law enforcement in search and seizure, including provisions that allowed federal agents to "sneak and peek," and to utilize national security letters to circumvent warrant requirements. National security letters are letters issued by the Federal Bureau of Investigation (FBI) to access private information without a warrant. Recipients of such a letter, until later modifications of the Patriot Act, could not ever tell anyone of the letter. Thus, a librarian who received a letter demanding all Internet records for a particular patron, or a telecommunications agency that received a similar request, could not tell the target of the letter or even discuss the letter with their lawyers. It came to light that the FBI was issuing tens of thousands of these letters each year, and many may have involved violations of law or policy. Misuse of national security letters prompted an investigation by the Office of Inspector General of the Department of Justice and annual audits. The latest extension of the Patriot Act gave recipients at least the right to confer with a lawyer upon receipt of a national security letter, and required annual audits of the use of the letters (Kreimer, 2007).

The Bush administration had also pushed for several data-mining programs that basically sift through large amounts of information, tagging key words for further scrutiny (Kravets, 2003; Moss and Fessenden, 2002; Cole, 2002), although, as far as we know the programs were not put into operation. It also has come to light that President Bush authorized secret wiretapping by the National Security Agency. These wiretaps were conducted without warrants from the FISC. The Supreme Court refused to hear a legal challenge to the wiretapping, brought forward by civil liberties groups. In August 2007, the Protect America Act was passed, which allowed the government to wiretap, without a warrant, anyone suspected of being linked to a terrorist group. In effect, this gave approval to the secret wiretapping program after the fact.

The Protect America Act had an expiration date of February 2008, and, in that month, Democrats and Republicans could not come to terms on the elements of the extension, and the act expired without confirmation. However, in July 2008, Congress agreed to a bill that included legal immunity for telecommunications companies that cooperated with warrantless wiretapping. The bill also changes some elements of the FISC, expanding government's powers to invoke emergency wiretapping, and affirms the position that the FISC is the only legal authority to grant wiretaps (specifically opposing any presidential power in that regard) (Lichtblau, 2008b). Critics allege that, just as in the 1960s and 1970s, unfettered power to spy has been misused today in the indiscriminate use of national security letters and spying on groups that have no possible connection to terrorism but are merely left-leaning or groups that disagreed with the administration's actions (Harris, 2006). For instance, it has been reported that the Department of Homeland Security issued a "threat assessment" of pro-choice and anti-abortion groups for a local police department, and issued a report on a Muslim conference held in Georgia. These investigations of American citizens are outside the scope of the investigative powers of the federal government (because they do not involve espionage and terrorism) and cause concern for civil libertarians even though the reports were destroyed after concerns were raised (Savage and Shane, 2009). The Quote and Query box illustrates the concerns of many.

QUOTE & QUERY

We're protecting freedom and democracy, but unfortunately freedom and democracy have to be sacrificed.

—SOURCE: JETHRO EISENSTEIN, NEW YORK LAWYER, QUOTED IN MOSS AND FESSENDEN, 2002: A18.

Is this claim overstating the issue?

RENDITIONS AND SECRET PRISONS Other actions that the United States has taken in response to 9/11 have occurred overseas. Officials in Canada, Sweden, Germany, and Italy have declared that the CIA has kidnapped individuals in those countries and subjected them to torture to discover what they knew about terrorist activities. The practice, called rendition, is usually done with the host country's knowledge, but in some cases no notice was given or permission granted. When this happens, the country's leaders object to the U.S. practice of ignoring the sovereignty of the country and its laws (Whitlock, 2005; Weinstein, 2007).

Italy convicted *in absentia* CIA operatives who kidnapped a radical Egyptian cleric in February 2003 and smuggled him out on a U.S. military airplane. In an unusual turn of events, 26 CIA agents were prosecuted *in absentia* in Milan, Italy, for this kidnapping. In May 2008, the wife of the kidnapped man testified that, after he was kidnapped by CIA agents, he was taken to an Egyptian prison and held for 14 months. During those months, he was beaten, shocked over all parts of his body including his genitals, and tortured in other ways. Similar to others who were subjected to rendition, he was released with no explanation of why he had been taken in the first place (Associated Press, 2008c).

In some of the cases, the kidnapped suspects were sent to secret prisons run by the CIA in Eastern European countries. The existence of secret prisons run by the United States in formerly Soviet countries is an ironic and sad commentary on recent history. After the existence of such prisons was exposed in 2006, they were allegedly closed, with some of the detainees sent to Guantanamo (Whitlock, 2007). The Walking the Walk box describes how the secret prisons may have been exposed.

GUANTANAMO AND THE MILITARY COMMISSIONS ACT Soon after the United States military initiated hostilities in Afghanistan, "enemy combatants" were captured and sent to Guantanamo Bay in Cuba, a military installation that is considered American territory. The Iraq war began, and enemy combatants from Iraq were also sent there, along with suspected terrorists captured in other countries. Controversy continues over the legal status of these detainees and what due process rights they should receive. The initial arguments by the federal government were that the individuals did not deserve the due-process rights granted by the American Constitution because they were not Americans and were not on American soil; and they did not deserve the due-process rights granted by the Geneva Conventions (the agreements made by all the major world powers after World War II on how to treat war prisoners), because they were defined as enemy combatants, not soldiers.

In *Hamdi v. Rumsfeld* (542 U.S. 507 [2004]), the Supreme Court held that U.S. citizens could not be held indefinitely without charges even if they were labeled enemy combatants. In *Rasul v. Bush* (542 U.S. 466 [2004]), the Court held that detainees in Guantanamo could challenge their detention in U.S. federal courts. A related case was *Clark v. Martinez*

 **WALKING THE WALK**

Mary McCarthy was born in 1945. She received a Ph.D. in history from the University of Minnesota. In 1984, she began working for the CIA as an intelligence analyst. Her specialty was Africa, and she was known as an independent-minded analyst. She was promoted to director of intelligence programs on the National Security Council staff and was appointed as special assistant to the president and senior director for intelligence programs under President Clinton. In this position, she reviewed all clandestine operations. After President Bush was elected, she left that position in 2001, took a sabbatical, and obtained a J.D. In 2005, she was working for the CIA again, but in the Office of the Inspector General. That office investigates complaints about unethical or illegal actions by federal employees, and McCarthy's position involved investigating detainee treatment in Iraq and Afghanistan.

In 2006, she was castigated and fired over revealing governmental secrets. Although the whole affair continues to be murky, it seems that, weeks away from retirement, she spoke with Dana Priest, a *Washington Post* reporter who wrote a series of Pulitzer Prize–winning articles on the United States' practice of rendition and operating "black sites," which were secret prisons in Eastern European countries. These were the places where enemy combatants picked up in Iraq, Afghanistan, and in countries all over the world were taken for interrogation.

The Bush administration and CIA director Porter Goss launched an intensive investigation concerning the leak. McCarthy reportedly failed a polygraph and then admitted she talked to the reporter, according to CIA sources. McCarthy and her lawyer deny that she gave information to Priest about the black sites, and the reporter will only say that her information came from "multiple sources." McCarthy was fired 10 days before her planned retirement. Her colleagues were surprised since she was a veteran employee with decades of service. McCarthy has been described as "engaging, charming, persistent,

loud, and aggressive." She evidently could not be "snowed easily" and was, by nature, a skeptic. The reason she spoke with the reporter seemed to be, according to news stories citing her friends and colleagues, that she was disturbed that senior officials were not telling the truth to the Senate and House committees investigating CIA activities regarding interrogation. She and other CIA staff members were convinced that the interrogation tactics approved by the White House violated international treaties. Worse, congressional committees were not aware of the extent of the interrogation tactics used, at least from her perspective.

The news stories led to the decision to shut down the secret prisons and move the detainees (who were also known as "ghost detainees" since they never appeared on official lists provided to the International Red Cross) to Guantanamo. Whether Mary McCarthy is a hero or a traitor depends on one's perspective. It is still unclear whether or not she was the source for the reporter's story about the secret prisons. Some argue that her position at the Inspector General's office would not have given her access to such information. Others argue that she would have had access to the information only if there had been internal complaints from other CIA employees that laws were being broken. To some, she betrayed the secrets of her employer and country. Most CIA agents and other observers condemned her actions, arguing that you never leak secrets, no matter what the reason. To others, once McCarthy saw that the internal processes were not going to stop what she believed was unlawful and wrong, she did something that was much more effective—bringing the white light of public scrutiny to the activities. As the events such as Abu Ghraib, the secret prisons, and Guantanamo fade into memory, it is important to understand the dilemmas faced by those who saw wrong and tried to right it. They changed the pages of history.

Sources: Smith and Linzer, 2006: A01; Smith, 2006.

(125 S.Ct. 716 [2005]), which involved Cubans held for years in federal penitentiaries after illegally entering the United States. In this case, the Court held that the government may not indefinitely detain even illegal immigrants without some due process. In *Hamdan v. Rumsfeld* (125 S.Ct. 972 [2005]), the Supreme Court held that the military commissions, set up as a type of due process for the detainees, were outside the president's power to create and were, therefore, invalid.

Congress then passed the Military Commissions Act, which set up procedures similar to those struck down by the Supreme Court. In *Boumediene v. Bush* (553 U.S. 723 [2008]), the Supreme Court rejected the military commissions as a due-process substitute for federal courts and habeas corpus, and it further held that the Detainee Treatment Act with the provision of some form of appeal over the "enemy combatant" status was also not a substitute for habeas corpus rights. The Court's rationale is that Guantanamo is considered to be a legal territory of the United States and therefore is subject to United States law. Dissents by Chief Justice Roberts and Justices Scalia, Thomas, and Alito vigorously opposed the Court's rationale and predicted "devastating" consequences (Greenhouse, 2008; Savage, 2008b).

President Obama promised that Guantanamo would be closed within the first year of his presidency, but that has not occurred and what to do with the remaining detainees continues to be problematic. There are indications that the Obama administration will use military commissions that will respond to the due-process concerns raised by the Court, but there are also indications that some detainees will be tried in American courts.

TORTURE Many citizens probably would not have believed that the legality and ethics of torture would ever be a topic of discussion in the United States of America, yet it is. After World War II, commanders of the Japanese and German armies were tried for war crimes that included unnecessary killings of civilians, mistreatment of civilians, and the use of torture against captured soldiers. One of the forms of interrogation used by the Japanese that was later the basis for convictions was the "water cure." We know it today as waterboarding. In the 1940s, judicial officials assessing guilt in war crime trials called it torture and convicted the military officers who ordered it or allowed it to happen; in 2007 and 2008, the president of the United States called it legal and necessary.

Torture is defined as the deliberate infliction of violence and, through violence, severe mental and/or physical suffering upon individuals. Others describe it as any intentional act that causes severe physical or mental pain or suffering. Amnesty International considers all forms of corporal punishment as falling within the definition of torture and prohibited by the United Nations Convention Against Torture (McCready, 2007).

As new information about the government's activities in the wake of 9/11 comes to light, we now know that immediately after 9/11, certain individuals suspected of being involved in the planning of the attacks or of being members of Al-Qaeda were seized wherever they happened to be and taken to secret locations. At first they were sent to countries such as Egypt, which used torture in interrogation. Later they were taken to secret prisons run by the CIA in Eastern Europe. Finally, some were moved to Guantanamo. Evidently, by 2002, various forms of coercive interrogation techniques were being used at Guantanamo, as well as Bagram prison in Afghanistan. At these locations, allegedly, the suspects were subjected to extreme forms of coercive interrogations, including the following (Massimino, 2004: 74):

- Subjected to loud noises and extreme heat and cold
- Deprived of sleep, light, food, and water
- Bound or forced to stand in painful positions for long periods of time
- Kept naked and hooded
- Thrown into walls
- Sexually humiliated
- Threatened with attack dogs
- Shackled to the ceiling

In an ironic twist, it has now been revealed that military interrogators in Guantanamo were trained in the techniques of coercive interrogation techniques with material that was originally from a 1957 Air Force study of Chinese Communist techniques used during the Korean War. The original source detailed a continuum of coercive techniques that were used to obtain false confessions from U.S. soldiers, including practices such as semi-starvation, filthy surroundings, extreme cold, and stress positions. At some point, the chart was taken from the original source, which described how such techniques could "brainwash" American soldiers into falsely confessing war crimes, and became included in training materials on how to conduct coercive interrogations to obtain evidence against suspected insurgents (Shane, 2008b).

At the Bagram prison in Afghanistan, a young taxi driver was killed by interrogators who suspended him from the ceiling and beat his legs so badly that an autopsy revealed his leg bones were pulverized (see the Quote and Query box). It was discovered that Dilawar, the taxi driver, had no association at all with insurgents and that his taxi and the passengers in it had been picked at random by an Afghan guerrilla commander who told the Americans that they were responsible for bombing a U.S. camp. Later it was discovered that the commander himself was responsible for the bombing (Golden, 2005).

QUOTE & QUERY

It became a kind of running joke, and people kept showing up to give this detainee a common peroneal strike just to hear him scream out "Allah." ... It went on over a 24-hour period, and I would think that it was over 100 strikes.

—SOURCE: STATEMENT BY MILITARY GUARD. QUOTED IN GOLDEN, 2005: A16.

How does the utilitarian ethical system justify this treatment? Does any ethical system justify it?

There were troubling indications that interrogation techniques being utilized in Guantanamo, starting in 2001 through 2003, were contrary to the Military Field Manual and American law. FBI agents who were at Guantanamo to assist in interrogations wrote memoranda to their superiors objecting to what they saw, as did some military lawyers and other officers. By the time the Abu Ghraib prison scandal erupted, such techniques had been used in Guantanamo and in Bagram prison in Afghanistan. Far from being the isolated acts of a few sadistic soldiers, these techniques were the subject of memos written and signed by officials in the Office of Legal Counsel and at the Pentagon.

We now know that a legal memorandum authored by lawyers John Yoo and Robert Delahunty from the Office of Legal Counsel had provided a 2002 opinion that the president could authorize waterboarding and other forms of torture,. Yoo also wrote a 2003 memorandum with Jay Bybee that basically reiterated the justification that the president had the legal right to order torture as long as it did not result in organ failure or death (Shane, 2008a).

Critics today argue that these legal memoranda ignored other sources of law, including international treaties such as the Convention Against Torture, which the United States ratified in 1994, that also bar such acts (Gillers, 2004). As these memos came to light, the authors, Bybee and Yoo, faced an investigation from the Department of Justice's Office of Professional Responsibility and possible sanctions from their respective bar associations. However, the final report concluded that they exercised flawed legal reasoning, but were not guilty of professional misconduct, and recommended that they not be referred to their state bar associations for discipline. Steven Bradbury, associated with four memos providing legal support for the interrogation techniques, was also found not to have committed professional misconduct. Bybee is now a federal appeals court judge, and Yoo is a law professor (Lichtblau and Shane, 2010).

As far as can be determined, many of those who were tortured were not insurgents. Some had stolen from military supply trucks, some had engaged in civilian crimes, some had been captured after tips suggested that they were involved. Soldiers in Abu Ghraib and Bagram evidently felt comfortable using extreme interrogation techniques because they knew or had seen military interrogators use them. Once human rights are discarded for one group, it is hard to preserve them for others.

The Quote and Query box sums up the message in the above points.

QUOTE & QUERY

We take this moral high ground to make sure that if our people fall into enemy hands, we'll have the moral force to say, "You have got to treat them right." If you don't practice what you preach, nobody listens.

—SOURCE: SENATOR LINDSEY GRAHAM, IN SUPPORT OF AN AMENDMENT BANNING TORTURE TO MILITARY PRISONERS, QUOTED IN GALLOWAY AND KUHNHENN, 2005: A4.

Is this argument against torture a utilitarian argument or an ethical formalist argument?

The argument that we should not use torture because our enemies then will feel free to use torture against American soldiers is a utilitarian argument (greatest benefit), but it also has elements of the categorical imperative (act in such a way that you will it to be a universal law) and the religious imperative (do unto others as you would have them do unto you).

Kleinig (2001a) and others, even before the worst abuses were revealed, examined the weak justification for torture and abusive practices during interrogation and also pointed out that they have been used in Northern Ireland, Israel, South Africa, and South America, among many other countries. The so-called "doctrine of necessity" is purely utilitarian, as is the argument of some that there must be secrecy concerning interrogation tactics so they can be more effective. To the contrary, Kleinig (2001a: 116) points out that torture dehumanizes both victim and oppressor: "There is a loss of the moral high ground, a compromising of values that supposedly distinguish a society as civilized and worth belonging to."

Whether torture is effective or not is a utilitarian argument. Some argue that it is not effective because people will say anything to stop the torture, and interrogators can't tell when someone is lying (Rejali, 2007). Some military interrogators are speaking out now, describing how they had obtained good information from high-value detainees using standard techniques and then other interrogators took over, used torture, and the detainees stopped talking. The same sources indicate that the information that has been said to have come from coercive interrogation tactics actually was obtained much earlier when such techniques were not in use (Margasak, 2009). Others argue that torture does work in getting information out of individuals. Even those people, however, admit that using torture to interrogate may damage the interrogator as well as the detainee. Individuals may find the dark corners of their soul when they realize that they get some form of excitement from inflicting pain on others. They may suffer guilt that destroys their peace of mind and

in the **NEWS**

WAR CRIMINALS?

The same Spanish court that prosecuted and convicted Augusto Pinochet, the Chilean dictator who was responsible for thousands of murders by death squads in the 1970s, has agreed to hear charges against Bush administration officials, including former Attorney General Alberto Gonzales, David Addington, Jay Bybee, and John Yoo. Spanish law allows courts to address cases of torture or war crimes wherever they may occur, under a doctrine of universal justice.

SOURCE: Haven, 2009.

affects them long after the detainee's wounds have healed. It has been reported that some interrogators are suffering post-traumatic stress syndrome (Blumenfeld, 2007).

Alan Dershowitz (2004) offers a utilitarian argument for torture—he writes that sometimes the greatest benefit is to torture, but that it should be limited to situations in which the benefit is so great that it overwhelms the harm to the individual. He also proposes, however, that any torture should be done under the auspices of a court or objective hearing body that issues a type of "torture warrant." Others (e.g., McCready, 2007) dispute the feasibility of this proposal, arguing that any need for torture would be immediate and, if there was time to pursue a warrant, there probably would be other ways to get that information. Another thing to consider about the terrible effects of torturing for information is that the innocent who knows nothing suffers the most pain. The movie *Rendition* is a fictionalized account of what might have happened in real life in the months and years following 9/11.

When individuals such as Dershowitz present justifications for torture, they invariably use the most extreme situation—the "ticking bomb" scenario in which one *knows* that the person being tortured has information about a bomb that is going to go off soon, killing many people. Whether one accepts the utilitarian equation for such a scenario does not necessarily justify the actual incidents of torture that have taken place. There is a world of difference between the ticking bomb scenario and torturing a suspect accused of stealing from the U.S. military, or torturing a suspect to obtain his confession so that he can be punished.

The In the News box describes how the United States' actions have been perceived by other nations.

Crime Control versus Rights-Based Law Enforcement

Utilitarianism is the ethical justification for all the counter-terrorism measures we've discussed. These practices are justified as preventing or deterring terrorism, but the argument is crime control revisited. Fourth Amendment limits were justified as necessary in the war on drugs, and we see the same argument justifying extreme methods in the war on terror. We have also seen the same type of abuses. Just as a few police officers felt they could justify planting evidence and lying to get drug dealers off the street, and some decided they could also steal from drug dealers because they were outside the protection of the law itself, we have similar scandals in the war on terror. Whenever there is a threat to the peace and safety of the population, there is the temptation and tendency to use illegal and unethical means for protection.

Utilitarian reasoning is accepted as an ethical rationale, but it does not justify all actions just because they may protect us. Cohen (1987: 53) uses a utilitarian approach in the following justification for police action:

1. The end must itself be good.
2. The means must be a plausible way to achieve the end.
3. There must be no alternative and better means to achieve the same end.
4. The means must not undermine some other equal or greater end.

crime control approach The law enforcement concept that uses means–end or utilitarian thinking to determine good by the result, which is crime control.

As we discussed in Chapter 5, the **crime control approach** is utilitarian and justifies actions that otherwise would be wrong for the end of crime control. In the **public service approach**, which can also be described as the human rights model, values and ethics focus on human rights, including the right to due process, and the fundamental duty of all public servants is to protect those rights. In this approach, the protection of rights is more important than the end of crime control.

public service approach The law enforcement principle whereby the values and ethos of law enforcement and justice professionals focus on human rights, including the right to due process, and the fundamental duty of all public servants is to protect those rights.

A **rights-based model** of policing recognizes police officers as servants of the public good. Although crime control is important, protection of civil liberties is the fundamental mission. A crime control approach is utilitarian, and a rights-based approach is not. Under the rights-based approach, which is deontological, no end would justify taking away human rights.

This discussion can obviously be applied to the discussion of what are acceptable responses to terrorist threats; the threat may be great, but the loss of liberty may be greater if we succumb to fear. Although racial profiling has been legally and ethically condemned as a violation of rights when it is used to catch drug dealers, it has been resurrected as an appropriate and justified response to catching terrorists. Our Supreme Court has held that privacy is more important than catching criminals, so wiretaps have been used sparingly and with judicial oversight. However, the prevention of terrorist attacks has changed this balance, and many are willing to give up their privacy rights in order for the government to protect them from terrorism.

rights-based model The policing approach that recognizes the police as servants of the public good; although crime control is important, protection of civil liberties is the fundamental mission.

Some argue that it is a false argument to weigh privacy or any civil liberty against security. Writing before the attack on the World Trade Center, Alderson (1998: 23) presented a prescient argument against the "end" of security as a justification for taking away liberties:

I acknowledge that liberty is diminished when people feel afraid to exercise it, but to stress security to unnecessary extremes at the price of fundamental freedoms plays into the hands of would-be high police despots. Such despots are quick to exploit fear in order to secure unlimited power.

Alderson also addressed terrorism directly: "It is important for police to maintain their high ethical standards when facing terrorism, and for their leaders to inspire resistance to any degeneration into counter-terrorism terror" (1998: 71).

Protection of rights can also be framed as a utilitarian argument. In the effort to prevent future terrorism by Al-Qaeda or other radical Muslim groups, the greatest ally of law enforcement in any country is the Muslim community. If the Muslim community is cooperative with preventive efforts, it is because this community believes in the legal system and the integrity of those within it. Observers noted that one of the reasons that British police were able to identify the subway bombers so quickly in 2005 was the cooperation of the Muslim community, but that later actions enraged community members and hardened opinion against the police; thus, it is possible that their assistance in identifying future perpetrators may not be forthcoming (Buchholz, 2005; Emling, 2005).

The major problem in the utilitarian ethical system or means–end thinking is that we are unable to know the outcome of our actions. Justifying otherwise unethical means by arguing that these means will lead to a good end depends on the ability to know that the means will result in the desired outcome. Unfortunately, this is not possible. In our haste to protect ourselves from terrorists, it is at least conceivable that we may create more terrorists (Bender, 2005). The current generation of Middle Eastern children may identify the United States only as an aggressor. Our actions, if misunderstood, could create many times more terrorists than the number we are trying to control today.

In engaging in renditions, operating secret prisons, and defending the right to torture, we lose allies around the world and, in the process, threaten our future security. In this country, those of Arab descent who came here for freedom now find that their heritage denies them that precious gift. In detaining Arab American men without the due process that protects most citizens, we may germinate the seeds of future destruction in the children who watch their fathers being taken away. In fact, the new threat seems to be "home grown terrorists" who were born in the United States or have lived here most of their lives. By engaging in acts that are associated with oppressive countries, such as torture and secret prisons, we make it easier for radical clerics and others to convince adherents that this country deserves to be a victim of terroristic acts.

By parceling out human rights for some and not for others, we also weaken civil liberties for all citizens. Once we start parceling out human rights and justice differentially, it opens the door to those who look for an excuse to abuse and victimize.

The premise of rights-based law enforcement is that some acts are never justified. No end is so important that governments can stoop to slavery, genocide, or torture. No situation ever justifies sexism, racism, murder, rape, or intimidation. There is a suspicion of state power in rights-based law enforcement and a fear that police will be used to oppress the powerless. The way to avoid this is to place the protection of rights, rather than crime control, as the central theme of policing, because the definition of crime and the identification of who is a criminal may be subverted for political ends. The United Nations Code of Conduct for Law Enforcement Officials illustrates the values and premise of the rights-based approach: "In the performance of their duty, law enforcement officials shall respect and protect human dignity and maintain and uphold the human rights of all persons" (Article 2, reported in Kleinig, 1999).

Neyroud and Beckley (2001: 62) describe the police standards of the United Kingdom as reflecting an emphasis on human rights. Standards include the following provisions:

- To fulfill the duties imposed on them by the law
- To respect human dignity and uphold human rights
- To act with integrity, dignity, and impartiality
- To use force only when strictly necessary, and then proportionately
- To maintain confidentiality
- Not to use torture or use ill-treatment
- To protect the health of those in their custody
- Not to commit any act of corruption
- To respect the law and the code of conduct and oppose violations of them
- To be personally liable for their acts

Because European police have had a longer history of dealing with terrorism, it is interesting that the trend there evidently has been to move toward a rights-based model of policing. For instance, British police have had their share of noble-cause corruption in dealing with Irish terrorists; Spain has dealt with Basque terrorists; Germany dealt with the Baader-Meinhof gang in the 1970s and, more recently, with neo-Nazi groups; and so on.

In Chapter 10, we discussed the importance of an independent judiciary. This concept is an essential element of the discussion here as well. It is no coincidence that the United Nations and the European Union both mandate that a country have an independent judiciary in order for that nation to be considered protective of human rights and thus eligible to join the European Union. The way to freedom and democracy is through the recognition of human rights, and the way to protect human rights is through an independent judiciary (Keith, 2002, 196–197).

Why are we discussing terrorism and the Iraq war in a book on the criminal justice system? The answer is that the war on terror has replaced the drug war, and the crime control perspective has morphed into a much broader government mandate of national security. In response to that mandate, government's powers of investigation and control were expanded to address terrorism. However, Crank and Gregor (2005) note cases where the arsenal of responses against terror has been used against ordinary criminals, such as a federal law against terroristic threats applied to a lovesick woman who wanted the cruise ship she was on to turn around, the use of a law against weapons of mass destruction against a methamphetamine "cook," and the use of federal subpoena power to investigate members of an antiwar group that sponsored a rally with signs reading "Bring the Iowa Guard Home." As mentioned previously, once rights and liberties are taken away from some groups, they become more tenuous for us all.

Ethical Dilemmas and Decisions

This last chapter has focused on the war on terror because it is the greatest challenge facing this country today, but it also illustrates in dramatic ways how ethics is an unspoken and largely unanalyzed but powerful element in how events unfold. This last section reiterates the idea that ultimately ethics is about facing a dilemma and making a decision. Like police officers, CIA and FBI agents may be tempted to use illegal and unethical means to accomplish their mission. Like prosecutors, lawyers in the Justice Department and the military justice system have been pressured to skirt the law to pursue a good end. Like correctional officers, personnel who worked in Guantanamo and Bagram are exposed to a subculture where prisoners are considered not worthy of basic respect and humane treatment.

Throughout this book, the Walking the Walk boxes have presented individuals facing ethical dilemmas. Some of them were involved in the war on terror, such as Charles Swift, who was assigned to defend Salim Ahmed Hamdan against the president and the Pentagon; Mary McCarthy, who might have exposed the secret prisons; James Yee, who defended the rights of the detainees in Guantanamo and was labeled a traitor as a result; and Joe Darby, who revealed the abuses occurring at Abu Ghraib.

There are also others who might be labeled whistleblowers because they came forward with information about governmental actions they believed to be wrong. Babak Pasdar, a computer security expert, was hired to conduct a security audit of a major telecommunications carrier. In the course of his audit, he found a mysterious circuit that others called the "Quantico circuit," which was sending all information about telephone and e-mail from subscribers to Quantico, Virginia. When Pasdar asked about it and objected that it was a threat to the security of the system, he was told to forget that he ever saw it. He could not forget it, though, and, because of his concern, ended up testifying before Congress about what he witnessed and went public in March 2006. Pasdar is now affiliated with an organization that seeks to protect the privacy of Americans from secret governmental spying (Devine, 2008: 4A).

Lieutenant Commander Matthew Diaz was a JAG lawyer for the joint military task force at Guantanamo, in charge of holding and interrogating enemy combatants. He supported the 2004 Supreme Court decision *Rasul v. Bush*, granting detainees the right of habeas corpus, and thought they should be allowed lawyers to represent them. He disagreed with the government's refusal to supply the names of the detainees after a civil rights organization had filed a request under the Freedom of Information Act to obtain them. On January 15, 2005, he mailed a list of detainees to the Center for Constitutional Rights in New York. In 2006, a federal court declared that the list of names was public information, and the government released it to the Associated Press, but Diaz was still prosecuted for his disclosure with the government, arguing that he exposed the United States to danger. Diaz was convicted and sentenced in May 2007 to six months' imprisonment and was given a dishonorable discharge (Wiltrout, 2007).

Coleen Rowley was the FBI lawyer who made headlines when she publicly reported that officials in Washington ignored reports from the field about Zacarias Moussaoui, who has since admitted conspiring with Al-Qaeda. Rowley retired from the FBI in frustration over the bureaucratic practices that punished those who criticized superiors who were not doing their job in sharing and analyzing important information (Carr, 2005: A1, A6).

It is not only whistleblowers, however, who face ethical dilemmas. Sometimes, ethics simply means doing one's job. General Antonio Taguba was tasked with preparing a report on Abu Ghraib. He was criticized informally, evidently for the comprehensiveness of the report and his strong condemnation of the practices he found there. According to reports, his career was derailed by doing his job too well in investigating and chronicling the abuses at Abu Ghraib and documenting the lack of leadership that lead to the abuses.

Pasquale D'Amuro was the chief of counterintelligence at the FBI when he directed FBI agents in Guantanamo Bay in 2002 to have nothing to do with interrogations that included the techniques that became the focus of scandal later. There are many others—some known, many more unknown—who faced difficult decisions about what was right.

How we face and resolve dilemmas is influenced by our ethical systems and understanding that doing the right thing is not always easy, nor is it necessarily easy to determine what is right. Some of the individuals above were and still are criticized bitterly over their decisions. While some consider them heroes, others consider them traitors. We cannot deny, however, that they faced their dilemma courageously and chose to do what they considered was right, knowing they would face consequences for doing so.

In the final analysis, the approach we have taken throughout this book is perhaps the best one when faced with any type of ethical dilemma. To review, when faced with a dilemma one should consider law, policy, and then consider the ethical systems such as utilitarianism and ethical formalism.

- Is there relevant law?
  Are you being asked to do something or observing something that is contrary to state, national, or military law?

- Is there relevant policy?
  Does the action violate company or agency policy? If you feel the policy is wrong, can you use official channels rather than violate the policy?

- Finally, what do ethical systems tell you to do?

Although utilitarianism may be the most pervasive ethical system used in the war on terror and when responding to other national challenges, there are limits to what can be done for a "good end." One could apply ethical formalism or ethics of care to consider the action, or, even the simpler "front page test," which basically just asks you to consider how you would feel if your action was described on the front page of a newspaper. If you would not want that to happen, there may be problems with your action.

CONCLUSION

The World Trade Center attack and other assaults on U.S. targets around the world have created a sense of vulnerability and fear. The response to this fear has been to reduce civil liberties through law, policy, and individual practices. This "end justifies the means" thinking is insidious—even more so now that that threat is so much greater. If utilitarianism is used to justify actions, then one must also show what facts exist to prove that the desired end will be brought about and that negative side effects do not outweigh the good that one seeks. This step seems to be missing in many current discussions. However, ethical formalism and other systems would conclude that even if one could prove the good end outweighs the bad means, some acts cannot ever be justified. Certain human rights belong to everyone—even terrorists. In the crime war, drug war, or war on terror, the most important element of making ethical decisions is to apply ethical reasoning and not succumb to fear. Our final Quote and Query box makes a case for political liberty.

QUOTE & QUERY

Political liberty, which is one of the greatest gifts people can acquire, is threatened when social order is threatened. It is dismaying to see how ready many people are to turn to strong leaders in hopes that they will end, by adopting strong measures, the disorder that has been the product of failed or fragile commitments. Drug abuse, street crime, and political corruption are the expression of unfettered choices. To end them, rulers, with the warm support of the people, will often adopt measures that threaten true political freedom. The kind of culture that can maintain reasonable human commitments takes centuries to create but only a few generations to destroy.

—SOURCE: JAMES Q. WILSON, CITED IN COLE, 2002: 234.

Although Wilson's statement is discussing the sacrifice of due process in the drug war and crime control, it has incredible relevance to the issues of terrorism. Interestingly, it was made by a noted conservative. How do we meet the threat of terrorists?

Most of us are lucky in that we will never have to decide whether or not to participate in torture, violate laws against wiretapping, or expose secrets in a way that could be considered a threat to national security. Criminal justice professionals, however, will probably encounter at least some of the dilemmas that have been described in previous chapters. The power of discretion, authority and power, and the duty of protecting public safety create dilemmas for these professionals that are quite different from those that most citizens encounter. Ultimately, for criminal justice professionals as well as everyone else, the way you resolve dilemmas throughout the course of your career will constitute, in no small measure, the person you are.

CHAPTER REVIEW

1. Identify the basic themes of the book.

The presence of authority, power, force, and discretion exists in each of the subsystems of the criminal justice system. Informal practices and value systems among criminal justice actors may vary from formal codes of ethics. The importance of ethical leadership exists in each area of the system. The tension between deontological ethical systems and teleological or "means–end" ethical analysis also exists in each area of the system, as well as in the war on terror.

2. Describe the basic elements of the "just war" debate and the "just means" discussion.

The traditional justification for war comes from natural law, and the second comes from positivist law. Natural law gives sovereigns the right to use force to uphold the good of the community, when unjust injuries are inflicted on others, and to protect the state. Positivist law justifies war when agreed upon by international bodies such as the United Nations.

3. Describe the responses to 9/11.

Since 9/11, the nation has been involved in moral debates over such responses as detainments and governmental secrecy, wiretapping and threats to privacy, renditions and secret prisons, Guantanamo and the military commissions, and the use of torture.

4. Compare the crime control approach to the human rights model of policing.

The crime control approach is utilitarian and justifies actions that otherwise would be wrong for the end of crime control. In the human rights model, values and ethics focus on human rights, including the right to due process, and the fundamental duty of all public servants is to protect those rights. In this approach, the protection of rights is more important than the end of crime control.

5. Present a method to resolve ethical dilemmas.

The method used throughout the book has been to evaluate the choices of action based on relevant law, policy, and ethics. A short ethical test is the "front page test."

KEY TERMS

crime control approach
positivist law

principle of double effect
public service approach

rights-based model
terrorism

STUDY QUESTIONS

1. What are some actions the federal government has taken in response to terrorism?
2. What are the arguments in support of torture? What are the arguments against torture?
3. What are some rights recognized by the United Nations and the European Union?
4. Explain why "means–end" thinking leads to criminal actions.
5. What are the two justifications for a just war?

WRITING/DISCUSSION EXERCISES

1. Write an essay on (or discuss) the most difficult ethical dilemma in this chapter, and try to answer it by considering law, policy, and ethics. Also, use the "front-page test." This is a quick ethics test that asks if you would feel comfortable if your action were published on the front page of the newspaper. If you would not want it to be, there may be an ethical problem with your action.

2. Write an essay on (or discuss) an ethical or moral dilemma from your own life. Try to solve it by using any guidelines derived from this book. Be explicit about the procedure you used to arrive at a decision and about the decision itself.

3. Write a code of ethics for yourself.

ETHICAL DILEMMAS

Situation 1

You are a member of Congress, and the Patriot Act is coming up for a vote to renew its provisions. What would you do, and why?

Situation 2

As a soldier in Iraq, you have pictures of fellow soldiers engaging in various acts of abuse and torture. What, if anything, would you do with the pictures?

Situation 3

You are a new police officer and are talking with other officers before roll call. The group is loudly and energetically proposing various gruesome torture techniques to get Al-Qaeda operatives to talk. There is some hyperbole in the discussion, but also the sincere belief that torture is justified by the circumstances. What do you think about this position? If you object to torture, would you make your position known?

Situation 4

You live next door to an Arab family, and you hear the husband talking negatively about the United States. Your friends at work tell you that you should report him to the police because he might be a terrorist. What would you do? Why?

Situation 5

You are the president of the United States, and there has been another terrorist attack using passenger airplanes. One has crashed into the Pentagon, and another is heading for the White House. You have deployed fighter jets to surround the plane, and whoever is flying it refuses to acknowledge the command to turn around. Your military commanders are advising you to shoot down the plane—an act that would kill the 353 people aboard. What would you do? Would your answer be any different if it were heading toward the Statue of Liberty? Toward an athletic stadium filled to capacity?

Glossary

act utilitarianism The type of utilitarianism that determines the goodness of a particular act by measuring the utility (good) for all, but only for that specific act and without regard for future actions.

applied ethics The study of what is right and wrong pertaining to a specific profession or subject.

asset forfeiture A legal tool used to confiscate property and money associated with organized criminal activity.

attorney–client privilege The legal rule by which an attorney cannot disclose confidential information regarding his or her client except in a very few specified circumstances.

authority Unquestionable entitlement to be obeyed that comes from fulfilling a specific role.

blue curtain of secrecy Another name for the code of silence or the practice of police officers to remain silent when fellow officers commit unethical actions.

bureaucratic justice The approach in which each case is treated as one of many; the actors merely follow the rules and walk through the steps, and the goal is efficiency.

burnout The condition in which a worker has abandoned the mission of the organization and is just "going through the motions."

categorical imperatives The concept that some things just must be, with no need for further justification, explanation, or rationalization for why they exist (Kant's categorical imperative refers to the imperative that you should do your duty, act in a way you want everyone else to act, and don't use people).

civil disobedience Voluntarily breaking established laws based on one's moral beliefs.

civilian review/complaint model The use of an outside agency or board that includes citizens and monitors and/or investigates misconduct complaints against police.

code of silence The practice of officers to not come forward when they are aware of the ethical transgressions of other officers.

cognitive dissonance Psychological term referring to the discomfort that is created when behavior and attitude or belief are inconsistent.

community corrections A term that encompasses halfway houses, work release centers, probation, parole, and any other intermediate sanctions, such as electronic monitoring, either as a condition of probation or as a sentence in itself that takes place in the community rather than prison.

community policing A model of law enforcement that creates partnerships with the community and addresses underlying problems rather than simply enforcing the law.

confirmatory bias Fixating on a preconceived notion and ignoring other possibilities, such as in regard to a specific suspect during a police investigation.

conflict paradigm The idea that groups in society have fundamental differences and that those in power control societal elements, including law.

consensus paradigm The idea that most people have similar beliefs, values, and goals and that societal laws reflect the majority view.

correctional officer The term that replaced the old label of guard, indicating a new role.

crime control approach The law enforcement concept that uses means–end or utilitarian thinking to determine good by the result, which is crime control.

criminalistics The profession involved in the application of science to recognize, identify, and evaluate physical evidence in court proceedings.

cruel and unusual punishment Punishment proscribed by the Eighth Amendment.

cultural relativism The idea that values and behaviors differ from culture to

culture and are functional in the culture that holds them.

cynicism A trait of those who work in corrections, characterized by a pessimistic view of human nature and their ability to change.

deontological ethical system The study of duty or moral obligation emphasizing the intent of the actor as the element of morality.

developmental theories Approaches to behavior proposing that individuals have normal growth phases in areas such as morality and emotional maturity.

Dirty Harry problem The question of whether police should use immoral means to reach a desired moral end (taken from a Clint Eastwood movie).

discretion The authority to make a decision between two or more choices.

due process Constitutionally mandated procedural steps designed to eliminate error in any governmental deprivation of protected liberty, life, or property.

duties Required behaviors or actions, i.e., the responsibilities that are attached to a specific role.

egoism The ethical system that defines the pursuit of self-interest as a moral good.

enlightened egoism The concept that egoism may appear to be altruistic because it is in one's long-term best interest to help others in order to receive help in return.

entrapment When an otherwise innocent person commits an illegal act because of police encouragement or enticement.

ethical dilemmas Situations in which it is difficult to make a decision, either because the right course of action is not clear or the right course of action carries some negative consequences.

ethical formalism The ethical system espoused by Kant that focuses on duty; holds that the only thing truly good is a good will, and that what is good is that which conforms to the categorical imperative.

ethical issues Difficult social questions that include controversy over the "right" thing to do.

ethical system A structured set of principles that defines what is moral.

ethics The discipline of determining good and evil and defining moral duties.

ethics of care The ethical system that defines good as meeting the needs of others and preserving and enriching relationships.

ethics of virtue The ethical system that bases ethics largely upon character and possession of virtues.

expiation Atonement for a wrong to achieve a state of grace.

Federal Sentencing Guidelines Mandated sentences created by Congress for use by judges when imposing sentence (recent Supreme Court decisions have overturned the mandatory nature of the guidelines).

force The authority to use physical coercion to overcome the will of the individual.

generalization principle The principle that all decisions should be made assuming that the decision would be applied to everyone else in similar circumstances.

Good Samaritan laws Legislation that prohibits passing by an accident scene or witnessing a crime without rendering assistance.

graft Any exploitation of one's role, such as accepting bribes, protection money, or kickbacks.

gratuities Items of value received by an individual because of his or her role or position rather than because of a personal relationship with the giver.

halo effect The phenomenon in which a person with expertise or status in one area is given deference in all areas.

hedonistic calculus Jeremy Bentham's rationale for calculating the potential rewards of a crime so the amount of threatened pain could be set to deter people from committing that crime.

human service officer The corrections officer who perceives the role to include influencing and interacting with the offender.

hypothetical imperatives Statements of contingent demand known as if-then statements (if I want something, then I must work for it); usually contrasted with categorical imperatives (statements of "must" with no "ifs").

imperative principle The concept that all decisions should be made according to absolute rules.

imperfect duties Moral duties that are not fully explicated or detailed.

informants Civilians who are used to obtain information about criminal activity and/or participate in it so evidence can be obtained for an arrest.

Innocence Project An organization staffed by lawyers and law students who reexamine cases and provide legal assistance to convicts when there is a probability that serious errors occurred in their prosecution.

integrity testing "Sting" operations to test whether or not police officers will make honest choices.

internal affairs model A review procedure in which police investigators receive and investigate complaints and resolve the investigations internally.

interpretationist An approach to the Constitution that uses a looser reading of the document and reads into its rights that the framers might have recognized or that should be recognized as a result of "evolving standards."

just deserts model Fogel's conceptualization that the punishment of an individual should be limited by the seriousness of the crime, although treatment could be offered.

justice The quality of being impartial, fair, and just; from the Latin "jus." concerning rules or law.

justice model Von Hirsch's conceptualization that the punishment of the individual should be purely retributive and balanced to the seriousness of the crime.

Kohlberg's moral stages The view that moral development is hierarchical; each higher developmental stage is described as moving away from pure egoism toward altruism.

laws Formal, written rules of society.

legal moralism A justification for law that allows for protection and enforcement of societal morals.

legal paternalism Refers to laws that protect individuals from hurting themselves.

lex salica A form of justice that allows compensation; the harm can be repaired by payment or atonement.

lex talionis A vengeance-oriented justice concerned with equal retaliation ("an eye for an eye; a tooth for a tooth").

mechanical solidarity Durkheim's concept of societal solidarity as arising from similarities among society's members.

meta-ethics The discipline of investigating the meaning of ethical terms, including a critical study of how ethical statements can be verified.

modeling Learning theory concept that people learn behaviors, values, and attitudes through relationships; they identify with another person and want to be like that person and pattern themselves after the "model."

moral pluralism The concept that there are fundamental truths that may dictate different definitions of what is moral in different situations.

morals Principles of right and wrong.

natural law The idea that principles of morals and rights are inherent in nature and not human-made; such laws are discovered by reason but exist apart from humankind.

natural rights The concept that one has certain rights just by virtue of being born, and these rights are not created by humans, although they can be ignored.

net widening The concept that some intermediate sanctions are used for those who would not have received any formal correctional sanction before, so instead of diverting those who would have been sentenced to harsher sanctions, the program increases the total number under correctional supervision.

new rehabilitationists Theorists and researchers who believe that evidence shows that rehabilitative programs do result in lower recidivism.

normative ethics What people ought to do; defines moral duties.

organic solidarity Durkheim's concept of societal solidarity as arising from differences among people, as exemplified by the division of labor.

passive time server The type of officer who does the bare minimum on the job to stay out of trouble.

peacemaking corrections An approach to corrections that depends on care and wholesight, or looking at what needs to be done with both the heart and the head.

peacemaking justice An ancient approach to justice that includes the concepts of compassion and care, connectedness and mindfulness.

penal harm The idea that the system intentionally inflicts pain on offenders during their imprisonment or punishment, because merely depriving them of liberty is not considered sufficiently painful.

persuasion The use of signs, symbols, words, and arguments to induce compliance.

plea bargain Exchange of a guilty plea for a reduced charge or sentence.

pluralist paradigm The concept that there are many groups in society and that they form allegiances and coalitions in a dynamic exchange of power.

pluralistic ignorance The prevalent misperception of the popularity of a belief among a group because of the influence of a vocal minority.

positivist law Human-made law.

power The right inherent in a role to use any means to overcome resistance.

prevention A rationale for punishment that views it as a means rather than an end and embraces any method that can avoid crime, painful or not (includes deterrence, rehabilitation, and incapacitation).

principle of double effect The concept that a means taken for a good end results in the good end but also in an inevitable but unintended bad result.

principle of forfeiture The idea that one gives up one's right to be treated under the principles of respect for persons to the extent that one has abrogated someone else's rights; for

instance, self-defense is acceptable according to the principle of forfeiture.

principle of the golden mean Aristotle's concept of moderation, in which one should not err toward excess or deficiency; this principle is associated with the ethics of virtue.

procedural justice The component of justice that concerns the steps taken to reach a determination of guilt, punishment, or other conclusion of law.

professional ethics Applied principles of right and wrong relevant to specific occupations or professions.

psychological egoism The concept that humans naturally and inherently seek self-interest, and that we can do nothing else because it is our nature.

public servants Professionals who are paid by the public and whose jobs entail pursuing the public good.

public service approach The law enforcement principle whereby the values and ethos of law enforcement and justice professionals focus on human rights, including the right to due process, and the fundamental duty of all public servants is to protect those rights.

punishment Unpleasantness or pain administered by one in lawful authority in response to another's transgression of law or rules.

punitive law enforcer The type of officer who perceives the role as one of enforcer, enforces every rule, and goes "by the book."

reciprocity Sykes's term denoting the situation in which officers become indebted to inmates and return favors.

recognition tests Paper-and-pencil tests that measure an individual's ability to recognize and/or agree with moral terms.

reinforcement Rewards.

reintegrative shaming Braithwaite's idea that certain types of punishment can lead to a reduction of recidivism as long as they do not involve banishment and they induce healthy shame in the individual.

religious ethics The ethical system that is based on religious beliefs of good and evil; what is good is that which is God's will.

repressive law Durkheim's view that law controls behavior that is different

from the norm (related to mechanical solidarity).

restitutive law Durkheim's view that law resolves conflicts between equals, as in commutative justice (related to organic solidarity).

restorative justice An approach to corrective justice that focuses on meeting the needs of all concerned.

retribution A rationale for punishment that states that punishment is an end in itself and should be balanced to the harm caused.

retributive justice The component of justice that concerns the determination and methods of punishment.

rights-based model The policing approach that recognizes the police as servants of the public good; although crime control is important, protection of civil liberties is the fundamental mission.

rotten-apple argument The proposition that the officer alone is deviant and that it was simply a mistake to hire him or her.

rule utilitarianism The type of utilitarianism that determines the goodness of an action by measuring the utility of that action when it is made into a rule for behavior.

sanctuary Ancient right based on church power; allowed a person respite from punishment as long as he or she was within the confines of church grounds.

self-efficacy Individuals' feelings of competence and confidence in their own abilities and power, developed by comparing self to others.

shadow jury A panel of people selected by the defense attorney to represent the actual jury; sits through the trial and provides feedback to the attorney on the evidence presented during the trial.

situational ethics The philosophical position that although there are a few universal truths, different situations call for different responses; therefore, some action can be right or wrong depending on situational factors.

situational model A conceptualization in which lawyers weigh the priorities in each case and decide each case on the particular factors present.

social contract theory The concept developed by Hobbes, Rousseau, and Locke in which the state of nature is a "war of all against all" and, thus, individuals give up their liberty to aggress against others in return for safety. The contract is between society, which promises protection, and the individual, who promises to abide by laws.

stigmatizing shaming The effect of punishment whereby the offender feels cast aside and abandoned by the community.

strict constructionist The view that an individual has no rights unless these rights are specified in the Constitution or have been created by some other legal source.

substantive justice Concerns just deserts—in other words, the appropriate amount of punishment for a crime.

superogatories Actions that are commendable but not required in order for a person to be considered moral.

systems model An absolute or legalistic model in that an attorney's behavior would always be considered wrong or right depending on the ethical rule guiding the definition.

teleological ethical system An ethical system that is concerned with the consequences or ends of an action to determine goodness.

terrorism The "deliberate, negligent, or reckless use of force against

noncombatants, by state or non-state actors for ideological ends and in the absence of a substantively just legal process."

three-strikes laws Sentencing legislation that imposes extremely long sentences for repeat offenders—in this case, after three prior felonies.

treatment Anything used to induce behavioral change with the goal of eliminating dysfunctional or deviant behavior and encouraging productive and normal behavior patterns.

treatment ethic The idea that all criminal acts are symptoms of an underlying pathology.

Tucker telephone An electrical device attached to the genitals of inmates that delivered severe shocks as a form of torture; formerly used at an Arkansas prison farm.

"tune-ups" "Lessons" taught to inmates by Texas prison guards that involved verbal humiliation, profanity, shoves, kicks, and head and body slaps.

utilitarian justice The type of justice that looks to the greatest good for all as the end.

utilitarian principle The principle that all decisions should be made according to what is best for the greatest number.

utilitarianism The ethical system that claims that the greatest good is that which results in the greatest happiness for the

greatest number; major proponents are Bentham and Mill.

values Judgments of desirability, worth, or importance.

veil of ignorance Rawls's idea that people will develop fair principles of distribution only if they are ignorant of their position in society, so in order to get objective judgments, the decision maker must not know how the decision would affect him or her.

wedding-cake illustration The model of justice in which the largest portion of criminal cases forms the bottom layers of the cake and the few "serious" cases form the top layer; the bottom-layer cases get minimal due process.

welfare/therapeutic worker The type of officer who perceives the role as one of counselor to the offender and who helps to effect rehabilitative change.

whistleblowers Individuals, usually employees, who find it impossible to live with knowledge of corruption or illegality within a government or organization and expose it, usually creating a scandal.

wholesight Exploring issues with one's heart as well as one's mind.

zero-tolerance policy The law enforcement approach whereby small violations and ordinances are enforced to the maximum with the expectation that this will reduce more serious crime.

Bibliography

Aaronson, T. 2005. "Hollywood's Finest: After Even a Police Chief Called Them Unfit, These Officers Continue to Patrol Hollywood's Streets." Broward Palm Beach.com, June 30. Retrieved 8/1/2009 from www.browardpalmbeach.com/content/printVersion/139221.

ABC News. 2009. "No Joke: Qld's Anti-corruption System a Hit Worldwide." October 9. Retrieved 10/13/2009 from www.abc.net.au/news/stories/2009/10/09/2710033.html.

Adams, V. 1981. "How to Keep Em Honest." *Psychology Today*, November: 52–53.

Alain, M. 2004. "An Exploratory Study of Quebec's Police Officers' Attitudes Toward Ethical Dilemmas." In *The Contours of Police Integrity*, eds. C. Klockars, S. Ivkovic, and M. Haberfeld, 40–55. Thousand Oaks, CA: Sage.

Alderson, J. 1998. *Principled Policing: Protecting the Public with Integrity*. Winchester, MA: Waterside.

Aleixo, P., and C. Norris. 2000. "Personality and Moral Reasoning in Young Offenders." *Personality and Individual Differences* 28(3): 609–623.

Allen, H., and C. Simonsen. 1986. *Corrections in America: An Introduction*. New York: Macmillan.

Allen, M. 2005. "DeLay Wants Panel to Review Role of Courts." April 2. Retrieved 10/1/2005 from www.washingtonpost xom/ac2/wp-dyn/A19793-2005Aprl?language=printer.

Alpert, B. 2010. "Impeached Judge Thomas Porteous Will Be Tried by Senate Committee." Nola.com, March 12. Retrieved 4/8/2010 from www.nola.com/crime/index.ssf/2010/03/impeached_judge_thomas_porteou.html.

Alpert, G., and R. Dunham. 2004. *Understanding Police Use of Force*. New York: Cambridge University Press.

Alpert, G., and J. MacDonald. 2001. "Police Use of Force: An Analysis of Organizational Characteristics." *Justice Quarterly* 18(2): 393–409.

American Bar Association. 2007. *Model Code of Judicial Conduct*. Retrieved 5/12/2008 from www.abanet.org/judicialethics/approved_MCJC.html.

American Bar Association. 2008. *Standards for Criminal Justice*. Retrieved 5/26/2008 from www.abanet.org/crimjust/standards/pinvestigate.html.

American Judicature. 2005. "Judicial Independence." Retrieved 8/17/2005 from www.ajs.org/include/story.asp?content_id=418.

American Psychological Association, "Ethical Principles of Psychologists and Code of Conduct." Available at www.apa.org/ethics/code/.

Amnesty International. 1999. *"Not Part of My Sentence": Violations of the Human Rights of Women in Custody*. London: Amnesty International.

Amnesty International. 2007. *Amnesty International's Concerns About TASER Use: Statement to the U.S. Justice Department Inquiry into Deaths in Custody*. London: Amnesty International.

Anderson, C. 2010. "John Connolly Gets 40 Years in Prison." WBZ38.com, January 15. Retrieved 5/15/2010 from http://wbtv.com/local/john.connolly.sentence.2.909001.html.

Anderson, P., and L. T. Winfree. 1987. *Expert Witnesses: Criminologists in the Courtroom*. Albany, NY: SUNY Press.

Arax, M. 1999. "Ex-Guard Says 4 Men Set Up Rape of Inmate." *Los Angeles Times*, October 14: A3.

Arax, M. 2004. "Guard Challenges Code of Silence." *Los Angeles Times*, January 20. Retrieved 1/21/2004 from www.lattimes.com/news/printededition/california/la-me-guard20jan20,l,5834171.story?coll=la-headlines-pe-california.

Arboleda-Florez, J. 1983. "The Ethics of Psychiatry in Prison Society." *Canadian Journal of Criminology* 25(1): 47–54.

Arbuthnot, J., and D. Gordon. 1988. "Crime and Cognition: Community Applications of Sociomoral Reasoning Development." *Criminal Justice and Behavior* 15(3): 379–393.

Archibold, R. 2009. "Hired by Customs, but Working for the Cartels." *New York Times*, December 18. Retrieved 12/22/2009 from www.nytimes.com/2009/12/18/us/18corrupt.html?pagewanted=2and_r=1.

Ariens, M. 2008. "American Legal Ethics in an Age of Anxiety." *St. Mary's Law Journal* 40: 343–452.

Ariens, M. 2009. "Playing Chicken: An Instant History of the Battle over Exceptions to Client Confidences." *Journal of the Legal Profession* 33: 239–300.

Armstrong, K., and M. Possley. 2002. "The Verdict: Dishonor." *Chicago Tribune* Reports, November 11. Retrieved 11/11/2002 from www.ishipress.com/dishonor.htm.

Aronson, R. 1977. "Toward a Rational Resolution of Ethical Dilemmas in the Criminal Justice System." In *Criminal Justice Planning and Development*, ed. A. Cohn, 57–71. Beverly Hills, CA: Sage.

Aronson, R., and J. McMurtrie. 2007. "The Use and Misuse of High-tech Evidence by Prosecutors: Ethical and Evidentiary Issues." *Fordham Law Review* 76: 1453–1538.

Arrigo, B., and N. Claussen. 2003. "Police Corruption and Psychological Testing: A Strategy for Reemployment Screening." *International Journal of Offender Therapy and Comparative Criminology* 47: 272–290.

Arrillaga, P. 2006. "Corruption Opens Holes in the Border." Associated Press, in *Austin Statesman*, October 1: A13.

Associated Press. 1997. "After Cash Rains Down in Miami, Finders Remain Quiet Keepers." *Austin American-Statesman*, January 10: A7.

Associated Press. 2000. "Prison Guards Suspected of Money Laundering." *Austin American-Statesman*, January 27: B3.

Associated Press. 2002. "Review of Prison Clinic Stumbles." *Austin American-Statesman*, November 21: A1, A12.

Associated Press. 2004. "FBI Apologizes to Lawyer Held in Madrid Bombings." MSNBC.com, May 25. Retrieved 6/17/2010 from www.msnbc.msn.com/id/5053007/.

Associated Press. 2005. "Study: Detroit Pays More in Police Misconduct Cases than Other Big Cities." Officer.com, July 15. Retrieved 4/9/2008 from www.officer.com/publication/printer,jsp?id=24773.

Associated Press. 2007a. "Focus Turns to Federal Probe in Hewlett-Packard Spy Scandal." *International Herald Tribune*, March 14. Retrieved 4/16/2008 from www.ihtxom/articles/ap/2007/03/15/business/NA-FIN-US-Hewlett-Packard-Directors.php.

Associated Press. 2007b. "Faith Based Prison Programs Multiply." CNN.com. Retrieved 3/27/2008 from www.cnn.com/2007/LIVING/wayoflife/10/15/god.behindbars.ap/.

Associated Press, 2007c. "Has Zero Tolerance Gone Too Far?" MSNBC, June 15. Retrieved 4/2/2008 from www.msnbc.msn.com/id/19249868.

Associated Press. 2007d. "Sexual Abuse Alleged at State Juvenile Prison." *Austin American-Statesman*, February 19: B1, B3.

Associated Press. 2008a. "Ireland Appoints Top Official to Field Complaints of Police Corruption, Malpractice." *International Herald Tribune*. Retrieved 4/9/2008 from www.iht.com/articles/ap/2008/03/ll/europe/EU-GEN-Ireland-Police-Corruption.php.

Associated Press. 2008b. "Report: Dallas County Inmate Cleared of Rape After 26 Years in Prison." *Austin American-Statesman*, January 3: B3.

Associated Press. 2008c. "Wife Says Cleric Tortured After CIA Captured Him." *Austin American-Statesman*, May 15: A4.

Associated Press. 2008d. "White House: Waterboard Technique Is Legal, Useful." *Austin American-Statesman*, February 7: A7.

Associated Press. 2008e. "Deal to Return Children to Parents Collapses." Reported by MSNBC.com, May 30. Retrieved 6/11/2008 from www.mdnv.mdn.vom/if/24887140.

Associated Press. 2008f. "Salaries: Wall Street Generous with its Workers."

Austin American-Statesman, October 5: H6.

Associated Press. 2009a. "Probation Was Most Common Punishment for Prison Smuggling." *Austin American-Statesman*, March 15: B1.

Associated Press. 2009b. "Imprisoned Man Talks About Prison Food Scandal." *Boston Herald*, November 14. Retrieved 11/17/2009 from www.bostonherald.com/news/national/west/view.bg?articleid=1211910.

Associated Press, 2009c. "Photo Catches N.Y. Prison Guard Sleeping on Job in Front of Inmate." Fox News Online, December 30. Retrieved 1/8/2010 from www.foxnews.com/story/0,2933,581411,00.html?test=latestnews.

Associated Press. 2009d. "Ex LAPD officer in Rampart Scandal Takes the 5th." *Mercury News*. Retrieved 4/12/2009 from www.mercurynews.com/breakingnews/ci_12120383?nclick_check=1.

Auerhahn, K. 1999. "Selective Incapacitation and the Problem of Prediction." *Criminology* 37(4): 705–734.

Austin, J., and J. Irwin. 2001. *It's About Time: America's Imprisonment Binge*. Belmont, CA: Wadsworth.

Axtman, K. 2003. "Bungles in Texas Crime Lab Stir Doubt Over DNA." *Christian Science Monitor*, April 18. Retrieved 4/21/2003 from www.csmonitor.com/2003/0418/p03s01-usgn.html.

Babwin, D. 2001. "In Chicago, Allegations Plague Police Department." *Austin American-Statesman*, April 22: A26.

Baelz, P. 1977. *Ethics and Beliefs*. New York: Seabury.

Baker, M. 1985. *Cops: Their Lives in Their Own Words*. New York: Pocket Books.

Baker, A., and J. McGinty. 2010. "NYPD Confidential." *New York Times*, March 26. Retrieved 3/28/2010 from www.nytimes.com/2010/03/28/nyregion/28iab.html.

Balko, R. 2009. "Report: New York State Crime Lab Tainted by Incompetence, Corruption, Indifference." Reason.com blog, December 18. Retrieved 12/22/2009 from www.reason.com/blog/2009/12/18/report-new-york-state-crime-lab.

Bandura, A. 1964. *Principles of Behavior Modification*. New York: Holt, Rinehart and Winston.

Bandura, A. 1969. "Social Learning of Moral Judgments." *Journal of Personality and Social Psychology* 11: 275–279.

Bandura, A. 1971. *Social Learning Theory*. New York: General Learning Press.

Bandura, A. 1990. "Mechanisms of Moral Disengagement in Terrorism." *Origins of Terrorism: Psychologies, Ideologies, Theologies, States of Mind*, ed. W. Reich, 161–191. Cambridge, England: Cambridge University Press.

Bandura, A. 1991. "Social Cognitive Theory of Moral Thought and Action." *Handbook of Moral Behavior and Development*, eds. W. Kurtines and J. Gewirtz, 44–103. Hillsdale, NJ: Lawrence Erlbaum.

Bandura, A. 2002. "Selective Moral Disengagement in the Exercise of Moral Agency." *Journal of Moral Education* 31(2): 101–119.

Barber, B., and H. Lassek. 2010. "Bartlett: Judgment Protection Needed." Tulsaworld.com, July 25. Retrieved 7/26/2010 from www.tulsaworld.com/site/printerfriendlystory.aspx?articleid=20100725_11_A1_Financ960321.

Barker, T. 1983. "Rookie Police Officers' Perceptions of Police Occupational Deviance." *Police Studies* 6: 30–10.

Barker, T. 2002. "Ethical Police Behavior." In *Policing and Misconduct*, ed. K. Lersch, 1–25. Upper Saddle River, NJ: Prentice Hall.

Barker, T., and D. Carter. 1991. "Police Lies and Perjury: A Motivation-Based Taxonomy." In *Police Deviance*, 2d Ed., eds. T. Barker and D. Carter. Cincinnati: Anderson.

Barker, T., and D. Carter, eds. 1994. *Police Deviance*, 3rd Ed. Cincinnati: Anderson.

Barnes, R. 2007. "High Court Reaffirms Leeway on Sentencing." *Austin American-Statesman*, December 11: A7.

Barrier, G., M. Stohr, C. Hemmons, and R. Marsh. 1999. "A Practical User's Guide: Idaho's Method for Implementing Ethical Behavior in a Correctional Setting." *Corrections Compendium* 24(4) (April): 1–3.

Barry, V. 1985. *Applying Ethics: A Text with Readings*. Belmont, CA: Wadsworth.

Bay City News. 2007. "Three Oakland 'Riders' Still Seeking Arbitration." *East Bay Daily News*, February 6. Retrieved 3/28/2008 from www.ebdailynews.com/article/2007-2-6-02-06-07-bcn89.

Bazemore, G., and D. Maloney. 1994. "Rehabilitating Community Service: Toward Restorative Service Sanctions in a Balanced Justice System." *Federal Probation* 58(1): 24–35.

Beauchamp, T. 1982. *Philosophical Ethics*. New York: McGraw-Hill.

Beccaria, C. 1977. *On Crimes and Punishment*, 6th Ed., trans. Henry Paolucci. Indianapolis: Bobbs-Merrill.

Beck, A., and P. Harrison, P. 2007. *Sexual Victimization in State and Federal Prisons Reported by Inmates*. Washington, DC: U.S. Department of Justice, Bureau of Justice Statistics.

Bedau, H. 1982. "Prisoners' Rights." *Criminal Justice Ethics* 1(1): 26–41.

Beecher-Monas, E. 2009. "Reality Bites: The Illusion of Science in Bite-Mark Evidence." *Cardozo Law Review* 30: 1369–1410.

Bellamy, A. 2004. "Ethics and Intervention: 'The Humanitarian Exception' and the Problem of Abuse in the Case of Iraq." *Journal of Peace Research* 41: 131–145.

Belluck, P. 2007. "Judge: US Must Pay Millions in Framing of Four Men." *New York Times*, reported in *Austin American-Statesman*, July 27: A13.

Bender, B. 2005. "War Turning Young Arabs into Terrorists, Studies Say." *Austin American-Statesman*, July 23: A21, A24.

Bentham, J. 1843. "The Rationale of Punishment." In *Ethical Choice: A Case Study Approach*, eds. R. Beck and J. Orr. New York: Free Press, 1970.

Bernstein, N. 2010. "Officials Hid Truth of Immigrant Deaths in Jail." *New York Times*, January 10. Retrieved 1/18/2010 from www.nytimes.com/2010/01/10/us/10detain.html.

Bloom, M. 2007. "Hays Near Deal in Groping Suit" and "Officer Accused of Fondling Child." *Austin American-Statesman*, July 7: B1, B2.

Bloom, M. 2008a. "Corruption Case Yields Guilty Pleas by Ex-officials." *Austin American-Statesman*, January 23: A1, A7.

Bloom, M. 2008b. "Chief Accused of Using Slurs, Abusing Power." *Austin American-Statesman*, March 18.

Bloom, M. 2008c. "Quit: Man Won't Seek Police Job, Lawyer Says." *Austin American-Statesman*, March 22.

Blumberg, A. 1969. "The Practice of Law as a Confidence Game." In *Sociology of Law*, ed. V. Aubert, 321–331. London: Penguin.

Blumenfeld, L. 2007. "The Tortured Lives of Interrogators." *Washington Post*, June 4: A01.

Bomse, A. 2001. "Prison Abuse: Prisoner-Staff Relations." In *Discretion, Community and Correctional Ethics*, eds. J. Kleinig and M. Smith, 79–104. Oxford, England: Rowman and Littlefield.

Bone, J. 2010. "Bernard Madoff 'Beaten Up in Jail'." Timeonline.com. Retrieved 6/14/2010 from www.timesonline.co.uk/tol/news/world/us_and_americas/article7066903.ece.

Bonner, R., and L. Vandecreek, 2006. "Ethical Decision Making for Correctional Mental Health Providers." *Criminal Justice and Behavior* 33: 542–578.

Book, A. 1999. "Shame on You: An Analysis of Modern Shame Punishment as an Alternative to Incarceration." *William and Mary Law Review* 40(2): 653–683.

Borchert, D., and D. Stewart. 1986. *Exploring Ethics*. New York: Macmillan.

Boss, J. 2001. *Ethics for Life*, 2d Ed. Mountain View, CA: Mayfield Publishing.

Bossard, A. 1981. "Police Ethics and International Police Cooperation." In *The Social Basis of Criminal Justice: Ethical Issues for the 80's*, eds. F. Schamalleger and R. Gustafson, 23–38. Washington, DC: University Press.

Bourge, C. 2002. "Sparks Fly Over Private v. Public Prisons." UPI. Retrieved 2/12/2002 from www.upi./com/view.cfm?storyID=20022002-064851-U221.

Bouza, A. 2001. *Police Unbound: Corruption, Abuse, and Heroism by the Boys in Blue*. Amherst, NY: Prometheus.

Bowie, N. 1985. *Making Ethical Decisions*. New York: McGraw-Hill.

Bowker, L. 1980. *Prison Victimization*. New York: Elsevier.

Boyce, W., and L. Jensen. 1978. *Moral Reasoning: A Psychological-Philosophical Integration*. Lincoln: University of Nebraska Press.

Boyer, P. 2001. "Bad Cops." *New Yorker*, May 21. Retrieved 1/17/2003 from www./newyorker.com/printable/?fact/010521fa_FACT.

Braithwaite, J. 2000. "Shame and Criminal Justice." *Canadian Journal of Criminology* 42(3): 281–301.

Braithwaite, J. 2002. "Linking Crime Prevention to Restorative Justice." In *Repairing Communities Through Restorative Justice*, ed. J. Perry, 67–83. Lanham, MD: American Correctional Association.

Braswell, M. 1996/2002. "Ethics, Crime, and Justice: An Introductory Note to Students." In *Justice, Crime, and Ethics*, eds. M. Braswell, B. McCarthy, and B. McCarthy, 3–9. Cincinnati: Anderson.

Braswell, M., and J. Gold. 2002. "Peacemaking, Justice, and Ethics." In *Justice, Crime, and Ethics*, eds. M. Braswell, B. McCarthy, and B. McCarthy, 25–13. Cincinnati: Anderson.

Braswell, M., B. McCarthy, and B. McCarthy. 2002/2007. *Justice, Crime, and Ethics*, 3rd ed. Cincinnati: Anderson.

Braswell, M., L. Miller, and D. Cabana. 2006. *Human Relations and Corrections*, 6th Ed. Prospect Heights, IL: Waveland Press.

Britt, C. 1998. "Race, Religion, and Support of the Death Penalty: A Research Note." *Justice Quarterly* 15(1): 175–191.

Brown, B. 2007. "Community Policing in Post-September 11 America: A Comment on the Concept of Community-Oriented Counterterrorism." *Police Practice and Research*, 8(3): 239–251.

Brown, J., and J. Gaines. 1990. *Justice Denied*. New York: Noble Press.

Brown, M. 1981. *Working the Street*. New York: Russell Sage Foundation.

Bryson, D. 2010. "South Africa: Mandela Marks 20 Years of Freedom." Associated Press, February 11. Retrieved through Yahoo.News on 2/10/2010 from http://news.yahoo.com/s/ap/20100211/ap_on_re_af/af_south_africa_mandela_anniversary.

Buchholz, B. 2005. "Innocents Are Dying, in the Name of Security." *Austin American-Statesman*, September 4: HI.

Buchholz, B. 2008. "Chaplain's Guantanamo Nightmare." *Austin American-Statesman*, March 23: Gl, G4.

Buckle, S. 1993. Natural Law. In *A Companion to Ethics*, ed. P. Singer, 161–175. London: Blackwell Publishing.

Bunker, R. 2009. "Should Police Departments Develop Specific Training and Policies Governing Use of Multiple TASER Shocks Against Individuals Who Might Be in Vulnerable Physiological States?" *Criminology and Public Policy* 8(4): 893–901.

Buntin, J. 2007. "William J. Bratton: Solid Brass." Governing.com. Retrieved 4/20/2008 from www.governing. com/poy/2007/bratton.htm.

Bureau of Justice Statistics. 1992. *Prosecutors in State Courts, 1990*. Washington, DC: U.S. Department of Justice.

Bureau of Justice Statistics. 2006. *Prison and Jail Inmates at MidYear 2006*. Retrieved 5/26/2008 from www.ojp. usdoj.gov/bjs/abstract/pjim06.htm.

Burrell, W. 2000. "How to Prevent PPO Stress and Burnout." *Community Corrections Report* 8(1): 1–2, 13–14.

BusinessInsider.com. 2009. "White Collar Criminals in Jail." July 16. Retrieved 2/10/2010 from www. businessinsider.com/white-collar-criminals-in-jail-2009-7#bernard-madoff-10.

Buttell, F. 2002. "Exploring Levels of Moral Development Among Sex Offenders Participating in Community-Based Treatment." *Journal of Offender Rehabilitation* 34(4): 85–95.

Butterfield, F. 2004. "Mistreatment of Prisoners Is Called Routine in U.S." *New York Times*, May 8. Retrieved 5/12/2004 from www.nytimes. com/2004/05/08/national/08PRIS. html.

Callahan, D. 1982. "Applied Ethics in Criminal Justice." *Criminal Justice Ethics* 1(1): 1, 64.

Carey, M. 2005. "Social Learning, Social Capital, and Correctional Theories: Seeking an Integrated Model." In *What Works and Why: Effective Approaches to Reentry*, ed. American Correctional Association, 1–33. Lanham, MD: American Correctional Association.

Carlyle, E. 2009. "Officer Who Shot Fong Lee Fired." Citypages.com, September 17. Retrieved 4/19/2010 from http:// blogs.citypages.com/blotter/2009/09/ officer_who_sho_1.php.

Carollo, R., and L. Kaplow. 2005. "In Iraq, Military Justice in Doubt," *Austin American-Statesman*, October 2: A1, A9.

Carr, R. 2005. "In Federal Job: Blow Whistle, Get Boot." *Austin American-Statesman*, December 11: A1, A6.

Carr, R., and Herman, H. "Attorney General Apologizes for Handling of Firings but Says He Can Do Job." *Austin American-Statesman*, April 14: A1, A7.

Carroll, L. 1998. *Lawful Order: A Case Study of Correctional Crisis and Reform*. New York: Garland.

Carter, D. 1999. "Drug Use and Drug-Related Corruption of Police Officers." In *Policing Perspectives*, eds. L. Gaines and G. Cordner, 311–324. Los Angeles: Roxbury.

Cassidy, R. 2006. "Character and Context: What Virtue Theory Can Teach Us About a Prosecutor's Ethical Duty to 'Seek Justice'." *Notre Dame Law Review* 82(2): 635–697.

Cauvin, H. 2009. "Inmates, Md. Prison Guards Face Drug Smuggling Case." *Washington Post*, April 17. Retrieved 4/20/2009 from www. washingtonpost.com/wp-dyn/ content/article/2009/04/16/ AR2009041604337.html.

CBS Chicago. 2010. "Cop in Infamous Bar Video Tests Positive for Drugs." CBS Chicago, February 26. Retrieved 4/8/2010 from www. cbs2chicago.com/local/Abbate.cop. bar.2.1524014.html.

CBS.news.com. 2005. "Praise for Iraq Whistleblower." Retrieved 3/12/2008 from www xbsnews. com/stories/2004/05/10/iraq/ main616660.shtml.

CBS.news.com. 2007. "Exposing the Truth of Abu Ghraib." CBSnews. com. Retrieved 3/12/2008 from www.cbsnews.com/ stories/2006/12/07/60minutes/ main2238188_page4.shtml.

Chanen, D. 2009a. "Corruption Trial Starts for Minneapolis Police Officer." StarTribune.com, May 10. Retrieved 5/10/2009 from www.startribune. com/local/44645887.html.

Chanen, D. 2009b. "Ex-strike Force Member Sues Minneapolis." StarTribune.com, August 31. Retrieved 9/2/2009 from www. startribune.com/local/56349982.html.

Chappell, A., and A. Piquero. 2004. "Applying Social Learning Theory to Police Misconduct." *Deviant Behavior* 25: 89–108.

Chattha, Z., and S. Ivkovic. 2004. "Police Misconduct: The Pakistani Paradigm." In *The Contours of Police Integrity*, eds. C. Klockars, S. Ivkovic, and M. Haberfeld, 175–194. Thousand Oaks, CA: Sage.

Chermak, S. 2009. "Conducted Energy Devices and Criminal Justice Policy." *Criminology and Public Policy* 8(4): 861–864.

Chermak, S., E. McGarrell, and J. Gruenewald. 2006. "Media Coverage of Police Misconduct and Attitudes Toward Police." *Policing: An International Journal of Police Strategies and Management*, 29(2): 261–281.

Chevigny, P. 1995. *The Edge of the Knife: Police Violence in the Americas*. New York: New Press.

ChicagoTribune.com. 2008. "Exorcising Officer Abbate." ChicagoTribune. com, March 19. Retrieved 4/10/2008 from www.chicagotribune.com/ news/chi-0319editlmarl9,0,6591244. story.

Christianson, S. 2004. *Innocent: Inside Wrongful Conviction Cases*. New York: New York University Press.

Claussen-Rogers, N., and B. Arrigo. 2005. *Police Corruption and Psychological Testing*. Durham, NC: Carolina Academic Press.

Clear, T. 1996. *Harm in American Penology: Offenders, Victims, and Their Communities*. Albany, NY: SUNY Albany Press.

Close, D., and N. Meier. 1995. *Morality in Criminal Justice*. Belmont, CA: Wadsworth.

CNN.com. 2010. "Jihad Jane, American Who Lived on Main Street." March 10. Retrieved 5/15/2010 from www.cnn. com/2010/CRIME/03/10/jihad.jane. profile/index.html.

Coady, T., S. James, S. Miller, S., and S. O'Keefe. 2000. *Violence and Police Culture*. Victoria, Australia: Melbourne University Press.

Cohen, E. 1991. "Pure Legal Advocates and Moral Agents: Two Concepts of a Lawyer in an Adversary System." In *Justice, Crime, and Ethics*, eds. M. Braswell, B. McCarthy, and B. McCarthy, 123–163. Cincinnati: Anderson.

Cohen, E. 2002. "Pure Legal Advocates and Moral Agents Revisited: A Reply to Memory and Rose." *Criminal Justice Ethics* 21(1): 39–55.

Cohen, H. 1983. "Searching Police Ethics." *Teaching Philosophy* 6(3): 231–242.

Cohen, H. 1985. "A Dilemma for Discretion." In *Police Ethics: Hard Choices in Law Enforcement*, eds. W. Heffernan and T. Stroup, 69–83. New York: John Jay Press.

Cohen, H. 1986. "Exploiting Police Authority." *Criminal Justice Ethics* 5(2): 23–31.

Cohen, H. 1987. "Overstepping Police Authority." *Criminal Justice Ethics* 6(2): 52–60.

Cohen, H., and M. Feldberg. 1991. *Power and Restraint: The Moral Dimension of Police Work*. New York: Praeger.

Cohen, R. 2001. "How They Sleep at Night: DAs Turned Defenders Talk About Their Work." *American Lawyer: The Legal Intelligence*, April 9.

Colarossi, A. 2009. "Lake County Prison Official Arrested on Drug Charge." Orlando Sentinel, September 4. Retrieved 9/15/2009 from www.orlandosentinel.com/news/local/breakingnews/orl-bk-prison-worker-arrest-090409,0,980900.story.

Cole, D. 1999. *No Equal Justice*. New York: Free Press.

Cole, D. 2002. "Trading Liberty for Security After September 11." *Foreign Policy in Focus Policy Report*. Retrieved 8/29/2002 from www.foreignpolicy-infocus.Org/papers/post9-11_body.html.

Cole, D., and J. Lamberth. 2001. "The Fallacy of Racial Profiling." *New York Times*, May 13: A19.

Cole, G. 1970. "The Decision to Prosecute." *Law and Society Review* 4, February: 313–343.

Coleman, S. 2004a. "Police, Gratuities, and Professionalism: A Response to Kania." *Criminal Justice Ethics* 23(1): 63–65.

Coleman, S. 2004b. "When Police Should Say 'No!' to Gratuities." *Criminal Justice Ethics* 23(1): 33–14.

Columbia Law School. 2002. "A Broken System, Part II: Why There Is So Much Error in Capital Cases, and What Can Be Done About it." *Columbia Law School Publications*. Retrieved 2/11/2002 from www.law.columbia.edu/brokensystem2/exe_summary.html.

Comas, M. 2010. "Federal Prison Boosts Security, Builds Relations." OrlandoSentinel.com, January 23. Retrieved 1/29/2010 from www.orlandosentinel.com/news/local/lake/os-lk-coleman-prison-tries-to-burnish-ima20100123,0,2675324.story.

Conlon, E. 2004. *Blue Blood*. New York: Riverhead.

Conti, N. 2006. "Role Call: Preprofessional Socialization into Police Culture." *Policing and Society* 16(3): 221–242.

Conti, N., and J. Nolan. 2005. "Policing the Platonic Cave: Ethics and Efficacy in Police Training." *Policing and Society* 15(2): 166–186.

Copp, T. 2006. "Renewed Patriot Act Could Limit Appeals." *Austin American-Statesman*, March 10: A1, A8.

Corey, G., M. Corey, and P. Callanan. 1988. *Issues and Ethics in Helping Professions*. Pacific Grove, CA: Brooks/Cole.

CourierPostOnline.com. 2010. "Fear Can Help Stop Corruption." January 28. Retrieved 3/16/2010 from http://beta.courierpostonline.com/section/archive?date=20100128.

Cox, D. 2000. "Grand Jury Inquiry into Death of Inmate Extended." *Sun-Sentinel* (Ft. Lauderdale), January 5.

Craig, G. 2003. "Suit Alleges Rampant Female-Inmate Abuse." *Rochester Democrat and Chronicle*. Retrieved 1/30/2003 from www.rochesterdandc.com/news/forprint/0129story2_news.shtml.

Crank, J. 1998. *Understanding Police Culture*. Cincinnati: Anderson.

Crank, J. 2003. *Imagining Justice*. Cincinnati: Anderson.

Crank, J., and M. Caldero. 2000/2005. *Police Ethics: The Corruption of Noble Cause*. Cincinnati: Anderson.

Crank, J., D. Flaherty, and A. Giacomazzi. 2007. "The Noble Cause: An Empirical Assessment." *Journal of Criminal Justice* 35(1): 103–116.

Crank, J., and P. Gregor. 2005. *Counter Terrorism After 9/11: Justice, Security and Ethics Reconsidered*. Cincinnati: Lexis/Nexis Publishing.

Criminal Justice Policy Council. 2003. "Initial Process and Outcome Evaluation of the InnerChange Freedom Initiative." Available at www.lbb.state.tx.us/PubSafety_CrimJustice/6_Links/IFIInitiative.pdf.

Crouch, B. 1980. *Keepers: Prison Guards and Contemporary Corrections*. Springfield, IL: Charles C Thomas.

Crouch, B. 1986. "Guard Work in Transition." In *The Dilemmas of Corrections*, 3d Ed., eds. K. Haas and G. Alpert, 183–203. Prospect Heights, IL: Waveland.

Crouch, B., and J. Marquart. 1989. *An Appeal to Justice: Litigated Reform in Texas Prisons*. Austin: University of Texas Press.

Cullen, F. 1995. "Assessing the Penal Harm Movement." *Journal of Research in Crime and Delinquency*, 32(3): 338–358.

Cunningham, L. 1999. "Taking on Testilying: The Prosecutor's Response to In-Court Police Deception." *Criminal Justice Ethics* 18(1): 26–40.

Curry, M. 2002. "Faulty Drug Cases Draw Police Inquiry." *Dallas Morning News*, February 21: 25A.

Daley, R. 1984. *Prince of the City*. New York: Berkeley.

Daly, K. 1989. "Criminal Justice Ideologies and Practices in Different Voices: Some Feminist Questions About Justice." *International Journal of the Sociology of Law* 17: 1–18.

Dantzker, M., and J. H. McCoy. 2006. "Psychological Screening of Police Recruits: A Texas Perspective." *Journal of Police and Criminal Psychology* 21(1): 23–32.

Dart, B. 2004. "Police Use Taser Guns 'Excessively,' Rights Group Asserts." *Austin American-Statesman*, November 30: A14.

Davies, N. 1991. *White Lies*. London: Chatto and Windus.

Davis, K. 1980. *Discretionary Justice: A Preliminary Inquiry*. Santa Barbara, CA: Greenwood Press.

Davis, M., and F. Elliston. 1986. *Ethics and the Legal Profession*. Buffalo, NY: Prometheus.

Dawson, J. 1992. "Prosecutors in State Courts." *Bureau of Justice Statistics Bulletin*. Washington, DC: U.S. Department of Justice.

Delaney, H. 1990. "Toward a Police Professional Ethic." In *Ethics in Criminal Justice*, ed. F. Schmalleger, 78–95. Bristol, IN: Wyndham Hall.

Delattre, E. 1989a. *Character and Cops: Ethics in Policing*. Washington, DC: American Enterprise Institute for Public Policy Research.

Delattre, E. 1989b. "Ethics in Public Service: Higher Standards and Double Standards." *Criminal Justice Ethics* 8(2): 79–83.

DeLeon-Granados, W., and W. Wells. 1998. "Do You Want Extra Police Coverage with Those Fries?" *Police Quarterly* 1(2): 71–85.

Dershowitz, A. 1982. *The Best Defense*. New York: Vintage.

Dershowitz, A. 2004. *Rights From Wrongs: A Secular Theory of the Origins of Rights*. New York: Basic Books, 2004.

Deutsch, L. 2001. "L.A. Police Corruption Probe Set to Wrap Up." *San Jose Mercury News*. Retrieved 11/12/2001 from www.mercurycenter.com/premium/local/docs/rampart08.htm.

Devine, T. 2008. "The Need for Privacy." *San Marcos Daily Record*, March 28: 4A.

Dewan, D., and B. Goodman. 2007. "Prosecutors Say Corruption in Atlanta Police Dept. Is Widespread." *New York Times*, April 27: A18.

Dial, K., and R. Worley, R. 2008. "A Quantitative Analysis of Inmate Boundary Violators in a Southern Prison System." *American Journal of Criminal Justice* 33: 69–84.

Dilulio, J. 1987. *Governing Prisons: A Comparative Study of Correctional Management*. New York: Free Press.

Donn, J. 2003. "Ex-Agents Say FBI Overlooked Informants' Violent Crimes." *Austin American-Statesman*, March 2: A16.

Donner, F. 1992. *Protectors of Privilege*. Berkeley, CA: University of California Press.

Dorschner, J. 1989. "The Dark Side of the Force." In *Critical Issues in Policing*,

2d Ed., 254–274. Prospect Heights, IL: Waveland.

Draybill, D. 2006. "Forgiveness in the Foundation of Amish Faith." *Austin American-Statesman*, October 11: A11.

Ducrose, M., P. Langan, and E. Smith. 2007. *Contacts Between Police and the Public, 2005*. Bureau of Justice Statistics Report, April 29 (web). Retrieved 5/15/2010 from http://bjs.ojp.usdoj.gov/index.cfm?ty=pbdetail&iid=653.

Dunningham, C., and C. Norris. 1999. "The Detective, the Snout, and the Audit Commission: The Real Costs in Using Informants." *Howard Journal of Criminal Justice* 38(1): 67–87.

Durkheim, E. 1969. "Types of Law in Relation to Types of Social Solidarity." In *Sociology of Law*, ed. V. Aubert: 17–29. London: Penguin.

Dwyer, J. 2005. "Videos Challenge Accounts of Convention Unrest." *New York Times*, April 12. Retrieved 4/19/2008 from www.nytimes.com/2005/04/12/nyregion/12video.html.

Dwyer, J. 2007. "New York Police Spied on Protesters." *New York Times*. Reported in *Austin American-Statesman*, March 25: A11.

Dzur, A., and A. Wertheimer. 2002. "Forgiveness and Public Deliberation: The Practice of Restorative Justice." *Criminal Justice Ethics* 21(1): 3–20.

Ecenbarger, W. 2009. "Luzerne's Youth-Court Scandal: How? Why?" Philly.com., October 25. Retrieved 10/27/2009 from www.philly.com/inquirer/front_page/20091025_Luzerne_x_youth-court_scandal_How_Why_html.

Edelbacher, M., and S. Ivkovic. 2004. "Ethics and the Police: Studying Police Integrity in Austria." In *The Contours of Police Integrity*, eds. C. Klockars, S. Ivkovic, and M. Haberfeld, 19–39. Thousand Oaks, CA: Sage.

Edwards, R. 2009. "Police in 'Water Torture' Inquiry." Telegraph.com, June 10. Retrieved 4/8/2010 from www.telegraph.co.uk/news/newstopics/politics/lawandorder/5489964/Police-in-water-torture-inquiry.html.

Edwards, R., and R. Smith. 2009. "Ian Tomlinson G20 Protests Death:

Police Officer Faces Manslaughter Charge." Telegraph.co.UK, April 17. Retrieved 5/13/2010 from www.telegraph.co.uk/finance/financetopics/g20-summit/5172206/Ian-Tomlinson-G20-protests-death-police-office-faces-manslaughter-charge.html.

Egelko, B. 2007. "Firing over Web Site of Nude Wife Upheld." SFGate.com, September 6. Retrieved 4/2/2008 from www.sfgate.com/cgi-bin/article.cgi?f=/c/a/2007/09/06/MN8ORVPD8.DTL.

Eggen, D. 2007. "White House Secrecy on Wiretaps Described." *Washington Post*, October 3: A05.

Elliott, A., and B. Weiser. 2004. "When Prosecutors Err, Others Pay the Price." *New York Times*. Retrieved 3/23/2004 from www.nytimes.com/2004/03/21/nyregion/21prosecute.html.

Ellis, L., and A. Pontius. 1989. *The Frontal-Limbic-Reticular Network and Variations in Pro-antisociality: A Neurological Based Model of Moral Reasoning and Criminality*. Paper presented at 1989 ASC conference, Reno, NV.

Elliston, F. 1986. "The Ethics of Ethics Tests for Lawyers." In *Ethics and the Legal Profession*, eds. M. Davis and F. Elliston, 50–61. Buffalo, NY: Prometheus.

Emling, S. 2005. "Terror Crackdown Upsets British Race Relations." *Austin American-Statesman*, August 6: A18.

Engel, R. S., J. Calnon, and T. Bernard. 2002. "Theory and Racial Profiling: Shortcomings and Future Directions in Research." *Justice Quarterly* 19(2): 249–273.

ESPN News Service. 2007. "Genarlow Wilson Released After Georgia Supreme Court Decision." ESPN.com, October 26. Retrieved 4/30/2008 from http://sports.espn.go.com/espn/news/story?id=3080331.

Ewin, R. 1990. "Loyalty and the Police." *Criminal Justice Ethics* 9(2): 3–15.

Fahim, K. 2009. "Lawyer Sentenced for Witness Tampering." *New York Times*, December 4. Retrieved 12/22/2009 from www.nytimes.com/2009/12/05/nyregion/05simels.html.

Fahrenthold, D. 2006. "Online Registry or Target List?" *Washington Post*, April 20: A03.

Farrell, G. 2005. "Sentence's Message: Crime Doesn't Pay." *USA Today*, July 14: B1–B2.

Fattah, G. 2005. "Complaints Against Utah Judges Rise." Desertnews.com. Retrieved 8/11/2005 from http://desertnews.com/dn/print/l,1442,600154724,00.html.

Fecteau, L. 1999. "Private Prisons Warned." *Albuquerque Journal*, August 27. Retrieved from www.albqjournal.com/news/2news08-27-99.html.

Feeney, J. 2005. "The Wisdom and Morality of Present-Day Criminal Sentencing." *Akron Law Review* 38: 853–867.

Feibleman, J. 1985. *Justice, Law and Culture*. Boston: Martinus Nijhoff.

Feinberg, J., and H. Gross. 1977. *Justice: Selected Readings*. Princeton, NJ: Princeton University Press.

Felkenes, G. 1987. "Ethics in the Graduate Criminal Justice Curriculum." *Teaching Philosophy* 10(1): 23–36.

Fenton, J. 2010. "Raid on Corrections Officer's Home Shows Links to Criminals." *Baltimore Sun*, July 9. Retrieved 8/7/2010 from www.baltimoresun.com/news/maryland/bs-md-bgf-search-warrant-20100709.0.3437837/story.

Fielding, N. 2003. "Integrity Is Non-negotiable: Cultural, Legal and Organizational Responses to Police Corruption in the United Kingdom." In *Police Corruption: Challenges for Developed Countries*, eds. M. Amir and S. Einstein, 53–74. Huntsville, TX: Office of International Criminal Justice (OICJ), Sam Houston State University.

Fink, P. 1977. *Moral Philosophy*. Encino, CA: Dickinson.

Finn, M., and L. Stalans. 2002. "Police Handling of the Mentally Ill in Domestic Violence Situations." *Criminal Justice and Behavior* 29: 278–289.

Fishbein, D. 2000. *Biobehavioral Perspectives on Criminology*. Belmont, CA: Wadsworth.

Fishman, E. 1994. "'Falling Back' on Natural Law and Prudence: A Reply to Souryal and Potts." *Journal of Criminal Justice Education* 5(2): 189–203.

Fitzgerald, G. 1989. *Report of a Commission of Inquiry Pursuant to Orders in Council*. Brisbane, Australia: Goprint Publishers.

Fitzgerald, P. 2009. "Thoughts on the Ethical Culture of a Prosecutor's Office." *Washington Law Review* 84: 11–35.

Flanagan, D., and K. Jackson. 1987. "Justice, Care, and Gender: The Kohlberg-Gilligan Debate Revisited." *Ethics* 97: 622–637.

Fletcher, D. 2010, "Why Is Pat Robertson Blaming Haiti?" Time.com, January 14. Retrieved 2/14/2010 from www.time.com/time/specials/packages/article/0,28804,1953379_1953494_1953674,00.html.

Fletcher, G. 1993. *Loyalty: An Essay on the Morality of Relationships*. New York: Oxford University Press.

Fogel, D., 1975. *We Are the Living Proof*. Cincinnati: Anderson.

Fogelson, R. 1977. *Big City Police*. Cambridge, MA: Harvard University Press.

Folkenflik, D. 2010. "Prosecutor Turns on Crusading Journalism School." NPR.org., January 11. Retrieved 1/18/2010 from www.npr.org/templates/story/story.php?storyId=122359627.

Foot, P. 1982. "Moral Relativism." In *Relativism: Cognitive and Moral*, eds. J. Meiland and M. Krausz, 152–167. Notre Dame, IN: University of Notre Dame Press.

Fountain, H. 2009. "Plugging Holes in the Science of Forensics." *New York Times*, May 12. Retrieved 5/12/2009 from www.nytimes.com/2009/05/12/science/12fore.html.

Fountain, J. 2001. "Former Top Chicago Detective Admits to Leading Theft Ring." *New York Times*, October 26: A16.

Foxnews.com. 2007. "Congressman William Jefferson Indicted on Bribery Charges." June 5. Retrieved 5/2/2008 from www.foxnews.com/story/0,2933,377774,00.html.

Freedman, M. 1986. "Professional Responsibility of the Criminal Defense Lawyer: The Three Hardest Questions." In *Ethics and the Legal Profession*, eds. M. Davis and F. Elliston, 328–339. Buffalo, NY: Prometheus.

Friedrich, R. 1980. "Police Use of Force: Individuals, Situations, and Organizations." *Annals of American Academy of Political and Social Science* 452: 82–97.

Fuller, L. 1969. *The Morality of Law*. New Haven, CT: Yale University Press.

Futch, M. 2009. "When Good Cops Go Bad." *Fayetteville Observer*, May 10. Retrieved 5/11/2009 from http://fayobserver.com/print?id=326020andtype=article.

Fyfe, J., and R. Kane. 2006. *Bad Cops: A Study of Career-Ending Misconduct Among New York City Police Officers* (Document #215795). Washington, DC: U.S. Department of Justice.

Galloway, J., and J. Kuhnhenn. 2005. "Senators Add Anti-torture Words to Bill." *Austin American-Statesman*, October 6: A4.

Gallup Poll. 2005. *Gallup Poll Online*. "Respect for Police." Retrieved 4/20/2008 from www.gallup.com/poll/19783/Confidence-Local-Police-Drops-10Year-Low.aspx#2.

Gallup Poll. 2006. *Gallup Poll Online*, May 8, 2008. Retrieved 5/5/2008 from www.gallup.com/poll/25888/Nurses-Top-List-Most-Honest-Ethical-Professions.aspx.

Galston, W. 1980. *Justice and the Human Good*. Chicago: University of Chicago Press.

Gamino, D. 2009. "A Giant of Texas History." *Austin American-Statesman*, October 15: A1, A11.

Garay, A. 2007. "Man's Innocence in Gang Rape Affirmed." *Austin American-Statesman*, April 10: B5.

Gardner, H. 2007. *Five Minds for the Future*. Boston: Harvard Business School.

Garland, D. 1990. *Punishment and Modern Society*. Chicago: University of Chicago Press.

Garner, J., C. Maxwell, and C. Heraux. 2002. "Characteristics Associated with the Prevalence and Severity of Force Used by the Police." *Justice Quarterly* 19(4): 705–745.

Gavaghan, M., K. Arnold, and J. Gibbs. 1983. "Moral Judgment in Delinquents and Nondelinquents: Recognition versus Production Measures." *Journal of Psychology* 114: 267–274.

Geis, G., A. Mobley, and D. Shichor. 1999. "Private Prisons, Criminological Research and Conflict of Interest." *Crime and Delinquency* 45(3): 372–388.

General Accounting Office (GAO). 1996. *Private and Public Prisons— Studies Comparing Operational Costs and/or Quality of Service.* Washington, DC: U.S. Government Printing Office.

Gershman, B. 1991. "Why Prosecutors Misbehave." In *Justice, Crime, and Ethics*, eds. M. Braswell, B. McCarthy, and B. McCarthy, 163–177. Cincinnati: Anderson.

Gershman, J., and M. Saul. 2010. "An Epic Spree of Mischief." *Wall Street Journal Online.* March 6. Retrieved 5/8/2010 from http://online.wsj.com/article/SB10001424052748704869304575103802953340446.html.

Getlin, J. 2002. "DA Suggests Overturning Convictions in Jogger Case." *Austin American-Statesman*, December 6: A16.

Giannelli, P., and K. McMunigal. 2007. "Prosecutors, Ethics, and Expert Witnesses." *Fordham Law Review* 76(3): 1493–1537.

Gibbs, J., K. Arnold, H. Ahlborn, and F. Cheesman. 1984. "Facilitation of Sociomoral Reasoning in Delinquents." *Journal of Consulting and Clinical Psychology* 52(1): 37–15.

Gillers, S. 2004. "Tortured Reasoning." *American Lawyer*, July: 65–66.

Gilligan, C. 1982. *In a Different Voice: Psychological Theory and Women's Development.* Cambridge, MA: Harvard University Press.

Gilligan, C. 1987. "Moral Orientation and Moral Development." In *Women and Moral Theory*, eds. E. F. Kittay and D. Meyers, 19–37. Totowa, NJ: Rowman and Littlefield.

Gilmartin, K., and J. Harris. 1998. "Law Enforcement Ethics: The Continuum of Compromise." *Police Chief*, January 1998. Retrieved 3/26/2008 from www.rcmp-learning.org/docs/ecddl 222.htm.

Giradeaux, J. 1949. *The Madwoman of Chaillot*, adapted by Maurice Valency. New York: Random House.

Glaser, B. 2003. "Therapeutic Jurisprudence: An Ethical Paradigm for Therapists in Sex Offender Treatment Programs." *Western Criminology Review* 4 (2): 143–154.

Glaze, L., and Bonczar, T. 2009. *Probation and Parole in the United States, 2008.* Washington, DC: U.S. Dept of Justice, Bureau of Justice Statistics.

Glendon, M. 1994. *A Nation Under Lawyers.* New York: Farrar, Straus and Giroux.

Glenn, L. 2001. *Texas Prisons: The Largest Hotel Chain in Texas.* Austin, TX: Eakin.

Glover, S., and M. Lait. 2000. "71 More Cases May Be Voided Due to Rampart." *Los Angeles Times.* Retrieved 4/20/2000 from www.latimes.rampart/lat_rampart000418.html.

Golab, J. 2000. "L.A. Confidential." Salon.com. Retrieved 1/17/2003 from http://dir.salon.com/news/feature/2000/24/rampart/index.html.

Gold, J., M. Braswell, and B. McCarthy. 1991. "Criminal Justice Ethics: A Survey of Philosophical Theories." In *Justice, Crime, and Ethics*, eds. M. Braswell, B. McCarthy, and B. McCarthy, 3–25. Cincinnati: Anderson.

Gold, S., and J. Rubin. 2009. "LAPD Gang Units Feel the Pinch of Financial Disclosure Rule." *Los Angeles Times* Online, December 28. Retrieved 12/30/2009 from www.latimes.com/news/local/la-me-gangcops28-2009dec28,0,1554614,full.story.

Golden, T. 2005. "Cruel and Unusual Punishment." *Austin American-Statesman*, May 21: A16.

Gonzales, S. 2009. "Tasered 72-year-old Gets $." *Austin American-Statesman*, October 6: B1, B3.

Gourevitch, P., and E. Morris. 2008. "Exposed: The Woman Behind the Pictures at Abu Ghraib." *New Yorker.* Retrieved 3/21/2008 from www.newyorker.com/reporting/2008/03/24/080324fa_fact_gourevitch.

Greene, J. 1999. "Zero Tolerance: A Case Study of Police Policies and Practices in New York City." *Crime and Delinquency* 45(2): 171–187.

Greene, J. 2001. "Bailing Out Private Jails." *American Prospect* 12(16): 23–27.

Greene, J., A. Piquero, M. Hickman, and B. Lawton. 2004. *Police Integrity and Accountability in Philadelphia: Predicting and Assessing Police Misconduct.* Washington, DC: U.S. Dept. of Justice, NCJRS, available at www.ncjrs.gov.

Greenhouse, L. 2007. "Supreme Court Took Big, Small Steps to Right." *Austin American-Statesman*, July 1: A15.

Greenhouse, L. 2008. "Justices, 5–4, Back Detainee Appeals for Guantanamo." *New York Times*, June 13.

Greenwood, P. 1982. *Selective Incapacitation.* Santa Monica, CA: Rand Institute.

Grezlak, H., and L. Strupczewski. 2009. "Pa. Judicial Corruption Probe Said to be Eyeing Criminal Cases." Law.com, June 1. Retrieved 4/6/2010 from www.law.com/jsp/law/LawArticleFriendly.jsp?id=1202431103066.

Grossi, E., and B. Berg. 1991. "Stress and Job Dissatisfaction Among Correctional Officers: An Unexpected Finding." *International Journal of Offender Therapy and Comparative Criminology* 35(1): 79–110.

Grotius, H. 2005. *The Rights of War and Peace. Book 1*, ed. Richard Tuck. Indianapolis, IN: Liberty Fund.

Guilfoil, J. 2010. "Ex-officer Admits to Obstruction of Justice." Boston.com, February 17. Retrieved 2/22/2010 from www.boston.com/news/local/massachusetts/article.

Haag, A. 2006. "Ethical Dilemmas Faced by Correctional Psychologists in Canada." *Criminal Justice and Behavior* 33: 93–109.

Hafetz, D. 2002. "Their Innocence Proved, Men Sue." *Austin American-Statesman*, November 8: B1.

Hall, H. 2008. "A Sentence Too Close to Death." *Los Angeles Times*, March 27.

Hall, M. 2002. Death Isn't Fair. *Texas Monthly*, December: 124–167.

Hamm, M. 1989. "Whistleblowing in Corrections." *Sociological Viewpoints* 5(1): 35–45.

Haney, C. 2008. "A Culture of Harm: Taming the Dynamics of Cruelty in Supermax Prisons." *Criminal Justice and Behavior* 35: 956–984.

Hanners, D. 2009. "Family Claims 'Massacre'; Cops Say Justified Shooting." Twincities.com, April 11. Retrieved 4/12/2009 from www.twincities.com/ci_12119906?nclick_check=1.

Hansen, M. 2007. "The Toughest Call." *ABA Journal*, August: 28–29.

Harmon, T., and Lofquist, W. 2005. "Too Late for Luck: A Comparison of Post-Furman Exonerations and Executions of the Innocent." *Crime and Delinquency* 51(4): 498–520.

Harris, C. 1986. *Applying Moral Theories.* Belmont, CA: Wadsworth.

Harris, C. 2010. *Pathways of Police Misconduct.* Durham, NC: Carolina Academic Press.

Harris, D. 2004. "Review Essay/Profiling: Theory and Practice." *Criminal Justice Ethics* 23(2): 51–57.

Harris, D. 2005. *Good Cops: The Case for Preventive Policing.* New York: The New Press.

Harris, D. 2006. "Do Something Before the Next Attack, but Not This." *Criminal Justice Ethics* 25(2): 46–54.

Harris Poll. 2008. Support for Capital Punishment. Harris Opinion Poll. Retrieved 5/24/2008 from www.pollingreport.com/crime.htm.

Hartman, V. 2001. "Implementing an Asset Forfeiture Program." *FBI Law Enforcement Bulletin*, 70(1): 1–7.

Hashimoto, E. 2008. "Toward Ethical Plea Bargaining." *Cardozo Law Review* 30: 949–963.

Hassine, V. 1996. *Life Without Parole: Living in Prison Today.* Los Angeles: Roxbury.

Hatamyar, P., and K. Simmons. 2002. "Are Women More Ethical Lawyers? An Empirical Study." *Florida State University Law Review* 31: 785–857.

Hauser, C. 2009. "Few Results for Reports of Police Misconduct." *New York Times*, October 5. Retrieved 10/13/2009 from www.nytimes.com/2009/10/05/nyregion/05ccrb.html.

Haven, P. 2009. "Spanish Court to Let U.S. Torture Case Proceed." *Austin American-Statesman*, March 29: A7.

Hays, K. 2005. "Report: Houston Crime Lab Was Long Neglected." *Austin American-Statesman*, July 1: B7.

Heffernan, W., and J. Kleinig. 2000. *From Social Justice to Criminal Justice: Poverty and the Administration of Criminal Law.* New York: Oxford University Press.

Heidensohn, F. 1986. "Models of Justice: Portia or Persephone? Some Thoughts on Equality, Fairness and Gender in the Field of Criminal Justice." *International Journal of the Sociology of Law* 14: 287–298.

Henriques, Z. 2001. "The Path of Least Resistance: Sexual Exploitation of Female Offenders as an Unethical Corollary to Retributive Ideology and Correctional Practice." In J. Kleinig and M. Smith, *Discretion, Community and Correctional Ethics*, pp. 192–201. Oxford, England: Rowman and Littlefield.

Hentoff, N. 1999. "Serpico: Nothing Has Changed." VillageVoice.com. Retrieved 11/4/1999 from www.villagevoice xom/issues/9944/hentoff.shtml.

Herbert, B. 2002. "In Tulia, Justice Has Gone into Hiding," *Austin American-Statesman*, August 13: A9.

Herbert, B. 2003. "Truth Has Been Told About Tulia, but Story Isn't Over Yet." *Austin American-Statesman*, April 29: A9.

Herbert, S. 1996. "Morality in Law Enforcement: Chasing 'Bad Guys' with the Los Angeles Police Department." *Law and Society Review* 30(4): 799–818.

Hermann, P. 2009. "The Murky World of Informants." BaltimoreSun.com., October 4. Retrieved 6/17/2010 from http://articles.baltimoresun.com/2009-10-04/news/0910030041_1_informants-fbi-agent-cops-and-crooks/3.

Hersh, F. 1979. *Developing Moral Growth: From Piaget to Kohlberg.* New York: Longman.

Hickey, J., and P. Scharf. 1980. *Toward a Just Correctional System.* San Francisco: Jossey-Bass.

Hickman, M., A. Piquero, B. Lawton, and J. Greene. 2001. "Applying Tittle's Control Balance Theory to Police Deviance." *Policing* 24(4): 497–519.

Hicks, W. 2004. "Constraints in the Police Use of Force: Implications of the Just War Tradition." *American Journal of Criminal Justice* 28(2): 254–270.

Hight, B. 2005. "In Atoning for Tragedy, a Former Navy Captain Finds His Voice." *Austin American-Statesman*, March 11: A11.

Hilzenrath, D. 2010. "Swiss Banker Turned Whistleblower Ended up with a Prison Sentence." *Washington Post*, May 16: G01.

Hinman, L. 1998. *Ethics: A Pluralistic Approach to Moral Theory*, 2d Ed. Ft. Worth, TX: Harcourt Brace.

Hobbes, T. 1651. *Leviathan.* New York: Penguin Classics (1982).

Hofer, P., K. Blackwell, and R. B. Ruback. 1999. "The Effect of Federal Sentencing Guidelines on Inter-judge Sentencing Disparity." *Journal of Criminal Law and Criminology* 90(1): 239–321.

Holley, P. 2010. "Second Officer Fired Over Alleged Misconduct." MySANews.com, March 20. Retrieved 4/7/2010 from www.mysanantonio.com/news/local_news/Officer_accused_of_sexual_assault_to_be_fired.html.

Holmes, M. 2000. "Minority Threat and Police Brutality: Determinants of Civil Rights Criminal Complaints in U.S. Municipalities." *Criminology* 38(2): 343–336.

Hook, M. 2001. "How and Why the System Is Failing Victims with Mental Impairments." *Crime Victims Report* 4(6): 81–82.

Hopfe, L. 1983. *Religions of the World.* New York: Macmillan.

Hornum, F., and F. Stavish. 1978. "Criminology Theory and Ideology: Four Analytical Perspectives in the Study of Crime and the Criminal Justice System." In *Essays on the Theory and Practice of Criminal Justice*, ed. R. Rich, 143–161. Washington, DC: University Press.

Houston, J. 1999. *Correctional Management: Functions, Skills, and Systems.* Chicago: Nelson-Hall.

Huberts, L., M. Kaptein, and K. Lasthuizen. 2007. "A Study of the Impact of Three Leadership Styles on Integrity Violations Committed by Police Officers." *Policing* 30(4): 587–607.

Human Rights Watch. 1998. *Shielded from Justice: Police Brutality and Accountability in the U.S.* New York: Human Rights Watch.

Hunter, R. 1999. "Officer Opinions on Police Misconduct." *Journal of Contemporary Criminal Justice* 15(2): 155–170.

Huspek, M., R. Martinez, and L. Jiminez. 2001. "Violations of Human Civil Rights on the U.S.-Mexico Border, 1997–1997: A Report." In *Notable Selections in Criminal Criminology and Criminal Justice*, eds. D. Baker and R. Davin, 183–202. Guilford, CT: McGraw-Hill/Dushkin.

Hylton, W. 2006. "Prisoner of Conscience." GQ.com. Retrieved 3/21/2008 from www.men.style.com/gq/features/landing?id=content_4785.

Institute for Law Enforcement Administration. 2008. Ethical Courage Awards. Retrieved 4/15/2008 from www.cailaw.org/ilea/pastwinners.html.

International Association of Chiefs of Police (IACP). 2008 (1999). *Ethics Training in Law Enforcement.* Retrieved 6/17/2010 from www.theiacp.org.

Isikoff, M. 2008. "The Fed Who Blew the Whistle." *Newsweek* Online. December 13. Retrieved 3/15/2010 from www.newsweek.com/id/174601.

Ivkovic, S., and C. Klockars. 2004. "Police Integrity in Croatia." In *The Contours of Police Integrity*, eds. C. Klockars, S. Ivkovic, and M. Haberfeld, 56–74. Thousand Oaks, CA: Sage.

Jablon, R. 2000. "L.A. Confronts Police Scandal That May Cost Tens of Millions." *Austin American-Statesman*, February 19: A18.

Jackman, T., and A. Kumar. 2009. "3 of 'Norfolk 4' Conditionally Pardoned in Rape, Killing." *Washington Post*, August 7. Retrieved 5/27/2010 from www.washingtonpost.com/wp-dyn/content/article/2009/08/06/AR2009080602065.html.

Jacoby, J., L. Mellon, and W. Smith. 1980. *Policy and Prosecution.* Washington, DC: Bureau of Social Science Research.

Janey, A. 2010. "First Posthumous Pardon Granted." *Austin American-Statesman*, March 2: B1, B6.

Javed, N. 2009. "Police Freebies Spark Resignation." TheStar.com, April 9. Retrieved 4/12/2009 from www.thestar.com/printArticle/616038.

Jeffrey, D. 2007. "How Prosecutors Go Bad." *Legal Times*, August 6: 1–2.

Jenson, E., and J. Gerber, 1996. "The Civil Forfeiture of Assets and the War on Drugs: Expanding Criminal Sanctions While Reducing Due Process Protection." *Crime and Delinquency* 42(3): 421–134.

Johanek, M. 2008. "Justice Department Scandal Almost Buried by Financial Crisis." *Toledo Blade*, October 10.

Retrieved 11/10/2008 from www.toledoblade.com/apps/pbcs.dll/article?AID=/20081010/COLUMNIST13/810109970/-1/NEWS508.

John-Hall, A. 2009. "Temple Reporter Was Shocked, Too." Philly.com, April 10. Retrieved 4/12/2009 from www.philly.com/philly/hp/news_update/20090410_Annette_john-Hall_Temple_reporter_was_shocked_too.html.

Johnson, C. 2009. "Justice Department Looks to Avoid Another." *The Washington Post*, October 15. Retrieved 10/15/2009 from www.washingtonpost.com/wp-dyn/content/article/2009/10/14/AR2009/.

Johnson, D. 2004. "Police Integrity in Japan." In *The Contours of Police Integrity*, eds. C. Klockars, S. Ivkovic, and M. Haberfeld, 130–160. Thousand Oaks, CA: Sage.

Johnson, J. 2010. "Probation Fraud Investigation Continues." OnlineAthens.com, May 3. Retrieved 6/2/2010 from http://onlineathens.com/stories/050310/new_631637628.shtml.

Johnson, R. 1996/2002. *Hard Time: Understanding and Reforming the Prison.* Belmont, CA: Wadsworth.

Johnson, R. 2005. "Whistleblowing and the Police." *Rutgers University Journal of Law and Urban Policy* 1(3): 74–83.

Johnson, R. 2006. *Hard Time: Understanding and Reforming the Prison.* Belmont, CA: Wadsworth.

Johnston, M. 1995. "Police Corruption." In *Morality in Criminal Justice*, eds. D. Close and N. Meier. Belmont, CA: Wadsworth.

Josephson Institute of Ethics. 2005. *Preserving the Public Trust.* Available at www.josephsoninstitute.org.

Josephson Institute of Ethics. 2008. 6 Pillars of Character. Retrieved 3/19/2008 from www.josephsoninstitute.org/MED/MED-2sjosephsoninstituteixpillars.html.

Josi, D., and D. Sechrest. 1998. *The Changing Career of the Correctional Officer: Policy Implications for the 21st Century.* Boston: Butterworth-Heinemann.

Juozapavicius, J. 2008. "Oklahoma Sheriff Charged with Using Inmates as Sex Slaves." Retrieved 4/26/2008

from www.officer.com/publication/printer.jsp ?id=41064.

Kamisar, Y., W. LeFave, and J. Israel. 1980. *Modern Criminal Procedure: Cases, Comments, and Questions.* St. Paul, MN: West.

Kane, R. 2002. "The Social Ecology of Police Misconduct." *Criminology* 40(4): 867–896.

Kane, R. 2005. "Compromised Police Legitimacy as a Predictor of Violent Crime in Structurally Disadvantaged Communities." *Criminology* 43(2): 469–498.

Kane, R., and M. White. 2009. "Bad Cops: A Study of Career-Ending Misconduct Among New York City Police Officers." *Criminology and Public Policy* 8(4): 737–769.

Kania, R. 1988. "Police Acceptance of Gratuities." *Criminal Justice Ethics* 7(2): 37–49.

Kania, R. 1999. "The Ethics of the Death Penalty." *The Justice Professional* 12: 145–157.

Kania, R. 2004. "The Ethical Acceptability of Gratuities: Still Saying 'Yes' After All These Years." *Criminal Justice Ethics* 23(1): 54–63.

Kant, I. 1788. *Critique of Practical Reason*, trans. Lewis White Beck. Chicago: University of Chicago Press (1949).

Kant, I. "Ethical Duties to Others: Truthfulness." In *Lectures on Ethics*, ed. L. Infield, 224–232. Indianapolis: Hackett (1981).

Kaplan, M. 1976. *Justice, Human Nature and Political Obligation.* New York: Free Press.

Kappeler, V., R. Sluder, and G. Alpert. 1984/1994. *Forces of Deviance: Understanding the Dark Side of Policing.* Prospect Heights, IL: Waveland.

Karp, D. 1998. "The Judicial and Judicious Use of Shame Penalties." *Crime and Delinquency* 44(2): 277–295.

Kassin, S., S. Drizin, T. Grisso, G. Gudjonsson, and R. Leo. 2010. "Police-Induced Confessions: Risk Factors and Recommendations." *Law and Human Behavior* 34: 3–38.

Katz, M. 2010. "Camden Police Scandal Has Widespread Consequences." Philly.com, February 21. Retrieved 3/5/2010 from www.philly.com/philly/news/homepage/20100221_Camden_police_scandal_has_widespread_consequences.html.

Katz, M., B. Boyer, and G. Anastasia. 2010. "Camden Officer Admits Role in Rogue Cop Operation." Philly. com, March 20. Retrieved 3/22/2010 from www.philly.com/philly/news/homepage/20100320_Camden_officer_admits_role_in_rogue_cop_operation.html.

Kauffman, K. 1988. *Prison Officers and Their World.* Cambridge, MA: Harvard University Press.

Keith, L. 2002. "Judicial Independence and Human Rights Protection Around the World." *Judicature* 84(4): 195–200.

Kelly, J., and P. Wearne. 1998. "Tainting Evidence: Inside the Scandal at the FBI Crime Lab." *New York Times.* Retrieved 5/15/2010 from www.nytimes.com/books/first/k/kelly-evidence.html.

Kennedy, T., and P. McEnroe. 2009. "On a Collision Course." StarTribune.com, April 23. Retrieved 4/18/2009 from www.startribune.com/local/43318822.html.

Kessler, G. 1992. *Voices of Wisdom: A Multicultural Philosophy Reader.* Belmont, CA: Wadsworth.

Khanna, R. 2009. "New Tests Show Man Jailed in 1987 Attack Is Innocent, Defense Attorney Says." Chronicle.com, April 24. Retrieved 6/17/2010 from www.chron.com/disp/story.mpl/front/6391280.html.

Kim, V., and J. Leonard. 2010. "Justice Department Seeks Police Reform in Inglewood." LATimes.com, January 11. Retrieved 1/11/2010 from www.latimes.com/news/local/la-me-inglewood11-2010jan11,0,7526464,full.story.

King, R., and M. Mauer. 2001. *Aging Behind Bars: Three Strikes Seven Years Later.* Washington, DC: The Sentencing Project.

King, R., and M. Mauer. 2002. *State Sentencing and Corrections Policy in an Era of Fiscal Restraint.* Washington, DC: The Sentencing Project.

Kipnis, K. 2001. "Health Care in the Corrections Setting: An Ethical Analysis." In J. Kleinig and M. Smith, *Discretion, Community and Correctional Ethics,* 113–124.

Lanham, MD: Rowman and Littlefield.

Kirchmeier, J., S. Greenwald, H. Reynolds, and J. Sussman. 2009. "Vigilante Justice: Prosecutor Misconduct in Capital Cases." *Wayne Law Review* 55: 1327–1385.

Kleindienst, L. 1999. "Florida Prison Guards Twice as Likely as Police to Commit Violations." *Sun-Sentinel* (Ft. Lauderdale), August 25: A1.

Kleinig, J. 1986. "The Conscientious Advocate and Client Perjury." *Criminal Justice Ethics* 5(2): 3–15.

Kleinig, J. 1999. "Human Dignity and Human Rights: An Emerging Concern in Police Practice." In *Human Dignity and Police: Ethics and Integrity in Police Work,* ed. G. Lynch, 8–40. Springfield, IL: Charles C Thomas.

Kleinig, J. 2001a. "National Security and Police Interrogations: Some Ethical Considerations." In *Policing, Security and Democracy: Special Aspects of Democratic Policing,* eds. S. Einstein and M. Amir, 105–127. Huntsville, TX: Office of International Criminal Justice (OICJ), Sam Houston State University.

Kleinig, J. 2001b. "Professionalizing Incarceration." In *Discretion, Community and Correctional Ethics,* ed. J. Kleinig and M. Smith, 1–17. Oxford, England: Rowman and Littlefield.

Klockars, C. 1983. "The Dirty Harry Problem." In *Thinking About Police: Contemporary Readings,* ed. C. Klockars and S. Mastrofski, 428–438. New York: McGraw-Hill.

Klockars, C. 1984. "Blue Lies and Police Placebos." *American Behavioral Scientist* 27(4): 529–544.

Klockars, C., S. Ivkovic, and M. Haberfeld. 2004. *The Contours of Police Integrity.* Thousand Oaks, CA: Sage.

Klockars, C., S. Ivkovic, W. Harver, and M. Haberfeld. 2000. *The Measurement of Police Integrity? NIJ Research in Brief.* Washington, DC: U.S. Department of Justice.

Knudten, M. 1978. "The Prosecutor's Role in Plea Bargaining: Reasons Related to Actions." In *Essays on the Theory and Practice of Criminal Justice,* ed. R. Rich, 275–295. Washington, DC: University Press.

Kohlberg, L. 1976. "Moral Stages and Moralization." In *Moral Development and Behavior: Theory, Research and Social Issues,* ed. T. Lickona, 31–53. New York: Holt, Rinehart and Winston.

Kohlberg, L. 1983. *Essays in Moral Development, Vol. 2. The Psychology of Moral Development.* New York: Harper and Row.

Kohlberg, L. 1984. *The Psychology of Moral Development.* San Francisco: Harper and Row.

Kohlberg, L., and D. Candel, 1984. "The Relationship of Moral Judgment to Moral Action." In *The Psychology of Moral Development,* ed. L. Kohlberg, 498–582. San Francisco: Harper and Row.

Kohn, S. 1997. "Testimony of Stephen Kohn, Attorney for Frederic Whitehurst." Retrieved 5/14/2010 from www.fas.org/irp/congress/1997_hr/h970513w.html.

Kottak, C. 1974. *Anthropology: The Exploration of Human Diversity.* New York: Random House.

Kramer, M. 2004. *Where Law and Morality Meet.* New York: Oxford University Press.

Kramer, R. 1982. "The Debate Over the Definition of Crime: Paradigms, Value Judgments, and Criminological Work." In *Ethics, Public Policy and Criminal Justice,* eds. F. Elliston and N. Bowie, 33–59. Cambridge, MA: Oelgeschlager, Gunn and Hain.

Kraska, P., and V. Rappeler. 1995. "To Serve and Pursue: Exploring Police Sexual Violence Against Women." *Justice Quarterly* 12(1): 85–111.

Kraus, C. 1994. "Poll Finds a Lack of Faith in the Police." *New York Times,* June 19: A1.

Kravets, D. 2003. "ACLU: Privacy Rights Diminished." Salon.com. Retrieved 1/16/2003 from www.salon.com/tech/wire/2003/01/16/aclu/.

Kreiger, M. 2009. "A Twenty-First Century Ethos for the Legal Profession: Why Bother?" *Denver University Law Review* 86: 865–900.

Kreimer, S. 2007. "Rays of Sunlight in a Shadow 'War': FOIA, The Abuses of Anti-Terrorism, and the Strategy of Transparency." *Lewis and Clark Law Review* 11(4): 1141–1220.

Kreytak, S. 2008. "No Excess Force Used in Police Beating in Austin." *Austin American-Statesman*, March 28, A1.

Kreytak, S. 2010. "3-Year License Probation for Gesturing Lawyer." *Austin American-Statesman*, May 6: B1.

Krisberg, B. 1975. *Crime and Privilege: Toward a New Criminology*. Englewood Cliffs, NJ: Prentice Hall.

Krogstand, J., and J. Robertson. 1979. "Moral Principles for Ethical Conduct." *Management Horizons* 10(1): 13–24.

Kronenwerter, M. 1993. *Capital Punishment: A Reference Handbook*. Santa Barbara, CA: ABC-CLIO.

KTRK. 2009. "Man Walks Free After 22 years." KTRK News, April 30. Retrieved 5/25/2010 from http://abclocal.go.com/ktrk/story?section=news/localandid=6789190.

LaForgia, M. 2010. "Inmates Describe Illicit Marketplace in Palm Beach County Prisons." *Palm Beach Post*, February 13. Retrieved 3/8/2010 from www.palmbeachpost.com/news/crime/inmates-describe-illicit-marketplace-in-palm-beach-county-231581.html.

Lait, M., and S. Glover. 2000. "LAPD Chief Calls for Mass Dismissal of Tainted Cases." LATimes.com. Retrieved 2/1/2000 from www.latimes.com/news/state/200000127/t000008518.html.

Laitinen, A. 2002. "Corruption of the Police: Is It Not at All a Problem in Finland?" Paper presented at ACJS, Anaheim, CA, March.

Laitinen, A. 2004. "Corruption and Policing in Finland." In *Police Corruption: Challenges for Developed Countries*, eds. M. Amir and S. Einstein, 383–413. Huntsville, TX: Office of International Criminal Justice (OICJ), Sam Houston State University.

Laker, B., and W. Ruderman. 2010. "D.A.'s Pick for Top Detective Oversaw 'Tainted' Unit." *Philadelphia Daily News*, January 6. Retrieved 1/7/2010 from www.philly.com/philly/news/homepage/80773697.html?cmpid=15585797.

Land, K., Teske, R., and H. Zheng. 2009. "The Short Term Effects of Execution on Homicides: Deterrence,

Displacement or Both?" *Criminology* 47 (4): 1009–1039.

Lane, C. 2006. "Scalia's Récusai Sought in Key Detainee Case." *Washington Post*, March 28: A06.

LaPeter, L. 2004. "Torture Allegations Dog Ex-police Officer." *St. Petersburg Times*, August 29. Retrieved 4/1/2010 from www.truthinjustice.org/jon-burge.htm.

Larrabee, M. 1993. *An Ethics of Care: Feminist and Interdisciplinary Perspectives*. New York: Routledge.

Lavoie, D. 2007. "Wives Struggled After Husbands Were Wrongly Convicted of Murder." *Austin American-Statesman*, August 15: A19.

Lee, H. 2004. "Oakland 'Riders' Lied, Brutalized Man, Ex-Rookie Testifies." SFGate.com December 14. Retrieved 4/16/2008 from www.sfgate.com/cgi-bin/article.cgi?file=/chronicle/archive/2004/12/14/BAG75ABBITl.

Lehr, D. 2009. *The Fence: A Police Cover-up Along Boston's Racial Divide*. New York: Harper.

Leiser, B. 1986. *Liberty, Justice and Morals*. New York: Macmillan.

Lendman, S. 2009. "'Hizzhonor:' Chicago Politics Under Richard M. Daley." *Baltimore Chronicle and Sentinel*, Wednesday, April 22. Retrieved 4/27/2009 from www.baltimorechronicle.com/2009/042209Lendman.html.

Lersch, K. (ed.). 2002a. *Policing and Misconduct*. Upper Saddle River, NJ: Prentice Hall.

Lersch, K. 2002b. "All Is Fair in Love and War." In *Policing and Misconduct*, ed. K. Lersch, 55–85. Upper Saddle River, NJ: Prentice Hall.

Levenson, M. 2010. "Probation Uproar Fuels State Campaigns." Boston.com, May 20. Retrieved 6/2/2010 from www.boston.com/news/local/massachusetts/articles/2010/05/29/probation_department_scandal_puts_incumbants_on_defensive/.

Levine, C., L. Kohlberg, and A. Hewer. 1985. "The Current Formulation of Kohlberg's Theory and Response to Critics." *Human Development* 28: 94–100.

Lewis, M. 1999. "Corcoran Guards Launch Ads." *Fresno Bee*, September 17: A1.

Lewis, N. 2005. "In New Book, Ex-Chaplain at Guantanamo Tells of

Abuses." *New York Times*, October 3. Retrieved 5/14/2008 from www.nytimes xom/2005/10/03/politics/03yee. html.

Lichtblau, E. 2008a. "Debate and Protest at Spy Program's Inception." *New York Times*, March 30. Retrieved 3/31/2008 from www.nytimes.com/2008/03/30/washington/30nsa.html.

Lichtblau, E. 2008b. "Senate Approves Bill to Broaden Wiretap Powers." *New York Times*. Retrieved 7/10/2008 from www.nytimes.com/2008/07/10/washington/10fisa.html.

Lichtenberg, L., H. Lune, and P. McManimon. 2004. "'Darker Than Any Prison, Hotter Than Any Human Flame': Punishment, Choice, and Culpability in 'A Clockwork Orange'." *Journal of Criminal Justice Education* 15(2): 429–449.

Lichtblau, E., and S. Shane. 2010. "Report Faults 2 Authors of Bush Memos." *New York Times*, February 19. Retrieved 6/17/2010 from www.nytimes.com/2010/02/20/us/politics/20justice.html.

Lin, A. 2006. "New York Panel Disbars Defense Lawyer for 14 Actions." Law.com, August 14. Retrieved 3/5/2007 from www.law.com/jsp/article.jsp?id=1155303323211.

Lindell, C. 2006a. "When $25,000 Is the Limit on a Life." *Austin American-Statesman*, October 30: A1.

Lindell, C. 2006b. "Sloppy Lawyers Failing Clients on Death Row." *Austin American-Statesman*, October 29: A1, A8.

Lindell, C. 2006c. "Lawyer's Writs Come Up Short." *Austin American-Statesman*, October 30: A11.

Lindell, C. 2007a. "Effort to Reform Death Penalty Appeals Falters." *Austin American-Statesman*, June 9: A1.

Lindell, C. 2007b. "Criticism Grows for Judge Over Execution." *Austin American- Statesman*, October 11: B1.

Lindell, C. 2008. "Sex Tainted Man's Trial for Murder, Appeal Says." *Austin American-Statesman*, June 13: A1, A11.

Lindell, C. 2009. "Man Executed Over Arson that Wasn't, Scientist Says."

Austin American-Statesman, August 26: A1, A5.

Lindell, C. 2010a. "Ex-deputy, Dogs Facing Court Test Over Scent Evidence in Murder Case." *Austin American-Statesman*, April 11: A1, A8.

Lindell, C. 2010b. "Panel Hits Judge with $100,000 Ethics Fine." *Austin American-Statesman*, May 1: A1.

Lindell, C., and Embry, J. 2009. "Governor Shakes Up Forensic Agency." *Austin American-Statesman*, October 1: A1, A8.

Lindquist, C. 1994. "Criminalistics in the Curriculum: Some Views from the Forensic Science Community." *Journal of Criminal Justice Education* 5(1): 59–68.

Liptak, A. 2003. "Houston DNA Lab Worst in Country, Experts Say." *Austin American-Statesman*, March 11: B1.

Liptak, A. 2004. "Study Suspects Thousands of False Convictions." *New York Times*, April 19. Retrieved 4/20/2004 from www.nytimes. com/2004/04/19/national/19DNA. html.

Liptak, A. 2005. "Date Missed: Court Rebuffs Low IQ Man Facing Death." *Austin American-Statesman*, December 17: B1.

Liptak, A. 2007. "Study Reveals Gap in performance of Public Defenders." *Austin American-Statesman*, July 14: A7.

Liptak, A. 2010. "Group Gives up Death Penalty Work." *New York Times*. Retrieved 1/5/2010 from www. nytimes.com/2010/01/05/us/05bar. html.

Liptak, A., and R. Blumenthal. 2004. "Death Sentences in Texas Cases Try Supreme Court's Patience." *New York Times*, December 5. Retrieved 12/7/2004 from www.nytimes. com/2004/12/05/national/05texas. html.

Lombardo, L. 1981. *Guards Imprisoned: Correctional Officers at Work*. New York: Elsevier.

Lombardo, L. 1989. *Guards Imprisoned: Correctional Officers at Work*. Cincinnati: Anderson.

Lombardo, L. 1997. "Guards Imprisoned: Correctional Officers at Work." In *Correctional Contexts*, eds. J. Marquart and J. Sorensen, 189–203. Los Angeles: Roxbury.

Loo, R. 2003. "Are Women More Ethical Than Men? Findings from Three Independent Studies." *Women in Management Review* 18(4): 169–181.

Lord, V., and B. Bjerregaard. 2003. "Ethics Courses: Their Impact on the Values and Ethical Decisions of Criminal Justice Students." *Journal of Criminal Justice Education* 14(2): 191–211.

Lucas, J. 1980. *On Justice*. Oxford, England: Oxford University Press.

Luscombe, B. 2001. "When the Evidence Lies." Time.com, May 13. Retrieved 4/9/2008 from www.time.com/time/ printout/0,8816,109568,00.html.

Lush, T. 2007. "The G-Man and the Snitch." MiamiNewTimes.com, February 8. Retrieved 4/26/2008 from www.miaminewtimes.com/2007-02-08/news/the-g-man-and-the-snitch/ print.

Lutwak, N., and J. Hennessy. 1985. "Interpreting Measures of Moral Development to Individuals." *Measurement and Evaluation in Counseling and Development* 18(1): 26–31.

Maas, P. 1973. *Serpico*. New York: Viking.

Maas, P. 1983. *Marie*. New York: Random House.

MacIntyre, A. 1991. *After Virtue*. South Bend, IN: University of Notre Dame Press.

MacIntyre, A. 1999. *Dependent Rational Animals: Why Human Beings Need the Virtues*. Chicago: Open Ct.

Macintyre, S., and T. Prenzler. 1999. "The Influence of Gratuities and Personal Relationships on Police Use of Discretion." *Policing and Society* 9: 181–201.

Mack, K. 2009. "Former US Marshal Sentenced for Leak in Witness Protection Program." Chicagotribune. com. October, 28. Retrieved 11/3/2009 from www.chicagotribune. com/news/chi-marshal-leaked-secrets-senteoct28,0,7908466.story.

Mackie, J. L. 1977. *Ethics: Inventing Right and Wrong*. New York: Penguin.

Mackie, J. L. 1982. "Morality and the Retributive Emotions." *Criminal Justice Ethics* 1(1): 3–10.

Maestri, W. 1982. *Basic Ethics for the Health Care Professional*. Washington, DC: University Press.

Magid, L. 2001. "Article: Deceptive Police Interrogation Practices: How Far is Too Far." *Michigan Law Review* 99(5): 1168–1210.

Main, F. 2009. "Ex-Chicago Police Cmdr. Jon Burge: Move My Perjury Trial Out of Chicago." Suntimes. com. April 30. Retrieved 5/5/2009 from www.suntimes.com/news/24-7/1552339,jon-burge-trial-move-chicago-043009.article.

Malloy, E. 1982. *The Ethics of Law Enforcement and Criminal Punishment*. Lanham, NY: University Press.

Mandak, J. 2010a. "PA Police: Trooper Can't Work for Roethlisberger." Associated Press, April 21. Retrieved 7/18/2010 from www.huffingtonpost. com/huff-wires/20100421/ us-roethlisberger-police/.

Mandak, J. 2010b. "Police Ties to Roethlisberger Still in Question." Associated Press, April 17. Retrieved 7/18/2010 from http://abcnews.go.com/Sports/ wireStory?id=10401108.

Manning, P. 2009. "Bad Cops." *Criminology and Public Policy* 8(4): 787–794.

Marculli, J. 2010. "NYPD Cops Acquitted in Michael Mineo Sodomy Case Will Face Civil Trial in June." *New York Daily News*, March 1. Retrieved 5/14/2010 from www.nydailynews.com/news/ ny_crime/2010/03/01/2010-03-01_ nypd_cops_acquitted_in_michael_ mineo_sodomy_case_will_face_civil_ trial_in_june.html.

Margasak, L. 2009. "Harsh Methods Useless, Ex-interrogator Says." *Austin American-Statesman*, May 14: A4.

Marks, F., F. Raymond, and D. Cathcart. 1986. "Discipline Within the Legal Profession." In *Ethics and the Legal Profession*, eds. M. Davis and F. Elliston, 62–105. Buffalo, NY: Prometheus.

Marquart, J., M. Barnhill, and K. Balshaw-Biddle. 2001. "Fatal Attraction: An Analysis of Employee Boundary Violations in a Southern Prison System, 1995–1998." *Justice Quarterly* 18(4): 877–911.

Marquart, J., and J. Roebuck. 1986. "Prison Guards and Snitches." In *The Dilemmas of Corrections: Contemporary Readings*, eds. K. Haus and G. Alpert, 158–176. Prospect Heights, IL: Waveland.

Martin, D. 1993. *Committing Journalism: The Writings of Red Hog*. New York: Norton.

Martin, M. 2003. "Corrections Director Summoned to Testify: Federal Inquiry Seeks Pelican Bay Answers." SFGate.com. Retrieved 11/7/2003 from www.sfgate.com/article.cgi?file=/c/a/2003/ll/03/MNGJJ20R5Q1.DTL.

Martinelli, T. 2000. *Combating the Charge of Deliberate Indifference Through Police Ethics Training and a Comprehensive Risk Management Policy*. Paper presented at the Annual Meeting of the Academy of Criminal Justice Sciences, New Orleans, LA.

Martinelli, T. 2007. "Minimizing Risk by Defining Off-Duty Police Misconduct." *Police Chief*, June: 40–45.

Martinez, P., and J. Pollock. 2008. "The Impact of Type of Attorney on Criminal Sentencing." *Criminal Law Bulletin* 5(44).

Martyn, S., L. Fox, L., and W. Wendel. 2008. *The Law Governing Lawyers: 2007–2008 Edition*. New York: Aspen Publishers.

Marx, G. 1985a. "Police Undercover Work: Ethical Deception or Deceptive Ethics?" In *Police Ethics: Hard Choices in Law Enforcement*, eds. W. Heffernan and T. Stroup, 83–117. New York: John Jay Press.

Marx, G. 1985b. "Who Really Gets Stung? Some Issues Raised by the New Police Undercover Work." In *Moral Issues in Police Work*, eds. F. Elliston and M. Feldberg, 99–129. Totawa, NJ: Rowman and Allanheld.

Marx, G. 1991. "The New Police Undercover Work." In *Thinking About Police: Contemporary Readings*, eds. C. Klockars and S. Mastrofski, 240–258. New York: McGraw-Hill.

Marzulli, J. 2010. "NYPD Cops Acquitted in Michael Mineo Sodomy Case Will Face Civil Trial in June." NYDailyNews.com, March 1. Retrieved 8/18/2010 from www.nydailynews.com/news/ny_crime/2010/03/01/2010-03-01_nypd_cops_aquitted_in_michael_mineo_sodomy_case_will_face_civil_trial_in_june.html10.

Massimino, E. 2004. "Leading by Example? U.S. Interrogation of

Prisoners in the War on Terror." *Criminal Justice Ethics* 23(1): 2, 74–76.

Mastrofski, S., M. Reisig, and J. McCluskey. 2002. "Police Disrespect Toward the Public: An Encounter-Based Analysis." *Criminology* 40(3): 519–551.

Mather, L. 2003. "Ethics Symposium: What Do Clients Want? What Do Lawyers Do?" *Emory Law Journal* 52: 1065–1088.

Mauer, M., M. Chesney-Lind, and T. Clear. 2002. *Invisible Punishment: The Collateral Consequences of Mass Imprisonment*. New York: The Sentencing Project.

McAnany, P. 1981. "Justice in Search of Fairness." In *Justice as Fairness*, eds. D. Fogel and J. Hudson, 22–51. Cincinnati: Anderson.

McCabe, D., and L. Trevino. 1996. "What We Know About Cheating in College: Longitudinal Trends and Recent Developments." *Change*, 28(1): 28–33.

McCaffrey, S. 2007. "Release of Sex Video Draws Fire." *Austin American-Statesman*, July 13: A6.

McCarthy, B. 1991. "Keeping an Eye on the Keeper: Prison Corruption and Its Control." In *Justice, Crime, and Ethics*, eds. M. Braswell, B. McCarthy, and B. McCarthy, 239–253. Cincinnati: Anderson.

McCarthy, B. 1995. "Patterns of Prison Corruption." In *Morality in Criminal Justice*, eds. D. Close and N. Meier, 280–285. Belmont, CA: Wadsworth.

McCarthy, B. 2010. "Danziger Bridge Case Suggests Culture of Corruption at NOPD." (Originally published in the *Times-Picayune*.) Nola.com, March 21. Retrieved on 3/25/2010 from www.nola.com/crime/index.ssf/2010/03/danziger_bridge_details.html.

McCready, D. 2007. "When Is Torture Right?" *Studies in Christian Ethics*, 20: 393–398.

McDonald, W. 2000. *Testilying: The Psychological and Sociological Determinants of Police Testimonial Deception*. Dissertation. City University of New York. Ann Arbor, MI: University of Michigan Dissertation Abstracts.

McGurrin, D., and V. Kappeler. 2002. "Media Accounts of Police Sexual

Violence." In *Policing and Misconduct*, ed. K. Lersch, 121–142. Upper Saddle River, NJ: Prentice Hall.

McKinley, J. 2007. "Mexico Purges 284 Police Commanders in Antidrug Effort." *New York Times*, June 26. Retrieved 4/9/2008 from www.nytimes.com/2007/06/26/world/americas/26mexico.html.

McKoski, R. 2008. "Charitable Fundraising by Judges: The Give and Take of the 2007 ABA Model Code of Judicial Conduct." *Michigan State Law Review* 2008: 769–841.

McRoberts, F., and S. Mills. 2004. "From the Start, a Faulty Science." *Chicago Tribune* Online Edition. Retrieved 10/19/2004 from www.chicagotribune.com/news/specials/chi-041019 0150octl9,l,2959538,print.story.

McRoberts, F., S. Mills, and M. Possley. 2004. "Forensics Under the Microscope." *Chicago Tribune* Online Edition. Retrieved 10/19/2004 from www.chicagotribune.com/news/specials/chi-0410170393octl7,1,7219383,print.story.

Medwed, D. 2009. "The Prosecutor as Minister of Justice: Preaching to the Unconverted from the Post-conviction Pulpit." *Washington Law Review* 84: 35–66.

Meekins, T. 2007. "Risky Business: Criminal Specialty Courts and the Ethical Obligations of the Zealous Criminal Defender." *Berkeley Journal of Criminal Law* 12: 75–135.

Meincke, P. 2009. "Cops Plead Guilty, Sentenced in Corruption Cases." ABC.com. September 25. Retrieved 10/1/2009 from www.abclocal.go.com/wls/story?section=news/localandid=7033273andpt=print.

Memory, J., and C. Rose. 2002. "The Attorney as Moral Agent: A Critique of Cohen." *Criminal Justice Ethics* 21(1): 28–39.

Menninger, K. 1973. *Whatever Became of Sin*. New York: Hawthorne Books.

Mesloh, C., R. Wolf, and M. Henych. 2003. "Perceptions of Misconduct: An Examination of Ethics at One Correctional Institution." *Corrections Compendium* 28(5): 1–19.

Messner, S., and R. Rosenfeld. 1994. *Crime and the American Dream*. Belmont, CA: Wadsworth.

Metz, H. 1990. "An Ethical Model for Law Enforcement Administrators." In *Ethics in Criminal Justice*, ed. F. Schmalleger, 95–103. Bristol, IN: Wyndam Hall.

Micucci, A., and I. Gomme. 2005. "American Police and Subcultural Support for the Use of Excessive Force." *Journal of Criminal Justice* 33: 487–500.

Mieczkowski, T. 2002. "Drug Abuse, Corruption, and Officer Drug Testing." In *Policing and Misconduct*, ed. K. Lersch, 157–192. Upper Saddle River, NJ: Prentice Hall.

Milgram, S. 1963. "Behavioral Study of Obedience." *Journal of Abnormal and Social Psychology* 67: 371–378.

Miller, J., and R. Davis. 2007. "Unpacking Public Attitudes to the Police: Contrasting Perceptions of Misconduct with Traditional Measures of Satisfaction." *International Journal of Police Science and Management* 10(1): 9–22.

Miller, K., and M. Radelet. 1993. *Executing the Mentally Ill.* Newbury Park, CA: Sage.

Mills, S. 2005. "Texas May Have Put Innocent Man to Death." *Chicago Tribune*, April 20: A7.

Mills, S., and F. McRoberts. 2004. "Critics Tell Experts: Show Us the Science." *Chicago Tribune*, October 17: A18.

Mitchum, R. 2009. "Chicago Mob-Leak Trial: Witness Tells of Undercover Recordings in Case Against Marshall." Chicagotribune.com. April 17. Retrieved 4/17/2009 from www.chicagotribune.com/news/local/chi-us-marshal-trial-17apr,0,2223865.story.

Mobley, A., and G. Geis. 2002. "The Corrections Corporation of America, a.k.a. the Prison Realty Trust, Inc." In *Justice, Crime, and Ethics*, eds. M. Braswell, B. R. McCarthy, and B. J. McCarthy, 329–349. Cincinnati: Anderson.

Moll, J., R. Zahn, R. de Oliveira-Souza, F. Krueger, and J. Grafman. 2005. "The Neural Basis of Human Moral Cognition." *Nature* 6: 799–809.

Monahan, L., J. Monahan, M. Gaboury, and P. Niesyn. 2004. "Victims' Voices in the Correctional Setting: Cognitive Gains in an Offender Education Program." *Journal of Offender Rehabilitation* 39(3): 21–34.

Monroe, J. 2006. "Applying the Responsible Corporate Officer and Conscious Avoidance Doctrines in the Context of the Abu Ghraib Prison Scandal." *Iowa Law Review* 91: 1367–1395.

Moore, M. 1997. *Police Integrity: Public Service Without Honor.* Washington, DC: U.S. Department of Justice.

Moore, S. 2009. "Judge Ends Monitor of the Los Angeles Police." *New York Times*, July 18. Retrieved 4/6/2010 from www.nytimes.com/2009/07/18/us/18lapd.html.

Morain, D. 2010. "Private Prisons? A Sweet Deal for Some." *Sacramento Bee*, January 8. Retrieved 1/8/2010 from www.sacbee.com/opinion/story/2443722.html.

Moran, J. 2005. "'Blue Walls,' 'Grey areas' and 'Cleanups': Issues in the Control of Police Corruption in England and Wales." *Crime, Law and Social Change* 43: 57–79.

Moran, R. 2009. "Ramsey Acknowledges Rift with Latinos." Philly.com, April 8. Retrieved 4/12/2009 from www.philly.com/inquirer/local/pa/20090408_Ramsey_acknowledges_rift_with_Latinos.html.

Moreno, S. 2007. "In Texas, Scandals Rock Juvenile Justice System." *Washington Post*, April 5: A03.

Mores, T. 2002. "Police Misconduct: A Global Problem." *Crime and Justice International*, January: 9–10, 24–26.

Morris, R. 2000. *Stories of Transformative Justice.* Toronto: Canadian Scholars Press.

Morrison, G. 2009. "Conducted Energy Weapons: Learning from Operational Discretion and Encounter Outcomes." *Criminology and Public Policy* 8(4): 915–925.

Moscoso, E. 2007. "Lawmakers Seek Review of 2 Border Agents' Cases." *Austin American-Statesman*, October 17: A7.

Moss, M., and F. Fessenden, 2002. "War Against Terrorism Stirs a Battle Over Privacy." *Austin American-Statesman*, December 11: A17–A19.

Muir, W. 1977. *Police: Streetcorner Politicians.* Chicago: University of Chicago Press.

Mulhausen, M. 2010. "A Second Chance at Justice: Why States Should Adopt ABA Model Rules of Professional Conduct 3.8(g) and (h)." *University of Colorado Law Review* 81(1): 309–341.

Murphy, C. 2002. "Monitor Gives DC Police Mixed Review." *Washington Post.* Retrieved 8/8/2002 from www.washingtonpost.com/wp-dyn/articles/A52807-2002Aug6.html.

Murphy, J. 1985/1995. *Punishment and Rehabilitation.* Belmont, CA: Wadsworth.

Murphy, J. 1988. "Forgiveness, Mercy, and the Retributive Emotions." *Criminal Justice Ethics* 7(2): 3–15.

Murphy, K. 2002. "States Get Grants to Help Ex-Offenders." Stateline.org. Retrieved 7/17/2002 from www.stateline.org/story.do?storyID=248888.

Murphy, P., and D. Caplan. 1989. "Conditions that Breed Corruption." In *Critical Issues in Policing*, eds. R. Dunham and G. Alpert, 304–324. Prospect Heights, IL: Waveland.

Murphy, P., and K. Moran. 1981. "The Continuing Cycle of Systemic Police Corruption." In *The Social Basis of Criminal Justice: Ethical Issues for the 80's*, eds. F. Schmalleger and R. Gustafson, 87–101. Washington, DC: University Press.

Murphy, S. 2009. "Families Awarded $8.5 m in Mob Case." Boston.com, May 2. Retrieved 5/5/2009 from www.boston.com/news/local/massachusetts/articles/2009/05/02/families_awarded_85m_in_mob_case/.

Murray, J. 2005. "Policing Terrorism: A Threat to Community Policing or Just a Shift in Priorities?" *Police Practice and Research* 6(4): 347–361.

Murray, J. 2009. "Ex-drug Cop's 25-year Sentence Among Longest for Local Police." Indystar.com, September 24. Retrieved 9/28/2009 from www.indy.com/posts/ex-drug-cop-s-25-year-sentence-among-longest-for-local-police.

Murton, T. 1976. *The Dilemma of Prison Reform.* New York: Irvington.

Murton, T., and J. Hyams. 1969. *Accomplices to the Crime: The Arkansas Prison Scandal.* New York: Grove.

Nakashima, E. 2007. "GOP Opposes Attempt to Revise Wiretap Law." *Washington Post*, October 10: A04.

Nash, L. 1981. "Ethics Without the Sermon." *Harvard Business Review*, November–December: 81.

National Institute of Justice. 1992. "Community Policing in the 1990s." *National Institute of Justice Research Bulletin*, August: 2–9.

National Institute of Justice. 2008. *Study of Deaths Following Electro Muscular Disruption*. Washington, DC: Office of Justice Programs.

Nelson, J. 2000. *Police Brutality*. New York: Norton.

Nettler, G. 1978. *Explaining Crime*. New York: McGraw-Hill.

New York Inspector General. 2009. *Inspector General Finds Misconduct at State Police Forensic Crime Lab*. Inspector General Report, December 17. Retrieved 6/22/2010 from http://readme.readmedia. com/Inspector-General-Finds-Misconduct-at-State-Police-Forensic-Lab/1000392.

New York Times. 2002. "Three Guards Acquitted in Death of Inmate." February 16: A13.

New York Times. 2010a. "Lingering Questions About 'Stop-and-Frisk'." February 19. Retrieved 2/19/2010 from www.nytimes. com/2010/02/19/opinion/19fri3. html.

New York Times. 2010b. "Editorial: Tasers and Liability." January 4. Retrieved 1/5/2010 from www.nytimes. com/2010/01/05/opinion/05tue3. html.

New York Times. 2010c. "Justice in the Jury Box." June 4. Retrieved 6/6/2010 from www.nytimes. com/2010/06/06/opinion/06sun2. html.

Newman, G. 1978. *The Punishment Response*. New York: Lippincott.

Newsweek. 2001. "A Captain's Story." April 2.

Neyroud, P., and A. Beckley. 2001. *Policing, Ethics and Human Rights*. Devon, England: Willan.

Noddings, N. 1986. *Caring: A Feminine Approach to Ethics and Moral Education*. Berkeley: University of California Press.

Nola.com. 2009. "New Orleans Police Department Shootings After Katrina Under Scrutiny." December 12. Retrieved 5/10/2009 from www. nola.com/law_and_disorder/index.

ssf/2009/12/nopd_acts_under_fire. html.

Nola.com. 2010. "Mayor Mitch Landrieu Asks U.S. Department of Justice to Assess Troubled NOPD." May 5. Retrieved 5/6/2010 from www.nola. com/crime/index.ssf/2010/05/ mitch_landrieu.html.

Novak, T. 2009. "Crooked Cop Still Gets His Pension." Suntimes.com. September 21. Retrieved 9/24/2009 from www.suntimes.com/news/ watchdogs/1781215,CST-NWS-watchdogs.

NY1.com. 2008. "Seven Corrections Officers Face Corruption Charges." April 24. Retrieved 6/14/2010 from www.ny1. com/?SecID=1000andArID=80875.

Ogle, R. 1999. "Prison Privatization: An Environmental Catch-22." *Justice Quarterly* 14(3): 579–600.

Olson, R., and D. Chanen. 2009. "Minneapolis Police Told to Watch Video, Talk About Force." StarTribune.com, August 31. Retrieved 8/31/2009 from www. startribune.com/local/55489727. html.

Oppel, R. 2009. "Corruption Undercuts U.S. Hopes for Improving Afghan Police." MercuryNews.com, April 11. Retrieved 4/13/2009 from www. mercurynews.com/nationworld/ ci_12125802.

Packer, H. 1968. *The Limits of the Criminal Sanction*. Stanford, CA: Stanford University Press.

Paoline, E., S. Myers, and R. Worden. 2000. "Police Culture, Individualism, and Community Policing: Evidence from Two Police Departments." *Justice Quarterly* 17(3): 575–605.

Papke, D. 1986. "The Legal Profession and Its Ethical Responsibilities: A History." In *Ethics and the Legal Profession*, eds. M. Davis and F. Elliston, 29–49. Buffalo, NY: Prometheus.

Parenti, C. 1999. *Lockdown America: Police and Prisons in the Age of Crisis*. New York: Verso (New Left Books).

Pasztor, D. 2003a. "Lawyer, Ex-Judges Fear Texas About to Kill an Innocent Man." *Austin American-Statesman*, March 6: A1, A11.

Pasztor, D. 2003b. "Rejected Appeals Leave Inmate with Execution Date

a Day Away." *Austin American-Statesman*, March 11: A1.

Patrick, R. 2009. "St. Louis Police Officer Gets Prison Time." Stltoday.com, September 17. Retrieved 9/22/2009 from www.stltoday.com/blogzone/ st-louis-crime-beat/2009/09/17/ st-louis-police-officer-gets-prison-time/.

Payne, D. 2002. *Police Liability: Lawsuits Against the Police*. Durham, NC: Carolina Academic Press.

Payne, B., and W. Guastaferro. 2009. "Mind the Gap: Attitudes About Miranda Warnings Among Police Chiefs and Citizens." *Journal of Police and Criminal Psychology* 24: 93–103.

Pearson, F. 2002. "The Effects of Behavioral/Cognitive-Behavioral Programs on Recidivism." *Crime and Delinquency* 48(3): 476–497.

Pellicotti, J. 1990. "Ethics and the Criminal Defense: A Client's Desire to Testify Untruthfully." In *Ethics and Criminal Justice*, ed. F. Schmalleger, 67–78. Bristol, IN: Wyndam Hall.

Perez, E. 2001. "For Profit Prison Firm Wackenhut Tries to Break Shackles to Growth." *Wall Street Journal*. Retrieved 5/15/2001 from www. msnbc.com/news/570728.asp.

Perry, J. (Ed.). 2002. *Repairing Communities Through Restorative Justice*. Lanham, MD: American Correctional Association.

Perry, S. 2006. *Prosecutors in State Courts, 2005*. Washington, DC: U.S. Dept. of Justice, Bureau of Justice Statistics.

Perksy, A. 2009. "A Cautionary Tale: The Ted Stevens Prosecution." *Alaska Bar Rag* 33: 1–8.

Personal Communication. 2010. Conversation with a police chief (identity not revealed), May 3.

Philadelphia Inquirer. 2010. Editorial: "Shouldn't Delay Justice." August 11. Retrieved 8/11/2010 from www.philly.com/inquirer/ opinion/20100911_Editorial_ Shouldn_t_delay_justice.html.

Philly.com. 2010. Editorial: "Can't Call it Justice." February 20. Retrieved 2/22/2010 from www.philly.com/ inquirer/opinion/20100220_ Editorial_Can_t_call_it_justice.html.

Pierce, C. 2009. "Crooked and Crookeder." Boston.com. Retrieved

10/1/2009 from www.boston. com/bostonglobe/magazine/ articles/2009/09/27/crooked_and_ crookeder/.

Piller, C. 2003. "FBI's Crime Scene Bullet Analysis Test Flawed." *Austin American-Statesman*, November 21: A28.

Piller, C. 2010a. "Bee Investigation: Guards Accused of Cruelty, Racism." *Sacramento Bee*, May 9: 1A.

Piller, C. 2010b. "California Prison Behavior Units Aim to Control Troublesome Inmates," *Sacramento Bee*, May 10: 1A.

Piller, C. 2010c. "Prison Officials Open 'Full Investigation' into Abuse Claims." *Sacramento Bee*, May 10: 1A.

Piller, C., and R. Mejia. 2003. "FBI's Bullet Analysis Method Is Flawed, Studies Suggest." *Austin American-Statesman*, February 4: A8.

Pimentel, D. 2009. "The Reluctant Tattletale: Closing the Gaps in Federal Judicial Discipline." *Tennessee Law Review* 76: 909–957.

Pinkele, C., and W. Louthan. 1985. *Discretion, Justice and Democracy: A Public Policy Perspective*. Ames: Iowa State University Press.

Pioneer Press. 2009. "A Stain on Good Police Work." TwinCities.com. August 22. Retrieved 8/24/2009 from www.twincities.com/opinion/ ci_13179756?nclick_check=1.

Pistone, J. 1987. *Donnie Brasco: My Undercover Life in the Mafia*. New York: Hudder and Stoughton.

Pistone, J., and C. Brandt. 2007. *Donnie Brasco: Unfinished Business*. New York: Running Press.

Platt, A. 1977. *The Child Savers*. Chicago: University of Chicago Press.

Plohetski, T. 2006. "Consent Searches in Austin Plummet." *Austin American-Statesman*, March 11: A1, A8.

Plohetski, T. 2007. "From Officer's Order to Taser: 45 Seconds." *Austin American-Statesman*, September 30: A1, A6.

Plohetski, T. 2008. "Officer Accused of Filing False Report Not Indicted." *Austin American-Statesman*, March 20: B3.

Plohetski, T. 2010. "Report: Officer's Force Excessive." *Austin American-Statesman*, May 8: A1, A10.

Pogarsky, G., and A. Piquero. 2004. "Studying the Reach of Deterrence: Can Deterrence Theory Help Explain Police Misconduct?" *Journal of Criminal Justice* 32: 371–386.

Pollock, J. 2004. *Prisons and Prison Life: Costs and Consequences*. Los Angeles: Roxbury.

Pollock, J. 2010. *Measuring the Ethical Climate in a Police Department*. Paper presented at the ACJS annual meeting in San Diego, February 22–27.

Possley, S. 2004. "Arson Myths Fuel Errors." *Chicago Tribune* Online Edition. Retrieved 10/19/2004 from www.chicagotribune.com/news/ specials/chi0410180222octl8,l,1517744, print.story.

Possley, S., S. Mills, and F. McRoberts. 2004. "Scandal Touches Even Elite Labs." *Chicago Tribune* Online Edition. Retrieved 10/25/2004 from www.chicagotribune. com/technology/chi- 0410210285oct21,l,2398403,print. story.

Post, L. 2005. "FBI Bullet Test Misses Target: Court Rejects Test." Whistleblowers.org. Retrieved 4/16/2008 from www.whistleblowers. org/hljFjP.htm.

Postema, G. 1986. "Moral Responsibility in Professional Ethics." In *Ethics and the Legal Profession*, eds. M. Davis and F. Elliston, 158–179. Buffalo, NY: Prometheus.

Poveda, T. 2001. "Estimating Wrongful Convictions." *Justice Quarterly* 18(3): 689–708.

Powell, J. 2009. "Priest Able to Forgive After Brutal Stabbing in South Texas." *Austin American-Statesman*, October 7: B6.

Power, C., and L. Kohlberg. 1980. "Faith, Morality, and Ego Development." In *Toward Moral and Religious Maturity*, eds. J. Fowler and C. Bursselmans, 311–372. Morristown, NJ: Silver Burdett.

Prendergast, A. 2003. "Cowboy Justice." *Denver Westword*, June 26. Retrieved 4/1/2008 from www.westword. com/2003-06-26/news/cowboy- justice/4.

Prenzler, T. 1995. "Police Gratuities: What the Public Thinks." *Criminal Justice Ethics* 14(1): 15–26.

Prenzler, T. 2000. "Civilian Oversight of Police: A Test of Capture Theory." *British Journal of Criminology* 40: 659–674.

Prenzler, T. 2006. "Senior Police Managers' Views on Integrity Testing, and Drug and Alcohol Testing." *Policing: An International Journal of Police Strategies and Management* 29(3): 394–107.

Prenzler, T., A. Harrison, and A. Ede. 1996. "The Royal Commission into the NSW Police Service." *Current Affairs Bulletin*, April/May: 4–13.

Prenzler, T., and J. Ransley. 2002. *Police Reform: Building Integrity*. Sydney, Australia: Hawkins.

Prenzler, T., and C. Ronken. 2001a. "Police Integrity Testing in Australia." *Criminal Justice* 1(2): 319–342.

Prenzler, T., and C. Ronken. 2001b. "Models of Police Oversight: A Critique." *Policing and Society* 11: 151–180.

Presser, L. 2003. "Remorse and Neutralization Among Violent Male Offenders." *Justice Quarterly* 20(4): 801–825.

Prior, W. 1991. "Aristotle's Nicomanchean Ethics." In *From Virtue and Knowledge: An Introduction to Ancient Greek Ethics*, ed. W. Prior, 144–193. New York: Routledge, Kegan Paul.

Puonti, A., S. Vuorinen, and S. Ivkovic. 2004. "Sustaining Police Integrity in Finland." In *The Contours of Police Integrity*, eds. C. Klockars, S. Ivkovic, and M. Haberfeld, 95–115. Thousand Oaks, CA: Sage.

Putman, Y. 2008. "Retired Navy Officer Reflects on Honesty, Responsibility." *Chattanooga Times Free Press*, February 27. Retrieved 3/19/2008 from http://timesfreepress.com/ news/200 8/feb/27/retired-navy- officer-reflects-honesty-responsibility.

Quinn, M. 2005. *Walking with the Devil*. Minneapolis: BooksbyQuinn.

Quinn, P. 2006. "Detentions Called Unjust." Associated Press, reported in *Austin American-Statesman*, September 18: A1, A7.

Quinney, R. 1974. *Critique of the Legal Order*. New York: Little, Brown.

Radelet, M., H. Bedau, and C. Putnam. 1992. *In Spite of Innocence: Erroneous Convictions in Capital Cases*. Boston: Northeastern University Press.

Raeder, M. 2007. "See No Evil: Wrongful Convictions and the Prosecutorial

Ethics of Offering Testimony by Jailhouse Informants and Dishonest Experts." *Fordham Law Review* 76: 1413–1452.

Raftery, I. 2010. "6-Year Sentence for Guard in Rikers Island Beatings." *New York Times*, August 6. Retrieved 8/6/2010 from www.nytimes.com/2010/08.07/nyregion/07guard.html.

Ramsey, R. 2007. "Perceptions of Criminal Justice Professionals Regarding the Frequency of Wrongful Conviction and the Extent of System Errors." *Crime and Delinquency* 53, 3: 436–470.

Raphael, D. 1980. *Justice and Liberty.* London: Athlone.

Rawls, J. 1957. "Outline of a Decision Procedure for Ethics." *Philosophical Review* 66: 177–197.

Rawls, J. 1971. *A Theory of Justice.* Cambridge, MA: Belknap.

Rawstorne, T., and S. Wright. 2009. "Special Investigation: Waterboarding at the Met and Why the Force Faces the Biggest Police Scandal in Decades." DailyMail.com. Retrieved 7/4/2009 from www.dailymail.co.uk/news/article-1197427//SPECIAL-INVESTIGATION-Waterboarding-Met-force-faces-biggest-police-scandal-decades.html.

Rayman, G. 2010a. "The NYPD Tapes: Inside Bed-Stuy's 81st Precinct." *Village Voice*, May 4. Retrieved 5/11/2010 from www.villagevoice.com/2010-05-04/news/the-nypd-tapes-inside-bed-stuy-s-81st-precinct/5.

Rayman, G. 2010b. "The NYPD Tapes, Part 2: Bed-Stuy Street Cops Ordered: Turn This Place into a Ghost Town." *Village Voice*, May 11. Retrieved 5/12/2010 from www.villagevoice.com/2010-05-11/news/nypd-tapes-part-2-bed-stuy/.

Reasons, C. 1973. "The Politicalization of Crime, the Criminal and the Criminologist." *Journal of Criminal Law, Criminology and Police Science* 64 (March): 471–477.

Reichel, P. 1997. *Corrections.* Minneapolis: West.

Reiman, J. 1990/2004. *Justice and Modern Moral Philosophy.* New Haven, CT: Yale University Press.

Reiman, J. 1984/2005/2007. *The Rich Get Richer and the Poor Get Prison:*

Ideology, Class, and Criminal Justice. Boston: Allyn and Bacon.

Reiman, J., and P. Leighton. 2010. *The Rich Get Richer and the Poor Get Prison.* Boston, MA: Allyn and Bacon.

Reisig, M., J. McCluskey, S. Mastrofski, and W. Terrill. 2004. "Suspect Disrespect Toward the Police." *Justice Quarterly* 21(2): 241–268.

Reisig, M., and R. Parks. 2000. "Experience, Quality of Life, and Neighborhood Context: A Hierarchical Analysis of Satisfaction with Police." *Justice Quarterly* 17 (3): 607–630.

Rejali, D. 2007. "What Torture Tells Us (And What It Doesn't)" *Washington Post.* Reprinted in *Austin American-Statesman*, December 23: Gl, G4.

Reuss-Ianni, E. 1983. *Two Cultures of Policing: Street Cops and Management Cops.* New Brunswick, NJ: Transaction.

Rimer, S. 2000. "Lawyer Sabotaged Case of a Client on Death Row." *New York Times*, November 24. Retrieved 11/11/2002 from www.againstdp.org/sabotage.html.

Rodin, D. 2004. "Terrorism Without Intention." *Ethics* 114: 752–771.

Rossmo, K. 2008. *Criminal Investigative Failures.* Boca Raton, FL: Taylor and Francis.

Roth, A., and J. Roth. 1989. *Devil's Advocates: The Unnatural History of Lawyers.* Berkeley, CA: Nolo.

Rothbart, M., D. Hanley, and M. Albert. 1986. "Differences in Moral Reasoning." *Sex Roles* 15(11/12): 645–653.

Rothlein, S. 1999. "Policy Agency Efforts to Prevent Abuses." In *Human Dignity and the Police: Ethics and Integrity in Police Work*, ed. G. Lynch, 15–27. Springfield, IL: Charles C Thomas.

Rothwell, G., and J. Baldwin. 2007. "Whistle-Blowing and the Code of Silence in Police Agencies: Policy and Structural Predictors." *Crime and Delinquency* 53(4): 605–632.

Rousseau, J. 1983. *Discourse on the Origins of Inequality.* Indianapolis, IN: Hackett Publishing.

Rowe, M. 2009. "Notes on a Scandal: The Official Enquiry into Deviance and Corruption in New Zealand

Police." *Australian and New Zealand Journal of Criminology* 42(1): 123–138.

Rubicam, M. 2009. "Former Pa. Judges Indicted in Kids-For-Cash Scheme." *Austin American-Statesman*, September 10: A1.

Ruggiero, V. 2001. *Thinking Critically About Ethical Issues* (5th Ed.). New York: McGraw-Hill.

Ruiz, J., and C. Bono. 2004. "At What Price a 'Freebie'? The Real Cost of Police Gratuities." *Criminal Justice Ethics* 23(1): 44–54.

Ryan, J. 2002. "The Appearance of Ethics." *Austin American-Statesman*, November 16: A11.

Sabol, W., H. West, and M. Cooper. 2009. *Prisoners in 2008.* Washington, DC: U.S. Department of Justice, Bureau of Justice Statistics.

Sallah, M., and R. Barry. 2009. "Allen Stanford Ponzi Scheme Puts Lawyers in New Light." MiamiHerald.com, October 3. Retrieved 10/4/2009 from www.miamiherald.com/news/florida/story/1265650.html.

Saltzburg, S. 2008. "Changes to Model Rules Impact Prosecutors." *Criminal Justice* 23: 1–36.

Saltzman, J. 2010. "Former Stoughton Detective Pleads Guilty to Lying to FBI Agents." Boston.com, January 6. Retrieved 1/6/2010 from www.boston.com/news/local/breaking_news/2010/01/former_stoughto_2.html.

San Antonio Express News. 2002. "Lawyers Should Not Aid, Abet Wrongdoers." December 29: 2H.

Sanders, B. 2008. "Using Personality Traits to Predict Police Officer Performance." *Policing: An International Journal of Police Strategies and Management* 31(1): 129–147.

Sapp, A. 1994. "Sexual Misconduct by Police Officers." In *Police Deviance*, 3rd Ed., eds. T. Barker and D. Carter, 187–200. Cincinnati: Anderson.

Savage, D. 2008a. "High Court Won't Hear Surveillance Program Challenge." *Austin American-Statesman*, February 20: A10.

Savage, D. 2008b. "Court: Detainees Have Rights." *Los Angeles Times.* Reprinted in *Austin American-Statesman*, June 13: A1, 13.

Savage, C. 2008c. "Report Weighs Impact of Political Selection of Judges."

Austin American-Statesman, August 24: A9.

Savage, C., and Shane, S. 2009. "Intelligence Improperly Collected on U.S. Citizens." *New York Times*, December 16. Retrieved 8/23/2010 from www.nytimes.com/2009/12/17/us/17disclose.html.

Schafer, J. 2002. "Community Policing and Police Corruption." In *Policing and Misconduct*, ed. K. Lersch, 193–217. Upper Saddle River, NJ: Prentice Hall.

Schaper, D. 2007. "Former Illinois Gov. George Ryan Heading to Prison." NPR. Retrieved 3/17/2008 from www.npr.org/templates/story/story.php?StoryId=16051850.

Schehr, R., and J. Sears. 2005. "Innocence Commissions: Due Process Remedies and Protection for the Innocent." *Critical Criminology* 13(2): 181–209.

Schehr, R., and L. Weathered. 2004. "Should the United States Establish a Criminal Cases Review Commission?" *Judicature* 88(3): 122–145.

Scheingold, S. 1984. *The Politics of Law and Order*. New York: Longman.

Schoeman, F. 1982. "Friendship and Testimonial Privileges." In *Ethics, Public Policy and Criminal Justice*, eds. F. Elliston and N. Bowie, 257–272. Cambridge, MA: Oelgeschlager, Gunn and Hain.

Schoeman, F. 1985. "Privacy and Police Undercover Work." In *Police Ethics: Hard Choices in Law Enforcement*, eds. W. Heffernan and T. Stroup, 133–153. New York: John Jay Press.

Schoeman, F. 1986. "Undercover Operations: Some Moral Questions About S. 804." *Criminal Justice Ethics* 5(2): 16–22.

Schreck, C. 2009. "Russia's YouTube Craze: Exposing Police Corruption." Time.com, November 20. Retrieved 11/24/2009 from www.time.com/time/printout/0,8816,1941620,00.html.

Schweigert, F. 2002. "Moral and Philosophical Foundations of Restorative Justice," In *Repairing Communities Through Restorative Justice*, ed. J. Perry, 19–37. Lanham, MD: American Correctional Association.

Sellin, T. 1970. "The Conflict of Conduct Norms." In *The Sociology of Crime and Delinquency*, eds. M. Wolfgang, L. Savitz, and N. Johnston, 186–189. New York: Wiley.

Serrano, R., and R. Ostrow. 2000. "Probe of FBI Lab Reviews 3,000 Cases—Affects None." LATimes.com. Retrieved 8/21/2000 from www.latimes.com/news/front/20000817/t000077169.html.

Shaffer, T., and R. Cochran. 2007. "'Technical' Defenses: Ethics, Morals, and the Lawyer as Friend." *Clinical Law Review* 14: 337–353.

Shakespeare, W. *The Merchant of Venice*, Act 4, Scene 1. *William Shakespeare: The Complete Works*. Baltimore: Penguin (1969).

Shane, S. 2008a. "Waterboarding Inquiry Focuses on Legal Advice." *Austin American-Statesman*, February 23: A10.

Shane, S. 2008b. "China Inspired Interrogations at Guantanamo." *New York Times*. Retrieved 7/2/2008 from www.nytimes.com/2008/07/02/us/02detain.html.

Sheley, J. 1985. *Exploring Crime*. Belmont, CA: Wadsworth.

Sherman, A., and D. Moskovitz. 2009. "Hollywood Aims to Fire Six in Police Department." MiamiHerald.com. January 5. Retrieved 1/7/2010 from www.miamiherald.com/news/broward/breaking-news/story/1412599.html.

Sherman, L. 1981. *The Teaching of Ethics in Criminology and Criminal Justice*. Washington, DC: Joint Commission on Criminology and Criminal Justice Education and Standards, Law Enforcement Assistance Administration.

Sherman, L. 1982. "Learning Police Ethics." *Criminal Justice Ethics* 1(1): 10–19.

Sherman, L. 1985a. "Becoming Bent: Moral Careers of Corrupt Policemen." In *Moral Issues in Police Work*, eds. F. Elliston and M. Feldberg, 253–273. Totawa, NJ: Rowman and Allanheld.

Sherman, L. 1985b. "Equity Against Truth: Value Choices in Deceptive Investigations." In *Police Ethics: Hard Choices in Law Enforcement*, eds. W. Heffernan and T. Stroup, 117–133. New York: John Jay Press.

Shermer, M. 2004. *The Science of Good and Evil: Why People Cheat, Gossip, Care, Share, and Follow the Golden Rule*. New York: Times Books, Holt and Co.

Shukovsky, P. 2006. "Gitmo Win Likely Cost Navy Lawyer His Career." *Seattle Post-Intelligencer*, July 1. Retrieved 4/2/2008 from http://seattlepi.nwsource.com/national/276109_swift01.html.

Siegal, N. 2001. "Sexual Abuse of Women Inmates Is Widespread." In M. Wagner, *How Should Prisons Treat Inmates? Opposing Viewpoints*, ed. M. Wagner. San Diego: Greenhaven Press.

Silberman, M. 1995. *A World of Violence: Corrections in America*. Belmont, CA: Wadsworth.

Simmons, A. 2006. "Immigration Judges' Abusive Antics Prompt Review." *San Antonio Express News*, February 12: 6A.

Skolnick, J. 1982. "Deception by Police." *Criminal Justice Ethics* 1(2): 40–54.

Skolnick, J. 2001. "Corruption and the Blue Code of Silence." *Police Practice and Research* 3(1): 7–19.

Skolnick, J., and J. Fyfe. 1993. *Above the Law: Police and the Excessive Use of Force*. New York: Free Press.

Skolnick, J., and R. Leo. 1992. "Ideology and the Ethics of Crime Control." *Criminal Justice Ethics* 11(1): 3–13.

Slobodzian, J. 2009. "FBI Report Finds Pattern of Police Misdeeds." April 25. Retrieved 4/28/2009 from www.philly.lcom/philly/news/homepage/20090425_FBI_report_finds_pattern_of_police_misdeeds.html.

Smilansky, S. 2004. "Terrorism, Justification and Illusion." *Ethics* 114: 790–805.

Smith, B., and M. Holmes. 2003. "Community Accountability, Minority Threat, and Police Brutality: An Examination of Civil Rights Criminal Complaints." *Criminology* 41(4): 1035–1063.

Smith, M., and G. Alpert. 2002. "Searching for Direction: Courts, Social Science, and the Adjudication of Racial Profiling Claims." *Justice Quarterly* 19(4): 673–703.

Smith, R. 2006. "Fired Officer Believed CIA Lied to Congress." *Washington Post*, May 14. Retrieved 6/2/2010 from www.washingtonpost.com/wp-dyn/content/article/2006/05/13/AR2006051301311.html.

Smith, R. 2009. "Police Cameras Don't Lie, but Did Fla. Cops?" CBSnews.com. August 6. Retrieved 8/7/2009 from www.cbsnews.com/blogs/2009/08/05/crimesider/entry5216150.shtml.

Smith, R., and Linzer, D. 2006. "CIA Officer's Job Made Any Leaks More Delicate." *Washington Post*, April 23: A01.

Smith, R., and D. Linzer. 2006. "Dismissed CIA Officer Denies Leak Role." *Washington Post*, April 25. Retrieved 6/17/2010 from www.washingtonpost.com/wp-dyn/content/article/2006/04/24/AR2006042401601.html.

Smith, S., and R. Meyer. 1987. *Law, Behavior, and Mental Health*. New York: New York University Press.

Sniffen, M. 1997. "FBI Suspends Agent Whose Charges Led to Critical Report." *Austin American-Statesman*, January 28: A5.

Solomon, A. 1999. "Wackenhut Detention Ordeal." *Village Voice*. Retrieved 3/3/1999 from www.villagevoice.com/features/9935/solomon.html.

Solomon, J. 2007a. "Former N.C. Chief Justice Takes Up Prisoner's Case." *Washington Post*, November 28: A07.

Solomon, J. 2007b. "FBI Fails to Tell Convicts of Ruling that Could Help Their Cases, Investigation Finds." *Washington Post*, reprinted in *Austin American-Statesman*, November 18: A11.

Sourcebook of Criminal Justice Statistics. 2007. "Respondents' Ratings of the Honesty and Ethical Standards of Police, Table 2.20." Retrieved 4/23/2008 from www.albany.edu/sourcebook/pdf/t2202007.pdf.

Souryal, S. 1992/2007. *Ethics in Criminal Justice: In Search of the Truth*. Cincinnati: Anderson.

Souryal, S. 1996. "Personal Loyalty to Superiors in Public Service." *Criminal Justice Ethics*, Summer/Fall: 44–62.

Souryal, S. 1999a. "Corruption of Prison Personnel." In *Prison and Jail Administration: Practice and Theory*, eds. P. Carlson and J. Garrett, 171–177. Gaithersburg, MD: Aspen.

Souryal, S. 1999b. "Personal Loyalty to Superiors in Criminal Justice Agencies." *Justice Quarterly* 16(4): 871–906.

Souryal, S. 2009. "Deterring Corruption by Prison Personnel: A Principle-Based Perspective." *Prison Journal* 89: 21–45.

South, N. 2001. "Police, Security and Information: The Use of Informants and Agents in a Liberal Democracy." In *Policing, Security and Democracy: Special Aspects of Democratic Policing*, eds. S. Einstein and M. Amir, 87–105. Huntsville, TX: Office of International Criminal Justice (OICJ), Sam Houston State University.

Spence, G. 1989. *With Justice for None*. New York: Penguin.

Spencer-Wendel, S. 2010. "Corrections Officer Sentenced to 1 Year in Jail for Bringing Contraband into South Bay Prison." *Palm Beach Post*, January 5. Retrieved 1/6/2010 from www.palmbeachpost.com/news/correction-officer-sentenced-to-1-year-in-jail-163507.html.

Stace, W. 1995. "Ethical Relativity and Ethical Absolutism." In *Morality and Criminal Justice*, eds. D. Close and N. Meier, 25–32. Belmont, CA: Wadsworth.

Staples, W. 1997. *The Culture of Surveillance*. New York: St. Martin's.

Star Tribune. 2009. "Racial Tension Still Plagues the MPD." *Star Tribune* Editorial, May 7. Retrieved 5/7/2009 from www.startribune.com/opinion/editorials/43819812.html.

Stefanic, M. 1981. "Police Ethics in a Changing Society." *Police Chief*, May: 62–64.

Stein, J. 2010. "Whitehurst's Legacy Still Haunts the FBI Lab." *Spytalk: A Washington Post Blog*, March 25. Retrieved 5/14/2010 from http://blog.washingtonpost.com/spy-talk/2010/03/whitehursts_legacy_still_haunt.html.

Steptoe, S. 2007. "Can Bratton Survive May Day?" Time.com, May 31. Retrieved 4/20/2008 from www.time.com/time/nation/article/0,8599,1627076,00.html.

Sterba, J. 1980. *The Demands of Justice*. Notre Dame, IN: University of Notre Dame Press.

Sterngold, J. 2000. "Los Angeles Police Admit a Vast Management Lapse." *New York Times*, March 2: A14.

Stevens, D. 1999. "Corruption Among Narcotics Officers: A Study of Innocence and Integrity." *Journal of Police and Criminal Psychology* 14(2): 1–11.

Stickels, J. 2003. *The Victim Satisfaction Model in Criminal Justice*. Ph.D. dissertation, University of Texas.

Stohr, M., C. Hemmens, R. March, G. Barrier, and D. Palhegyl. 2000. "Can't Scale This? The Ethical Parameters of Correctional Work." *Prison Journal* 80(1): 56–79.

Stover, R. 1989. *Making It and Breaking It: The Fate of Public Interest Commitment During Law School*, ed. H. Erlanger. Urbana: University of Illinois Press.

Sulzberger, A., and J. Eligon. 2010. "2 Officers, 2 Courts, and Charges of Eliciting Sexual Favors." *New York Times*, May 18. Retrieved 5/19/2010 from www.nytimes.com/2010/05/19/nyregion/19cops.html.

Swift, C. 2007. "The American Way of Justice." Esquire online, June 26. Retrieved 4/2/2008 from www.esquire.com/print-this/features/ESQ0307swift.

Swisher, K. 2009. "The Judicial Ethics of Criminal Law Adjudication." *Arizona State Law Journal* 41: 755–828.

Sykes, G. 1980. "The Defects of Total Power." In *Keepers: Prison Guards and Contemporary Corrections*, ed. B. Crouch. Springfield, IL: Charles C Thomas.

Sykes, G. 1989. "The Functional Nature of Police Reform: The Myth of Controlling the Police." In *Critical Issues in Policing*, eds. R. Dunham and G. Alpert, 292–304. Prospect Heights, IL: Waveland.

Talbot, M. 2003. "Catch and Release." *Atlantic Monthly*, February.

Tanay, E. 1982. "Psychiatry and the Prison System." *Journal of Forensic Sciences* 27(2): 385–392.

Tanner, R. 2002. "Central Park Case Puts Focus on Confessions." *Austin American-Statesman*, December 7: A9.

Tanner, R. 2006. "Bad Science May Taint Many Arson Convictions." *Austin American-Statesman*, May 3: A1, A5.

Taylor, W. 1993. *Brokered Justice: Race Politics and Mississippi Prisons 1798–1992*. Columbus: Ohio State University Press.

Terrill, W. 2001. *Police Coercion: Application of the Force Continuum*. New York: LFB Scholarly Publishing.

Terrill, W. 2005. "Police Use of Force: A Transactional Approach." *Justice Quarterly* 22(1): 107–139.

Terrill, W., and S. Mastrofsky. 2002. "Situational and Officer-Based Determinants of Police Coercion." *Justice Quarterly* 19(2): 216–248.

Terrill, W., and E. Paoline. 2007. "Non-arrest Decision Making in Police-Citizen Encounters." *Police Quarterly* 10: 308–331.

Terrill, W., E. Paoline, and P. Manning. 2003. "Police Culture and Coercion." *Criminology* 41(4): 1003–1034.

Texas Bar Association. 2000. "Muting Gideon's Trumpet: The Crisis in Indigent Defense." Report by the Committee on Legal Services to the Poor in Criminal Matters, Texas State Bar. Retrieved 2/2/2005 from www.uta.edu/pols/moore/indigent.

Thoma, S. 1986. "Estimating Gender Differences in the Comprehension and Preference of Moral Issues." *Developmental Review* 6: 165–180.

Thompson, D. 1980. "Paternalism in Medicine, Law and Public Policy." In *Ethics Teaching in Higher Education*, eds. D. Callahan and S. Bok, 3–20. Hastings, NY: Hastings Center.

Thompson, D. 2004. "Prison System Blasted by Lawmakers, New Administration." Sandiego.com, January 20. Retrieved 1/22/2004 from http://signonsandiego.com/news/state/20040120-1658-ca-prisonhearings.html.

Tilove, J. 2009. "William Jefferson Sentenced to 13 Years in Prison." Nola.com, November 13. Retrieved 5/13/2010 from www.nola.com/politics/index.ssf/2009/11/william_jefferson_sentenced_ye.html.

Timerman, J. 1981. *Prisoner Without a Name, Cell Without a Number*, trans. Toby Talbot. New York: Knopf.

Toch, H. 1977. *Living in Prison*. New York: Free Press.

Toch, H. 1997. *Humanistic Corrections*. Guilderland, NY: Harrow and Heston.

Tonry, M. 2005. "The Functions of Sentencing and Sentencing Reform." *Stanford Law Review* 58: 37–67.

Trainum, J. 2008. "The Case for Videotaping Interrogations." LATimes.com, October 24. Retrieved 10/28/2008 from www.latimes.com/news/opinion/commentary/la-oe-trainum24-2008oct24,0,7918545.story.

Transparency International. 2008. "Annual Report." Retrieved 3/27/2008 from www.transparency.org/policy_research/surveys_indices/cpi/2007.

Transparency International. 2009. "Corruption Perception Index, 2009." Retrieved 7/29/2010 from www.transparency.org/policy_research/surveys_indices/cpi/2009/cpi_2009_table.

Trautman, N. 2008. "The Ethics Continuum." Retrieved 4/7/2008 from www.ethicsinstitute.com/pdf/Corruption%20Continum.pdf.

Tuchman, G., and K. Wojleck. 2009. "Texas Police Shake Down Drivers, Lawsuit Claims." CNN.com, May 6. Retrieved 5/26/2010 from www.cnn.com/2009/CRIME/05/05/texas.police.seizures/.

Turner, C. 2007. "Ethical Issues in Criminal Justice Administration." *American Jails* (January/February): 49–53.

Turner, A. 2010. "Panel Cites 'Flawed Science' in Arson Case." *Houston Chronicle*, July 24. Retrieved 8/9/2010 from www.chron.com/disp/story.mpl/metropolitan/7122381.html.

Tyler, T. 1990. *Why People Obey the Law*. New Haven, CT: Yale University Press.

Tyler, T., and L. Wakslak. 2004. "Profiling and Police Legitimacy: Procedural Justice, Attributions of Motive, and Acceptance of Police Authority." *Criminology* 42(2): 253–281.

Umbreit, M. 1994. *Victim Meets Offender: The Impact of Restorative Justice and Mediation*. Monsey, NY: Criminal Justice Press.

Umbreit, M., and M. Carey. 1995. "Restorative Justice Implications for Organizational Change." *Federal Probation* 59(1): 47–54.

Umbreit, M., R. Coates, and B. Vos. 2002. "Peacemaking Circles in Minnesota: An Exploratory Study." *Crime Victims Report* 5(6): 81–82.

United States Attorney's Office. 2008a. "Boston Police Officer Pleads Guilty to all Charges." News Release: November 8. Boston: U.S. Dept. of Justice, U.S. Attorney's Office, Michael J. Sullivan.

United States Attorney's Office. 2008b. "Correctional Officer Pleads Guilty to Bribery and Carnal Knowledge." News Release: June 23. Retrieved 6/14/2010 from www.justice.gov/oig/reports/press/2008_06_23.pdf.

United States Department of Justice. 2005 (July 28). Retrieved 10/7/2005 from www.usdoj.gov/usao/fls/050728-02.html.

Valentine, D. 2009. "Police: Officers Under Investigation Removed from Patrols." *Gazette News*, July 20. Retrieved 4/6/2010 from www.gazette.net/stories/07202009/prinnew140235_32543.shtml.

Van Maanen, J. 1978. "The Asshole." In *Policing: A View From the Street*, eds. P. Manning and J. van Maanen, 221–240. Santa Monica, CA: Goodyear.

Van Ness, D., and K. Heetderks Strong. 1997. *Restoring Justice*. Cincinnati: Anderson.

Vaughn, M., and L. Smith. 1999. "Practicing Penal Harm Medicine in U.S. Prisons." *Justice Quarterly* 16(1): 175–231.

Vaznis, J. 2008 "Ex-Officer Gets 18 Years in Drug Plot." Boston.com. Retrieved 4/9/2008 from www.boston.com/news/local/articles/2008/03/1l/ex_officer_gets_l8_years_in_drug_plot.

Vedantam, S. 2007. "If It Feels Good To Be Good, It Might Be Only Natural." WashingtonPost.com. Retrieved 5/28/2007 from www.washingtonpost.com/wp-dyn/content/article/2007/05/27/AR2007052701056.html.

Visser, S. 2009. "Ex-cop Sentenced in Corruption Case." *Atlanta-Constitution*, June 20. Retrieved 4/6/2010 from www.ajc.com/services/content/printedition/2009/06/20/stallings0620.html.

Vodicka, D. 2009. *The Green Wall*. Bloomington, IN: iUniverse Inc.

Vogelstein, R. 2003. "Confidentiality vs. Care: Re-evaluating the Duty to Self, Client, and Others." *Georgetown Law Journal* 92: 153–171.

Von Bergen, J. 2006. "Graft Probe Mushrooming in Chicago." *Philadelphia Inquirer*, August 10: A1, A13.

Von Hirsch, A. 1976. *Doing Justice*. New York: Hill and Wang.

Von Hirsch, A. 1985. *Past or Future Crimes.* New Brunswick, NJ: Rutgers University Press.

Von Hirsch, A., and L. Maher. 1992. "Can Penal Rehabilitation Be Revived?" *Criminal Justice Ethics* 11(1): 25–31.

Walker, L. 1986. "Sex Difference in the Development of Moral Reasoning." *Child Development* 57: 522–526.

Walker, S. 1985/2005. *Sense and Nonsense About Crime.* Monterey, CA: Brooks/Cole.

Walker, S. 2001. *Police Accountability: The Role of Citizen Oversight.* Belmont, CA: Wadsworth.

Walker, S. 2007. *Police Accountability: Current Issues and Research Needs.* Paper presented at National Institute of Justice, Policing Research Workshop: Planning for the Future, Washington, DC, November 28–29, 2006. (Available through National Institute of Justice, Washington, DC.)

Walker, S., and G. Alpert. 2002. "Early Warning Systems as Risk Management for Police." In *Policing and Misconduct,* ed. K. Lersch, 219–230. Upper Saddle River, NJ: Prentice Hall.

Walker, S., C. Spohn, and M. Delone. 2000. *The Color of Justice.* Belmont, CA: Wadsworth.

Walsh, A. 2000. "Evolutionary Psychology and the Origins of Justice." *Justice Quarterly* 17(4): 841–864.

Ward, M. 1996. "State Approves Faith-Based Pre-release Program for Texas Inmates." *Austin American-Statesman,* November 16: B12.

Ward, M. 2004. "Echoes of Texas' Sordid Past in Iraq Prison Abuse." *Austin American-Statesman,* May 12: B4.

Ward, M. 2006a. "Arrests of Prison Workers Climb." *Austin American-Statesman,* April 23: A1, A9.

Ward, M. 2006b. "Prison Workers' Rap Sheets Run Gamut." *Austin American-Statesman,* April 28: A1, A12.

Ward, M. 2006c. "Secrecy of Parole Files Opens Door for Abuses." *Austin American-Statesman,* March 18: A1, A11.

Ward, M. 2007a. "Privately Run Prisons Come Under More Fire at Capitol." *Austin American-Statesman,* October 13: B1, B3.

Ward, M. 2007b. "Inquiries Spring Up in Abuse Scandal." *Austin American-Statesman,* March 3: A1, A14.

Ward, M. 2008. "Inquiry: New Trial Had Been Ordered by Federal Appeals Court Last August." *Austin American-Statesman,* April 23: A1, A9.

Ward, M. 2009. "Court Cases Forcing Change at Texas Parole Agency." *Austin American-Statesman,* August 31: A1, A9.

Ward, S. 2007. "Pulse of the Legal Profession." *ABA Journal* (October). Retrieved 5/8/2008 from www.abajournal.com/magazine/pulse_of_the_legal_profession/.

Ward T., T. Gannon, and J. Vess. 2009. "Human Rights, Ethical Principles, and Standards in Forensic Psychology." *International Journal of Offender Therapy and Comparative Criminology* 52(2): 126–144.

Warren, J. 2004a. "Guards Tell of Retaliation for Informing." LATimes.com, January 21. Retrieved 1/22/2004 from www.latimes.com/news/local/la-me-prison?Ijan21,l,1780985.story?coll=la-headlines-california.

Warren, J. 2004b. "State Penal System Is Hammered in Report." LATimes.com. Retrieved 9/19/2004 from www.latimes.com/news/local/la-me-prisonsl6Janl6,l,6085723.story?coll51a-home-headlines.

WBZtv.com. 2007. "Boston Cop Pleads Guilty to Drug, Gun Charges." November 8. Retrieved 4/21/2008 from http://wbztv.com/topstories/Boston.Police.Department.2.605024.html.

Webb, J. 2009. "Now Is the Time to Reform our Criminal Justice System." *Criminal Justice Ethics* 28(2): 163–167.

Webby, S. 2009. "Two San Jose Police Officers Face Firing for Suspected Cover-up." *San Jose Mercury News,* September 21.

Weinstein, H. 2007. "ACLU: Company Aiding Torture." *Los Angeles Times.* Reprinted in *Austin American-Statesman,* May 31: A8.

Weisburd, D., and R. Greenspan. 2000. *Police Attitudes Toward Abuse of Authority: Findings from a National Study (Research In Brief).* Washington, DC: U.S. Department of Justice.

Weitzer, R. 1999. "Citizens' Perceptions of Police Misconduct: Race and Neighborhood Context." *Justice Quarterly* 16(4): 819–846.

Weitzer, R., and S. Tuch. 2000. "Reforming the Police: Racial Differences in Public Support for Change." *Criminology* 38(2): 391–116.

Weitzer, R., and S. Tuch. 2002. "Perceptions of Racial Profiling: Race, Class, and Personal Experience." *Criminology* 40(2): 435–156.

Weitzer, R., and S. Tuch. 2004. "Race and Perceptions of Police Misconduct." *Social Problems* 51(3): 305–325.

Wells, W., and J. Schafer. 2006. "Officer Perceptions of Police Responses to Persons with a Mental Illness." *Policing: An International Journal of Police Strategies and Management* 29(4): 578–601.

Wendle, J. 2009. "New Rules for Russia's Cops: No Bribes or Wild Sex." Time.com, April 15. Retrieved 4/15/2009 from www.time.com/time/printout/0,8816,1891215,00.html.

Westmarland, L. 2005. "Police Ethics and Integrity: Breaking the Blue Code of Silence." *Policing and Society* 15(2): 145–165.

Whistleblowers Australia. 2007. *The Whistle: Newsletter of Whistleblowers Australia* 50, April: 4–10. Also see Government Accountability Project website: www.whistleblower.org.

White, J. 2005. "Documents Tell of Brutal Improvisation by GIs." *Washington Post,* August 3: A1.

White, M., and J. Ready. 2009. "Examining Fatal and Nonfatal Incidents Involving the TASER." *Criminology and Public Policy* 8(4): 865–891.

White, R. 1999. "Are Women More Ethical? Recent Findings on the Effects of Gender on Moral Development." *Journal of Public Administration Research and Theory* 9: 459–472.

Whitehead, J. 1991. "Ethical Issues in Probation and Parole." In *Justice, Crime, and Ethics,* eds. M. Braswell, B. McCarthy, and B. McCarthy, 253–273. Cincinnati: Anderson.

Whitlock, C. 2005. "CIA Role in Abductions Investigated." *Austin American-Statesman,* March 13: A5.

Whitlock, C. 2007. "Officials Remain Reticent About Fate of 'Ghost

Prisoners'." *Washington Post*, reprinted in *Austin American-Statesman*, October 27: A3.

Whitman, J. 1998. "What Is Wrong with Inflicting Shame Sanctions?" *Yale Law Journal* 197(4): 1055–1092.

Wiley, L. 1988. "Moral Education in a Correctional Setting: Reaching the Goal by a Different Road." *Journal of Offender Services and Rehabilitation* 12(2): 161–174.

Williams, H. 2010. *Are the Recommendations of the Braidwood Commission on Conducted Energy Weapons Use Sound Public Policy?* Paper presented at the Academy of Criminal Justice Sciences Meeting, February, San Diego.

Williams, M., Holcomb, J., Kovandzic, T., and Bullock, S. 2010. "Policing for Profit: The Abuse of Civil Asset Forfeiture." Available at the Institute for Justice, www.ij.org/images/pdf_folder/other_pubs/assetforfeituretoemail.pdf.

Wilson, J. Q. 1976. *Varieties of Police Behavior*. New York: Atheneum.

Wilson, J. Q. 1993. *The Moral Sense*. New York: Free Press.

Wiltrout, K. 2007. "Naval Officer Sentenced to Six Months in Prison, Discharge." McClatchy-Tribune Information Services, May 18. Retrieved 3/19/2008 from www.accessmylibrary.com/coms2/summary_0286-30808288_ITM.

Witt, A. 2001. "Allegations of Abuses Mar Murder Cases." *Washington Post*, June 23: A01.

Wolfe, C. 1991. *Judicial Activism*. Pacific Grove, CA: Brooks/Cole Publishing.

Wood, D. 2009. "In Stunning Reversal, LAPD Goes from Reviled to Respected." *Christian Science Monitor*, June 24. Retrieved 4/8/2010 from www.csmonitor.com/USA/2009/0624/po2517-usgn.html.

Wood, J. 1997. *Royal Commission into the New South Wales Police Service, Final Report*. Sydney, Australia: Government of the State of N.S.W. (cited in Prenzler and Ronken, 2001b).

Worden, R., and S. Catlin. 2002. "The Use and Abuse of Force by Police." In *Policing and Misconduct*, ed. K. Lersch, 85–120. Upper Saddle River, NJ: Prentice Hall.

Worrall, J. 2001. "Addicted to Drug War: The Role of Civil Asset Forfeiture as a Budgetary Necessity in Contemporary Law Enforcement." *Journal of Criminal Justice* 29(3): 171–187.

Worrall, J. 2002. "If You Build It They Will Come: Consequences of Improved Citizen Complaint Review Procedures." *Crime and Delinquency* 48(3): 355–379.

Wren, D. 2010. "Safety Official's Lie Could Hurt North Myrtle Beach." TheSunNews.com. Retrieved 1/4/2010 from www.thesunnews.com/news/local/story/1241980.html.

Wren, T. 1985. "Whistle-Blowing and Loyalty to One's Friends." In *Police Ethics: Hard Choices in Law Enforcement*, eds. W. Heffernan and T. Stroup, 25–17. New York: John Jay Press.

Wright, K. 2001. "Management-Staff Relations: Issues in Leadership, Ethics, and Values." In *Discretion, Community and Correctional Ethics*, eds. J. Kleinig and M. Smith: 203–218. Oxford, England: Rowman and Littlefield.

Yee, J., and A. Molloy. 2005. *For God and Country: Faith and Patriotism Under Fire*. New York: Public Affairs Press.

Yen, H. 2009. "Survey: Hispanics Skeptical of Police Fairness." Associated Press, April 22.

Retrieved 4/22/2009 from www.finalcall.com/artman/publish/printer_5950.shtml.

Yost, P. 2010. "FBI Looking Into Deadly Coal Mine Explosion." *Austin American-Statesman*, May 1: A9.

Zacharias, F., and B. Green. 2009. "The Duty to Avoid Wrongful Convictions: A Thought Experiment in the Regulation of Prosecutors." *Boston University Law Review* 89: 1–59.

Zamora, J., H. Lee, and J. van Derbeke. 2003. "Ex-Cops Cleared of 8 Counts." SFGate.com, October 1. Retrieved 4/16/2008 from www.sfgate.com/cgi-bin/article.cgi?file=/c/a/2003/l0/01/MN20967.DTL.

Zapotosky, M. 2009. "Officers' Finances Demand Frequent Scrutiny, Experts Say." *Washington Post*, August 18. Retrieved 8/18/2009 from www.washingtonpost.com/wp-dyn/content/article/2009/08/17/AR2009081702795_pf.html.

Zhao, J., N. He, and N. Lovrich. 1998. "Individual Value Preferences Among American Police Officers." *Policing: An International Journal of Police Strategies and Management* 21(1): 22–37.

Zimbardo, P. 1982. "The Prison Game." In *Legal Process and Corrections*, eds. N. Johnston and L. Savitz, 195–198. New York: Wiley.

Zimring, F., G. Hawkins, and S. Kamin. 2001. *Punishment and Democracy: Three Strikes and You're Out in California*. Oxford, England: Oxford University Press.

Zitrin, R., and C. Langford. 1999. *The Moral Compass of the American Lawyer*. New York: Ballantine Books.

Zohar, N. 2004. "Innocence and Complex Threats: Upholding the War Ethic and the Condemnation of Terrorism." *Ethics* 114: 734–751.

Name Index

Subject Index

Case Index